Alhazred

DONALD TYSON

Author of the Necronomicon

Llewellyn Publications
Woodbury, Minnesota

FIRST EDITION
First Printing, 2006

Cover design by Kevin R. Brown
Edited by Tom Bilstad

Library of Congress Cataloging-in-Publication Data

Alhazred / Donald Tyson.— 1st ed.
     p.   cm.
     "H.P. Lovecraft's compelling character, Abdul Alhazred, is brought to life in this epic tale detailing the mad sorcerer's tragic history and magical adventures."
     ISBN-13: 978-0-7387-0892-8
     ISBN-10: 0-7387-0892-5
     1. Magicians—Fiction. I. Lovecraft, H. P. (Howard Philips), 1890–1937.

     PR9199.3.T94A79 2006
     813'.45—dc22   2006040921

Llewellyn Worldwide does not participate in, endorse, or have any authority or responsibility concerning private business transactions between our authors and the public.

All mail addressed to the author is forwarded but the publisher cannot, unless specifically instructed by the author, give out an address or phone number.

Any Internet references contained in this work are current at publication time, but the publisher cannot guarantee that a specific location will continue to be maintained. Please refer to the publisher's website for links to authors' websites and other sources.

Llewellyn Publications
A Division of Llewellyn Worldwide, Ltd.
2143 Woodale Drive, Dept. 0-7387-0892-5
Woodbury, MN 55125-2989, U.S.A.
www.llewellyn.com

Printed in the United States of America

PART ONE

Chapter 1

The day began like any other. I awoke to the distant cry of a peacock on the lawn of the palace garden, and lay listening to the plash of the marble fountain below my chamber window while one of my slaves brought in a basin of warm water scented with rose petals for me to bathe, and another laid out on the foot of my bed my day robe. Naked beneath the silk sheet, I arched my back and wiggled my toes, unwilling to leave the soft embrace of the down-filled pillows that had molded themselves to my shape.

My slave Anu stood beside the bed with the steaming copper basin in his hands, a white linen towel draped across his black arm, patiently waiting. He was an Ethiopian, sold into slavery at the age of five years by his father, and was generally held to be the best attendant in the palace, although I had my eye on a man who presently served the king's bedchamber. Anu was a trifle too silent and serious for my taste. I needed attendants who could appreciate my wit when it burst forth spontaneously at odd times. Then my remarks would be repeated and would find their way into the harem, and my reputation among the wives and concubines of the king would grow, and eventually the praise would reach his ears.

"Stop staring at me and put the basin down. Your arms are beginning to shake."

Wordlessly, Anu set the basin on the marble tiles of the floor beside the bed and stood with arms folded across his massive chest. His dark eyes were upon me, yet unfocused, as though he stared into the distance at some unseen vision. He often did that to irritate me. With a deep sigh, I slid the sheet off my limbs and pushed myself to my feet in front of the window. The cool morning breeze made my skin tingle. My manhood stood in a rampant condition, something that often occurred in the morning. The other slave, a boy from the Lebanon with the absurd name of Dodee, ran to get the glazed chamber pot and held it under my prick. I always felt the need to urinate after rising, having invariably drunk wine just before going to bed the night before.

"I'm too stiff to piss, Dodee. Wait a few moments."

Dodee smiled in his half-witted way, prepared to wait all morning and into the afternoon if necessary. At least he was affable, which made me like him better than distant Anu, who paid no attention to my magnificent display of manhood, though he must have noticed from the corner of his eye. I was proud of the size of my prick. Several women of the palace, including the youngest wife of the king, had assured me that it was uncommonly huge for a man of my height. I wondered if I were larger than Anu. My head only came up to his chin, and his shining black arm where it projected from the short sleeve of his unbleached cotton tunic was thicker than my calf, but these were not always true indicators of manhood.

Staring at my prick as though it were a rearing cobra, Dodee grinned and revealed his blackened teeth. He was my own age, nineteen years, with barely a fuzz of hairs beginning to sprout from his narrow chin, but he had a passion for sweets that rotted his teeth and caused his breath to stink.

"A minute more, Dodee."

Just before waking, the princess Narisa had held me tight in her embrace and whispered honeyed words into my ear, tickling its depths with the pink tip of her tongue and catching the lobe playfully between her teeth. The dream was still with me. I stared up at the intricate interlocking pattern of colored tiles on the ceiling, thinking of a theorem of geometry from Euclid, and soon my piss began to tinkle into the chamber pot. Dodee carried his prize away.

My arms spread slightly, I allowed Anu to wash my entire body with a linen cloth that floated in the basin and pat my white skin dry on the fluffy cotton towel. It was our daily ritual together. He worked with speed and efficiency.

The intricately carved sandalwood screens that shuttered the window had been thrown open, as they always were at first light. My gaze wandered unobstructed down to the splashing fountain in the garden below, formed in the shape of two dancing marble dolphins with thin jets of water erupting from their opened mouths. Clusters of red roses grew all around the circular base of the fountain. Already, a slave assigned to maintain the palace grounds was watering the flowers with a wooden water bucket, while another slave pulled a reservoir behind him on a small cart. Periodically the second slave dipped a pitcher into the reservoir and poured water into the bucket, from which it streamed out through countless holes drilled in its bottom. One day without water and the flowers would wilt; in three days they would die. The same sun that shone down its rays into the walled garden of the king raised dust devils and shimmering mirages on the sands of the desert only an hour away at the walking pace of a horse.

Amid the green lawns and spreading shade trees of the garden, the desert was no more than a distant illusion, yet seven years before, when first brought to the palace of King Huban by my father, the richness and diversity of forms in the palace had seemed a waking dream or a mad fantasy created by the spell of a djinn. My father was a herder of goats, his house a one-room hovel with mud-plastered walls and a roof of crooked sticks. In those days, dimmed by the passage of time but never to be forgotten, my bed had been a few discarded sacks on the hard clay floor, riddled with lice and fleas. I could never stop scratching my scalp, no matter how many times my mother hit me on the crown of my head with her knuckle. Her knuckle grew callused through overuse and made a dry sound as it struck my skull, like a walnut thrown into an empty wooden bowl.

My life would have settled into a predictable routine of nit picking and goat herding, indistinguishable from the lives of my father and his father before him, but through some caprice of fate I was gifted at birth with a talent for poetry and the voice of an angel. My early spontaneous songs aroused the wonder of our village. In my twelfth year, my father and I were summoned to audience with King Huban ibn Abd Allah of Yemen at his palace in Sana'a. He had heard the fame of my poetry and wished to learn if it was more than the idle gossip of a small village.

Strangely, I felt no fear when I stood barefoot in my patched shirt and newly scrubbed face to sing my poetry for the king. I never feel nervous when I recite or sing. A deep calmness comes over my soul, and I seem to rise out of myself and listen as though to the performance of some admirable stranger. The philosophers of the

Greeks held that all poetry descends from the gods, or as we would phrase it in our more enlightened times, now that the Prophet has lifted our race out of barbarism, from the one God through the mediation of his angels.

So charmed were the king and his advisors by my song, he entered into agreement with my father that I should remain and live within the palace, to be instructed by the tutors who taught his eldest son, the crown prince Yanni. With these few words, my life changed. My vermin-infested sleeping sacks were handed on to my less fortunate brothers and sisters, who no doubt gave thanks for the additional space created in the cramped little house by my absence. I was forced to become accustomed to sleep beneath sheets of milk-colored silk trimmed with arabesques of golden thread and on pillows filled with the down of swans.

"Has the Princess Narisa arisen?" I asked without turning to look at Anu, who rubbed the towel down my back and buttocks.

"I do not know, lord." His voice was so deep it held the rumble of distant thunder. It grated on my teeth each time he spoke.

"You have not forgotten my instruction to watch for her each morning?"

"I remember, lord. I have not seen the princess today."

With a shrug, I left him and went to Dodee, who knelt with my white cotton surwal held open between his hands so that I could step into it. He pulled it up my legs and tied the drawstring at my waist. It was of Persian design, baggy but gathered at the cuffs just below the knees, and tastefully embroidered along the seams in rust-colored woolen thread with alternating leaves and flowers. Dodee lifted my thawb from the bed and held it high in his outstretched arms so that I could slip it over my head and shoulders. Of late I had adopted the robe of a scholar, a plain thawb of white silk with long sleeves and a hem that touched the ground, unadorned save for a few filigrees of gold thread worked with black seed pearls about the neck and tiraz bands around the sleeves.

The Arabic script on the tiraz bands carried the words "In the name of God, the compassionate, blessing from God and mercy upon the Caliph, Yazid ibn Muawya, slave of God, the prince of believers." I cared nothing either for God or the Caliph, but a pious verse on the tiraz bands lends a young man a modest appearance. The recent austerity of my clothing was the talk of the palace, which amused me greatly. In the harem, whispers spread that I meant to become a philosopher and forsake women altogether. This rumor served my purpose, since of late my attention was devoted to Narisa, and I had neither the energy nor inclination to lie with the slatterns who had polluted my bed in the past.

Besides, it would injure the feelings of the princess were I to be unfaithful. I had sworn to her that we would be wed, and meant to broach this delicate subject with the king at the first opportunity. Even though my blood was common, the king could easily have me adopted into a noble family, which would render me fit for marriage to his eldest daughter. He had a great fondness for me and treated me in all things as though I were his own son. How to approach the subject of my marriage with the princess, I was uncertain. The question played through my mind each morning with no satisfactory conclusion. There would be only one chance to win the approval of the king, and if he denied the match, he would be alerted to my interest in his daughter and would have my movements watched.

Our midnight meetings in the arbor beside the dolphin fountain would cease. To know the soft surrender of her parted thighs, gleaming like polished ivory in the moonlight, the palpitations of her heart beneath her breast, her warmly panted kisses, the bite of her nails into my back as she clutched me closer in the height of passion, and then to be driven apart from her and forced to pretend that I felt nothing when I looked at her—it would be more than I could endure, and would surely lead to some hasty and ill-conceived action that would end my life. The word of the king was law, and once spoken could not be revoked.

Dodee drew yellow leather stockings over my bare feet and tied them above my calves, then slipped my feet into Persian slippers of dark blue felt. The toes were in the latest fashion from Baghdad and narrowed to upturned ends almost as sharp as the point of a dagger. Their tops were decorated with flowers of green and red glass beads. In my opinion, one of the blessings of the Sassanian rule of Yemen had been the introduction of Persian clothing, so much more colorful and graceful than the mundane garments of this land. The armies of Mohammed conquered the Sassanian Empire some ten years before I was born, but it was still possible to buy Persian styles, even though they were frowned upon by disapproving mullahs.

Without prompting, Dodee held up an oval mirror of polished silver in a black ebony frame. My beardless face was undoubtedly handsome in a boyish way, my changeable gray-green eyes mysterious and penetrating, my nose narrow like the beak of a hawk, my full lower lip tinged with pink. Though my father was dark of complexion, some freak of nature had given me a pale skin that resisted browning beneath the sun. There was a rumor in my village, never spoken before the face of my father, that my mother had lain with a djinn on her journey to the village to be wed, and that I was the spawn of an evil spirit of the desert. The intense devotion of my mother to the teachings of the Koran refuted this slander, yet each time I gazed at my pale skin, the fable returned to my thoughts.

For a moment I debated whether I should renew the black lines of kohl around the rims of my eyelids, then decided that they would serve until tomorrow. I abhorred vanity. My dark hair was beginning to curl over my ears. I reminded myself to have Anu summon the royal barber some afternoon later in the week, when I was bored and could find no more interesting occupation. Two women of the palace had expressed the desire to possess locks of my hair, which they intended to enclose in silver and crystal pendants, and I saw no harm in gratifying this whim.

It was not my custom to eat in the morning. I wandered into the adjoining room that held my books and sat at my desk to finish writing the letter I had begun the previous night by lamplight, before the wine made me sleepy. It was addressed to a book merchant at Damascus. He had written describing a new addition to his wares that might interest me, and I intended to include payment in gold with this letter so that the book would be sent to Sana'a on the next caravan east. The work was a rare Greek text on necromancy, difficult to obtain here in Yemen since such books were forbidden to be read or possessed on pain of death. It was fortunate that no mullah would dare to apply these laws to a chosen favorite of the king, since many books of a similar type lined the shelves of my writing room.

Sealing the letter in wax with my carnelian seal ring, I entrusted it to Anu, who bore it silently from my chambers to place with the rest of the royal mail. I took a black leather volume from a shelf and carried it under my arm down the stairs and out into the garden, meaning to sit in the bower by the fountain and read until Narisa came forth to make her morning circuit of the lawns, with her ever-present maids trailing their dark veils behind her. It would not have been decorous for her to stop and speak with me, but she would glance across at the bower as she passed, and if she saw that my legs were crossed, it was a signal that she should steal from her sleeping chamber that night and come to the bower, where I would be waiting to make love. Today my legs would be crossed.

The polished marble seat of the bower, shaded from the rising sun by the leaves of the over-arching vines, felt cool against my back and thighs through the silk of my thawb. I opened the black cover of the book and began to read with some difficulty the crabbed Hebrew characters, so inelegant when compared with our own flowing script. In six months, I promised myself, I would read Hebrew as easily as I read Greek. Hebrew was rich in magical texts, and no serious student of the arcane arts could afford to be ignorant of its meaning.

"Necromancer! Come out into the sun. You're as white as a frog's belly."

My displeasure did not reveal itself as I closed the book upon my index finger and looked up at Prince Yanni's plump insolent face. He stood at the entrance to the bower, arms raised to the arch of the trellis that supported the vines.

"You know the rays of the sun have no effect on my skin."

"Then come out and let me put some color in your cheeks. I want to wrestle."

Yanni was two years older, and had always been bigger and stronger. He enjoyed wrestling with me because he invariably won.

"The last time we wrestled you broke the bone of my arm."

"Bruised. The physician said the bone was merely bruised, not broken. You always exaggerate, Abdul."

He would not go away until he got what he wanted. The look in his eyes said that he wanted to humiliate me by throwing me to the grass and holding me there until I could not breathe and lost consciousness. No one defied the wishes of the crown prince, not even the court poet.

Closing the book and setting it on the stone bench, I walked to an open patch of sunlit grass, far enough away from the path of pink gravel that Yanni would have difficulty throwing me onto the stones. He followed with a swagger in his step, anticipating the pleasure of his victory. We stripped off our clothing. Yanni took off his jeweled rings and gold neck chains. His paunch was larger than the last time I had viewed it under a similar circumstance. It pleased me to note that his prick, so much more diminutive than my own, was nearly hidden beneath the bulk of his belly.

He shook his head at my thawb, lying discarded on the grass, while I bent to pull off my leather stockings.

"Why do you dress like a Persian?"

"I don't know what you mean," I murmured in irritation as I freed myself from my surwal and dropped it on the grass.

"You wear nothing on your head. You shave your beard. You wear silk that trails across the ground. All these things are expressly forbidden by the Prophet, upon him peace."

"When did you become so religious, big brother?"

He shrugged, a slight smile quirking the corner of his mouth.

"One day I will be king. A king must set an example for his people, especially with the appointed governor of the Caliph constantly peering over his shoulder."

We grappled, and our naked bodies slapped together. His arms about my shoulders were tight on my dry skin, so that I could not twist away from them.

"Still reading forbidden books, little brother?" he grunted in my ear. "One of these days father will have your head cut off."

My knee blocked his thigh as he tried to sweep me from my feet. He arched his back and lifted me from the grass. I let my body go limp, and the shift of my weight forced him to renew his hold. When he relaxed momentarily, I slipped away with a spinning motion.

"The king approves of my studies."

"Father values knowledge, but does he approve of the books in your library?" He named several texts of black magic.

"How do you know what books are in my library?"

My fury made me forgetful. He lunged and caught my leg in his hand. We fell to the grass, fighting for the upper position. Yanni spun his body deftly and covered my back, his arms around my chest. I struggled to keep my hands and knees beneath me.

"You have the favor of the king," he hissed in my ear. "That will not save you from a charge of sorcery."

"Why should you care what books I read?" I retorted.

"I care about the honor of my sister."

His words chilled me like a dagger of ice through my heart. How much did he know?

With a cry, he turned me on to my back and pinned me, his arm across my throat. It began to tighten. I slapped his shoulder with my hand.

"Enough. The first fall is yours."

Reluctantly, he let me slide from his hold and climb to my feet. My left shoulder throbbed and my left arm felt numb from the elbow to the fingertips, but I could still use my hand. I worked my fingers open and closed, eyeing him warily as he stood.

"Did you really believe no one would notice your eyes on Narisa, or that your slaves would keep silent?"

Anu. It must have been Anu. I had been discreet. My eyes never strayed to Narisa when we passed on the lawns or in the halls of the palace. Was the slave truly my property, or had he belonged to Yanni these many months he had tended to my needs? Still, he could say no more than that I had asked about the movements of Narisa.

Yanni slapped with playful brutality his cupped hands against my shoulders and head, trying to hit my ears as we circled each other. One blow could rupture the eardrum and cause deafness. I kept my shoulders hunched.

"I've come to warn you, necromancer. There has been talk."

"Harem gossip." I spat into the grass. "No man would listen to it."

The sound of female laughter drifted from one of the windows of the east wing of the palace, where the harem was kept. I glanced across the lawn and saw the brief flash of a bright blue scarf passed through the fretwork of a shut screen and drawn back as the breeze filled it. Our wrestling match provided diversion for the royal wives and concubines. The window was too distant for our words to be overheard.

"Anyway," I continued, "what harm would there be were I to admire Narisa? Your father could grant me a noble title."

Anger clouded his eyes. He lunged, but his arms slipped off my sweating torso before they could lock together. I spun and grasped his waist from behind, trying to throw him. He sought to hook my leg with his ankle. I blocked him with my knee, cursing inwardly the bulk of his fat that made him too heavy to lift.

"You're a goat herder, little brother," he said with scorn, trying to use his elbows against my upper arms to break my hold and digging at my hands with his powerful fingers. "Do you think a proclamation granting you a noble rank can change that?"

My heart became leaden. Narisa and I so often shared the dream that a grant of noble title would enable our union, I had almost come to believe it myself. The king was liberal in his opinions, and valued both talent and learning, but the prejudice of rank ran deep. Would he even consider giving the hand of his daughter to a common herder?

Anger lent my limbs renewed strength. I lunged up and back, drawing Yanni off his feet so that he fell with me, but before we struck the lawn I twisted and gained the upper position. His body absorbed the blow, which knocked the wind from his lungs. Quickly, before he recovered, I applied a lock and held him. He struggled furiously, but soon began to tire. I could hold the lock all day and he knew it. In disgust, he slapped my arm.

"This fall goes to you. How did you turn so quickly? You writhe like a serpent. Let me up."

We gained our feet and circled, both breathing hard and streaming sweat. He rubbed his left elbow, his eyes never leaving mine, and with a fierce exultation I knew that I had hurt him. That could be used to my advantage. I ceased circling to my left and began to move in the opposite direction, so that his weakened left arm would be exposed. Yanni saw what I was doing and turned his torso to shield his left side.

"Keep your eyes to the study of your black books and your barbaric tongues," he muttered. "My sister is not for you."

"She can speak her own words."

"I like you, Abdul. For these past seven years you've been like a brother to me. But we are not brothers. You are a singer of songs and a maker of verses. I am the crown prince of Yemen. Do not think to tie my blood to yours through my sister."

I could not oppose his strength or skill. My only weapon was guile.

"Narisa is a playmate of my childhood, nothing more."

"She has become a woman, and your time of playing with her is past."

He threw himself upon me, intending to use his sheer power to force me to my knees. Instead of resisting, I drew him to my breast and fell backward, my right foot planted in his stomach. His own weight threw him over my body as I straightened my leg, adding to his flight. He struck the gravel path with the flat of his back and slid across the stones cursing, then rolled to his side. Quickly, before he could stand, I darted after him and fastened a chokehold around his neck, forcing his face into the gravel. It was the same hold Yanni had taught me in our childhood, when he delighted to throw me across the lawn again and again until I could no longer rise to my feet.

The pink stones, though not sharp, cut his cheek and forehead. Blood streamed from his nose, and his lower lip began to swell. My forearm tightened on his thick neck. He struggled to throw me off, cursing and spitting a spray of blood from his cut lip. At last, he relaxed and slapped my arm. I tightened the hold, thinking of the many times he had used it to render me unconscious. Again he slapped my arm, and again with a frantic motion.

Reluctantly, I released him and stood quickly before he could vent his annoyance with a petty blow. Yanni got up rubbing his throat and tried to smile, but his swollen lip made the expression grotesque. He spat blood into the grass.

"You've gained skill since the last time we wrestled."

"A man can improve himself."

He laughed and gathered up his necklaces and rings. With quick, angry tugs at his white cotton thawb, he dressed and walked away without speaking.

Putting on my clothes without haste, I returned to the bower, only to find that it had lost its charms. My mind refused to interpret the Hebrew characters opened before me, so I sat pretending to read while my thoughts raced within my skull.

Yanni was correct that by the laws of Yemen, the mere possession of the book I held in my hands was death. It had never occurred to me that so foolish a law could affect me, the king's own favorite, within the palace, but should the king himself choose to apply it, the law was grounds for my execution by decapitation. I had watched such executions many times with great interest, observing how the fountain of blood sprang from the stump of the neck and the eyes rolled up so that only their whites showed in the sockets of the tumbling head, after the executioner's sword fulfilled its fatal arc. I had no wish to play the central part in such a tragedy.

Narisa's face arose in my imagination, playful with seduction, the countenance of a houri of paradise promising infinite delights. We loved with equally mingled passion of the flesh and purity of the heart. It was impossible to think of forsaking her. On a more pragmatic level, marriage with Narisa presented the opportunity to become a member of the royal family, which would protect my future ease and security. Who knew when the king might grow weary of my songs, and dismiss me from the palace? Marriage with his daughter would ensure that it would remain my home forever. Not even Yanni could cast me out when he ascended to the throne.

I glanced up through the leaves at the sun. The morning grew late. Narisa should have made her promenade of the garden. She was punctual in her habits. I wondered what might have delayed her, or whether she had fallen ill during the night.

Preoccupation with these thoughts made me ignore the approach of a member of the palace guard, who crossed the lawn with purposeful steps, his polished bronze breastplate gleaming in the sun and his short military sword slapping against his thigh in its sheath. Only when he stopped at the entrance to the bower did I look at him. His scarred face seemed familiar, and I realized that he was a guard of the throne room, sworn to protect the security of the king. It was unusual to see a throne room guard walking about in the garden.

"The king requests your presence, lord."

My heart began to beat faster as my thoughts raced. Yanni must have spoken his concern over my attentions toward Narisa to his father, and the king had decided to question me about the rumor. It was the opportunity I had waited for these past months, a chance to confess my love for the princess and my desire to have her hand in marriage. I would ask the king to bless our union, and to enable it by granting me adoption into a noble family, along with a rank and title.

"Immediately, my lord."

I became aware of my book. It was not the sort of text to leave lying around in the garden, yet neither was it a book I wished to parade before the king while asking for the hand of his daughter in marriage.

"May I return to my rooms to prepare?"

The guard's battered features expressed no emotion. He was a veteran twice my years, granted throne room duty as a reward for his faithful service.

"You are to accompany me at once to the presence of the king."

Sighing, I tucked the book under my arm. It was in Hebrew, after all. What chance was there that any of the courtiers in the throne room would be able to read a single word of it? True, the king's chief advisor was a Jew, but in the mornings he occupied himself drafting state documents.

The guard kept half a step ahead, glancing over his shoulder to ensure that I followed. He did not lead me to the large and ornate throne room, where the king spent much of his day surrounded by his advisors and nobles, but to a smaller and less ostentatious audience chamber in the rear of the palace. Evidently the king did not wish to make a public display of our interview. This suited my purpose, as it would allow me to express my intentions toward Narisa without the risk of embarrassing her or the king. We could speak man to man, or son to father.

The two guards standing on either side of the audience chamber door seemed oddly tense, but I thought little of it. My mind was preoccupied with the eloquence of the speech I composed. I have always had a talent for extemporaneous composition, and concentrated on casting the words I intended to utter before the king into the most persuasive pattern I could devise. Only one chance would be offered to me to win his agreement to the union.

My escort opened the featureless and uninviting door and stood aside to let me pass. The sound of weeping came from within the chamber, which was not large, with a low tiled ceiling and a floor of plain slate. I went forward with curiosity into the dim room, wondering who wept. The guard entered after me and closed the door, then stood stiffly at attention in front of it with a grim expression, as though to bar my exit.

Broken light shone through the closed screens of three windows along the outer wall and cast geometric patterns across the slates. The only furniture was a simple wooden chair at one end of the room in which the king sat. To the left of the chair stood his principal advisor, a tall gaunt figure in black with a gray beard that hung almost to his waist, and on the right my slave Dodee, who eyed me with bright awareness. Several of the king's personal guards were ranked at attention along each side wall, swords drawn and held at the ready.

These details I gathered from the edge of my vision, but my attention was fixed upon the pitiful figure of Narisa, who crouched on her hands and knees on the bare slates in front of the rough throne, her head hung low so that her long dark hair fell about her face and concealed it. Sobs shook her whole body.

With an effort of self-control, I resisted the urge to run to her and pull her up from the floor. Her hair dangled loose and uncombed, and she wore a simple white cotton shift of the kind a woman might wear for sleeping. Blood stained its hem. She did not look at me, but kept her head lowered.

"Here he is," the king said in a booming voice, so unnaturally bright. "The young man who has defiled the virtue of my daughter."

Chapter 2

Even seated as he was in an ordinary wooden chair, unburdened by his ornate robes of office and far removed from the grandeur of the gilded throne room, King Huban made an impressive figure. With back and head erect, hands resting on the carven arms of the chair, feet planted flat against the slates of the floor, his deeply lined features exuded an authority beyond contradiction. He wore a purple tunic girdled at the waist military fashion by a black sash, to raise its hem to a level just below his knees. Plain white bands embroidered the hem, cuffs, and neckline. On his head, a white turban of no great length wound around a conical cap of red felt. Black military boots with high shin guards of hard leather encased his legs.

It was said that in his youth, the king had been a great warrior. He still liked to affect military attire, although the Spartan appearance was somewhat spoiled by three lines of pearls braided across his square-cut, glossy beard, which was reddened with henna.

He motioned me forward with his finger until I stood alone in the center of the chamber, some three paces from the princess.

"You must forgive Narisa if she does not rise to greet you. She has endured a difficult night."

Stepping nearer, I saw that the whites were visible all around the umber centers of his widely staring eyes, and the smile that stretched his cheeks had the rigor of a funeral mask. A sense of fatality crossed my heart like a shadow and stifled any impulse to protest.

"Is she injured?" I asked, my voice so subdued I was not certain he heard me.

He cocked his head and seemed to listen to the air.

"Injured? You mean the blood? No, not injured, at least not in any permanent way."

I glared at Dodee, who seemed to find amusement in my rage. His eyes, no longer vague and wandering, met mine with insolence. Had he always been the king's spy? I had never troubled to conceal my purposes from him, thinking him too simple-minded to comprehend them. There could be no better cloak for a traitor than the pose of an idiot.

The king muttered a few words into the ear of the bearded advisor who bent at his side, and the old Jew cast me a malignant glance from the corner of his gray eye as he listened. He wore the yellow turban that was by law the required color for his race, but his thawb was lavishly embroidered with all hues of the rainbow, its low hem trimmed with threads of gold and silver, and rings covered every finger of both his hands. Jews were numerous in Yemen. They controlled the making of jewelry and other crafts that employed precious metals, and their collective wealth purchased them a measure of influence with the king.

The old man walked behind the chair to a closed door and rapped once upon it. Two figures came out bearing between them a wooden table. Hoods of soft black leather covered their faces, and were tied about their necks to prevent accidental removal. Over plain gray tunics they wore tanned leather aprons bound about their chests that hung down to their ankles. With a sickness in the pit of my stomach, I saw that the aprons were stained with what appeared to be brown rust.

They placed the table at my left side, slightly in front of where I stood with trembling knees. It bore an assortment of knives, pricks, hooks, and pinchers, all made of iron. Among them was a large pair of shears. Silent as ghosts, they slipped back through the door behind the king. The stillness of the chamber was broken only by the sobs of the woman at my feet.

"Why have you done this to her?" I could not keep a note of outrage from my voice.

He raised the palm of his hand as though to still my anger.

"I have done nothing," he said with unnatural mildness. "It is you who have done all. This morning before dawn, when the princess awoke in her bed, she complained of cramps and began to bleed. I was summoned from sleep to her bedside by the imploring of her frightened old nurse, and watched her give birth as she sat upon her chamber pot. The midwife called to treat her estimates that the fetus was some four months of age. The abomination began to mewl, lying amid the blood and urine, so I silenced it with this very hand. I instructed that my daughter be questioned, and she revealed that since the beginning of the winter just passed she has been giving her body to you for your pleasure."

Narisa lunged forward and hugged my ankles with her arms, pressing her wet cheek against my slipper.

"Forgive me, Abdul. They forced me to tell all. At first I would not speak, but they threatened to do terrible things to me."

I did not dare to bend and touch her head with my fingertips. The king nodded, and two guards dragged her away and flung her down on the floor in front of his chair, where she lay with her face buried in her arms.

"My lord, I love Narisa as I love my own life."

"Do you, indeed? That is fortunate."

His odd choice of words distracted me from my plea. I hesitated still longer as I watched the two hooded men carry on poles an iron charcoal brazier that shimmered with heat and sent up a thin plume of smoke to curl across the black and white tiles on the ceiling. They set the brazier on its tripod before me. Through the iron grill that covered it, embers glowed with the redness of hellfire, and I felt their scorch against my cheeks and lips.

As I took a step backward, the book fell from beneath my arm. The king noted it with mild interest.

"What is that?"

"Nothing, my lord. A book of my studies."

"Bring it here."

The tall Jew came forward, and eyeing me with profound distaste, bent at the knees and retrieved the book without removing his gaze from my face. He carried it to the king, who flipped its pages carelessly. In wonder I watched his lips move as he read. He glanced up and caught my eye.

"You did not know I could read Hebrew? There are many sides of my nature you have never seen."

My legs trembled so violently that I could barely stand. I had no control over the muscles in my thighs and calves. I felt my bowels begin to open, but fortunately they were empty and nothing came forth. One of the hooded men returned to the room behind the king while the other busied himself in front of me with the iron implements on the table. For the first time I noticed that Prince Yanni was not present in the audience chamber. I realized that he must know nothing of his sister's miscarriage, or he would certainly have tried to kill me in the garden. His father had not bothered to inform him of the proceedings, either to spare his feelings, or simply in contempt for his opinion.

"Dodee said you were a sorcerer," the king murmured, studying the page before him. "I did not believe him. I have greatly misjudged you, Abdul."

A protest died in my throat. What could I say that would make any difference to the outcome? Events moved forward with the slow inexorability of a nightmare from which there is no escape.

The hooded man returned bearing a silver tray covered with a silver lid. He stood beside the brazier, slightly to one side so as not to obstruct the king's view.

"I understand you have not yet eaten breakfast. You must be hungry."

Balancing the tray upon one hand, the man lifted the lid and exposed its contents. My heart quailed with a mingled horror and sadness. The bloody fruit of Narisa's womb, harvested before its ripeness, lay before me, impaled upon an iron skewer. It resembled a skinned rabbit on a spit. The other aproned man picked the fetus from the tray by the ring at the end of the skewer and laid it upon the grill of the brazier. A hiss and crackle of white smoke arose, and the air filled with a sweet scent.

Unable to restrain her curiosity, Narisa pushed herself up to her knees and looked at the grill. She began to shriek in a high keening and struck herself repeatedly in the face with her fingernails so that her cheeks bled, unable to turn away. At the king's harsh command, Dodee caught her arms and held them at her sides, preventing her from further injuring herself. He did not attempt to turn her face from the horror that sizzled on the coals. There was madness in her eyes as her shrieks mounted unceasing.

To my surprise, I felt nothing. My body quaked in terror, yet this fear was so deep, so far removed from my center of thought, its effect was entirely of the flesh, and almost seemed to be the affliction of some other unfortunate man.

The hooded figure with the empty tray replaced the lid and bore it away through the doorway behind the king. The other used the skewer to turn the meat, exposing a side that had become golden in the heat of the fire. His silent companion returned and took up a place behind me, but as yet refrained from touching me. A knife and prick were used to cut out a section of flesh from the fetus. I stared in fascination at its tiny hands, so human. A piece of steaming flesh was raised on the point of the iron prick to my lips, and its savor filled my nostrils, making the gorge rise in my throat.

"Aren't you hungry?" the king roared, for the first time revealing anger in his voice. "Eat!"

A strange calm came over me and stilled the racing of my heart. I drew a slow breath and accepted my mortality.

"No, I will not eat."

They forced me to my knees and pried open my mouth with iron hooks, loosening some of my teeth in their violence and filling my mouth with the salt taste of blood. The flesh of the dead thing was thrust down my throat, then another sliver, and another, until only bones remained on the brazier. Narisa had fallen silent. Abruptly she did what my burned and swollen throat would not allow me to do. Her vomit stained her shift as it gushed from her lips and splashed on her bare foot.

"Was the meal to your liking?" The king's eyes held a glitter that I had never before seen.

So damaged was my mouth, I could not have spoken had I wished. I tried to catch Narisa's gaze, but her face held the vacancy of a newborn infant, and I realized that she no longer saw what transpired before her.

"It was a meager feast. I think you must still hunger."

One of the hooded torturers held my arms folded behind my back in such a way that I could not twist loose. The other grasped my left ear between his thumb and forefinger, and with a deft stroke of a knife severed it from my head, then tossed it onto the grill. The other ear followed. He used iron pincers to hold my nose while he cut it off, presumably to safeguard his fingers from the blade. These bits of my body were forced between my teeth and down my throat, so that I was compelled to swallow to keep from choking. My stomach made no effort to reject the meat. My ear-holes filled with blood, so that it became difficult to hear the king's words.

"What? Are you still hungry? Very well, you shall be satisfied."

They tore my blood-stained thawb and surwal from my body, leaving me naked save for my leather stockings and slippers. The torturer drew my prick and testicles out from between my thighs with the pincers and prepared to apply his knife.

"No. Use the shears."

For the first time, I screamed. Why the shears struck me with greater horror than the knife remains mysterious. It may have been the anticipation of having my tightly stretched prick snipped off like a lock of hair by their chill iron edges. Gratification filled the face of the king. He had been waiting for my scream. After I screamed the first time, it was easy to scream again and again. He remained until my prick and balls had been roasted and fed to me, then left with his advisor and his spy, taking Narisa with him. I do not believe she saw me as she was led out from the chamber. Her mind was elsewhere.

They cauterized my wounds with heated irons to stop the flow of blood. Then they burned off all the hair from my body, including my eyebrows and eyelashes, slashed open my cheeks so that I might have thrust my tongue through the holes had I wished, and branded me with the blunt points of the irons all across my chest and back. This continued for several hours, until the coals in the brazier had almost extinguished themselves. I passed in and out of a dreaming state, so that I knew only part of what was done to my body.

At some later time I awoke naked in a cell. Even my feet were bare. It was a part of the palace I had never seen. A thin layer of dirty straw covered the rough stone floor. The only light came through a slit high in the wall, for the iron-bound door of the cell lacked a window or other opening. In one corner rested a wooden bucket, and beside it a clay pitcher. Too weakened and racked with pain to sit up, I lay with my cheek against the coolness of the stone, peering around and feeling the fullness in my stomach. Though I tried to vomit, my perverse flesh refused to give up its nourishment. Hours later, when I could crawl, I found that the pitcher was filled with water. The bucket stood empty, but the stink of its former contents conveyed its intended use.

Three days and nights passed, marked by the fall of darkness and the coming of the light through the slot in the wall. My jailer brought no food, but the pitcher was refilled each morning, and the bucket emptied. The first time I pissed, I could not stifle a scream of agony. White pus spurted out before the urine. After that, the pain was less. On the second day my bowels emptied the remnant of the obscene food I had been forced to eat, and it was silently taken away and discarded. I began to

21

believe that the king intended I should starve to death in the cell, but he had another purpose.

Around noon of the fourth day the bolt of the door clicked, and crown prince Yanni entered bearing a brass oil lamp in his hand. He wrinkled his nose in disgust at the stench.

"Abdul? Come forward to the light where I can see you."

Someone laughed, a ghostly sound. Abdul? Who was Abdul? I knew no one of that name. Even so, I shuffled forward until the glow of the lamp fall across my face.

Yanni's eyes narrowed. He began to draw back, then caught himself and continued to stare with an expression of revulsion, and something more that I could not define.

"I knew nothing of what my father planned for you."

His words lacked meaning. I struggled to suppress the giggle that rose in my throat.

"You are to be exiled from Yemen. Never return to this land, or you will surely be put to death."

There was something I must ask. Desperately I searched for the thought. It eluded me like a fish in the shallows. At last I caught it.

"The princess?" The burned tissues of my throat turned the words into a croak.

Anger drove the uncharacteristic softness from his expression. I thought he would not reply, but finally he spoke.

"She will not be harmed."

He turned, and the door slammed shut behind him, leaving me once again in the dimness.

The hunger gnawed at me as I sat in the straw. Not since childhood had my stomach been so empty for so long. In the beam of light that slanted through the wall slit, I watched black beetles crawl around the rim of the bucket, feeding on the dregs of my waste. Unable to resist the temptation, I caught one and crunched it between my teeth. The taste was foul. I spat it out. Later, I chewed another, and sucked upon the mass of its body until it was dry, then let the hard parts of its shell and legs fall from my lips. I ate them all.

Someone was to be released. But who, and from where? The question did not seem important. I slept.

The sand dunes of the desert stretched like silver waves to the horizon beneath the light of the full moon. I walked along the crest of a dune, my bare feet sinking into the soft sand. The quiet of the night filled with a chittering, such as might be made by the wings of a thousand insects. It was all around me. I stood and turned in a circle but could see nothing. In the distance a shadow moved upon the sand. I walked toward it, straining my eyes to discern its shape. The chittering intensified. As I drew nearer, the shadow became the figure of a man shrouded in a long black cloak, the hood of his monkish robe pulled over his head. He walked with a slow pace, his face averted, and seemed lost in meditation. When I stood almost near enough to touch his shoulder, he turned and regarded me.

He was taller than any man I had ever seen, and exceedingly slender. A cowl of thin black silk covered his face, hiding his features but not obstructing his vision, for it is possible to see through the weave of silk when it is held close to the eye.

He raised his arm and pointed into the desert, the skin of his hand so black that it appeared to be gloved. Upon his bony fingers gleamed the jewels of several rings.

"What do you see?" His hollow voice held a slight sibilance, like the hiss of a serpent.

Staring into the distance, I tried to discern the thing he pointed at, but could see nothing apart from the moonlit dunes.

"A wasteland."

"Your eyes are open but you do not see."

I made no attempt to dispute the statement.

"What do you hear?"

The sound of insects filled the night.

"The chirping of beetles."

"Your ears are open but you do not hear."

The thought came to me that I should strangle him and steal his cloak to cover my nakedness. Echoing laughter filled the night. Suddenly, he stood behind me. I had not seen him move. He laid his hand on my shoulder, his fingers impossibly long and slender, and I felt a burning cold.

"This is my kingdom," he whispered into my ear.

He was gone. I turned around bewildered and saw him standing on the summit of a high dune some distance away. With labored steps I ascended the sand. He waited until I stood before him.

"What do you seek?"

"Knowledge."

His bony hand unhooked his cowl at the side and let the black silk fall away. Fear and wonder filled my heart. He had no face, but only a darkness that was like the shadow in the depths of a deep well.

"What is your name?"

I hesitated, my mind filled with confusion. Once, I had known the answer to this riddle, but I had forgotten it. The beetles tried to tell me with their chirps and buzzing. I almost understood, but still the name eluded me.

"You are Alhazred," he said in his hollow voice.

In fascination I continued to stare into the emptiness that was his face. Something flickered in the depths. Stars. His face was filled with distant stars. I reached out my hand to touch them.

The rattle and bang of the door awoke me from my nightmare. I blinked and shielded my eyes from the glare of the oil lamp held in the hand of my jailer, who stepped back to scratch his bald head as two men I had never seen before entered my cell. They wore the loose cream-colored garb of Bedouins and had faces like hawks beneath the hanging folds of their ghutras. At their waists, short straight swords dangled in worn scabbards from baldrics that looped over their shoulders.

Wordlessly, they took me by each arm and raised me to my feet, then dragged me out of the cell and along a corridor. My legs were stiff and would not carry my weight, but my captors did not pause. They carried me up a flight of stone steps and into a courtyard, where a two-wheeled cart drawn by a horse waited in the darkness. A chain with locking iron bands at its ends was put on my legs, and I was thrown without gentleness into the open cart. The chain was fixed at its middle with a padlock to an iron ring in the bed of the cart so that I could not escape.

They walked on either side of the horse, leading it by its bridle out the archway of the courtyard and through the deserted streets of Sana'a, silent save for the creaking of the wheels and the distant barking of dogs. Not a single word passed between them. I felt no impulse to speak or question where they might be taking me. Wherever the cart was going, it lay beyond my power to help or hinder. A fatalism, so absolute it almost stifled the urge to breathe, gripped my heart. What thing could they do to me more horrible than the indignities I had already endured?

The gatekeeper regarded me curiously as we passed beyond the wall of the city, but he did not challenge my silent hosts. Evidently he had received orders not to obstruct their exit or question their purpose. We continued along the road toward the east at a walking pace. As the light of dawn cast its pearl glow across the horizon, we came upon the encampment of a ragged caravan that was preparing for its departure. It consisted of no more than a dozen wagons and twice that many camels. The men of the caravan were dressed in the same desert thawbs as my captors. They ignored me as they went about loading their goods upon the backs of their animals. The women, shrouded about the shoulders in black abayas and head scarves and veiled in black boshiyas up to their eyes, cast me occasional glances, but did not speak. Only the children who ran about between the campfires pointed and laughed behind their hands.

The cart in which I rode was heavily laden with sacks and bales. This was a band of desert traders, and to them I was no more than an object they had been paid to transport from one place to another. I realized that I would find scant compassion among them. They had doubtlessly been told that I was a criminal sent into exile. To what strange city or port would they carry me? I wondered if they would sell me into slavery at the oar of a galley, or digging at the end of a pick in a salt mine. I would bring a poor price as a household servant, but I could still do work in spite of my disfigurement.

We traveled east along a little-used caravan road, beyond the border of Yemen and into the great wasteland that is known only as the Empty Space. Never in my life had I gone beyond the bounds of Yemen. I recognized the rolling sand dunes, higher than the tallest building, from my strange dream, but saw with a shock of wonder that beneath the light of the sun the sand was a most delicate pink, like the blush of a virgin's cheek. The heat became unbearable. The Bedouins stretched a canopy over the cart in which I rode, and I lay beneath its shade in a daze, watching the miles of desert unwind beneath the turning wooden wheels that shrieked at each rotation. The axle of the cart needed grease, but its protest went unheeded.

The Bedouins conserved their strength just as jealously as they husbanded their water. They never walked when they were able to ride, and seldom spoke unless to convey necessary information. Women and children they ignored, but they paid close attention to the health of their animals. After five or six days, I lost track of the passage of time. I was given just enough food and water to survive, but nothing more, not even a rag to cover my nakedness. My daily meal was a single piece of flat bread, which I gnawed greedily with my chipped and aching teeth. My wounds began to heal without infection in the open air. The slits in my cheeks closed and scabs covered them. My hair and beard began to grow back, and even my eyebrows.

The ruin of my manhood was absolute. When the dried blood began to flake away, I saw that everything was gone. All that remained was a wrinkled hole akin to a second anus. One night, lying in the cart and unable to sleep due to the biting of the flies that followed the beasts of the caravan like their shadows, I chanced to glance down between my legs, and what I saw illuminated in the flicker of a nearby campfire made me weep silently so that my chest heaved and tears ran down my cheeks. It was the first true sorrow over my condition that I had felt. I thought of Narisa, but strangely could not remember her face. In place of her features there was only a black shadow.

The desolation of the Empty Space stretched to the horizon in all directions. Heat rising from the sand made whirlwinds spring up and race with a dancing motion across the crests of the dunes, so that they almost appeared alive. For some reason they seemed to follow the road, as though watching the progress of the caravan. The road itself became invisible. It could be identified only because it was the sole way of progress between the dunes and the low rocky hills that thrust up among them. The horizon shimmered with silver, as though wet with the waves of some distant sea, but it was no more than a mirage. High above, vultures circled the caravan in the hope that one of the animals would sicken and die, but the tender care the Bedouins took of their beasts cheated them of their banquet.

One day when the sun was at its height, the chain was removed from my ankles and I was pulled from the cart. The caravan began to move forward. I stumbled after it, thinking that my captors wished me to walk for exercise, but one of them confronted me and pushed me backward so that I fell upon the sand.

"You stay here," he said, the first words spoken to me since my removal from my cell.

I looked around in bewilderment. There was nothing in sight, not even an outcropping of rock. The great dunes rolled endlessly across the world. I scrambled to my knees and clasped my hands in front of my breast, tears springing to my eyes.

"Please, let me come with you. Do not leave me here to die."

A trace of pity touched his harsh features.

"We do as we are commanded."

I understood. To defy the order of the king of Yemen was death. He had given instructions that I be taken into the midst of the Empty Space and released. The Bedouins did not dare disobey.

Knowing it was fruitless, I wrapped my arms around his ankles and begged for my life. He tried to pull away, and then kicked me in the face with his sandal when I would not release him. Leaning down, he grasped the ivory hilt of his dagger and pulled the blade half out of its sheath. His meaning was clear. If I followed the caravan, I would be killed and the vultures would get their feast.

I sat naked upon the road, my arms and legs spread loosely, salt blood dripping from my cut lip where I had been kicked, watching the wagons and camels of the caravan dwindle between the distant hills and vanish from view behind the rising heat mirages. Then I was alone.

Chapter 3

During the time of my madness, I was not aware that I was mad. I ran off the caravan route through the hollows between the dunes, babbling in words that belonged to no human language. I fell a hundred times, each time climbing wearily to my feet, until I had no strength to stand, and then crawled with the sun blazing down on my bare back. Strangely, my skin was not burned, not even the soles of my feet. Rolling on the ground covered me with a layer of dust that shielded my pale body from its blistering rays.

No water had passed my lips since early morning. Awareness of my peril pierced my madness, and I knew in a wordless way that if I did not find shelter I would surely die. The vultures circled ever lower, taunting me with the cooling touch of their swift shadows. Sweat ceased to spring from my skin, and I began to pant in short hot breaths. At last I collapsed and lay still, too weak to raise my hand and shield my eyes from the glare of the dunes.

Something moved across my unfocused view. I blinked and saw that it was a lizard, no longer than my finger. It sat upon the hot sand, staring at me with open mouth as though recognizing me. With quick motions of its legs and tail, it began to dig itself into the sand. In moments the sand covered it.

For a time I lay staring at the place it had vanished, no thought in my mind. Then I began to rock my body, pushing the sand away with my arms and legs as I had seen the lizard push the sand with its feet. Action gave me a sense of purpose. I realized what I was doing and began to move the sand with more efficient strokes. Several inches beneath the surface of the desert, it was cool against my skin. I piled the sand high all around my body until I lay in a shallow trench on my back, then began to cover my legs and torso with the sand. When only my face remained exposed, I put my left arm across my mouth and nose, closed my eyes, and used my right hand to pull the sand over me.

The thought came that I was burying myself while still alive. In a moment it was lost amid the chaos of my mind. I forced myself to breathe slow and shallow breaths against the skin of my arm, and slept.

In my dream the faceless man beckoned, and I followed him across the dunes toward the angled crescent of the waxing moon that hung near the horizon, its lower horn pointing eastward. The droning beetles spoke to me through the darkness, whispering blasphemous secrets just beyond the boundary of my comprehension. I felt the power of their buzzing words, but each time I grasped for them with my mind they flew away in all directions. When I fell behind, the tall man waited patiently, his hands folded within the sleeves of his robe. Through the gap of his cloak I saw that it resembled the robes of the Christian monks who sometimes came from the west to convert the faithful to the strange teachings of the prophet Jesus. Years ago I had seen such a monk stoned to death in the marketplace at Sana'a, his emaciated body completely hidden beneath a pile of cobblestones and potsherds except for his cheek and staring, sightless eye. I remembered the blueness of his eye that was akin to the sky at its zenith.

The hooded figure stood upon the crest of a low dune and pointed beneath the horns of the moon at a cleft in a line of rocky hills. Through the gap ran a caravan road. It glowed with silver like a winding river against the darker ground of the desert.

Pain broke my mind from the dream. Something sharp cut the flesh of my palm, and for a moment I was again beneath the knives of the torturers. I clenched my fingers, and felt in their grasp a writhing, twisting serpent. With a cry I sat up from my bed of sand and shook the dust off my face. Twilight paled the sky. In my left fist I saw that I clutched the neck of a vulture. It squawked its fury and pecked with its hooked beak at my hand, pounding its wings against my arm. My fingers tightened, and I heard the bones of its neck crunch. The beating of its wings ceased.

Drawing it close to my face, I bit through its neck and sucked the spurting fountain of its blood. It was foul with salt but so dry was my body it had the sweetness of well water on my cracked lips. When I could suck no more blood from its neck, I bit off one of its feet and used its talons to cut open its belly. I ate its heart and liver before discarding the carcass.

Stars brightened like windblown sparks in the darkening sky. The thin crescent of the waxing moon made me remember my dream. Strengthened by my sleep and by the blood of the bird, I walked toward it. Unseen night insects droned their approval. Somewhere in the distance a desert fox barked for its mate. The cooling air made walking less of an ordeal. At times I glanced up from the ground to glimpse the tall figure in black disappear over the crest of the dune before me. I ran to confront the fleeting shadow, but always the emptiness of the desert mocked me.

Panting to catch my breath, I paused on the crest of a dune and spied in the south beneath the horns of the moon the cleft between the hills of my dream. The caravan road was not illuminated with silver, but I knew it must run through the gap, since there was no other way to progress with wagons past the high dunes except between the hills. I stumbled and slid down the slope to the edge of the road. At my right hand, the road wound westward to the border of Yemen, from which I had come. To the left, it passed between the hills and bent itself eastward into the depths of the wasteland. I judged its direction from the star Mismar that is set like a nail in the heavens, around which turns the glittering canopy of the firmament.

Nothing awaited me in the land of my birth but death. I turned toward the left-hand path and followed the road between the hills. As I passed between them, I noticed a shadow on the ground. To my crazed imagination it looked first like a giant spider poised to jump, and then like the severed head of a man, but as I drew near I saw that it was a leather water skin. Falling to my knees with a cry, I grasped it up in my hands. It was heavy to lift, and fat.

A Bedouin of the caravan, perhaps the man who had warned me against following, had felt a moment of compassion and had left the water behind on the road for me to discover. It was a treasure more precious than gold. I wept at this simple act of charity, cursing the weakness of my spirit that squandered the moisture of my tears in the dry dust. After my tears ceased to fall, I slung the strap of the water skin over my head and shoulder so that it hung at my right hip, and continued to walk eastward in the wheel ruts and camel tracks of the caravan.

When the paling of the stars alerted me to the coming of day, I sought shelter from the sun beneath a ledge of stone that would cast a shadow over the depression beneath its lip. As I lay down and prepared to make the water skin my pillow, a hiss betrayed the presence of a viper. It coiled its slender body like a necklace of shining black pearls, and reared its head with opened mouth. Again it expressed annoyance that its resting place had been violated. Some caprice of madness kept me from grabbing up a stone to kill it. I lay and watched it with sleepy eyes, my body motionless. When it felt no threat, it gradually undulated its way nearer, until it lay coiled against the skin of my thigh. We slept together, and I did not dream. When I awoke at dusk, the serpent had already departed to hunt for prey. I realized that I must do the same, or I would starve.

To the casual eye, the caravan road appeared barren, but this was an illusion. In comparison to the emptiness of the dunes, its path lay littered with useful items. I found a bright silk scarf striped with red and green, trodden into the sand, that was ragged on only one corner, and tied it about my neck. A dried melon rind retained some of its sweetness. In my extremity of hunger I ate all of it, even its tough outer skin. Hidden in the ashes of a campfire I discovered a bone that I judged to be from a goat, and cracked it between two rocks for its marrow. It was not enough, but for a short time it took away the gnawing emptiness. Nothing else remained between the stones of the hearth but bits of charcoal. Firewood, carried into the desert on wagons or the backs of camels, was too precious to leave behind.

As dawn approached, I searched for a natural shelter along the side of the road but found nothing. I was forced to waste the strength of my body building a cave with flat stones. It was barely large enough to lie in, but it shadowed me from the sun as I slept. The chinks in its sides allowed the breeze to pass freely through, making it more comfortable than expected. I rose after sunset refreshed, but my hunger was so great that it caused my belly to cramp in agony. Each time this happened, I was forced to crouch with my hands on my knees and wait for the pain to pass, panting as though giving birth.

The yelp of jackals through the darkness alerted me to a new prize, though what it might be I could not guess. The sounds drew me off the road and into the hollow of a small valley. In the moonlight I watched two jackals dance around a mound of rocks and scratch the ground with their paws. I approached carefully, hoping to kill one of the beasts with a thrown stone, but their ears were keen, and they fled with yips of frustration over the crest of a hill. Gazing down at the mound, which was marked with a large oblong rock at its head and another at its foot, I realized what had attracted them. Their noses had scented carrion. It was a grave. Someone had died upon the road and been buried here with scant ceremony.

My eager fingers pulled the stones aside and dug into the soft soil. The body was not far beneath the surface. Had it been buried deeper, the jackals might have failed to locate it, but who wasted strength digging in the desert for the benefit of the dead? It was wrapped in a shroud of white cotton sewn with coarse thread along its seams, and tied tight with lengths of cord. Trembling with eagerness, I untied the cords and opened the shroud. As I had hoped, it was the corpse of a man, and his relatives had dressed him for Paradise. I pulled his bloodless face toward mine and in the light of the moon recognized him as one of the Bedouins of the caravan that had abandoned me. I could not be far behind their wagons, since his flesh was quite fresh. The memory came that two days before my separation from the caravan this man suffered a sudden numbness in the left side of his body and had been unable to walk without help.

He was near my height, perhaps a trifle shorter and broader through the chest. I stripped off his cream-colored desert thawb and removed my water skin to put it on. Though frayed at the cuffs and hem, the cotton was clean and unpatched. His family had dressed him in his best attire for the grave. As expected, he wore no undergarments. It was not the custom of desert-faring men to cover their legs with the Persian surwal, which they considered a clothing fit only for women. I debated whether to place his ghutra over my head, then at last set the diagonally folded square of white cotton aside with its double-looped black agal. I have always preferred to leave my head uncovered, in defiance of fashion. The knots in the laces of his sandals came free with difficulty, and I discovered that they were slightly large for my feet. I drew the soft stockings of tan leather over my calves, and laced the sandals around my ankles. The touch of leather felt strange after so many days barefoot.

From a beaded and embroidered baldric of woven red wool that had been placed beside the corpse in the grave hung a dagger in its undyed leather sheath. The bone hilt of the old knife was cracked, and its blade well worn from years of use, but it bore a razor edge. It was an easy matter to cut with it several squares of cotton from the shroud. Such rags might be useful. I kissed its broad straight blade in my joy before returning it to its sheath, and slung its woolen strap over my head so that it dangled against my left hip. The water skin I hung on the opposite side, so that the baldric and the strap of the water skin crossed on my chest.

Coins jingled within a hidden pocket at the left breast of the thawb. It took me moments to locate its mouth, easily reached through the open neck of the garment that extended down almost to my navel. I drew them out and regarded them. Three silver Sassanian dirhams of the smallest of the three sizes, bearing the profile of the late shah Yazdegerd the Third. They were all good coins that showed scarcely any sign of clipping at their edges. What caprice had caused the family to bury silver with the corpse I could not imagine, but I reflected that I might use them on a future occasion to buy food or water. The same consideration made me decide to transfer the gold ring on the left hand of the corpse to my own hand.

The plain gold band would not come loose from its finger after much tugging, so I used the dagger. I stared at the red stump of the detached finger, turning it in my hands until the whiteness of the bone was visible at its center, and a terrible hunger rose within me. Still, I hesitated. No man could do what I contemplated. Yet I had already eaten human flesh, and therefore could no longer call myself a man. With a cry of surrender I fastened my teeth in the flesh and chewed it from the bone. After the finger was stripped clean, I cut a piece of meat from the inside of the thigh of the corpse and ate until my belly was full.

The night air felt strangely thick around my head as I feasted. I glanced up but could see nothing. It was as though a thousand moths pressed their soft wings against my face, in a futile attempt to stifle my breath. Petulantly, I waved my arm through the air above my head as though to drive away a fly, and the smothering sensation lessened. I sensed the presence of unseen creatures but gave them little thought. If they lacked the power to kill me, they were unimportant. Using a large stone from the grave, I cracked open the skull of the corpse and sampled its brain. As I had hoped, it was filled with wetness, almost like the juice of a ripe melon, but oily on the tongue rather than sweet. There was enough moisture in the skull to keep me alive for a day. It was a useful matter to know.

After cutting enough meat from the thighs to last me two days, and wrapping it in one of the cotton rags from the shroud, I left the remainder of the body for the jackals. It was unfortunate that I could not carry more, but in the heat of the desert the meat would have spoiled before I could have eaten it in any case. The knife was a great prize, as was the thawb and leather sandals. The grave had proven to be a treasure trove of riches. My water skin was growing slack, and somehow I would have to find a way to replenish it before the passage of several days, but at least I would not starve before I died of thirst.

The road led ever deeper into the Empty Space. There must be wells along its length, or no caravan could survive the journey. The prospect of a well drew me eastward like a lodestone. There was also hope that water could be stolen from the caravan that followed the road ahead, were I able to overtake it. I traveled by night, the caravan by day, and the days were longer than the nights in the spring of the year. Still, the Bedouins moved slowly, unwilling to exhaust their beasts by pressing them forward under the heat of the sun, and they paused to eat and rest. They wasted part of the day making camp at evening, and another part breaking camp at dawn.

By the sky glow of early morning, while ranging along a ridge of hills that followed the road, I saw the black shadow of a cave entrance between two boulders, at the end of a narrow valley. A deep cave held the prospect of water and could not be overlooked, but whether deep or shallow it would provide shelter from the sun. Since other creatures might well have had the same intention, I drew my knife and held it in my hand as I forced my body forward between the boulders and into the darkness. The roof of the cave pressed low, but the cave extended far into the hill, sloping downward. The chance for water seemed good. The entrance to the cave was located at the low end of the valley, and any rain would flow toward it. Once collected in the depths of the cave in a pool, it would persist for months.

The smell of water that rose up from the depths filled me with such joy I cried out in triumph. It was curious that even without a nose I could discern scents. Whatever part the torturers had cut off, it was not the part required for smelling. Even had I not been able to smell it, I would have known the presence of water by the dampness in my throat as I breathed. A bend in the cave shut out the last faint glow of light from the entrance. My lust to rush forward was tempered by my fear of smashing my head on a projecting point of rock. I continued to wriggle deeper into the passage on my belly, soiling the cleanliness of my newly stolen thawb in the dust that lay on the cave floor.

The pupils of my eyes widened to the darkness. In the depths ahead, a faint glow reflected from the walls, so pallid that it vanished when looked at directly, but returned when viewed from the edge of sight. It became stronger as I approached, a greenish-yellow hue like the color of festering pus. A sound reached my ears, more welcome than any other I had ever heard, the drip of water into a pool. My passion made me intemperate, and I slid rather than crawled the last dozen feet down a slope that opened into a cavern. The natural dome of the space was high enough for standing. In a depression in the center of its floor lay a pool of clear water. Drops condensing upon the dome fell into the pool and disturbed its mirror surface with rings.

Every part of the ceiling and walls, and much of the floor, was covered by a glowing carpet of fungi. I put my hand to it and found it moist to the touch, with the softness of fur. As my palm brushed it, I heard a faint crackling such as might be made by dry grasses thrown onto a fire, but so faint that it could scarcely be distinguished even in the deep silence of the cave. The crackling produced a fine orange dust that hung in the air above the stems of the fungi. I touched one stem and saw the small ball at its end break open and emit the dust, which had the pleasing scent of spice. Amid the stalks of glowing fungi moved spiders of the purest white, in size no larger than the ball of the thumb. As the body of a spider brushed the stalks, the spore pods at their ends split and showered dust over the spider's back and legs.

In my fascination, I forgot the pool of water for a time. Plucking a few stalks of the fungi, I put them into my mouth. The taste was bitter and burned my tongue, so I spat them out without chewing them. One of the white spiders crawled onto my finger and over my hand. It made no attempt to bite, even when I poked at it. Its back was covered with a layer of the orange dust. Reflecting that it might provide a source of nourishment in time of need, I put it into my mouth and chewed it. The taste was rich and resembled the flavor of almonds. I swallowed, then ate another spider, and a third. Caution made me stop. It would be best not to consume more than a few spiders, until the experiment revealed whether or not they were poisonous.

Cupping my hand, I dipped it into the pool and brought the water to my lips. It was pure and cool, with a faint sweetness on the tongue, as fine as any water I had ever tasted. By comparison, the brackish water of the Bedouins was like camel piss. I emptied the rest of the contents of the water skin into a hollow in one corner of the cavern and submerged the skin in the pool to fill it. Then I lowered my lips to the pool and drank until my stomach could hold no more.

By the glow of the fungus I saw my face for the first time and jerked my head away, heart racing. My appearance was worse in its reality than had been painted by my imagination. The dried and scabby skin of my face, stretched tight over the cheekbones and jaw, had the gauntness of death, and the illusion of a skull come to life was enhanced by the gaping black hole where my beautiful nose had resided, and the lack of hair and ears. Unwilling but resolute, I forced myself to gaze long at my reflection. I must know what others saw when they looked at me. No wonder the children of the caravan had laughed behind their hands.

Weariness overcame my body. I withdrew from the pool and found a bare ledge of rock upon which to sleep. The damp of the cavern made me shiver, and it amused me to think that it was cooler than I would have wished, after so recently enduring the killing heat of the desert. The spiders posed no threat. They did not leave the carpet of fungus, and in any case showed no trace of aggression. They had never been hunted and knew nothing of how to defend themselves. So it is with all soft and coddled creatures. So I was myself until the judgment of King Huban descended upon me. I felt pity for the innocence of the frail white things as I drifted into uneasy sleep.

In my dream I stood in the open desert beneath the sun, not naked but clothed in the garment of the dead man, and watched a spinning column of dust approach. Its dancing motions aroused only curiosity, until I realized that it moved directly toward where I stood. Then I tried to run from it, but the spinning pillar was faster. It roared as it approached with the howling voice of a demon, and glancing over my shoulder as I fled, I saw the brightness of countless eyes within its serpentine body. The column of wind enveloped me and bore me upward to the heavens.

I found myself standing unharmed in the center of a round chamber with a floor of black glass and walls of roughly cut stones that curved together overhead to form a pointed dome. From the center of the dome hung down a barbed lance of black metal. Its base appeared firmly fixed into the stonework, but I moved from beneath its point with unease. It radiated a kind of black light no brighter than starlight that made the air dance. As my eyes grew accustomed to this dim illumination, I noticed shifting shadows in the floor, and bent closer to look.

With a cry of fear, I leapt away and pressed my back against the wall, seeking to grip the stones with my fingertips and lift my feet. Beneath the floor was a vast chamber larger than the greatest cavern. Were the glass of the floor to shatter, the fall would be fatal, yet there was nowhere else to stand. I peered down in fascination, standing on my toes with the wall at my back. Dimly through the dark glass, tiny figures moved. I observed these vague specks as does a man who towers like a giant over the mound of ants and watches their insignificant comings and goings, before dashing down his heel to obliterate them. They were ranked in circular bands in a kind of amphitheater, but so great was the distance, of their appearance or purpose I could discern nothing.

The air at the center of the chamber, directly beneath the barbed lance, shimmered like rising heat and became a cloud of black mist. Or it may be that the mist was always there, and in my fascination for the chamber beneath the floor I merely failed to notice. This sooty cloud pulsated and grew larger, descending to the floor, where it assumed the shape of the faceless man who haunted my dreams, seated in an ornate chair of gleaming ebony. Again, I looked from side to side for a door. It was a futile gesture. There was no door.

"You have unlocked one gate," he said in his hollow, hissing tones. "Swear allegiance to me, and all other gates will swing wide."

"Why do you care for my allegiance? I am nothing to you."

"I collect men. Once I gathered other things to my service, but now, in this time, I collect men."

"Are you a god?" I asked in wonder, greatly fearing to hear the answer.

He made a scornful sound in his throat.

"Your gods dance beneath my feet at my pleasure. I am much more than a god of this sphere."

A memory came into my mind, a fragment from a book that I had read years before, a book of mad fantasy and necromantic spells. It had been written by a Jew at Babylon during the time of the captivity of that people, but the name of the scribe escaped me. Only a part of a single fable remained, the story of a race of gods who were not gods, and who were said to rule the gods of earth and to make them dance at their pleasure. It was curious that such an obscure fable should rise in my thoughts at this moment.

He lifted his arm, all except the fingers of his hand concealed within his long sleeve, and I shrank away in fear, but some power compelled me to walk toward his throne on stiffened knees. When I stood at his feet, he reached toward me. His fingernails were black and elongated, like the talons of a hawk. Using the tip of his first finger, he scratched the skin of my forehead so that my blood ran down on either side of the hole that had been my nose.

"By this mark my worshippers shall know you as one of my own."

"What is your name, lord?" I asked, my voice quavering.

He reached up to unhook his black silk caul, and let it fall from the dark well of his face. I stared at the stars in its depths. Something stirred there, approaching upward from the blackness with terrifying haste. Before I could draw away, a million flying black beetles erupted from the shadow and surrounded me in a spinning column. Their droning wings thundered in my ears. I heard the dark man speak, but his words were overwhelmed by the sound of wings.

Chapter 4

I woke in the spider cavern, the soft drip of the water echoing in my ears. My body felt refreshed, a sure indication that I had slept many hours. Dusk could not be long away. For some reason, I hesitated to piss within the cavern, and decided to wait until I reached the entrance to the cave, where I would lie until the coming of night. There was a lightness to my head, as though I had drunk half a bottle of wine, and my tongue tingled. If it was an effect of the spiders I had consumed, it was uncommonly pleasant.

Rising to my feet, I untied the silk kerchief from my neck and shook out its wrinkles above the rock that had served as my bed. My body swayed slightly, but it was not difficult to retain my balance. I began to collect spiders from the walls of the cavern, laying them on the outspread cloth and slapping them lightly with my hand to kill them without destroying their bodies. In a short while over a hundred spiders lay upon the striped silk, their legs curled under their bodies in death. I tied up the cloth with care to form a purse and placed it within an inner pocket of my thawb. The desert robe contained four pockets, two in each breast arranged one above the other.

When I crawled from the cavern and up the long channel of the cave, I discovered with surprise that dusk was falling. The entire span of the day I had slept without waking. I emerged and relieved my bladder, then sat for a time watching the stars appear one by one in the sky. The world seemed strangely altered, the air more alive, the stones and sand softly glowing. With unsteady steps I left the valley and made my way to the caravan road. I stopped on the side of a hill overlooking the road and stared down at it in wonder. The road glowed bright silver, as though it were a channel of water flowing beneath the moon. A desert mouse ran past, and I saw that its body also glowed silver. I raised my hand to my face. Light danced upon my fingers, faint but impossible to deny.

The urge to laugh was almost too strong to suppress. It would not be wise to surrender to it. Sounds carried far across the desert, and who knew what might be hunting in the darkness? I descended to the road and followed it with slow steps eastward, pausing from time to time to turn myself in a complete circle and gaze in admiration at the subtle alteration in the world. There was no danger of wandering off the road through carelessness. It shone like a beacon.

A flicker upon the sands drew my attention to the north. It danced and floated, a cloud of moonlight that changed its shape moment by moment as it moved across the desert with the irregular darts and pauses of a butterfly. Never had I seen any similar creature, nor did I remember hearing such a thing described. The thought came that it must be some kind of djinn.

As I watched, my eyes distinguished its form from the obscuring glow. Elongated legs that folded beneath its haunches allowed it to hop across the sand. A large head with expanded mobile ears like those of a bat surmounted its slender body, and framed enormous black eyes and a wide mouth filled with needle-like teeth. The forelegs of the djinn were gracefully tapered, its hands like those of a woman. It was a creature of the airy element, beautiful in its delicacy. I gazed at it in admiration as it hopped and darted nearer. It became aware of my attention, and its movements quickened as though with interest. While I continued to walk along the road it circled me, always remaining at a distance as though attracted yet at the same moment frightened by my awareness of its presence.

It was to be a night of surprises. Walking around a bend in the road, I saw standing beside a small mound of stones the figure of a woman. Her body glowed even as mine. She stood naked with her back to me, unaware of my approach. As I drew near, the strangeness of her nature revealed itself. Through the glowing mist of her transparent torso I was able to distinguish the rocks that lay beyond her on the desert.

Stopping behind her almost near enough to touch, I spoke. She trembled and slowly turned. Her face lacked all expression, and her open eyes showed only the whites, without their centers. Her lips parted and a faint sound came forth. I leaned nearer to hear. She stepped toward me and raised her hand to touch my face before I could draw back, but her hand passed through the flesh and bone of my head. I felt it go through me like a cold splash of water. Again she reached out, and put her hand through my chest. Her fingers brushed my heart but did me no harm. With an expression of regret, or perhaps disappointment, she slowly turned back to face the mound of stones at her feet.

She was a ghost, and the mound her grave. Never before had I seen a ghost, yet I felt unafraid. What could not touch my skin threatened little harm. I realized that my ability to see her must be due to the white spiders I had consumed the previous morning, and that the same was true for the darting djinn that watched and circled. I passed my hand through her naked back. She shuddered but did not step away, as though lacking the strength to respond. How many years had she stood alone, guarding her remains in the night? The grave was old, its stones scattered and weathered, almost hidden by sand. Even so, it might contain something of value.

When I had thrown aside the large stones, I drew my dagger and dug into the sand. It had packed beneath the stones over time and came away in pieces that crumbled in my hands. The ghost of the woman became agitated. She tried to grasp my shoulders and pull me away, but her hands passed through my body. Her shrieks of frustration sighed in my ears like the wind. I ignored her and went on with my digging until I exposed the shroud of the corpse. It ripped as I drew it from the hole, spilling its burden of bones. The grave was very old. With disappointment, I picked through the bones for any pieces of gold or silver. The grave clothes of the corpse had rotted away. Any jewelry of base metals had corroded to nothingness with the years. There was no gold.

A cloud of light surrounded me, pressing over my face and stifling my breath like a layer of cloth. I recognized the sensation, having felt it before after opening the grave of the Bedouin. The djinn had wrapped its arms around me and was pressing its hands over my mouth and the ruin of my nose in an attempt to suffocate me. With a shrug of annoyance, I cast it off and went on with my search, but it returned like a buzzing fly, pressing its body through mine. At last, I reached the end of my patience and stood.

"You want the corpse?" I asked the spirit. "Very well, take it."

The creature appeared to understand me. At once it ceased its futile efforts to stifle my breath and descended on the pile of brown bones. The ghost gave out a piteous wail and tried to push the djinn out of the grave, but the djinn ignored her. As it passed its slender fingers through the bones, I saw a golden mist arise from the bones and enter the spirit's gaping mouth. For a moment the mist swirled within the gaunt torso of the spirit, like smoke in a bottle, contrasting with the more silver radiance of its own essence, then it faded and spread through the djinn's limbs, making them glow more brightly. The ghost of the woman cried out once and vanished upward into the night sky in a streak of light.

"At least one of us has fed."

Disappointment at the lack of any useful object in the grave made me bitter. Leaving the spirit to digest its meal, I continued along the road, my head still spinning pleasantly from the effects of the spiders. I had not walked a dozen steps when I saw it from the corner of my eye, hopping in graceful bounds on its long hind legs as it kept pace beside me. I ignored the creature, thinking that it would lose interest and go away, but it began to dance in circles around me. After walking more than an hour, I stopped and faced it.

"What do you want with me?"

As though it had waited for me to speak, it loped nearer with graceful little hops and put its face close to mine, staring directly into my eyes. I saw that its face, and indeed its entire body, was covered in a fine fur. Its eyes had no lids, and were completely black and nearly as large around as my fists. Its lipless mouth quirked up at the corners, revealing its curved teeth, like the teeth of a comb.

"I may be ugly," I said, "but you are no houri of Paradise yourself."

It moved its face forward without warning so that its head passed into my own. I cried out in disgust and tried to pull my head away, but it held my neck and head in its arms and followed my motions, so that its spectral head remained embedded in mine. Dimly but clearly, I heard in my thoughts a single whispered word.

Friend.

I stopped struggling to free my head from its embrace, since the effort was futile.

"Did you speak?"

Friend to wanderer.

"I don't need any friends."

Useful to wanderer.

"How can you be useful?"

I will teach you. I know many secrets. Many places of concealment. Hidden things.

My interest quickened. With sufficient wealth I could buy the things I needed to survive from passing caravans, and would not need to scavenge the desert.

"Do you mean treasure? You know were treasure is hidden?"

Yes, if you wish. Treasures.

"What do you want in return for leading me to these treasures?"

You dig the earth. You move the stones.

Understanding came, and I felt the wordless affirmation of the djinn. It fed on corpses, or on the lingering life essence of corpses, but it possessed no physical body with which to dig them from their graves.

"Why can't you just pass your head and arms into the earth, as you pass them through my flesh?"

Holy words seal the ground.

In the books of necromancy I had studied, it was written that words were tangible to the djinn, and might be used as barriers or as weapons. A thing described in the correct words became real to the fleshless beings who dwelt in the realm of air that encircled our world. The words of the Koran must possess potency against devils. This surprised me, as I had always dismissed the holy texts sung by the mullahs as the meaningless diversion of fools.

"Very well. Show me a treasure, and the next grave I encounter will be opened for you."

No treasure lies here. Soon we reach treasure.

"Where is this treasure to be found?"

In the city between the hills.

"There are no cities in the Empty Space. What city?"

The city has no name.

My cynical laughter floated on the night breeze.

"You want me to continue feeding you, but you give me only promises in return?"

A sense of protest stirred in my mind. The dignity of the creature was offended by my lack of faith. With my hand I batted away its assurances as though they were beetles buzzing around my head.

"First show me treasure, then I will open a grave for you."

When I continued to ignore its thoughts in my head, the creature uncoiled its arms from my neck and pulled its face from my skull. It hopped gracefully to the ground and slipped away into the desert, pausing to look back at me.

"First the treasure, then the grave," I repeated.

Almost sadly, as though my words had injured its feelings, it darted and flitted behind the dunes and was lost from my sight.

As I walked onward alone, the silver glow of the road began to dim, and the dizziness that I had felt since waking left me. The night regained its customary appearance. I raised my hand in front of my face, but my fingers no longer gave off their own light. If the djinn hopped on the road behind me, it was invisible to my normal vision. The effect of the spiders persisted for less than a day. Idly, I wondered if I would still be able to hear the djinn speak were it to thrust its head through mine, even without the influence of the spiders.

The light breeze fell still. A faint sound made me stop and listen. Ahead a human voice murmured through the darkness, and a camel grunted. Taking care to walk silently, I climbed a hill near the road for a better vantage. Upon the black expanse of sand beside the road several campfires glittered like a scattering of rubies. The fires were small—no caravan made large cooking fires in a land without wood, where anything that burned must be carried by cart or on the backs of beasts. Yet by their light I saw several dozen large wagons and many smaller carts, numerous camels, and as many horses. It was not the caravan that had abandoned me, but a more prosperous group of merchants. Since I had not seen their tracks on the road, I knew it must be making its way west, to Yemen.

Descending the far side of the hill, I walked southward away from the road and into the moonlit dunes, then made my way east until I crouched behind the encampment, where the arc of wagons shielded me from the light of the fires. There would doubtless be many useful things to steal, if I could approach undetected. No dog barked. Since I was not able to move over the loose sand and pebble-strewn ground with absolute silence, there must be no dogs in the caravan, a token of good fortune from the fates. Most of the caravan lay sleeping, the poor on the ground in their blankets, the more prosperous in their wagons. Only a few men sat huddled before one of the fires, muttering to each other as they shared a leather-covered flask of wine.

Making my way to the wheel of a large wagon, I stood in its shadow and listened for several minutes. Nothing stirred within its cover. I sniffed the air. It was laden with a curious sweet fragrance. The point of my dagger easily penetrated the thick felt. I sawed the blade back and forth slowly to avoid noise, then climbed onto the hub of the wheel and pushed my head through the slit. Within the wagon it was very dark. Had the enhancement of my vision caused by the white spiders endured, I would have been able to see its contents easily, for the spiders made radiant not only anything having life, but anything formerly alive such as the very wood of the wagon, or anything possessed of life force, such as the djinn.

My eyes adapted to the nearly absolute darkness, which was broken only by a beam of light from the moon that shone between the imperfectly closed curtains at the front of the wagon. I saw an elongated box of wood that filled the bed of the wagon, and beside it two simple stools, both empty. Upon a small table the stub of a candle stood, most of its length melted to a puddle of wax at the base of its brass holder. The tang of the burnt wick still hung on the air, mingled with the overpowering sweetness of honey. Curiosity would not permit me to leave the wagon without learning its contents. It was not difficult to squirm through the slit in the covering. The flat lid of the box had been fastened with only two nails, neither of great length. I pried it gently up to avoid the protest of the wood as the nails pulled loose and slid it aside.

Within lay a bundle of linen that could be nothing else but a burial shroud, yet it was unnaturally bulky, as though layered beneath its surface. I slit away its binding cords and cut it open. The exhalation of honey and spices that welled up from the rent cloth almost made me retch, it was so overpowering. Beneath it was a body entirely swathed in bands of linen that were saturated in honey and spice. I smelled cinnamon clearly, and myrrh. My hands quickly became covered in the sticky honey, which had partially dried to a kind of paste. As I unwrapped the corpse, I cursed silently and periodically scrapped my fingers clean with the edge of my blade.

The unwinding swaths removed from the head revealed the face of a young woman of beautiful countenance, aged no more than eighteen years. Her flesh was perfectly preserved, so that she looked as though she had died only moments before. I realized the purpose of the honey. A wealthy family transported the corpse of their daughter to Yemen for burial, and the honey was intended to keep the body from decay on the long journey across the desert. I could not help but admire how well it fulfilled its service. Had I still retained my manhood, I might have been moved to lust, but in my butchered condition the only motive I felt in my heart was greed. With quick tugs at the windings, I exposed the hands of the corpse. The fingers of the girl were covered with gold rings, in many of which glittered pearls and jewels.

It was easier to cut through their thin bands with the point of my knife than cut off her fingers. Even the rings were sticky. Brush them as I would on the outer covering of the shroud, I could not get them completely clean. Reflecting that the sand of the desert would scour them, if I hung them in the wind while I slept, I cut a small square of the outer shroud and wrapped it around the rings. It needed no tie to keep it closed. More impatiently, I cut through the swaths around the breast of the girl and was rewarded with a silver medallion inscribed with holy texts. No doubt her family had placed it there to ward off the djinn. How effective it might be against spirits I could not guess, but it held no power over me. I scrapped as much of the sticky mess from it as would come away and forced it into a pocket of my robe.

Almost I turned away from the corpse, then thought to cut the shroud from her feet. Around each of her slender ankles glittered a fine chain of gold. Nicking through the gold links with my knife, I peeled them away and thrust them into my pocket against the honeyed mass of the medallion. Her feet and ankles were so graceful in their shape, I could not resist tracing their outlines with my fingertips. Narisa had just such ankles as these, but her anklets had been of silver, with tiny silver bells that tinkled as she walked. A pang touched my heart. It was the first time since my expulsion from Yemen that I remembered the loveliness of my beloved.

The only other prize in the wagon was the tinder box and flint that had been used to light the candle on the table. There was little on the open desert to burn, but the ability to make fire might prove useful were I able to find a store of candles, or an oil lamp. The wax stub on the table, though no longer than the width of two fingers, would burn for another hour. It slid easily into the same pocket that held the tinderbox. I took one last lingering gaze at the face of the corpse in the moonlight. She possessed a great beauty and would not have been out of place in the harem of King Huban. Yet here she lay, in the morning of her life, a corpse wrapped in honey, whereas I, wretched though I might be, continued to draw breath. Wondering at the mystery of being, I squeezed out the rent in the side of the wagon.

The few other covered wagons that I could approach without danger of immediate discovery were all occupied. Their inhabitants snored or stirred restlessly in sleep. The wagon with the corpse had been placed some distance away from the others, making it easier to approach. No one wished to remain near the dead, except perhaps the mother or brother or sister who had burned the candle and sat chanting prayers over the honey-wrapped corpse, and even that conscientious watcher had chosen to sleep elsewhere. I wondered if the ghost of the girl had been present in the wagon while I robbed her body.

The caravan proved as rich a prize as I had hoped, but there would be other prizes. It was an easy matter to steal from those who thought themselves alone in the desert, even for a man new to the trade. Another epithet to add to my name, whatever it might be. The name given me in my dream by the faceless walker across the dunes returned to me. Very well, I would be Alhazred, eunuch, monster, cannibal, grave-robber, and now, thief. What other titles would increase this list before my days ended?

Thinking bitter thoughts, I almost passed without notice a shadow upon the dunes, and would have done so had it not stirred as my eyes slid across it. I stopped and stared, and even then it appeared no more than a pool of darkness. I prepared to continue on, when something gleamed in the shadow. It was a moment before my mind identified it—the reflection of starlight in an eye. With an instinctive snarl I drew my dagger and backed away, holding the broad blade where it might be easily seen. Other shadows began to creep toward me across the sand. They were all around, closing inward. I turned, my teeth barred.

My eyes fixed upon the nearest of the shadows, but my mind refused for several seconds to make sense of its shape. At last, as though with reluctance, its form emerged under the moonlight. It was shaped like a man, but smaller and wizened, with slender limbs and a distended belly, a blackened corpse sprung to unnatural life. In its mouth sharp yellow teeth gleamed, and black claws adorned its elongated fingers. The nakedness of its body showed that it was male. A fragment of fable arose from my childhood, concerning ghouls that haunted the places of the dead, and had the ability to move unseen through the night. Now that I discerned the shape of the thing, I saw it in all its hideous clarity, and wondered that I had been about to pass it unaware.

A cry would bring the men from the caravan to investigate, but when they discovered the state of the dead noblewoman and found her rings in my thawb, they would undoubtedly kill me. The ghouls seemed to know that I would not raise an alarm. At least a dozen surrounded the place where I stood slashing the air with my knife in futile threat. They showed no fear of the blade, and in truth their claws were fearsome weapons, as deadly as any hooked talon of the hawk. More than any other thing, the silence of the creatures unnerved me. I considered crying out and testing my fortune with the men of the caravan, but it was too late—one loud sound and they would fall upon me and tear me to pieces. The men with their lamps would discover only bloody chunks of flesh on the sand.

As I turned to ward off a female ghoul that tried to creep nearer than the others, the heavy silver medallion I had stripped from the corpse of the young woman knocked against my breast. Instinctively, I thrust my hand into the pocket and drew it forth, holding it aloft in the moonlight. Soft hisses of dismay filled the night. The creatures put their taloned fingers up to shield their faces and backed away. Whether there was power in the charm, or whether my use of it caused them to fear it as an unknown weapon, I could not guess, but I thanked the fates that I had taken it from the corpse.

"What are you?" I whispered, speaking to the nearest of the monsters, the same one that I had first seen.

He was larger than the others and appeared less afraid of the talisman.

"We are ghouls," he hissed quietly.

"Why do you seek to attack me? I am not of the dead."

"This is our land. No one else may hunt here."

The only prey hunted by ghouls was corpses. They must be aware of the dead girl in the wagon. Perhaps they smelled her decay beneath the sweetness of the honey.

"I hunt nothing."

"You lie," he said, cocking his grotesque head to one side. "We saw you open the grave of the man whose robe and sandals you wear, and watched you feast."

A great shame rose within me. Another being knew that I had willingly eaten human flesh. Almost as quickly I felt a flash of anger at my irrational weakness, and buried it deep within my heart.

"I was starving. I would have died."

"You are not of our clan. You must die."

"Wait!"

The leader of the ghouls halted his approach.

"If I bring you the corpse in the wagon of the caravan, will that buy me the right to hunt in your land?"

The leader paused to consider, his black eyes narrowed in thought. He withdrew a few paces, and several other ghouls clustered around him. Their whispers reached my ears, but they spoke in a strange language unknown to me. He returned, the others following at his heels. I raised the knife, fearing a rejection of my pact.

"Bring the meat away from the fires and the men, and you may hunt in our land."

I realized that they feared the firelight. Perhaps they could only remain invisible beneath the natural light of the stars and the moon, or the brightness of the flames hurt their eyes. There was no choice but to trust them. I sheathed the knife and put away the medallion.

"You are not like other men," the leader of the ghouls murmured, sniffing at my thighs.

Silent laughter rose in my throat.

"I am ugly and no longer a man at all."

"That is not what I mean. You saw me."

"You are difficult to see. I almost walked past you."

"But you saw me. Other men would not have seen me."

To this, I had no answer. Leaving the ghouls behind the dunes, I returned to the wagons. The first glow of dawn tinged the horizon to the east. In less than an hour the sun would rise. I climbed into the wagon through the slit in its side and lifted the corpse of the girl from her box, thankful for the outer cover of the shroud that protected me from the worst of the honey. With care I slid the body through the slit and followed it to the sand. It was the work of only a few minutes, since I already knew what the wagon contained, and how to enter and leave it. The corpse was not heavy. I slung it over my shoulder and made my way back to the dunes where the ghouls waited. Laying the girl on her back on the sand, I parted her shroud and stood back.

The leader came forward eagerly, his nose snuffing the air. He peeled away the swaths from the belly of the corpse and bit the exposed white flesh, tearing off a chunk with his teeth and chewing. The motion of his powerful jaw stopped. He spat the flesh out on the ground.

"Poison," he hissed, glaring at me.

"I can scrape off the honey, " I said quickly.

"Not the honey. The meat. The meat is poison."

For a moment I wondered what the preparers of the corpse had done to taint its flesh. Then I comprehended the creature's meaning. Ghouls were carrion feeders. The preserved flesh of the corpse was too fresh. Evidently they could not digest fresh meat. The leader took a threatening step toward me, and the others followed.

"I can fix the meat, so that you can eat it," I said in haste.

The ghouls stopped and waited.

"The honey and spices keep the flesh from corruption. If I scrape off the honey and set the body out under the sun, by tomorrow night it will be fit for you to eat."

The leader considered these words and nodded his head. He spoke in his own language to the others, and all melted into the darkness.

Chapter 5

Knowing that the men of the caravan would search for the corpse at first light, I carried it far into the desert, taking care to erase my tracks when I crossed soft sand by beating the ground behind me with my thawb, which I removed and wound about my forearm for this purpose. The morning breeze would soon do the rest, obscuring even the faint marks left by my garment from the sand. There was no chance the searchers would discover where I took the body, and in a day they would be forced to move on. I found a rift between two rocky hills with an overhanging ledge that offered me shade from the sun, laid the corpse on an exposed stone, and put my thawb back on. With care, I stripped the shroud and wrappings from the body and used my knife to scrape away all the honey that clung to the naked skin. It was necessary to shave her head, beneath her arms, and between her thighs, in order to remove the honey that saturated her hair.

My work finished just as the first rays of the sun found their way between the hills and touched the corpse. I crawled under the ledge and prepared to sleep, but first ate three of the white spiders so that when the ghouls came I would have the advantage of enhanced vision, in case they were not true to their pact. The honey on my fingers improved their taste, and I licked them contentedly as I settled my head on my water skin. The corpse rested near enough that I would hear any attempt by bird or beast to disturb it.

Twice during the day I awoke at the sound of wings, and crawled out to frighten away a pair of persistent vultures, who continued to circle high above. The second time I remained in view to discourage the birds. The flesh of the corpse began to blacken in patches beneath the rays of the sun, and the flies swarmed over it, clustering most thickly upon its open eyes. It felt unnatural to be exposed to the light of day, and the heat wearied me. When at last the carrion hawks flew beneath the horizon in search of easier prey, I returned to my den and slept deeply.

My veiled companion stood beside me on the crest of a high dune beneath the shimmering sun and pointed with a bony hand at a whirlwind that danced across the desert.

"All turning things are gates. That which turns defines a center and opens it. All centers are at unity. To travel through a gate, you must go to the center and return from it. Yog-Sothoth is the way. I give you his seal. Use it to open the gates."

He bent and drew a symbol in the sand. I stared at it. He recited words in an obscure tongue, harsh and guttural to my ears. The sand began to turn beneath my gaze and a black pit opened. I felt it tug at me like a hungry mouth. With a cry of dismay I tried to pull back from its widening lip, but was drawn into the darkness.

The croaking scream still vibrated in my throat when I jerked awake and found myself lying beneath the ledge, the corpse beside me. Night had fallen, but a night filled with glowing forms. Several dozen ghouls crouched around the corpse, their bodies lit with silver, their eyes like burning lamps. The largest who was their leader stood beside the ledge staring down at me. He cocked his head in curiosity.

"I dream of a dark man who has no face," I said, wiping cold sweat from my forehead with my palm.

"What is a dream?" the ghoul asked.

"A dream is an illusion, a thing that seems to happen but has no reality."

"Nyarlathotep is real. We have watched him walk beneath the moon."

"Is that his name? What can he want with me?"

The ghoul made a motion with his shoulders that I interpreted as a shrug.

"Who can know the ways of the Old Ones? Always Nyarlathotep has wandered the desert. It is unlucky to meet him."

Crawling from under the ledge, I approached the corpse, and noticed the naked ghost of the girl standing some distance from the circle of ghouls, making anxious gestures with her hands, as though trying to brush them away.

"Do you see her?" I asked my companion.

The ghoul followed the direction of my gaze, then turned his head with disinterest.

"The shade always watches over the meat. It has no power. We ignore it."

The others parted and allowed us to approach the hairless corpse. Its belly had distended with the gases of decay, giving it a pregnant look. The rays of the sun had shriveled its eyes.

"What is your name, human?"

My mind sought for the name of my father, but still it eluded me. I smiled bitterly in the darkness.

"Alhazred."

"I am Gor, leader of the Black Spring Clan. All gathered here share my blood. We are few in number but strong in the hunt."

What was the proper response to such a salutation? I spoke the first words that came to my tongue.

"May your bellies always be filled."

A murmur of surprise arose from the creatures.

"You know the polite words. Have you been with my kind before?"

Silently I shook my head. The ghoul curled his lips away from the gums to reveal his sharp teeth and flicked out his long tongue, which glistened in the moonlight.

"As leader, it is my place to feed before the others. I give that place to you."

Gor's words held the cadence of ritual. I would not have dared to refuse, and in any case hunger gnawed within my bowels. Searching around the ground, I found a large stone that rested comfortably in my hand and used it to smash open the skull of the corpse. The trembling ghost of the dead girl vanished upward in a flash of light. With a broken piece of skull I scooped out the moist brain and ate it while the ghouls made approving sounds.

Their leader used his claws to slash open the swollen belly, releasing a gust of foul gas, and buried his face in the exposed intestines. With hooting cries the other members of the clan closed in and began to take pieces of the corpse. The largest fed first, but not even the smallest was denied a share of the flesh. In a few minutes nothing remained on the rock but a disordered pile of reddened bones. Even these the ghouls began to crack open with stones to release their marrow, which they sucked as though it were cream.

"You call yourselves the Black Spring Clan," I said to Gor. "Is there meaning in the name?"

He gnawed and sucked the broken end of a thigh bone as he nodded.

"We draw our water from a spring of the same name. It is unknown to men. You are one of us now, so I will show it to you."

Gathering up my few possessions, I went with them across the desert. I took my bearing from the star Mismar so that I could find my way back to the caravan road alone, though with my spider-enhanced vision it would have been difficult to become lost, since our footprints in the sand glowed with a pale light. Gor gestured to a low line of rocky cliffs near the northern horizon as he loped easily over the uneven ground.

"All the land to the cliffs is ours. What lies beyond belongs to the Red Hill Clan."

"How do you know the language of men?"

"When a caravan camps for the night, we gather near in search of meat. We watch and listen."

The ghouls moved quickly, making almost no sound. Mothers carried their infants on their backs, with each young clinging by its arms around its mother's neck. Not all the ghouls were naked. A few wore belts with leather pouches, and many had strings of beads around their necks or bands of brass on their arms. Their smell was earthy, but not unpleasant, resembling the smell of dogs.

A flash of light attracted my notice at the corner of my eye. It was the djinn who had communicated with me the night before, keeping pace with the ghouls.

"We are being followed," I muttered to Gor.

He looked around alertly, his ears moving as he listened for sounds in the night.

"Can't you see it? A spirit creature."

He made a rough, coughing noise that I realized must be laughter, and said something in his own tongue to the rest of the clan. More of the ghouls laughed and glanced at me.

"That is one of the *chaklab'i*. We pay them no attention. They are vermin who feed on the remnants of the feast. This one follows you, Alhazred."

Another of the large male ghouls spoke to Gor, and both laughed.

"He said perhaps it wants to mate with you."

"If so, it will be disappointed," I said, staring at the djinn as it danced along the crest of a dune and vanished on the far side.

After two hours of hard travel northward we entered a kind of great pit, shallow but of broad expanse, where the ground had fallen. In its center, well shielded by hills from the sight of any observer who might pass casually on a camel, grew a grove of date palms and grasses. The Black Spring was well named. Its waters were the color of pitch in the moonlight and appeared completely stagnant. The spring was narrow enough to leap across. Tiny bubbles ascended in its center, betraying the presence of moving water.

"It looks foul," I said, eyeing the water with disappointment.

"It has sustained me all the nights of my life, and the bodies of all the clan for countless generations." Gor spoke with a tone of veneration.

I recognized my error. To these creatures, the spring was more than water. It was the living heart of their world.

"You have done me great honor to show me this place," I told him. "It is a kindness that will not be forgotten."

He nodded, watching me with his large eyes.

"When I saw you feast on the man-corpse, I knew you were one of us. I am glad we did not need to kill you."

The rest of the clan separated and wandered to their homes, which lay within small fissures between rocks or in holes dug in the ground beside sheltering boulders. A cry rang up, and then another. Those who had entered the holes issued forth babbling in their guttural tongue. Gor left my side and went to learn the reason for this confusion. He listened to several of the ghouls, making no more than grunts by way of comment, then issued a rapid series of commands that sent the larger males of the clan scurrying in and out of the holes. He returned, a grim expression on his misshapen features.

"While we hunted, the Red Hill Clan raided our places of rest and stole our possessions. This cannot go unavenged. I will follow with my best warriors and punish the raiding party."

"I will accompany you," I said on sudden impulse.

He gazed at me for a moment, then nodded.

"We will have use for your claw."

Taking only small skins of water, a party of nine ghouls assembled on the rim of the pit, and at Gor's command separated and began to search the sandy ground.

"They look for the tracks of our enemies," Gor explained.

I glanced over the desert and saw faintly glowing the footprints of a number of travelers leading away from the pit, on the side opposite where we had entered.

"There." I pointed at the tracks. "They went east."

Gor barked an excited command to one of the ghouls, who ran over to investigate the place I had indicated. He smelled the ground and threw back his head, howling. Several others ran over and lent their voices to his. It was like the cry of wolves, and chilled the blood in my heart. We started on the track, moving at an easy run.

"You have good eyes," Gor said.

"They are not always so keen."

I explained to him the effects of the white spiders, and told of the cave where I had found them.

"We have a legend of the spider cave," he said when I finished. "None of my clan knows where it is located."

"Someday, I will show it to you," I promised. "It has clean water in abundance."

We ran without pause for more than an hour. The tracks we followed gradually bent their way north toward the hills. I realized that we would never catch the raiding party of hill ghouls unless they chose to stop for rest, since they could move as fast as us across the desert. The only chance we had was the long distance they had traveled to reach the spring. They might be weary, and were likely to pause at some time during the night. I did my best not to slow down the others. They appeared tireless. I could run faster for a brief while and gain the front of the pack, thanks to the advantage of my longer legs, but they seemed able to continue their regular pace all night and never exhaust their strength. Unless we came on the raiders soon, I would be forced to fall behind to catch my breath. Already I panted in the cool night air, my cotton thawb soaked with sweat against my skin. I considered casting it away and running naked to my sandals, but I might never have the chance to return for it.

Gor raised his hand and hissed quietly. The ghouls dropped from a run to a slow walking pace, their heads tilted back as they snuffed the air through wide nostrils. The cooling night breeze touched my face. Gor put his lips near my ear.

"Ahead of us, on the other side of the sand hill," he sighed.

Listening intently, I caught a murmur of voices, and coughing laughter.

Gor began to motion the ghouls forward, but I touched his arm and leaned close to speak. He listened to my words and nodded his head in agreement.

Leaving the others, I walked left for several minutes, then began to work my way around the place where the hill ghouls had stopped. It was my intention to come at them from as nearly opposite Gor's band as possible, while still being mindful of the direction of the wind. If I crossed upwind of the raiders they would surely scent my approach.

I saw them glowing against the darker sand as I surmounted the crest of an intervening dune, and quickly counted. There were fourteen males, all larger than Gor, although their bodies did not appear as powerful as those of the Black Spring Clan. Some would stand as tall as my shoulder on their thin legs. At present they squatted in a circle on the ground and drank from water skins, passing objects back and forth and admiring them.

Dropping to my hands and knees, I began to crawl toward them. I touched my sweating cheek to the ground so that the sand would stick to it. When I came closer, I emitted a piteous moan. They leapt to their feet with snarls and whirled to face me. I let myself collapse onto the ground, then panting heavy breaths that I was sure they would hear, I pressed my body once more to hands and knees and continued to approach, as though unaware of their presence.

They hissed in alarm and darted keen glances all around at the crests of the dunes, nostrils flaring as they scented the breeze, but when they saw nothing and smelled nothing, they silently approached and surrounded me. They moved with caution, knees bent and long fingers spread to expose their hooked claws. I raised my head and widened my eyes, as though seeing them for the first time.

"I am lost." My voice croaked as though with dryness. "Where is the caravan? Where is the road to Yemen?"

A tall ghoul who seemed to be their leader spoke a few soft words to his companion, and the other laughed a coughing laugh. The leader relaxed and approached without haste.

"Water," I croaked, hoping that my water skin was not visible hanging beneath the folds of my thawb. "Have pity, water."

The ghoul put his broad foot on my shoulder and pressed down experimentally, testing my strength. I pretended to collapse into the sand. He grunted and turned away, speaking a few words in his language to his companion. The other approached with a purposeful attitude, his right hand working as he flexed his fingers. It was plain that he intended to tear out my throat. I wondered if these ghouls would be as fastidious as the Black Spring Clan, or if they would consume my flesh immediately after my death. My right hand slid beneath the shadow of my belly to the scabbard of my dagger and closed around the hilt of my weapon.

The ghoul grasped my robe at the shoulder and pulled me to my knees to expose my throat. As I rose from the ground, I drew the dagger and in the same motion plunged it into his belly. His cry resembled that of a hawk. I twisted the broad blade of the knife and pulled it loose, then buried its point between his ribs, where I hoped to find his heart. The ghoul dropped to his knees in the sand so that our eyes were on the same level and stared at me in amazement.

This sudden violence froze the others for a few moments. Two began to rush toward me, when the air was rent on all sides by a shrill howling. My attackers stopped and whirled around with uncertainty. One started to run, then hesitated, not knowing which way to flee. By then it was too late. The warriors of the Black Spring Clan fell upon them, cutting with teeth and slashing with claws at any exposed vital place.

I backed away from the ghoul I had killed, still on my knees, blood streaming from the point of my dagger. To my enhanced sight it looked like milk as it pooled on the sand. Something struck me hard upon the shoulder and knocked me over. At least one of the raiders had not forgotten me. I rolled with the creature, grasping his wrists instinctively to keep his deadly talons from my face. In the process my dagger was lost. The strength of the ghoul was greater than mine. His reeking breath filled my face as his teeth snapped for my throat. I could not cast the weight of his body from me, but was pinned to the sand.

A bright light suddenly surrounded the head of the ghoul and covered his snapping mouth and flared nostrils. He shook his head in irritation as though unable to see clearly and barked. One of his hands pulled loose from my grasp and began to bat at the air above his head. With my free hand I pressed him away and rolled from beneath him. I saw the bone hilt of the dagger glowing where it had fallen and snatched it up just as the ghoul charged with claws outstretched. The bloody blade sank deep into the pit of his throat. One of his hands grazed my neck and drew blood, but I had no leisure to concern myself with the wound. A spray of blood coughed from his gaping jaws blinded me. In desperation I pulled myself close to his naked chest, inside the sweep of his claws, and ground the point of the dagger against the bones of his neck. He fell limp against me, and I realized that he was dead.

I blinked the blood from my eyes and looked around. The battle was over. Two of the hill ghouls fled up the side of a dune, both seriously wounded and pursued by several of the Black Spring Clan, but before they could pass from sight, Gor called back his warriors with a barked command. I pushed myself to my feet and stood swaying. With my fingers I examined the wound on my neck. It stung to the touch but was shallow. Twelve raiders lay dead, most with their throats or bellies ripped out. Four of Gor's followers were also dead, and most of the others had suffered wounds. Gor himself, though covered with the blood of his foes, was not injured.

He approached and looked down at the two hill ghouls I had killed. An expression of intense joy illuminated his grotesque face. His lips writhed back from his teeth and his tongue flicked out with excitement.

"A good battle. The Red Hill Clan will remember this night to their shame."

He began to whoop and dance around the bodies of the fallen foes, and his clan members imitated him gleefully. The fervor of their emotions intoxicated me. I found myself dancing with the rest, waving my bloody dagger in the air and singing wordlessly.

When the excitement subsided, the ghouls began to gather up their looted possessions. They stripped the bodies of their enemies of valuables, then prepared to carry their own dead back to the spring.

"Your lover waits for you," Gor said in a jovial mood, pointing with a thumb at the dancing ball of light that hovered and pranced some distance away.

"Tonight it saved my life."

I told him how the djinn had distracted the second hill ghoul long enough for me to kill it. He gazed at it more seriously.

"I have never known a spirit of this kind to help a creature of flesh."

As though aware that it was the subject of conversation, the djinn danced nearer.

"Talk to it," Gor said. "I will leave you two alone."

He ambled off, choking with laughter, to direct the preparation of his dead clan members for removal. Their gaping wounds were being sewn up with thread so that they could be carried without dripping blood across the desert.

The djinn approached with caution. As it drew nearer, its face emerged from the glow of light that masked its body. The fine details of its features could only be distinguished when it stood near enough to touch. I allowed it to grasp my head in its hands and thrust its tooth-filled mouth through my face.

"I thank you for my life," I told it.

You are a fierce warrior.

"Without your help I would surely have died."

Grant me a wish.

I paused before answering. This spirit had saved me from certain death. Whatever it desired, I could not in good honor refuse it. The djinn sensed my unspoken thoughts.

Let me accompany you on your wandering.

"You have already been doing so," I pointed out.

Let me unite with you.

An image of what the djinn wanted entered my thoughts. It sought to reside within my flesh, where it would be enabled to draw upon my life energies for its continuing nourishment. This it could not do without my explicit consent.

"You will drain me of vitality and kill me."

No. Only I will take a little of your fire. Leave you all the rest.

The prospect of having a djinn of the desert dwelling within my body as a kind of parasite did not appeal to me, but the debt I owed the creature could not be denied.

"I will consent, but only for the present. If at some future time I demand that you leave my flesh, you must obey."

Agreed.

I drew a deep breath as the spirit surrounded my upper body, hugging me with its long limbs, and seemed to squeeze itself through the barrier of my skin. Its movements in my muscles and along my nerves were clearly to be felt, and resembled the caresses of invisible hands. They fluttered over my heart, which stumbled in its regular beats, then regained its rhythm.

"Where is your companion?" Gor asked when he returned.

I explained the pact I had made with the djinn. He pressed a hand flat on the bald top of his skull and blinked, as though unable to contain his amazement.

"Never have I heard of such a thing, and all the secrets of the world are known to my clan."

"It has not told me why it is so interested in me," I said.

Gor writhed his lips in a grin and licked them, coughing with laughter.

"That should be obvious."

"How so?"

He realized that my puzzlement was genuine.

"Surely you noticed that the djinn is female?"

Still laughing softly to himself, Gor left me to ponder his words.

Chapter 6

We were greeted as heroes by the clan when we returned to Black Spring. There was much hooting and shouting as Gor told the battle to the assembled throng of ghouls. What he said in their language was obscure, but by his gesturing and intonations he might have been describing the fall of Troy to the armies of the Greeks. I felt no cynicism, but only satisfaction that turned to pride when I heard my own name spoken, and the females and young of the clan looked at me with wide eyes. After consulting with the elders, Gor gave me a dwelling place that had belonged to one of the slain, a hole dug beneath a sheltering ledge of stone that guarded the opening from the sun.

"What will you do with the dead?" I asked him, as we watched the four corpses carried into the entrance to a larger cave near the spring.

"Tomorrow you will see for yourself."

With these enigmatic words he left me. The sun glowed just beneath the eastern horizon and the stars had all but vanished when the members of the clan began to steal noiselessly into their dens. Soon the bottom of the pit was deserted. The exertions of the night made themselves felt in my body, now that the excitement had died, and I discovered that my neck throbbed where the claws of the hill ghoul had slashed it. With weary limbs I crawled headfirst into the hole that was my new home and found myself in an arched chamber the length and breadth of my extended body, with a floor of soft sand. It was empty save for a few twists of rope, an empty leather pouch, a stone tool probably used to crack bones for marrow, and a skull that did not look quite human.

Perhaps the skull had served its owner as a drinking vessel, I reflected, as I prepared myself to sleep in the dimness of the cave. Only enough morning light found its way through the elongated entrance tunnel to enable me to see the shapes of my limbs as I stripped off my sandals, leather stockings, and thawb. The influence of the white spiders had faded, leaving me with a slight headache. The robe I arranged on the sand for a bed, beside my water skin that served as a pillow. I lay upon them and put my arm across my face to block the gloom from my closed eyelids.

Something soft touched me on the side, near my armpit. I jerked to wakefulness and stared around with sleep-dry eyes, thinking to find that some small desert creature had sought refuge from the sun in my den. I was alone. Lying back, I rearranged my body and let myself drift toward sleep once again. This time the touch came more gently on my belly. I raised my arm and peered down the length of my chest but saw nothing, even though the sensation of a hand pressing on my skin was unmistakable. It began to move slowly down toward my groin.

"What are you doing?" I murmured.

The response came whispering into my mind.

Do not be frightened.

Where the invisible hand of the djinn touched my skin, it excited a tingling in my muscles and a sweetness that ran along my nerves. I felt the pressure of a body stretch itself along my chest and thighs with a palpable weight. Had I not seen with my own eyes that nothing pressed against me, I would have sworn that a woman lay atop me. The erect nipples of her firm small breasts brushed my chest, and her soft thigh found its way between my parted legs. Hands pressed against my back, as though this unseen lover reached through the sand to embrace me.

Close your eyes.

Hesitantly, I did as the voice in my thoughts instructed. At once I saw the face of a beautiful woman leaning over me. Her widely spaced eyes glowed like the finest dark amber. They turned up slightly at the corners, reminding me of the eyes of a desert fox. Scarlet henna tinted moist, full lips above a rounded chin. Egyptian kohl darkened her eyebrows and eyelashes, and lined her eyes, making them seem even larger. The unblemished skin of her domed forehead and cheeks possessed the delicate tan of desert sand.

She positioned herself on top of me, rocking gently on the bones of my hips. I drew a gasp of breath.

"This cannot be."

She touched cool fingers to my lips, smiling, and bent to kiss me. As desire built in my loins, I clearly felt my erect prick within her, sliding gently as she moved her hips with a swaying undulation akin to that of a dancing serpent. Pleasure built within my flesh, causing me to arch my back and raise my hips. I spread my arms, eyes still tightly shut, and clenched the sand between my fingers. The sensations came in waves that rolled from my groin to the extremities of my limbs. My toes curled and the taste of honey came to my tongue as my lover kissed my open mouth with hungry desire. The pleasure intensified with each succeeding wave yet seemed to have no peak. My head became dizzy with intoxication and my body floated on the sand as though on a gently flowing river.

"Enough!" I gasped. "I cannot bear any more."

Ecstasy erupted in my loins and overwhelmed my senses. For a time I ceased to exist. A shuddering inhalation made me aware that I had stopped breathing. My heart pounded with the slow, deep strokes of a blacksmith's hammer, and my entire body trickled with sweat. The soft weight of my invisible lover still nestled against my right side, as though resting with me, and I felt her arm across my chest.

"This cannot be," I repeated more calmly. "I am no longer a man."

Your mind remembers the ways of love.

I closed my eyes and saw her, smiling gently.

"What is your name?"

I have no name.

"You are a *chaklah'i*?"

Chaklah'i is the word for all my kind. I am a chaklah, yes.

"I will give you a name," I said with sudden determination.

An expression of delight illuminated her features.

No one has ever given me a name.

"You will be Sashi to me," I said as the name sprang into my thoughts without meditation.

Sashi, she repeated with pleasure. *It is good.*

"Can all of your kind give pleasure to men, as you gave to me?"

She shook her head, gazing down at me within the darkness of my closed eyelids.

When a man is damaged as you are, only one of my kind welcomed within your skin can do this.

"It cannot be done from outside?"

It cannot.

"Is that why you wished to be within my body?"

She lowered her gaze as though with modesty.

It is one reason.

A great weariness swept over me, yet it was not unpleasant. I allowed it to send me deep into the gentle vortex that opened beneath my mind.

Sleep, Alhazred.

When I awoke it was late afternoon, and the worst heat of the sun had passed. I dressed and crawled from my hole to relieve myself. None of the ghouls stirred in the great pit that surrounded the spring. I explored it with curiosity. The ground had fallen in upon itself in a large circle, leaving here and there irregular rocky ledges and hills. It was not deep, no more than the height of a tall palm tree below the desert, yet it was so broad that several minutes were required to walk from one side to the other. The spring occupied the center of the depression, bubbling slowly upward within an irregular circle of large rocks and overflowing to spread upon the sand for a short distance before being absorbed once again into the ground. Its waters looked foul but its taste was not unpleasant. By some trick of nature it was as cold as ice, numbing the tongue when drunk too quickly.

I occupied the end of the day washing my thawb and stockings, which had accumulated much dust and filth. First I saturated them in the spring, then took them to a flat rock and beat them against it until they were almost dry. This process I repeated several times. Leaving them spread in the slanting rays of the sun, I returned to the spring and slid my body into it to wash. To my surprise, I discovered that it had no bottom. Treading water, I rubbed my limbs and chest with my hands until I could no longer stand the freezing chill and crawled out on the rocks that surrounded its margin. The injuries to my body were healing well, without swelling or pus. I probed them gently with my fingertips. Soon they would be only scars.

As twilight fell, I dressed and sat upon a stone to await the coming of night. There was nothing to reveal that the pit was more than a vacant fault in the surface of the desert. The ghouls kept all their possessions below ground. No traveler who happened upon the pit while the sun was above the horizon would suspect their existence. As night came, they began to silently appear, emerging from their holes and making their way to the spring to drink and talk together in hushed voices. A curious peace lay over my heart, and I felt little impulse to stir from my place.

Gor emerged from the entrance to the larger cave and approached me.

"How did you sleep, Alhazred?"

"Well enough."

His eyes sparkled and he laughed his choking laugh, but whatever thought was in his mind he kept to himself.

"Where do we hunt tonight?" I asked him. The prospect of the hunt appealed to me. His amusement vanished away.

"No hunt tonight," he said solemnly. "Tonight we honor the dead of the clan."

"I did not know ghouls honored their dead."

"No man has ever seen it, so how should you know?"

The members of the clan began to make their way into the entrance to the large cave, which I gathered from Gor's remarks served them as a kind of mosque or holy place. Gor seemed in no hurry to join them, but remained beside me and talked.

I learned that he had been leader of the clan for three years, having claimed that place after the death of his father, who had been caught on the open desert during a sandstorm and killed. His father had been a great leader who ruled the clan for more than twenty years. No one had challenged Gor's claim to lead, even though it was the custom for those seeking to lead the clan to defend their claim in combat. Everyone had recognized his fitness to replace his father. He explained this with a quiet pride. In three years no other male had challenged him.

He listened without comment while I told him the story of my life. When I said I was a singer, he asked me to sing, and I found myself voicing the melody of a frivolous love ballad that was filled with vanity and deceit. The words, so cleverly adapted to the cynical listeners at the royal court, sounded alien as they echoed from the rocks in the night. The insects fell silent while I sang, as though they also listened. When I described how King Huban had forced me to consume the corpse of my own unborn son, Gor's eyes danced with interest.

"It was fated. He made you one of us, so you could come here and share our meat."

"Yes, he made me a ghoul," I agreed. Strangely, I said it without bitterness in my heart.

Gor pushed himself from the rock where he had sat beside me.

"Come. It is time to honor the dead."

We went together to the large cave, where all the clan had assembled. Its entrance was narrow enough to be touched with outstretched hands, but four times the tallness of a man, tapering to a pointed arch. The roof fell for the first dozen paces inside, then rose and widened into a great cavern with a floor broken into several rock ledges of different elevations, so that it formed a kind of natural amphitheater. Enough moonlight shone through the entrance to show the four corpses of the fallen warriors, arranged side by side on the bare rock at the center of the cavern. I noted a large pile of bones at the back of the cave near an opening, and judged them to be the bones of ghouls by their color and shape, but saw no skulls. Nothing in the cave resembled an altar or idol, nor was there anything to reveal why it served as a sacred space.

Gor left my side and went between the bodies, which were spaced apart so that it was possible to walk around each of them. In resonant tones he addressed the clan in his own guttural language. They sat and squatted on the ledges, listening to his words with solemn expressions. He moved to stand at the feet of the first corpse and spoke for several minutes, then did the same for the three others in turn. When he finished, he spoke a name, and one of the male ghouls came forward and took his place between the corpses. I recognized him as a member of the war party. He moved to the foot of the first corpse and spoke a few words, then did the same for the others. He called by name another male ghoul who had fought the raiders from the northern hills, and the ritual repeated itself.

When all the warriors who had fought beside the dead had spoken, I assumed the eulogy was ended, but Gor approached me.

"It is fitting that you praise the dead. I will translate your words into the language of the clan."

We stood between the corpses. As has been true from my earliest childhood, I found no need to struggle for words. It is a blessing of my divine gift that words always come easily to me. My heart swelled with a storm of feelings, and I knew that mere spoken praise would be insufficient to express my sense of kinship with these fallen creatures who lay at my feet. I sang and composed the verses of my song simultaneously, pausing at the end of each line for Gor to call out the meaning of my words. When I was done, there was silence. At first I thought I had offended some custom of the clan, but then a roar went up, and I realized that my song had stirred fierce pride in the ghouls. Their eyes flashed in the dim light and their tongues licked across their writhing lips as they stomped their naked feet against the stone ledges, filling the cave with a sound like thunder.

"You spoke well," Gor told me over the roar.

His approval moved me more than any I had received from the king or his courtiers for similar extemporaneous songs.

A female and a young male ghoul who was nearly grown to maturity came down from the ledges and knelt at the side of the first corpse. Several more ghouls knelt beside the second, two beside the third, and only a lone female beside the fourth. They looked at Gor expectantly. He spoke a word, and they began to feed.

"It is always my place to feed first," he murmured to me as we stood side by side and watched. "When the dead are honored, I give that place to the near-blood kin of the corpse."

"Do you always eat your dead?"

"What else should we do? Bury them in the ground and waste the meat, as men do?" He made a sound of disgust in his throat.

After the close kin of the dead had eaten their fill, Gor approached and drew me with him. I saw the other survivors of our war party gathering around. He ate a bit of flesh from each body and moved on to the next, and I emulated him. When we were done, the other males who had fought did the same. Then the rest of the clan fed until only bones remained. Ghouls discard no part of the dead—even the intestines are consumed. Indeed, they seem to relish the bowels more than any other part of the corpse.

"The bones will not be broken, but piled with the others," Gor explained.

"Why are there no skulls in the pile?"

"The skull is given to the mate or first-born child of the dead, to keep as a vessel of memories."

The purpose of the skull in my sleeping place became clear. I spoke of it to Gor.

"Would it not be best for the skull to be given to the nearest kin of the dead ghoul?"

He nodded with an expression of approval, and called over the female who had stood beside the last of the four corpses. He spoke to her in their own language, and a look of happiness entered her face. She nodded to me, grinning until her yellowed teeth were exposed. Her breasts hung so low they rested on the dome of her rounded belly, and her large nipples appeared purple in the dimness.

"This is Kall, sister of the ghoul whose cave you took. The skull of his father was overlooked in the sorrow of his death. It is right that it be given to her."

I nodded while meeting her eyes to show her that I understood, and she went away trembling with happiness.

We watched as the bones of the fleshless corpses were separated from each other and transferred to the bone pile. The skulls were stripped of their skin, flesh, and tongues by the near relatives of the dead, who used their teeth, holding the heads between their claws while they peeled them. A wooden hook that resembled a curled spoon, specially fashioned for the purpose, was employed to pull the brain out through the hole in the base of the skull, and to extract the eyeballs. Everything was eaten, and the blood-smeared skulls were carried reverently from the cave.

"One more secret I must show you," Gor said, beckoning for me to follow.

He made his way through the irregular ledges of stone to the rear of the cave, where the bones were being carefully piled. Without pausing he ducked his head and entered the small passage beside the bones. I followed, blinking and widening my eyes in the deeper gloom. For a moment I wished that I had eaten the white spiders, even though I did not think it was good for my body to consume them every morning, so potent was their effect. More by sound than sight I followed Gor with my hands raised to protect my face from sharp rocks that might hang from the ceiling. My feet told me that the passage led steeply downward, but it was so narrow and twisted there was little risk of stumbling.

The way ahead began to lighten with a soft glow almost too faint to see, yet it was enough to show the moving outline of the ghoul as he walked in front of me. As we followed the convoluted passage, it grew brighter, until at last we emerged on a ledge in the side of a vast chamber many times larger than the cave of the dead. Its walls shone with a natural gray light, though what caused this radiance was not evident—it seemed to emanate from the very surface of the rock. Dimly, high above, the roof of the chamber was a blur of shadow, but the chamber had no floor. Leaning over the end of the ledge to gaze downward, I could see only deepening blackness, as the distance itself defeated the light from the walls.

A staircase descended from the ledge around the curving side of the chamber, cut into the solid rock. The steps were unnaturally large, as though made for the legs of giants, and wide enough to have accommodated three or four men walking side by side. In their centers a deep trench was worn by the feet of countless users over the span of eons. As they spiraled ever deeper, they dimmed and were at last lost to sight in the blackness of the depths.

"No clan of ghouls carved this stair," I murmured.

The vastness of what I looked upon, so obviously made for the use of creatures with dimensions greater than the human body, awoke within me a vague terror that hushed my voice.

"It has always been here," Gor spoke in a whisper. "No one knows who made it."

"Where does the stair lead?"

He looked at me, and I saw in his eyes something I had not seen there before. Fear.

"No one knows."

I tried to force a smile on my lips, but it felt false and I let it fade.

"Has no ghoul ever descended the steps?"

"Many have descended. None has ever returned."

It is the work of the Old Ones.

"The *chaklah* in my head says it was cut by the Old Ones," I told Gor.

"So it may be. No one knows."

I stared down in wonder at the spiral of the stair. Never had I imagined such a creation. Only a race of gods could fashion such steps.

"This stair is the greatest marvel in the world, surely," I said.

Gor laughed, a hollow choking deep in his chest. He pointed with a claw at the side of the chamber, near the ledge where we stood. I looked, wondering what he wished me to see. Then at once I did see, and the blood left my head. Had he not grasped my shoulder, I would have fallen from the ledge. My knees shook with a terror so primal it had no source.

From within the darkness of the bottomless pit a groan arose, deep enough in pitch that it made my chest vibrate, but whether it was from the movement of stone on stone in the bowels of the earth, or the cry of some vast living thing, I could not tell, for it was unlike any sound I had ever heard.

"What is that?"

Gor shrugged, but the shadow of fear did not leave his eyes.

"My father said it was the voice of the earth itself, beckoning us to our deaths. He was the bravest of our clan, but he never went down the stair."

I gazed again at the stone wall, letting my eyes trace it downward below the level of the ledge where we stood. All along its surface were the marks of tools, where the stone had been cut and shaped. As far as the eye could distinguish above, below, and on either side of the ledge in the chill gray glow were the same marks.

Chapter 7

The approach of summer was unwelcome to the Black Spring Clan. We depended on the caravans for our meat, and as the days grew hotter, the caravans became fewer. In the extremity of starvation, a ghoul will feed upon the carrion of beasts, and even upon fresh meat, but no ghoul can remain in good health without the putrefying flesh of human corpses. Animal flesh, which their stomachs have great difficulty digesting, contains little nourishment for a ghoul. The people of the dwindling caravans grew wary, since it was not uncommon for a man to wander out of the glow of the campfires to relieve himself, never to be seen again.

It was around the time of the solstice, by my rough reckoning of the heavens, when the entire clan followed a ragged caravan for three days and nights in the hope of a death, either of man or beast; but though the camels staggered as they walked and the men were thinner than the ghouls who stalked them, no one died. I hunted during the day, while the clan sought shelter from the sun, keeping a constant watch for anyone who wandered away from the wagons while the caravan was on the move. At night the clan caught up with me, and I slept for several hours while the caravan made camp and the mature ghouls hunted just outside the glow of the fires. The men kept guard with uncommon vigilance. At least four of them remained awake all night, armed with swords and bows, and wearing armor. No one ever left the fires alone.

"The light would blind us," Gor murmured as we lay together on our bellies on the crest of a dune, gazing down at the encampment. "If we attacked, we could not see to fight, and they would slaughter us with their bows."

He spoke in his own tongue. I had acquired the language of the ghouls, although I could not yet speak it perfectly.

"I will try to steal into a wagon and kill a woman. Maybe I can drag her corpse away without being seen."

Gor shook his head.

"They watch too closely. Someone must have warned them at the last well."

"We need meat," I reminded him.

He made a clucking sound with his tongue.

"This part of the year is always hard. There will be better hunting when the days grow cooler."

"The caravan road is dying. What will you do when the camels cease to pass through the land of the Black Spring Clan?"

"Who can say? Perhaps we will hunt the villages that lie to the north."

"They are owned by the Red Hill Clan. There will be war."

"There has always been war between our clans."

"If I had a bow, I could kill a man from here. They would have to bury him and leave him behind."

"You do not have a bow, Alhazred."

"Why do the ghouls never use bows, or swords?"

He thought for a few moments in silence.

"They are the things of men. We are not men. It is not our way."

"Such weapons could help you in the hunt."

"It is not our way," he repeated.

I did not pursue the argument. There was a fatalism in the nature of the ghouls that could not be moved by any rational demonstration. They lived as they had always lived. They could not imagine change.

"We need meat," I repeated after a while.

Gor merely grunted.

I will hunt for you, Sashi said in my mind.

"You?" I told the djinn in a scornful tone. "What can you do? You have no strength."

Gor looked at me.

"The *chaklah* talks to me in my head."

His black eyes widened slightly, but he said nothing.

I can stop the breath of a man. It is our way of hunting.

"Yes, when you hunt in packs. A man would cast you off if you hunted alone."

A woman, then.

"A woman would cast you off, also."

An idea came into my head. I turned to Gor, who watched me with an indulgent expression, as though observing the antics of a mad relative.

"Last night, did one of the clan say he had seen a child in the white wagon?"

"Two children," Gor said. "They keep them in the wagon. My ghoul only caught a glimpse of them just before dawn, when the wagon curtains were opened."

"How old are they?"

Gor slid down the dune and walked to a hollow where a group of male ghouls crouched on their flanks, talking amongst themselves. He spoke to one of the ghouls, then returned.

"The boy is perhaps seven years. The girl is younger, five or four years."

Hope surged in my heart. Sashi felt it and began to hum with happiness within me.

"Hunt the girl first. If you are successful, then try the boy."

She had never left my body from the time of her entry inside my skin. There was a stirring within my chest and bowels that raised a sickly sensation and made me swallow my spittle. My skin expanded as though all my limbs were filled with air, and suddenly the pressure vanished. I had not eaten the white spiders, so I could not see her.

"Is she outside of me?"

Gor nodded, grinning at an empty patch of the night air.

A gentle touch brushed my cheek, and I realized that Sashi had kissed me.

The wait seemed long, but could not have been more than a quarter of an hour. Hope raised impatience in my heart. After three days and nights of frustration, at last something was being tried.

"The *chaklah* returns," Gor murmured.

A tingling covered my skin, and with an inward pressure pierced it like a thousand fine needles. It was not painful, merely strange. I closed my eyes and saw Sashi's smiling face. She nodded in delight.

Both are dead. The boy struggled, but became tangled in his sleeping blanket. I sealed their mouths and noses and cut off their breath.

I conveyed this good news to Gor, who closed his eyes and released a long puff of wind between his lips.

"The meat will not be much," I reminded him. "They are scarce more than infants."

"It will be enough."

The alarm came before dawn. Within the white wagon a woman began to shriek. The men guarding the camp ran to the wagon babbling their confusion, and the shrieks of the woman, who must have been the mother, gave way to long wails that rose and fell on the desert air.

There was nothing else for the men of the caravan to do but bury the corpses near the road and move on. After the clan retreated beneath the earth from the sun, I watched at a distance as the graves were dug and two small shrouds were lowered into their hungry mouths. A woman in black threw herself on the larger of the two corpses, and had to be pulled away screaming. Her boshiya came loose from her face, and I saw by the blue dots and crosses and stars tattooed on her chin and the lower part of her cheeks that she had been born a Bedouin, for it is only the wandering desert tribes that tattoo their women, in defiance of the laws of the Prophet. A man held her in the circle of his arms, and stared around at the hills that lined both sides of the road, as though seeking an enemy he could slay with his eyes. The harsh expression on his sun-darkened face was a blend of frustration and fury.

He knows.

"Yes, Sashi, he knows," I agreed. "The knowledge does him no good."

The caravan moved on in mid-morning. When it was certain that no archers remained behind to watch over the graves, I came down from the hills and unearthed the bodies from between the marker stones at their head and foot. It was an easy matter to carry them a safe distance from the road, since they weighed little. My knife cut through the bindings of the cotton shrouds. Their flesh had not begun to darken. The face of the girl was angelic in its purity. Never have I seen a more beautiful child. By contrast, the expression of the boy was distorted by a remnant of the terror that had gripped his heart in death.

71

I stripped the bodies and set them naked on the sand for the sun to ripen, then sat in the shade of a boulder and watched over them to ensure that no jackals or vultures tried to steal the prizes.

After sunset, the ghouls began to arrive. They danced and sang in their rough voices, so great was their joy. Starvation for the entire clan had not been more than a few days away, or at most a week. The body of one child would not have been enough to feed the clan, but two made a satisfying meal.

Gor gave me the honor of eating first. I used my dagger to slice a piece of meat from the inside of the girl's thigh, having a care not to take too much. My belly was as empty as all the rest, but a human can endure hunger better than a ghoul, and can go longer without food before becoming too weak to hunt.

I chewed the tender meat while the rest of the ghouls clustered around the corpses and tore off their portions. Nothing would be wasted, not even the marrow of the bones.

Gor squatted on his haunches beside me, a happy grin on his black lips, his chin and curved teeth stained with blood. He licked his lips with relish.

"We must go into the land of the Red Hill Clan," he said. "There is no more hunting here until the season changes."

"I agree. We must hunt in one of the villages in the north."

"The Red Hill Clan will not be happy to share their land."

I grinned back at him, still chewing.

"If they attack, we will kill them all."

He laughed his choking laugh and nodded.

There was a curious bitterness on my tongue as I swallowed. I rolled my tongue around in my mouth and examined the flavor. It was not like anything I had tasted before.

"How was the meat?" I asked Gor.

"Good. Good meat. Bitter, but good."

I remembered the face of the father, staring up at the crests of the hills as he clasped his screaming wife, how his dark eyes had glittered like the eyes of a serpent poised to strike. Horror swept through me. Leaning over, I vomited and spat repeatedly.

"Are you mad?" asked Gor, watching my performance with incomprehension.

"The meat is poison," I gasped.

Drawing forth my water skin, I rinsed my mouth and spat again, but the bitterness remained on my tongue. Indeed, it grew stronger with each passing moment.

"You must throw up the meat," I told him. "It was poisoned to kill us."

He stared into my eyes, comprehension at last dawning in his mind. Other ghouls paused in their feast to watch curiously.

"You cannot be sure. The meat may be good."

"It is too great a risk. The bitterness is unnatural. You must vomit it up. Everyone must vomit."

He laughed his choking laugh and looked at me with sadness in his eyes, and something more, a kind of love.

"If we cast off the meat, we will starve."

"No. I will follow the caravan and kill a man. Tomorrow night you will feast again."

"They would be watching," Gor said, and I knew he spoke the truth. "They would kill you, and we would still starve."

In the extremity of my concern, I grabbed his wrist. He did not pull away.

"I tell you, the meat is poisoned. You must vomit it forth."

"Alhazred, you know so little of us."

"What is there to know that concerns this poison?"

He smiled sadly, watching me.

"Ghouls cannot vomit."

I fell back on the sand as though struck and released his arm. He patted my knee in a comforting way.

"Perhaps it is not poisoned. We will see."

In an hour, the cramps began. I felt them in my stomach, clenching and relaxing, like a fist closed and opened. They moved down into my bowels, all the way down to my anus. My throat and tongue became numb. The younger ghouls began to murmur their distress. Gor had talked to the elders, and they remained silent as they squatted on the sand around the bones and remaining flesh of the two corpses and endured the discomfort that soon turned to pain, and then to agony. They hugged each other in their arms as though chilled, even though the night was hot, and shivered together.

I held Gor in my arms as he died. The tight, knowing smile never left him. He seemed almost to enjoy the joke the men had played on his clan.

"You are one of us," he told me after his sight failed him. He clutched my arm and drew blood with his talons, but I let him grip my flesh.

"We are the same," I agreed.

My words seemed to comfort him. He died with his eyes open, reflecting the starlight, a breath still issuing from his mouth.

I stood between the bones of the corpses and stared around at the bodies of the ghouls, distorted by their death agonies. Not one survived. How had the men of the caravan known which poison would be effective, and how had they possessed it? They must have procured the poison for just this purpose at some village or oasis on their journey. It was a terrible retribution. The Black Spring Clan was no more. No, I corrected myself, that is untrue—I am Black Spring Clan.

So sorry, my love, I am so sorry.

"You could not have known, Sashi. It is fate."

Had I possessed the strength, I would have taken all the members of the clan back to the pit, but I was starving and the pit was three days away. I could not bear to think of the vultures feasting on the corpses, as they surely would when the smell of death reached them, so I searched the hills until I found a cave large enough for my purposes. Through the last of the night and all through the following day I carried or dragged the ghouls into the cave, arranging the bodies in rows so that they lay one on top of the other. When all except Gor was in the cave, I closed its mouth with large stones, which I rolled into place with the last of my strength. Then I found a shadow to lie in and slept.

When I awoke it was dark. Gor's corpse lay beside me, bound up in the shrouds that had held the bodies of the children. It was not heavy on my shoulder. The bodies of ghouls are lightly framed except for their bellies, which are large to hold several days of meat, in the same way the camel holds a reservoir of water. By traveling both beneath the stars and the sun, I reached the pit in the night of the second day, my water exhausted, my belly still hungry.

I drank deep from the black cold water of the spring. It was necessary to see to my own hunger, or I would not be able to finish what I intended. Hunting was easy at the spring, since it was the only open source of water for many miles. I killed a snake and a desert rat and ate their flesh. Humans can eat anything, Gor had once said to me. That is our strength.

Unwrapping his body in the cave of the dead, I stood over it and let the muse that has always been a part of me find the words to sing in his honor. How long I sang, I could not tell, but my voice became hoarse, and the darkness gave way to dawn. When I had used all the words to praise him, I cut a small portion of flesh from his back, where I judged the poison would be weak, and ate it. The bitterness was slight. I would not have vomited the flesh, even had it been strong. With my dagger I sliced the flesh from his limbs and trunk, and set it aside, then cut through the sinews that connected the bones. His brain and eyes I drew forth with the wooden spoon that was kept for the purpose within the cave. I piled the bloody bones with care on the bone heap of his ancestors, but his skull I bound around my waist over my thawb with a piece of cord from the shrouds. The binding raised the hem of the garment from the ground.

What will you do, my love?

"We will see why the earth moans so piteously in the depths," I told Sashi with determination. Until that instant, I had not realized what I planned.

The great cavern was as I remembered it, rock sides glowing with chill radiance, when Gor and I had viewed it together from the ledge. I began to descend the awkward steps that wound around its curving interior, so broad and deep that each was an effort for human legs. From time to time a thundering moan issued up from the darkness. This should have aroused fear, but my heart was empty. I felt an impatience to reach the bottom, so that I could learn the secret that had forever been lost with the ghouls who had ventured down the stair before me. Gor's father had been the bravest of his clan, but he had never descended into the bowels of the earth, nor had Gor walked this path. Now I walked it for him, and with him.

For hours I descended the stair. The journey was monotonous, and the cavern appeared to have no bottom. Before long the vaulted roof had been lost in darkness above, just as the depths were concealed in shadow below, so that it was all but impossible to be aware that progress was being made. My legs ached. How much more they would complain on the ascent, I thought, and laughed softly. No one had ever ascended the stair.

The unvarying tedium coupled with my fatigue lulled me into a kind of dream, so that I nearly stepped onto empty space before I realized that the stair had ended. Not ended, I corrected myself, falling backward from the abyss. I could see it continuing further down the vertical wall of the cavern. There was a great gap where many of the projecting stones that formed the steps had fallen away. In the pallid light shining from the rock, I could see the irregular broken patches where the treads of the stairs had once joined the side of the cavern. The stairs had been shorn away as though from some titanic impact.

I peered downward, feeling disappointment. The damage did not appear recent. No sign of the floor of the cavern was visible at the end of the shadowed cylinder of its walls. Another moan rumbled up from the depths, mocking me. The gap was far too wide to leap across, and the wall between the two ends of the stair looked smooth apart from the marks of the tools that had cut the great cavern from the earth.

Something stirred at the opposite side of the gap in the stair, and I narrowed my eyes to better see through the dimness. There was a kind of gray bulge attached to the wall of the cavern just above the steps on the far side of the gap. I had not noticed it before because its color was almost identical to the color of the wall itself. As I looked upon it, the rounded side slowly opened, and a creature of nightmare stepped forth.

How does a man describe what the mind refuses to see? It was in size twice my height, and of the color of polished jet so that its limbs shone with a luster in the wall glow. Its chitinous body was shaped all in angles and folding lengths, like the body of a mantis. Four limbs supported it from the stones of the stairs, and two smaller limbs waved before its face as though testing the air. In its tear-shaped head numerous tiny eyes glittered. A ring of ropelike tentacles surrounded its mouth, which opened and shut from the sides and dripped a kind of dark ichor.

The thought came to me that I should flee, but I reflected that the same great gap that kept me from descending further prevented the monster from ascending. What a blessing this gap was to the men who dwelt on the surface of the earth, if such things as this lived in its depths. How fortuitous that the stair had become divided.

"You are not the thing that rumbles in the depths," I told it in a loud voice, seeking to raise my courage, for the sight of the monster stirred a tickle of fear within me.

"You are different from the others," it hissed and sighed, its mandibles clacking.

The words, though clearly expressed, were not in any language known to me, yet I understood their meaning in my mind.

"I am Alhazred, of the Black Spring Clan."

"You are not the same. Your shell is white instead of black."

"The others were ghouls. I am a man."

"I will feed on you as I fed on those who came before you."

I forced a laugh from my throat.

"You cannot ascend."

"True, I cannot ascend," the monster agreed.

It came into my mind to wonder why, if the thing could not cross the gap, no ghoul had ever returned up the stair.

With a whizzing like that of flat stones flung through the air, the ring of black tentacles around the mouth of the monster spun out and surrounded me. They felt like wire when they wrapped themselves about my arms and legs, and I know I would never break loose from them by force. They were eight in number. Effortlessly, they lifted me from my feet and drew me across the gap toward the opening and shutting jaws of the nightmare. I cursed myself in my mind for my stupidity. It was not difficult now to imagine how the ghouls had died.

Heat radiated from its armored body. It transferred me from its mouth tentacles to its forelimbs with surprising delicacy and held me close to its glittering little eyes to examine my head. I felt the exhaust of its breath on my cheek as it pulled me toward its mouth. It stopped and held me motionless, regarding my face.

"You bear the mark of Nyarlathotep," it said.

Remembering my dream, I touched my forehead, which was smooth and unblemished.

"I have no mark. It was a dream."

It ignored my words.

"You belong to Nyarlathotep," it said to itself in its strange clicking language, as though meditating in its own mind what to do with me.

Before I could speak in response, it returned me to its black tentacles and extended me across the gap in the stair to set me on the steps with a light touch.

"Tell your master that Nee'sak'hela always repays her debts."

"I have no master," I shouted in anger.

The chitinous thing turned away as though I had said nothing and entered the gray bulge on the wall above the stair. The aperture of the sack closed like an anus behind its body. A deep groan echoed up from the depths of the cavern, vibrating the stone beneath my sandals. For a while I stood staring at the place where the thing had vanished, but when it failed to emerge, I realized that I had been dismissed without ceremony, as a man dismisses a small child or pet animal, and would gain no second audience for my unanswered questions. With weary legs, I turned and began the long climb.

Chapter 8

There was nothing to keep me in the pit of the Black Spring. Even had I felt inclined to remain there, sooner or later a raiding party from the Red Hill Clan would come, and when they found me they would kill me. I had been content merely to live from one night to the next, taking what fierce joy I could find in the hunt, but the death of the ghouls made me question why the fates had blighted my life and filled it with so much sorrow. Was it a punishment for my transgression, or a test of my resourcefulness? That I had managed to endure for so long despite the hardships of my circumstances seemed more than natural.

As I leaned over the waters of the spring in the light of early morning, using its surface for an obsidian mirror while I shaved off the stubble of my beard with the edge of my knife, I studied my reflection. Hair and eyebrows had grown back upon my head, and the wounds on my cheeks were no more than thin scars. Suppose it were possible through the arts of necromancy to restore my face and body to wholeness? Could I then return to the world of men and live as a man? Perhaps even find a way to become reunited with Narisa? I dismissed these thoughts with bitter laughter, yet they would not entirely withdraw from my mind.

One last time I slept in my little cave, then filled my water skin at the spring and set forth at twilight toward the northwest. I had eaten the white spiders, and my head swam with their power.

Where are you going, my love?

"Long ago you had told me that the nameless lost city contains treasures and secrets."

That is so.

"Once while hunting, I spoke of the nameless city, and Gor pointed to a line of hills and said it lay behind them, although he was afraid to take me there. He called the place Irem."

How can a nameless city have a name?

"That is a mystery," I agreed. "We will seek the answer together."

I traveled quickly across the darkening sands after the manner of ghouls, by turns walking and running. It was, I had discovered, the way to cover the greatest distance in the shortest time with the least expenditure of strength. A dozen steps I walked, then a dozen steps I ran, and did this over and over as the ground fled beneath my sandals.

The land in this region of the Empty Space was more desolate than elsewhere. It is a strange truth that windblown sand can by its mere shape express sensuality, or peace, or restlessness. In this place the sands held the shape of sorrow. My inner pain was perfectly mirrored by its tortured starlit forms, so that I felt at one with the desert, as though it had shaped itself to echo my heartbeat.

On the crest of a dune a man dressed in a black robe stood with his back turned, gazing across the desolation. His body revealed itself by the silhouette it cut in the starry heavens. I stopped running and stood silent, my breaths stilled in my throat. The sight of his tall form on the dune awoke a sense that I had seen the same scene before, but when I tried to remember where, it eluded my thoughts. What man would walk alone across the desert at night? He must be mad. It was only later that it occurred to me that I was a man, walking across the desert at night, alone. At the time, instinct prevailed, and I saw only meat. I drew my dagger and approached on soft steps up the gentle slope of the dune.

As I raised my blade to plunge it between his shoulders, he turned, and I recognized the faceless figure of my dreams. My limbs stiffened and became heavy, as though cast in molten lead. I found it impossible to move. Black silk covered his features within his hood, if indeed he possessed features. I quailed inwardly at the thought. So he was real after all, just as Gor had told me. What else had he said? That it was bad luck to encounter Nyarlathotep walking abroad across the sands. I heard his breath beneath the caul, like a distant wind, and felt it cold against my cheeks. Two points of light glittered beneath the silk. He lifted his bony hand, the skin like black leather, and extended it toward my face, and I sensed that he intended to slay me. I babbled the first thing that came into my head.

"Nee'sak'hela pays her debts!"

The hand stopped. For a moment it hung motionless, and I saw the gleam of a star reflected in the stone of one of the rings that sheathed its elongated fingers. A shadow like the wing of a hawk crossed my eyes, and he was gone. My trembling legs refused to support me. I fell to my knees, relief so great that silent tears sprang from my eyes and streamed down my cheeks, wondering if I had merely dreamed again of the faceless wanderer. When I stood and looked down at the sand, I knew it was no dream. Footprints led up the dune from the opposite side. They ended in front of my dust-covered toes, only a step away. Whatever made them had been solid, but had vanished into the air. Wondering at this strange meeting, so soon after the monster in the cavern voiced the name of the ancient god, I continued on my quest for the forgotten city.

The moon in her last quarter had just risen when I saw the hills indicated by Gor. I approached them at a walk as I studied the sheer walls. They were more ramparts than hills, and there seemed no pass through their barrier. I began to circle them, seeking some opening or a way of climbing over their peaks. As I walked, I became aware that the ground beneath my feet glowed faintly. It was like the glow of the caravan road, but less bright.

My head hummed pleasantly from the effect of the spiders, so it was some time before I noticed the sounds that accompanied me on the still night air. Over the soft crunch of my sandals came the faint grind of pebbles beneath the hooves of camels, the jingle of a bridle bell, the rub of leather against leather, the flutter of cloth in the breeze. These sounds grew more distinct as I walked in a kind of dream. I knew them at once, having heard them many times. They were the sounds of a caravan. Yet it was obvious that no caravan had traveled this ancient road for centuries.

The drug of second sight dulled my curiosity. I looked idly around, and saw with faint surprise that a man walked beside me leading a heavily laden camel. The edges of both flickered with pale radiance. He observed me watching him and nodded with a knowing glance. He spoke but no words came from his moving lips. Looking away,

I saw a wagon before me, and almost at the same instant I heard its wheels grinding the sand. A babble of voices arose from somewhere in front of its obscuring bulk. With growing wonder, I glanced over my shoulder and saw more wagons and more camels with men seated upon them or leading them. The clothes of the men were strangely cut, of a style I had never seen. Evidently the caravan was rich, for they wore much silver and gold.

With each passing moment their forms grew more solid, and I both heard and saw them with increasing clarity. The sharp scent of camel dung filled the air. It was strange that none of the men showed surprise at my sudden appearance among them. They seemed to accept me without comment as one of their own. I might have continued to walk with them, and no doubt would be walking with them still, had I not noticed that as the men and camels and wagons grew more solid, the desert on either side of the ancient caravan road became transparent and pale.

With a curse I shook myself from my dreaming trance and thrust through the bulk of the camel on my left. I felt it separate and reform after my passage like smoke as I stumbled off the glowing strip of ground. At once the ghostly caravan vanished as though it had never existed, and the night fell silent, save for the quiet drone of beetles. What might have happened had I continued to walk the road, I cannot know, but there are many kinds of portals, and not all take the form of whirlwinds.

I followed the road more carefully toward the hills, walking beside it but avoiding its touch against my feet, and suddenly what had by a trick of angles appeared sheer rock in the moonlight opened into a narrow pass that cut through the hills like the blade of a knife.

So narrow was the pass, two laden camels could not have walked along it side by side. The rock walls above the pass leaned inward and nearly touched. As I entered beneath them, the soft flutter of bats came from their heights as they hunted the unseen but ever-present buzzing beetles. Shadows lay deep at the bottom of the pass as it wound its way through the hills, but the ground offered no pitfall. It had been beaten flat and smooth by centuries of travelers. No doubt the very ghost caravan I had seen on the road had walked between these stone buttresses long ago, when its men possessed bodies of flesh.

The way ahead widened and brightened, and I discovered that within the ring of cliffs lay a small valley. The pass was located at its narrow end at a slight elevation. I stood gazing across the valley floor, and wondered to see a glowing city of many tall pillars and towers that rose up from the sand like some fable of paradise. Though the city covered no great extent, the perfection of its shining white spires was a marvel to behold. A wall surrounded it, and in the wall was set a pointed gate of impressive dimensions of which I could not be certain in the moonlight, but I thought I saw the measured pacing of guards as they walked the top of the wall on either side of the projecting arch of the gate.

Surely this must be fabled Irem, said by storytellers to have been the most beautiful city in all the world, with a thousand towers that rose higher than any other towers built by men, yet so wicked in its ways that God cast it down in a great storm and buried it beneath the sand for eternity. The last part of the legend at least must be untrue, I reflected, as I crossed the valley floor toward the gate. The towers still stood. Yet as I drew nearer, I felt uncertainty. There was a disturbing silver light that played over the city, making it waver like heat rising from the desert beneath the sun. The same thinness that I had noticed in the wagons and camels of the ghost caravan showed itself in the walls and pillars, and grew more distinct with each step.

The illusion persisted almost within touching distance of the gate. As I reached out my hand, everything dissolved into shadows and ceased utterly. Before me lay only a few scattered stones and a broad sinkhole where the sand sloped gently inward. I stalked forward through the place where the gate had stood, cursing in a loud voice all ghosts and all mirages, both those under the sun and those beneath the moon. No doubt the treasure was a mirage also, I thought as I sat in discouragement on one of the rounded stones and drew up my water skin to drink.

In idle frustration I picked up a pebble and threw it at a rounded stone that projected from the sand a few paces away. I picked up a second pebble with the same intention, but the regularity of its surface made me hold it before my face. It glowed with its own light, and I realized that it was not a stone, but a fragment of pottery. I stood and looked around the sinkhole with greater care. The rounded boulders were glowing also, but very faintly. Crossing to one that was more exposed than the others, I dug with my hands around its base. Its sides were straight, and continued unbroken into the depths of the sand. It was not a boulder but the top of a stone pillar. The roughness of the weathering where the stone was exposed had deceived me. All around me were buried pillars.

"We have reached Irem. Show me its treasures."

I cannot.

"Then what use are you?"

The bitterness in my voice earned me a reproving glance from Sashi when I closed my eyelids.

The nameless city is a place of wealth and secrets. So it was whispered on the wind.

"I believe djinn are more credulous of travelers' tales even than men," I told her.

Wandering into the shallow bowl that lay in the center of the irregular ring of pillars, I kicked at the sand and heard its soft rustle as it slid down the slope. The rounded hollow of the ground magnified it in my ear-holes. My annoyance was not with Sashi but with myself for placing trust in a fable. There was nothing here but sand. The dry rustle of the tumbling grains drew my gaze downward, and I saw that the sand had ceased to move where I had kicked it, yet the sound of its sliding had not ceased. Here was a mystery, though it seemed unlikely to make my fortune. I walked down the slope and stood in the center of the depression, turning slowly to find the source of the sound.

The rustle came from a shadow midway up the eastern slope. I approached it curiously, thinking the noise must be made by a serpent or other small burrowing creature. Only when I stood close was I able to see that the shadow was an opening at the side of a pillar that barely showed its top above the sand. I fell to my knees and crawled forward, listening. When my head came near the hole, I heard a faint echo of sifting sand, and felt coolness on my moist lips. I made a click with my tongue and heard the echoes dance beneath the earth. Beyond the hole lay a cavern of no small dimension.

For a moment, I hesitated. It was possible that I might be able to squirm my way into the narrow opening, but that did not mean I would be able to squirm my way out. The vent sloped downward, and it was always easier to slide down soft sand than climb up it. The absurdity of my qualms made me smile. It was not as though I could go back along the path I had traveled. What did life offer behind me? Very well, I thought, I would go forward, and take what chance fate provided.

Extending my arms, I slid them into the vent, then my head. It was taller than it was wide, so I turned my body on to its side and was able to force in my shoulders, and after them my hips. The sheath of my dagger ground against my thigh until I shifted it out of the way, along with Gor's skull. As the opening narrowed, I felt a brief panic that I would be trapped upside down in the earth with only my sandal-clad feet projecting when the sun rose, a pretty sight for the vultures to pick at and puzzle over. I inched forward with my fingers by digging them into the sides of the passage, which had some firmness, and at last was rewarded when my body slid with sudden release down a slope of sand and came to rest a dozen feet beneath the hole, the outline of which glowed faintly with moonlight when I looked behind.

It was plain at a glance that I would never get out the way I had come in, therefore there was nothing else to do but search for some other passage from the cavern. When I moved from the slope of sand I discovered that the walls shone with tiny lights resembling stars. Looking more closely, I saw that the light came from small seashells embedded in the rock, each one glowing with its residual life-force to my enhanced vision. The glow was not enough to illuminate the cavern, but was sufficient to keep me from bumping into the walls of the cave, which sloped downward and widened as it descended.

The cave opened outward to a vast space that had been shaped by intelligent labor. At intervals massive pillars supported its vaulted roof. I stopped and held my breath, listening. From the darkness came the faint splash of a drop of water falling into a pool from a great height. Sniffing the air, I tried to discern the scent of water, but it if was present, it was so faint that I could not be sure whether I smelled it, or only imagined it. The space was like a great underground cistern, but many times larger than those I had seen at Sana'a. At intervals, openings led away through the curving wall to other chambers similar in design.

The entire ground beneath the lost city of Irem had been hollow, and it came to my mind that the thousand pillars of legend were perhaps not merely the pillars of its towers, but also the pillars that supported this hidden reservoir. It was a work of construction to rival the seven wonders of the world. I studied the slope of debris behind me, a mingling of sand and shaped blocks. Evidently the great voids beneath the city had collapsed, drawing down its buildings and forming the sink pit through which I had gained entry, but many chambers yet remained.

How many centuries had passed since water lapped at these stones? The same disaster that had buried the city deep under the sand must have cracked and emptied the underground cisterns that contained its riches—for the true wealth of a city in the midst of the Empty Space was water, and this wealth Irem had possessed in unimaginable abundance. I bent and rubbed the dust of the floor between my fingers. There was no trace of moisture. Again in the distance came the sound of a drop falling and striking the surface of a pool. It was not possible to determine its direction, and I wondered if it was the ghost of a sound, even as the glowing shells embedded in the stones were the visible ghosts of the dead creatures of an ancient sea.

A squeak and rustle in the dust aroused me from this meditation. The glowing form of a large rat approached without hesitation and began to nip and worry at the stocking-covered tip of my large toe, exposed between the bands of my sandals. A very obliging creature, I thought as I bent quickly to snatch it up and break its neck. Its blood was hot and sweet where I bit its throat. Tasting it on my tongue, I knew it would sustain me in the absence of water. I tore its fur with my teeth and was pleased to discover its flesh layered in fat. To a man accustomed to the meager fare of the Empty Space it was a feast. After eating until I was no longer hungry, I cut the best pieces that remained from the carcass and stored them in a folded rag in one of my pockets.

A bat flew silently past above my head, its wings bright against the darkness of the arched roof. Looking around with greater attention, I noticed a snake uncoiling itself from beneath a stone, and several spiders clinging to a pillar. This place, lost and forgotten though it might be, was far from lifeless. Scattered in irregular piles and drifts, as though left by the receding water, were pieces of wood. I picked up a small stick. It felt hard and dense, and exuded age. The wood must have formed part of the cistern's structure when it had been in use, and been cast down along with the rest of the city by the cataclysm that buried it.

Keeping a wall close enough at hand that its glow did not vanish in the general gloom, I set off to explore the perimeter of the caverns. There were many rats, but they kept a polite distance. No doubt they smelled the blood of their kin on my fingers and face. Their glowing bodies bobbed like torches, winking in and out as they moved behind fallen stones or piles of old wood. Soon the effects of the spiders would wear off, and the darkness would be absolute. This prospect did not alarm me. I had grown used to the dark on the open desert, though the desert never knew so deep a blackness as subsisted below the earth. It would make exploration more difficult. I wondered if I should risk a second feeding on the spiders.

With a shrug, I opened the silk scarf in which I carried them and put three of the shriveled bodies in my mouth. I chewed them slowly as I wrapped the rest with care and returned them to their pocket. The only ill effect I had ever suffered from their use was a headache. Surely that was a small price to pay for the gift of second sight.

The first indication that I was not alone in the cisterns was the tang of wood smoke on the air. Following it with what was left of my nose, I saw the redness of firelight reflecting from the pillars before me and approached without sound, as I had learned to do by watching the ghouls. I peered around the edge of the wall into a secondary chamber. Flames danced in a hearth of stones on a low ledge of natural rock that the architect of the cisterns had not taken the trouble to remove during construction. The wall behind the ledge was hollow, so that the space above it formed a shallow cave.

The fire glowing in its bed of embers gave off almost no visible smoke, nor did the dense ancient wood crackle, but burned with a quiet hiss. Before it rested what appeared to be a disordered pile of sticks and old rags, until the heap moved, and I realized it was a living being. The creature sang to itself in a cracked voice, and muttered words. Some of the words I recognized as an ancient dialect of my own language, but others were wholly strange in my ears. I crept nearer, the better to hear what the creature said. It seemed wrapped up in its mutterings and did not notice my approach.

The face lined by the flames was human, but so leathered and creased with age that it appeared a grotesque carving in stone. Rank white hair matted in filth hung down its shoulders and back and sprouted from its pointed chin. About its hunched shoulders the creature clutched a dirty cloak of heavy wool of some indeterminate brown color. The hand that held the edge of the cloak was unnaturally large, like the hand of a giant, and the same was true of the creature's shoulders, but by way of compensation the bulk of its legs beneath the folds of the cloak appeared withered.

My fascination was almost the cause of my death. As I worked my way around the side of a pillar to approach behind the creature, it sprang and twisted in the air, throwing itself backward toward me with its great arms outstretched and a ferocious expression on its face. I had time to notice the absence of teeth in its blackened gums as I darted backward. The thing rustled and scurried after me, but its stunted legs were no match for my quickness. It soon became tired of the chase, and stood hunched almost double, its hooked nose near the dust as it wheezed for breath.

"Wicked boy, to creep up on I'thakuah without bringing her a gift," she croaked and spat, for by her words it was plain the creature was female.

"What gift would you have from me?" I asked.

She cackled and bent until her head touched the stones at her feet, and she looked like nothing more than an oddly shaped boulder, apart from the shaking of her sides.

"No gift, yet already he asks for payment," she muttered, her tiny dark eyes glittering at me from under heavy lids. "Ungrateful brat."

With a sniff, she gathered her cloak about her and hobbled back to the ledge, then hopped up on it like a frog and settled herself on the flat stone that served her as a seat by the fire.

I approached warily, intent on probing the madness of this hag to determine whether she possessed anything of value. She was scarcely worth killing, and I doubted her blood would be as sweet as that of the rats.

Reminded by this thought of the meat I carried, I drew the rag that contained it from my robes and offered it to her.

"Here is a gift," I told her. "Fresh meat. Eat it if you wish."

Respect for her surprising quickness caused me to toss the bundle onto the ledge beside the fire. She snatched it up and unwrapped it eagerly. Drool oozed from the corners of her toothless mouth as she chewed and tore at the red meat with her hardened gums. In less than a dozen breaths the meat was gone.

"Was the gift to your liking?" I asked, marveling at the voraciousness of her appetite.

She leaned back and cackled until the spittle sprayed from her lips into the fire.

"Yes, yes, a perfect gift, you wasteful boy."

"I had no need for it," I told her. "The rats are many and easy to kill."

"Easy for one whose limbs are long and quick," she said with sudden bitterness, and the glance she cast me was filled with hatred.

"Do you live alone in this place?"

"No!" she roared, and slapped the ledge with her hand. It made the sound of brick striking brick. "One question. One question for one gift. That is the bargain."

Moving sideways so that the fire would be between us as I approached the edge of the ledge, I considered this curious pronouncement. She must value her knowledge highly if she considered a single answer worth a full day's meat.

I noticed in the shadows of her cave, at the edge of the fire glow, a pile of what appeared to be white stones. As I came near the ledge, I saw that they were skulls. The hag marked the direction of my gaze and nodded.

"My keepsakes," she said, eyeing the skull tied to my waist. "You collect them also."

"Only one," I corrected her. "This is the skull of a friend. A ghoul of the Black Spring Clan."

"Ghoul's skull," she muttered, the eagerness departing from her features. "No good, no good."

Peering closer at the pile of skulls in the cave, I saw that they were all human. Those on the bottom of the pile were brown with age and repeated handling, but the one on top still had bits of flesh clinging to its surface.

"Where do you get these skulls, old woman?"

She raised her long finger and wagged it at me.

"You can't trick me, boy. One question, one gift. That is the bargain."

I stumbled and caught myself on the edge of the ledge. In the excitement of avoiding her attack, I had not noticed my increasing dizziness, or the sickness in the pit of my stomach. The shadows had begun to pulsate with each throb of blood through my brain, and my headache had grown more intense moment by moment, but I had ignored these signs in my preoccupation with the hag. With surprise, the realization came to me that I must be ill. The remains of the chewed rat spewed from my spasming belly onto the dust of the floor and I fell forward, unconscious before my face struck the stone.

Chapter 9

In my disordered dreams, the tall man in black bent over me and spoke, but I could not understand his words. Each time he raised his bony hand to draw aside his silk caul, I ran away into the darkness, but there was no escape. He always found me. At last he cornered me and removed his veil. It was the face of the witch I'thakuah, peering down into mine. Something cold and wet pressed against my lips. I sucked on it, and it washed the sour taste from my tongue. Closing my eyes, which I had not realized were open, I slept.

The warmth of the fire radiating against my side woke me from an unconsciousness as deep as death. My mind floated, detached from the lifeless doll of flesh and blood that lay on its back with its head turned toward the fire. With effort, I tried to lift my hand and felt one of my fingers twitch, then two. Life returned slowly to my limbs. I tilted my head upward and saw the witch seated in her customary place, watching me with keen black eyes that were like black raisins set in pastry. The memory of my sickness and collapse returned. I was able to raise my hand to my face. My right cheek felt bruised, but nothing else appeared damaged.

The witch held up the red and green silk cloth that contained my storehouse of spiders.

"You ate these?" she asked.

I nodded.

"You ate too many."

My hand feebly fumbled around my waist in what I hoped was an unobtrusive movement. With relief I touched the bone hilt of my dagger. Why I felt relieved, I would not have been able to say, since I was so weak a child might have taken it away from me and used it to slit my throat. I wondered why the witch had not killed me. My water skin lay beside the fire, and I realized that it had not been a dream when I had seen her face leaning over mine, and had felt wetness on my lips.

"How long?" I asked.

She threw back her head and laughed harshly as though I had made a fine jest, then she spread her long arms to indicate the space around the fire.

"Do you see a water clock? A sun dial? There is no time here, fool."

Forcing my shoulders up so that I sat supported on my arms behind me, I looked at the wall of the cistern beyond the firelight. Nothing glowed in the surface of the stone. The effects of the spiders had worn off. That meant at least a day had passed. My head began to throb. I closed my eyes, and in a few moments the pain between my eyebrows became less intense.

Through the gap in her dirty woolen cloak I saw her breasts hanging down her chest like two empty leather bags. A tangle of curly white hair covered her groin, which she made no attempt to conceal by closing her knees. I turned to the hissing embers of the fire. The wood in this place was so hard and dry, it burned almost without flame, like charcoal.

"Why do you live here?" I asked.

"No more questions," she barked. "The bargain is—"

"I know, one question for one gift. No questions. Conversation."

She seemed to consider this, her ugly head cocked to one side. I thought she had forgotten me. She began to sing to herself in a toneless voice.

"This is my place," she said at last, as though speaking to herself. "No danger here. No time. I do my work."

What work this ancient hag could possibly perform alone in a hole beneath the earth was beyond my imagination.

"Long ago I lived in the city above. After the earth shook and the buildings fell, I came here. There are many fat rats. The rats in the valley were few and scrawny."

The coherence of her speech surprised me. She was not so senile as I had supposed.

"You lived in Irem before it fell," I said, voicing it as a statement.

She glanced at me coyly.

"I am older than I look."

A single white louse dropped from her tangled hair. She picked it up in her quick fingers and turned it over in the firelight, then ate it.

"You do your work," I said, hoping to induce her to speak more freely.

"I listen at the crack to the ones who dwell below in the nameless place. I gather information and sift it."

"You gather information," I repeated tonelessly.

"Many secrets are mine of things above and below. I teach them to those who bring me gifts."

"You might have killed me, but you did not."

She moved so quickly, I had no chance even to flinch away before my jaw was cupped in one of her enormous hands. Upon her stunted legs she might be awkward, but within the length of her body she could stretch with the speed of a striking serpent. Her hand forced my chin up as she regarded me with her black eyes.

"You are the only man I'thakuah has ever seen who is uglier than she."

With a cackle like the rasp of a dry hinge, she released me and leaned back to her sitting stone. I glanced at the pile of skulls. She followed my gaze with her own.

"Pretty boys. All so pretty. I ate their faces."

Picking up my water skin, I slung its strap over my shoulder. It did not feel lighter than it had before. Perhaps the hag did not need to drink, I reflected. With greater care I picked up the silk cloth containing the spiders from beside her, but she appeared not to notice. She sat gazing into the embers, muttering to herself in some language I had never before heard spoken.

"I will hunt, and bring gifts."

She nodded.

"Good. Go hunt. Bring gifts."

Strength had returned to my limbs, though my thighs still trembled when I stood. Climbing from the ledge, I felt my way into the darkness of the cisterns beyond the glow of the embers. It was necessary to move slowly to avoid tripping on stones fallen from the roof and tangles of wood. No doubt the witch knew every step of the cisterns with her eyes closed, having dwelt here for so many unnumbered years. I would be at a fatal disadvantage without the second sight of the spiders, should she decide to kill me and eat my face, ugly though it might be. Even so, I could not risk becoming poisoned by taking the spiders so soon after having been overcome by their effects. They were more dangerous than I had supposed.

It was not possible to become lost in the cisterns if the outer wall was kept continually within touching distance on one side. There were many round chambers, linked by short arched passages to a larger central space. Access must have been obtained by the city dwellers from openings in the roof. Doors in the walls would be useless when the cisterns were filled with water. I wondered how the water had entered to fill this vast space, and what its source might have been.

At one place where the wall of an outer chamber was natural rock rather than shaped stones, I came upon a fissure that ran up from the floor higher than I could reach. A faint breeze stirred the hairs of my eyebrows as I put my face into the opening. The way was narrow, but by turning my body to the side I found that I could slide between the rough walls of stone. The bottom of the cleft had filled with rubble and dust, and gave support for walking. I might have gone further, but a rustle in the darkness and the quiet sounds of a large creature sniffing the air quelled my curiosity. I slid backward and emerged to continue my exploration by touch of the water chambers. In my mind I noted the location of the crack so that I could return to it more quickly when I wished to probe its depths.

The care I took in my blind progress was repaid when I crossed to the middle of the central chamber. As I slid a foot forward, the stones of the floor ended on empty space. Dropping to my knees, I crawled to the void and felt the edge with my hands. It curved around and eventually returned to itself. Within the center of the space was the mouth of a well. It seemed unlikely to me that such a well would be used to drain the chambers, so I reasoned it must be one of the inlets for the spring or fountain that had kept them filled, before the failure of the water source. I dropped a pebble into the well and heard nothing.

For my own future security, I dragged some pieces of wood from a pile of rubble and laid them at the edge of the well so that they completely surrounded it. At least I would not wander over the edge in the darkness without some warning of my peril.

If the water had fountained up from this vent to fill the cisterns, there must be an outflow, or several outflows, high in the walls to maintain a constant level, but I had not encountered any in my partial circuit of the chambers. Perhaps they were well above my head, if they existed, and might for all I knew be too narrow to crawl through. Thus far, the only potential safe exit from this place I had found was the fissure. I might, with much work, dig my way out the way I had entered, but long before I escaped to the surface I'thakuah would have me by the heels. I could slay her when she slept, I thought, if indeed she ever did sleep. She seemed not to require water, and there was something inhuman in the shape of her body, shriveled with age though it might be. Surely no common woman could live the centuries she claimed to have lived. It might be dangerous to attempt to kill her. I decided to wait and learn what I could before I took this course.

The rats were easy to catch, even in total darkness. I heard them squeaking and the rustle of their long naked tails in the dust. They were accustomed to avoid the lunges of the witch, and knew enough to stay just beyond her reach, but did not move quickly enough to flee when I dashed forward and fell on them, clutching them to my chest. I took care to explore the space where I hunted before attempting these sudden rushes, so that I would not dash out my brains on a pillar or some angled beam. I killed four rats, one for myself and three for the witch. Mine I ate standing in the darkness with the other carcasses at my feet. The water in the eyeballs was almost tasteless. Moving with greater confidence, I returned the way I had come, the rats swinging by their tails in my hand.

She still sat before her fire, feeding small bits of wood into it. Somewhere she must have hidden flint and tinder, and a blade for shaving the ancient wood into slivers of kindling, or she would never be able to restart the fire were it to burn itself out. The fire would keep the rats at bay while she slept, if she ever did sleep. Perhaps she needed its heat for her crippled limbs. At the scuff of my sandals in the dust she raised her head and sniffed the air with her hooked nose.

Climbing onto the ledge, I dropped the rats beside the fire.

"Three gifts."

"You shall have three answers," she said, gazing up at me with what I guessed was intended to be a smile.

Without ceremony, she tore out the throat of each rat in turn with her powerful fingers and sucked its blood, then gnawed the flesh from one of the carcasses. The other two she set aside. I watched in fascination. So powerful were her fingers, she had little need for a knife. Were she to grip my throat in her enormous hands, she could snap my neck as easily as I had snapped the necks of the rats.

"Ask your first question, and I will teach you."

On the return across the cistern floor, I had considered what to ask. One question seemed more pressing than any other, so I asked it first.

"Is there a safe way out of this place that leads to the surface?"

"Yes."

I waited for her to continue, but she merely stared at me with glittering eyes, an expression of amusement on her face. I realized that I would need to phrase my questions more carefully if I was to gain any useful elaboration. The witch had played this game for centuries, but I was new to its rules.

"What are the directions that would allow me to leave this place and make my way to the surface?"

Amusement turned to annoyance, when she found she could not answer my second question with a single word.

"Go to the crack in the wall and enter it, provided your body is thin enough to fit," she said, eyeing me with an appraising glance. "Descend to the nameless city and go out from it through the gates of golden light to the dry river. By following the riverbed, you will emerge from under the ground."

The directions were clear and easy to comprehend. I wondered what she was not telling me. Almost I asked it as my third question, but curiosity at her mention of the city without a name overcame my prudence.

"What is the nameless city?"

She nodded with satisfaction, knowing that I could not resist asking about the city. It must have been a favorite topic, since she chose to speak at length.

"Before men came to this place, a race of creatures unlike any other dwelt here beneath the surface in a city of countless rooms and halls cut into the solid rock. Ages past they raised their herds in the valley above, but when the land became blighted by a great catastrophe, they retreated underground and began to shape their city. Though their wisdom was vast, after uncounted ages their crafts began to fail them, until they could no longer raise sufficient food in their tunnels. They needed a new source of meat, for they ate only meat, and devised a plan to attract men to the valley. With their arts they channeled upward a portion of the mighty river that flowed beneath their city so that it formed a spring in the valley. Men who happened upon the water settled beside it and eventually a city of many pillars arose that was called Irem.

"For uncounted generations the two races lived together, one city above the other. The dwellers below hid themselves from the dwellers above. The men shaped natural cavities already present in the rock to make these great chambers to hold their precious water. The other race, that has no name in the languages of men, took their food by stealth from among the people of Irem, at first only a few, but as their arts failed them, more and more in order to survive. A cult of the lower dwellers grew up among men, who offered sacrifices to those rarely glimpsed things of the nameless city that ventured up to the foundations of Irem. Travelers passing through the city on the caravan road sometimes went to their beds, and were never seen again.

"The kings of Irem were ruthless and full of craft. They made laws against dealing with the dwellers beneath, and killed all those who defied them, yet when they wished to learn of the magic that only the dwellers below possessed, they trafficked with them in secret and offered their own slaves, children, and concubines as meat. The nameless race took care never to offend the kings too greatly, but it is said that they made the mistake of abducting a king's favorite wife. This so enraged the king, he ordered his army to enter the city below and exterminate all that lived in its halls. The older race fought back but were no match for the soldiers. Just as they were on the point of defeat, the earth shook and drew the city of Irem into itself, so that not a second life was spared of citizen or slave, nor even of beast. I alone survived. In terror the soldiers fled the halls of the nameless city and were slaughtered from behind by the dwellers beneath. With no source of meat, they dwindled and at last abandoned their city, and now all is dead both above and below, as you see."

The way she told this tale showed that it was not the first time she had related it. I wondered how many other disciples had sat by her fire and listened to the same words. Probably as many as the number of skulls that composed her pyramid of trophies. Sooner or later, she would try to kill me as she had killed all the others.

Weariness overcame me in a wave and left my limbs trembling with fatigue and my eyelids heavy. I stretched out beside the fire on my side and continued to watch her through the shimmerings of heat that rose from the embers, still mumbling to herself as though she talked to invisible visitors. Drawing my dagger, I slid it close to my chest and held its hilt in my curled fingers as my eyes closed.

When I awoke, there was silence. Without changing the rhythms of my breaths, I parted my eyelids barely enough to see that the witch was gone from her place and the fire had burned low from lack of tending. A rustle came from the shadows at the back of the shallow cave. Tilting my head slowly so that the movement would not be noticed, I saw the witch squatting over an exposed cleft in the floor that had been covered by a flat stone. She cackled softly to herself and took from the hole something that flashed and shimmered. Light danced over the roof of the cave and the face of the witch. It was a mirror of no great size in an ornately wrought frame of silver.

Setting the mirror upright against a stone where she could see herself in its depths, she reached again into the hole and drew forth a shimmering chain set with jewels that seemed to glow with their own inner fire. They were of many colors, like the opal, not smoky within but clear and bright as diamond. The witch fastened this chain around her neck and admired herself from several angles in the looking glass, making little mewing sounds of pleasure. From the hole she took a thing like a tiara made of heavy gold set with rubies and balanced it upon her tangled thicket of hair. It did not sit firmly but wobbled as though about to fall, and I saw that it had not been shaped for a human skull. Several rings set with jewels she took from the hiding place and slid over her fingers. Even her giant hands were too small for their hoops. They slipped around under the weight of their stones, so that she repeatedly had to turn them to admire her hands in the mirror.

You see, my love, there is treasure here.

I will never doubt you again, honorable spirit, I said to the djinn in my mind.

As though she had heard my thoughts, I'thakuah hissed and turned to look at me. Her eyes glittered like black pearls, framed by the glowing multicolored stones of the chain and the rubies in her hair. I let the slits beneath my eyelids close and continued to draw slow breaths, my heart thudding in my chest. The bone hilt of the dagger still pressed against my fingers near my chest, but I did not dare to close them more tightly around it. After several breaths, I parted my eyelids and saw the witch replacing her treasures into their hole. She put the mirror in last, after gazing for a long while at her face in its depths, then covered the hole with the flat rock.

With uncanny silence she pushed herself up to her feet and hobbled to the fire, where she gathered up the two uneaten rats by their tails. Moving to the edge of the ledge, she let herself down to the floor of the cistern. A single backward look she cast me to assure herself that I had not stirred, then like a shadow she merged into the darkness. I heard the soft rustle of her cloak as its hem dragged behind her in the dust.

How good her ears were I had no way of knowing, or whether she could truly see through the utter blackness of the artificial caverns, but my curiosity compelled me to rise and follow the sound of her cloak, moving with what I hoped was greater stealth. She did not hug the wall but set out boldly across the open floor, avoiding the debris with the skill of repeated practice. It helped my progress that I followed in her path, since she chose the easiest way for her stunted legs, walking around anything she might have to climb over. Even so, it was difficult to follow noiselessly. I could not approach too near or the smell of my body would betray my presence. When I hung back, I sometimes crept into the stones or beams she had skirted. By walking bent over with my hands extended in front of my body at the level of my shins to feel my way, I somehow avoided stumbling.

The sudden silence made me halt and still my breaths. To my eyes the darkness was absolute, but for all I knew I stood in plain sight of the witch. I bent lower in an attempt to make my body appear no more than another pile of stones. The silence lengthened, and I began to worry that the crafty hag was creeping around to steal upon me from behind, when she spoke aloud in a strange guttural language that echoed, as though she were speaking into a great bell. She could not be more than six paces in front of where I stood. Cool air touched my cheek, and I realized that the witch had made her way to the fissure in the rock wall and was speaking into its depths.

A second voice replied in the same strange language. It was deeper than the voice of the witch yet soft, and slurred as though the mouth that formed the words had not been designed for speech. I'thakuah spoke again more briefly. A rustle came from the fissure as something was thrown into its depths, and soon after a second similar sound. I heard the click of claws on stone and the slither of a heavy body. Something was grabbed up from the loose rubble at the floor of the crack. A moment later came the unmistakable tinkle of silver striking the stones that lined the floor of the cistern. The witch made a little noise of delight in her throat and felt about in the dust until she located the object, which I took to be a ring or some similar trinket.

I knew by experiment that the misshapen body of the witch was too broad to fit into the fissure. Evidently whatever dwelt beyond its opening was too large to pass out. In return for meat it gave her adornments. Yet this was not the only commerce that passed between them.

They began to converse, the thing in the depths talking at length and the witch making short remarks, but more often listening in silence as it spoke. My body tensed as I heard the name Nyarlathotep framed in its inhuman mouth. The witch spoke, repeating the name of the faceless god who stood upon the dunes in the desert and stared up at the darkness of the heavens. A prickling came over my skin when I heard the sound of a flute, until I realized it was made by the voice of the thing in the fissure. The witch answered with a similar piping music, which I reasoned must be another form of language.

The voices ceased, and the sound of a heavy body sliding across loose rubble receded into the depths of the fissure. I began to creep backward and to the side, in the realization that the witch would probably retrace her steps, now that her meeting with the whistling thing was concluded. I heard no sound, which made me nervous, since she had not taken care to move silently on her way to the fissure. Why should she do so now, unless she sensed my presence? Or perhaps she was hunting rats, I told myself to calm my nervousness.

Backing around and stepping over obstructions on the floor of the cistern, I soon became hopelessly lost. The blackness was like liquid pitch poured into the eyes, and the only sounds were the squeak of rats amid the loose rocks and the maddening phantom drip of water that seemed to come from everywhere and nowhere.

Sashi, can you see in this darkness?

Not through your eyes.

What if you leave my body?

If I leave your flesh, I will no longer be able to talk to you.

I understood. If she left me, she could see in the darkness, but she would need to enter my skin once again before she could tell me the way, and that was a matter requiring some effort. It would not be practical for her to guide me across the floor of the cistern if it meant she would have to exit and enter my flesh every dozen paces.

A hiss of breath behind me made me whirl and clutch for my dagger on its baldric. My heel caught against a piece of wood and I stumbled backward in an effort to keep my balance. All at once there was nothing under my sandals but empty space. I uttered a silent curse in my mind when I realized that I had stumbled over one of the beams I had set around the well in the central chamber to warn me of its precipice. I began to fall, and time seemed to lengthen endlessly.

A hand caught my flailing arm at the wrist and stopped my plunge. The huge fingers felt as hard as stone and ground the bones of my forearm together. For a few moments it held me over the abyss while my toes kicked against the side of the well and scrabbled for footholds that did not exist. Slowly I was lifted upward and set onto the paving blocks that lined the floor of the cistern. The foul exhale of the witch touched my cheeks.

"Clumsy fool, this place is dangerous. Follow me and I will lead to where it is safe."

Silently, I returned my dagger to its sheath. The strength of the witch was even greater than I had imagined. I wanted to kill her, but if she died she could never teach me about the faceless man in black. It was surely more than chance that he haunted my dreams, and also that his name was on the lips of the hag and the clawed thing in the fissure. I must learn more about this god or devil, and why he interested himself in my existence, since I felt with inner certainty that I would meet him again.

Chapter 10

For what seemed the span of several lifetimes but could not have been more than a cycle of the moon, I stayed with the witch, hunting her rats and gathering her wood while I asked my carefully chosen questions. She never lied, or refused to respond, but the length of her answers depended on her capricious moods, which changed without cause from sun to storm. One moment she might be cheerful in her grotesque way, and the next sullen and resentful, as though I had committed an injury against her. That she was mad there was no doubt, but her madness came and left her by turns.

One day I would ask the wrong question, and she would answer it truthfully, and then she would kill me. I became certain in my own mind this was what had happened to all her other disciples whose naked skulls adorned her cave. The unknown question hung over my head like a sword suspended on a single hair, ready to fall at any moment, yet I continued to seek answers, while wondering at the extent of the hag's knowledge of ancient and secret matters long hidden from the awareness of men. What the schools of scholars and scribes of books had forgotten, or never learned, was known to the creatures that made their abode in the darkness under the earth, and passed on in communication to the witch.

I'thakuah did not object when I accompanied her on her periodic excursions to the fissure, and sat a little distance away on a stone as she haggled with the slithering thing in its depths. She reasoned that I could not comprehend its languages, and so let me listen as they conversed, or sent me to hunt for the rats she used to bargain with it for information or trinkets. Without betraying my interest, I listened with attention. I have always possessed an uncanny skill with tongues, the ability to learn those unknown to me with a swiftness that my royal tutors regarded as a divine gift. Over time the slurred words of the creature in the crack began to make sense in my ears, until at last I could understand its speech as well as the witch. I took care to show no sign of my ability.

The conversation of the slithering thing consisted of talk overheard on its wanderings beneath the world—not the talk of men but of other races older than ours that have inhabited the tunnels and caverns under the surface from a time before our creation. It spoke often of Nyarlathotep, and others of the Old Ones whose names I began to recognize. Nyarlathotep, I learned, was a kind of messenger or emissary of the Old Ones, chosen for this task because he alone could walk upon the surface of our world beneath the stars unharmed by the conflux of their rays, although the other gods were able to endure the surface for brief periods to accomplish specific necessary actions. They preferred to confine themselves to the depths of the seas, or the sumps of the earth, or to withdraw through portals into other realms that lay beyond the sphere of the fixed stars.

One exchange in particular caught my interest. The witch threw a rat into the slit, and for a time there came the sound of gristle and bone cracking between teeth, and the chewing of flesh and sucking of blood. Then silence fell, and I thought the thing had withdrawn.

"The Dark Chaos is restless. He walks each night and searches," it hissed so softly, I almost failed to hear its words.

"What is he looking for?" I'thakuah demanded.

"Who can know the purposes of the Old Ones? Those who watch him afar from clefts in the rocks say only that he searches. And that he stands and looks up at the stars."

"He waits for when they are right in their places, and their light becomes pure," the witch said.

"Perhaps. Or he worries that they will not cleanse themselves soon enough."

"He fears nothing," she snapped petulantly.

The creature maintained a moment of silence, as though to avoid argument.

"It is spoken in deep places that an army of men gathers in the north."

"An army of men," she said, making a sound of disgust. "What can men do?"

"They study the Old Ones to learn their ways. They seek weapons against them, and prepare themselves for a great battle. This is why the Dark Chaos ponders the stars."

"Weapons, you say?" The witch considered silently. "What kind of weapons?"

"No one knows. They prepare them in secret behind the walls of their sanctuary."

"Pah! What weapon can harm mighty Cthulhu, who is deathless? Or Yog-Sothoth, who has no form?"

"Cthulhu lies dead-dreaming."

"When he rises the ground will tremble."

The creature made no response. The witch chuckled to herself in reassurance.

"These are fables. My lord fears nothing."

Again, it seemed to me that the thing in the slit had withdrawn, but the witch did not stir from her place.

"What does he search for?" she muttered in a low croak, speaking as though to herself.

"He walks with head bowed, looking for tracks in the sand," came the soft voice from the darkness. "At times, he lifts his head to smell the air."

"Tracks, you say?" The witch considered. "Tracks of men?"

"Who can know the purposes of the Old Ones?"

I'thakuah grunted in disgust, and the creature on the other side of the cleft withdrew, its heavy body sliding over the stones with the sound of a leather cloak drawn across the floor tiles, punctuated by the click of its claws.

I considered what I had learned. The dark man was growing increasingly restless. He walked the desert searching for something, and studied the pattern of the stars with concern. Forces were gathering against his kind, who were vulnerable at this time because some poison in the rays of the stars prevented them from using their great powers to defend themselves. The leader of their armies lay sleeping beneath the sea, or lay dead—I was not certain which, since the word used by the creature seemed to signify both states. One day the stars would align in such a way that the poison would vanish, and the Old Ones could appear on the surface and dwell there as rulers of creation. The concern of the dark man was that an attack would be launched against them before the skies cleansed themselves, while they were still vulnerable. So much I gathered from this conversation and other fragments of talk.

Do you know what the faceless man looks for in the sand? I asked Sashi, speaking within my own mind so that the witch would not hear.

It is said by my kind that he is angry. We flee away whenever we see him approach.

The djinn could tell me nothing, I realized, and neither I'thakuah nor the creature in the cleft knew more on the matter than I had gathered from their words.

The witch left the open space in front of the slit and made her way deeper into the central cistern to hunt. I followed the sounds of her shuffling progress with nervous steps, unable to resist my fascination. When first I had come to the cisterns, I assumed that she could catch rats only with difficulty on her stunted legs, but I had discovered that she knew her own way of ensuring a constant supply of meat.

She began to whistle, a strange keening in the air that mounted and fell with a kind of music, yet never ceased. In some way she was able to sustain the sound while drawing in breath. I felt a prickling on my arms and neck. The whistle exerted a kind of compulsive attraction that I was able to resist only with difficulty, and perhaps only because it was not directed at me. From the darkness came a rustle in the dust as the rats, drawn against their will, approached the hag as though to offer adoration. She waited until they were almost at her feet. The whistle stopped, and before the rats could recover their wits and scurry away, she fell upon the nearest and snapped its neck in her massive hands.

By touch, I gathered bits of wood for the fire as we made our way back to the ledge. It had become evident to me that I'thakuah did not need me for her survival. Why, I sometimes wondered, did she want me with her? Merely to gather wood? That seemed an insufficient reason. Perhaps she welcomed a disciple to whom she could trickle out her wisdom, and thereby make herself feel wise. It must be lonely in the darkness, with no one to talk to but the inhuman thing beyond the cleft in the wall. Yet all her past disciples were dead. A use she might have for them, but it was not a purpose that endured forever.

While the witch ate her meat and tended the fire, I went off to hunt in my own way, with stealth and quickness. The first rat I killed and ate where I stood, then caught and snapped the necks of three more as gifts for I'thakuah, for I wished to ask particular questions that pertained to my departure from this place of endless darkness. I had learned as much as I wished to learn from the witch, or as much as I felt secure in learning. The longer I remained in the cisterns, the greater my sense that she would spring at my throat and try to kill me. The mute testimony of the pyramid of skulls did nothing to allay my growing anxiety.

She nodded and chuckled to herself at her place by the fire when she saw the rats swinging by their tails in my hand. I mounted the ledge and cast them beside her. She let them remain where they fell, watching me with glittering eyes as I took my usual cautious seat on the opposite side of the fire and composed my thoughts. The ember glow, shining upward on her immobile face, lent her ancient features the aspect of carven stone. With no attempt at polite talk, I asked my first question.

"What is the nature and history of the creature that dwells on the other side of the cleft in the wall?"

She grinned sourly at my attempt to combine two questions into one, but did not object.

"Long ago, when the Old Ones came, they found a race already ruling this world," she began without haste, turning her gaze to the embers of the fire as she searched the depths of her memory. "Some say the first race was always here; others that it came to this world in so ancient a time that nothing lived on the rocks nor in the seas. The Old Ones made war against these Elder Things, shaping life itself into their weapons, and the earlier race fought back in the same way, raising fearsome monsters from the slime and filling them with unnatural awareness, the better to wage battle. The creature beyond the gap in the rock is a *chandr'ah*, a siege horse you would call it. Were it narrow enough to fit through the crack, it would kill us both in an instant. But I keep it fat with rats, so that it cannot fit."

She cackled with amusement at her own joke, throwing back her snowy head and showing her blackened gums.

I took a slow breath, reviewing my second question in my mind to make certain I had it worded rightly.

"What is the way to safely bypass the *chandr'ah* without being injured?"

She answered at once, as though she had expected the question.

"Use the Elder Sign."

I looked at her with raised brows. She imitated my expression, mirth seething below her features, and met my gaze across the fire. I frowned at her, hoping she would not think of a way to evade my third question.

"What is the way of making the Elder Sign?"

Silently, she raised her right hand and touched her first finger to the tip of her thumb to form a circle. With surprising agility in her long fingers, she crossed her second finger on top of her third, then raised her fifth finger so that it pointed almost straight up into the air. She held this sign out before me so that I could memorize its formation, and when I imitated it with the fingers of my right hand, she nodded.

Something changed in the depths of her eyes, and I realized that I had spoken the fatal question. Each disciple before me had asked the same thing, just before his fleshless skull decorated the trophy pile. I let no hint of my awareness betray my face, but looked aside as though unconcerned. When she lunged, I was ready and sprang to the side off the ledge, my feet running before they touched the dust on the floor of the cistern. I left nothing behind. Always prepared for this day, I had adopted the habit of carrying all my possessions whenever I was awake. I ran directly toward the cleft, avoiding the rubble with the skill of long practice in the dark.

A trilling whistle cut the air behind me and made me stumble. My legs became so weak, I was barely able to walk, and could no longer move them fast enough to run. The shrill note rose and fell, weaving its weird song. With each step my legs grew heavier, until at last I stopped and swayed as though rooted to the stones of the cistern floor, my shivering body damp with icy sweat. It took all my will to resist walking toward the sound that approached ever nearer in the blackness. I heard the shuffle of the hag's stunted legs through the dust.

With sudden inspiration, I clapped my hands over the holes of my ears and began to sing so loudly, my throat became raw in a few moments. It was more bellowing than song, but it was loud enough to drown out the infernal whistle of the witch. My legs regained some measure of their strength, and I stumbled onward across the floor of the great cistern, avoiding obstacles without the need to feel for them since the whole of it was impressed on my memory. My speed was not great, and I wondered if the hag gained on me, but the only way to know would be to remove my hands and listen for her steps, and this I dared not do.

I miscalculated and rebounded from the wall of stone on my shoulder as I twisted in a senseless effort to look behind through the black. The impact knocked my hands away. I heard the whistle of the witch, not close but coming nearer. With desperate haste, I felt across the surface of the rock. The cleft had somehow sealed itself. Crying out in frustration, I felt toward my left side. As the whistling grew ever louder and sapped the strength from my limbs, at last I encountered the familiar gap and with a mad laugh of relief slid my body into it.

The whistling stopped, and I'thakuah began to curse as she realized I had entered the crack. She could not follow. Her body was too bent and grotesque for so narrow a space. Something knocked against my sandal. Leaning awkwardly to the side, I felt and discovered that it was a bone. Too large to be the bone of a rat, it must be the bone of a man. I knew then what the witch had done with the bodies of her disciples, after saving their skulls for her trophy pile. I picked the bone up and threw it over my head behind me out the gap, and was rewarded with a torrent of curses from the witch.

"Find someone else to kill your rats and carry your wood, bitch of Tartarus," I shouted.

The cursing stopped. There was a silence.

"Come back to me, pretty boy, and for the sake of the mark of our lord you bear on your face, I promise not to kill you."

"I bear no mark, only scars."

She cackled softly.

"I saw it when you came to me, and knew the dark man had sent you to me to be instructed. For his sake I took care of you."

"You would keep me forever, or kill me," I said.

I'thakuah began to chant in a language still unknown to me. I realized she was attempting to cast some spell and pressed my hands against the sides of my head, singing so loudly that my lungs felt about to burst. As I sang, I worked my body deeper into the cleft, which became so narrow, no part of my body could avoid the rasp of its sides. The rough stone scraped my back and thighs through the sturdy cotton of my thawb, and I was forced to duck my head and bend my knees to pass under a stone spur that pressed on my skull. The ordeal was brief. Not far beyond the wall of the cistern it widened, so that I could turn my chest to face forward.

Chill sweat did not cease to prickle my face. Every instant I expected to walk into the claws of the *chandr'ah*. I dared not hurry, or I might dash my brains out against a projecting point of rock. In the total darkness, with my hands pressed over my ears, there was no way to gain warning of the monster's approach, and my bellowing song would surely act as a beacon to it, no matter how far it might have strayed away from the cleft.

At last I risked removing my palm from my left ear. There was only silence. Either I'thakuah had given up, or I was too deep in the fissure to hear her frustrated curses. I continued more quickly, one hand sliding over the wall and the other held out in the air before my face. The floor of the fissure was oddly smooth, and I realized it must be due to the constant dragging of the *chandr'ah*'s heavy body to and from the entrance over a span of centuries, or even millennia. Every so often my sandals crunched on a piece of bone.

The floor of the fissure inclined always downward, and bent this way and that until I could no longer tell which direction was back and which was front, other than by the hand that touched the rock side of the passage. I dared not allow it to drop from the wall for more than a few moments, in the fear that I might get turned around and begin to retrace my steps back into the cistern where I'thakuah waited. Walking on the toes of my sandals so as to make little noise, I paused every few steps and listened for the sound of sliding leather, or the click of claws on stone.

"Are you a gift from I'thakuah?"

The deep hiss directly in front of my face made me jump back like a startled mouse. I crouched with my dagger in my hand, and wondered if there was anything to be gained by flight back to the cisterns.

"I am not a gift," I said in the language used by the creature. "I am a traveler."

It stirred its massive body, and I realized it must have sat in silence and waited for me to walk directly up to it. Probably it could see in the darkness.

"You speak the ancient tongue," it murmured in a voice like water seething in a pot. "What are you?"

For a moment I had no answer. My left hand chanced to brush the skull tied at my waist.

"I am a ghoul, a warrior of the Black Spring Clan."

A snuffling sound came on the darkness.

"You do not smell like a ghoul. You smell human."

"True, I was human, but I am human no longer."

"Such a thing cannot be," it said. "No beast can change its essential nature."

Relieved that the monster had chosen to converse rather than dine, I explained my unhappy circumstances, and the manner in which the king of Yemen had punished my body. It listened with interest, making slight sounds of attention that were like the puffing of a fire bellows. When it exhaled, a cloud of its hot breath surrounded my face.

"A good story," it said as I concluded my tale of woe. "Tell me this, ghoul who was a man, why should I not eat you?"

I jumped back another step and slashed the air with my dagger, trying to pierce the darkness with my eyes. The black was so thick, I might as well have had my head in a sack. Transferring the dagger to my left hand, I made the Elder Sign with my right.

The monster made a rumbling noise. It was a moment or two before I recognized it as laughter.

"Did the witch give you that?"

"She did," I admitted.

"It is true, some of the dwellers in the deep places recognize the sign of the Elder Race, and respect its power, but regrettably for you, I am not among them."

It began to slide forward, grinding the pebbles beneath its belly and scratching the dirt with its claws.

"Wait! I bear the mark of the dark man on my face."

Something so cold that it burned closed around my waist and drew me forward. I stabbed and cut at the encircling ring with my dagger, but the sharp blade might as well have been made from wood, and slid harmlessly from the hide of the creature. Grasping at the cold flesh, I realized with terror that it was some kind of giant hand, but one possessed of only two fingers and a thumb. The breath of the thing blew into my face like the snort of a horse as it bent near to study me. I saw, or thought I saw, two dim objects glowing with a faint green in the air before me, and realized they must be the eyes of the *chandr'ah*, burning with their own internal fire.

"He has marked you on the inside of your skull," it said at last. "Why would he do that?"

"Clearly, he has chosen me to fulfill an important task," I replied with a show of anger. "He will not be pleased if you prevent its accomplishment."

I hoped the creature would not ask what task I was to perform, since I had no answer. It spent what seemed a long time in consideration. At last, its massive fingers relaxed and slid from around my waist.

"Go in peace, servant of the Dark Chaos, and be mindful of your steps. There are things dwelling below that respect neither the Elder Sign nor Nyarlathotep."

It slid and contracted itself against one side of the passage so that I had barely enough room to squeeze past its bulk. The sliding touch of its leathery side as I worked my way down its length made me tremble, but it was impossible to avoid. When I was free of its loathsome press, I paused and turned.

"Tell I'thakuah she is a lying hag."

"For what reason?" it rumbled, slithering away down the passage. "She knows this already. Everyone knows I'thakuah is a liar. Only a fool would trust her."

I continued along the floor of the fissure in the opposite direction until the sounds of the monster's movements faded to silence.

Chapter 11

The complete absence of light made the journey through the fissure seem endless. I passed an opening on the right that led almost straight downward, and exhaled a reptilian odor of dankness. For a few moments I paused and considered whether to follow it, but the smell was not to my liking, so I continued forward. Beyond this rightward opening the floor of the fissure became more irregular, indicating that the *chandr'ah* usually took the right-hand path. With slow and cautious steps I felt the ground in front of my feet. The mishap at the well had made me timid about testing the way ahead before walking into the darkness. Just as I was wishing, for perhaps the tenth time, that I had taken the white spiders earlier, so that I would have the benefit of the luminous shells in the rock walls to guide me, I saw a faint green glow ahead.

As I approached the light, it became stronger and showed me that the natural fissure had given way to an artificial passage cut through the rock with vertical walls and a gently arched ceiling. I rounded a bend in the passage, and my eyes were dazzled by brightness. It shone out of a small doorway at the end of the passage that was so low, I was forced to crawl through it on my hands and knees. The ceiling of the chamber beyond was high enough that I could almost stand upright, if I kept my head bowed forward. The glow emanated from the ceiling. It could not have been very strong, but to my eyes, accustomed as they were to weeks of total darkness, it seemed for the first few minutes like the noonday sun.

The room was not large, and empty save for a single stone slab in its center, but it raised the hairs on my neck and made my heart quicken. There was something alien in its dimensions, something unsuitable and uncouth, that evoked a primal and undefined apprehension. The doorway through which I had crawled and the identical opening in the opposite wall were too low and wide, the ceiling was too low, even the stone slab that had the look of a sacrificial altar was nearer the floor than it should have been. Either the room had been cut for a race of dwarfs, or it was made to accommodate bodies not even remotely human in shape.

Dust of ages lay thick over the floor except where the *chandr'ah* had dragged its long body around the altar and through the opposite doorway on its explorations. A gleam caught my eye from the corner of the room. I knelt and saw that it was a jewel, very pale in color but beautifully faceted.

"The treasure of the nameless city," I murmured, picking up the stone and placing it in a pocket of my robe.

Even as promised, my love.

"The monster must have dropped it while carrying similar trinkets to give to the witch."

I crawled through the opening on the far side of the altar and found another long corridor with doorways along its sides that branched into rooms and halls. They had a more habited appearance than the antechamber with the altar. The walls of the rooms were covered in a patterned plaster with the texture and appearance of carved stone, into which had been impressed abstract geometric designs. The floors were tiled in bright colors. Remnants of furniture remained, but scattered in disorder as though the inhabitants of the rooms had been forced to make a hasty departure. There were chairs and couches of unnatural shape, massively constructed and low to the floor. Some were made of the same hard black wood that lay littered in the cisterns, while others were of cast bronze that had gone green with age. In one room I found a cracked hand mirror, and in another some kind of curved scraper the purpose of which I could not even guess.

Everywhere the dragging track of the *chandr'ah* showed in the thick dust over the tiles of the floors. It had explored all the rooms in its search for trinkets with which to buy rats from the witch. Marks of vermin were absent from the dust. The monster had exhausted its food supply, which explained its eagerness to receive the offerings of I'thakuah. Following its track through a low arch, I could not suppress a cry.

Jewels lay scattered across the dust, so many that I had to step with care to avoid them. They glittered with many colors, brightness undimmed by the passage of centuries. In a corner lay an overturned silver chest, the source of this outpouring. I picked up the box and more jewels tumbled out. I laughed and filled my hands with them. With this wealth, I could return to the cities of my own race. No man is an outcast who has money, regardless of his deformity. I gathered the bulk of the jewels and tied them into one of the shroud rags I carried, then concealed them securely within a pocket of my thawb.

Another discovery in a room near the end of the central corridor made me pause. In the dust beside a kind of flat bed, the wooden frame alone of which survived, lay a skeleton with a sword between its ribs. It could not have been the skeleton of a man, even a man severely deformed. The skull was much too large and elongated, the arms and legs unnaturally short and angled incorrectly from the spine. The straight bronze blade of the sword was leaf-shaped and deeply pitted with corrosion, and the leather wrapping of its hilt had perished. The blade had snapped a hand's breadth from its point, but the broken tip was not to be found among the bones. Picking up the weapon, I tried its hilt. It was of unconventional design, but there was no doubt that it had been fashioned for the hand of a man. With regret, I tossed it aside. It might once have been a useful weapon, but was of little value without its point. How anyone had managed to swing it in battle beneath the low ceiling of the room was difficult to imagine.

A heavy door of cast iron occupied the end of the main corridor, the first door of any kind that I had seen. It had jammed partway open and was not to be moved, and it was only with difficulty that I squeezed my body through the gap. A similar corridor lay on the other side, well illuminated by the greenish glow from the ceiling. It no longer seemed so bright to my eyes, or so green, for I had become accustomed to the color and was ceasing to notice it. With relief I saw that the dust lay undisturbed down the length of the passage. Evidently the *chandr'ah* had not been able to move the iron door, and was too large to slip through its opening. For the first time since leaving the cisterns I ceased to worry about what slithered behind me, and was able to devote all my anxiety to what might hide waiting in front.

There was a subtle difference in the chambers and connecting halls on the far side of the iron door. The ceilings were higher, allowing me to walk upright. At intervals, bright frescos decorated the walls. The disordered furnishing of the chambers appeared more costly in appearance, and the rooms were larger. Still there were no individual doors dividing room from room. Whatever creatures had dwelt in these halls had not valued privacy. I found more jewels, and gold in the form of small rectangular blocks. A few of the gold pieces I pocketed, but left the gemstones where they lay scattered, since I could not easily carry more.

The deadness of the air began to unnerve me. Even my footfalls were muffled in the thick dust. Nothing stirred. It was a distinct relief to notice the tracks of rats and spiders in the dust. At least I was not the only living thing in these empty spaces. The signs of these vermin increased as I progressed deeper into the unnamed city. I descended a stairway with steps too shallow and broad for human feet, and discovered a lower level of halls and rooms very similar to the level that lay above. The city was like a great maze, but by observing my footprints in the dust there was little chance of becoming lost.

On the lower level, signs of habitation became more numerous. In one room upon a low slab of stone that I identified in my own mind as an altar rested a wooden box the length of a man, but wider. Its top was composed of a transparent glass panel that had been broken inward, but its interior stood empty. It was a strange shape for a display case, and I wondered what it had held. The dense wood was beautifully carved and polished. Could all of the altars I had seen be intended to support similar cases? If so, what had become of them?

The frescos that decorated the walls occupied my attention with the hope that I could determine the appearance of the inhabitants of the underground city. Many were abstract swirls and polygons of bright color, but others depicted in a more natural style strange landscapes of mountain ranges and great forests and fantastic cities of spires rising from dense jungle. One painting showed small figures that had the shape of men, but they were naked and like apes, with hair growing from their bodies and long arms that brushed the ground. The bodies of these ape men did not match the furniture in the chambers of the city.

In several frescos I noticed the forms of lizards, ceremonially arrayed in colorful robes and jeweled neck bands. They were much like the descriptions I had read of the crocodiles of the Nile, with thick legs extending down from their reptilian bodies, and long snouts filled with teeth, but their heads were domed rather than flat, and some of them were shown standing upright on their hind legs, balancing with the aid of their tails. I dismissed them from my mind as depictions of the god of the race, but some correspondence with something I had seen nagged at my thoughts. At last I realized that the bodies of the brightly clothed reptiles were the same as the skeleton I had found in the upper chambers. I decided they must be a type of pampered pet of the inhabitants of the nameless city, draped in robes and adorned with jewelry in the same way that wealthy noblewomen sometimes put garments on a lapdog.

Descending even lower into what I sensed was the heart of the city, I came upon a large circular chamber with a domed roof. It was completely unlike any other room, save only that it had two doorways located almost opposite each other, a feature universal throughout the city. Even these were rounded by a tall arch rather than square, and much larger than common entranceways. The vault of the dome was painted a deep blue, and, inset at irregular intervals over its surface, colorless jewels gave off a chill radiance, so that they resembled stars set in the night sky. On the curved wall of the chamber seven frescos had been painted with such vitality of detail and color that they resembled doorways. The paint was textured and raised from the surface of the wall, and when stared at for more than a few moments, it seemed to squirm with its own life.

A great disk of translucent green stone filled the center of the floor to the height of my knees. Many interlocking triangles were deeply carved in its surface, and in a circle at the center was set a seal unfamiliar to me, somewhat like the branch of a tree, and somewhat like the splayed fingers of the human hand. Seven brass pins stood up at the edge of the green disk, each pin as thick as my wrist and rounded at its top. I noted that they were opposite the frescos, though what function they might be intended to serve was obscure. The chamber had an air of importance that made me think it must be a place of worship.

Weariness overcame me as I sat on the edge of the green disk, the stone of which had a waxy feel beneath my fingers, similar to that of carnelian. I had gone longer than usual without sleep, though how much longer was impossible to determine in the absence of any indicators of the passage of time. My neck and shoulders ached from walking hunched over under the low ceilings. I decided to sleep before exploring for a way out of the city. Now that I possessed the treasure I had come seeking, I wanted only to leave these halls and chambers as quickly as I could discover a way back to the moonlight and the natural stars of the heavens.

Something brushed my cheek, like a puff of air. I looked around and saw nothing. In a few moments the sensation repeated itself, and I felt a twinge in my heart, as of some nebulous object passed through my body. I swung my feet up on the dais of green stone and stood, turning slowly on my own axis. A bat flitted silently through one entrance and out the other, but it evaded the space above the stone. I knew the sensations had not been caused by a bat. For several minutes I waited, but the touches did not repeat.

"I do not think we are alone," I said to Sashi.

There are ghosts here, she agreed. *They cannot harm us.*

"Would it be safe for you to leave my body in this place?"

I would be safe. I move quickly, and ghosts are no threat to me.

"While I sleep, I want you to explore and learn what you can about this chamber. Perhaps there are more of your kind, or other types of djinn, who might tell you its purpose."

I will learn what I can, and share it with you when you awake, my dear one.

A gentle pulling sensation came across the front of my chest and face as she forced her tenuous body through my skin, followed by a soft touch on my cheek that I recognized as a kiss.

Some impulse made me take three of the white spiders and eat them before preparing myself to sleep. I had learned to disregard ghosts, but if this chamber was haunted by the ghosts of the inhabitants of the city, it was an opportunity to study their form. The green stone felt oddly warm against my skin, as though heated from within. Scant moments after my eyelids closed, I slept.

The tall man in the black cloak walked beside me across the sand, which resembled frozen silver waves beneath the moonlight. He had been speaking for some time, but my mind was unfocused, so that I did not comprehend his words. With an effort I brought my awareness back from where it drifted and listened.

"If you are to walk among men as my agent, you must pass unremarked. This your present disfigured state will not allow."

"Make me whole again in face and body," I said.

"I cannot."

"Is there no magic that can restore my manhood?"

"Perhaps. It is a work beyond my capacity under these poisonous stars. They weaken my power."

"When will the stars come right?"

"Soon, Alhazred. In the meanwhile, I give you this glamour to deceive the senses of other men. While you wear it, you will appear to be whole in face and body, even though you are unchanged."

He stopped and turned to me, then made several gestures upon the air and spoke a word.

"It will fade in the space of a dozen hours unless you renew the force of the spell."

I imitated the gestures and spoke the word, which sounded harsh and strange on my tongue. My skin tingled.

"Look upon your own appearance," the dark man said.

He raised an ebon hand and drew aside his shadowy caul of silk. In the oval of his hood, as in a mirror, I saw my own face restored to its former beauty. I cried out and reached to touch my cheek.

The cry in my throat awoke me on the green stone disk. Opening my eyes to the chill glow from the jewels in the dome, I saw ringing the stone dais a throng of palely glowing spirits. In form they resembled Nile crocodiles, but they stood upright on their short hind legs and slashed at me with their transparent fore claws, each as long as a curved dagger blade. At the same time they snapped at my face with their massive jaws, expressions of fury blazing in their reptilian eyes, which had pupils in the shape of slits like those of snakes.

The silent savagery of their expressions terrified me. I shrank to the center of the stone disk. Then I reflected that they were only shades of the dead, in spite of their ferocious appearance, and noticed that their teeth and claws never passed beyond the edge of the disk. Some invisible barrier kept them from climbing onto its surface. I stood up and looked over their heads. They were all pressed against the stone, leaving the rest of the chamber empty except for Sashi, who crouched on the folded legs of her djinn body and watched with her enormous eyes.

"Can you come to me?" I asked her above the snapping snouts of the ghosts.

She shook her grotesque head.

"Then I will come to you."

With more confidence, I stepped from the green stone disk through the bodies of the ghosts and walked to where she squatted, ignoring their attempts to slash at me with their claws. I felt them pass through my body like cool puffs of air. Sashi grinned, showing her needle-sharp teeth, and leaped upward to embrace me, pressing her face into mine. In moments she was once again inside my flesh.

"These are the inhabitants of this city," I said to her.

The ghosts are everywhere. They do not stand guard over their corpses, but wander the halls and haunt the chambers.

"Why are they so angry?"

This was for them a holy place. Your presence defiles it.

"Just as well for me that they have no power. What did you learn?"

There are levels below this level. In them dwells a creature that once lived in the desert, and knows the language of the djinn. It says that this chamber is a kind of gateway for traveling to distant places in the soul body while the body of flesh remains empty.

"A soul portal?" I looked around at the painted murals. "How is it activated?"

The creature did not know, or would not say.

"Can you go back and ask it again?"

No.

"Why not?"

I ate it.

I closed my eyelids. The lovely human face of Sashi gazed back at me and shrugged in apology.

I was hungry.

"No matter. Perhaps the creature knew nothing more."

Talk of food awakened my own appetite, but I decided to examine the stone disk more closely. If the chamber was a portal, there must be some way to activate its function. Ignoring the attempts of the ghosts to prevent my progress, I knelt on the disk and traced with my fingers the deep grooves of the carving in its surface. No opening or hidden lever revealed itself to my touch. Grasping one of the brass pins at the edge of the disk, I tried to pull it up but found it immobile. As I released it, my palm pressed against its rounded surface, and it slid down smoothly into the stone. Immediately, the light was extinguished from the majority of jewels in the domed ceiling of the chamber. Those that remained aglow were angled in such a way that their rays illuminated the painted panel on the wall nearest the depressed pin. The other six paintings lay in shadow.

Sitting back up and crossing my legs so that my thawb formed a tent over my thighs, I studied the lit panel. It showed a plateau ringed by the snow-capped peaks of distant mountains. Nothing grew upon the plateau but tall grass. In the foreground clustered a dozen tents beside a herd of beasts with shaggy coats and short horns that twisted downward at the sides of their heads. In the distance beyond the tents a large black building with red tile roofs was visible, surrounded by a stone wall. Tiny figures rode across the plain on horses. As I gazed at them, they began to move, and I saw with detachment of mind that the grass was blowing in the wind. I smelled dung, and heard the howl of a beast that might have been a wolf, or a dog.

There came a great rushing noise in my ears, and a sense of falling from a high place down a tunnel, as though propelled by an irresistible waterfall. With a shock I regained awareness of my surroundings, and realized that I stood in the midst of an endless expanse of grass that grew as high as my waist. A horse munched the tender seedy heads of the grass stalks beside me. It wore a saddle and bridle of strange design, though the purpose of their parts was clear enough. The horse was no taller than a donkey, and the bristling hairs on its black mane stood straight up from its neck. Its brown coat was shaggy and hung in patches on its sides, as though it were shedding its hair.

I reached out to touch its neck. It did not try to pull away, and I felt its flesh warm against my fingertips. With surprise I saw that the shape of my hand was not my own, but that of another man. The fingers were thick and short, whereas mine are slender and long. I felt my face, and discovered that I possessed a nose. That alone was sufficient to convince me that I inhabited a different skin.

Sashi, can you hear my thoughts?

No response came from the *chaklah*. Whatever power had impelled my soul through the painting on the wall had not carried the djinn along with me. That I had traveled through one of the portals in the round star chamber I had no doubt. My present concern was how to return to my own body before it was eaten by vermin. Of the ghosts I had no fear, but the rats and scorpions and bats that lived in the underground city would find my senseless flesh a banquet, unless Sashi was able to defend it. I decided the most important course was to learn whether a similar disk of green stone existed in this grassland by which I might return to my own body.

I mounted the horse and sent it trotting through the grass toward the cluster of tents, which in shape were round, with conical roofs, and made of leather skins sewn together.

A squat, ugly woman with black eyes and greasy black hair tied behind her head in a long rope emerged from under one of the tent flaps as I rode past. She wore a shirt of undyed leather belted at the waist, and had leather leggings lashed tightly around her calves and thighs. She looked at me in surprise, hands on her ample hips.

"Back so quickly, Yoliff?"

"A sickness in my head," I murmured, and found that I could both understand and speak the language of the place.

"You should see the shaman," the woman said with disinterest, and set about tending her cooking fire, upon which boiled a copper pot filled with something that resembled stew.

"Yes, I will see the shaman," I told her.

Looking around to orient myself, I pointed my horse at the distant walled building with the red roofs, and kicked the flanks of the placid horse to make it trot in that direction. After a few moments I heard a puffing behind me and the thud of running feet in the turf. The woman's fat hand caught the bridle of my horse and jerked it to a stop.

"Yoliff, have you gone mad?" The woman stared at me with fear in her eyes. "Where are you going?"

"To visit the shaman."

She cursed and spat into the grass, then turned the head of the horse around until it faced the other direction and began to pull it along beside her as she walked back toward the tents.

"You must be very sick, not to dread the monastery of the priests. Just as well that you ride off the edge of the plateau, as ride within their walls."

Saying nothing, I allowed myself to be led back to the encampment. She made me dismount and had a young child stand beside me and watch me so that I did not wander off while she went into one of the tents. It was larger than the others, and pitched some distance away as though for privacy. When she came out, it was in the company of a short man with a broad chest who was very like her in appearance. His slitted eyes were black, his hair black and standing up from his head much like the mane of the horse. His moustache and beard were both trimmed short, showing most of his sallow, wind-burned face, which was covered with the blue whorls of an elaborate tattoo. The white streaks in his beard indicated that he was not a young man.

He wore the same rough leather shirt and leather breeches as the woman, but around his neck on a cord of woven grasses hung a curiously carved pendant of green stone. I recognized it as the same type of stone that composed the disk in the round chamber of star jewels. It was as large as the palm of my hand, and carved in the shape of a winged hound with a snarling mouth and blazing eyes, that sat upon its haunches as though on guard.

The man stood close and stared into my eyes for several moments. He stepped away and gestured for me to follow before ducking back into the tent. I looked at the woman, who stood without moving, a stolid expression on her face. Perhaps women were forbidden to enter the dwelling of the shaman, I reflected. With a shrug, I pulled up the flap and left her. The interior of the tent was dark and hot. Smoke rose in a thin stream from a fire that smoldered under a great iron kettle and exited through a hole in the center of the roof, through which I could see the blue sky. A younger man sat on his haunches, stirring the kettle with a long wooden ladle. He grinned up at me, and I saw that he lacked two front teeth. The same blue whorls that adorned the cheeks of the older shaman also decorated his face.

I crossed the floor to approach the elder man, and noticed the arm of a small child floating in the bubbling kettle. The shaman drew me close and passed a burning clay oil lamp back and forth in front of my face, watching my eyes. Setting down the lamp, he took up a bone wand with feathers tied to its end and shook it over my head while chanting meaningless sounds.

"You have changed, Yoliff. Something is different about you."

"It is a sickness in my head. It will pass."

"No, it is something else."

His skillful thumbs pressed the flesh of my temples and lifted my eyelids. The younger shaman rose from the fireside and came over curiously. The older man stepped back and let the young man go through the same motions he had just completed. The young man waved the bone wand over my hair and probed my skull with his thumbs, then merely shook his head.

"Go back to your tent and sleep, Yoliff. If you are still sick in the morning, come to me again."

I nodded and left the tent. It was my intention to find my horse and ride to the monastery to investigate its inhabitants. Surely a place so feared by these peasants must have features of interest for a student of necromancy. Instead, I stopped and gazed across the plain in gap-jawed wonder. The sun had set while I was being examined in the shaman's tent. In the gray of twilight a shimmering city of impossibly tall spires and vast obelisks floated above the grass. Several women and a group of children had also paused to gaze at the phantom city. The heavy woman who had taken me to the shaman came over to stand beside me.

"I've never seen the Elder City clearer than it is this night."

"Have you seen it often?" I asked.

She snorted and looked at me as though I were joking.

"Morning and evening, all my life, just as you."

I smiled at her to show that I had only been making a jest, and she raised her eyebrows, staring at me strangely.

"Who dwells there, I wonder?"

"Whoever it is, they have been dead since before the beginning of time," she said with disinterest, and wandered away.

The light became dim, and the city began to fade into the growing murk. A single star appeared in the heavens. From somewhere across the plain a dog howled, and the call was echoed by another, and another as the pack gathered. I saw them, slinking through the tall grass at the horizon, beyond the edge of the herds of shaggy beasts that clustered together as though seeking warmth, although the night was mild. The backs of the hounds projected above the waving tops of grass, so they must have stood as tall at the shoulder as my breast. I marveled at their size as I watched them skulk around the edge of the herds, hounds larger than wolves.

The young shaman carried out six clay jars with clay lids while I watched the circling hounds and set them down on the ground in a line. The elder shaman emerged from the tent with his bone wand, his shoulders covered in a feathered cape that had a hood attached. At the brow of the hood was the head of a hawk. Claws of hawks dangled from the hem. The older man went to the line of clay jars and removed their lids, then began to chant over their opened mouths.

From each jar a cloud of bright points of light, like sparks from a fire, swirled into the darkening air, and solidified into the shape of a man. Each ghostly figure carried a naked sword in its right hand and wore a round shield on its left forearm. They were not as solid as flesh, but more dense than the ghosts I had seen with the second sight. In some way difficult to define they felt menacing, and I took a step backward when the gaze of one glowing warrior passed across my face. The shaman made a silent gesture. All six turned and stalked quickly from the camp in different directions. I watched one of the spirits as it approached the herds. The shaggy beasts did not appear to notice its approach, but the lurking hounds backed away and vanished in the long grass. The spirit reached the nearest herd and stood like a statue, staring outward at the place the hounds had been.

The thought of crossing the plain by horse in the darkness with the hounds trailing at my heels did not appeal to me, so I decided to wait until morning before investigating the monastery of the priests. Even as this thought came to my mind, I felt dizzy, as though dropped from a great height, and the sky and plain closed into a narrow passage through which I rushed on a great roaring wave.

Chapter 12

The ghosts had vanished from the domed chamber. I looked slowly from side to side, my neck stiff from sitting so long in the same position, and reasoned that they were probably still present, but that the effects of the white spiders had worn off. I noticed that the depressed bronze pin had returned of its own accord to its former position.

Welcome back, Alhazred, Sashi said in my mind.

I closed my eyes, and she smiled at me, relief evident in her face. Studying my arms, I saw they were unbitten.

"You kept my body safe from vermin while I traveled."

There was no need. A barrier surrounds this stone that only you can cross.

"You crossed it."

Because you carried me here inside you. When I was outside, I could not cross inward.

I passed my hand beyond the edge of the stone disk, and felt nothing. If such a barrier existed, it was subtle. It made a kind of sense. No one would wish to leave their body to soul travel if there was a danger that it might be eaten by rats. The magic of the barrier must distinguish between lower and higher forms of life.

When I tried to unfold my legs, I could not move them. I found that they had no more sensation than blocks of wood. Using my hands, I lifted each and extended it at the knee, then massaged their flesh with my fingers. After several minutes the feeling of a thousand pinpricks came under the surface of my skin. It grew in intensity until it was agonizing, but I endured it silently. When it reached its peak, it began to fade. I slid from the green stone disk and stood. My weakened legs functioned well enough to bear my weight.

The next time I attempt soul travel, I will need to adopt a more comfortable sitting posture, I reflected. That there would be a next time, I had no doubt. I could never leave this place until my curiosity had been satisfied concerning all seven portals. At present, the pangs of hunger outweighed the lust for knowledge. I left the round chamber in search of rats.

Those that lived in the halls of the city were smaller and more wary than the rats dwelling in the cisterns, but months of practice had made me skillful in hunting the creatures, and it was not long before I caught one. I ate its flesh and eyes, then caught another and did the same. Their blood was not as wholesome as the blood of the rats in the cisterns, but I knew it would suffice. My body had adapted to the lack of pure water and was able to tolerate the blood and fluids of the creatures despite their salts. The third rat that I caught I cut into strips and stored away in a rag for later use.

How long I remained in the unnamed city I had no way to measure, but I traveled through each of the seven portals in the star chamber many times, seeking to perfect my knowledge of the places on the other side. I learned that the grassland plateau was called Leng in the language of its inhabitants. Each time I went there, I entered a different body, but always a body of the herders, never the body of a shaman or a priest of the monastery. Charms of magic such as the hound of green stone worn around the necks of the shamans had the power to prevent the displacement of a soul. I approached the monastery only once, and was rewarded by a glimpse of its priests standing along the top of its wall. One of them killed the female herder whose body I wore with a bolt of force that was similar to lightning, but not before I saw that the robed priests were of a different race than the herders, and had short horns growing from their heads.

As I began to comprehend the working of the soul portals, and to gain knowledge of their destinations, I realized that they spanned both distance and time. At least two of the places were not even of this world, but the others, strange though they were, seemed to be located on the earth, either as it presently was or as it had been in the past.

One portal led to a fantastic city beneath three suns of different colors that made the air shimmer with the changing hues of the rainbow from moment to moment. It opened on to a high balcony edged by a metal balustrade of strange cast images depicting the inhabitants of the city. They possessed no fear of heights for they were able to fly through the air on their wings that spread like fans from the seams of their barrel-shaped bodies. I was never able to control them. Their minds were too powerful. Indeed, they seemed amused at my efforts, and spoke among themselves in their curious piping language, which I could not understand since I was not in full possession of my soul vessels. They were obsessed with their own forms, and placed their images throughout their city, as men might place religious icons.

Another portal opened on a great island city on the eve of its destruction by revolution. I could not control its inhabitants, though they were human, but was forced to watch at each visit as the sun crossed the afternoon sky, and the war began that would cast the island beneath the waves with the rays of its terrible crystalline weapons. Upon the third or fourth visit to this place, I realized that it must be the Atlantis written about by the Greek philosopher Plato. Why the reptilian creatures of the nameless city were so fascinated with its downfall was not clear, but it occurred to me that they might be studying the energy weapons that wrought such utter destruction during the brief uprising of its slaves.

One gate opened on a world without a sun, but with a great moon many times the size of our own that was deep purple in color. The creatures who dwelt there were crab-like in appearance, the hard shells of their bodies covered in a white fungus that resembled fur. Yet another portal led deep beneath the ocean to the ruins of a great city upon a hill. At the crown of the submerged hill rose an obelisk covered with strange hieroglyphics, and even more curious, the same branching sign that was carved into the circle at the center of the green stone disk in the round star chamber was set as a seal upon the vast door of the monolith. I explored it in the bodies of deep-dwelling sea creatures with many tentacles, but learned little of its enigma.

Another gate gave entrance to a vast palace that was located high on the peak of a mountain. The throne room was like an enormous cavern with a floor of polished onyx, and walls and columns inlaid with shimmering jewels. It contained not one, but many thrones arranged in a series of crescents, and those who sat in them were gods and goddesses. Some were giants, while others were no larger than men. Their faces shone with radiance, their features were pure and perfect, and their voices beautiful to hear, yet they seldom spoke and never laughed. Thousands of attendants, some of human form and others monstrous in shape, served these curiously silent and morose deities. A brooding oppression hung over their heads, and more than once while inhabiting the body of an attendant, I saw a god stop in conversation and glance upward with apprehension, as though fearing some punishment from above for imprudent words.

Wondering what could cast such gloom over so exalted an assembly, I decided to explore the upper rooms of the palace at the first opportunity. The attendants were closely watched and given constant tasks to perform, so it was not always possible to move freely. When, after passing through the portal, I found myself inhabiting the body of a young man with no immediate work who was not under observation from the overseers, I slipped out of the throne room into the back passageways of the palace and found a narrow wooden stair that led to its summit. It was a servant's stair. I was familiar with such passages from my life in the palace at Yemen. All great houses have hidden halls and stairwells to allow slaves to move about unobtrusively and perform their work.

At the top of the stair was a plain door of polished wood with no lock. I opened it, making as little noise as possible, and peered around its edge. When nothing stirred in the space beyond, I pushed it wider and entered. At first there was only darkness, and I had a sense that the walls of the place pressed close on every side, like the walls of a tomb. Gradually, the shadows retreated as my eyes accustomed themselves to the gloom, and I saw that I stood in a curved corridor paneled in ebon, and ringed on its outer wall with great windows of clear crystal. Each window showed a night sky filled with stars that glittered unnaturally bright.

On hushed feet I walked along the curve of the hallway, tracing its full circle. I glanced fearfully through each window as I passed, but saw nothing except stars. The wall on the other side was featureless save for a single symbol inlaid in ivory or bone at the level of my heart on a panel nearly opposite the door through which I had entered. It had the shape of three interlocking rings. I raised my hand and traced its outline with my fingertip, wondering at its meaning. It shimmered, and my hand passed through the panel. Although I tried to draw my arm out, my body was pulled forward through the wall.

I found myself in a small chamber with a floor of polished obsidian and walls of unadorned stone blocks. From the center of its vaulted stone ceiling hung a kind of lance with three barbed edges. Its flat black metal glowed, giving off a kind of light that illuminated the chamber well enough for me to see that it was empty. I walked to the center of the room and stood beneath the lance, feeling a sense of familiarity but unable to remember where I had seen it. As I pondered, the silence was broken by a shrill piping, like the notes of a flute, and suddenly I remembered the room in my dream. It was here the dark man had marked my brow with his fingernail.

The air above my head began to glow and swirl, forming a kind of whirlwind, and I knew that he was coming. With frantic haste I returned back to where I had entered and felt over the surface of the rough stones in the wall with my hands. They bore no mark, and I wondered if I had mistaken the place of my entry into the chamber. My pressing palm slid through the hard block. I had only an instant to cast a glance over my shoulder at the glowing cloud that formed itself into a solid shape, before I was drawn through the wall and out of the chamber.

Stepping lightly to make no sound, I left the hall of windows and closed the wooden servant's door softly behind me, then descended the stair and returned to the great onyx throne room. The reason for the pervasive gloom of the gods was evident. They feared the wrath of Nyarlathotep. I wondered if it was true, as asserted by I'thakuah, that he compelled them to dance for his pleasure? The thought made me uneasy. When my time in that hallowed place ended, and the star portal drew me back into my own flesh, I never again entered the palace on the mountain, but left it to its unhappy lords.

The portal that most fascinated me led to a browning grassy plain in the season of early winter, where stood an ancient temple of massive squared pillars set in a ring. It was difficult to imagine how such stones had been erected by human ingenuity, but as impressive as they were, even more amazing were the lintel stones that rested flat across their tops and joined them together. How such great blocks had been lifted high into the air and set above the pillars could not be conceived. Even more massive pillars of a different type of stone stood within the ring, and one lay flat on the sod like a great altar. Remnants showed that a roof had once covered the temple, but nothing remained except some rotting beams that had fallen in from long neglect.

The race of tattooed barbarians dwelling near the temple wore roughly woven skirts of wool and animal skins, and lived in huts made of mud and sticks that were thatched with reeds. It was plain at first glance that such a crude people, who were scarcely above the level of the beasts, could never have built the temple, yet they continued to worship there and to offer blood sacrifices to the stones. I returned to this winter place repeatedly and sought to discover the mysterious origin and function of the round temple. Each time, I found myself in the body of one of the villagers, sometimes a man, sometimes a woman, or a child, and according to the abilities of my vessel, I asked my questions.

"Father, why do the priests make sacrifices at the temple?"

It was late in the afternoon, and the sun setting behind the great stones on the horizon cast long shadows across the village. My father, who was both a farmer and a hunter, studied me shrewdly from under bushy brows while fledging an arrow upon his crossed knee. We sat outside our hut, enjoying the last warmth of the sun. No doubt the question surprised him, coming as it did from a girl no more than five years of age. He decided to humor me.

"Blood feeds the earth, child. The earth is our mother. To keep her fertile, we must feed her."

"Would not the blood of a goat do as well as the blood of a man?"

"If we fed her only the blood of beasts, she would grow restless and unsatisfied, and the ground would quake, and the stones of the hills would roll down and fill up the rivers and lakes."

"Then why do we feed her only at the temple?"

He smiled at me, a gleam of indulgent pride in his eye.

"You are full of questions today. The temple is the heart of mother earth. Just as our own heart beats and pumps blood to our fingers and toes, so does the temple send the blood of sacrifice to distant lands along lines that spread out from the temple like the lines of a spider's web spreading from its center."

"Why do the priests make sacrifice only on certain days of the year?"

He dropped his eyes to his work, his patience exhausted.

"Enough questions. Go inside and help your mother."

That was all I learned of the temple while residing in that young vessel, but I had many other opportunities to pursue the matters that interested me.

The lords of the barbarians spoke in the language of the Romans, and by listening to their conversations I discovered that the place was an island that the Romans had called Albion due to the whiteness of its sea cliffs, for in the Latin tongue *albus* means white. Rome conquered the isle in the time of Julius Caesar and made it a part of the Empire. It was said by the common men and women that a priesthood called druids had built the temple, but some of the lords disputed this belief, on the grounds that the few druids who remained were all poets, not builders. After many transitions through the portal, it became clear to me that the barbarians knew nothing of the making of the temple or its use.

The priests who ruled the land worshiped a god they called Janus, having two faces, one for arrival and the other for departure. I remembered from my reading that Janus was a Roman god, and reasoned that the name had merely been applied to an older god of the temple with similar attributes. Janus was the god of portals, and the lord of the Old Ones who presided over the gateways between worlds was Yog-Sothoth. If Yog-Sothoth was the true god of the round temple, as I suspected, then it must be a great gateway.

I wasted many visits in the futile effort to learn the way of opening the gate, but the religion of the people had fallen to such a decadence that it consisted of nothing more than a set of superstitious observances to avert disasters. The priests knew only that the stones of the temple must be fed with the blood of human sacrifice on particular days of the year, or great rumblings and shakings of the ground would take place all over the world that would result in much loss of life. They looked upon themselves as guardians of the health of mother earth, and viewed the soil beneath their feet as a living being that was everywhere connected by common feeling. However misplaced their efforts, their devotion to what they perceived as their sacred duty was admirable.

In all my visits to Albion I had never found myself in the body of a priest, and naturally assumed that the priests of the isle were protected from such intrusion, as had been true of the shamans of Leng. Imagine my surprise when, after flying through the soul portal to the isle in the usual way, I found myself inside the body of the high priest, standing within the temple before the altar stone, the sacred dagger of sacrifice raised over my head in both my hands. I knew I must be the high priest because no one else could wield the sacred blade of polished obsidian. Before me on the altar lay a naked youth, staring up at my face with terrified blue eyes. Curling hair that shone like spun gold hung low on his forehead and covered his ears. His arms were bound and extended above his head by a taunt leather cord, held firmly in the hands of a young priest at one end of the stone. A similar cord held his bound ankles, so that his body stretched helplessly across the surface of the stone.

The silence seemed to echo, as though someone had just stopped speaking. I lowered the dagger slightly and glanced around in confusion. The people stood in two crescents on either side of the altar stone, watching with solemn eyes. In addition to the two priests who held the youth on the stone, six other priests in white linen robes stood beside me, three on either side. I had witnessed similar gatherings around shallow pits dug outside the circle of the temple, into which were cast the freshly slain corpses of sacrifices, but this was the first sacrifice I had seen on the great altar. Turning to the east, I noticed that the red sun was just rising above the plain.

A few of the men who stood across the stone with hands clasped and heads bowed peered at me curiously. At my right shoulder, a priest cleared his throat. I turned to him, and he nodded meaningfully, a slight frown upon his serious features. I recognized him as the second in the hierarchy of the sect. The realization came that I was the man who had been speaking, and that I had not finished the litany. I cursed to myself and rifled through my memory for the words I had overheard uttered on the occasions of other sacrifices. If I could complete the words, I had no qualms about performing the sacrifice. I was curious to see what, if anything, would happen on what must be one of the high holy days of the year.

"We offer to the mother of all life the blood of her child, that the redness of the soil shall never fade or blacken . . ."

I ceased to speak when I saw the second priest shake his head in horror, and the other priests stare at me with mouths gaping. Troubled murmurs arose from the crowd of assembled villagers. A different litany was used for this high rite, and having never witnessed it, I had no shadow of a notion what it might be. Desperately wondering what to do, I decided to feign sickness as a cover for my strange behavior. With a moan I lowered the obsidian blade and pretended to stumble. Just before I fell, I caught myself on one hand on the edge of the altar.

The transformation in those around me was immediate. Faces that had held uncertainty and concern turned first white with shock, then red with rage. With homicidal cries the priests beside me drew their daggers and lunged. The wide blade of black glass fell from my hands and embedded itself in the frozen turf at my feet. I had no place to flee, so I leapt upward onto the altar stone, straddling the terrified naked youth. He scrambled off the stone on bound hands and feet, no longer kept in place by the leather cords of the priests, who were intent only on my death. They ringed the stone, slashing at my dancing legs with their blades, but careful not to touch the stone with their own bodies. What would happen were I to be killed while away from my flesh, I did not know, but I feared the death of the high priest would prevent my return to the star chamber.

One blade cut through my right palm as I caught it, and laid open the flesh down to the bone. Another stabbed my left hip, and a third passed between my ribs just under my heart. Crying out in agony, I fell to my hands and knees on the stone. The daggers rose above me like a thicket of thorns. The progress of time slowed. In my mind I saw the seal of Yog-Sothoth, and remembered the words of opening spoken to me upon the desert by the dark man of my dreams, so many months ago.

"Aye, Yog-Sothoth!" I cried, making the seal of the god upon the surface of the altar stone with the blood that streamed down my finger. "Na f'tng ha-ngloa yah!"

The name of the Old One froze the priests as though they had been petrified by the gorgon. They backed away from the altar on stiff legs, faces distorted in terror. They did know the true name of their god, I thought, struggling to remain conscious under the tide of agony that washed over my borrowed body. It was only that it was forbidden to them to utter it aloud. My blood rained down upon the altar stone beneath the tent of my linen robe, which was brightly stained with crimson in the morning sunlight. I felt life ebb from my body. A great turning began in the air around the altar. With screams of fear, the villagers and the priests alike fled the circle in all directions. The naked youth who had been intended as the sacrifice had managed to free his ankles, and ran with the others, his wrists still lashed together. For the first time in uncounted generations, the portal of the temple was opening.

Struggling to remain conscious as my life gushed onto the stone, I concentrated my thoughts on the star chamber in the unnamed city, and upon my own true flesh that sat there, senseless and unaware. It must be possible to direct the destination of the portals opened in the name of Yog-Sothoth, or what good was there in opening them? With all the strength of my will I aimed the opening whirl on the star chamber. The last breath rattled in my throat, my heart ceased to beat, and I knew that I was dead. At the same moment I felt my soul caught up and carried at such speed through the air that the world became a blur. I opened my eyes in my own body, and found it as I had left it, seated on the green stone disk.

The great rushing noise was still in my ears. I shook my head to clear it, but instead of fading it became louder. I looked up at the dome of the chamber, and my heart quailed. The air of the dome was filled with a turning vortex of gray and black mist that had its focus directly above my head. It somewhat resembled a lidless eye. Within its dark center sparks of brightness danced, and the shadowy outline of a form. I squinted up at it, but could not distinguish its shape, which changed from moment to moment as though struggling to manifest against some hindrance.

You must flee this place, Alhazred. Go now, before it is too late.

Sashi's anxious words, spoken into my mind, broke me from the trance into which I had fallen. I slid from the green disk and stumbled to my knees on my nerveless legs. Cursing, I snatched up my empty water skin and slung it over my shoulder. I touched my hand to the pocket that held the jewels I had gathered, and was relieved to feel their bulge through the cotton of my thawb. As my legs began to tingle, I was able to force myself to my feet and stagger back from the green disk. In fascination, I saw that the seal of five branches cut into the center of the disk glowed with red light that was the color of fresh blood. Each time the vortex in the dome strengthened and widened, the seal glowed more brightly.

Somehow the seal prevented the passage of whatever tried to follow me through the vortex. I dared not wait to see whether it would be strong enough to hold the second traveler at bay. What glimpses of its shape I caught in the dim swirling of the eye of the vortex were enough to teach me that I had no wish to see its body perfected. For a moment, I stood looking at the two entrances to the star chamber in turn, wondering which to take. The same consideration that had caused me shortly after my banishment to turn my steps east on the caravan road, rather than west, came to my mind with renewed force. The past held nothing for me but pain and death, therefore I must choose the unknown future. I ran on trembling legs out the far archway of the domed chamber and did not look back.

Chapter 13

The passages and rooms west of the star chamber I had not explored with care, but had gone only so far into them as had been necessary to hunt for food. I soon found myself walking across dust undisturbed by any human foot. The rooms increasingly appeared never to have been used as dwelling spaces. They were unfurnished, and the stone walls seldom bore decorative paintings. Most were completely empty with no sign to show that they had been used even for storage. As the inhabitants of the city became fewer due to the difficulty in finding sufficient meat, they had no doubt been forced to abandon large areas, and these may have remained empty for centuries. So I reasoned as I moved with light footsteps down eerie deserted halls past the doorways to empty rooms, the brush of my sandals against the floor tiles muffled by the ever-present carpet of dust.

As I approached what must be the western extremity of the city, even the rats and other vermin ceased to show themselves. My eyes were intent on the dust for tracks, so it was not until I was midway down a long hall that had no doorways in its sides that I noticed the faint glow emanating from its far end. The light that shone down uniformly from all the ceilings of the city was green in color. My eyes had adapted to it so that it appeared colorless. By contrast, the light at the end of the hall was a deep golden, more yellow than sunlight yet paler than the light of a lamp. The hall ended in a large chamber with a low ceiling, completely empty save for one of the flat stone altars that occupied various rooms throughout the city. The light shone from an open doorway on its opposite side, dazzlingly bright.

Shielding my eyes with my hand, I moved around the altar, my head bowed and shoulders hunched due to the low ceiling. The doorway stood at the top of a flight of stone steps narrow enough that I could touch either wall by spreading my arms. The brightness emanated from the featureless walls of the stairwell, but reflected so strongly from the sloped ceiling and even the steps themselves, that I could not see the bottom of the stair when I squinted. The steps appeared to descend into a golden mist that concealed them from view. When I put my palm flat on the radiant stone wall, I felt a gentle warmth. The steps were too shallow and too wide for easy progress, but by moving with care I felt my way down them. Much of the way I kept my eyes shut to rest them, but the glare found its way through my closed lids, as does bright sunlight.

The walls at the base of the stair opened into a chamber of no great size, with a very high ceiling. Set in the wall opposite the stair was an ornate door of cast bronze, twice the height of a man. Its surface was divided into twelve ornamental panels arranged in two columns, each panel a square somewhat less than a cubit in size, which is a measure equivalent to two Roman feet. An inherent property or applied treatment of the polished bronze preserved it from corrosion. Each panel was a work of art displaying considerable skill, and together they told the history of the race that had constructed the nameless underground city. I stopped to study the door in detail, for the light from the stair was behind my back and not so bright against the brass that it blinded.

The panel on the upper-left corner depicted the earliest beginning of the race, and showed them dwelling naked on the bank of a river beside small round caves that evidently served them as dens. One of the crocodile creatures caught a fish between its jaws, while another stood upright on its hind legs and short tail, holding a stone knife in its hand. The second panel on the right was the market square of a populous city of low buildings made of mud. The inhabitants thronging the square wore simple garments of white cloth. They stood beside hairless beasts with round bellies and short thick tails, that had great flat ridges of bone around their heads and three horns projecting from their faces, but whether these were herd animals or beasts of burden was not evident.

The next pair of panels contained more complex and larger cities, and were intended to convey the progress of civilization. In the first, the creatures navigated the broad river in boats without sails or oars. I saw no mechanism to drive them, and could not imagine how they were moved, unless they were pulled on ropes by beasts walking along the banks. The second panel had an even more fantastic figure of one of the creatures flying through the air above the city in some kind of machine with wings like those of a bird. I dismissed this as a scene of myth rather than history.

A kind of disaster formed the subject of the third pair of panels. On the left, some vast explosion was shown uprooting mountains and boiling away the seas. Such destruction has been known to occur when the fires deep within the earth erupt from under mountains, but it appeared in the illustration to fall from the heavens. The second panel was a scene of utter waste and desolation. Nothing grew, nor was there any bird or beast. The rivers and lakes perished, and the seas lay stagnant. Roiling clouds filled the dark sky.

The left side of the fourth pair of panels showed starvation among the crocodile race. With bodies so gaunt, the bones showed along their sides, they gazed sadly at stunted plants that refused to grow, and at their feet was the decayed body of one of their horned beasts. Rows of oblong boxes with windows set in their lids, similar to the box I had seen in the upper chambers, stood on their ends like sentinels, and within each was the corpse of one of the race. On the right panel a long line of these creatures, their scant possessions tied to their backs or filling small carts that they pulled with their hands, wound its way into the mouth of a cave. Evidently this was their self-imposed exile from the surface of the earth.

The left side of the fifth pair of panels showed a construction beneath the ground consisting of mines and chambers, the making of the very city in which I wandered. With their mechanical arts the reptilians caused the waters of a mighty underground river to flow through all their halls and moisten long chambers in which grew plants in troughs of soil that extended the full length of the rooms. Other large caverns were used to house their strange livestock, which they fed with the plants. Whereas their beasts ate only growing things, the race of the city fed on the meat of the animals they nurtured beneath the surface. In the right panel, some hardship or blight had fallen over the plants, so that not enough remained to feed the herds of horned beasts. Their corpses lay rotting in great piles.

On the left of the final pair of panels at the base of the door, the underground race, greatly diminished in number, used their skills to direct the water of the river upward, so that it fountained onto the floor of the valley above. Men stood around the fountain, their hands raised in celebration. Behind them the beginnings of a city were being erected on the sands. The scene on the right panel was more sinister. Men, their heads bent beneath the low ceiling of an altar chamber, passed across the surface of an altar to one of the underground race a squirming human infant. In return, the crocodile things gave the men weapons and cloth and open caskets of jewels. Hidden from the view of the men in an adjacent chamber, the crocodiles gathered around an infant and tore it to pieces, feeding on the fragments of its flesh.

Such was the state of affairs between the decadent men of Irem and the race dwelling in the chambers below its foundation at the time the great door had been cast. The attack upon the underground city by the soldiers of the king, and the destruction of Irem in retaliation, had occurred long after the making of the door. I had only I'thakuah's tale as a guide to these events, and as I knew now, the witch was a liar. Yet her story seemed to match the conditions of Irem. Some shaking of the earth had cast it down. Her story did not explain the utter desertion of the halls and rooms of the city by the inhabitants after they had defeated the army of Irem.

With the expectation that the door was bolted, or so corroded on its hinges that it would be immobile, I took in my hand the ring of bronze that hung in its center at the level of my chest and pulled lightly. To my amazement, the heavy metal slab swung silently toward me with almost no resistance. I had learned respect for the craftsmanship of the reptilian race, but this was more than natural, and I wondered for the first time if the polish on the door was truly the result of some protective coating, or if it was maintained in that condition.

An exhalation of cold air blew into my face from the shadows beyond, indicating that the way led to a large cavern or series of chambers. The slanting tunnel in the rock that extended on the other side of the door was too deep to be illuminated by the golden glow shining from the stairway behind me, and I saw that if I entered, within a score of steps I would walk in darkness as deep as that of the cisterns. I stood with my hand on the edge of the door, wondering what to do. I might gather wood in the chambers above to shave and split into kindling that could be bound together to make torches, and these could be sustained by the fat of rats, but the corridors and rooms behind me were empty alike of furniture and vermin. It would take considerable time to go back to where I could hunt, catch and kill the rats, and prepare the wood.

I decided to take three of the fungoidal spiders and sleep. When I awoke, my second sight would allow me to see any living creature in the tunnel beyond the door, and would illuminate scraps of wood that might serve for torches. Even if there was no wood, I preferred to move forward rather than back. It was possible that whatever creature had struggled to follow me through the portal I had opened from Albion to this place had succeeded in entering the city, and if so, I felt no wish to encounter it.

Shutting the door with care so that it would not boom in its frame, I sank to the floor with my back against it and took from a pocket of my thawb the red and green striped silk scarf holding the white spiders. Almost a hundred remained, for I had not felt like consuming them after my sickness. I crunched three of their dried bodies between my teeth and swallowed them, their pleasant almond taste tingling on my tongue. Putting the rest away, I ate a strip of the dried rat meat I carried, then lay on my side and draped my arm across my face to shield my eyelids from the light shining down the stair.

My thoughts wandered to the mystery of the lack of a bolt or catch upon the door. Why build any door, and especially one so substantial, yet not provide it with a means by which it might be securely fastened or locked? What good was a door without a lock? In all the rest of the city I had seen only the single small door of iron by which I had entered the ornate living chambers of its noble citizens. The crocodiles had not used doors as men use them. Their sleeping rooms and living rooms had no doors that could be closed. Yet these two doors existed, one a humble and low door of iron, unadorned in any manner, and the other a magnificent work of art in brass.

Not all questions that may be asked receive answers. My mind drifted into sleep, and I dreamed a curious dream. I saw myself, lying asleep with my back against the brass door. In my dream vision, I floated through the door and was able to look at the tunnel on the far side. Even though it was dark, in my dream I saw clearly a gathered throng of the former race of the city, their bodies white as though covered in chalk dust, their eyes red. They knelt on their short hind legs in ranks, filling the tunnel with their grotesque faces turned toward the door, and bent their upper bodies forward with their arms extended until their snouts touched the floor stones, as though praying before the idol of some unseen god.

Sashi's caresses tingled upon my skin when I awoke, feeling languid and much rested. I closed my eyes and saw her smiling face lean forward to kiss my lips. We made love without haste, neither of us feeling a need for words. I rose from the floor and passed through the bronze portal, leaving it opened wide behind me to gain as much benefit from the light of the stairway as was possible. Having decided what I would do before sleep, there was no cause for hesitation, yet as I ventured deeper into the darkness I felt a stirring of fear that was borne of ignorance of what might lie ahead. The breeze now came from behind me, and I reasoned it must change its direction from day to night.

The rough stone walls of the passage were lit with a sprinkling of silver sparks, generated by tiny shells embedded in the stone. They were not so numerous as they had been in the walls of the cisterns, but were enough to define the shape of the tunnel, which showed less marks of the stonemason's chisel as I advanced, until it became entirely natural and irregular, a cave that sloped ever downward. A great sound like thunder made my heart stumble and almost cast me from my feet in my terror. After a moment, I began to breathe again as I realized its source. I laughed aloud, my voice echoing from the stone. The breeze had slammed shut the bronze door. It made no difference to my progress, since I had already moved beyond the reach of its light.

As I went forward, the walls and roof of the cave widened, and I found myself walking across the floor of a vast cavern. The floor was strewn with small stones. I bent and picked one up to feel its shape in the darkness. It was smooth, like a pebble from the bed of a river. An infinite number of similar stones lay heaped across the cavern in regular ridges similar to the dunes of the desert, no doubt deposited there by a great flood of waters in the distant past. The cavern was not one simple space but convoluted in shape, and divided by natural pillars and buttresses that rose from its floor like islands in a lake. Large spiders the size of my palm dwelt there in abundance, as did other creeping forms of life. I saw the glow of their bodies, clustered most thickly around piles of ancient tree roots and stumps swept from the surface of the earth into the cavern on the floods of its vanished river.

I stood still and listened, holding my breath. After a minute or so I was gratified to hear the faint squeak of a rat. There was meat in the cavern. It would not be necessary to subsist wholly on the spiders and other vermin. I bent quickly and caught one of the spiders. It struggled in my grasp, its hairy legs digging into my skin like wires. Sharp pain stabbed through my thumb, and I realized it had bitten me. Annoyed at my careless handling of the creature, I pulled off its head and tossed it away, then tore its body open with my teeth. As I had hoped, it held a large amount of fluid that was pure enough to suck. I chewed some of its flesh. The taste was mild and not unpleasant. As I ate, the pain in my thumb grew less. To my good fortune, the spiders were not venomous. I picked up the head from where I had thrown it and examined it closely. The curved fangs, sharp as needles, continued to spasm open and shut.

Another sound reached my ears as I stood silent. At first I thought it was nothing more than the pulse of blood in my head, but it came like the flow of water over stone, a continuous rushing murmur that rose and fell but never entirely ceased. I wondered if the white spiders I had taken to enhance my vision had also sharpened my ears, so that I was able to hear sounds that had echoed from the walls of the cave in the distant past, when the river still made its way beneath the nameless city.

High above my head I noticed at intervals glowing irregular masses, as if some kind of moss grew upon the rock. A portion of one glowing cluster detached itself and circled downward through the air toward me on silent wings. It was shaped somewhat like a bat, but having long forelimbs with great claws like daggers and a sinuous tail that rippled like the body of a serpent upon the air as it flew. Evidently it thought I could not see it, since it came directly toward me with its claws extended. I drew my dagger and as I dodged aside cut upward into its belly. Its shriek of pain filled the darkness, and I felt wet upon my fingers. The thing flapped awkwardly to rise from where I stood and flew away, dripping out its life blood with each beat of its wings.

I raised my hand and tasted on the tip of my tongue the blood that had spilled down my dagger blade. The bitter foulness nearly made me retch. Spitting it out, I wiped both my hand and the broad blade clean on the pebbles at my feet. High in the air, others of the creature's own kind attacked it, striking with their talons and circling away repeatedly until at last it fell to the cavern floor. They flew down like the vultures of the desert and began to tear it to pieces with their beaks. If its flesh was as poisonous as its blood, which I had no reason to doubt, they were welcome to the carcass.

Leaving them to their feast, I made my way around a line of connected natural pillars that formed a kind of curved wall arising from the floor of the cavern. Four glowing masses lay on the ground before me. I thought they were ancient logs, and began to walk past. The one nearest stirred and lifted itself from the pebble bed on four short legs. I stopped, and in the intervals between my heartbeats heard the dry rustle of breathing. Looking upon the thing directly, I saw that it was one of the inhabitants of the underground city. It appeared a great deal more threatening than it had in the wall paintings that depicted its form. Its jaws were shorter than those of a crocodile, but massively muscled and filled with pointed teeth. Intelligence of a kind glowed from the eyes set on either side of the prominent dome of its skull. The other three creatures lifted themselves upon their legs and began to move around me, with the intention of cutting off my retreat.

I pulled my dagger and slashed the air in what I hoped was a menacing manner. The monsters ignored the gesture. Cursing, I put it away and formed the Elder Sign with my right hand. Even as I did so, I wondered if the things could see in the darkness, or if they hunted by smell. The Elder Sign provoked no more response than the dagger. My curses gained a purpose, as I added the name I'thakuah to them. Was there any creature that did fear the sign she had shown to me? In desperation, I tried to think of some token or act that the creatures would respect. If they could not see, perhaps they could hear.

"Yog-Sothoth protect me, Cthulhu protect me," I cried into the darkness. "My lord Nyarlathotep, guard the life of your faithful servant."

At the pronunciation of the name of the dark man, the creatures made hissing noises and scampered back several paces. Evidently they could hear, and this Old One was not unknown to them.

"Yes, Nyarlathotep is my lord. I serve his will and he protects me in all things."

Inwardly, I hoped voicing the name of the god would not invoke him, as I had no more wish to meet him than the crocodile monsters.

They withdrew a short distance and gathered to converse, speaking in a language of grunts and snorts punctuated by the snap of their jaws. I waited patiently, wondering if I could outrun their short legs. Their movements were surprisingly quick. I noticed that, unlike their depictions on the city murals, they were naked and wore no jewelry or adornments. Nor did they carry tools or weapons. That they were descended from the original builders of the city I could not doubt, since the resemblance was exact.

When I stepped to one side, they ran in front of me and blocked my path, though not so aggressively as at first. Again I tried to walk around them, and this time they allowed me to go forward unhindered, but fell into step on either side and behind me. Feeling like a herded goat, I went forward with as much a display of confidence as I could manage, on the assumption that if they could not see it in my posture, they would hear it in my steps. In this way they guided me along. I might have run in a different direction, but my curiosity was aroused, and I wanted to learn what they intended.

We made our way toward the edge of the cavern, where the wall met the floor at an angle formed a kind of roof. Here, the stones were heaped up in a long ridge, so that behind them there was a cave within the larger cavern. As I approached this hill of pebbles, more of the creatures appeared at its crest, emerging from the sheltered space behind it. They descended the side of the hill without hesitation, snuffing the air with their snouts. One came quite close to me and nipped with its jaws the air beside my left hand, but my guards warned it away with grunts, swishing their thick tails across the loose stones so that they rattled. There were perhaps two dozen of the creatures, all approximately the same size. I saw no young, and could not distinguish male from female.

They turned themselves expectantly to the crest of the hill and waited. After a few minutes, a crocodile slightly larger than the others, robed in a tattered cloak of some woven cloth and wearing a jeweled metal bracket on the dome of its head that resembled a kind of crown, descended slowly. It paused at each few steps as though tired, but none of the others moved to assist it. One of my escorts spoke to it at length in their grunting tongue, and it regarded me in silence. With an effort, it reared itself up on its hind legs and tail so that its head was on the same level as mine, and stood swaying, as though unaccustomed to the posture.

"Are you a man of Irem?"

Its words were slurred and strangely accented, but I had no difficulty understanding them. They were articulated somewhere in the creature's throat, not with its mouth as we pronounce our words.

"I am not of the city."

"You are not of A'zani."

"What is A'zani?"

"This place is A'zani. The place of rushing waters. Or so it was, long ago."

I understood. The dry river had been called A'zani by the people of Irem.

"No, I am not of A'zani."

It regarded me as though pondering my words.

"Where do you come from?"

"The desert."

The creature spoke in its own language to the assembly of its people, and they responded with grunts.

"You speak the name of the lord of chaos," it said to me.

"I am the servant of Nyarlathotep," I lied.

The utterance of the god's name made all the creatures scurry away from me. Even their robed leader withdrew a step before remembering its dignity.

"Have you come to punish us?" There was a note of fatality in its growling throat.

"No. I am a traveler passing through this place."

The tenseness of the creature's limbs relaxed and its back sagged. It grunted and clicked a few words, and a similar relief ran through the others like a wave across the water.

"Tell the god whose name is not to be uttered that we have kept faith with him, and have not returned to the city of our ancestors. We remain outside the portal, as we promised."

"When next I see him, I will convey this message."

The response of the leader was lost in a roar that came from behind me. I turned and saw a large number of crocodiles rushing toward the hillside. There were twice as many as those that stood placidly around me. Cries of confusion and dismay arose from the gathering. Some turned to confront the charge, while others ran wildly up the hill toward the mouth of the cave, disregarding the harsh commands of the leader.

Had I been perceived as a threat by the attackers, I would surely have died in the first few moments of the battle, but they ignored me as they grappled with others of their own race. I backed slowly away from the midst of the conflict and stood without moving in the hope that the crocodiles could not see me through the darkness and would miss my scent in the disorder of battle. They were intent only on killing each other. The battle inspired both terror and awe in my heart. The creatures were even more powerful than I had imagined. They grappled with their clawed hands and threw each other upon the ground with their powerful tails. Yet despite the ferocity of the fight, scant blood was drawn. Neither side used weapons, and their thick leather skins protected them from all but the most savage of bites.

The outcome was never in doubt. The attackers overwhelmed the defenders by their superior number and drove them away from the hillside, all save a few who lay bleeding or dead. One of those killed was the leader. Its throat had been torn out in the first savage moments of the battle, and the crocodile that had killed it had put on its cloak and crown, and danced in glee around the corpse. The victors wasted no time in rushing up to the mouth of the cavern. They vanished into its dark hollow, and I wondered what treasure it contained that could explain so brutal and sly an attack. I had not long to wait for an answer. In minutes they emerged, each carrying on its back one of the wooden boxes with a glass lid that held the corpse of an ancestor. They bore them quickly away, not pausing to hunt down the scattered remnants of the defenders.

Before they passed beyond my sight, an angry cry went up from somewhere in front of them, and I saw them cast down their boxes and flee back in confusion, pursued by a force of their own race. The newcomers charged after them with great fury, and though they were less in number, the concentration of their attack unnerved the craven looters, who perhaps had anticipated an easy victory. Cries went up around me as the defeated guardians of the cave rallied together, and the unhappy predators became the prey, caught between two hostile bands. I realized that the attack on the cave had been planned for a time when the force of the defenders was weakest, but the attackers had been surprised by the untimely return of the others, who probably had been off hunting for food.

These hunters made no attempt to catch or slay the attackers. All their concern was for the boxes that lay scattered around in confusion where they had been dumped. They began to carefully tip upright these cases and to brush with gentle fingers the dust from their glasses, all the while making a strange lament that was like a gulping noise deep in their throats. They seemed not to care about those who lay dead or dying from the attack, but only for those who had died centuries ago and lay like dry sticks within their cases.

With quick but careful steps I moved away from the place of battle. None of the creatures looked in my direction, giving me reason to believe they truly were blind in the darkness. Whether there might be any other apart from the slain leader who could speak human language, I did not seek to discover. With their bloodlust aroused, the returned hunting party might be more disposed to kill than to talk, and I was not confident that the name of Nyarlathotep alone was sufficient to ensure my security. I did not stop until I was well beyond the sound of the creatures. I reasoned that my hearing was probably as good as theirs, or better, and if I could not hear their deep grunts, it was unlikely they would hear the crunch of my sandals upon the pebbles.

I stood breathing deeply, thankful for my escape, and wondered which way I should travel. The faint breeze that touched my cheek decided my course. It must come from an opening to the surface, no matter how far away it might lie. I began to follow it, letting it lead me up and down the piled mounds of stones and around the tangled wrecks of ancient tree trunks. How many days I walked, there was no way of reckoning. I continued to eat the white spiders, on the reflection that the ability to see the bat-like things and other threats to my life was more important than the risk of possible poisoning. I found that when I ate only three spiders at each sleep, my body did not reject them.

The soles of my sandals became ragged on the stones, and I grew to loathe the juice of the great spiders on my tongue even though it sustained my life. The journey through the depths seemed without end. Only the faint breeze that touched my lips like a kiss kept me from becoming hopelessly confused in the winding dry riverbed, which twisted from side to side like the body of a serpent, and sometimes bent back upon itself. When I felt that madness must surely descend to carry away my reason beyond all recovery, I saw ahead a light that I had not glimpsed in many months. It was the light of the sky.

I emerged between a jumble of great boulders and stood swaying in the cool salt breeze of early morning that swept in from the ocean, for the mouth of the cave was located at the base of a cliff separated from the sea by only a narrow strip of sand. Even though the sun had not yet risen, the light was so intense it made tears gush from my eyes. I closed my lids to slits and laughed aloud from the sheer joy of release from the womb of earth. On stiff knees, the soles of my sandals flapping on the beach, I walked to the edge of the water and let it wash with a cool touch over my toes while I stood staring at the crests of the waves that rolled gently toward me.

Chapter 14

In a daze, eyes clenched against the brightness of the sky, I left my possessions and thawb on the beach and walked naked save for stockings and sandals into the waves of the ocean. When I stood up to my waist, I splashed the cool water over my face, and finally bent and submerged my head completely. I used my fingers to scrub out the dust and fleas and lice from my hair and beard, then washed the rest of my body. A group of sea birds floated upon the water near a jut of rock, some distance from the sand. They watched me with curious tilts of their heads but did not fly away. Laughing to myself from the simple joy of being clean once again, I imitated their cries and made faces at them that must have been horrible to contemplate, although they did not appear disturbed.

Only when my body was scrubbed red did I emerge from the water. I used one of the rags I carried to wipe myself so that the salt of the ocean would not dry on my skin, then stood naked to the knees, enjoying the morning sunlight. Gathering up my thawb, I removed everything from it, including the honey-covered jewelry of the dead girl that was stuck fast in one of the pockets, and washed the garment in the ocean until its original cream color returned by repeatedly wetting it and beating it against a smooth rock that rose above the waves. When it was clean I draped it over flat boulders to dry and rinsed off the jewelry. I shaved my face with my knife in the reflection of a small tidal pool between the rocks, then lay upon the sand on my back. I felt renewed, as though I had died under the earth and been reborn.

From the position of the rising sun, I judged I must be somewhere on the shore of the Sea of Aurmia, that is called the Red Sea, on a deserted part of the coast of Yemen. Were I discovered and recognized, it would mean execution, but there seemed little chance that anyone believed me still alive. I had been sent out to the desert to perish. To be left alone and naked in the Empty Space, without food or water, is to be dead. Only the disfigurement of my face might betray me should I encounter a soldier or officer of the government who had heard the story of my torture. I remembered the dream in which the dark man had given me a spell of glamour to cause my features to appear normal, and wondered if it was a fancy of my imagination.

Untying the cotton rag that held the jewels and gold pieces gathered in the underground city, I examined them in the sunlight. Each stone was of the finest quality. Sold with care, there was sufficient wealth in my two hands to last the remainder of my lifetime. It was more than enough to travel out of this nation, for I had decided to leave Yemen and become a wandering seeker of knowledge in distant lands. There was nothing to keep me here, and every reason to leave. The thought of the dark man, pacing the desert and sniffing the air with his head down in search of footprints, made me nervous. The single encounter with him outside my dreams convinced me that I did not wish to meet him again.

When my thawb dried, I shook it to beat out the sea salt and put it on. The plain but honest cotton threads had stood up well to the ordeals of the desert and the places under the earth, but the same could not be said for my sandals, the soles of which flapped as I walked. There was nothing to do but endure it, or go barefoot, since the thin leather of my stockings had worn in holes on the bottoms. The slippery rocks along the shore were sharp enough that I wanted some protection from them, and ragged sandals were better than nothing. Collecting my few possessions, I walked north with the rhythmic plash of the waves on my left hand and the low cliffs on my right.

In late afternoon, just as I began to wonder whether it would be wise to find a place to sleep, I came upon a kind of loading dock built of timbers sunk into the beach to form a shallow box filled with rocks and sand. There were no habitations attached to it. Evidently it had been constructed by the king to allow traders in this sparsely populated region of the coast to transfer their goods to ships, saving them the expense and danger of carrying them overland to a port city. A single ship was tied to the outer side of the dock, and its crew used the crane attached to the dock to transfer bales into its hold. The traders who had deposited the cargo on the dock had already departed. A road extended away from the shore and wound between two hills to disappear from sight. It was marked by the footprints of many camels, still easy to see in the sand, although the wind would surely cover them before nightfall.

As I approached along the margin of the ocean around a headland that put the setting sun over my left shoulder, members of the crew peered at me from beneath their hands, which they raised to shield their eyes against the glare. I made the gestures upon the air the dark man had taught me in my dream, and spoke the word aloud. I saw and felt nothing. Whether the spell worked, I would soon discover. It would be easier to converse with the captain and meet his mariners with a normal face, but if he saw me as the monster I was, I must still attempt to convince him to take me aboard as his passenger. The sight of even the smallest of the jewels I carried would be persuasive, but the thought came to me that it would be better not to display my treasure. There was always a chance the captain might decide to slit my throat and steal it, and little way I could defend myself against so many foes.

One of the men on the ship jumped down from the rail to the dock as I approached and waited for me. The crew that worked with ropes the stone counterweight on the heel of the long boom of the wooden crane gave me curious glances, but there was no horror in their eyes, as there surely would have been had they gazed upon my true face. I wondered what my mask of glamour resembled, and with a certain vanity hoped that I was handsome. The man who waited wore a skirt of white linen trimmed with blue that covered his knees, and over it a vest of striped red and gold silk that left his muscular arms free. Its bright colors contrasted with the simple white skirts of the other men, most of whom labored bare to the waist. Like them, he wore a turban but went barefoot, and he carried in its scabbard at his leather belt a short sword with a blade as broad as my hand.

The weathered lines of his sun-browned face gave an initial impression of harshness, but his gaze as he watched me approach was direct and neutral. I saw as I drew nearer that his head reached only as high as my shoulder.

"I am called Alhazred," I said, stopping to face him. "Will you give me passage aboard your ship?"

He smiled at my directness, and at once his expression became less intimidating.

"You don't even know where we are going."

I spread my arms and turned in a circle.

"Wherever you sail, it is surely more hospitable than this coast."

He gazed up the shore, upon which nothing but a scattering of sea birds moved, and grunted his agreement.

"We sail north, to the port of Suez. Will that suit you?"

"I can wish for no finer destination."

He dropped his glance to my tattered sandals and met my eyes.

"How did you plan to pay for your passage?"

Working from my finger the gold ring that I had worn since stealing it out of the grave of the Bedouin of the caravan that had abandoned me in the Empty Space, I handed it to him. He held it up to the sunlight and studied its plain band, which was thin enough. With a shrug, he tried it on his third finger, and finding it too tight, transferred it to his smallest.

"Have you got anything else?"

I felt through the breast slit of my thawb to an inner pocket, and drew out the silver medallion I had taken from the dead girl wrapped in honey. He made a sound of appreciation and squinted to read its Arabic text, then tucked it in his belt so that its neck chain dangled. His eyes rested on Gor's polished white skull at my waist.

"A keepsake I found in the desert."

He grunted.

"My name is Jabir ibn Abdullah. This is my ship, the *Eye of Mecca*." He waved a negligent finger at the crew on the dock. "These are the laziest and most worthless fools I've ever had the misfortune to sail with."

His words aroused a sullen chuckle from an old man with a white beard, who did not pause in his work. Another turned and spat onto the sand.

The captain clapped me on the back in a friendly fashion.

"Come into my cabin. We will share a flask of wine while these malingerers finish their work."

He spoke a few short words of instruction to a large man who labored with the rest, and the man nodded. He looked at me for a moment before bending to jerk tight the rope around the bale of wool he was about to load, and I saw worry in his expression. Jabir noticed my eye upon him.

"That's Ulik, my first mate. The only thing that keeps this scum from robbing me and slinking off into the night is the fear that he would bash their heads together. And he would."

The *Eye of Mecca* was broad in her beam and low in the water. Her bottom must have been completely flat, or she would never have been able to load her hold in so shallow a mooring. Painted on the starboard side of her curving bow was a large eye. Though I could not see the opposite side, I assumed a similar eye adorned it. Her square sail was furled on its angled cross arm at the base of the mast. Along the side, shuttered ports showed where oars could be lowered into the water in times of calm, though to move such an ungainly craft by oars alone would be an agonizing labor. Stacks of cargo rested everywhere, making it awkward to move across the deck to the small cabin at the stern of the ship. The roof of this cabin was an elevated deck where would stand the steersman who held the great oar that acted as the rudder of the ship. At present it was not occupied.

Ducking my head and following the captain into the shadowed interior of the cabin, I saw him pull the cork from a leather-covered bottle and pour its contents into two brass cups he had set on a small table. He dropped the bottle on the table unsealed and passed me a cup, then sank into a chair. I took the only other chair on the opposite side of the table and sampled my drink. In the months since my expulsion from the palace I had nearly forgotten the taste of good wine, and this swill did nothing to remind me. It had a woody flavor and a slight sourness. I drank deep and smiled my appreciation to my companion, who must have been well accustomed to the taste since he could drink the wine without grimacing.

"Alhazred? That's a strange name."

"My father was a fanciful man," I lied. "He named me after a djinn."

Jabir raised his glossy black brows over the rim of his cup.

"Better if you don't say that to the men. They are a superstitious lot. They won't like me taking a passenger as it is."

"Why would they object to a passenger?"

"Not just a passenger, a man from the desert. You gave them quite a scare when you appeared on the beach. Ulik thought you were a djinn when first he looked at you—said you had the face of a monster."

I laughed to cover my discomfort. The first mate had keen eyesight.

"In the twenty or more years we've been coming here, no one has ever appeared alone from the desert. No one lives here for many leagues in all directions."

It was plain he wanted my story, so I told it to him.

"I was in a caravan, making my way to Sana'a, when we were attacked by bandits, who intended to hold me and others for ransom. They took us with them when they fled into the Empty Space to avoid the soldiers of the king of Yemen, and I managed to escape on a camel. The poor beast died of thirst. My own water ran out just today."

I patted my empty water skin at my waist to lend credence to my tale.

"I've been walking along the coast, hoping to see a ship. It was fortunate I found you."

"Very fortunate. Allah be praised."

He drained the last of his wine and refilled his cup from the bottle.

"You said you were traveling to Sana'a? Don't you want to go there?"

"Can you take me to Sana'a?"

He laughed.

"Sana'a is an inland city. My ship doesn't sail over sand. Nor can I take you to the ports of Qizan or Maida, which are not far from Sana'a, because they lie down the coast to the south, and I must sail north at once. I can let you off as we pass the port of Jidda, which isn't too far from Mecca. You could make your way back to Yemen overland, if you have money for the journey, or friends who will lend you money."

I spread my hands and put on a look of sorrow.

"My family was killed in the bandit raid on the caravan. I have no family or friends in Mecca. However, I do have an uncle living in Alexandria who I am sure would be happy to see me, and would lend me the money to make my way home."

"Egypt it is, then," he said with a tone of finality.

When the cargo had filled the hold and been tied down to every available open space on the deck, we waited for the turning of the tide. As the sun settled into the western sea, we cast off and began to sail north on a favorable wind. The captain offered me space beside him in his bunk, but I declined, saying that I preferred to sleep under the stars. The truth was that I did not wish to reinfest myself with fleas after so soon cleaning them from my hair and thawb.

Before our sailing, I filled my water skin with a wooden dipper at the ship's water barrel, and had a chance to gaze upon my altered features. The magic of the dark man had restored my lost face. It stared back at me from the still surface of the water, a little more tanned and lined than it had looked in the mirror that, in another life, Dodee was accustomed to hold up for me each morning, but otherwise unchanged. So great was my longing for that face, my tears fell into the barrel like rain, and I took myself to the private place I had managed to find near the bow of the ship between two high piles of horsehides, where I sat squinting at the setting sun until it disappeared beneath the horizon.

The night was mild. The constant breeze drove away flies. I fell asleep on the deck, listening to the shouts of the seamen, who labored unseen behind the piles of cargo. The rocking of the ship did not trouble me. I slept longer and more deeply than I had in months, with my right hand not closed around the hilt of my dagger.

A scream woke me. I sat up and squinted through the morning light in the direction of the sound. An old man with a bald head and long white beard stood between the piles of skins, staring at me with his mouth agape. His scalp looked pale where it was usually protected from the sun by his turban, which he clutched in both his hands in front of his chest. I saw that he had no teeth, and it reminded me of I'thakuah. I grimaced. The old man screamed again, then turned and stumbled away between the bales and barrels.

As the sleep left my head, I realized that the dark man's glamour had ended. It endured only a single day, and must be renewed daily. He had spoken a term of hours in the dream. Searching my memory, his words came back to me. Twelve hours. Less than the span from sun to sun, at this season of late summer. I made the gestures and uttered the word of the spell under my breath, as a babble of frightened voices approached the place I sat. Quickly, I lay down on my side with my head on my arm, my back turned to the sounds.

"You! Stand up," a deep voice ordered.

I waited for the man to repeat his words before slowly rolling over and pushing myself erect. As I turned to show my face, I let it express puzzlement mingled with annoyance.

The five seamen, among them the old man and the first mate, Ulik, stared at me in silence, their bodies tense with fear. The first mate shook himself from his paralysis and cuffed the old man on his bald head with an open hand.

"What are you playing at, Kabassa, you old fool? There's nothing wrong with his face."

"It was the face of a djinn, I tell you," the old man babbled as he rubbed his crown. "It was horrible, Ulik, the face of a monster."

The first mate glared at me. I met his gaze calmly with just the right amount of bemusement.

"Back to work," he roared at the others, who cleared a passage for him when he turned and stalked away without another glance. The other three seamen looked at me and at each other uncertainly, then backed away. The old man scowled in anger, but he was too fearful to remain alone and shrank back with the rest.

"I know what I saw," he said fiercely, staring at me with defiance.

When I was once more unobserved, I turned to the open sea and urinated over the rail.

I am puzzled, Alhazred.

"Why is that, Sashi?" I murmured, wondering what the outcome of this little drama would be.

He said you look like a djinn. You look nothing like a djinn.

I laughed in spite of my misgivings.

"These men have never seen a djinn. To them, djinn is just another word for monster."

After a while, the boy who helped the black cook prepare the meals poked his head around the edge of one of the piles of skins and nervously told me that the captain wished me to share his morning meal. He was kneeling on his prayer rug on the deck above his cabin when I approached. I waited in silence for him to finish. He rolled up the rug and we entered the cabin together without exchanging a word. Laid out on his table were plates of dried figs and apricots, a hard biscuit with the texture of wood, smoked goat meat simmered in oil, and brass cups of the same sour wine we had shared the previous day. I relished the dried fruit, but the smoked meat was not to my liking, so accustomed I had become to the raw flesh of rats. I pretended to enjoy it.

"My first mate still claims that you are a djinn," Jabir said, smacking his lips with enjoyment as he drank his wine.

"Has he ever seen a djinn?"

"Not to my knowledge."

"There, you see?" I said to Sashi.

I spread my hands and smiled, as though I had been talking to the captain, and he nodded.

"I perceive your point. Still, probably best if you avoid the crew for the rest of the voyage. I've given orders that you are not to be bothered."

I kept to myself, and when I could not avoid a seaman, I smiled pleasantly and nodded, even though my smile was never answered with anything other than a glare. They were afraid of me, that much was obvious. On a ship, it is nearly impossible to avoid human contact, but I found myself able to be alone most of the day and night.

Each morning and each evening I renewed the spell of glamour to conceal my true features. The trouble might have ended had not the wind died. For three days we lay in the middle of the sea, becalmed, the water as flat as a polished marble table. I heard it muttered among the crew that the captain had sailed too far from land and had lost the wind. Some of them cursed me and swore I was the cause of the error.

When the sail was hoisted in a futile effort to take advantage of the passing ghost of a breeze, and one of its supporting ropes snapped, the discontent swelled into open discord. All morning, the anger of the crew had gathered strength, and when the rope broke, their patience snapped along with it. The captain sent the cook's boy to call me to his cabin. He stood in the open doorway, his sword naked in his hand and a grim expression on his face.

"Get inside," he snapped, his distaste at seeing me obvious.

Silently, I slid around him and entered the cabin.

"Shut the door and bolt it. Whatever happens, don't come out."

"I have a dagger," I said. "You may need me beside you."

"No. If you stab one of the crew, they will fall on you and tear you to pieces. They are close enough to doing that as it is."

It was not my place to argue with his judgment. I took a moment to admire both his principles and his courage, then shut the door and bolted it while he continued to stand guard on the outside of the portal. Through the carved wooden lattice of the door I was able to look over his shoulder and saw the crew approach in one mass, murder in their eyes. The first mate went before them with his arms outspread and tried to slow their progress, but they ignored his gruff words and pushed him onward with the tide of their bodies.

"Stand, you dogs!" he roared. "Show some respect."

"No, let them approach," Jabir said in a steady voice that carried across the deck. "If my crew is troubled, I will hear their complaint."

This moderated the anger of the seamen. They milled around, uncertain who to send forward to speak to the captain. At last they shoved the unwilling Kabassa in front of them until he stood alone. He eyed the sword and licked his lips.

"Have you a grievance, Kabassa?" Jabir asked.

"Not against you, Captain," the old man stuttered.

"What is it, then? Speak your mind, if you have one."

The insult seemed to annoy the old man, and stiffened his nerve. He pointed over the captain's shoulder directly at my face.

"That's not a man, it's a djinn. We have to cast it over the side or this ship is doomed."

The rest of the assembled crew murmured their agreement. I saw the flash of a knife blade between their tightly pressed bodies as they shifted and surged forward. Jabir raised his sword.

"Hold! There'll be no murder on this ship as long as I command."

He lowered his sword and swung his finger in an arc to point at each of the seamen.

"You've had your say, now it's my turn. I say this man is not a djinn. I say he is a passenger who has paid his way to Suez."

He showed the ring on his hand to indicate the payment.

"We are bound by honor to take him to Suez, as was agreed."

Another man whose name I did not know stepped forward in anger.

"He's a monster. Kabassa saw his face. So did Ulik. We have to get him off the ship or we're all dead men."

The captain looked at his first mate.

"Ulik, tell them you didn't see any monster."

The big man remained silent with a stubborn expression. The captain waited. At last Ulik shook his head.

"I did see a djinn. Kabassa is right, we have to get it off the ship."

The body of the captain sagged as he realized that the first mate would not stand with him against the crew. He was alone.

I had seen and heard enough. I stepped back from the door into the shadows of the cabin and dug into my thawb, drawing forth the rag that held the jewels. With care I took out one jewel at random and tied up the rag, putting it back in its pocket. I placed the stone into my mouth and held it under my tongue.

"Sashi, I want you to leave my body," I murmured under my breath. "Stay close to me, and go where I point. Do you understand?"

I will do as you ask, my love.

The familiar pulling sensation on the surface of my chest informed me when the djinn vacated my flesh. Even though I could not see her, I knew she remained near at hand.

The captain was losing the battle of words. As his mutinous crew prepared to pull him aside and rush the cabin, I unbolted the door and stepped into the sunlight. They let forth a roar of rage and started toward me like a single beast. I raised both my hands.

"It is true," I cried. "I am not like other men."

This admission halted them. The captain turned with a puzzled expression.

"I am not a djinn, but a necromancer."

A murmuring sigh ran through the crew. In a few moments they would gather their anger and rush forward. I spoke quickly.

"What was seen was not my face, but the face of the familiar spirit that serves me. With this spirit I can work wonders. I can raise a breeze."

As I spoke, I gestured with my index finger across the line of men who faced me. One by one their eyes widened as they felt the cooling touch of the djinn on their skin when she passed through their bodies.

"It's true," Ulik rumbled in wonder, stepping away from me. "I felt it. A breeze."

"I can do more than this," I said. "I can shape and harden the very air itself into anything I desire."

With theatrical gestures I shaped my hands into a horn and raised them to my lips. I blew a long noisy breath out between my curled fingers, then another, and another. On the third breath I let my hands close together and passed the jewel into my palms on the tip of my tongue. Lowering my cupped hands from my face, I held them out and slowly opened them to show the sparkling stone. The gasps of wonder came from almost every throat. Carelessly, I tossed the jewel to Ulik, who caught it before he could think, then held it up on his outstretched palm as though it were hot and burning him.

"Keep it," I told him in an indifferent tone. "I can make another any time I wish."

The captain backed away from me, terror in his eyes, his sword raised in front of his body in defense.

"You are a necromancer," he breathed. "What have I brought onto my ship?"

"Nothing that will harm you, unless you attack me. It is true, I could kill you all with a few words, but if you do not molest me, I will summon a breeze and we will continue our voyage. I will even make a few more jewels for you as tokens of my good faith, before we reach Suez."

"If you can summon a wind, do it," the captain said.

I laughed as though he had spoken in a childish manner.

"I will summon a wind, but it cannot be done in an instant. It is a great work of magic to call a wind big enough to move this ship."

"How much time do you need?" Ulik asked, fingering the jewel. Part of his anger had turned to fear, and another part to greed, as I had hoped.

"A night and a day. By sunset tomorrow you will have your wind."

All backed as far away from me as the crowded deck of the ship allowed. They looked at each other, uncertain what to do. Many eyes turned to the jewel between Ulik's thick fingers, and the eyes of the captain were among them.

"You swear you will summon this wind?"

"I swear it."

"And that you will make more jewels for my men, as compensation for carrying an unclean thing on this ship?"

"I swear it, and this also I swear. I will slay with a word the first man who tries to harm me."

With as much dignity as I could muster, I turned and entered the cabin, slamming the door behind me. There I stood in silence, listening to the low murmuring of voices as my fate was decided. I had done as much as lay within my power. When a knock came on the door, I knew I had won the battle.

"Enter," I said carelessly.

The captain opened the door, but did not come into the cabin. He looked at me as though seeing some demon in the shape of a human being. His sword still hung drooping in his hand.

"We will wait to see whether you summon the wind, as you have sworn to do. If the wind comes, I will take you to Suez, as we agreed."

"I can ask for no more from an honorable man."

I started to leave the cabin. He put up his hand in alarm.

"No, you must remain here. The crew would not work if they saw you walk the deck. You will be safer here."

I knew he spoke the truth, and nodded my agreement. Silently, he closed the door behind him, leaving me alone in the gloom. I was unclean, a monster. As much as I had tried to pass as a man among men, they had perceived my taint. I almost cried out with relief when I felt Sashi enter my body, so gladdened was my heart by her company.

That night and the following morning I waited, listening to the sound of the rigging and the sail, which hung limp on its mast. Either a breeze would rise up, or it would not. If no breeze came, it was almost certain that I would be killed. Since there was nothing I could do to change this, I was not as frightened as I might have expected, but the uncertainty robbed me of sleep.

Around noon on the following day, a steady wind began to blow from the south and filled the sail. I listened to the movements of the crew in the rigging and the shouted commands of the captain, and at last I was able to sleep for a few hours. When I woke, I found food placed just outside the door of the cabin. I opened the door, but saw no member of the crew. They must have hidden themselves at the sound of the door's latch being thrown. Somewhat to my surprise the food was not poisoned.

Toward sunset I left the cabin and stood on the upper deck, to the terror of the steersman, who could not leave his post at the tiller of the ship.

"Men of the *Eye of Mecca*," I cried. "Gather to witness the working of a miracle. I will fashion a jewel from thin air, as I promised. Each day I will make another jewel, so that you may share in their value when your captain sells them."

The jewel was already prepared beneath my tongue. I repeated my strange performance of the previous day, and produced another glittering stone. Since none of the crew, including the captain himself, would approach me, I set the jewel on the deck and returned to the cabin. Each afternoon saw the production of another gem. The crew would have little to complain about when the total payment for the passage was added together, I reflected, and wondered how much of the money the captain and the first mate would share with the others.

It was as though a great weight lifted from my shoulders when the captain knocked on the door of the cabin to announce that we had entered the port of Suez. I wasted not a moment leaving the ship. It appeared deserted, but looking back just before I stepped over its rail onto the planking of the dock, I saw several faces twisted in hatred as their eyes tracked my movements. One man spat and mouthed a silent curse at me. I could not resist making a meaningless gesture in the air as I returned his glance. He paled and fell stumbling as though struck in the face.

I walked away from the *Eye of Mecca* without a backward glance.

Chapter 15

The whispers would never cease. They would spread from mouth to ear like a disease, pursuing me wherever I went. The best I could hope to do was stay in front of them by moving quickly. It had been my intention to go first to Alexandria, but having told Jabir that I had an uncle in Alexandria, it seemed prudent to avoid it for the present, since he would assume that to be my destination. Alexandria would still be there, whenever I chose to enter its walls. The reputation as a great wizard was not such a burden in Egypt, where wizards were common, as it would have been in Yemen, but the Christians might see it as a reason to persecute me, and denounce me to the soldiers of the Caliph. Decades after the conquest of the Nile, the greater part of the people remained Christian, though the rulers were Muslim.

After leaving the dock in Suez I entered a wine shop, and by asking discreet questions was able to learn the residence of a Jewish money lender, scarcely taller than a ghoul, who impassively exchanged for silver dirhams the rings and ankle chains I had stolen from the corpse of the girl in honey. He refrained from asking the source of the ornaments, and made no comment on the dagger cuts through the bands of the rings and the links of the chains. I realized that I would need gold dinars if I was to pay my way through Egypt, so reluctantly I sold one of the jewels from the nameless city. The little man grunted in appreciation when he held it up to the light from his window and peered at the red flashes of fire in its heart through a round lens of clear glass. It would not be long before he was evaluating the others I had given to the crew of the *Eye of Mecca*, since he was the only person in Suez who traded gems for gold, or so I had been told.

In the market place I bought a pair of leather boots and a leather purse to hold the coins. The boots came up to the middle of my shins, and were trimmed on the outside with brown rabbit fur. For no obvious reason, the leather laces had been dyed a bright green. I thought my worn stockings and sandals worthless, but the cobbler was happy to give me a trifling reduction in the price of the boots in exchange for them. Though not really new, the boots were a pair in good condition sold to the cobbler that day, their owner having died of a convulsion the week before. They fitted my feet almost perfectly, and were not as hot or uncomfortable as I expected.

My dagger I had polished and sharpened by a tinker who sat before his grindstone under a stripped awning while his son, who could not have been more than twelve, fashioned a copper pot over his knee while squatting on the ground. The tinker told me that he could not match the quality of steel in my dagger with any knife on his table, which was my own private judgment, though I said nothing. He made no attempt to sell me a knife, but removed the rust from my own blade and put an edge on it that was as sharp as any razor. Watching him grind the steel on his stone, which he turned by spinning a wooden wheel under his table with his bare foot, I was reminded that I had not shaved my beard since boarding the *Eye of Mecca*, and after leaving his table I located a barber in the marketplace and had my head and chin shaved clean.

Even though I had washed in the sea scarce more than a week ago, the only way to ensure that the hatchlings of the lice did not return was to remove all traces of my hair. I watched it fall around my feet without regret, listening to the snip of the barber's shears close to my ear holes, and the scrape of his razor. At first I wondered how the spell of glamour would endure a close scrutiny of my head and face by both sight and touch, but after a few minutes I realized that it was proof against the closest examination. The barber gave no sign that he felt anything amiss, but chattered unceasingly while he snipped. He was one of the hairiest men I have ever seen. Both the long braids of his head, and the thicket of a beard that almost covered his face, were black as jet. Seeing his lack of attention to his hands, I was not sorry that my ears were already gone, for pieces of them would surely have fallen to the ground beside my locks of hair.

The babble of voices and the milling of bodies in the market, the bleat and cackle of the animals penned for slaughter, the shrill cries of the vendors, the smells of cooking and human sweat, the flashing colors of the awnings and robes, so bewildered my senses that at intervals I had to close my eyes and concentrate to still the spinning of my head, but after a time I grew able to endure them. Even so, my discomfort never left me. I felt vulnerable, as though naked. The hostility of these noisy human beings seethed just below the surface, and I feared it would suddenly erupt against me for some trifle. This did not occur, but my sense of danger never left me. Though I walked among men, I no longer felt myself to be one of them. I knew that if they sensed how alien I truly had become, they would turn and rend me to pieces like a pack of wolves.

I did not seek a lodging for the night in Suez, but immediately made arrangements to travel to the Delta. By asking discreet questions, I learned that it was possible to go by small boat along the course of ancient waterways which the Egyptians had dug centuries ago to link the head of the Red Sea to the mouth of the Nile. This system of canals had been allowed to decay and fill with silt, but part of it was still navigable by flat-bottomed boats, which were drawn along by donkeys while their masters kept them from running aground by pushing the boats away from the bank of the channel with long poles. At several places, where the course of the canal had filled completely with sand, it was necessary to debark and walk or ride overland. Even so, water travel was always easier than land travel, so I chose to journey to the Delta by way of the ancient canals.

My departure was none too soon. As I sat in the stern of a boat with a triangular sail that would take me to the mouth of the first canal, gazing back at the outskirts of the port, I noticed several soldiers on the reedy shore of the gulf who pointed at me in animated conversation. It was with relief that I watched this group of gossips obscured behind the bank of a low hill. I crossed my legs and let my mind empty, lulled by the gentle rocking of the craft.

Transfer to the little pole boat that plied the canal system was the work of a few minutes. The water channel ran neither wide nor deep, and much of it was choked with plants, but the boatman had no difficulty finding a passage through the tall grasses. As twilight drew near, I felt a profound sense of peace. The only sounds were the tinkle of the bell at the bridle of the donkey, and the scrape of the boatman's pole against the stone blocks along the bank. The old boatman and the youth who led the donkey did not converse. Perhaps they had already said all they wished to say to each other. I welcomed their silence, and sat listening to the lazy buzz of flies in the gathering twilight.

After night fell and the stars spread their glittering cloak across the heavens, we continued on by the light of lanterns, one hung on the curved bow of the boat, the other carried by the youth who led the donkey. Fluttering white moths made a halo around his head. At last they stopped to rest their animal, and I found myself sharing a rough hut of woven reeds with the old man, the boy, and the beast, which the old man would not leave outside in spite of my attempted bribe. I was able to get a few hours of sleep on a dirty reed mat before the journey resumed at first light of morning. The canal system opened into a salt lake, the western shore of which we followed, then resumed on the far side of the lake. So we progressed the second day and night, but on the third day I left the canal and traveled overland on the back of a hired horse to the town of Bubastis, in the Delta of the Nile.

My first glimpse of the ancient land of Egypt was not impressive. Bubastis was a farming town on a lesser tributary of the Nile, surrounded by plowed fields irrigated by channels that let the waters of the river wet the crops. Barley and wheat appeared to be the primary produce. There were also many groves of fruit trees and an abundance of flowers that were natural to the place, but so large and bright in their colors, and so numerous, that they appeared cultivated. Oxen moved ponderously in the fields, drawing plows or pulling carts. The town itself was of no great size, but stone ruins on its outskirts showed that in the past it had been a more populous place. Much of the town was built of these old stones, which the residents had gathered and used to erect their houses and walls. Those too large to be easily moved had been left in the fields, and the farmers plowed around them.

It was the greenest land I had ever seen. Everywhere, something grew, and not only grew but flourished. Water flowed with such abundance, it formed an obstruction to progress, so that small bridges were constructed to allow the countless irrigation channels to be crossed. Many of the freshly plowed fields were wet with water, and the black mud of the earth stuck like excrement to the shoes of anyone foolish enough to attempt to walk through them, so that it had to be periodically scraped off with a stick or knife. Everywhere life thrived. The sunlight was thick with swarms of flies of all kinds, both those that were harmless and those that bit. Great flocks of birds nested in the reeds at the bank of the river, and when startled into flight, they blocked the sun and their wings made a sound like thunder.

Cats swarmed the paved streets within the walls of the town, displaying neither affection nor fear of the horses and wagons. They were curiously elongated and had very short hair, so that they appeared at a distance to be hairless. As I was making my way to the market place, after leaving my hired horse, as arranged, in a stable near the gate of the town, I saw a cat kicked by a donkey when it tried to run between the donkey's legs. Rather than ignore the animal and pass on, as I assumed he would, the portly merchant who sat astride the donkey dismounted with a horrified expression and knelt in the street. He tried to stand the cat on its feet, but it was too badly injured. A crowd gathered, their faces solemn. Anyone looking at them without seeing what lay at their feet would have assumed that the horse had struck a child. Eventually a woman came from one of the houses and took the cat up in her arms. The merchant opened his purse and gave her money. With tender care she carried it inside, and it was evident that she intended to nurse it back to health.

I watched all this with amazement. It was not as though there was any shortage of cats in Bubastis. On the contrary, it was scarcely possible to walk without brushing one with your toe, although the citizens took great care to avoid kicking the creatures or stepping on their tails. In any other city they would be treated like vermin, but here they were given greater affection than the hordes of dirty children that ran screaming at play through the narrow streets. I saw more than one merchant strike away with the back of his hand a naked beggar child that tried to steal from his cart, but the cats were allowed to walk and climb where they wished, and steal what they liked.

Shaking my head in puzzlement at this mystery, I entered the open gate of the market. I was hungry, and let my nose draw me to a vendor who cooked strips of lamb spitted with peppers on reeds over a charcoal grill. As I stood eating, I watched a juggler perform on the broad paving stones in the open space at the center of the square. Naked to the waist, he balanced swords by their points on his forehead and both outstretched palms while dancing from one foot to the other, to the sound of a flute played by his less muscular partner, who capered around him like a monkey. Accustomed as I was to performances at the royal palace at Sana'a, I was unimpressed. The townsfolk were easier to please, and paid him with applause and a few bronze fils, which they tossed into his upturned turban.

"You look like a man with a future."

I turned from the juggler, searching for the source of these words uttered in Greek. A grizzled man of middle years, in a dirty linen tunic slit down the front in the Egyptian fashion, who stood hunched under a back deformed by some accident of fate, or perhaps a misfortune of birth, peered up at me from beneath his turban with sharp brown eyes and an ingratiating smile. One shoulder was higher than the other, and I saw that one bare leg twisted, so that he limped when he moved.

The blue of his turban suggested that his faith was Christian, as laid down in the Covenant of Umar, in which it was required that Christians wear blue turbans and Jews yellow turbans, so that they might be more easily identified by members of the true faith, but the color laws were frequently violated, so it was no sure test. I gazed down at him without interest, and was about to walk away when he spoke again.

"Yes, you look like a young man with a future, but what use is a future unless it can be known in advance?"

"All futures are unknown, both mine and yours," I muttered in my own tongue, thinking to discourage his impertinence by revealing that I was Muslim.

With caution I glanced around the square, and wondered if he had accomplices who prepared to rob me while he distracted my attention, but I saw only a slender child clothed in a long black dress, who huddled behind the man with head bowed, so that I could not easily see her face within the shadow of the black wrap that swathed her hair and girdled her waist. By her stature and posture I judged her to be a girl of some fourteen years. She was the first girl approaching womanhood that I had seen in this green land without a veil. Perhaps that explained her shyness.

"Nothing is concealed from a master in the arts of magic," he whispered in Arabic, leaning close, so that I bent away from his stench.

There was wine on his breath, and I saw redness at the corners of his eyes. Even so, he did not appear drunk, but regarded me with a shrewd calculation, as though gauging the effect of every word. I knew I should simply turn and walk away, but some disordered humor made me remain. His knowledge of Arabic surprised me. It was the language used by the rulers of Egypt since the victory of the Prophet more than forty years earlier, but I had not expected to hear it spoken in the marketplace. The mention of magic on the tongue of so earthy a creature amused me. I wondered what his reaction would be if he saw my true face or felt the touch of the djinn passing through his body.

I pretended to look around the square.

"Where is the master of magic?" I asked. "Has one passed us while you were speaking?"

He laughed with his scarred lips, but his eyes glittered. I saw that my poor jest angered him, and resisted the urge to thrust him onto his buttocks on the dusty stones.

"He stands before you."

"You, a magician?"

"Not only a magician, but a seer. There is no man of greater skill in the arts of divination. You say your future is unknown, but to me it is an open book, waiting to be read."

I regarded him with a mild expression.

"If you are so great a seer, perhaps you can tell me how much the knowledge of my future will cost me."

He smiled broadly with his thin mouth, for these were the very words he had hoped to hear.

"A trifle, noble lord, a pittance, a nothing. No more than a silver coin, for the unveiling of the world to come."

Some caprice caused me to open my new leather purse and extract a dirham of the smallest of the three sizes. His eyes watched every motion of my hands, and I could see him estimate the weight of silver and gold coins that lay in the bottom of the purse by the sounds they made clinking together. I passed the coin to him and watched it disappear, indeed as if by magic.

"A piece of silver is little enough for a knowledge of the future. Show me your arts, master sorcerer."

He barked a harsh word in Coptic while continuing to smile with his mouth, and the girl emerged from behind him. I expected her expression to be nervous when she raised her head, but there was boldness in her wide-set eyes, which were the most startling bleached gray I had ever seen, and of uncommon largeness. They were almost white, so pale was their color. She looked at me without a tremor, and her cool gaze seemed to pierce into me.

Without a word, she jerked back the loose sleeve of her black gown and extended her right hand. The palm was filthy, as though she had been cleaning oil lamps and had not washed herself. I noticed that her fingernails were trimmed to points, instead of rounded in the usual way, and wondered if it was a style of the women of this strange wet land.

The bent man took from his clothing a small flask of clouded glass and uncorked it, then poured some of its contents into the girl's palm, where it formed a midnight pool of shining liquid. By its smell, I guessed it to be an oil mixed with lamp black to make a kind of ink. The girl held her hand with care, the fingers slightly cupped, as though the jet pool were precious. She bent her head over her palm, and a wisp of her black hair escaped from her wrap and fell across her thin cheek.

"I thought you were the magician, not your daughter," I said to the cripple.

He shrugged off my words the way a dog shakes water from its coat.

"She is only my instrument. It is I who call the spirits of the ink. It is I who compel them to reveal their secrets."

He made several passes with his forefinger over the girl's palm and began to chant in Coptic. It was a language unknown to me, so the words were meaningless. After a while, he spoke to her in Greek, for the benefit of my understanding.

"What do you see?"

She squinted into the ink and licked her lips.

"Nothing, I see nothing," she said in Greek.

With a curse, the man repeated his passes and incantations, his voice more demanding in its tone. For several minutes we stood in silence and waited. The body of the girl became motionless, and her breaths deepened.

"I see the desert," she said without expression. She spoke as though in a trance.

The man glanced up at me from the corner of his eye and nodded.

"What else?"

"A whirlwind comes sweeping across the sand. Now it stops and dies, leaving a man in its place, a tall man dressed in black, with a black hood pulled over his head."

My heart quickened. Could it be that this fool or his daughter possessed power? I peered into the ink but saw only reflections.

"What does the man do?" her father demanded with impatience.

"He stands. He lifts his head as though smelling the air. Now he walks forward, head bent to the ground, as though searching for something at his feet."

"Leave this dark man and look elsewhere," her father hissed into her ear. "Show our noble lord something of value."

She did not respond, and I saw that she had not heard him. All her attention was in the ink.

"He looks up, as though he has seen something before him. He walks forward with long strides, coming closer. He has seen me, but I cannot see his face. It is in shadow. He walks so swiftly, his feet fly across the sands."

Her voice became strained with emotion.

"The dark man speaks, and his voice rolls like thunder. I cannot understand his words, but he chants in some strange language. *Nf'tang li gok, Yog-Sothoth ngh'ah . . .*"

I struck her hand aside and sent the pool of ink flying off her palm. The effect was as though I had hit her on the cheek. She gave a faint scream and fell unconscious to the dusty stones of the square.

The conjuror knelt and shook her by her thin shoulders.

"Martala, wake up! Martala!"

She groaned and shuddered so that her entire body shook from head to toe. Her eyelids fluttered.

He glared at me with malice.

"You fool, you might have killed her."

"That would be tragic," I said without emotion. "How would you earn your living?"

I turned and left them on the ground, thinking that I should find a place to sleep for the night. I intended to spend the rest of the day in Bubastis, and the next morning to set out for Memphis, which lay some length of distance up the Nile, just above the Delta. From my readings, I had learned that Memphis was a city of mysteries. I hoped to learn something of value in magic while in Egypt, and Memphis seemed like the best place to begin. To the girl and her father, if indeed he was her father, for there was no likeness between them, I gave no further thought. She was possessed of the gift of seership, of that there was no doubt, but I was certain that neither of them had skill in the arts of necromancy that I sought to acquire. The divination by ink was a juggler's trick, nothing more.

The fat owner of the inn where I stopped to seek a bed for the night was happy to rent me his best room, an airy space on the second level that had a window opening over a walled garden.

"It is your fortune that you came at the end of summer, when the town is deserted. In spring you could not have found a room for any money," he told me in Greek.

"What happens in the spring?" I asked, walking around the bed and eyeing the window. A trellis stood below it, covered in orange flowers that left a delightful scent on the breeze that blew into the room through the carven wooden shutters.

He threw up his fat hands and rolled his eyes.

"The rites of Bast take place. This is her birthplace. Men and women come from all over Egypt, and even as far away as Rome and Athens, to celebrate the birth of the goddess."

My gaze was distracted by his hands, which had the same pointed nails I had noticed on the hand of the girl in the marketplace.

"Bast?"

"The goddess of cats." He looked at me with an expression of shock. "Have you never heard of Bast? Where do you come from?"

"Ah, the goddess of cats. Thank you for refreshing my memory."

"Every spring for two weeks her worshippers celebrate by dancing in the streets, feasting, singing, making love." He winked at me. "Many a young Greek has come to Bubastis during the spring rites, but not to celebrate the goddess."

"Forgive me, but wasn't Egypt a Christian land before it fell under the protection of the caliphate?"

He shrugged, and used his dirty fingernail to flick a fly from the lip of a pitcher that sat on a table, half filled with water.

"We are Christians, but we are also Egyptians. My people have celebrated the rites of Bast for thousands of years."

"If I am not being impertinent," I murmured, pointing to his hand.

He glanced at it and looked at me.

"Your fingernails. Why do you cut them to points?"

With a laugh, he wiggled his fingers and put his hand behind his back, as though in slight embarrassment.

"It is nothing. A fashion of this place. You will see it on others. It has no meaning."

Since he did not wish to explain, I let the question pass into silence. A boy entered to announce that the hot water I had requested upon renting the room was ready. I descended to the kitchen, where a large copper trough with rounded ends had been prepared for me in a back chamber that offered privacy. Through the open doorway I saw that it was half filled. The sullen-faced scullery drudge took from the stone hearth of the enormous kitchen fireplace a copper kettle, using a scorched cloth to protect her hands from its coiled handle, and emptied its boiling contents into the trough, holding the kettle away from her body in both hands with her legs spread wide until she poured off some of its weight. Before leaving me alone in the chamber, she dripped scented oil into the water from a glass vial.

At the palace in Sana'a I had grown accustomed to frequent hot baths. Not until my exile had I recognized the greatness of this luxury. I stripped and slid my naked body into the tub with a sigh of pure delight. As steam from the warm water rose around me, I breathed its dampness as though it were fine perfume. The feel of the rough linen wash cloth against my skin was like a caress. I soaked it in hot water and covered my face, leaving my mouth exposed, then slid down into the bath until the water came up to my chin. Only my knees stuck out above the surface of the water; the copper trough was not large enough to contain them.

A scuff behind me on the clay floor aroused me from my state of bliss. I had noticed a rough wooden door in the outer wall of the windowless little room, but had thought nothing of it. Without moving, I tried to think where I had put my thawb. My dagger lay beneath it. I remembered folding it across a workbench that stood against the rear wall of the room, no more than two paces from the back door. Whoever had entered stood between me and the table. I considered crying out with all the strength of my voice the word murder in both Arabic and Greek, but knew that I would be dead before help arrived. Instead, I grasped the sides of the trough and with one motion pulled myself to my feet and turned.

The girl from the market stood in front of the open door. Her hands were empty, I noted with relief. No one moved in the deserted yard beyond the doorway.

Her gaze dropped from my eyes to my groin. She stared at it, and I hoped the illusion she was seeing was as attractive as my own body had been before its mutilation. She met my eyes. Her lower lip bore a cut on its corner and her cheek had acquired an ugly purple bruise.

"You are in danger," she said in Greek. "I came to warn you. Leave Bubastis or you will be killed."

Stepping from the trough, I took down the dry linen towel that had been left for my use on a wall hook and wiped my body. My eyes never left her.

"Shut the door."

She closed the wooden panel and stood watching me with her hands clasped in front of her waist, hidden within her sleeves.

"Who would wish to kill me? I am a stranger in Egypt. No one even knows me."

"You have gold and silver. That is reason enough."

"Your father?"

She made a sound of disgust.

"He is not my father. He is a pig."

Picking up my thawb, I dressed. When I tied Gor's skull around my waist, I felt more comfortable. The weight of my dagger on its baldric was also reassuring.

"Whatever the man's connection with you, I do not fear him," I said as I pulled on my boots and laced them against the edge of the trough.

"He will not come alone."

"How does he know where I am staying?"

"He had me follow you."

I considered her words. Bubastis held no great interest for me, but I had not expected to be forced to leave the same day I arrived.

"Why are you warning me?"

"You must take me with you. I cannot stay here any longer. If I do Farri will kill me."

"Farri? That's his name?"

"Farri al-Asadi."

She glanced with unease at the door behind her, as though speaking his name might invoke him.

"He is watching the front of the inn. When it is dark and he thinks you are asleep, he plans to break in with two of his hired men and strangle you, then take everything you own."

"The innkeeper is not part of this plot?"

She shook her head.

"He is an honest man."

I considered her words. If I left the inn, I would be followed, and the robbers might seize the opportunity to kill me in some empty alley or shadowed doorway. If I remained, I would be killed in my room. At least there seemed no danger until the night, after the inn retired to sleep. I pointed to my lip and cheek, and raised my eyebrows. She touched her cheek with her fingertips, wincing.

"He wanted me to help him. I refused."

"Did he see you come here?"

She shook her head, her pale eyes wide.

"The garden in back has no gate, and the wall is very high. I climbed the wall. Farri would not expect anyone to come that way."

I did not trust her, but could see no purpose to her words if they were meant to deceive. In any case, it was safer for her to remain with me than to let her rejoin her companions and tell what she had seen.

"Go back into the garden. Hide out of sight from the inn. There is a wooden trellis under my window. I will open the shutters. When you see them open, and no one watches, climb to my room."

She nodded, gratitude softening her expression. I watched her pass out the door and close it softly behind her.

Chapter 16

While passing through the kitchen, I bought from the innkeeper's wife a loaf of bread, cheese, and a bottle of wine, and carried them up to my room on a wooden platter. Setting it on the table beside the door, I crossed to the window and cast wide its crudely carved wooden screens. The garden below appeared empty. Flowers grew in abundance, but hung over the paths, indicating that the tending of the plants had been neglected of late. Perhaps the girl had managed to enter without being seen, as she claimed. I tapped three times on the frame of the shutter with my knuckle. She extended her head around the edge of a wooden shed near the rear of the garden, and with a furtive glance toward the back door, ran across the grass and climbed the trellis beneath the window.

In spite of her long black dress, she had the nimbleness of a monkey and made no sound. Its hem rode up her legs as she climbed. I saw that she wore kuff boots of thin, soft leather that was scarcely thicker than a stocking bound just below her knees, and over them more substantial shoes that did not cover her slender ankles. Between the tasseled tops of the boots and the hiked hem of her white cotton chemise, I glimpsed the ivory skin of her thigh.

"I see how you were able to scale the wall," I murmured, shutting the screens.

She unwound her indigo head wrap and shook out her dark hair, letting both hair and wrap hang over her shoulders. Her hair showed highlights of red where touched by the beams of the afternoon sun that found their way through the holes of the screens. It had been oiled and brushed with greater care than I would have expected from a girl of her type.

"I am a good climber. Farri sends me up the trees to steal fruit."

Tearing the flat loaf of bread in two, I gave her the smaller portion. She bit into it eagerly. Without asking permission, she went to the table. A small knife appeared in her hand. It came from somewhere in the folds of her dress, but she drew it so quickly, I did not see where it was kept. She cut a piece from the block of cheese on the wooden platter and ate it in two bites.

"The cheese will make you thirsty. Have some wine."

She took up the pitcher of water that rested on the table and drank from its rim, then wiped her mouth with the back of her hand.

"I don't like wine," she said. "Water is better when you thirst."

I thought of the months I had survived on the blood of rats and the juice of spiders. She was correct, water was better than wine to quench thirst, but she had never known true thirst. How could she, living in this green land? Pulling the cork from the wine bottle, I sat on the bed and filled my mouth with its sourness, then began to gnaw at the tough outer crust of the bread. It had been left in the oven too long and was burned around its edge.

"What is your name?" she asked, watching me with her intense gaze.

"Alhazred."

"I am Martala."

"Your master spoke your name."

"Farri is not my master. Not any more."

It was a matter of no importance to me what she called him. Washing the last of the bread down with the dregs of the wine, I set the bottle aside and drew forth the glazed chamber pot from the opposite corner on the other side of the door, then hitched up the hem of my thawb and pissed into it. She did not blush or turn her face away. I hoped the spell of glamour provided her with a satisfying spectacle. When I finished, she pulled the pot to her and raised her dress and chemise, then squatted over it, facing me. Our anatomy was not dissimilar, though she had more hair between her legs.

The heat of late afternoon penetrated the room and made the air stifling. I recovered the pot with its lid and slid it back into the corner, then pulled my thawb over my newly shaved head and sat on the bed to remove my boots. Bundling everything together, I piled them on the seat of the solitary chair that stood next to the table. Silently, she began to take off her clothing. I paid no attention, but drew my dagger from its sheath and lay on my side upon the center of the bed, the knife cradled close to my chest, my fingers curled around its bone hilt. The mattress, no more than a sack of coarse wool filled with straw, itched through the linen sheets against my sweating skin. At least the sheets were clean. I thought about sliding between them, but the air was too warm.

"What are you doing?" she asked, standing with her dress in her hands.

I closed my eyes and rolled over so that my back was to her.

"Farri won't come until after dark. I'm getting some sleep."

After a few moments I felt her crawl onto the edge of the bed behind me. Her body pressed softly against my back and buttocks.

"It's too hot," I told her. "This bed is not large enough for two."

She stiffened against me. For a while she lay still, then slid away and got off the bed. A shadow crossed my face. I raised an eyelid. Still naked, she walked to the window and lay down beneath it, where the breeze from its screen would fall upon her, curling herself on her side like a dog with her face turned away from the bed.

I wonder if I can trust her not to murder me in my sleep? I said in my mind to Sashi.

Sleep, my love. I will watch and wake you if she threatens your life.

Comforted by the knowledge that the djinn would alert me to any danger, I slept deeply, and awoke after the sun had set and full darkness had fallen. The inn was utterly silent, so I knew the hour must be late. I had not intended to sleep so long. By the silver glow of the nearly full moon that filtered into the room, I saw the shadow of the girl standing beside the door, watching me. She had dressed.

"How late?" I whispered.

"Almost midnight," she said in a low voice, her face hidden within the folds of her head wrap.

I studied the angle of the moonbeams and judged that she was right. Farri and his accomplices would come soon. Swinging my bare feet off the bed on the side nearest the window and turning my shoulder so that my back would be to the girl, I made the gestures and muttered the word that would renew my spell of glamour. She uttered no comment when I rounded the foot of the bed. With my ears alert for a step on the stair or in the hall outside the closed door, I pulled on my boots and thawb, and slung the baldric of my dagger and strap of my water skin over my shoulders. She looked at the full skin as I returned the dagger to its sheath.

"Why do you carry that weight? We are beside the river."

"Habit."

She shrugged and started toward the window. I put a finger on her shoulder and stopped her. In the inn below us, I heard the mutter of a man's voice and a sharp hiss. We stood still and listened. After a while, one of the treads on the stair creaked.

"They are coming," I breathed into her ear, and felt her head nod against my lips.

If they were inside the inn, they could not be watching its doors from outside. That is why I had waited until the middle of the night before leaving. It was my hope that the shadows would conceal our departure from any spy that lingered in the street.

I had already taken note of which floorboards in the room gave forth noise when stepped on, and drew the girl around them so that we reached the window without a sound. The hinges of the screens swung silently. I motioned her to climb down to the ground. She was gone almost before I could turn back from a glance at the door. A boot scuffed in the hall and the wooden door latch made a faint rattle. It would be brief work to raise it with the blade of a knife slipped between the door and its frame. With a silent prayer that the trellis was strong enough to support my weight, I stepped over the sill and began to climb down its ladder-like rungs.

It had been well made, and carried me easily without even a groan of protest. The scent of flowers intoxicated me like wine on the night air, and the nearly full moon lit the garden brightly.

"Which way did you enter?" I whispered.

She led me to a corner where a lime tree grew near the wall and climbed its trunk without effort, then waited while I struggled to find a grip on its smooth bark. Its branches were well above my head. The only way I could reach them was to hug the trunk like a lover and inch my way upward with my cheek pressed against it. A muffled curse issued from the open window of my room. I echoed it in my mind, trying to hurry.

"Climb faster," the girl hissed. "Why are you taking so long?"

The urge to strangle her gave me renewed strength, and I was able to grasp one of the limbs of the tree before I slid down the trunk. I pulled myself up and with the support of the branch got my feet on the top of the wall, which I discovered was embedded with broken bits of glass and pottery to discourage climbers. They did not pierce the thick soles of my boots, but how the girl had avoided being cut while climbing into the garden was difficult to imagine. Another moment, and we would have been on the other side without detection, but I was too late. A cry sounded from the window.

There was a wooden thud as the girl dropped into the alley on the far side of the wall. Feeling my way downward with one leg in the shadows while hanging awkwardly from my arms, I discovered the head of a wooden barrel. I followed the girl into the street. Farri had left someone to watch the back of the inn, who heard our footsteps. Feet pounded toward us on the cobblestones. I ran down the street in the opposite direction and turned into another, the girl behind me. In the silence of the night, the noise of my boots might as well have been the beating of a drum. Our pursuer was joined by at least two others. I could clearly hear them running toward us, but as yet they had not come into view. I stopped, realizing that in the night and the unfamiliar streets, I was completely lost. I did not even know where the river lay.

"Which way, Alhazred?" the girl asked.

"The east gate."

That was the gate through which I had entered Bubastis, and I knew where the donkeys and horses were stabled not far from it. My intention had been to steal a horse and rise southward along the tributary of the river.

"No, they will expect you to flee to the gate. I know where we can conceal ourselves until morning."

Her meaning was obvious without the need to express it. Once the sun rose, and the streets thronged with people, the opportunity for secret murder would be lessened. We could ride through the gate in full view of Farri and his band of cutthroats so long as we kept in plain sight. They might follow, but would never attack us amid the crowd. Did I dare to trust that the girl would not lead me directly to him?

"Show me."

Night or day, she knew the streets as I knew the corridors of the palace at Sana'a. She led me swiftly down back alleys and through gaps in fences to a large building in an open square. It was an ancient structure of massive stone blocks, but the wooden pitched roof had a modern appearance. Carved into the roof gable was a cross. I realized the building must be a Christian church. She did not approach the closed front doors, but made her way around the back to a small door sheathed in green copper.

Innumerable copper nails held the tarnished metal in place, their heads arranged in a graceful pattern of lotus flowers. She struck this ornate portal three times with her fist, then after a pause, twice more. I was surprised to see the door open. The golden light of an oil lamp shone forth, outlining a plump woman of middle years in a white linen dress and head wrap.

"It's Martala," the girl said in Greek. "I've brought someone who needs the protection of the Goddess."

The round woman stepped aside, holding the door open, and I saw in the flickering glow that her wrinkled face bore a kindly expression.

"Enter in peace, and may the Goddess watch over you."

I smiled and nodded, noting that her hand had the same pointed fingernails I had observed on Martala's hands, and on the hands of the innkeeper. When she closed the door behind us and slid its iron latch bar home, I felt easier in my heart. It was not a latch that could easily be forced. We followed her down a narrow hallway, toward the sound of murmuring voices. I bent my head close to the ear of the girl.

"What is this place?"

"This is the temple of Bast. We will be safe for the night."

"It has a cross on its roof."

She laughed with derision.

"The Christians call it their church. For centuries they have tried to take over all the sacred places and make them their own. In the day it is a church, but at night it is the temple of the Goddess, and always will be."

We went down a flight of stone steps and emerged in a large chamber the flat roof of which was supported by massive pillars carved in the shape of lotuses. It was lit by oil lamps hanging on chains from the walls. The far end of the chamber was dominated by a black pedestal in the shape of a double cube that supported the figure of a cat carved from green translucent stone. The statue was the same size as a living cat, and so well had the artist rendered the figure that it seemed to breathe and watch in the flickering light of the lamps. Its eyes, formed from polished bits of lapis lazuli and jet, appeared alert. Fastened to its head was a milk-white crescent of polished moonstone. A dozen or so men and women knelt on woven reed mats before the statue and murmured prayers, while rhythmically bowing so that their foreheads touched the slates of the floor.

"This is a night of worship," Martala explained. "We adore the Goddess for seven nights when the moon is large."

A black cat, its fur shining like sable, jumped from the floor to the pedestal of the goddess and rubbed its face against the face of the statue. After a moment, it curled up and went to sleep with its tail tucked under its nose. Other cats moved in the shadows at the corners of the room. I noticed pewter plates of raw fish and wooden bowls of milk set on the floor at the feet of the statue. Through a small round channel in a wall, a cat entered and crossed to eat from a plate. The plump woman saw my eyes on the hole.

"She is their goddess, too, and they must be allowed to reach her."

"One sleeps at her feet," Martala said to the woman. "A good omen."

The woman nodded, a happy smile on her face.

"Your friend has brought us good fortune this night."

All those who knelt and chanted before the statue had pointed fingernails, and it was clear to me that it must be a sign of membership in the cult of the cat. I noticed that one elderly man had no fingernails at all, and asked Martala about it.

"The leaders of the town are Christian, and try to suppress the worship of the Goddess. They cannot punish us all, because we are many, but when we wear the points of our nails too long, they take it as an affront to Christ and petition the Muslim administrator to have our nails torn out by the roots, as a warning to others."

"Christians are barbarians," the fat woman said. "They fear what they do not understand."

"As do we all," I murmured in my own language. Neither gave any sign that they understood.

I remained in the back and watched Martala perform her ritual observances before the statue of Bast. When she was done, we sat together on a reed mat and waited for the dawn. All during the night, men and women came and left through the green copper door in a ceaseless trickle, depositing their offerings of silver dirhams at the feet of the statue and speaking their prayers. The offerings must have necessitated considerable sacrifice. With only a few exceptions, they were laborers or servants. The cult of Bast was for the poor.

A scattering of citizens walked the streets when we left the temple, even though the morning hour was early. I searched with care the mouths of alleys and doorways for any spy, but if Farri's men had followed us to the church, they stayed far enough back to remain undetected. Making the gestures and uttering the word of the spell of appearance, I renewed the glamour that concealed my features. I took my direction from the sun and set out at a brisk walk in an easterly direction.

174

174

The girl stood watching me for a few moments, then ran after me and matched my pace.

"What are your plans, Alhazred?"

I told her I would get a horse and ride to Memphis. Her laughter surprised me and made me stop in the street.

"This is Egypt," she said, staring at me as though I were a simpleton. "Egypt, the land of the Nile? Nobody rides here. We use the river."

I considered this, and had to concede that it made sense. Why endure the discomfort of a horse when I could take a boat? I looked around with uncertainty.

The girl rolled her pale gray eyes.

"Follow me. I will show you where we can hire a boat that will take us up river."

She led me across town to the bank of a tributary of the Nile where boats floated, moored to poles driven into the river mud so that they would not be pulled downstream on the sluggish current. Their owners sat under awnings, gossiping with each other, or maintaining their sails with needle and thread across their knees. They looked up as we approached with the same stare a cat uses to watch a mouse. Martala walked along the dockside, examining the brightly colored boats that bobbed on the water. They were all of the same design, constructed of countless reeds gathered together in tightly tied bundles and curved up at the bow and stern.

She found a boat she liked, then spoke in rapid Coptic. One of the older men, so thin and fleshless that he resembled a walking corpse beneath his dirty linen tunic, uncoiled himself from the ground and approached us with a broad but toothless smile in the bristle of his gray beard. He and the girl began to argue. The smile faded and was replaced by a look of outrage. He protested while the other boatmen murmured and laughed quietly, watching us as though we were a performance. At last the owner of the boat threw up his hands and stalked away, cursing under his breath.

"What went wrong?" I asked her in Greek.

"Nothing went wrong. We sail as soon as the man I talked to can prepare the boat."

He removed his long tunic and tied it into a bundle, which he balanced on his turban. He was not naked beneath, but wore a dirty loincloth around his groin. As I watched, he waded into the muddy water toward the boat, pressing through the reeds that grew in profusion along the riverbank. The water rose to just above his waist. With a practiced motion he threw his clothes over the side and lifted himself from the river with his hands. The boat rocked violently but did not capsize.

"I thought something you said offended him."

She laughed, a surprisingly musical sound.

"He was offended. I made him agree to take us to Memphis for less than half the fee he wanted."

"What makes you think you are going to Memphis?"

"I have to go," she said simply. "The boatman doesn't speak Greek."

Since I wished her to accompany me, I made no strenuous argument.

The boatman used a long pole to guide his craft to a plank dock extending from the shore on rough posts. It was designed so that passengers could enter the boats without getting their feet wet, but since it was of small size and there were many boats, the boats were moored in the river and had to be brought up to the dock. We climbed on board and sat in the bow facing the mast. He pushed the boat into the midst of the current and raised the dirty linen sail on its angled crossbeam. It was triangular in shape, as were the sails of all the other boats I saw moving on the river. The breeze filled it with a snap and the boat seemed to come alive beneath us as it pressed forward against the current.

The boatman set about rigging a blue and white striped awning in the bow to shield us from the sun. He slung it across four upright poles that he forced into gaps in the bundled reeds at the sides of the boat. When he finished, we slid under its welcome shadow. The awning had so many tiny holes, sunlight shining through it made small circles on the girl's shoulder.

"How long before we reach Memphis?" I asked her.

"Two days. We will have to stop tonight and sleep in a hut on the bank of the river."

As the green papyrus reeds at the edge of the broad tributary slid past, I was once again astonished by the sheer abundance of life in this land. Cultivated fields and villages were numerous, and between them the land flourished with birds and beasts of every description. The water birds, some as large as a dog, paid the boat no notice, but went about on their impossibly long legs, hunting fish in the shallows. They stood amid the reeds watching the mirror surface of the water with keen eyes, plumed heads cocked as though listening, then darted their long and slender beaks downward to pluck up a thrashing silver fish. One bird was especially beautiful. It had plumage of pure white and pure black, and a curved beak. I noticed that a long feather of similar black and white coloring hung from a cord in the bow of the boat.

"The feather of the ibis," Martala said, watching my eyes and divining my thoughts. "The ibis is the bird of the god Thoth, and foe to the crocodile, the beast of the god Set, who Thoth hates. No crocodile can harm the bearer of an ibis feather, or so it is said."

The reason for displaying the feather in the bow was soon apparent. Once we left the settlements at the outskirts of Bubastis, the river became wilder, and the crocodiles began to appear, sunning themselves on the muddy banks or floating like logs in the shallows. I had expected to see crocodiles on the Nile, from my reading, but had not anticipated how large they would be. Some were longer than the boat in which we sailed. When they opened their huge jaws, as though yawning, and allowed small birds to hop in and out of their mouths, I saw that they were capable of biting a man in half. The little birds pecked at their white teeth, searching for scraps of food. Why the crocodiles did not snap them up and swallow them, I could not imagine, unless they were too poor a prey to be worth the effort.

Martala leaned over the side of the boat for a better look as we passed no more than a dozen paces from a group of the creatures that lay on a mud flat. The boat dipped alarmingly. The boatman spoke a few sharp words to the girl in Coptic, and she reluctantly sat back.

In the afternoon, he fed us on flat bread and dried dates that lay protected from flies in a covered reed basket in the bottom of the craft. It was apparently a part of the service I had hired, since he did not ask for payment. We continued on until the sun was near the western horizon. As it began to set, the boat glided into a small cove that had several wooden posts standing up from the water. Dropping the sail, the boatman tied his craft to the post nearest the shore. He stripped to his loincloth and slid into the water, which rose to his breast, then with cheerful words spoke to Martala. She leaned over the side and hitched up her black dress to kneel upon his shoulders, balancing precariously by holding his turban. He did not seem inconvenienced, but carried her with sure steps through the water and onto the bank, where she slid to her feet. He came back into the water and made a gesture with his hands that he wished to carry me to shore.

I shook my head and drew off my thawb and boots. Bundling them in my arms with my other possessions and lifting them over my head, I sat on the side of the boat and let myself slip into the water. The mud felt soft and warm between my toes. The boatman laughed, showing his gums, and slapped me on the bare back as we waded ashore together, where I dressed. Martala had already gone along the path that led from the river over the crest of a low hill. I followed, and saw on the other side a small hut of reeds with a thatched roof. It was a poor accommodation, but it had a door that closed, offering some protection against animals during the night. The boatman did not follow me. I guessed that he intended to spend the night on his boat, perhaps because he thought I might wish privacy with the girl. In this he was correct, though not for the reason he supposed.

The hut had two beds, neither boasting a mattress. They were scarcely more than wood frames with a woven cover of reeds. When I reached the hut, I found the girl with her head wrap thrown back and her shoes off, stretched across the bed nearest the door, so I wordlessly accepted the other and pulled off my boots. We had eaten on the boat, but I chewed several of the dried dates I had kept from the meal in one of my rags. The girl sat up and licked her lips. I broke off a sticky date from the rest and threw it across to her. She caught it and popped it into her mouth with a smile.

"Why do you wear that skull at your waist?" she asked, chewing audibly.

"In memory of a friend."

When I said nothing more, she pursed her lips and looked down at her hand, then sucked her fingers.

"What do you hope to find in Memphis, Alhazred?"

"I am a traveling scholar. I seek wisdom."

"Wisdom?" She did not seem impressed. "Is that all you seek?"

"I am a necromancer. I go to Memphis to learn how to summon spirits."

"Then you go to the right place. Many sorcerers dwell near Memphis."

"How would you know?" I asked in irritation.

"I was born in Memphis. My family has lived there for a hundred generations. I came to Bubastis two years ago."

"Why did you leave your family?"

She shrugged and lay back on the bed with her fingers laced under her head, staring up at the ceiling.

"My father raped me. I told him to stop, but he wouldn't, so I killed him and left."

I lay back on the bed. The sun had set, and the shadows thickened rapidly in the hut as the twilight outside the unshuttered window deepened.

"Was Bubastis better than Memphis?"

She yawned, and I heard her scratch herself.

"No, but it was different."

Chapter 17

Iwoke in the night, listening. A creak from the leather door hinge made me turn my face. For a moment, the canopy of stars outlined the head and shoulders of the girl as she slid quietly out the door and closed it after her. Moving carefully to prevent any noise from the wickerwork of the bed, I got to my feet. I did not bother to put on my boots, but stepped to the door and eased it open by slow degrees, then slipped through the gap.

My first thought was that the girl was in collusion with the boatman, and that they intended to return and murder me in my sleep. I looked along the path that led over the crest of the hill to the river, but did not see her against the heavens. The crack of a twig drew my attention to tall grass behind the hut. I followed the sound, walking on my toes in the cool moss, the long stalks brushing my thighs through the fabric of my thawb. Fortunately, there was a light breeze that made the grass rustle, and this covered the sound of my progress.

As I approached the shadow of a date palm tree, I heard a faint grunt. The scent of shit filled the air, and I realized the girl had left the hut to relieve herself. I bent and felt the ground at my feet, digging my fingers into the moss until I located a stone the size of my fist, then approached the tree with care and peered around its trunk. She squatted with her dress and chemise drawn up over her head, her back to me. Stepping forward silently, I hit her on the skull with the stone through the cloth of her garments. It made a dry thud, and she fell on her side without a murmur.

I debated with myself how to dispose of her corpse. It was my intention to indicate by gestures to the boatman that she had run off in the night, after refusing to share my bed. He was likely to accept such a story, but only if he did not stumble across the girl's remains. Her body must be hidden in the undergrowth some distance from the hut, or it might be discovered. Grasping her chest to mine so that our faces almost touched, I pulled her limply to her feet, then before her legs collapsed, bent and caught her across my shoulder. Her dress fell back around her ankles. She weighed little. I carried her into the trees, directly away from the river, and hoped to myself that I was not unlucky enough to startle a leopard or other large hunting beast.

The rising moon offered a welcome light. I walked through the clumps of trees and dense stands of tall grass until certain I had gone further than the boatman would ever search for the girl. This part of the river seemed uninhabited. The only sound was the ceaseless chirping of insects on the night air. Carrying the corpse through a dense cover of low trees, I saw that I had entered a natural gully and judged it a good place of concealment. I let the burden slide from my shoulder onto the grass in a patch of silver moonlight, intending to drag it into the center of a thick growth of brush, where it would remain undiscovered for as long as no scavenger pulled it out.

A groan from the girl drew a curse from my own lips. She still lived. Her dress and undergarment around her head as she squatted had cushioned the blow from the rock. I drew my knife and knelt on one knee beside her, then laced my fingers in her long hair and pulled her head sideways to expose her throat. Her pale gray eyes met mine in the moonlight, but she did not struggle.

"I know a secret of value," she said.

Ignoring her words, I set the edge of my blade against her neck.

"If you kill me you will never find the tomb of Nectanebus."

The name made me pause. It had a familiar sound. I searched my memory, and remembered reading a tale about a wizard of that name who was also a king of Egypt.

"Why would I wish to find his tomb?"

"Many have sought it. The bodies of wizards contain power, and Nectanebus was the greatest wizard of them all."

I laughed at my own credulity for even listening.

"You would say anything to save your life."

"My family at Memphis were tomb robbers. They found the resting place of the wizard but feared to plunder it."

"They told this great secret to a child?"

"They told me nothing. I followed them and saw the entrance with my own eyes."

I stared into her unblinking eyes and considered her words. If there was any chance they were true, it was indeed a valuable secret. The bodies of wizards absorb their powers after death, and by consuming a portion of the corpse, these abilities may be transferred to the living. Wizards took great care that their tombs should never be discovered. They were known only to their disciples, into whom the wizards sought to transfer their spiritual essence after death, so that the wizard lived again in the body of the younger man by displacing his soul. Sometimes it happened that the disciple of a wizard feared this ritual of transference, and instead of attending on the tomb of his master after death, fled and left it unguarded.

With my left hand, I caught her thin wrist and squeezed it tightly.

"If I let you live, will you guide me to this place?"

"I will."

"Swear to me that you will not betray me or make any attempt on my life."

"I swear it, by Bast."

"If you break this oath, you will regret it. I am not the man you believe me to be."

"I know who you are."

The certainty in her tone angered me.

"I am a monster. If you ever looked upon my true face you would run screaming."

"I see your true face now. I have always seen it."

I frowned at her. Was this only a lie spoken to distract and confuse me, or could she see beyond the veil of glamour that hid my disfigurement from others? I had renewed it at dusk before entering the sleeping hut. That she was a seer, I did not doubt, after witnessing her power in the market square at Bubastis.

"If you can see my face, tell me what I look like."

Her pale eyes darted over my features.

"You have no ears, no nose, and your cheeks are deeply scarred. There are other scars, perhaps made by fire."

"What else have you seen?"

"That you are a eunuch."

I shook my head in amazement. She had known me all the time, yet had still come to my room at the inn to warn me. It made no sense.

"Why did you not run screaming the first time you saw me?"

She shrugged.

"I told you my family are grave robbers. I have seen worse."

Standing, I drew her to her feet by her wrist. She swayed and I was forced to hold her by the shoulder until she recovered well enough to keep her balance. Without speaking, I led her back toward the hut. She paused beside the tree where she had defecated and picked a handful of leaves to wipe herself clean. I did not wait but went into the hut and lay down to sleep on my cot. I heard her enter after me and lie down on the other bed.

"I would not have betrayed you, Alhazred," she spoke into the darkness.

Her words hung on the air and faded to nothingness as my mind entered sleep.

When the scrawny boatman carried the girl into the boat on his shoulders the next morning, he cast me a toothless leer. I smiled politely. Let the man believe anything he wished. As he poled us into the current and raised the sail, I knelt in the bottom of the rocking vessel and pulled on my thawb over my damp body. There was river mud between my toes, so I left them bare to dry in the sun. The girl sat beneath the awning, her head between her hands, her eyes closed. If her scalp had bled, it did not show beneath her head wrap. She felt me watching and met my gaze without changing her expression. I could not guess her thoughts, which troubled me.

The tributary we followed would itself have been a mighty river in most lands, but when it opened into the broad course of the Nile, I drew a breath of wonder that so much fresh water could be gathered in a single place. There was water enough to turn the Empty Space into a garden of paradise, were it possible to transport it into the depths of the desert, yet here it was allowed to make its way into the sea, where every precious drop was wasted on fishes. Why was it that the great rivers of the world always found their way to the ocean, which had enough water already, and avoided the deserts, where water was needed? Such is the inequity of all things under the sun.

The river stretched to the horizon both south and north, and on its breast sailed too many vessels to count. A few were large galleys, but most were smaller boats of wood or reeds with triangular sails, an innovation carried to this country by the armies of Mohammed, or so I had been told by a tutor. Before the conquest, all boats on the Nile had used the square sails still relied on by the galleys. These little craft were adept at sailing against the wind, and were able to follow a course that would force a ship with a square sail to shift its crew to the oars. Our boatman stayed close to the eastern bank as he steered us up river on a favorable breeze. The band of green that slid past our port side cut the blue of the sky and the blue of the water like a great sword. Everything was dwarfed by the Nile. The bare rock cliffs beyond the trees resembled the sand hills made by a child, and the crocodiles that sunned themselves on the mud seemed no larger than lizards that might be held in the palm of the hand.

I fell into a kind of waking dream, lulled by the rocking of the boat and the soft touch of the breeze against my cheeks. At noon we ate what remained in the basket without speaking. None of us felt the need for conversation, which was just as well. The girl remained in the shadow of the awning, preoccupied with the pain in her head, and since I knew no Coptic and the boatman understood no Greek, we could not communicate without her intervention. In late afternoon the splash of a jumping fish roused me from my reverie, and I noticed that we had drifted away from the shore and were making a slanting course across the center of the great waterway. The boatman displayed his gums and said a few words in his own language, pointing over my shoulder. Turning, I saw that we approached the docks of a city that stretched for some distance along the river.

"Memphis," the boatman said in answer to my look of inquiry.

I touched the knee of the girl. She had been dozing and jerked awake. A look of pain distorted her face, and she pressed her head between her hands.

"We've reached Memphis," I told her.

She glanced over her shoulder and shrugged.

"I've seen it before," she said, lowering her head between her knees.

"How bad is the pain?"

She looked at me with resentment.

"Why should you care?"

I shifted in the bottom of the boat until I sat facing her, our knees almost touching. Pulling her hands away from her head, I felt with my fingertips until I found the ridges in her skull that I sought and pressed upon them with an even force.

"While I lived at Sana'a, I learned a trick for curing headaches," I told her. "Look at my eyes."

She met my gaze with her large ice-gray eyes, and for a moment I felt discomforted, as though she gazed into my soul. Annoyed with myself, I cast the feeling away. It was a quality of her unusual eyes, nothing more, I told myself. I matched the slow rhythm of her breaths with my own breathing, and began to talk to her in a low and monotonous voice.

"Listen to my words. Think of nothing else, and keep your eyes upon my eyes. As I talk, you will feel yourself becoming light, as though you were filled with air, as though you were about to drift away, but have no fear, my hands will hold you safely in place. Concentrate on my words. Look into my eyes. Believe that what I tell you is true, for it is true. The pain in your head is going away. As I speak, it becomes less and less. You feel yourself becoming lighter, and the lightness has no pain. You float up and leave the heavy pain behind you. You drift apart from it where it cannot touch you. Less and less, it grows less and less with each word I utter."

I continued to talk in this way, pressing gently against her skull, for ten minutes or so, until I was certain by the pupils of her eyes that she had fallen into the trance I sought to induce. After repeating that the pain in her head was no more, and that she felt strong and good, I told her she would rest for a few minutes and then feel refreshed, with no pain at all. I took my fingers away from her head and left her sitting, staring into the distance with unfocused eyes and blinking slowly. After a few minutes she roused herself and smiled in amazement.

"How did you do that? The pain is gone."

"A trick I learned at Sana'a from a court physician. It is nothing of importance."

She laughed and spoke to the boatman, who watched us curiously. An expression of fear shadowed the hollows of his face.

"I told him you are a great necromancer."

"You should not have said that. Look at him—he is afraid of me."

"As he should be," she said more darkly.

Her words angered me. I turned my back on her to pull on my boots, then watched the docks of Memphis approach. The boatman took my dirhams in nervous hands, all of his smiling good nature banished by the careless remark of Martala. He helped us out of the boat and immediately left us to spend the silver coins on one of the whores in scarlet surwals who lounged in the doorways of the storehouses and inns that lined the dock, and periodically raised the hems of their dresses to flash their brightly colored undergarments. We could see them from where we stood on the stone quay, surrounded by piles of cargo being loaded or unloaded from a dozen large ships by a hoard of nearly naked laborers, who ran shouting in all directions like ants, their sun-browned backs and limbs gleaming with sweat. The air hung heavy with the stink of fish, and river birds wheeled and screamed in the sky, attracted by the odor.

"Do you know a safe inn that is clean?" I asked her above the racket of the docks.

"I know everything in Memphis."

Once we passed through the fish market, I discovered the paved streets of the city clean and the houses well kept. Whereas Bubastis had presented an appearance of slow but inevitable decay, Memphis bustled with an intensity of life that is a sure sign of health. Beggars mingled on the streets with merchants and nobles in their sedan cars, all in constant motion. I wondered where they were going with such frantic purpose.

The sound of drums and flutes stayed the crowd and opened a way down the center of the street. We pressed our backs against the stone front of a building along with the rest to allow passage of the strange procession that wound into view like an undulating dragon composed of dancing human bodies. Costumed in bright colors, and wearing the masks of cats of all imaginable colors and shapes, they spun and leapt into the air to the sound of the drums, shouting chants at the watching crowd, who laughed at them in good humor. The dancers were equally divided between men and women. All at once, the women lined themselves up and with a great shout, raised the hems of their dresses and spread their knees to display their hairy vulvas to the applauding onlookers, who far from being outraged at the spectacle, appeared delighted.

We waited until the procession was fully passed before continuing along the street in the opposite direction.

"Who were the dancers?" I asked Martala, since the girl gave no indication that she intended to explain what we had just seen.

"They worship Bast. Didn't you see the cat masks? The Goddess is strong in Memphis."

"Why did the women expose themselves?"

She laughed.

"Sometimes we say we do it to annoy the Christians, but really it is to celebrate the source of life."

"Is some great festival in progress?"

"No, it is only the rite of the full moon. The festival is not until the spring. If this were the festival, we would not be able to find a vacant room in any inn in the city, and we could not move through the streets, they would be so filled with people."

The inn she led me to was located in the heart of the city, and seemed to be of considerable age, although it was of no great size and had few guests. I took a small room on the second level that overlooked the street, or more properly the window of the house opposite, for it would have been possible to reach out the window, and by stretching the arm, touch the open screens of the house on the other side, so narrow was the street, and so projecting the second stories of the buildings.

The slender matron who showed us the room, dressed all in black and with a severe expression on her long face, looked from me to the girl with disapproval but held her tongue, which must have been difficult for her. Later, I heard her shouting at her cook, and it was evident that she did not hold her tongue often. I noticed that her fingernails were not pointed, but were cut straight across and close to the quick. She must be Christian. After she left the room, I spoke my thought to Martala.

"She thinks you brought me here to steal my virginity," the girl said, throwing herself back across the feather mattress on the bed with her arms spread wide.

I slung my water skin over a peg on the door.

"If she saw between my legs, she would have no such concern."

"If she saw between your legs, she would run screaming."

"Are all Christians so sour and unhappy with life?"

"Most of them. Those who are not fanatics about converting others to their faith."

Sitting on the only chair in the room, I pulled off my boots to relax my toes. They were beginning to take the shape of my feet, but I was still unaccustomed to wearing anything heavier than slippers or sandals. It felt warm in the room, though the sun was setting. The evening breeze between the open screens would soon cool the air.

"Have you ever danced in the festival of Bast?"

"Of course. It was great fun." She smiled at the memory. "My aunt helped me make my costume."

I stood from the chair and looked down into the street from the window. In the room across the way, a slender young woman in a faded blue dress bent to fold laundry upon a bed. Her white head scarf hung open, revealing an uncommonly attractive face. She did not bother to glance at me. Living where she did, I suppose she was accustomed to have strangers stare through her window. The men and women moving along the narrow street did not look up, and no beggars lounged in the doorways. It was probably too soon to worry about Farri or his band of cutthroats, since even if he had followed us to Memphis, he could not have arrived ahead of our boat, but the evident lack of interest paid to the inn by those who passed made me feel more relaxed.

"If Farri is the leader of lawless men, why does he pose as a fortuneteller in the marketplace?" I asked the girl.

"That isn't a pose, that is what he does. He has always been a teller of fortunes, as was his father before him."

"What else does he do?"

She rolled her eyes at the whitewashed ceiling beams and considered the matter.

"He hires children to cut purses and steal from wagons. He prostitutes young girls. He sells property that his men steal from houses. He extorts money from traders by threatening to maim them and burn their ships. He kidnaps the children of wealthy Christians. He does many things, but telling fortunes is his profession."

"Do you think he will follow us?"

"I am certain he will."

"Does he believe I carry that much wealth, to make such a trip worth the effort?" Her voice was drowsy.

"Even if he thought you had nothing, he would follow us. I betrayed him, and you escaped. He won't stop until he kills us both."

"Then I will have to kill him."

"Yes," she murmured. "I will help you."

I let her sleep on the bed. There seemed little reason to disturb her, since the air was cooler beneath the open window. Moving the chair to clear a space for myself, I lay upon the floor and watched the stars come out one by one in the darkening sky. They were oddly dimmed, as though obscured by a film of dust or soot. It was only when I was on the point of sleep that I realized it must be the smoke from the city, rising above the houses. To my surprise, I found myself wishing that I lay upon the open sand beneath the bright stars of the desert, far away from the cries of beggars and the smell of rotting fish.

In my dream, I stood at night on an elevated plain with great sloping mountains of stone blocks rising from the sands. I recognized the artificial mountains of stone as the pyramids of Egypt, although I had never seen them in a drawing but had only read their descriptions. The dark man stood beside me, silent and unmoving save for the hem of his cloak that undulated in the evening breeze.

"Why do you visit my dreams?"

"Would you rather I came while you were awake?" he said with a hint of sardonic amusement in his dry voice.

"I would rather you did not come at all."

Ignoring my words, he raised his long arm and pointed across the plain.

"Do you see that man?"

I looked where he indicated, and noticed a man robed in black creeping along a path. He carried a large gray jar under his arm, and gazed around furtively as though afraid of being observed. His pale face shone like a mirror in the moonlight, accentuating thick eyebrows and dark eyes. The lack of adornment on his hooded robe lent him a monkish appearance not unlike that of the dark man.

"He is my servant. Follow him."

I started after the creeping figure with the dark man walking beside me like a tall shadow. At first I stayed some distance behind my quarry, but when he gave no sign of noticing my footfalls on the stones of the path, I moved nearer. He made haste toward a hulking statue of some monster that squatted on its haunches, partly obscured by dunes of sand. It was much weathered, and larger than any statue I had ever seen. Though its body was that of a cat or lion, its head was human. I thought my quarry intended to approach it between its extended forepaws, but he moved around its side toward its hindquarters.

"Draw near and watch closely," the dark man said, making no effort to hush his voice.

The skulker with the jar did not turn his head.

"Why does he not hear us?" I whispered.

"You are dreaming, Alhazred. How shall he hear you, when you are not even flesh?"

I considered this as I quickened my steps so that I walked close behind the man.

"Are you flesh?" I asked Nyarlathotep.

"When I wish it."

The man with the jar, only a few years my senior, paused beneath the tail of the great statue and set his burden with care between his feet, as though fearful some djinn might run off with it. He pulled back his hood, and taking a black silk scarf from his pocket, wrapped it over his face so that it concealed his features completely, then lifted his hood back into place. His veiled aspect perfectly imitated that of the dark man. Having had a good look at his face in the moonlight, I knew I would recognize him were I ever to encounter it again, and I wondered why he chose to conceal his features.

He muttered three words and made a gesture with his right hand, then bent and clutched the jar to his chest as though it were a holy object. The air before the hindquarters of the statue wavered and melted to reveal a featureless door of stone. The hooded man touched a projection on the frame of the door. It opened inward soundlessly. From the interior flickered the red glow of a torch that flamed in a bracket on the wall. Without hesitation, the man passed through the door. It swung shut behind him, then disappeared as the air shimmered over its surface and concealed it. I marveled at the perfection of the glamour. No one would ever know a door existed.

"Shall we follow him?" I asked my dark companion.

"I cannot enter, unless I am invoked within."

Making the gesture I had seen the other man make in the air before the stone, I spoke the words he had spoken. Nothing happened.

"Remember what you have seen," the man in black said, his voice echoing strangely.

Chapter 18

woke with the babble of voices from the street in my ears, had I possessed ears, and the smell of cooking oils in my nose, had I owned a nose. On a flutter of soft wings, a white dove flew past my window. Blinking the dryness away, I sat up and looked over the sill. The bird had a perch on the ledge below the window, where it walked back and forth like a sentry on a city gate, preening its ivory wing feathers with its blunt beak, unconcerned by my presence.

Martala sat on the side of the bed, watching me.

"You talk in your sleep, Alhazred."

"What do I say?"

"This morning, you said that you would remember. Remember what?"

At once the dream came back to my mind in all its details. In my vanity, I had begun to believe that the god of chaos had lost my footprints in the desert, and had ceased to stalk my dreams, but his absence had only been a respite. What did he want from me? He treated me as his servant, yet he gave me no duties to fulfill.

"Have you ever seen a great statue of a cat on the plateau of the pyramids?"

She stared at me as though I had made a foolish jest.

"You mean the Sphinx?"

The moment she spoke the name, I remembered reading about the statue in the book of the Greek historian, Herodotus. I had not recognized it in my dream only because I had never seen it depicted.

We ate our morning meal of fresh bread and steaming mutton stew in the dining hall with the other guests of the inn, then set off through the crowded, narrow streets of the city, Martala leading the way. I was anxious to find the tomb of the great necromancer she promised to reveal, and she claimed to know where we could hire horses in good health for little money. How much the beasts might cost was of no concern to me, but I did not wish the girl to realize that I possessed wealth.

On the way we passed an open door that exhaled the most extraordinary mix of scents. I recognized cassia and myrrh and oil of cedar, but there were a dozen other rich odors strange to me. I grabbed the girl by the shoulder and pulled her back to the door.

"What is this place?"

She looked into the opening and wrinkled her nose. The delightful perfumes that so attracted me had on her the opposite effect.

"A house of the dead. It is full of corpses. Let us go, Alhazred, it is bad luck to enter here."

The odors were nothing like the stench of corpses, which I knew as well as any man. My curiosity made me draw her inside after me, even though she squirmed in my hand like a small child. As my eyes adjusted to the dim light, I saw several bodies on stone tables, partially wrapped in strips of white linen. In a basin beside the corpse of a woman lay a human heart, liver, and other organs. It was a tribute to the power of the incense that hung in the air that no trace of decay could be detected.

A smiling man with a bald head, naked to his thick waist and wearing only a simple white skirt and sandals on his feet, approached when he saw us loitering in the entranceway. As he passed a table, he picked up a cloth and wiped his hands, then dropped the cloth on another table.

"How may I help you, good sir?" he inquired in flawless Greek.

"What is this place?"

He seemed mildly surprised by my question, but he spread his arms in an affable manner to welcome me in.

"This is a house of embalming, as you can readily see. Here we prepare the bodies of the dead in the old way that was used by our forefathers."

What I had read in the texts of the Greeks concerning the preservation of the dead in this land arose in my memory, and I understood the purpose of the place. I stared around with renewed fascination. It was the custom of the ancients of Egypt to preserve their dead for eternity, so that they would never decay. This they achieved by means of a complex preparation and the treatment of the corpse with numerous costly spices and other substances that defied putrefaction.

"I am new to this land," I explained. "I thought the Christians had abolished these rites long ago."

A shadow of anger crossed his face. With an effort he forced his smile to return.

"It is true, some Christians disapprove, but they do not possess the authority to forbid the old ways, and many of our wealthy and powerful citizens prefer to have their family members made imperishable."

"There are only two places like this in Memphis," Martala remarked, edging with distaste toward the open door.

"Yes, your young friend is quite right," the portly embalmer agreed. "In the past, houses of the dead such as this were to be found throughout the city, but only two remain. Ours does the superior work, and employs the better materials, which are increasingly difficult to procure. If you are seeking a price for our services . . ."

"No," I said with a smile. "Not yet."

He hid his disappointment.

"I hope I have been able to satisfy your curiosity," he said more briskly, glancing back at the table he had vacated to talk with us.

"You have been very kind. Please, return to your work."

The girl breathed a sigh of relief when we emerged into the sunlight, as though escaping from a den of horror. I left the delightful scents with regret. I had not smelled such rare spices since my days in the palace at Sana'a. Corpses, in whatever condition, did not move me other than to quicken my appetite. I realized it had been some time since I had eaten human flesh, and discovered that I missed the savor.

The street opened into a plaza with an elevated well at its center. It was a pleasant place to rest. Wild flowers of the brightest purple grew up a rough stone wall on slender climbing vines. A pair of well-clothed children chased each other around the well, their laughter like the babble of a brook. Three old men with long white beards sat at a stone bench, deep in conversation. Martala leaned against the raised stone platform around the well and pulled off her left shoe from the fine leather kuff boot that sheathed her foot and shin, then turned the shoe upside down and beat it against the side of the stones as though trying to shake out a pebble.

"A man is following us," she murmured close to my ear as I lounged with my hip against the well and my arms crossed, watching her.

I glanced around the plaza but saw no one who appeared interested in my existence.

"Where?"

"Look the way we came. That beggar with the bad foot and the wooden stick."

I let my eyes slide in what I hoped was an unobtrusive way over my shoulder, and saw a beggar with ragged gray hair and a long gray beard, supporting himself on a forked stick propped beneath his armpit to relieve the weight from his twisted left foot. His head was wrapped in a rope of dirty white cloth in place of a turban, and he wore only a tattered shirt that ended midway down his thighs. While I watched, he asked all those who passed for money, and one merchant took a bronze fil from his purse and tossed it carelessly through the air. The beggar caught the coin with the skill of long practice and pushed it between the folds of his headdress. At no time did he glance my way.

"What makes you believe he follows us?"

"He was walking behind us when we went into the house of the dead."

"It is a public street."

"He was still walking behind us when we came out."

I pondered this information. It was possible that the beggar had happened to stop just as we entered the place of embalming, and had happened to continue just after we left, but I agreed in my mind with the girl, it was suspicious.

"Is he one of Farri's men?"

She shook her head.

"I haven't seen him before, and I know everyone Farri works with, but he may be someone Farri hired to watch us while we are in Memphis."

We continued onward to a stable near the western gate of the city. On the way I found pretext several times to stop, but the beggar did not show himself. If he still followed us, he was a master at his profession. I hired two mules that had a healthier look than the horses in the dirty stalls, and bought enough food and water for the girl and the beasts to let them survive two days in the desert. Martala claimed the tomb was no more than a few hours' ride beyond the walls of the city, but I decided to take more provisions than needed. It was wise to be prudent when dealing with the desert, and the desert was never far in Egypt, as I saw when we rode through the gate and into the low hills. The ground soon became dry and the grasses and low plants few. It was still a paradise compared with the Empty Space, but to the girl it must have appeared a wasteland.

"Are you certain you remember the way to the tomb?"

She gave a short laugh of contempt.

"I know these hills as well as I know the streets of Memphis."

There was no trace of anyone on the path before us or behind. I stared around at the crests of the hills, feeling disappointment. I had no intention of leading the beggar to the tomb of Nectanebus, and hoped to waylay and murder him in the hills. It would ensure our privacy. Without the certainty of his death, the best I could do was keep watch for any movement, and trust that no one could follow us without being seen. I told myself that I worried without cause. It was likely the beggar had not followed us at all, and that we aroused no interest when we left the city. Even so, my unease would not sleep.

The rising sun beat upon our heads with waves of heat that reflected from the rocks and dazzled my eyes. It is not often that I regret the lack of a turban, but this was such a day. The girl soon led me off the traveled path and into the hills themselves. We rode over ledges scarcely wide enough for a single human foot, and up steep inclines. I was glad I had resisted the impulse to hire horses. Few horses could follow this invisible trail, but a mule is more sure of foot than a man.

The girl often lifted the leather strap of her water skin off her shoulder and drank deeply from its spout, indifferent to my disapproving gaze. She drank too much, too quickly. Even so, I resisted the urge to criticize. What else could be expected from a child of the river? She had never been without water, and could not even imagine what it would be like to thirst and have nothing to wet her lips.

She drinks too much, Sashi said, echoing my thoughts.

"I know, my love," I murmured. "She is foolish."

The girl turned in her saddle and looked back at me with a frown on her face, as though she feared I was losing my mind.

"Who do you talk to?"

I hesitated, but saw no reason to be untruthful.

"I have a djinn living in my body. She speaks to me, and I answer."

The girl looked at me for a moment, then broke into peals of laughter. She laughed so hard I feared she might tumble from her saddle and roll down the steep slope that fell away from the narrow path on one side. I said nothing. After a time, she wiped the tears from her eyes and looked back at me.

"A djinn inside you!"

She slapped her thigh and began to laugh again, and continued to laugh for some distance. Whenever she stopped, she would glance back and begin anew. I marveled that my condition was so amusing, but it was clear that she thought I lied. Whether she believed me mad or possessed was of no importance, but for some reason her laughter irritated me.

"What is that mark?" I asked.

We rode past a boulder that had a small scrape upon it, such as might be made by rubbing its surface repeatedly with a stone. It was weathered but distinct.

"A marker to show the men of my family the way to the tomb," she said, barely glancing at it. "I don't need the markers. I know the way in the dark."

There was a chance that I could follow the invisible trail myself, now that I knew how it was marked, and I wondered if I needed the girl any longer. It seemed prudent to let her continue to lead, in case the markers ceased or the entrance to the tomb was difficult to find.

This proved a wise decision. After a time, she stopped her mule and looked at me with triumph, excitement shining in her ice-gray eyes.

"The tomb of Nectanebus," she said.

I looked around. We sat on our mounts in a small canyon between two hills, facing a rocky cliff. There was no way to ride further without climbing one of the hills, which would be impossible even for the mules, sure of foot though they might be. The cliff reared like a wall high over our heads, unbroken and unclimbable.

"Don't you see it?" she asked with amusement. "It's right in front of you."

She obviously enjoyed my inability to see the entrance to the tomb. Taking a breath, I calmed my irritation.

"Do you see the entrance, Sashi?"

There is an opening part of the way up the cliff. It looks like a shadow.

I searched the featureless face of rock, and for a time still could not see the opening, even though I stared directly at it. Then it seemed to leap out from the cliff, and became obvious. I pointed with my finger.

"There."

The features of the girl registered disappointment. She would have enjoyed emphasizing my dullness by pointing out the entrance herself, but I had robbed her of the pleasure.

"You have good eyes, Alhazred," she said, pouting.

It was possible to reach the slit of the entrance by standing on the saddle of my mule and pulling myself up with my arms. After hobbling both mules with short ropes tied around their forelegs, I balanced on the saddle of my beast while Martala held its bridle to steady it. I discovered a narrow ledge in front of the cave mouth, hidden from the ground. The girl had some trouble ascending, since there was no one to hold her mule, but I was able to pull her up just as it flinched and darted out from under her feet. We stood together on the ledge, peering with a mixture of eagerness and caution into the dark interior.

The girl took a tallow candle from the embroidered sash that girdled her waist, and I used my tinderbox to light the wick. Its flame flickered, almost invisible in the bright sunlight. We shielded it with our cupped hands, looking at each other.

"I will go first, if you wish," she said.

I nodded. It was possible that the tomb had pitfalls to catch the unwary.

Ducking her head, she carried the candle in front of her, and I followed close at her heels. Once we passed beyond the entrance, its flame became steady in the dead air. The tunnel was not entirely natural, but had been widened and smoothed with tools. Not far in, it sloped downward so steeply it became almost a vertical shaft. A stair that was really nothing more than a series of notches in the stone allowed us to descend with caution. One false step would have precipitated us to our deaths. The air smelled dry with the dust of ages. No rain had found its way into this passage for a long time.

"My uncle discovered this tomb by searching out landmarks mentioned in an ancient legend of Nectanebus," Martala said over her shoulder as she crept carefully downward. "He found it had been robbed centuries ago, but said it had not been entered in his lifetime. He knew this from the dust."

"Have you never seen the tomb yourself?"

She shook her head.

"I saw the entrance years ago, never the inside of the tomb. My uncle said it contained nothing of value. Everything had been stolen but the mummy of the king, and even that had been defiled."

"Defiled? How do you mean?"

"I don't know. My uncle told my father it had been defiled. My father came to look, but they carried nothing away with them."

"They didn't touch the body of the king?"

She stopped and looked up at me, her face in its head wrap shadowed from the flickering flame of the candle in her hand.

"Are you mad? If you disturb the body of a king, you are cursed for eternity."

"You believe that?"

"Yes, as did my father, and as do my uncles and their sons. Nobody has moved this mummy, Alhazred."

The steep shaft ended upon a wider passage that inclined down at a more gentle angle. Its stone floor showed scratches under its layer of dust, as though something heavy had been dragged down its length. The upper part of this passage was not shaped but natural—only the floor had been leveled. The taps of our boots and shoes echoed from the roof like gentle laughter.

At the end of the passage a doorway led into a square chamber in which I could stand upright. I straightened my back with relief. I had unconsciously been hunching my shoulders and bowing my head. A scent reached my nostrils, the same scent I had smelled in the house of the dead at Memphis, but much more faint. The room was empty save for a stone sepulcher that occupied the center of its floor. Its heavy lid lay shattered in three pieces on the floor beside it. Across these broken stone slabs lay a coffin lid of carven wood that had also been broken into pieces by the blows of a hammer.

We approached the sepulcher with small steps, alert for any traps. There seemed little to fear, since the robbers in ancient times who had broken the lids would have sprung them and died, had such traps existed, yet no skeletons were evident. As Martala raised the flame in her hand, I leaned forward to peer into the stone box. Within it was a second smaller box of carved and painted wood, and in this lay the linen-wrapped corpse of a man. The wrappings had been stripped away from his feet and his hands, which were crossed on his chest and appeared to clutch the air in frustration.

"Bring the light nearer," I said, frowning.

The candle revealed that all the fingers were missing from the right hand of the corpse, and that only the thumb, index and large finger remained on the left hand. Similarly, all ten toes were gone from the feet. Peering closely at the toes, I saw that the stumps showed the marks of teeth where they had been gnawed off.

"Rats," the girl said.

"No rat has teeth that large."

I pointed at the marks on the feet, and she drew a nervous breath.

"What monster would do such a thing?"

"Only a necromancer," I said, excitement building in my breast. "To a necromancer, the flesh of a wizard possesses power, and this force can be absorbed when the flesh is consumed."

She made a sound of disgust in the back of her throat.

"Why did they only take the fingers and toes, and leave the rest of the corpse?"

"The will and magical force of a wizard remain locked within his flesh after death. To eat of his flesh is to gain his power, but to eat too much is to risk being possessed by his spirit."

"How do you know so much of these dark matters?" she asked, staring at me with a trace of fear.

"It is a study of mine. I read it in a book."

"In Egypt, you can be burned for reading such books."

"As you can in Yemen."

She pointed to a medallion of carved green stone that lay over the groin of the mummy. It was the only ornament on the corpse.

"Perhaps we should take that trinket, so that our trip will not have been wholly wasted."

Glancing at it, I recognized the Elder Seal. It was the same symbol that had been carved in the middle of the disk of green stone in the star chamber of the nameless city. I caught her hand by the wrist before her fingers could touch it.

"It is bad luck to disturb the mummy of a king, remember?"

"Yes, but that disk is just lying there."

"It is not the disk that concerns me, but what it might uncover were it removed."

She leaned over to study it, and I saw her lips moving.

"Can you read the inscription?"

"These are the ancient writings of my people. I have some skill. Let me try."

Extending the candle above the stone sepulcher, she puzzled over the strange symbols for several minutes. Then she read the words aloud:

The bone and flesh which possess no writing are wretched, but behold, the writing of Nectanebus is under the Great Seal, and behold, it is not under the Little Seal.

"There must be a scroll beneath the seal," she said. "I wonder what it contains?"

The ache to know its contents burned in my heart, but I resisted the impulse to snatch the medallion aside. Some deep instinct told me it would be suicide, and since being cast into the desert, I had learned to trust my instincts. Instead, I quickly bent my head and caught the longest finger on the left hand of the corpse between my teeth. With a savage twist and bite, I severed the finger, its bone cracking like a dry stick. The girl shrieked with surprise, but I paid her no attention. Grasping the finger between my hands, I tore at its desiccated flesh, which was like ancient leather, and swallowed the bits. After sucking clean the finger bones, I put them safely away in a pocket of my thawb. When I found the chance, I would powder them and add the powder to my food.

The girl still crouched in the corner of the burial chamber when I finished, a look of mingled horror and disgust on her features. The tallow of the candle dripped unnoticed over her fingers.

"How could you do that? Truly, you are not human."

"I am a ghoul of the Black Spring Clan."

On another occasion, she might have laughed at this declaration, as she had laughed when I told her my body harbored a djinn. Her revulsion removed any impulse to mock me. She licked her lips, and I saw that she fought the urge to vomit.

"Drink some water," I told her.

She straightened her back and set the stub of the candle on the corner of the sepulcher, then uncapped her water skin to suck at its nipple, eyes vacantly staring down at the corpse.

"The others who came before us," she said, her gaze upon the stump of the finger I had eaten.

"Seventeen of them," I finished her thought. "All necromancers. I am the eighteenth."

"Do you feel its power within you?"

Holding my breath, I turned my attention inward. I felt nothing at all.

I shook my head.

She forced an unsteady laugh.

"Then my uncle was right, this tomb really is worthless, and we were fools to come here."

Picking up the candle, she left the chamber. As she progressed up the ramp and the light faded behind her, I looked around one final time to see if there was anything worth stealing. In the gathering darkness, I noticed a curious blue glow from the sepulcher. It came from the corpse. The entire body shone, but the light was brightest on its bare feet and hands, and brightest of all on the ends of the bones projecting from the stumps of its toes and fingers. Had the glow always been there, obscured beneath the brighter light of the flame, or was this the first sign of power acquired from the consumption of the wizard's flesh?

I waited for some other sign, but the glow continued as before, constant and unvarying. The only feature of the corpse that did not radiate light was the green stone disk on its groin. The temptation came again to snatch it up and see what lay beneath it. All parts of a great wizard were fabled to contained potency, but none so much as his sexual organ. I thrust the temptation away. Having eaten his finger, I could not even consider consuming his prick. It would be too much flesh, and I would be possessed by his angry spirit.

The irritated voice of the girl echoed dimly down the passage.

"Alhazred, I am at the shaft. Do you want me to leave you to climb it in darkness, or are you coming out?"

So adept had I become at moving through darkness, I knew I could climb the steep stair of the shaft with my eyes shut, but there was nothing to keep me in the burial chamber, so I left it and walked up the incline of the ramp to where Martala waited at the base of the shaft. She gripped the candle stub between her teeth and began to climb. I followed her without speaking, feeling vaguely dissatisfied. I had expected more after consuming the finger of the mummy. Perhaps the others who had gone before me in previous centuries had experienced the same unrest.

"Sashi, do you notice any change in me?" I murmured.

There is a difference, my love, but I am not sure what it means.

"Still talking to your djinn?" the girl asked, her words distorted by the effort to speak with her teeth clenched on the tallow shaft.

"It is a private conversation," I said to the soles of her shoes.

"Where are my manners? Continue to pretend to talk to your imaginary djinn, and I will pretend that I do not hear."

Her short temper puzzled me. She had expected nothing from the tomb, so why was she disappointed?

We let ourselves drop from the mouth of the tomb to the floor of the canyon and gathered in the mules. They had not strayed far, as there was neither grass nor water to attract them. I poured a cooling stream from my water skin into the mouth of each beast in turn. They turned their heads and lapped at it, rolling their brown eyes with silent gratitude. When they were refreshed, we mounted and started back toward Memphis, the girl riding in front as before.

I cast my eyes at the hills on either side of the almost invisible trail, wondering if Farri or his hired men were waiting to ambush us. As we rode further, and I saw no movement in the hills, I relaxed. It was evident that we had not been followed to the tomb. It would remain a secret place, and if at some future time I saw fit to return, I could expect the mummy of Nectanebus to be waiting.

We rejoined the well-traveled road that led eastward to Memphis. As we rounded a ridge of rock, the girl abruptly pulled back on the reins of her mule, causing the beast to bray and kick in protest. Four men sat on stones to one side of the road, out of sight of any rider who approached the city until the rider was upon them. Their saddled horses pawed the dust at their backs. My heart grew cold as I recognized the bearded beggar at the well plaza. He had put off his rag turban and torn shirt and donned a fur-trimmed cap, wool surwal, short linen tunic, and an open coat belted at the waist, of the sort favored by soldiers and mercenaries. The other three were unfamiliar but similarly garbed. All were armed with swords and knives hanging at their belts. They smiled at us as though we were the object of some jest.

"Greetings, Martala," the beggar said. "Farri apologizes for not being here, but he sends his love."

Chapter 19

The beggar spoke in Coptic, but I realized that I understood his words perfectly, even though I had never studied the language, or heard it spoken before coming to the Nile. This was not an opportune moment to consider my sudden gift for tongues. The four men walked toward us in a careless way with broad smiles on their faces, their arms swinging at their hips, to form a crescent with the purpose of surrounding our mules. Once they grabbed the reins, there would be no escape.

"Follow me," I said to the girl.

Digging my heels into its flanks, I wheeled the startled mule around and galloped toward the rocky hills from which we had just descended. I heard the hooves of Martala's mount behind me, pounding over an exposed bed of stone. The men who intended to waylay us began to curse. Casting a glance back, I saw them run toward their horses. They would be after us in seconds, and a horse is considerably faster than a mule.

I made no attempt to follow the trail to the tomb, which was in a blind canyon where we would become trapped. Instead, I set out across the hills toward the distant open desert that I glimpsed between their peaks. We had not gone far when the steel shoes of the horses clattered on the hard stone shelf. One of the men laughed. No doubt he thought us easy prey, and so we would have been had we fled along the road. A horse can outrun a mule, but a mule can outclimb a horse. I deliberately chose a steep and difficult path over the hill we ascended, and was gratified by curses of dismay behind us as the horses balked at the incline of the smooth rock. They were forced to lead their horses along an easier but less direct path up the hill, and this slowed them enough that they fell behind.

So it continued through the afternoon, with me driving the exhausted beast between my knees up slopes and along narrow ledges, the girl always close behind, and the four assassins now drawing near, and now falling more distant, depending on what path they were able to find. They could not pursue us directly, as they discovered to their sorrow. In an attempt to cross a steep and angled slab of rock, the horse of the old beggar slipped and fell, throwing him to the stones some distance below. His curses told me that he had not been killed, but I felt reason to hope he had been injured. After that, the four were more cautious, and took their time picking their way over the slopes.

The sun glared in my eyes, a huge red ball on the western horizon, when at last we descended from the heights into the desert expanse. We had gained enough ground on our pursuers that they were not in sight, but I knew they would never give up the chase. They were being paid to kill us, and would have to show some proof that they had accomplished their purpose, and that meant taking a trophy from our bodies. They had probably questioned the owner of the stables where we hired the mules, and he had told them we only possessed enough water for two days, assuming we rode at a walking pace. They would believe it suicide for us to stray far from the Nile. The tracks leading to our corpses would be easy to follow in the sand.

"What do you intend?" Martala asked.

Her face was flushed and her lips dry. She had tried to drink from her water skin, but I had snatched it away from her.

"We will ride into the desert until nightfall."

I sensed fear in her voice. She tried to keep it hidden behind her eyes when she looked at me, but it was obvious the desert terrified her. She had learned to deal with all the dangers that faced a young girl in a city of men, but the indifference of the dunes and the emptiness of the horizon were immune to her flatteries and deceits. The desert did not care whether she lived or died, or even that she existed.

My heart felt strangely light. I was returning home, and embraced the desert as a child hugs its mother. It would have been sensible to worry about the four assassins who followed our tracks, but I experienced only a deep joy and a sense of peace.

My mule stumbled and nearly fell. Its breaths came in gasps and snorts, and a white foam of sweat lathered its flanks. Martala's mount appeared stronger, but was equally exhausted. The beasts had been tired at the beginning of the chase, whereas the horses of the men who followed were rested and well-watered. We could not spare any more of our water for the mules. I slowed to a walking pace to conserve their strength. Every time we topped the crest of a dune, I turned in my saddle and cast a lingering glance behind us at the diminishing line of hills. As the sun flattened itself against the edge of the sky, I looked back and saw the dust of galloping horses.

Dismounting, I led my mule between two dunes. Martala also stepped down from her saddle and began to follow. I shook my head at her.

"Wait here."

Once hidden from the sight of the other beast, I drew my dagger and with a smooth stroke cut the mule's throat. It cried out in surprise and staggered, then fell to its knees. I pressed my lips to the scarlet fountain that spurted from its severed blood vessel and swallowed as much as I could before the beast fell over onto its side. Its legs twitched several times, and its brown eye rolled with a lack of comprehension. I cut the eyeballs from its skull, wiped my dagger on its hairy hide, and sheathed the blade.

The mule behind the girl snorted and tossed its head at the scent of blood on my face and robes. Drawing my dagger, I sliced the eyeballs open and handed them to the girl.

"Drink."

She looked at the bloody eyes of the mule with disgust, then at me. To her credit, she shuddered and raised the first eye to her pursed lips, sucking its contents into her mouth. With a grimace she squeezed shut her eyes and swallowed the liquid of the second, then cast the empty eyeballs from her in loathing. I took off my water skin, no more than a third full due to the water I had given to the beasts earlier, and slung it over her shoulder, retaining her nearly empty skin for myself. The dust of the four riders was much closer in the failing light. They were too distant to make out their individual forms, but that would change in the space of minutes. I indicated with a gesture for the girl to remount her mule, and threw my leg over its rump to sit behind her saddle. The mule brayed and stumbled in a half circle on stiff legs to show its displeasure. Reaching around the girl, I took the reins and rode due west at as fast a walk as the beast could manage burdened with the two of us.

"What have you gained, Alhazred?" she asked without turning. "We are slower than before."

"The mule I killed was at the end of its strength. So is this one, almost. The men who follow us know these beasts cannot be ridden back to Memphis until they are rested and watered, and they know we dare not give them our water. They think we flee from them in panic to our deaths in the desert."

"Are they right?"

"Perhaps," I conceded. "We will see."

The light fell rapidly, and the stars began to appear in the heavens. I saw what I had been looking for, a long ridge of bare rock that pierced the sands like the inverted keel of a great ship.

"Listen carefully," I told the girl. "Continue to ride west over the sand. Mark your course by the stars. Over the sand, not on the rocks."

I gave her the rest of my instructions and she nodded.

"I understand."

As we passed the ridge, I lifted my body on my hands against the rump of the mule and vaulted across to the rock. The girl held the animal under control and continued to ride west. I watched her until she passed from view behind a sand dune. Taking care to leave no recognizable footprints, I worked my way across the boulders and drifted sand until I found a small hill that I could hide behind.

It was not long to wait. In less than the quarter part of an hour, the four horsemen came at a walking pace along our trail, their heads bent over the necks of their mounts as they scanned the sand for marks. As I had anticipated, the failing light forced them to go slowly, or they risked losing sight of the tracks of the mule. The horses were lathered with sweat but did not appear at the limit of their endurance. At the saddle of each hung two heavy water skins. The assassins had come better prepared for the desert than I, who should have known better.

After they passed, I followed them with great caution, taking care to stay well behind and to one side of the lines of tracks made by their horses in case they lost the mule's prints and needed to retrace their path. It was an easy matter to follow with my ear-holes alone, since they talked and laughed loudly, but I kept them within sight. They were sure of their quarry. As I had hoped, the dead mule removed any worry in their minds that we might somehow escape. The bearded beggar said little, and appeared to sit his saddle with discomfort. I noticed a patch of blood drying on his tunic over his knee. I was not surprised to see his left foot unbandaged and showing no trace of its former twist. The largest of the other men, a giant with a huge belly, drank from a flask what must have been wine. His words slurred when he talked. He began to sing in a toneless voice that set my teeth on edge, and I was grateful when his companions cursed him to silence.

We came to a stony hill. The track of the mule led past it, but instead of running in a straight line due west, it began to wander from side to side, gradually curving southward.

"The beast has run mad from lack of water," I heard the beggar say in Coptic.

The night continued to deepen. Since the moon was just past full, it would soon rise, but until then riding would be increasingly difficult. At last the four reined their horses into a circle and began to debate. The giant wanted to continue, saying that he could follow the track of the mule by starlight, and anyway, it was plain that it was about to collapse. The beggar opposed him with the comment that they might lose the trail in the darkness, now that it wandered from side to side, and in any case the horses needed to be rested and watered. He said it was better to camp for the night, and continue to follow at the first light of dawn. The other two were inclined to side with the big man, putting forth the argument that a wind might arise and cover the tracks, but the beggar was their leader, and his pain made him stubborn. He cursed them and they fell silent.

They dismounted and hobbled the horses, then removed their saddles and bridles and gave the beasts water. After rubbing the weary creatures down with blankets, the men sat together on stones and shared two flasks of wine between them. I waited patiently for the wine to have its effect. One by one, they lay down on blankets they spread across the sand and went to sleep. They had not bothered setting a guard since they assumed by their reading of the boot prints around the dead mule that I had mounted behind the girl on the other beast. The rising moon bathed the hillside in silver.

Removing my boots, I crept toward the hill without a sound, dagger in my hand. The scent of dried blood on my thawb drifted to the horses, and one of them whinnied softly. It was a still night. I stopped and waited, breath held, but none of the men raised his head. The big man snored sonorously. His snores had better pitch and timber than his singing. Judging him to be the most dangerous, I rounded the sleepers and approached him from behind. He lay on his side, curled into a great ball. Pressing my left hand over his mouth and nose, I slid the blade of my knife into his back between his ribs, and through his heart.

His violent convulsion threw me away and forced me to jerk out the dagger or lose my grip on its bone hilt. Air from his collapsing lung made a wet sound as it escaped through the slit, and a loud moan issued from his lips. The horses scented his hot blood and shrilled in terror as they fought their fetters and clattered over the loose stones on the slope. It is needless to add that all three of the remaining men awoke and sat up.

Inwardly cursing my clumsiness, I ran behind the nearest and grabbed his head in my arm, then cut his throat with a sweeping stroke. The beggar and the other hired man were on their feet, their swords drawn. One glance in the moonlight showed me that the old man knew how to use a long blade. I snatched the sword of the man I had killed from its scabbard and danced to my bare feet, the moon behind me. Along with crown prince Yanni and the other noble youths who lived at the palace in Sana'a, I had received instruction in the use of the sword from a master swordsman. This was the first time I had ever found a need for it. I wondered how much of my lessons I remembered.

The two spread themselves apart and came at me in silence. This game might be new to me, but they were well practiced. I caught the down stroke of the beggar near the hilt of my weapon and deflected it with a circular motion, as I had been taught, then jumped to the side to avoid the thrust of the other man. Neither paused, but continued to hack and thrust at me, forcing me back over the treacherous rolling stones. The foot of the younger man slipped from under him and he struggled to keep his balance. I saw my chance and cut down diagonally across his breast with my point, slicing open his coat, tunic and chest alike. Blood gushed black in the moonlight.

Too late I saw the gleam of the beggar's sword descend toward my head. There was only a moment to cast myself backward. I lost my balance on the loose stones. An enormous impact knocked my sword from my numbed fingers, and I fell onto my back. He lunged forward without hesitation, and would have thrust his point through my heart, but the direction of my fall put the moonlight across my face. The wiry old man staggered and cried out in horror, his eyes twin circles of dark and light. He hung for an instant above me, frozen at the sight of my mutilations. When he recovered his senses and drew back his sword for a killing thrust, it was too late. My dagger was already in his belly. I twisted the blade and tore it viciously to the side to open his bowels. His thrust went wide and the point of his sword scraped the stones over my shoulder as he collapsed across my body, pouring out his life blood on my chest.

The shadow of the other man loomed above me. I struggled to free myself from the weight of the beggar, who clutched at me with his bare hands in his agony. The remaining assassin was less easily moved by appearances than the beggar. He stared down at my face without flinching, and prepared his sword to strike off my head.

An expression of surprise possessed his bearded features. He stood unmoving with his sword raised. It fell from his fingers and clattered at his feet as his mouth gaped to emit a black stream of blood, and he collapsed to his knees. I saw Martala standing behind him, tiny dagger in her hand, its blade stained with wetness that glistened under the moon. She kicked the dying man aside with the toe of her shoe and knelt to pull the beggar off my chest.

"You were supposed to jump off the back of the mule and hide in the hills."

She shrugged.

"I got tired of waiting."

We turned the beggar onto his back. His face was so pale it looked ghostlike, and I knew he was bleeding his life away inside his own body.

"Did Farri hire you to kill us?" I asked in Coptic.

He tried to look down at his open belly but did not have the strength to raise his head. Instead, he lifted his blood-soaked hands to his face and stared at them. His fingers shook. Impatiently, I pulled his hands aside and repeated my question.

His eyes met mine. The fight had drained from him even faster than his blood. There was no malice or deception, only fear. He nodded.

"Is he in Memphis?"

The old man shook his head.

"When will he arrive?" the girl asked.

He spoke but his voice was weak. I had to bend forward while he repeated his words.

"Three days."

"How many does he bring with him?"

We could not hear him. He raised a hand with four fingers extended.

"I know who he will bring," Martala said. "He will bring the best he has."

The beggar died before we could question him further. I searched his body and took the few bronze fils he wore in a purse at his waist, then did the same for the other three corpses. None of them carried enough money to have made killing them for it worth the effort. I regarded the beggar's sword, which was superior to the others, and wondered if I should take it for my own. Reluctantly, I decided to leave it on the rocks. It might be recognized in Memphis.

I retrieved my boots, and we spent a few minutes gathering the horses. The violence had terrified them, but their hobbles prevented them from running far. I collected the water skins and slung them over the saddles of the two strongest mounts. Everything else I left where it lay. Eventually the corpses would be discovered. It would probably be assumed that they had killed each other in a drunken brawl, though how their presence in the desert would be explained, I could not imagine.

"We can't be seen with the horses. We'll ride them back to the outskirts of Memphis, then release them. Someone will find them."

The girl nodded agreement.

"When did you learn to speak Coptic?"

"When I ate the wizard's finger."

"So it wasn't a lie," she mused. "I wonder what other skills you acquired?"

I shrugged. Time would reveal whether the potent flesh had changed me in any other way. It was not of immediate concern. Mounting the horse I had chosen, I indicated for Martala to do the same. She stared at me in outrage.

"What about the mule?"

"What of it?"

"Alhazred, you can't leave it here in the desert. It will die of thirst."

The impulse to cow her into silence with curses was replaced by amusement. She had just killed a man by running her knife through his heart, and she was concerned over the health of a beast. I had almost forgotten the capriciousness of a woman's favor.

"Very well. You take the other horses and lead them back toward Memphis. I will search for the mule."

"You promise," she said with the expression of a wounded child.

I laughed shortly and nodded. The sound of my laughter made her smile. It sounded strange in my ear-holes.

The moon rose higher in the sky and cast a good light on the sand. It was enough to see the serpentine track winding its way southward between the dunes. There was little breeze, and the hoof prints were still sharply defined. I watched Martala start back with the three horses toward the range of low hills, then turned the head of my own mount and went after the mule.

Its prints told the tale of its flight. At first it had run, but after a short distance its weakness and thirst had compelled it to slow to a walk. It had wandered aimlessly, picking the easiest path around the hills and between the low dunes. The further it went, the less steady the line of prints became, until they staggered like those of a drunkard. I expected at any moment to come upon its body, but when at last I reached the end of the trail, what I saw surprised me.

The mule lay upon its belly, its legs folded under it, watching me with tranquil eyes as I rode around the shoulder of a dune. It gave no expression of alarm at my approach, nor did it make a sound. As I drew near I saw that the corners of its muzzle were flecked with white foam, and that it breathed quick pants of air. Dismounting, I stepped forward and laid my hand on its neck, still sticky with dried sweat. The flesh was hot. Under my touch the mule turned its head to look at me.

Perhaps it was not too late to revive the beast, I thought. Fetching one of the water skins from the horse, I opened it and poured it into my cupped palm under the mule's nose. It sniffed the water but did not attempt to lap it up. I let a little of the stream flow over its muzzle, and it began to weakly lick at it with its tongue. After a few moments, its interest became more demanding. I let it have its fill, pouring the water into my hand so that it could draw it in with its soft lips, taking care that the beast did not nip off one of my fingers. At last I pulled the skin away, evoking a bray of protest, and poured some of the water over the mule's head and ears. With my hand I spread it across the neck of the creature, hoping to cool its blood.

"You have a strong heart," I muttered in my own tongue. "You carried the two of us well. Now you must stand up."

The animal rolled its brown eye at me. Horses are fabled to comprehend Arabic, but I have heard no opinion on this matter regarding mules. I picked the reins up from the sand and gently tugged at its head. After a few seconds, it lurched to its feet and stood on trembling legs. I gave it more water and watched it drink eagerly. It was a good sign, and I had reason to hope that it would be strong enough to walk back to the city through the cool night air.

The girl had not ridden far. I saw her outlined against the horizon, sitting on her horse and waiting. When she turned at the sound of my approach, she gave a cry of delight.

"All the beasts have been rescued from the desert."

"Except for the one you killed," she reminded me with reproach, running her fingers over the rough mane of the mule.

"That one would have died anyway," I said, but in my heart I was not sure it was the truth.

It was mid-morning before we reached the road leading to the western gate of Memphis. I did not dare ride my horse nearer, but dismounted and had Martala do the same. I gestured for her to get onto the back of the mule, which had become stronger on the walk back to the city. Taking the reins in my hand, I led it along the road. The horses tried to follow at our heels, but a few shouts and claps of my hands made them shy away. We left them nibbling a clump of grass that grew at the base of a hill, for as we approached the Nile the ground became fertile and alive with growing things.

"Are you sure they will be found?" the girl asked.

"This is a well-traveled road. They will be found before noon."

The gate was already standing wide when the city wall came into view. I drew the mule back along the road before we were seen by someone on the wall.

"Why have you stopped?" the girl asked.

Spreading my arms, I showed her my thawb. She regarded the blood that spattered its front as though seeing it for the first time.

"You must ride to the marketplace and buy me something to wear. I cannot enter the city looking like a butcher. When Farri's assassins are discovered, some quick-minded guard may connect the two events."

"What do you wish me to buy?"

"It doesn't matter. Wait, get something with pockets."

"Egyptian tunics don't have pockets," she said, as though explaining something to a child.

"Just buy clothing that will pass without notice."

I took out my purse and dug around in it until I found a gold dinar. Martala accepted the coin when I pressed it into her hand and closed her fingers over it.

From the crest of a low hill, I watched her ride slowly through the gate. No one challenged her passage. While I waited with growing impatience, several riders left the city along the road, forcing me to crouch from sight. Flies attracted to the blood on my thawb buzzed around my face. After what must have been nearly an hour, I heard the slow clop of the mule's hooves on the road. I clapped my hands to draw the girl's attention to the top of the hill, and gestured for her to lead the animal behind its shelter.

She appeared refreshed and happy. I saw that she had taken the time to wash her face, and guessed that she had already eaten breakfast. My stomach rumbled at the thought. Lifting down a tied bundle from the saddle of the mule, she tossed it toward me. I caught it to keep it from landing in the dust at my feet, and held it on my raised knee to untie it.

"Since you are Muslim, I brought what Muslims usually wear in this land."

Upon a slope of rock I laid out a tastefully embroidered white shirt with narrow sleeves and a long tail, a loose white surwal the cuffs of which hung below my knees at the length approved by the Prophet, and a long blue Persian coat of the kind that close by wrapping one side over the other. The flaps were held shut both by buttons and a leather belt, which seemed a needless degree of security. To my delight I discovered that the coat had pockets inside each breast.

"I had the tailor put them in," the girl said with satisfaction when she observed my expression. "That's why I took so long."

It was the work of a few minutes to cast off the stained thawb, which stuck to my skin in places with dried blood, and put on my new garments. The girl took my water skin from her saddle, and used it to wash a crust of dried blood from my forehead. I saw that she had refilled it. The weight of the water on my right hip reassured me. I slipped the baldric of my dagger over my head and shoulder, and tied Gor's skull to my belt next to my purse, then concealed the thawb beneath loose stones and walked alongside the mule toward the gate of Memphis, with the girl riding.

Just in time I remembered to renew the glamour that concealed my face. The gatekeeper watched us enter the city with evident curiosity, but made no remark. I could feel his eyes on my back as we passed, probably wondering about Martala's comings and goings, and why we had ridden out the day before with two mules and returned with only one. I reflected that it would be best to be away from this place before the corpses in the desert were discovered. Memphis seemed none the worse for being four ruffians fewer. Already the streets thronged with women carrying water pots of baked clay on their heads and merchants pushing their wares toward the market square in two-wheeled carts.

We were making our way toward the stables from which we had hired the mules when I caught a glimpse of familiar features in the corner of my eye. I stopped and looked after the man I had recognized, debating with myself what course to take. The contest was brief. Curiosity alone would never have allowed me to lose sight of the figure that moved so swiftly down the street. I gave the girl another dinar.

"Pay for the dead mule. Make up some plausible tale. I have other business."

She glanced down the street at the man I had recognized, and I saw by her expression that she would know him if she ever encountered him again.

"How will I find you?"

"Return to the inn. I will meet you there later."

Without waiting for her agreement, I hurried after the familiar figure. Sliding my body between the colorful mass of humanity that filled the street, while keeping my hand pressed over my purse, I drew nearer to my prey. He moved with quick but relaxed steps, unaware that he was being watched. I had not been mistaken. He had changed from his black monk's robe to a more common unbelted Egyptian tunic of white linen trimmed with red and blue wool, and wore a white turban in the modest style of a scribe, but his heavy eyebrows made him easy to recognize. It was the young servant of the dark man, whom I had seen in my dream enter through the secret door beneath the tail of the Sphinx.

Chapter 20

The young man continued through the twisted streets of the merchant district with a relaxed stride, completely at his ease. Several times he paused to exchange words with prosperous-looking sellers he chanced to encounter outside the doorways of their shops. I judged him to be either a scholar or a priest not only from the wrap of his turban, but from the pallor of his complexion and the smoothness of his hands, which bore no calluses that I could see at a distance. His clean and polished fingernails were rounded in the usual fashion, proving that he was no worshipper of Bast. I followed and watched all he did, puzzling to myself over his purpose.

He gave a cloth purse of coins to a sunburned Greek seaman with a harsh countenance who loitered in the shadow beneath an archway as though he had been waiting for the scholar. It was no small purse. The Greek wore a costly vest of red silk embroidered with flowers of gold thread over a white shirt, and a billowing white silk surwal, the cuffs of which were tucked into the tops of high boots of soft yellow leather, so I knew he must be the captain or mate of a trading vessel, since no ordinary seaman could afford such apparel.

As I watched the exchange from a street corner, while trying to appear as though I had merely paused to rest my legs, an elderly Egyptian with a white beard who sat beside the threshold of a tailor's shop pushed himself up with the aid of a walking staff and gestured to the stone block upon which he had been sitting.

"Why did you stand?" I asked in Coptic.

He grinned, showing a gap where several teeth were missing from his mouth.

"You are a follower of the way of the Prophet, are you not?"

I nodded, though in truth I cared nothing for either the Prophet or his teachings.

"It is required that we stand and offer you our seats."

"Required? Who requires it?"

He looked at me with a faint confusion, as though I were testing him.

"The Amir of Egypt, Alquama al-Azdi, enforces the law of the Caliph at Damascus, Yazid the Great."

I had heard the Caliph called many things while passing the council chambers of the palace at Sana'a, but great had not been among them. He was more usually referred to as Yazid of the Wines, for he had given up his former love of rose sherbet in favor of the blood of the grape since rising to power three years ago in the place of his father, Mu'awiyya. He was reputed to be cruel and debauched, but could not be all bad, for like the ancient Roman emperor Nero he was also a musician.

"Forgive me," I said with a smile. "I am new in Egypt, and unfamiliar with its laws."

Gesturing for him to return to his seat, I continued to follow my quarry as both he and the Greek captain made their way north.

Most of the houses and public buildings were abandoned in the northern section of Memphis, and the stone temples had been pulled down to their foundations, their stones dragged away, so that only their outlines remained on the ground. I stayed well back to avoid being seen, but the pair remained deep in conversation and took no precaution. There were more people, and more signs of industry, as we approached the river where a dozen ships rode the current on their moorings. I judged their cargos of questionable legality. Why else tie up so far from the heart of the city?

They walked onto a stone quay where a ship with a single tall mast and two banks of oars was tied up close to the dock. The Greek barked orders to the seamen who labored to unload numerous oblong crates of wood over the side. Each box was about four cubits in length, and broader than it was deep. It seemed a perfect size to conceal a corpse. Also being unloaded were large-bellied jars of glazed gray clay, similar to the jar I had seen the young scholar carry beneath his arm in my dream, and slender cylinders of polished copper. Whatever the latter held, it must be in the form of a liquid or powder since the mouths of the cylinders were quite narrow.

For a few minutes the two stood together on the dock and watched the work. The scholar, if such he was, spoke a few parting words to the Greek seaman and left him to supervise the unloading. As he made his way back into the street that ran along the riverside and turned his face again to the north, I fell into step behind him.

He pulled aside the dirty linen flap of a door cover and ducked his head to pass beneath the wood lintel of the entrance. Approaching the portal with caution, I guessed from the sound of drunken conversation and the sour smells that drifted out of the interior of the red clay building that it was a wine shop. I took a deep breath, wishing for a nose that I might plug it, and ducked through the doorway. Inside was dark, but cooler than outside. The only light shone through a tiny window in the rear wall. The long and narrow room had a ceiling so low that my short hair, still scarcely more than the fuzz on a peach, brushed one of the rough wooden beams. Straw lay strewn across the floor, but I saw that it was clean straw, probably scattered on the clay that very morning.

A score of seamen and laborers sat at square tables, lost in drink and talk. They turned when I entered, the scholar among them, but soon resumed their muttered conversations. A few were Egyptians, the rest Greeks. None of them offered me his seat. Since there were several empty places, this was of no concern. The young man left the wooden counter at which he stood with a tin cup in his hand that almost overflowed with red wine, and made his careful way toward the tables, so intent on preserving his drink that he took no further notice of me. I caught the eye of the owner across the room and pointed at the cup the scholar held, indicating with gestures that I wished the same. The owner nodded.

The scholar sat himself at an empty table and sipped his wine. He raised his thick eyebrows with curiosity when I approached. I was reasonably sure from his guileless expression that he had not noticed me follow him through the streets.

"You look like a man of rank and learning," I said in Greek. "May I sit with you? I have no wish to talk about bilge buckets and sail mending."

He shrugged his narrow shoulders with a faint smile.

"Hardly a man of rank, but I am a seeker after wisdom."

I lowered myself onto a rough stool and regarded him across the table with what I hoped was a disarming expression.

"I myself am a traveler from the city of Sana'a, but newly arrived on the Nile. My father wished me to view the world before I took up my duties in the palace administration of King Huban ibn Abd Allah, the ruler of Yemen, so I have no purpose here other than to watch and learn."

"Your father is a wise man. I can imagine no better preparation for life than a journey to distant nations. Are you alone?"

"Yes, apart from a single servant I acquired in Bubastis."

"My name is Drunellu," he said. "Everyone calls me Dru."

"I am called Alhazred."

The owner of the shop brought a tall tin cup filled to the brim with red wine and set it before me. I took out my purse and gave him one of the bronze fils I had stolen from the corpses of the assassins, taking care that Dru saw the weight of the purse before I put it away.

"Why do you drink here?" I asked when the shop owner was out of hearing. "Surely there are better places?"

"Alas, no, not in the northern section of Memphis."

"The part I walked through did have a desolate aspect," I agreed.

He took a deep drink from his cup.

"Little wonder. The Amir is having the buildings pulled apart, and the stones shipped down river to the new city of Fustat."

"What of the people who live in them?"

He shrugged philosophically, with the air of a man who is sure that he has a roof waiting for him at the end of the day.

"They are cast out, and must fend for themselves. Most have gone down river to Fustat, where there is much work to be had for laborers and craftsmen."

"Surely those who have lived all their lives here resent this destruction of their city?"

"What can we do? You are our lords and masters."

He smiled faintly in apology, and waved his hand.

"I don't mean you personally, of course, but the army of Mohammed that rules this land from Babylon."

"Babylon? Don't you mean Damascus?"

He laughed.

"There is an old fortress at Fustat that they call Babylon. That is where the Muslim troops are quartered."

All this was useful information, but had nothing to do with his reasons for being under the tail of the Sphinx by moonlight. I wondered how to approach the subject. His furtive movements in my dream, and the care with which he had taken to conceal his face before entering under the Sphinx, indicated that it was a matter of great secrecy. He would never speak of it in casual conversation, and I did not believe he was a man I could easily cause to become drunk.

Glancing around to be sure no one else in the wine shop was near enough to hear, I leaned forward.

"I have not been completely honest with you. Like yourself, I am a seeker after wisdom. Indeed, it was the quest for arcane knowledge that drew me to this land."

"What do you consider arcane?" he asked with a wary smile, studying my face.

"You are a man of sophistication, so I will speak freely. The arts of sorcery and necromancy."

"These arts are forbidden, as I am sure you know," he said.

"Forbidden, but not forgotten, not in this ancient land."

He pursed his lips and considered whether to answer.

"True. There are necromancers on the Nile, just as there were in the age of the pharaohs. They conceal their identities, for discovery to the authorities means swift execution."

"I wish you to introduce me to them."

His eyes widened under his heavy brows, and he laughed.

"What makes you believe that I know anything about such forbidden matters?"

When I held up my index finger, he fell silent. I waited until his gaze rested upon the tip of my finger, then lowered it to the surface of the table and traced the symbol I had seen him use to expose the hidden door beneath the tail of the Sphinx.

With a choked cry, he leapt to his feet, knocking over his wine cup in the process. He stared around wildly, his eyes lingering on the door. Smoothly, so as not to frighten him, I stood and laid my hand on his shoulder.

"Do not fear. Your secret is safe," I murmured.

Everyone in the shop stopped talking to watch our little pantomime. Dru realized he was the object of attention and forced an unconvincing smile onto his face.

"How clumsy," he said in a loud voice. "I've spilled wine all over myself."

The proprietor of the shop bustled over with a rag, making sympathetic noises, and brushed off the hem of the scholar's tunic, then wiped the table. We sat down as though nothing had happened, smiling and joking as two old friends. When he saw that we no longer held the attention of the other patrons of the shop, Dru leaned across the table.

"How do you know that symbol?"

"It was revealed to me in a dream."

"Alhazred, this is nothing to jest about."

In a few words I described my dream, telling him how I had gone in the company of a tall man wearing a caul of black silk to the plateau of the pyramids, where I had seen Dru enter beneath the tail of the Sphinx. When I described the dark man, his face became even paler than normal, so that I was sure he would faint. I pushed my cup across the table.

"Take a drink, my friend."

He shook his head, staring at me with mingled terror and awe.

"This dark figure in your dream, does he have a name?"

"Nyarlathotep," I whispered.

He clutched my hand and squeezed painfully. I do not believe he was even aware of doing it.

"Never utter his name aloud, Alhazred."

"I know nothing of him, other than that he appears in my dreams," I said carelessly, extracting my hand from the vise of his fingers.

"Why would he visit your dreams?" he said, more to himself than to me.

"He wants me to serve him in some way, but of what way I can be of service, I am ignorant."

He nodded, thinking furiously to himself. He had the look of a man about to lapse into a fit, and I thought it best for us to leave the wine shop before we attracted more attention. I drew him to his feet and led him out the door with my arm around his shoulder, as though supporting him in his drunkenness.

"The leader of my order must speak to you. The god of chaos has called you to Egypt for a purpose."

"I am eager to meet with your leader, who must be a man of great wisdom."

"So he is," Dru said. "And he is my father."

"Take me to him, then."

The scholar shook his head.

"He is in Fustat, along with most of the members of my order. I am only in Memphis on a buying mission. My ship will sail down river as soon as it loads the cargo that is presently being readied for it on the docks, but that will not be until tomorrow morning."

"Very well. I will meet you on the northern docks in the morning, after I collect my belongings and my servant from the inn."

He seemed reluctant to allow me to go out of his sight, but at last agreed to my arrangement. I left him standing in the street and made my way back toward the inn.

Martala sat with crossed legs on the floor of our room beneath the coolness of the open window. On the other side of the street, through the open screens of the opposite house, I saw the young householder's wife sweeping with her broom. She glanced at me with an expression I could not define and continued with her work. Martala had already eaten, but had possessed the forethought to buy an extra plate of roast breast of fowl and boiled peppers, along with a piece of bread. I sat on the edge of the bed facing her and ate this cold fare from my lap while she watched.

"The stable keeper was distraught over the death of his best mule," she said. "He wept when I told him how it fell from a ledge of rock and broke its neck."

"The gold coin will solace him."

She averted her pale eyes for a moment, and I realized she had not given him the coin, but had divided it and paid for the mule with only part of the money. The rest she had kept for herself.

I tore with my teeth at the meat of the fowl. It was from a bird I could not identify, and as tough as old boot leather, with the same dryness and lack of flavor. Having experimentally gnawed at the leather of my sandals while hungry in the desert, I knew the taste well. The bread was a day old and dried out, but more tender than the bird. Even so, it was food, and would nourish my body.

Martala took amused notice of the uncommon time I spent chewing a shred of the fowl.

"The cook left the service of the inn yesterday. Your meal was prepared by the innkeeper's wife—she of the long face and disapproving expression."

I swallowed with difficulty, reminding myself that I was a ghoul.

"Tomorrow morning I sail for Fustat. You may come with me if you wish, since it serves my purpose to have a servant."

"I am no one's servant," she said hotly, ice-gray eyes blazing.

"It is a pose, nothing more. I have presented myself as a man of wealth. Such a man would not travel without at least one servant."

"Why do we go to Fustat?"

In few words I described my dream, and how I had recognized the man in the street as the same who had passed under the Sphinx. To my surprise, she did not scoff, but merely nodded.

"I have had such dreams, not about this dark man but about matters of importance in my life. It is always wise to heed them."

"It is for my own purposes that I go. This order of sages may possess knowledge I can turn to use. Let the dark man believe I am his servant, while I pursue my own ends."

"What are those ends?"

I gestured with my greasy fingers at my face and then to my groin.

"I was not always as you see me with your scryer's vision. Once I was a whole man, and I will be whole again. I seek the magic to restore my body."

She nodded, satisfied with this explanation. The restoration of my body was a quest material enough for her comprehension, as I had known it would be.

"Very well, Alhazred, I will pretend to be your servant, even as you pretend to serve the dark man." She smiled to herself. "I wonder who he pretends to serve?"

To this, I had no answer.

The night was uncommonly warm. I took off my Muslim coat, undershirt, and surwal, then lay upon the feather-filled mattress of the bed on my back. Martala curled up naked on the floor beneath the open window, its screens wide to admit any faint trace of a breeze. As the sweat trickled from my chest and rolled down my sides beneath my arms, I envied her whatever coolness of the night air found its way over the windowsill, and considered giving her the bed and taking her place on the floor, but decided it was not fitting for a man of wealth to give his bed to his servant. With a silent laugh, I rolled on to my shoulder, facing the window, and let myself sink into sleep.

Through the vague depths of some troubled dream the beautiful face of Sashi swam into view. I thought she had come to make love to me, and in my imagination opened my arms to receive her, but the expression in her almond eyes remained serious.

Wake up, my love, there is danger.

"What danger, Sashi?" I muttered in my sleep.

With urgency, she reached forward and grabbed me by the hands. Her strength was strangely out of proportion for her slender body. She jerked me forward until my teeth rattled.

221

Wake up, Alhazred!

I started to awareness on the mattress and opened my eyes, listening. The night was as silent as it ever becomes in the midst of a city. A faint moon glow shone through the open window, illuminating the huddled form of Martala where I had last seen her. Slow deep breaths gave indication that she slept. For a minute or two I lay still, my heart thudding in my chest. No sound came from outside the bolted door. At last I relaxed and allowed myself to breathe normally. I was about to say something harsh to Sashi when a shadow moved outside the window.

At first I thought someone climbed from the street on a rope or ladder, but the motion that attracted my eye was further away than the windowsill, and I realized the wooden screens of the window across the street were slowly widening. So gradual was their movement that it could not be seen at a glance, but only by the change in the position of the edges of the screens over the span of seconds. I observed their parting with fascination, and wondered what they might reveal.

A shadow shifted in their gap, the same dark shadow I had seen move through their latticework before the screens parted. As it leaned outward, it resolved itself into a man in a dark cloak. The cloak parted momentarily, and polished silver at his waist caught the moonlight and gleamed with a chill radiance. His shoulders were narrow, his arms thin. More than this I could not observe, for his eyes were covered by a visor that hung from a kind of skullcap of black metal, leaving only the lower part of his nose and his mouth exposed. His masked face and dark clothing merged well with the night, but not well enough to deceive the eyes of a ghoul.

The visor must have obstructed his vision in the uncertain moonlight, which did not penetrate far into my room. He raised a slender white hand and tipped it away from his face, locking it upright to reveal a soft countenance and large dark eyes lined with kohl. With surprise, I realized that it was not the face of a man at all, but a young woman of some twenty years. She might have been beautiful, were it not for a hardness around her thin mouth when she clenched her square jaw.

She drew back, and I heard a strange sound, a kind of creaking such as might be made by a dried reed when it is bowed. Her arm extended through the window, with something upright in her clenched fist, and there was the sound of tightening twine.

Even before I realized what the noises signified, I rolled off the opposite side of the bed and threw myself to the floor. My naked body made a sound like a sack of turnips when it struck. The air whistled, and something cut into the feather mattress where my back had pressed only a moment before.

"Alhazred?" Martala's voice was faint with sleep.

"If you value your life, keep your head down," I hissed.

Crawling on my belly around the foot of the bed, I saw her crouched on hands and knees under the window. No sound came from across the street. Was the assassin waiting for a second chance, or had she fled? I slid to the wall and gained my feet, then approached the window from the side. With caution, I peered around the edge and immediately drew back my head. The thrum of the bowstring and the hiss of the arrow were followed immediately by a thud as the arrow embedded itself in the brick wall of the room on the opposite side of my bed.

Through the window I heard a door rattle open, followed moments later by a second door, and running footfalls on the paving stones of the street. I risked another look. Nothing moved in the oblong of shadow that was the opposite window.

"What's going on?" Martala murmured, drowsiness blurring her voice.

I pulled her to her feet and drew her across the floor to the bed. The arrow had passed into the mattress at an angle so that it had vanished from sight, but when I pulled the mattress out of its frame, we saw it embedded in the side rail of the bed. I worked it back and forth to remove it, taking care not to touch its metal tip. Perhaps it had not been poisoned, but there was no reason to assume so. Handing Martala the arrow, I extracted the other from the wall. It was identical. Both were flat black in color, even to their fledging and tips, and bore no marking or symbols of any kind.

"Farri is persistent," I murmured.

"Yes, that is his only virtue."

She nodded with a grim expression when I described what I had seen in the moonlight, before leaping to the floor to preserve my life.

"Zayna, Farri's daughter. At one time she was his chief assassin. If she is in Memphis, Farri cannot be far behind."

"You told me nothing about a daughter."

She shrugged her white shoulders.

"I've never met her. She lives in Alexandria. Before I came to Bubastis, she had some sort of argument with her father and left in anger."

"It seems they have reconciled."

There would be no rest for me until I knew what had taken place in the house across the street. Peering down from my window, I saw that its front door hung ajar. I told the girl to remain in the room and out of sight as I threw my coat over my naked limbs, and made sure that my dagger was still in its sheath when I slung its

223

baldric around my head and shoulder. I worked my way softly down the stairwell of the inn and unbolted the front door. The hour was late enough that nothing stirred in the street.

The gaping front door gave the house across the way an abandoned look. Feeling the grit of the paving stones against my bare feet, I stepped over the sewage channel in the middle of the street and eased my shoulders sideways through the gap in the door, then drew it shut behind me. I had to feel my way through the black interior toward the stairs, listening all the while with my breath stilled in my throat. What I expected to find, I do not know, but when I felt a sticky wetness under my toes in the upper hallway, it was without a sense of surprise. I leaned over and touched the face of a woman. Her cheeks were cold beneath my fingers. They told me what my eyes could not. I felt her long black hair spread around her head like a halo, half of it soaked in the blood that had gushed from the slash in her throat.

Standing in the darkness in her drying blood, I remembered the curious expression on her face when I had seen her sweeping the room, after my return to the inn. Had the assassin been in the room, watching her? Had she heard my talk with Martala, and learned that we sailed to Fustat in the morning? There was no way to know, but it would be safest to assume that in one way or another Farri would learn we had traveled to Fustat. The time for carelessness was past. I found myself curiously eager that Farri did know my destination. It was apparent that the only way to end these attempts on my life would be to kill him.

Chapter 21

Fustat had the chaotic look of a city not grown from natural roots, but imposed upon the land. Everything remained half finished. The roads were muddy tracks. The docks consisted of wooden logs that held frames of rutted, compressed earth. Elegant buildings of polished stones stolen from the temples of Memphis rose beside rude huts of clay or tents of camel hair. Despite its rough face, the new city held an air of purpose. Men labored or hurried about on errands with the inner assurance that their work was important. Memphis, for all its grandeur and beauty, lacked this frantic energy. That it was being built upon the eastern bank of the river, the direction of the rising sun, whereas Memphis occupied the west bank where the sun sets, only seemed to emphasize the distinction.

The sole structure with an air of permanence was the stone hulk of Babylon, looming over the city as though to intimidate the lesser buildings. It was not so ancient as the temples of Memphis, but it was far older than anything else in the city, which had been build around it. The high walls of the fortress bristled with soldiers, and through its open gates streamed a column of spear-carrying Muslims led by an officer on horseback, their ongoing mission to impose the will of the Amir, Alquama al-Azdi, upon the Christians. I watched the sunlight gleam from their spear points.

There were more of my own race gathered here than I had seen anywhere else in Egypt.

Dru left the sweating and cursing seamen who unloaded his cargo of oblong boxes and jars from his ship, and crossed the dock to where I stood with Martala. He noticed my gaze upon the fortress.

"It has been here for centuries," he said in Greek. "It was built to guard the entrance to the canal that links the river directly with the Red Sea. When your people conquered Egypt and drove the Roman Christians out of Alexandria, they chose this old stronghold as the site of their capitol."

"I thought the only canal was the one I followed to the Delta."

"No, that canal is much older, and has fallen into disuse."

"Where does the Amir live?" the girl asked.

Dru glanced at her with irritation. He was not accustomed to questions from servants. She did not drop her gaze, but confronted him with defiance.

"Your servant is impertinent, Alhazred."

"Answer her, to humor me."

He shrugged and smiled, pointing at a cluster of imposing walled buildings not far to the south of the fortress.

"Alquama's palace is there, along with the fine houses of his counselors and advisors."

He gestured to the north, where the outskirts of the city met the river. Between the naked masts of the ships tied up along the docks, I saw several large buildings on a slight eminence of land, surrounded by shade trees.

"My father's house is there, in the better part of the Coptic section of the city. I will take you to meet him."

He whistled and barked an order. Two sedan chairs that sat waiting on the quay were picked up by their well-muscled negro carriers, who were naked to the waist, and brought to where we stood. The carriers set them down side by side without speaking. Each consisted of a box containing a chair that was shaded from the sun by a canopy of cloth. The canopy extended down on either side for privacy, but the sides contained small slits for peering out. I waited for Dru to choose one, then drew aside the flap of the other and stepped into it. My life in the palace at Sana'a had accustomed me to this mode of transportation. The chair rocked as the bearers raised it.

"Where do I sit?" Martala asked.

I laughed, and Dru could not resist joining me.

The mud in the streets made walking difficult. Our bearers stumbled and slid in its slickness, even though they were experienced in dealing with it and tried to avoid the worst ruts. Water was continually carried in open wagons from the docks to various building sites in the city, and as it slopped out of huge urns in the wagons, it drenched the roads, which otherwise would have dried in the hot sun. I heard Martala cursing in her native Coptic as she stumbled and plodded behind my chair.

Once we crossed the bridge that spanned the canal and progressed from the heart of the city, the roads improved. The house of Dru's father nestled amid groves of fruit trees and flower gardens, overlooking the broad sweep of the Nile. It was situated to catch the breeze from the river and commanded an unobstructed vista.

The bearers set the sedan chairs down inside the walled courtyard of the house. Dru was greeted as he emerged by a noisy old servant, evidently the head of the house staff, who fluttered his wrinkled hands like a woman. Dru listened with patient indulgence for a short while, then murmured a few words into the ear of the talkative house master, who went away and returned leading a more imposing man of some fifty years' age. Dru embraced him with affection, so I guessed it must be his father, the head of the sect of sages who knew the secret of the Sphinx.

While seeming to admire the architecture of the house, which indeed was impressive, I studied the elder man. This was a dangerous moment. He might decide to have me put to death as an expedient way of ensuring the secret of the entranceway beneath the great statue. In his place, it is what I would have done.

He was a man of strength, both in body and will. One of the few I had seen in Egypt taller than myself, he stood with his back straight as a river reed. He had the economical yet proud walk of a military officer, an impression reinforced by his air of authority. I wondered if he had fought in the war to drive the Roman Christians out of Egypt. He was old enough, and even today would be formidable in battle.

As the two approached, he looked keenly at me but asked no questions of his son. Dru must have sent a runner from the docks to the house with the story of our meeting as soon as his ship moored.

"This is Feisel ibn Malik, my father," Dru said to me. "Father, this is the man I sent word to you about, Alhazred, a nobleman of Sana'a."

His eyes were like chips of flint as he studied my features, but they held no condemnation, and I allowed myself to relax.

227

"We will eat and talk," he said in a voice accustomed to obedience.

For the first time since my expulsion from Sana'a, I ate a civilized meal. We reclined on thick pillows covered in cloth of gold, before a table so laden with fruits, wine, and delicacies that I had no place to set my silver goblet. Musicians played behind a carved screen upon strings and flutes. The smoke of incense made from rose petals hung sweet upon the air.

I looked over my shoulder at Martala, who stood silently behind me, and tossed her a half-gnawed leg of fowl. She caught it from the air and set her teeth in the flesh while glaring at me. The pose of servant was not to her liking, but she had resigned herself to play the part.

"For a man of wealth, you travel lightly," Feisel observed.

"Why tempt robbers and cutthroats? Possessions are a burden."

"The only possession worth having is knowledge," Dru said, drinking deeply from his wine cup.

"Forgive my impatience, Alhazred, but I am eager to hear the tale of your dream. My son sent a messenger with the story you told him, but I wish to hear it from your own lips."

In a few words, I described the appearances of the dark man in my dreams, how he had marked my brow with an invisible mark, and how he had told me to seek out his son. It felt contrary to my natural caution to be so candid, but since the god had described these men as his servants, I wished them to know that I also had been marked in his service. That I did not consider myself Nyarlathotep's servant was something I thought better to conceal. Let them believe I worshiped the strange god who walked the desert. It would cause them to feel greater kinship with me.

Feisel leaned across his cushion and studied my brow, searching for any sign of the mark. The glamour that concealed my disfigurements resisted his scrutiny, though I had the sense that his sharp gray eyes were piercing my very soul.

"I see no mark."

"Yet how else could Alhazred know of the spell of opening?" Dru said.

"That is true." His father nodded to himself in decision. "I believe your story, Alhazred. The god of chaos has sent you to us for a purpose. Who are we, his humble servants, to question his actions? Today you will be made one of our order. Tomorrow you will share in our work. The purposes of the god in bringing you to us will unfold themselves at their own pace."

I bowed in acknowledgement. He glanced at Martala.

"Can your servant be trusted?"

"She owes me her life, and has pledged herself in obedience to me unto death."

"Still, perhaps it would be wisest to cut out her tongue, so that she cannot betray our secrets?" Dru languidly observed, spitting out the pit of a date into a wooden bowl on the table.

"She is educated, and knows how to read and write. It would be necessary to cut off her hands, and that would be inconvenient."

Feisel nodded in agreement.

"We will not deprive you of the usefulness of your solitary servant."

I heard an almost inaudible sigh escape the lips of the girl behind me, and hid the urge to smile in my wine goblet.

"We must be cautious," Dru explained in apology. "Of late secret documents have been disappearing."

"You suspect a thief?"

"Worse," Feisel said. "We have a spy in our sacred order. I am certain of it, though who sent him and for what purpose, we have been unable to fathom."

"What is the nature and labor of your fraternity?" I asked.

Feisel smiled without humor.

"Patience, Alhazred. Soon you will learn everything. It will suffice to say that we call ourselves the Order of the Sphinx. We are an ancient brotherhood of sages that existed long before the conquest of our land by the Greeks. When the Nile was a young river, and the nation of Egypt no more than rude huts of mud along its length, our forefathers worshiped the god of chaos beneath that great idol on the plain, and drank deep of his knowledge, which is vaster than the space between the stars. Only we know the true riddle of the Sphinx. It is a secret we have kept for thousands of years."

"Shall I be taught this secret?"

"You shall," Dru said, eyes shining with fanatical intensity.

"The god has chosen to make you one of us, for his own purposes. You will be shown all that we know."

At this admission from Feisel, my heart quickened, for the knowledge of occult secrets has always excited my desires. Regardless of what the dark man intended me to accomplish, I would learn of arcane matters that might later be turned to practical use, and this prospect of gain made me eager.

Later, I was taken to a chamber by Dru, who watched while a pair of attendants stripped me of my coat and undergarments, then robed me in black. Both were young men with serious expressions who fulfilled their task in silence. The long linen robe was the same costume I had seen Dru wear in my dream, an imitation of the garb of the dark man, with a tasseled sash at its waist. They gave me a caul of silk and showed me how to wrap it around my head, so that it would not slide off my face beneath my hood. It was very thin, and quite easy to see through, nor did it impede my breathing. After wearing it for a few minutes, I almost forgot that it existed.

"Now you look like one of us," Dru said, slapping me on the shoulder.

"When will I meet the others of our order?"

"You won't. None of us knows the identities of the brothers except my father, who is our leader. We meet only beneath the Sphinx, and always we wear this caul to conceal our faces. That is the source of our strength. Even were we to be captured by the Muslim soldiers and tortured, we could not betray each other."

"But you know the identity of your father," I pointed out.

"Each of us knows two others by name. It is necessary for purposes of communication when we go with faces exposed in Fustat. Only Feisel knows all of us."

"If you knew two before, then I am the third."

"True, but you are a special case."

He ordered the impassive attendants to wait outside the chamber, and shut the door behind them.

"Now I must show you something. Pay attention, your very life depends on it."

Raising his right hand, he formed a sign in the air, then made it again more slowly. I imitated it.

"No, you got it backwards. Here, stand by my shoulder and watch again."

I stood beside his right shoulder and watched him make the sign, then made it myself. He nodded with approval.

"This is the sign of passage into the chambers of our order. Never reveal it, and never forget it."

Before escorting me to my room, Dru offered to replace my drab Muslim coat with a new tunic of native Egyptian cut, more elegant in appearance and of finer cloth. I declined with thanks. My camel hair coat, though simple in design, was strong and well adapted to use in the wastelands. I could see at a glance that the Egyptian tunic was less practical. It would not have held together from one moon to the next under hard wear.

He summoned back the attendants, who took off my caul and order robe and showed me how to fold them into a leather travel pack designed to be worn over the shoulders. I dressed, and with pack in hand, followed Dru along the tiled hallways and up a marble stair to my bedroom. Martala was already waiting there as we entered, standing demurely by the side of a huge bed in a robe of flowered yellow silk that tied at the waist, with fingers folded together over her groin and head bowed. She had been washed, and her glossy dark hair bound up with tortoise shell combs. For the first time I realized the grace of her neck. She was quite an attractive young woman, with the dirt scrubbed from her face and hands, and had I possessed anything between my legs I might have found her enticing.

"I will leave you two alone," Dru said, eyeing the bed and smiling at me. "Don't stay up too late. We depart the third hour after midnight."

He closed the door behind him as he left. I tossed my pack to Martala, who caught it by instinct.

"Put this away. Then fetch the chamber pot. My bladder is stretched like a drum."

As I sat on the bed and pulled off my boots, the pack hit me in the side of the head.

"Put it away yourself! I am sick of being a servant."

"If you weren't my servant, you would be dead," I reminded her.

"I am not your servant," she said in a voice louder than necessary. "Remember that, Alhazred. This is a pose, nothing more. I am no man's servant."

"Why not open the window screens and shout it to the world?"

She frowned at me. With a petulant thrust of her lower lip, she stalked around the bed, reached beside it, and banged the brass chamber pot down between my feet. It rang like a bell. Fortunately, it was empty.

"A good servant anticipates her master's wishes," I said as I hiked up my coat and urinated into the pot.

She went to the window and threw open the screens, and for a moment I thought she actually would shout out our deception, but she merely stood there, staring west across the ribbon of the Nile, which shimmered in the rays of the setting sun.

"They branded me," she said in a small voice.

"What?" I thought I had heard her incorrectly. "They did what?"

Frowning but not looking at me, she slid the loose neck of her robe down her right shoulder, to reveal a small scarlet mark no larger than my thumbnail. With a shrug, she covered herself once again. Having felt the touch of hot iron on my own bare skin, I remained silent, not knowing what to say to cheer her.

"It is a mark of admission," I murmured at last. "It must be the practice of the order to brand all servants of its members."

"What are we doing here?" she asked in a normal tone. "It is dangerous."

"I came to Egypt to learn, and there is great wisdom in this Order of the Sphinx, I can sense it."

"Little good it will do if they kill us."

"Haven't you heard? I am the chosen instrument of the dark man."

This brought a smile to her lips. She turned to face me, leaning back on her hands against the window sill.

"How do you like being a servant?" she asked.

"As little as you."

The bed was filled with pillows of down so soft and thick, I almost sank from sight when I stripped naked and lay among them. Martala curled herself in her silk robe on the floor under the window, without being instructed to do so. I almost spoke to ask her to share the bed, since it was ample in size for two, but I held my tongue. Better not to accustom her to such luxury, as we were unlikely to encounter it often in our travels. I lay wondering to myself how I had come to acquire a traveling companion, and could find in my memory no single moment when I had agreed to such an arrangement.

My dreams were broken, and troubled by bubbling vats of noxious liquids and distant screams from throats that seemed less than human. Robed priests stood in groups around the vats with long wooden paddles, or hurried down dark corridors with obscure objects in their arms. I stood in a dimly lit chamber of stone, before walls lined with row upon row of cylindrical jars of translucent green glass, each bearing a label of papyrus, but what was written on the labels, I could not read in the shadows.

"Invite me in, Alhazred."

I recognized the dry voice of the dark man, and turned to seek him, but the dim chamber had vanished and I saw only utter darkness and felt a fluttering breeze against my face. Through the void a tapping reached my ears. Walking forward, I puzzled to myself what might create such a curious noise, but before I could reach a conclusion, the rattle of a door woke me.

The old man with the fluttering hands entered carrying an oil lamp followed by two serving maids. He led me to a bath chamber and supervised my bath while the women scrubbed me, then made sure that I was given everything I desired to eat and drink for my breakfast. Martala was scrubbed in the same water after I left it, and was allowed to forage in the kitchen while I ate. No doubt she found something to chew on. In the coolness of the night we left the house with our packs on our shoulders, along with Dru and his father, and descended the hill to the riverside, where a ferry waited at a private dock to carry us to the west bank. It was already laden with boxes and jars. Dru noticed my gaze upon them.

"They will be taken to a secure place not far from the Sphinx, and carried into our halls under cover of darkness."

He spoke in Greek, presumably so that his words would not be understood by the two boatmen in sleeveless vests and linen skirts who stood as his elbow, hoisting the sail on a wooden pulley badly in need of grease. I answered in the same language.

"What do the boxes contain?"

He merely smiled.

The ferry master was the elder of the two, a short man with a bulging belly and a black beard that bristled down his chest. He hugged the tiller and barked orders while his more agile companion handled the trim of the linen sail. For all his ill humor, the short man was competent at his task. He guided the boat upriver on the light breeze and let the current carry it back toward its landing place on the western side.

Four horses stood restlessly pawing the ground on the slope of the bank, their reins held in the hand of a patient servant boy. As our boat glided to the dock, a group of a dozen or so laborers tied it up and immediately began to wrestle the boxes and jars off the deck. They worked silently, without the usual jests and curses. We mounted and left them behind, riding westward away from the river.

"It surprises me that servants are permitted beneath the Sphinx," I told Dru when our horses chanced to walk close.

"We are all men of wealth, who could scarcely be expected to labor with our own hands, even in the sacred chambers."

"Each brother is allowed a single servant," said Feisel, who overheard my remark.

"Then you spoke in error when you said that each brother is known to only two others, for surely his own servant knows him."

"True, but a matter of no significance," said the elder man. "Once the servants enter beneath the Sphinx, they never leave its chambers."

I saw Martala's spine stiffen in the starlight.

Before approaching the Sphinx, we stopped in a small gully and changed into our order robes. It was with regret that I put Gor's polished skull into the travel pack, wrapped inside my blue coat. I had worn the skull so long, it felt strange not to have it dangling at my hip, but it would be instantly recognized by any brother who might have seen me walking in Memphis or Bubastis. Almost I put my dagger into the pack along with my other possessions, then thought better of it and slid its sheath into the top of my right boot, where it fitted snugly against the outside of my calf. The hem of the black robe fell to the ground, and even when I tied its sash around my waist, it was not pulled up enough to reveal the toes of my boots.

Martala pulled a white robe over her head, evidently the standard servant garb of the order, then folded and tied her long hair behind her neck as she had been instructed so that it hung in a kind of lobe, held into place by several silver pins. She approached and pretended to assist me in tying the sash at my waist.

"I don't want to be trapped under the Sphinx for the rest of my life," she hissed in my ear.

"Patience," I murmured.

She wound the caul of silk around my face, and I flipped up my monk's hood, just as Feisel emerged around a boulder in similar attire. I recognized him by his erect posture.

"Once we enter the chambers beneath the Sphinx, we do not speak. We communicate only by gestures of the hands. It is an ancient language known only to our order. You and your servant will learn it as you dwell among us."

The horses were left in the gully, tethered to stakes that had been driven into the earth. We continued on foot to the base of the great monument just as the first rays of morning light were striking its face. Its head seemed curiously small for its crouching lion body. I mentioned this to Dru as we walked across the sands toward the front paws of the beast.

"The statue has suffered many indignities over the centuries," he said. "It is reported in legend that when the Egyptian pharaoh Kephren dug it from the sands that had buried it, long before the coming of the Christians to this land, he found its head so worn by the wind that its features were unrecognizable, and had his own likeness carved in their place."

"To judge by your tone of contempt, I would say that you believe the legend false."

"When Kephren uncovered the Sphinx, its face was as clear as yours or mine. He had it chiseled away because he could not bear to look upon it."

"Why is that?"

"You will learn it in time. Have patience."

Although I had said much the same thing to Martala, it was irritating to hear it myself. Patience has always been one of my virtues. I contented myself with studying the serene profile of Kephren in the red morning light as we walked around the paws of the beast and approached its hindquarters. He had a fine nose for an Egyptian.

We stood in the chillness of the shadow beneath the buttocks of the monster and looked at the featureless, weathered stone. It was impossible to believe that a door existed, even though I knew this to be so. When Feisel made the gesture that dispelled the glamour, and the door appeared, I had to suppress an impulse to cry out in amazement. Martala caught her breath so suddenly, it made a noise in her throat. She stared at me, face pale, body shaking with terror. Dru pressed a stud in the doorjamb that opened the portal, and we watched it swing soundlessly inward. The flicker of torchlight beckoned from the corridor beyond.

Feisel entered, followed by Dru. I made a motion with my hand for Martala to follow. She hesitated and glanced across the desert, and I saw that she was considering a dash for freedom. This would surely prove fatal to both of us. Gently, I laid a hand on her shoulder. This touch steadied her nerves. She eyed my veiled face and took a deep breath, then stepped into the Sphinx. I followed behind her. Feisel, who waited for us, pressed a stud of stone on the inner edge of the door frame, and the massive slab swung shut, making a sound like the tone of a great drum as it sealed out the morning light.

Chapter 22

Ornate torches of cast brass flamed in iron brackets on either side of the door. The fluted design on their shafts had an ancient look, and was worn almost smooth by centuries of handling. Dru took one from its socket and led the way down a passage with a flat ceiling of unadorned stone. In a few steps we left the feeble glow at the entrance behind us and walked through complete darkness in the wavering pocket of torchlight between featureless stone walls. Only a faint gleam at the far end of the tunnel provided a sense of direction to our progress.

The passage appeared level, but the backward slant of our bodies as we walked showed that it sloped downward. I found myself raising my gaze, even though there was nothing to see on the ceiling apart from the marks left by the tools of the masons. The weight of the great creature crouched on the desert above our heads was palpable. It pressed on my chest like the hand of a god.

"When you leave this entrance tunnel, you must not speak," Feisel told me in a low voice. "Observe with attention all that you see. Tonight, I will teach you some of our hand language."

At the end of the passage, two brass torches burned in brackets of black iron on either side of a double door sheathed all over its surface in beaten gold. I looked back the way we had come, and saw only a tiny square of faint light. We had walked the full length of the Sphinx, and must be standing somewhere beneath its paws. Dru set his torch into an empty socket. With a light touch, Feisel pushed the doors inward. They swung open to reveal a long chamber illuminated by oil lamps along both walls.

We walked forward down a central aisle of green stone paving blocks the surface of which was raised a fingerbreadth above the slate-colored stone on the rest of the floor. On each side of this aisle rows of black columns supported the low flat ceiling. They were not the lotus columns so common to Egyptian temple architecture, but were square in shape and of massive thickness. I counted eleven pillars on each side. The ceiling was painted the deep blue of lapis lazuli, with numerous stars in gold leaf scattered across its surface.

As impressive as these features of the long chamber were, my gaze was immediately drawn to small plaques of gold mounted in the sides of the pillars facing the central aisle. Each was no larger than the flat of my hand, yet they were strangely compelling. I paused and leaned close to examine one of them. Its surface had been chased and carved into an illustration that showed a great tower struck by a blast of lightning. The crown of the tower crumbled to the earth, carrying with it the flailing bodies of a man and a woman. Flames licked up from the ruin.

Each of the black pillars had an image on its gold plaque, and all depicted scenes pregnant with allegorical meaning. I had time only to glance at the others, but resolved that when I found leisure, I would study them in detail.

Feisel stopped before a door of cedar wood. In contrast to the imposing double doors of gold through which we had entered the pillared hall, it was unadorned, and no larger than the entrance to the most humble of houses. Either it was formed of a single piece of wood, or the joints between its boards were too cunningly made to show themselves. Beside it stood a tall man in the black hooded robe of the brotherhood, his arms folded across his massive chest. The index finger and thumb of his right hand wore a harness of leather straps that held a curved steel blade. It jutted out from the tip of his index finger like the talon of a hawk. His cauled face betrayed no sign of his intentions.

With his right hand, Feisel made a series of gestures. I observed them with interest, and discovered that they were familiar. This was impossible, since I had never seen such gestures before, yet I understood their meaning. The desiccated flesh of the wizard Nectanebus had given me the gift of this strange tongue that was not spoken with the voice.

The master of the order conveyed through his gestures that I was a new member seeking admission to its inner chambers. The impassive sentry made a sign signifying that I should approach. I gave no indication that I understood, but waited for Dru to motion me forward. From the corner of my eye I saw Martala shift about on the balls of her feet like a nervous fawn, and wondered where her little dagger was hidden in her white servant robe.

The slender curved blade on the tip of the sentinel's finger gleamed with a blue luster in the lamplight. It could only be poison that caused the azure hue. He laid his right palm over my heart, and I felt the faint pressure of the tip of the blade against my chest. With great care, I raised my right hand and drew upon the air the sign of passage Dru had shown me the previous evening.

The guard did nothing, and fear chilled my heart that I had made a mistake and had inverted the symbol. After what seemed an eternity, but could have been no more than a few moments, he turned and took up a key that hung at his sash on a chain. Inserting it into the brass lock of the cedar door, he pushed it open and stepped aside to allow us to pass. Martala was not challenged, or even noticed. She stepped quickly around the guard, her eyes never leaving the tiny blade on his finger.

A strange smell hung in the air beyond the door of cedar. It was unlike anything I had smelled before, having something of the sweetness of incense smoke and something of the sourness of a leather tannery. We stood in a spacious square chamber, gawking upward at a lofty ceiling unsupported by pillars. It rose in the shape of a narrow vault, each level of stones along its sides stepped in further than the level below, their meeting place lost in shadow high over our heads. The sheer height of the roof inspired awe.

The unobstructed slate floor beneath the vault was dominated by a recumbent stone block half a dozen paces long and as high as my shoulder, upon which rested a replica of the Sphinx that was around ten cubits in length from its extended paws to its hindquarters. Flaming lamps on brass posts illuminated each corner of the pedestal. The idol crouched facing the cedar portal, so that it confronted all who entered the chamber as though in challenge. I looked at it more closely, and realized it differed in its details from the great statue above. Unlike the larger monument, its head was in correct proportion to its body, and did not bear the features of the pharaoh Kephren.

I stared at its face, trying to make sense of its pattern of curves and planes. In some obscure way they eluded my comprehension. I saw the face, yet did not understand it, and when I looked away it left no memory, only a vague unease that crawled at the base of my spine.

Two members of the brotherhood entered through a side passage as we stood before the idol. Ignoring our presence, they knelt on the slates beneath its extended paws with their arms crossed on their breasts, and murmured prayers in such low voices that I could not discern the words, periodically bowing their heads to the floor. They jerked open the fronts of their robes to bare their chests, and drawing small daggers from sheaths at their hips, slashed themselves between their nipples, then fell gasping forward so that their blood dripped between their hands. Only then did I notice the dried rust stains, imperfectly cleaned from the cracks between the slates. The pair pushed themselves to their feet with their black robes still gaping. Touching their right hands to the wetness on their chests, they then reached up to daub blood on the paws of the idol.

I would have continued to watch, but Feisel motioned us to follow and walked around the idol and through an archway on the opposite wall of the chamber. Beyond it stretched a corridor with numerous openings along both its sides. He took us into one of the rooms, where several oblong wooden boxes similar to those unloaded from Dru's ship lay on the floor. A bald man of middle years and a young woman whose hair was bound behind her neck with silver pins, both wearing the white garb of servants, knelt over one of the boxes, and with practiced skill opened its lid with hammers and chisels. The wooden pegs that secured the lid released their hold with a groan, and the lid clattered aside to reveal the linen-wrapped form of an ancient mummy, still covered with a thick layer of dust from its tomb.

Without ceremony, the man began to unwrap the bandages from the body. I saw that in addition to the corpse, the box held dried and blackened objects that had the look of human organs. After the final strip of linen had been pulled away, the man seized up an ax, and while the woman held the corpse in place, began to hack it into pieces. When the corpse was dismembered and beheaded, he lifted the parts, including the detached organs, with care from the box and transferred them to a large copper bin set on a two-wheeled cart. After them were thrown in the linen bindings. The pieces from the body were dropped into the bin with no regard to how they fell, but when the box had been emptied of the larger pieces, the servants took scrupulous care to transfer every tiny fragment that remained from the box to the bin.

With a gesture, Feisel indicated that we should follow the pair as they pushed the cart from the room and along the corridor to another larger chamber, in which four gigantic copper kettles filled with greenish-gray liquid bubbled over low fires. The kettles were round on the bottom, and rested on the rings of tripods inset with little metal wheels that allowed the kettles to be tilted. A dozen or so servants moved purposefully about the kettles, supervised by two black-cauled members of the order. The shaved heads of the male servants gleamed in the lamplight. Oil fed the flames beneath the kettles, giving off no smoke. Above each, a square vent opened into the stone ceiling to carry away the fumes from the burning.

The servants who had dismembered the mummy stopped their cart before the first kettle, which was being stirred by a short, fat man using a wooden paddle almost as long as the oar of a boat. Without speaking, they began to transfer the pieces of the corpse into the steaming liquid, having a care to let them slide in gently so that none of the liquid splashed onto their skin. The reason for this caution was at once apparent, when the floating body parts began to soften as though they were lumps of wax held to the flame of a candle. Even the linen bandages were added. All the while, the bald servant with the paddle never ceased to stir this stinking brew.

At another kettle that had evidently been boiling for an extended period, since its thickened liquid filled only half its volume, servants used metal rods to fish out bandages that had been whitened by the scalding water, then wrung them with iron pinchers to extract every drop from them before discarding them into an open barrel. One of the brothers watching over the second kettle took from a wall shelf a slender vial of red glass and a small tin cup, and carefully poured a measure of the dark potion held by the vial into the cup. He sprinkled this over the top of the kettle, just as though he were a master chef seasoning a stew.

Surely the brotherhood did not consume these ancient corpses, I thought as I watched. I felt no reluctance at eating human flesh, but the smells rising from the kettles turned even my strong stomach and made the gorge rise in my throat. I licked my lips and swallowed my saliva to keep myself from gagging, and behind me I heard Martala cough against her hand.

Feisel led us back along the corridor into an identical chamber where four round-bottomed kettles sat on tripods over fire places, but no fires burned beneath them. We watched servants tilt one of the kettles onto its side, and I saw that it was empty save for a scum of white powder that clung to the bottom. A brother of the order knelt with a wide-mouthed bottle of green glass in his left hand and a small spatula of lead in his right. He scraped with great care at the crusted whiteness and transferred it into the bottle. When not a trace remained in the kettle, he closed the bottle with a lead stopper and took it with him from the chamber.

We followed him into a long hall lined on both sides with shelves that were cut into the rock of the walls. Hundreds of similar green bottles, their tops sealed with lead plugs, rested on the shelves, each bearing a label of papyrus. With surprise, I recognized the room as the same that I had seen in my dream. I leaned close, and in the dim lamp light saw that the labels on the bottles were lettered both in Greek characters and in Egyptian hieroglyphics. The one I looked at bore a name, but it was unfamiliar.

Feisel led us down a narrow passage off from the main corridor into what I took to be the private living quarters of the brotherhood. We entered a large and well-furnished living hall. The servant who admitted us had a head so closely shaven that his hair resembled the stubble on the chin of a man just returned from the barber. He closed the door, shutting out the rustle of movement from the public passage. Feisel and Dru threw back their hoods and unwrapped the scarves from their faces with evident relief.

"We can talk here," Feisel said. "These are my private living chambers. This is my personal servant, Tanni, who attends to all my needs while I am beneath the Sphinx."

The slender young man bowed at me with a solemn expression and withdrew through an archway. I put back my hood and peeled away my scarf, then handed it to Martala, who shook it and folded it. Feisel sat on a pillow-covered couch and gestured for me to take a seat beside him. Dru threw himself carelessly into a chair opposite and regarded me with interest.

"What do you think of our work?" the older man demanded, studying me with his flint-gray eyes.

"You are rendering the bodies of the ancient Egyptian dead into their essential salts, and storing them in glass vessels."

"Why do you think we do this?" Dru asked.

"The bodies of the dead have curative value in healing disease, and may be used for certain potions and unguents to produce occult effects."

Dru made a sound of disgust in his throat, and Feisel suppressed a smile. We waited while his gloom-faced servant returned with a tray containing bread and cheese, and a leather-covered flagon of red wine. He poured wine into three silver cups and set them before us, then withdrew.

"You don't really believe that is our work?" Dru said.

I shook my head, looking at the two of them over the rim of my cup.

"If that were so, you would not store the salts separately, or label them with such care."

"You will learn our secret soon enough. Today, there is no work for you. I wish you only to wander the halls and acquaint yourself with the processes we use to render out the essential salts of the dead. Tomorrow, I will assign you some plausible task that will justify your presence to the other members of our order. Watch and learn all you can. The dark god to whom we give service has placed you here for a reason. Let it unfold itself."

"May I ask you a few questions?"

Feisel stretched his legs and regarded me with an indulgent smile.

"What is it that puzzles you?"

"When we entered the chamber of worship, I saw that the idol on the pedestal was the same as that of the great Sphinx above us, save only for its head. Why does the head differ?"

"The Sphinx is old. Only our order has any comprehension of how ancient it truly is. Legend teaches that it was carved by Kephren, who built one of the three pyramids it seems to guard, but this is false. Kephren merely uncovered it from the sands that had buried it up to its neck, and had its face recarved in his own image. What you saw in our hall of worship is the true visage of the Sphinx. It is the face of a god from beyond the stars, he who wanders the desert regions of the world, the herald and messenger of the Old Ones."

"Do not speak his name," Dru cautioned with a finger to his lips, smiling in apology. "We never speak his name in these halls. It is a superstition, but we have adhered to it for centuries."

"The face is curiously uncouth, and difficult to hold in the memory," I said.

Feisel nodded his agreement.

"It depicts the true face of the god, which is not a thing of our time or place. Our human minds are too frail to comprehend it. Those who gaze long upon it without turning away invariably go mad. It was for this reason that the pharaoh Kephren had it chiseled away, and replaced it with his own features."

"That single act of hubris earned Kephren the enmity of the dark god for eternity. Long have we searched for his linen-wrapped corpse," Dru said, a redness in the depths of his dark eyes.

"What would you do if you found it?"

"All this, you will learn in time. It is best that you become acquainted with our work in stages, so that it will not overwhelm you."

"Let me ask another question," I said, changing the subject. "What are the gold plaques I saw in the hall of pillars?"

Feisel tore a piece from the loaf of bread and tossed it to me. I tore it into two parts and cast one at Martala, who caught it and began to chew at it. I observed with approval that she had not spoken since entering Feisel's private chambers. She was leaning her place. Perhaps she would make a useful servant after all.

"The golden tablets are said in the annals of our order to be as old as the Sphinx itself," Feisel told me. "What they depict, no one knows. What their purpose may be is a matter of conjecture, but one view is that they show scenes of prophetic importance."

"They are obscure," Dru said carelessly, a piece of cheese between his fingers. "Do not waste your time with them."

"They interest me. That one depicting the collapse of a great tower—"

"Perhaps the fall of the Tower of Babel, who can say? What does it matter, when that event took place countless generations ago?"

"The pillars are inscribed with the Hebrew letters," I observed to Feisel.

"It is an ancient language. Some say it was the original language of the angels in heaven, that was taught to Adam and Eve before they were expelled from the Garden of Eden."

"The golden tablets are a relic of the past," Dru said, drinking deeply. He did not see, or chose to ignore, the disapproving glance of his father. "No member of our order pays them any attention."

"Yet we draw our strength from the past," Feisel said, more to his son than to me. "We honor it for the wisdom it teaches."

"The living past, yes," Dru said. "Not the dead past. When we make the past live it yields up its secrets, but the mystery of the golden tablets is lost in time."

Feisel spent the next hour teaching me the rudiments of the sign language used by the brotherhood. Since, as I had discovered, I already knew it thanks to the ingestion of the finger of Nectanebus, I proved an apt pupil, and he praised my quickness and my memory.

"Tell me what you can about the traitor in your brotherhood," I said when opportunity presented itself. I cared not a fig about this traitor, but I was eager to present the mask of a loyal servant of the dark god.

243

"Our most precious scrolls have been vanishing from our scriptorium," Feisel said, his face darkening. "Last month, we lost two, the month before, three."

"What do these scrolls contain?"

"They are a record of our work, as you shall learn in the course of your stay with us."

"Not ancient wisdom?"

"In a manner of speaking, but the scrolls themselves are quite new."

"The ink is barely dried on them before they vanish," Dru said bitterly.

"It must be one of the brotherhood, since the servants never leave," I said.

Feisel nodded.

"Of that we are certain. We have instituted a rigorous search of the clothing and packs of all brothers who leave these halls, but as yet it has provided no hint of the traitor."

"I do not know how I am to find this traitor," I told him with a shake of my head. "I have no knowledge of spying or treachery. I am only a young man of the household of the king of Sana'a."

Feisel startled me by leaning forward and taking my hand between his. His fingers felt dry and cold against my skin.

"Our lord has faith in you. He has placed you among us, as a cunning wolf among the goats. You will not fail."

I clasped his hands in mine and smiled reassurance, inwardly wondering what barbed trap I had allowed myself to wander into in my arrogance. What would Feisel's regard for me be when I failed to produce his traitor? Perhaps it was in my interest to search for this spy. Even if I could not identify him, I could always accuse some innocent member of the order. That would satisfy the bloodlust of Feisel and his son. It would not placate Nyarlathotep, and I was more concerned about the wrath of the dark man than about all the secret brotherhoods in Egypt. I did not wish to give him reason to seek me out. It was bad enough that I had to endure his presence in my dreams.

Dru showed me to my own private rooms and left me alone with Martala. All their illumination came from oil lamps that hung on iron brackets set into the stone of the walls, the severity of which was softened by hanging tapestries depicting Egyptian pastoral scenes. There were two rooms, an outer work chamber with a writing table and several chairs set on a rug of good quality from Persia, and an inner sleeping room containing a comfortable bed, a wooden wardrobe, and a side table with a basin and pitcher of water for washing. It was Martala's task to empty the chamber pot and replenish the water in the pitcher, as well as to sweep the floor and make up the bed. No other servant would enter our rooms, Dru had assured me with a sidelong leer at the girl. I wondered if his own servant was a woman.

"What do we do now?" Martala asked, sitting on the bed. She bounced up and down on its mattress to test its softness.

"We play our parts. I wander about like a curious brother and learn the work I am to do, and you go among the drudges in the kitchens and laundry and acquire the skills of a good servant."

"Do we search for the spy?"

I saw the eagerness in her ice-gray eyes, so like the eyes of a wolf, and suppressed a smile.

"Why not? Learn what you can. Be discreet. If you discover any matter of interest, let me know."

The prospect of spy hunting made her cheerful. It would distract her mind from the less elevated aspects of her present situation, and she might even learn something useful.

Time was kept in the chambers beneath the Sphinx by means of water clocks. Each hour a bell rang in a small alcove at the end of the main corridor, the number of strikes signifying the hour of day. There were no locks, and indeed no doors, in the public halls and chambers. Each brother and his personal servant roamed freely where duty required, as did the members of the working staff of the kitchen and other rooms run by the general servants. They fulfilled the same utilitarian tasks necessary in any large institution or palace, as well as a number of others peculiar to the order.

Bread was baked and meat roasted in the ovens. Plates, cups, and knives were set out on the long tables in the public dining hall, where the brothers ate by raising their cauls to the level of their noses. These dishes required scouring after the daily meals. Dirty robes and bed linen were collected and washed in the laundry. Slops were emptied into the pits in the hall of defecation, and periodically these had to be cleaned out with buckets. The oil lamps that provided light were in constant need of replenishment. Those who maintained the bubbling kettles fed them an endless stream of water and various chemicals that came from jars and metal cylinders similar to those I had seen unloaded from Dru's ship. The scriptorium, where the scrolls of the order were copied and stored, required its own supply of lamps, pens, ink, and papyrus rolls.

While Martala was off discovering the joys of manual labor, I walked the length and breadth of the corridors and halls until I gained a fair sense of the location of everything of importance. The size of the brotherhood surprised me. There must have been several hundred members of the order dwelling beneath the desert in these interlocking rooms, each with his own servant, and many general servants besides, so that the total number in the chambers beneath the Sphinx could not have been less than half a thousand. All their purpose appeared to consist of nothing more than rendering down corpses in the great copper kettles into neatly labeled glass jars filled with powdered gray salts. How this was of any interest to Nyarlathotep, or indeed to the brotherhood itself, was not apparent.

I returned to my rooms at the sounding of the bell for the eighth hour of evening. Martala awaited me. She had procured a tray with wine from the kitchen, but I had already eaten an evening meal in the dining hall and was not thirsty. I waved it off, and she set in on my writing table.

"What have you learned?" I asked wearily. The effort to comprehend all the details of the order chambers taxed my mind.

"This is a mad place," she said. "Everyone labors here to no purpose. All they do is cut up corpses."

"I am inclined to agree. Perhaps we will learn more tomorrow."

When I went into the bedchamber, she followed and began to disrobe me without being instructed. I allowed her to strip me naked. She folded my black robe and put it away on a shelf of the tall wardrobe with care. Closing its doors, she turned and noticed me watching her.

"What?"

"I was wondering if some djinn had stolen away your soul and replaced it with another."

"If I am to be your servant, I may as well act like it."

"You will get no argument from me."

She prepared scented oil and clean linen cloths by the wash basin, and proceeded to use a cloth to wash my body. The water, though unheated, refreshed me. More than once I saw her eyes wander to the ruin between my thighs. I let it pass without remark. Little wonder she would be curious. Although my renewed glamour veiled me from the eyes of most men, Martala's gift of scrying vision allowed her to pierce it, so I knew she saw me as I really was, not as I appeared to others. Once, her hand strayed to my groin with a gentle touch, almost of pity.

She disrobed and prepared herself to lie for the night upon the rug beside the bed. I crawled onto the bed and slid myself beneath its soft sheet and woolen blanket. The air in the chambers under the desert was not cold, but neither was it warm. She cupped her hand around the flame of the last table lamp that burned in our rooms and blew it into darkness with her breath.

"No, don't lie on the floor. You may as well share the bed, since it is large enough for two."

Her warm body pressed against my naked back and buttocks. Her foot slid down my calf as she made herself comfortable, and a sigh of contentment escaped her lips. I felt it on the back of my neck. Reflecting that it was poor practice to give favors to servants, I allowed myself to sleep.

It was utterly dark when I woke. For a moment I strained for some glimpse of moonlight or starlight, then remembered where I lay and almost laughed. No light would shine into these rooms for the rest of eternity, unless it was lamplight. A faint cry caught my attention. I stilled my breath and listened. It came again, very distant and almost inaudible, but I recognized it without difficulty. It was the scream of a man undergoing torture. Had not similar cries sounded from my own lips? It was not a sound that I would ever mistake.

"What is it?" Martala whispered in my ear, or where my ear should have been.

Some impulse made me cast off the blanket and slide my feet over the bed.

"Strike tinder and light a lamp. We will see."

She was able to find my tinder box where she had set it in preparation the evening before, and soon had a hand lamp flickering. I dressed quickly in my order robe and cauled my face, then waited for her to finish putting on her servant robe. My dagger sheath I slid into my boot, but my dagger I carried in my hand. We left the outer chamber and crept down the passageway. Most of the lamps had been extinguished at that late hour. Not another person stirred. All the doors to the private chambers remained shut.

The cries guided us. We crossed the central corridor without encountering anyone and entered a series of connecting halls that looked little used. Dust lay upon the floors. The screams of agony became louder. They led us to an unlit room containing several crates. Another scream slit the air like the blade of a knife, and seemed to come from the blank wall at the far side of the room. I stared at it in bafflement as Martala raised her lamp. There was obviously no secret passage. The wall was a solid slab of rock.

Yet the floor was not completely solid. I noticed a faint flicker from the edge of one of the crates, and moving around it, saw that it half covered a tarnished bronze grate in the floor. The grate was no more than a cubit square. Taking the lamp from Martala, I set it on the opposite side of the wooden box so that its light would be shadowed, and approached the floor grate. We both dropped to our hands and knees.

A wave of heat washed over my cauled face. It was like the air that rises from a fire. With disappointment, I saw that the grate was baffled with a plate a few inches below it so that it was impossible to see into the lower chamber. A faint lamp glow leaked around the edges of this baffle. I had not even suspected that the chambers beneath the Sphinx had two levels.

I heard a sound that I recognized all too well as the sear of red-hot iron applied to living flesh. A man shrieked involuntarily as pain drove the air from his lungs.

"Where is the location of the urn?" someone asked in a strange language. The tongue was unfamiliar, but I knew its meaning thanks to the flesh of the wizard's finger.

"Horus will flay the skin from your bones and burn your flesh to ashes," another man gasped in the same tongue.

His voice held a hollow echo, and his accent seemed utterly alien in my ears. The very sounds were as ancient as time-weathered stones. He spoke a string of words at his tormentor that could only have been curses. These were cut off by the hiss of hot iron against flesh. Another brother spoke a sharp word of caution, and whoever held the iron reluctantly removed it.

"He knows nothing more," the second man said in Greek.

"Can we be certain?" the inquisitor asked.

"I am certain. He knows nothing of value."

The clatter of the iron rod as it was cast down rang loudly through the grate and sent a wave of heated air upward. For a few moments there was an ominous silence.

"Horus will avenge me," the tortured man spat in his ancient tongue.

The brother who seemed to have authority chanted an incantation in the language I recognized, from the few phrases I had encountered, as the guttural tongue of the Old Ones. A sound came that was difficult to describe, a soft sound, like a sack of salt upturned and poured onto the floor. No further word was spoken.

Martala stared at me, her face strangely lit from below by the redness from the grate. I saw the thought in my mind mirrored in her eyes.

"Necromancy," she whispered.

Chapter 23

The days passed with the regular monotony of the drips from a water clock. I was assigned the task of copying scrolls in the scriptorium, and labeling and keeping close records of the collection of green glass cylinders filled with corpse dust, which numbered in the thousands. Feisel's purpose was to place me close to the scrolls, so that I would become immediately aware when one of them was stolen. He did not reveal to any other members of the order that I was an agent of Nyarlathotep, since he feared alerting the spy.

As a new brother, I was not permitted access to the locked storage room at the rear of the scriptorium where the more important documents were kept. I spent my days seated on a high stool, bent over an angled table stained with centuries of spilled ink, squinting in the uncertain lamp light with my reed pen poised over parchment or papyrus sheets. There were four rows of similar tables. The documents I copied were of minor significance. Only the elder scribes handled the more precious scrolls, which were closely watched whenever they were taken from the locked room.

I was assigned a number for identification. All brothers of the order under the Sphinx were known only by numbers. As the head of the order, Feisel bore the number two. The god himself was the monad. Each time two brothers communicated with sign gestures, they identified themselves by their numbers. This was necessary since no personal jewelry or emblems were worn on their black robes. It was apparent to me that it would be an easy matter for a spy to adopt the number of some other brother, and in this way penetrate to chambers beyond his usual duties. I mentioned this weakness in the procedure to Feisel, but he was reluctant to change a system of identification that had served the order well for so many generations.

Martala and I spoke little about what we had overheard through the floor grate that first night, since we had so little information upon which to speculate. That it was necromancy, I had scant doubt. No living man had spoken that ancient tongue for at least a thousand years. In some way the work involved the bottles of essential salts. After the mummies were reduced to their dust, they waited on their shelves until called for by one of an elite group of brothers. Which bottle was chosen depended on its perceived importance, as I learned by studying the records. The corpse of a king or court magician seldom waited on the shelf more than a few days after its preparation, but the corpse of a minor nobleman of the pharaoh's palace might remain neglected for years, as the dust covering its lead seal attested.

The particular bottle chosen was carried down a concealed back stair to the lower level by one of the elite brothers, who did not participate in the work of the upper level, and always remained aloof and apart from the rest of us. Regular members of the order were never permitted to descend the stair to the deeper level. Its cedar door was concealed behind an elaborate tapestry that depicted a battle between the Egyptian gods Horus and Set, and no brother ever spoke of it, even though the youngest and most recent knew of its existence. The removal of the bottles to the lower level invariably occurred during the hours of night when most of the brothers lay in sleep.

At last, after several weeks as a copyist of scrolls beneath the Sphinx, Feisel decided that I was ready to be shown the true work of his brotherhood. It was with keen curiosity that I accompanied him through the door and down the hidden stair. The lower level was not as large as the upper level. Six archways on either side led off from the central corridor. Oil lamps hanging from wall brackets provided ample light, but the corridor possessed a utilitarian air, being unadorned by furniture, paint or tapestries.

It was shortly after ten of the clock. Feisel led me to the third opening on the left wall, and waited for me to enter the chamber ahead of him. I saw no one in the other rooms into which I glanced as I passed their archways. However, this room was almost crowded. It was not large, and square in shape. Set in its center was a chair made of wood. I noted that it was unusually sturdy in construction, including its arms, and also that it was stained with a small amount of dried blood on the back. The chair rested within a flat pan made of copper that had been scoured so clean, its inner surface gleamed in the lamp light. This odd piece of furnishing had a rim no higher than the span of a hand that ran all the way around its four sides.

Behind the chair, a brother sat at an angled writing desk similar to those used in the scriptorium, his reed pen in hand, a blank scroll spread before him. Two other brothers looked up from the glowing iron brazier they were tending to nod with deference at Feisel. I wondered how they recognized him when he had not delivered his identifying hand signal, then realized that his uncommon height and military bearing set him apart. He moved with a posture of authority, as one in complete command. The brazier rested on an iron tripod. Heat emanated from its orange bed of embers in waves, though the glowing charcoal made almost no smoke. I looked up and saw a square vent hole in the ceiling above the brazier. No doubt it led to a bronze grill similar to the one through which Martala and I had listened.

One of the two white-robed servants in the room took a green glass cylinder from a table against the wall and removed its lead stopper. He tilted the vessel and poured out its contents in a pile on the flagstones of the floor just in front of the chair. Several camel-hair hand brushes and a hand sweeper of pig's bristles lay on the table beside a coil of fine white ropes that appeared to be made of silk. The floor was uncommonly clean, so clean that I noticed its cleanliness, even though it is not my habit to pay attention to such things. Indeed, the entire chamber had been so dusted and swept and scoured that any of its surfaces might have served as a banquet table. No speck of dust, no wisp of straw, no spider's web, was to be found in the corners.

One of the brothers stepped toward the pile of dust, but Feisel waved him aside, and he withdrew backward with a bow. Feisel motioned me to approach. I stood behind his right shoulder. The two servants stepped nearer and stopped on either side of the mound of dust, all that remained of the corpse of a once-living human being. Feisel raised his hand, and I watched closely as he drew a symbol in the air. I recognized it as the sign of the *caput draconis*, the Head of the Dragon, an astrologer's glyph used to designate the point of intersection of the path of the moon with the path of the sun, when the moon is ascending. He uttered a brief incantation in the language of the Old Ones.

My ear for such things has always been good. I had no trouble committing the words of the chant to memory. However, the effect of its utterance startled me to such an extent that I almost allowed the words to slip away, even though I had expected to see precisely what transpired under my gaze. At the last word, the mound of essential body salts became molten, as though transformed to liquid wax, and began to expand into an irregular mass. The air grew distinctly cooler. I wondered as I watched if it were only my imagination, but I realized later that the coolness was due to the extraction of moisture from the air, which was drawn into the reddening and obscene wetness that lay quivering on the floor.

It resembled nothing I had ever seen, save perhaps the aborted fetus of a horse I had chanced to observe at the age of fourteen in the royal stables at Sana'a. Wetly glistening with blood and other fluids similar to the clear slime from the nose that only comes with sickness, it quivered and quaked, opening before my wondering eyes into the body of a woman. In seconds the bloody mass covered itself with white skin, and gray hair sprouted from its skull. Its eyelids sprang open, and its parting lips emitted the most repulsive shriek it has ever been my misfortune to hear. It was a woman of some fifty years or more of age. The shape of her head and the bones of her face were unnatural yet strangely familiar. It was several moments before I recognized them as the same features I had seen on the ancient temple statues at Memphis. She lay naked but an instant, then leapt to her feet.

Only the quickness of the two servants prevented her from dashing out the archway of the chamber. They caught her upper arms with practiced precision and forced her backward until she was compelled to step over the rim of the flat copper pan and sit in the wooded chair. She babbled in the language of the old race of Egypt, which was not unknown to me thanks to the flesh of Nectanebus.

"What is happening? Holy Mother Isis save me."

The brother I judged to be of lesser authority took up the coil of ropes and bound her arms and ankles to the chair. Her agitation soon gave way to bewilderment. She stared around at us as though we were all demons from hell. In truth, she was a pitiful sight, sitting naked, her flat breasts sagging over her wrinkled belly, her gray hair disordered upon her bony shoulders. Yet I felt nothing. Any pity I might have possessed had been beaten from me by the rays of the sun upon the anvil of the Empty Space.

Feisel stepped back and allowed the brother who seemed to be in command of the night's entertainment to approach the shivering woman.

"What do you know of magic?" he demanded in the same ancient language she had spoken.

She shook her head and stared at his black caul. His accent must have sounded strange in her ears. He repeated the question more slowly.

"Nothing, I swear. It is forbidden. I know nothing of such things. Are you a demon?"

"What do you know of hidden treasure?" he asked, ignoring her words.

"Nothing. I do not understand, what treasure? Where am I?"

It would be tedious to describe the entire interrogation, which was of a routine order. During life, the woman had been attached to the nursery of the Egyptian pharaoh Tethmosis, in charge of the many nursemaids who provided milk for his dozens of infants, born from the wombs of his many concubines. Her name was Nemeruma. It was asked of her only to verify her identity, not so that she might be addressed in a more personal way. Throughout the interrogation she was treated as a slave, or less than a slave—an object. The extended list of questions had two primary purposes, exemplified by the first two questions. One was to learn any fragment of magical lore that might be gleaned from the thrashing floor of history, and the second to discover the hiding places of ancient treasures.

This was the source for the great wealth of members of the Order of the Sphinx, I reflected as I watched the hot iron applied to her sagging breast. In so ancient a land as Egypt, gold and other treasure must lie everywhere, buried in the earth, hidden in caves in the hills, beneath the foundations of forgotten temples. In the ordinary course of events, when those who hid treasure died, it remained in its hiding place undiscovered. Hence the popularity of the necromantic arts. All other necromancers were as children in comparison with this black-robed brotherhood. Individual necromancers sought the treasures of individuals, but the order pursued the treasures of an entire race.

Gold was the prize that fueled their lamps and paid for their fine houses and rich city apparel, but knowledge was even more coveted than gold. For this reason, the most sought after mummies were those of necromancers and sorcerers. Almost as valued were the mummies of kings and queens, since they were privy to many secret things, and to the methods of worship and compulsion of the gods that had been lost in time. The ancient Egyptians had not merely adored their gods, but had commanded them. Methods for controlling the gods were the most valued of all secrets.

As this last thought passed through my mind, I realized it might have some bearing on the theft of the scrolls, and resolved to examine the records of the resurrections at the first opportunity.

When the interrogator believed he had extracted all the information of value possessed by the woman, who had fainted from the pain of the burning iron, he turned to Feisel. The head of the order nodded his permission. Stepping close to the chair so that the hem of his robes almost touched the lip of the copper pan, the chief torturer made the sign I recognized as the *cauda draconis* of astrologers, the Tail of the Dragon, which is used to signify the crossing of the path of the moon downward through the path of the sun. He uttered the same brief chant that Martala and I had listened to through the floor grate, and the woman instantly collapsed into a sifting of gray dust.

Sweat beaded my forehead beneath my silk caul. The air had suddenly become moist. The two servants, who stood ready with brushes in their hands, came forward and used great care to sweep the dust from the chair into the copper pan beneath it. They removed the chair and collected the dust from the pan. It was transferred on small lead scrapers back into the glass bottle, then resealed for future use.

As I watched, I meditated on this ultimate indignity. It was not sufficient to resurrect the dead in their terror and confusion, and torture their bodies for secrets that most of them did not possess, but this same procedure could be repeated again and again, as often as the bottle was opened and the incantation uttered. If a king did not give up the resting place of his treasury during the initial questioning, he might on the second occasion, or the tenth. Even to my jaded sense of morality this repetition of outrage had an evil air.

I accompanied Feisel back to his private rooms. Dru was absent in Fustat, supervising another cargo of mummies, and Martala was occupied with servant work. We were alone save for Feisel's own servant, who did not emerge from the inner rooms. Feisel gestured for me to sit and I complied silently. The habit of not speaking was difficult to relinquish.

"Now you know everything about our work, Alhazred."

"I had surmised much during the past few weeks, but now I have seen everything."

Feisel laughed, something he did rarely. His throat rasped with the effort.

"You have yet to see the interrogation of a sorcerer. What we witnessed today was nothing."

"Will the woman be awakened from death again?"

"Probably not. She knows little of value. Still, she will be preserved with the others in case at some future time her knowledge should prove of use."

"How many times can a corpse be resurrected?"

"There is no limit of times in the abstract, but in practice impurities always find their way into the dust, no matter how much care is taken to keep it clean. After a dozen restorations, the thing that is brought back is not coherent enough to offer useful answers."

Finally I asked the question that had burned in my mind throughout the interrogation.

"Is it possible to resurrect the body of a man who has suffered the loss of a limb or other mutilation during life, so that once reborn, his body becomes whole?"

Feisel's keen gray eyes narrowed in thought.

"An interesting question. No, it is not possible. Flesh lost cannot be reconstituted from nothing. That is why we take such care that every spec of dust be gathered up and placed in the glass vessel. Should the dust that forms the head, for example, be lost, the next resurrection would result in a headless monstrosity."

My heart fell with his first few words. I listened to him expound on the need to keep contamination away from the salts, but my thoughts were elsewhere. I could not restore my face and manhood merely by dying and being resurrected. For a few days I had cherished this hope. I allowed it to pass from me with a philosophical shrug. I would find a way. If not this, then some other.

"I have a boon to ask of you," I said when he finished his discourse. "Give me access to the records of your resurrections, so that I may study them."

Interest quickened in his flint-gray eyes.

"Does this pertain to the thefts?"

"An idea, nothing more," I said with a shrug. "Let me prove it out or disallow it, as the fates decree."

To this, he gave ready agreement.

Deep in thought, I returned to my chambers. Martala sat waiting. She rose and washed me silently, having learned to respect my moods. Though my mind raced with speculations, I fell asleep in my bed in a few minutes, the warmth of the girl radiating against my bare back. Again I dreamed of vats, and dismembered mummies, and the screams of the tormented. This dream had been my constant companion while living under the Sphinx. The most maddening part was that tapping noise, which never had a source and seemed without meaning.

The next morning, I made my way to the scriptorium and spent the entire day reviewing the records of the resurrections conducted within the last year. By referring to historical documents kept by the order, I was able to verify the identities and stations in life of almost all the men and woman raised from the dust. As I suspected, the thefts were not random crimes of opportunity. Each had been carefully planned. I sought Feisel to inform him of my discovery, but he was absent from his usual haunts, so I went to speak with his son after the conclusion of the evening meal in the dining hall.

Dru sat lounging on a cushion-covered divan in his outer chamber when I entered. His servant, a slender young woman of African blood whose name was Vanoo, took my caul and escorted me to the seat. He was intoxicated, not an unusual condition for him at this hour of night, since he began his drinking in the morning, but the dreamy clouds left his eyes when I told him what I believed I had discovered.

"This is excellent work, Alhazred," he said slowly with the effort of keeping his words unslurred. "We should have noticed it before."

"You are accustomed to trust within the brotherhood. It has made you complacent."

"Perhaps. No traitor has defiled our ranks for centuries. It is a problem strange to our experience."

"When is the next necromancer assigned for resurrection?"

"Tonight." He smiled at me and waved his hand vaguely. "It is a matter usually concealed from the common ranks of our order, but my father chooses the times, and he keeps nothing from me."

He motioned Vanoo to him and drew her down to kiss her full lips. She glanced at me with an expression of complacent satisfaction as she held her mouth to his.

"Fetch my father. Say only that his son needs to have words with him."

She bowed her head slightly, answering him with the hand sign language of the order, and slipped out the door into the public corridor, closing it behind her.

"She can neither speak nor write, but her skills in the arts of love are unsurpassed," Dru said, drinking from his cup.

"A valuable servant."

"Just like your little Martala. She is young, that one. I don't sleep with children."

"She has other talents that serve me."

"Too intelligent," he said, laughing softly to himself. "You can't trust a servant with wits."

"Indeed."

When Feisel followed Vanoo into the chamber and exposed his head, his disordered gray hair and inconvenienced expression said that he was not happy at being summoned to his son's rooms like a servant. To curb his irritation, I told him my suspicions at once while Dru sat in silence. Feisel's face became somber. He seated himself beside his son and nodded as I made my points.

"Your reasoning is sound, if the records bear out your speculation."

"They do."

He put the tips of his index fingers together and pressed them to his upper lip beneath his hawk-like nose, deep in thought.

"You are the agent of the dark god. Therefore I am yours to command in all things. What do you require?"

"To be present as scribe at the interrogation tonight. Along with my servant," I added, as an afterthought.

"But you do not know the ancient tongue."

I told him that I had acquired it in the course of my private studies. He regarded me with surprise, and something more, a trace of fear.

"You are a man of many talents, Alhazred."

I described the rest of my plan, simple as it was, in a few words.

"It shall be so," he said.

The interrogation was set to commence at midnight. Neither Dru nor his father would be there, since it was not the custom, and I did not wish to alarm the thief by changing the natural order of things too greatly. Feisel went to arrange that I should replace the scribe scheduled to record the words spoken during the questioning. In all other respects, the interrogation would unfold in the usual way, save that this time it was no shivering matron who faced the ordeal of hot iron, but a potent magician well versed in all the black arts.

When I returned to my chambers, Martala prepared to wash me before bed, as was her custom. She became alert the moment she noticed my haste.

"Gather our possessions and conceal them somewhere near the cedar door that leads to the hall of pillars."

"Are we leaving this place? Thank the Goddess."

"Perhaps, perhaps not. If events fail to unfold as I anticipate, you can retrieve our things before morning, and no one will know they were ever there."

Once the thief was exposed and captured, my purpose beneath the Sphinx would be at an end. I had little reason to believe that Feisel would allow me to live. Why should he, when my silence would be assured by my murder? It was with this consideration I wished to prepare for the possibility of escape. It would have been wiser, I reflected as I shoved my dagger in its sheath into my right boot, to have allowed the thefts to continue, yet when faced with such a puzzle, who could resist seeking its solution? I had already learned as much as I would learn from the practices of the order. It seemed a good time to think about leaving.

Chapter 24

The torturers eyed Martala curiously when she entered the interrogation chamber with my writing instruments and blank scroll in her hands. It was not usual for the scribe to be accompanied by his servant, but the commands of Feisel were never questioned. She laid out the scroll along with my pens and ink on the ledge of the angled surface of the small wooden writing desk while I seated myself on the stool, then stood behind my left shoulder, hands folded before her groin in the manner expected of a female servant of the order.

Events proceeded as they had for the other resurrection I had witnessed, but with significant differences. Brothers and servants alike were armed with swords and daggers at their waists. There were seven brothers present, and five servants, all standing near enough to rub against each other, The closeness of the many bodies made the air stifling, an impression not helped by the heat that radiated from the glowing coals in the brazier on its iron tripod. Perhaps for this reason, a larger room had been selected than that in which I had witnessed the previous resurrection.

The senior brother poured the salts of the necromancer upon the stones before the chair and made the sign, then spoke the words. I had described to Martala what would follow, so she was able to control her terror. The sound in her throat was faint enough that only I heard it.

The wizard's flesh reconstituted itself as had the flesh of the matron, but he was neither frightened nor confused. He stood instantly with the agility of a cat and seemed to take in and comprehend his situation at a single glance. A tall man of cadaverous thinness, his ribs showed clearly on his chest and the muscles in his arms and legs stood out like ropes beneath his swarthy skin. His shaven head had the nobility of royalty, but cunning lurked in his wide-set dark eyes. As the servants stepped in from either side to seize his arms, he made a gesture with the spider-like fingers of his right hand. One of them fell back clutching his throat and collapsed to his knees. Another instantly took his place. Before the necromancer could act again, his arms were forced behind his back. One of the brothers held the point of a naked sword to his throat as a leather gag with a projection that was covered in a wad of linen was roughly jammed between his teeth. They thrust his hands into leather gloves and bound them behind his back. Rendered impotent by these measures, he could only glare as he was compelled to sit, then tied into his chair.

A brother took a glowing iron spike from the brazier. He used his thumb to peel back the necromancer's eyelids, and with efficient jabs poked out both eyes. The necromancer did not scream but endured it stoically. Heat from the iron cauterized the wounds so that they remained black holes when he raised his eyelids. A dagger was held to his throat until he felt its bite against his skin, and the gag on his mouth loosened just enough so that he would be able to speak around it. While all this was going on, the servant who had fallen holding his throat had become a corpse, and been dragged from the room without ceremony.

Apart from this single death, the interrogation of the ancient magician went smoothly. I copied down the questions, and the words that came from his lips, translating them into Greek as I wrote as was the usual practice. Each time the gag was loosened, the dagger was pressed to his throat, and he knew that any aggression would bring about his immediate death. He seemed resigned to his fate, with the calmness of a philosopher. He told his secrets freely, and only on a few occasions needed the prompting of the hot irons. At the conclusion of the affair, he was not reduced to his salts, but led away to some holding place with his arms still bound behind his back and the gag in his mouth, presumably to be questioned again on the following night.

The scroll never left my hands. This had been my purpose in asking Feisel to make me scribe. The ink had not yet completely dried upon its yellow-white surface of closely pressed papyrus strips as I carried it up the steps to the main level of the chambers and along the corridors to the entrance of the scriptorium. Martala walked beside me, her feet making even less noise than my own on the carpets that covered the stone floor. She carried my writing instruments, a pretext for her presence. I did not anticipate attack, since this was not the manner of the traitor, who worked by stealth rather than force. Even so, the skin of my back prickled and I listened for the slightest sound of a following footfall. Due to the late hour, the corridors were empty.

Since the beginning of the thefts, guardians had been assigned to stand watch at the entrance to the scriptorium at night when it was otherwise deserted. The cauled man who lounged beside the archway with back against the wall and crossed arms received my identifying hand signs impassively and allowed us to enter the outer chamber. On his right hand he wore the leather harness that supported the tiny poisoned dagger extending from his index finger, the usual weapon of the guardians beneath the Sphinx, who were few in number but who fulfilled their tasks with scrupulous attention. He turned to watch us through the archway as we crossed the main chamber, where the copying was done on rows of angled tables, to the iron-bound door of the locked rear room where the scrolls were stored.

I took out the key Feisel had given to me and unlocked the door, leaving it wide open as we passed into the vault. The scrolls were stored in sturdy wooden racks ranked along the stone walls. From where he watched, the guardian saw me slide the scroll I carried into one of the numbered niches in a rack. Locking the door behind us as we left the room, I crossed to the central writing table and gestured for Martala to open my ink well and hand me my pen, so that I could note the name, date, and location of the scroll in the record book. I ignored the guard, who laid his hand on the side of the arch and tapped the stone with the tip of his little poisoned dagger, as though impatient for us to be gone. The tapping sound was familiar, and I paused and smiled to myself when I recognized it.

Martala gathered up my writing instruments and put them away with care. As we left the scriptorium I made the sign of parting. The guard responded indifferently with the same sign. Martala did not look at him, but I saw a slight tremble in her shoulders as she passed. We walked the length of the corridor under his gaze and turned in the direction of the personal chambers.

Feisel and Dru waited for us in the archway to an empty room just around the corner, as we had prearranged. Both carried naked swords. I drew my dagger from my boot, and Martala made her little blade materialize from somewhere within her white servant robe. We had not long to wait. The sound of a single set of boots echoed distantly from the corridor we had just quitted. I heard a faint murmur. After a few moments, two pairs of feet made the carpeted stones speak, moving in the opposite direction.

"We have only a minute or two," Feisel whispered through his caul.

On our toes we made our way back to the scriptorium. The guard was absent. What subterfuge Feisel had arranged to draw him briefly from his post, I did not know, but it was essential to my purpose that he return quickly, so that his suspicions would not be aroused. I unlocked the sturdy door to the rear room, and we entered it together, all of us holding our breath to better hear the sound of approaching feet. I locked the door behind me, leaving us in complete darkness.

Due to an irregularity in the floor of the room, the storage racks along the walls did not touch them, but stood away from them a few palms. I had verified to my satisfaction earlier that there was enough room to squeeze behind the racks along the rear wall, although the space was tight. Feeling my way, I found the rack I had chosen and slid my shoulders against the wall until my chest pressed the wooden back panel of the rack. As arranged, Feisel did the same on the opposite side. Dru and Martala hid behind a second rack also located along the rear wall. I could hear Martala's excited breaths, but although we stood only a few feet apart I could see nothing in the darkness, nor could I even turn my head, so tight was the space.

The guardian returned almost before we were completely settled into our hiding places. I listened to his heavy footfalls on the stone floor of the outer chamber as he entered and walked around it. They came nearer, and the lock on the storage room door rattled. He was not supposed to possess a key. Feisel hissed softly when the door opened, spilling lamplight upon the wall. I stilled my own breath. It would be a poor time for a sneeze. The guardian cleared his throat harshly, so that I knew he stood directly in front of me, separated only by the thickness of the rack. I had deliberately hidden myself behind the niche where I had placed the latest scroll.

The rustle of fingertips against papyrus and the slide of the scroll against wood informed me when he took it from its place. So silent was the room, I distinctly heard the sound of the ties that bound it released, and the scroll unrolled as he examined its contents. Soft footsteps echoed from the other chamber, growing louder as they approached.

"Here it is," the guard said in a deep voice. "I watched where he put it."

"Give it to me," said a lighter voice. "Here is the false scroll. With luck, it will be a few days before the fools notice the theft."

"Now," I said calmly, and stepped out from the edge of the rack.

My three companions did the same, and before the two traitors could think to act, our blades were at their backs and throats.

A choked curse exploded from Feisel, as he glared at the slender man who stood at the point of his sword.

"When Alhazred voiced his suspicion, I refused to believe it."

His servant Tanni rubbed the short stubble of hair on his head and smiled in mock apology.

"Who is better placed to learn the secrets of the order than the servant of its leader?"

"How did you anticipate us?" the guardian demanded through his caul.

"Every theft was discovered within a few days after the interrogation of a wizard," I told him. "I reasoned that enemies of the order would seek its most precious secrets, the forbidden ways of commanding gods, which only were known to magicians of the black arts. It was easy to deduce that the thefts took place at night, since there are always brothers working here during the day, and because the scriptorium is guarded at night, that the guardian must be involved."

"I still don't understand," Dru said, keeping his sword between the shoulder blades of the veiled traitor. "The guardians never go to the surface. Tanni is forbidden from leaving, as are all servants. In any case, everybody is searched before we are permitted to depart. How did they get the scrolls out from under the Sphinx?"

Tanni stared at Dru with a silent sneer.

"Is it true that all are searched?" I asked Feisel.

His body stiffened as understanding came to him.

"All but the leader of the order. I am not searched. I alone pass out unchallenged."

Tanni laughed, enjoying the moment. I could not help but admire his coolness in the face of certain death.

"It was so easy to sew the scrolls into the lining of your robes. You carried them out yourself, old fool."

"Your confederate in my father's household will die," Dru said.

"We do not fear death," rumbled the sentry. "Our cause is righteous. You do the work of an alien demon from beyond the seventh sphere."

"You will both die," Feisel said in a voice like rasping steel. "Before you die, or after you die, you will tell us everything."

Tanni spun deftly away from Feisel's blade and plucked a dagger from beneath his robes.

"Ishtar protect us!" he cried out in a loud voice that echoed from the stones.

Dru laughed.

"No one will protect you."

"Drunken rake," Tanni said as he backed toward the archway. "Did you think we came alone?"

The cry from his lips was echoed by other voices. In moments the sound of many feet pounded in the corridor, and I heard the scrape of steel on stone. They fell upon us almost before we could turn to confront them. Four in number, all wearing the white robes of servants, they attacked like fiends from hell. For the next several minutes all my attention was occupied with avoiding the many blades that flashed in the dim lamp glow from the other room. The close quarters of the storage chamber worked to my advantage. It was too small a space to conveniently swing a sword, but ideal for the use of a dagger. I killed one man outright with a thrust through his heart, and disabled another with a cut across his forehead, which gushed blood and blinded him.

In the grappling madness I heard Dru scream in rage, and Martala's unending stream of curses. From outside the scriptorium came the sounds of running feet and the clash of weapons. For an instant my mind registered that the traitors had been prepared for discovery, and that they were far more numerous than anyone could have imagined. Then I was occupied dodging a vicious sword thrust that would have disemboweled me. I slipped in blood, and from my bent position saw Dru on the floor with his throat cut. Martala fought like a wildcat, spinning, leaping and slashing with her little blade. Tanni had lost his dagger. Feisel held his servant before him with an arm around his throat, using him as a shield while he fought with his free right arm.

A random sword cut knocked my dagger from my bloody grasp. There were others in the chamber fighting, but whether loyal members of the brotherhood or traitors was not evident in the chaos. I turned at a shadow of movement in the corner of my eye and saw the cauled guardian rush toward me. In desperation I pulled up the hem of my robe and wrapped it around my left forearm. It was a poor shield but better than nothing. He cut at me with his venomous right hand, trying to scratch my face, and I knocked it aside with the wadding of my robe.

The butt of a flailing sword hit me in the temple. I reeled backward. My shoulders and head struck the stone wall between two racks of scrolls, and I slid in a daze to the floor, numbness in my limbs. For a moment I thought of crawling behind a rack, but my body would not obey. The guardian bent over me. He ripped aside his silk caul to reveal his triumphant bloodlust. His youthful features were handsome beneath his shaved scalp, but neither Egyptian nor Arab. I had never seen one of his race, and had an instant to wonder at his origins.

"Our cause is just," he said harshly, his face almost touching my own. "We will triumph in the end."

By way of answer, I chose to bite his cheek. He howled in fury and pulled back, blood streaming down his chin and neck.

"Nyarlathotep!" I cried with all the strength in my lungs.

The effect was astonishing. The fighting ceased in the scroll room and in the large outer chamber of the scriptorium. For several heartbeats everyone stood frozen in place and held their breath. The sound of more distant battles echoed from the corridor. Then time moved again, and the fighting resumed.

"Your god is a fraud," the guardian said with a sneer on his lips.

He thrust his tiny poisoned blade deep into the flesh of my neck. There was almost no pain, only a prick like that of a thorn. Before he could remove it, Martala grasped him by the collar with her left fist and pulled him backward, ripping the blade away.

"Take care," I called to her, my voice strangely weakened. "His hand is deadly."

She did not even look at me, but kept her eyes fixed upon him as she searched for a vital place to bury her knife. As fast as she was, he was quicker. He regained his feet in an instant and while she watched his right hand to avoid the poisoned steel, he struck her with his left fist in the side of the face. She fell without a sound and lay motionless.

From the corridor came irregular cries. They were not the same as the former shouts of battle, but were screams of terror, each cut off as it reached its height of intensity. My mind strangely calm, I observed that the screams drew nearer. A kind of heat pulsed through my heart and moved in my veins. It made me weak, so that it was an effort merely to hold up my head.

The enraged face of the guardian loomed over mine, his left cheek a mass of bloody flesh.

"I would like to stay and watch the poison take its effect, which will be the work of only a few minutes," he hissed. "You will be intrigued by its action upon your body. Alas, I must carry this scroll to my masters."

He turned his hand so that his little blade was on its side and prepared to draw it across my throat. I found myself unable to raise my arm in defense, but could only meet his gaze with my own.

The sudden stillness was so absolute, it made him hesitate and turn to look over his shoulder at the rest of the room. Glancing past him, I saw Feisel standing with his back against one of the racks, bloody sword limp in his hand. It slipped from his fingers and clattered to the floor. Everyone stood as though carved from stone, staring at the doorway, which was filled with the body of a tall brother of the order. Yet it was not a member of the brotherhood, I corrected myself. The robe he wore beneath his cloak was of a different cut, and faded by wind and sun. Its dusty hem swept the floor and stirred the air into a breeze that touched my face with chillness. In it was the dryness of the desert and the scent of death.

With swift steps he walked in a circle around the perimeter of the room, touching with his black hand now this man, now that man as he passed, yet sparing them scarce a glance. As his bony fingers reached out, the man he was about to touch screamed, and as the touch was made, the cry cut off in his throat, and he fell to dust, so that his robe collapsed to an empty, rumpled pile on the floor.

The traitor who had been about to kill me found strength to leap to his feet and confront the dark man as he approached with his hand outstretched.

"I defy you, demon," he shrieked.

The dark man brushed his cheek, and he became dust.

He was about to continue past me, when I made a noise in my throat. He paused to regard me, as though with mild curiosity.

"I am your agent," I croaked. It was almost impossible to talk. My throat had swollen. "Cure me."

"That is not in my power," he said in a hollow tone.

Bending at the waist, he reached down to touch my head, and I thought my end had come. The touch did not kill me, but seemed to have no effect.

"I have delayed the action of the poison. What would have taken minutes will now take days. Travel above the Cataracts. That is where the poison was brewed. There you will find its antidote."

"Wait! How will I find it?"

He had already passed on, killing as he went. In seconds he departed from the scriptorium, and I heard the death cries of the traitors echoing in the corridors.

I tried to stand but found myself too weak even to move my legs.

Let me help you, my love, Sashi said within my mind.

Closing my eyes, I saw her beautiful face near mine. She breathed her perfumed breath into my parted lips, and strength returned to my limbs. The pain in my joints that had been increasing in intensity vanished.

Opening my eyes, I pushed myself to my feet. My head felt strange, as though it were a hollow bell. I recognized my dagger where it lay a few steps away, and retrieved it.

"How long can you counteract the effects of the poison?"

Not long. It is powerful and seeks your death. You must hurry.

The servants and brothers of the order who remained in the scriptorium stood or stumbled about as though entranced. Feisel knelt over the body of his son, weeping with such force that his square shoulders shook. He had torn away his caul. As I bent to the pile of clothing that had been the traitorous guardian and extracted my scroll, he watched me with wild eyes that streamed tears, but he seemed powerless to speak or act. I shoved the scroll under the sash of my robe and gathered the unconscious Martala into my arms. Her weight was slight. Not wasting a word or glance on Feisel, I left the scriptorium and walked along the corridors, making my way toward the cedar door that led to the hall of pillars and freedom from this accursed place.

Everywhere, the halls were littered with the bodies of the dead and wounded, and with little piles of clothing that had once been living men. Screams still echoed from the corridor of the private chambers, but my path led away from it. None of the brotherhood attempted to question or stop me. They were unhinged by the presence of their living god, and probably could not have remembered their own names. From the piles of remains, I saw that the traitors had not been great in number, but their uprising might have succeeded due to the late hour at which it occurred, had not the intervention of the god of chaos ended it.

At least now I knew how important I was to Nyarlathotep's purposes, I reflected with bitterness. My self-appointed master was quite willing to let me die rather than inconvenience himself. If I was to avoid death, it must be by my own efforts.

I spent a few precious minutes searching around for where Martala had hidden our possessions. At last I set her down and gently began to slap her cheeks and rub her hands. She sighed a deep sigh and opened her pale eyes. They did not focus on my face.

"Where did you put our belongings?"

She seemed not to understand my words. I repeated them. With an effort, she lifted her head and looked around.

"That room," she said, pointing at an archway. "Behind the red clay pots."

In moments I returned to her side with our belongings, which she had packed into the travel packs given to us by Feisel. Slinging my arm through their straps, I bent to pick her up, but she waved me off and stood on her own feet. Her balance was still not certain. I held her elbow.

"Wait," she said, stopping abruptly and patting her robe. "Where is my knife? We must go back for it."

"Damn your knife," I said, pushing her forward. "I'll buy you a new knife, if I live to see another moon."

Cursing weakly, she allowed me to push her through the cedar door and into the deserted hall of pillars. I could not resist pausing before one of the gold plaques on the pillars and prying at its corner with the point of my dagger. The thick gold plate bent but did not come free, and I saw it was fastened too securely to be removed in haste without damaging it. With regret I left the enigmatic plates behind us.

Chapter 25

Away from the moon shadow of the Sphinx, we opened our packs, stripped off our robes, and changed into our common clothing. The serpent who sheds his old skin must feel the same relief that I experienced once more to stand in my sturdy Muslim coat, Gor's skull at my belt, my water skin hanging from its shoulder strap at my right hip, and my dagger on its woolen baldric at my left hip, where a sword would have hung, had I possessed such a weapon. Knowing my eccentricity, the girl had filled the water skin. I patted it with contentment.

Martala balled up her white servant robe and cast it away from her with a sound of disgust.

"No, put it into the pack."

She did not question, but retrieved the robe and stuffed it into her travel pack. When I slung mine over my shoulders on its straps, she did the same.

Luck was with us. Brothers had arrived at the Sphinx that very night, and had left their horses in the usual hollow, where they had not yet been retrieved but stood pawing the ground and tugging at their tethers. They were three in number. We took the best two and rode at a canter to the ferry. It had completed the unloading of its cargo, and the stout ferry master was about to cast off and sail back to Feisel's private dock on the eastern bank of the river.

I stopped behind a screen of dense brush and dismounted, then pulled off my pack and took from it my caul of black silk. Martala regarded me curiously from her saddle.

"Wrap this around your head," I told her, handing her the scarf.

She did as ordered, and I felt a small satisfaction that she had ceased to question every command I gave her. With my knife, I notched the hem of my black robe and tore off a thin strip of cloth. I used this to bind the girl's hands loosely in front of her, then closed and donned my pack. Before remounting, I took a moment to renew the glamour that concealed my disfigurements. It was easy to forget, after living for weeks in a place where my face had so seldom been seen, save by my servant. I mounted, took the reins from her saddlebow, and led her horse beside mine toward the landing place of the ferry.

Before the ferry master could speak, I held up my hand.

"I have urgent business in Fustat. I must get this bitch across the river immediately."

He glanced at the girl, and saw that her hands were bound. Still he hesitated. He was the same stocky man with the bristling black beard who had carried me across the river with Feisel.

"Your master commands you to obey me in all things."

I made the sign of greeting used between brothers of the Order. To my great relief, the boatman appeared to recognize it.

"We are just casting off," he said gruffly. "Get your horses on board."

When we were underway, I caught the eye of the ferry master and beckoned him over. He left the tiller in the hands of the younger man who helped manage the boat. He was not happy at being given orders by a stranger, but he would obey me as long as he thought I had Feisel's authority.

"Your master wants me taken to the main docks of the city. He has ordered that you are to arrange for passage in a ship sailing upriver to the First Cataract. He will compensate you when he returns."

The man stroked his beard and thought. The effort must have been painful, since it caused him to narrow his eyes and distort his mouth.

"I know of a ship sailing to the Cataract at first light. They may have room for you. Do you mean to take the girl?"

"That's why I'm going." I lowered my voice to give it a conspiratorial tone. "It is necessary for the good of the brotherhood that she be conveyed to the Cataract."

He began to ask a question, saw me shake my head, and closed his mouth.

"The captain is a friend of mine. I'll make sure you get passage."

With the brotherhood in disarray beneath the Sphinx, I judged that I had several hours to escape Fustat before I was pursued. Once Feisel recovered from his grief over Dru's death, he would want me apprehended, not only to get back the scroll I had stolen, but to make certain that neither Martala nor I ever betrayed his secrets. He had overheard Nyarlathotep's words, as had others, so there seemed no reason to conceal our destination. Delay was death for me. I must get up the Nile as quickly as possible, though what I was expected to do there I had not the faintest notion.

The first rays of the morning sun that broke over the roofs of the muddy and unfinished city of Fustat saw us glide away from the docks on board a flat-bottomed and wide-beamed trading vessel that was aptly named the *Elephant's Foot*. The sunlight lit the edges of the fortress of Babylon with fire and gave its looming stone walls an evil aspect. Soldiers moved along its battlements, no larger than ants, their helmets glinting like sparks cast off from a blacksmith's hammer. It was a place that knew no rest. Somewhere below its foundations, in the bowels of its dungeons, men groaned in despair. I was delighted to turn my back upon it and gaze southward toward the unseen and unguessed fountains of the Nile.

"How far up the river must we go?" Martala asked, as though she had read my thoughts.

"The dark man said to sail above the Cataracts. How many are there, anyway?"

"Many. But it is uncommon for anyone to venture above the first two. The people there are black-skinned and barbarous of custom. It is a dangerous land, Alhazred."

In spite of myself, I laughed, and she responded with a smile.

"Perhaps I will take the risk, even so, since the alternative is death by poison."

I looked down into her pale eyes. A bruise discolored her left cheek. The traitorous guardian had struck her a hard blow, and it was a wonder that the bones of her face had not shattered.

"You are not bound to me. If you wish, you may depart at the first landing. I will give you money so that you can make your way back to Memphis, or anywhere else you desire to travel."

"I am your servant," she said with an angry tone. "When the poison begins to act, you will have need of my help."

To this practical if somewhat callous observation, I had no argument. In a few days I might not even be able to walk under my own strength.

271

In spite of her ponderous name and broad beam, the *Elephant's Foot* glided swiftly against the sluggish current of the Nile when there was a good breeze behind her to fill her enormous square sail. When the breeze died, slower but constant progress was maintained by rhythmic sweeping of the banks of long oars on either side of the ship, for she was a galley, and chained slaves sat on benches below her deck. Her half-Greek captain must have overseen the construction of the craft, which mingled in her details both Greek and Egyptian ornaments.

Captain Critias was the son of a Greek trader and an Egyptian merchant's daughter, as I learned in the course of our many conversations. He loved to talk almost as much as he loved his ship. He was a man of small size, but athletic and active, with great strength in his arms. The top of his bald head gleamed with sweat in the sunlight as he darted about, barking orders to his crew, for he wore no turban. He was shaven on the chin, a style not uncommon among the Coptic Egyptians, but by way of compensation, he had allowed his fringe of brown hair to grow long down his back, and kept it in order by braiding it like the lash of a whip. It hung almost to his buttocks, and swung from side to side as he moved.

His fat young Egyptian wife shared his cabin. She spoke seldom, and then in so soft a voice that it was barely to be understood, but she smiled often and was a great favorite with the crew, who numbered nine Egyptians and four Greeks. They did not dislike their captain, but were afraid of him, and leapt on the instant he gave an order without a grumble, even those twice his size. This was a matter of curiosity to me, since Critias seemed even-tempered and fair in his ways. As was true of most of the Greek traders I had seen in Egypt, he liked to make a display of his wardrobe. Rich silk trim and gold embroidery ornamented his long white tunic, and his belt, broad as my hand, was made of oiled crocodile skin. Jewels caught the sun on the hilt of his sword, which he wore with the assurance of a soldier.

Martala and I were given a reasonably clean rolled rug to lie upon at night, and an open place near the stern of the ship, a favorable location for sleeping as we soon learned. The breeze was usually behind us, and blew the clean scent of the river into our nostrils. There is no stench so foul as the stench of a slave galley. Even though the slaves were always kept below deck, unless one fell ill, their odor found its way to every part of the ship. Accustomed as I was to the fragrance of human corpses, this did not trouble me greatly, but I was glad for Martala's sake that most of the stench would be blown away from us during the nights.

Everything aboard the *Elephant's Foot* took place in the open air, except the ordeal of the rowers. The captain's cabin, located just astern of the mast, consisted of little more than a roof that kept off the sun. He spent much of his time on top of it, scanning the river for signs of drifting logs or other obstructions. When a difficulty was seen, he darted down his ladder and took the long tiller in his own hands. Watching him work it, I understood why his arms were so massive. The ship and the river did not fight each other, but when it was necessary to tack across the current they held a conversation. It could be heard in the lap of the water against the bow and in the creak and groan of the rigging.

The savor of flat loaves of bread baking in pans, and of strips of mutton frying in oil as the captain's wife, Fatima, prepared the midday meal, almost overpowered the stench from the hold. She cooked for all the crew working above deck. The evil-looking stew eaten by the slaves was prepared by a slave master near the bow and carried down through the forward hatch in wooden buckets. When the meal was ready, she spoke soft words to her husband, who bellowed to his first mate, and the crew assembled with pans to receive their portions and carry them wherever they wished to enjoy them. Martala and I, as the only passengers aboard the ship, were favored with a bench at the table, and sat facing the stern opposite Critias and his first officer. His wife never sat, but seemed in constant motion as she supplied the table with food and drink.

I had untied Martala and unveiled her face shortly before boarding. There had been no reason to continue with the subterfuge that she was my prisoner once the ship left the dock at Fustat. What the ferryman had told Critias I did not know, but both he and Fatima seemed to regard Martala as my servant and lover. It might have been expected that the wife of the captain would show disdain for the girl, but instead she displayed affection in her quiet way, smiling at Martala and even speaking to her. Martala returned her warmth, and spent much of the meal on her feet helping with the serving.

As we sat drinking wine after our meal, I asked the question that had concerned my mind since boarding. The language at the captain's table was Greek.

"How far do you plan to sail up river before putting in to a port?"

"We sail to Thebes, and from there to the Cataract."

"How long will it take us to reach Thebes?"

Critias shrugged to show that it was not a matter in his control, then looked at his mate.

"What do you think, Hannis?"

"If the winds favor us all the way, four days," his long-faced mate said after a moment of silent calculation.

Hannis was a curious contrast to his master. A full head and shoulder taller, his face and skull appeared to have been compressed on the sides and narrowed. He sat hunched over the table, his back rounded to bring his eyes down to the same level as ours. He had almost no eyebrows, merely small tufts of black hair directly above his dark eyes, and his beard was so thin as to be transparent. Around his head he wore a single rope of linen that might have been dyed red at some point in the distant past, but was now a sun-bleached pink.

"The winds won't hold, since they never do." Critias turned to me. "Five days, if we are fortunate."

My heart fell. The dark man had said that the minutes of the poison had been extended to days, but how many minutes were there? I had no way of knowing the rapidity of its usual action, or how greatly Sashi had inhibited its working.

"Must we stop at Thebes? I would be willing to compensate you, were you to sail past directly to the Cataract."

Critias and his mate stared at me. They both broke into laughter at the same moment.

"Forgive me, Alhazred," Critias said, patting my arm in a companionable way and grinning. "If we didn't stop at Thebes, we couldn't unload that part of our cargo destined for that port. Unless that cargo is removed, we will not have enough room on the decks to take on all the goods we intend to receive at the Cataract. We would have to throw the Thebes cargo into the river. It would be very costly."

"I can pay your costs."

His eyes widened slightly, and the smile slipped from his lips.

"You must be a very wealthy man. Even so, no, it is impossible."

From his tone, I saw the futility of argument and let the matter lie. Perhaps I could hire a faster boat at Thebes. My eyes wandered past the man who worked the tiller to a white triangular sail on the river behind us. A smaller and more maneuverable craft was bound to be able to out speed a great ship laden with cargo. Had I possessed the forethought, I would have hired such a boat at Fustat, but it had been imperative to escape from the city before we were hunted by the Order of the Sphinx.

Critias looked over his shoulder at the object of my attention. He continued to regard the small boat. Hannis turned on the bench and the two of them sat with their backs to us, watching the sail.

"What do you think he's playing at?" Hannis muttered.

"What does it matter? There can't be more than three or four men on such a small boat."

For another minute they watched the little craft as it tacked. Critias turned to drink from his tin cup, and seemed to remember that I was sitting at the table.

"What is so interesting about that boat?" I asked mildly.

"Whoever's piloting it is a fool, or up to no good," Hannis said before his master could speak. He scowled, and the little furry dots of his eyebrows descended close to his eyes.

"He's been behind us all morning," Critias explained.

"He's faster than this ship, isn't he?" Martala said, watching the sail over his shoulder.

"Much faster. He should have overtaken us long ago."

"Is he following your ship?" I asked, trying to keep my voice casual.

"Who knows? I don't see why he would, since it can gain him nothing."

For an hour after we left the table, I sat on the rail near the stern and watched the little boat. Martala busied herself helping the captain's wife with her cleaning, and seemed to have forgotten the craft, but now and then her eyes darted back and searched the river until she found it. She stared at it for a few moments before going on with her work. As the sun crawled across the heavens into the west, and the boat continued to pace the ship with unvarying monotony, I lost interest and amused myself by examining the cargo.

Much of it was cloth brightly colored and coiled in huge bolts around woven reed spindles. There were many large amphorae of wines and oils, mirrors, strings of beads, wool rugs, iron axes and spades. Most of the cargo consisted of manufactured things that were utilitarian rather than of fine workmanship. This was not to be wondered at, since we were bound for barbarian lands where even the simple furnishings and tools of a city such as Alexandria would be regarded as precious possessions. The deck was crowded, but enough space had been left between the bound piles to permit progress through the maze they created. Bales of dried spices scented the air and almost overpowered the stench from below.

I paused beside the open forward hatch, listening to the rhythmic creak of the oars in their locks. None of the seamen paid any attention to me. It was too dark to see into the opening. Some wayward impulse made me climb down the steep stair into the hold. The moist heat and choking stench enveloped me like a damp blanket that has been warmed beside the fire. I stopped at the base of the stair and blinked as my eyes adjusted to the gloom.

The galley slaves were ranked two abreast on either side of the ship. They sat on benches naked or wearing soiled clouts around their hips, chained at the ankles. Sweat gleamed on their backs and dripped from their beards. A man who was a slave, to judge by his lack of clothing, moved along one bank of oars with a bucket and a dipper and gave each rower a drink in turn. They drank without pausing in their work or removing their hands from the oars, which swung back and forth with the regularity of a pendulum. A slave master, unsatisfied with the pace, called out for attention and used the butt of his short lance to beat time on the walkway that ran between the benches. The oars swung marginally faster in their locks.

The slaves who sat forward of the hatch, and who faced the stern of the ship, saw me descend the stair and continued to watch me with curiosity rather than hostility in their expressions. They did not seem in ill health. Here and there a wet cough rose above the sounds of the oars. Most of the backs were unmarked by the whip, and their bones were covered with muscle and fat. There was no conversation between the rowers. Either they were forbidden from speaking, or they had said all they wished to say, and heard all they wished to hear, from their bench mates long ago.

One of the overseers noticed me and approached with mingled hostility and impatience.

"This is no place for an honest man," he barked in Coptic. "Best get up on deck where you belong."

"I am Mohammedan," I told him mildly. "I walk where I please."

Even in the dimness of the hold, I saw the color leave his cheeks. He stepped backward and bowed awkwardly.

"Forgive me, lord, I did not see your face. You may remain as long as you wish. How may I help you?"

"I have seen enough."

Resisting the urge to smile, I turned away and ascended the ladder. Being a member of the ruling race in a captive nation had its advantages, and I saw no reason to deny myself their benefits.

The sun painted the sky with red and orange and reflected from the sliding water of the river as it settled below the western hills. I went to the sleeping place I had been given and found that Martala had already unrolled the rug between the high piles of textiles. The space was as close to private as any place on a ship could ever be. We stood unspeaking at the far end against the rail and watched the sunset fade into night, and the stars begin to emerge.

"How are you feeling?" the girl asked after full dark had fallen.

"Normal."

This was not entirely true. My heart was beating faster than was natural, and my body felt warm. There was no pain, but I sensed its presence. In some way Sashi shielded me from it. I wondered how long she would be able to continue doing so with success. My neck where the tainted little saber had entered was swollen and tender to the touch. Reflexively, I raised my hand to my throat.

"Let me see," Martala said, a mothering tone in her voice.

She pushed my hand aside and drew apart the collar of my coat. She frowned and said nothing.

"What?"

"It looks like the sting of a wasp. It's white around the wound, then red in a ring."

I shrugged and turned to the rail. Leaning as far out as I could, I tried to catch sight of the little white triangle. Either the boat had ceased to follow us, or it was hidden behind the mass of the ship. The lingering glow in the western sky and the starshine gave sufficient light to see the river. It was by this pale illumination that Critias or his first mate would navigate until the round face of the rising moon provided a more reliable guide. Somewhere on the distant, reed-hemmed bank, a beast grunted, and water splashed.

My sleep was peaceful, untroubled by dreams, until the sweet countenance of Sashi came gliding towards me through the darkness, wearing an expression of concern.

There is danger, Alhazred. You must wake.

I started and caught my breath, then slowly opened my eyes and breathed deeply. The moon cast her silver beams over the wall of cloth bolts before me. I heard Martala sigh in her sleep at my left side. Apart from the ever-present creak of ropes in wooden blocks and the splash of water on the bow, the ship was silent.

Closing my eyes, I waited until Sashi approached where I could see her.

What is the danger? I asked in my thoughts.

I know not, my love. I sense some threat approaching. It is very strong.

After the alert the djinn had given in my hotel room at Memphis, I knew better than to disregard her concern. I drew up my legs and pushed myself slowly to my feet, trying to move soundlessly. The girl remained asleep. Not bothering to put on my coat or boots, I went in my surwal and shirt to the rail and scanned the side of the ship in both directions, then walked around the stacks of cloth that bordered our sleeping place. One of the crew passed down the central walkway without seeing me in the shadow, intent on some task of his own. I peered around the edge of the cloth bales and saw the tall form of Hannis at the tiller of the ship. He had his eyes fixed on the near bank of the river and did not notice me.

A strange sound cut the night air, a hiss like that of an angry serpent. This was immediately followed by a soft impact, and at once the ship was lit by a flickering redness, as though the hood had been removed from a giant oil lamp. I looked up, and saw the square linen sail on fire, the thin black length of an arrow dangling from it by its fletching. Even as I watched, another flaming arrow joined it, and a third. The fire enlarged and began to gutter and roar. Hannis gave a deep cry of alarm, which was taken up by other members of the night watch. Above the mounting din came the hiss of more arrows. One stuck in a stack of cloth bolts and began to blaze furiously.

"Alhazred? Where are you?" Martala called.

"I'm here. The ship is under attack."

Crossing to the burning cloth bolts on the opposite side of the ship, I grasped the arrow and tried to pull it loose. Its barbed head resisted, but finally came free of the burning linen. The arrow blazed with a fury that was unnatural, and I held it well away from my face so that none of the sparks showering off its fiery end would fall upon my skin. Martala came to my shoulder to look at it. I cast the arrow over the side and watched it float on the water of the Nile, still burning. A seaman shoved me aside and threw a bucket of water over the burning cloth, but it continued to blaze with a strange persistence, as though something sustained the fire with secret vitality.

I forced my way to the stern, Martala following close at my back, jostled by frantic crew members who sought to lower the sail and douse the flames that had sprung up in a dozen places on the deck. The air rang with cries of confusion and terror. Critias stood naked with his legs braced, his sword in his right hand, glaring back at the river. For the moment, no one held the tiller. In the moonlight the small boat was easy to see. It had drawn nearer than before. Two tiny flames shone like stars along its side. One after the other, they flew through the air, and thudded into the cargo on the ship behind us.

Critias began to curse the boat in Greek. He waved his sword impotently in the air. No answering cry came from the boat, which seemed ghostly in the moonlight. Slowly, it tacked and moved away. The captain's wife emerged from under the roof of their cabin with a blanket clutched around her fat body and put her hand on her husband's shoulder.

I grabbed his arm, and he whirled at me with murder in his eyes. Suddenly I knew full well why his crew paid him such respect.

"The tiller," I said calmly.

Reason returned to his gaze. He stared at the lolling shaft of the tiller and threw down his sword, then ran and grasped it in both hands.

"Help me," he snapped in a voice of command.

I lent the strength of my back to the task of swinging the tiller over. Above the cries of the crew and the dull roar of the flames, some sound was missing, a sound I had grown so accustomed to that it had become a part of nature. Critias realized its absence at the same moment.

"Hannis," he bellowed, his voice carrying above the confusion. "Get those slaves back to their oars. We're drifting."

The slave masters had come up to the deck to help fight the fire, and the slaves, in their terror at being burned alive, had ceased to row. I saw the slave master who had spoken so uncivilly to me running with a bucket of water. He slipped and fell, and the water spilled across the deck and washed over the side.

Hannis, lost somewhere amid the burning bales on the deck, added his deep roar to that of his captain. In a short time the rhythmic splash of the oars resumed, but it was too late.

The deck of the ship shuddered under my bare feet. Somewhere deep in the hold, wood groaned against wood. There was a slight lurch, and all motion stopped. So accustomed had I grown to the slight roll of the deck that its stillness was difficult to walk across.

Hannis appeared, his long face streaked with soot. An ugly red burn marred the underside of his left forearm, but he did not seem to notice it. His expression was grim.

"We've run aground," he said.

Chapter 26

In the chill light of dawn, the damage was less than had appeared the previous night. A dozen of the bound stacks of cargo were singed, but were tied so tightly that flames had been unable to penetrate to their hearts to consume them. We lay about thirty paces off the reedy western bank of the river in a small cove where grew a profusion of white lilies. Pink waterfowl on long legs watched us with concern from the edges of the reeds, and I realized this must be their feeding place. If not for the clouds of biting insects that came and went as the breeze quickened or died, it would have been quite pleasant.

Under the shouted directions of Hannis, the crew removed the blackened sail from the mast in two pieces. The fire from the first arrow had burned up its center, rendering it useless. They hoisted in its place the spare sail, patched and discolored by age, but still functional. It filled in the morning breeze. The ship trembled but refused to stir from its bed of mud.

All morning the crew and the galley slaves labored to free the ship. Had the breeze been stronger, the force of the wind alone might have been enough to move her, but it came and went fitfully, as though determined to mock their efforts. The bow of the ship pointed southeast, almost directly across the river at this point in its course, which bent somewhat to the west.

As the sun neared the zenith, Critias finally became aware of his naked condition and took a minute to dress himself, the last person on the ship to do so. His face bore a haggard look. His wife tried to feed him, but he waved the proffered bowl of dates and nuts aside without even seeing it. Finally, when it was well after midday, he acknowledged to himself that nothing would be gained by frenzied effort, and allowed the crew and the slaves to rest and eat.

"We're not stuck hard," he said to Hannis. "If we had a real wind we could rock her loose."

"Or more oars," Hannis agreed. "A few more rowers would do it."

"We'll have to unload the cargo to lighten the ship. With only a single boat to do the work, we'll be here for days."

We sat at the table, eating fresh bread and strips of goat meat fried in oil. The meat had the consistency of uncured leather, so that my jaw became tired as I chewed it.

"If I had two more boats," Critias said.

He had no need to finish the thought. Hannis nodded. All morning the single rowboat that was usually kept inverted on the deck of the *Elephant's Foot* had toiled in the water, attached to the bow with a stout hemp rope, its crew of six rowing for all their strength to add their pull to that of the galley slaves.

Martala turned her head to spit out a piece of gristle. She waved her table knife at Critias.

"Why don't you push the ship off the mud?"

"If only we had two banks of oars on each side," Hannis went on. "We don't have enough oars."

"Had the new sail not been burned in the fire, I could rig a second mast and that would do it," Critias muttered into his wine cup.

"Why don't you push the ship off?" Martala said in a louder voice. There was a tone of impatience. She disliked being ignored.

"Don't be foolish, girl," Hannis said, his worry making him forgetful of his manners.

"How do you mean, push it off?" I asked her.

She shrugged, chewing on the tough goat meat, a gleam of grease clinging to her lips.

"The oars used by the slaves must be very long to reach all the way into the water from inside the ship. Why not release the slaves, and have them stand along either side of the deck, then use the oars like poles to push into the mud at the bottom of the river? That's what the boatmen do at Bubastis when they get stuck in the mud."

Critias stared at Hannis. They both stopped chewing.

"The mud is probably too soft," Hannis said.

"Maybe not. When she struck, it felt solid to me."

"It just might work, if there's anything to push against."

Both men stood and left the table without wasting a word or a glance at either of us. Martala grinned at me.

"If it works, I want ten percent of the profits from the sale of the cargo."

In less than an hour, everything had been made ready for the attempt. The small boat held its place against the current of the river, ready to apply the full force in the arms of its crew when the word was given. The sail filled with the fitful breeze. On both rails of the galley the nearly naked slaves stood blinking against the unaccustomed brightness of day, their long oars held upright like poles. Their shoulders and backs shone white from years without sun. The remaining members of the crew stood guard over them with swords and daggers in their hands, which Critias had passed out to them from his storage locker. He was wise enough not to risk a slave uprising in such awkward circumstances.

Critias flexed his fingers and renewed his grip on the tiller. He gave the word, and all the slaves strained their powerfully muscled arms and shoulders at the same moment. The angled oars sank into the mud of the river bottom, and for a moment I thought they would continue to sink until they were too low for the slaves to hold them, but before they had descended half their lengths, they met solid resistance and kept their places. The slaves strained. The crewmen in the boat churned the water. By a fortunate chance, the wind chose that moment to freshen, and the old patched sail billowed and made the rigging creak and groan.

A shudder ran through my feet. The motion of the boat was almost too slight to notice. Again the breeze blew stronger, and a longer and more violent shudder vibrated through the planks of the deck. There was a stirring that increased in speed, and the ship began to move.

"We're free," Hannis called, a deep note of satisfaction in his voice.

"The sail will hold us," Critias replied as he bent to the tiller. "Get those slaves back to their places."

The *Elephant's Foot* continued her ponderous course up the river, none the worse for her ordeal. The mud bed had been flat enough that not a single plank in her bottom had sprung. Apart from the destruction of the new sail and minor damage to some cargo, the only consequence of the attack was the loss of twelve hours or so of sailing, and that was a matter of scant consequence, except to a single passenger slowly dying of poison.

For the rest of the day Critias made Martala his darling. He proclaimed her genius to his wife, his first mate, and the members of his crew, until we were all sick of hearing it. He only stopped when Martala raised the suggestion that she might merit a portion of the profits from the sale of the cargo. At this notion, he became thoughtful and serious, and resumed his naturally aloof bearing, which was a great relief to everyone.

We made good progress the rest of the way to Thebes, and the voyage passed without incident. A sharp lookout was kept for the small boat that had tried to destroy us, but though many similar boats with triangular white sails passed us going up river and down river, Hannis swore that none of them was the boat that had attacked us. I was forced to accept his judgement, since I could not tell them apart. Even had the boat returned, there was little we could do except stay vigilant against another assault. The ship's rowboat had no sail, and the vessel of our unknown foes was so fast and maneuverable, compared with the *Elephant's Foot*, that it might have sailed circles around us with impunity, as long as it stayed out of arrow range.

Critias had a Greek war bow among his armaments, and spent some time oiling it and testing the strength of its string. From the way he handled it, I had no doubt that he knew how to use it with competence. It would have been a fine justice to kill one of our attackers with the same weapon that had almost burnt the ship to the waterline. He had no occasion to test his marksmanship.

On the afternoon of the fifth day the gleaming walls of Thebes came into view on the western bank of the river. Responding to the holler of the lookout in the bow, Martala ran forward and stood leaning out over the rail, staring at the city with wide eyes. I approached behind her more slowly. My muscles had begun to ache, making rapid movement painful.

"This is where the pharaohs lived," she said without turning. "This is where they had their greatest temples."

"Have you ever been this far up the Nile before?"

She shook her head.

"My uncles used to talk about the riches of Thebes. Once they heard about a tomb in a valley not far from the city, and they traveled up river to rob it, but they found nothing."

As the *Elephant's Foot* rode the wind across the river, I saw that the city extended to the eastern bank, though most of its dwellings were on the western side. Marble pillars gleamed white in the sunlight, rank upon rank of them standing like stalks of ripe wheat. It was an impressive sight, far more intimidating in its aspect than Memphis. The walls and temples of Thebes stretched heavenward and sought to touch the blue vault of the sky, whereas the temples of Memphis seemed to hug the ground as though to make love to the black earth.

Only as the ship made its slow and cautious approach to the stone docks with its sail furled did the grandeur dissolve and vanish like a fortress in the clouds. The nearer we approached the city, the more evident its fallen state became. Some of the pillars were cracked or missing from their places. Grass crowned the heads of the great statues of the gods, and windblown sand cloaked their shoulders. The roofs of several temples visible from the riverside had collapsed inward many years ago and had never been repaired. Some buildings stood partly dismantled, like those I had seen at Memphis, robbed of their stones by laborers who found it cheaper to steal than to quarry.

Critias was occupied with the details of bringing the vast bulk of the ship against the dock without damage. I waited patiently beside him as he bellowed his commands to the men of his crew who hauled on the heavy ropes. The side of the *Elephant's Foot* struck the dock with a gentle thud that trembled through the soles of my boots, and I saw that it had been secured to the stone pylons. Critias began to yell orders to the men who scrambled over the side of the ship and manned the timber-frame cranes. Almost immediately they began to lift cargo off the deck.

"How long before we continue up to the Cataract?" I asked when the captain had fallen uncharacteristically silent.

"Tomorrow around midday," he said curtly without looking at me. "My men will work all night to make up for the time we lost in the mud, but that's as quickly as they can unload and load the cargo for this port."

"Martala and I will stay on shore overnight."

"Suit yourself. Be sure to be back on board before noon. We can't wait for you."

I gestured to attract the girl's attention. When she approached, I took her aside where we could speak privately and told her to gather our belongings. She stared at me with surprise.

"Are we leaving the ship?"

I nodded.

"By the Goddess, why? The men who tried to wreck us will be looking for you."

"That is very likely. Even so, I need to make inquiries about our destination, and I want to try to hire a faster ship that will take us up the river."

After wandering the dockside of Thebes for an hour in the blazing sun, it became evident that fortune would not hurry our progress. Several ships offered passage down river over the next day or two, but none except a few small boats were to be hired to take us in the opposite direction. After the attack we had suffered, it would have been madness to sail in a boat crewed by one or two men, and make ourselves easy prey for the bowmen who had sent fire arrows into the *Elephant's Foot*.

Following the scents of food upon the air, I made my way to the market square, which was not far from the dockside. As I expected, an armorer had his wares displayed on a long table beneath a striped awning of green and white that fluttered in the dusty breeze. He was grinding an edge on a sword as we approached. At a younger age, he had been a soldier, the numerous scars on his weathered face and bare arms testified. He stopped when he saw us standing on the opposite side of the table.

"I need a knife and a sword," I told him.

Martala wandered down the table, picked up a blade, and tapping it with her fingernail. She made a sour face. The armorer lowered his bushy eyebrows in a scowl and frowned in the depths of his curling white beard.

"Take your pick," he said, nodding at the blades ranked on the table.

"Do we look like jackals?" Martala demanded with hands on hips.

The armorer glared at her, but she met his eyes calmly.

"No," he said, hunching his shoulders.

"Good, because what you have here is trash, and only a jackal picks through the dung heap."

Before he could express his rage, I laid a silver dirham of the middle size in front of him.

"Show us your best wares. I will pay a fair price for fair blades."

He swallowed his indignation and pocketed the coin, then drew out from beneath the table a long box bound with iron. It required all his considerable strength to lift it onto the table. When he opened it, Martala made a soft noise in her throat.

"These are all Damascus blades," he told me. "There are none finer in Thebes."

Examining the swords and knives, I felt inclined to believe him. The steel was even better than that of my dagger.

For myself, I selected a sword with a blade as narrow as a ribbon of silk, slightly curved near its end. It felt light in my hand when I cut the air with it. The armorer nodded with appreciation as he watched me.

"It looks thin but it won't break, I promise you. Only the finest steel in the world could be used for a blade that thin."

The scabbard was simple black leather unornamented with jewels or gold, which suited my tastes. It had no baldric, so I slid my belt through it and buckled it on my left hip, then sheathed the sword.

Martala pulled her head out of the depths of the trunk, a gleam of delight in her eyes. I expected her to have found another tiny blade to match the one she had lost, but she held in her hands a more serious weapon, a straight dagger half a cubit in length sheathed in a leather wrist strap. I took it, and saw that it was designed to be worn with the hilt of the knife toward the hand, yet was so tight that the thin blade of the dagger would not slide out on its own. The weapon itself was feather light.

"You're sure?"

She nodded without hesitation.

I paid the price the armorer asked without haggling, and we left his table better able to defend ourselves. The feeling was almost as satisfying as a good meal. Turning toward a wall of red brick to shield my actions with my body, I drew two dirhams from my purse and pressed them into Martala's hand.

"Go and find us a place to sleep. Make sure they can supply a hot bath."

She put the silver coins inside the embroidered girdle of her black dress.

"What will you be doing?"

"Seeking information. Meet me here in the market in an hour or so."

I caught her arm as she started to turn away.

"Be careful. The assassins sent by Feisel will be on watch for us."

There was no trace of fear in her disdainful shrug.

"You don't think it was Farri's men on the boat?"

"Perhaps. Who knows? Just be sure to guard your back."

"Yes, father."

I watched her walk out of the market square, an insolent roll to her slender hips beneath her flowing dress. She was overdue for a whipping, to remind her of her manners. Still, arrogance was a part of her nature, and nothing would be gained by breaking her spirit.

My purse had begun to grow light. It was time to sell another jewel or two in exchange for coins. The bulk of the gems remained safely tied in a rag inside one of my breast pockets, but I had placed several in my purse before leaving the ship with the hope that I might find a money lender or dealer in jewels who would buy them at Thebes. I began to ask the merchants at their tables where I might find a fair dealer in precious stones, and as I expected, soon obtained directions to the house of a Roman trader who would buy any stone of value, though it was said he drove a hard bargain.

Strolling through the broad streets of Thebes would have been a pleasant diversion except for the growing pain in my joints, which had begun to swell from the relentless attack of the poison. The city was a strange combination of the grand alongside the humble. Towering obelisks rose from the spacious yards of abandoned temples, their interiors gutted and roofs decayed. Many of the statues of gods and goddesses had been toppled or defaced with hammers, but here and there a pagan deity gazed down from its pedestal, serene and perfect, as it had when Thebes was the center of the universe. The inhabited streets were lined with houses and shops constructed of mud bricks, a sad contrast to the well-shaped blocks of stone that formed the temples. Even on the most populous streets many of the buildings stood vacant. Thebes was a city in decline, just like Memphis, although the followers of the Prophet had not looted it for its stones, leaving the majority of its ancient temples looking much as they had looked a thousand years before, provided you did not look too closely.

A grave-featured servant of some twenty years' age, dressed in a white tunic and turban, listened to my inquiry at the door of the house on the Street of Olives to which I had been directed. The house was no different from any other on the street, and had it not been for its bright red door, I would not have been able to locate it unaided. There was no sign or number, nothing to show that it was the shop of a trader.

The beardless Egyptian opened wide the door, averting his eyes from mine, and with a bow of his head led me into the depths of the house to a room at the back where an obese man sat behind an enormous table studying a ring through a magnifying lens of clear glass. Light streamed through the great window behind him, making me blink at its brightness. It was difficult to see his face, but the gold-embroidered green silk of his robe shone in the sunlight like the wing of a dragonfly.

"Are you Michael Lucellus?"

He did not reply for a few seconds. Reluctantly, he put the lens down and laid the ring aside in a patch of sunlight. I saw that it was a seal ring of carnelian.

"I am," he said in a cultured tone, turning his attention to me. "Have you something to show me?"

"I do."

Without ceremony, I extracted the smallest of the three jewels in my purse and laid it on the table in front of him. As I leaned forward, I saw that his eyes were an intense blue, and his lips fleshy and red, like the painted lips of a harlot. He wore no beard, and kept the hair on his head unusually short, so that the bald patch on his crown had nowhere to hide itself. Sweat gleamed on his corpulent cheeks in spite of the breeze that found its way past the carved wooden screens of the open window.

He picked up the jewel with little interest, but when he raised it into the sunlight and applied his magnifier to it, his breathing slowed and deepened. It was a clear and unfaceted stone with just a trace of green in its depths. I smiled to myself, wondering how he would disparage the jewel, which I knew to be almost flawless. To my surprise, he made no slighting remark, but merely laid the stone on the table between his hands and looked up at me with his keen glance.

"Where did you get this?"

"That is surely a private matter that need not enter into our transaction."

"Are you a tomb robber?"

I said nothing, meeting his eyes with mine.

He chuckled and relaxed slightly, waving his hand.

"Forgive my curiosity. I only ask because this jewel is unknown to me. I thought I had seen every kind of gem stone in the world, but I have never seen this before."

"I obtained it in trade from a caravan master in Arabia Petra."

"That is a large place."

"It was in the region of Sana'a, on the Roba el Khaliyeh."

He waited with widened eyes, but when he perceived that I did not intend to speak further about the finding of the jewel, he smiled in a genial way.

"I will buy it, of course. Because it is unique, I cannot offer as high a price as the quality of the stone merits. I may have trouble selling it if I cannot say what it is."

He spoke his price, and I realized that I had no need to sell a second stone. The silver would fill my purse. I agreed without haggling.

"Have you more of these stones?" he asked casually.

"One or two. But I do not intend to sell them unless my needs become pressing."

From the floor beneath the window he took a small strongbox of cedar wood bound with iron and opened it. I was surprised to see that it was unlocked—although the box was of a size that would allow a thief to carry it away under his arm, so perhaps a lock was deemed superfluous. He counted from its depths my silver dirhams and set the box back into its place.

"There is another matter you may be able to help me with," I said as I slid the coins from the table into my open purse.

He merely raised his brows and spread his fat hands in invitation.

"I am seeking information about a deadly type of poison, or more specifically, about the antidote to the poison, which I have reason to believe is manufactured above the Second Cataract."

"There are so many poisons."

"This one is used by the Order of the Sphinx. Have you heard of them?"

His body stiffened for an instant as I spoke the name, then relaxed.

"Rumors only. I have no dealings with them."

"You are wise," I murmured, and a look of understanding passed between us. "Do you know where the antidote to their poison may be found?"

"Unfortunately, no. However, I know of someone you might ask, if you are not a man timorous in heart."

His eyes wandered to my belt, where hung Gor's polished white skull. I had worn it so long, I no longer noticed its weight.

"Are you acquainted with the feeders on the dead?"

"I am of the Black Spring Clan," I said, and was surprised to note that proclaiming the words still carried with it a feeling of pride.

"That clan is unknown to me. Even so, you are clearly a man who would not shirk from confrontation with these creatures of the night. Their knowledge is vast on matters pertaining to death and burial customs both modern and ancient."

"Tell me how to find them. I will pay for the information."

"They frequent a valley that lies between steep hills no great distance from the city. It is said that many ancient and noble tombs are hidden in this valley, though it is perilous to search there, for the Stone Valley Clan, as they name themselves, claim it as their hereditary territory, and have dwelt there since before the rise of the pyramids, or so they boast."

"You seem uncommonly knowledgeable about ghouls."

He laughed, so that the slabs of fat hanging from his cheeks jiggled.

"You would be surprised what precious objects are found in forgotten graves, and those who find them always have need to sell them."

Less surprised than you imagine, I thought to myself, but said nothing. I took five large dirhams from my purse and laid them on the table. He slid three toward him and let the other two remain. I returned them to my purse. In a few words he described how to find the valley of the dead. It was near enough to be reached on foot.

I left the house of the red door and returned to the marketplace. The sun hung low in the west, indicating that more than an hour had passed, but to my surprise Martala was nowhere to be found. Since I had no idea which inn she might have chosen, or what might have delayed her, I waited in the market until the sellers began to close up their awnings and put away their wares for the night.

I stood in the lengthening shadows, watching the fitful wind blow sheets of dust around the hem of my coat, and the red gleam from the dying sun crawl its way up the eastern walls. Should I begin a search of all the inns in Thebes, with the hope of finding Martala? If she was at the inn she had chosen, she was in no danger, I reasoned, and if she was not at the inn, there was scant chance that I would find her. Perhaps she had been delayed by some harmless necessity, although it seemed likely that she would have sent word to me by messenger.

Cursing silently, I set off in the direction I had seen her walk with that arrogant swagger of her hips, which now seemed more endearing than insolent. I was surprised to feel genuine concern over her safety, and wondered at my sudden weakness. If she were killed, what of it? I told myself. She was only a servant.

At the fifth inn where I made inquiry, the proprietor admitted to renting a room to the young woman I described. She had paid for the room with silver, told him to prepare hot water for two baths at nightfall, and had departed. He had not seen her again, nor had his wife or any of their servants. He asked me what he was to do with the water boiling in kettles on the fire, and I told him to let it cool. No one in the vicinity of the inn had noticed Martala either coming or going. It appeared that she had rented the room, then vanished from the earth.

Chapter 27

I wasted another hour searching for the girl before I forced myself to admit the futility of it. She had vanished completely, and not one man or woman I questioned had seen how. Time was short. Since I could not find Martala, I decided to make my way to the valley of the dead alone, and resume my search after my conversation with the ghouls, for I had no doubt that they would be easy to locate at night in the confines of their own valley. They would undoubtedly seek to kill me as soon as I strayed into their territory.

It was fortunate that the moon rose early. The path to the valley did not show signs of recent use, but was well cut into the stone-covered ground by countless centuries of the feet of those who had traveled to and from Thebes along its serpentine length. The valley was as the Roman gem trader had described, narrow and hemmed in by looming walls that rose steeply to pyramidal hills of broken rock. To walk into it during the day would have been like crawling into a bread oven, but already the heat was departing from its scattered stones, which littered the floor of the valley in such a multitude that it was scarce possible to take a step without risking a twisted ankle or a stumble.

My footfalls echoed like the vacant laughter of a lunatic from the hills. I made no attempt at stealth. They waited until I reached the midst of the valley floor, making a hasty retreat impossible, then showed themselves as shadows that moved. Only their motion enabled me to distinguish them from the dark shapes of boulders. They slid beneath the moon with no sound at all, and I found myself admiring their skill. No doubt they knew the location of every stone in the valley with their eyes shut. Swiftly they closed their ring around me. Moonlight glinted on their eyes, their barred teeth, their black claws.

I drew my sword. The ring of its steel on the brass guard of its scabbard made them pause. Slowly I turned in a circle, seeking the leader.

"I am not food," I said clearly in the language of the Black Spring Clan. "I am a ghoul."

A murmur of surprise stirred the air. They glanced with uncertainty at each other. One who was taller than the rest stepped forward, his shoulders hunched and taloned hands spread wide to slash. I pointed the tip of my sword at his naked breast.

He was strongly built, bigger and heavier of limb than the members of my own desert clan had been. This told me that food was not in short supply. These ghouls were fat with meat, and unaccustomed to having to hunt to survive. His dark skin had a yellow cast, as did the skins of the others. Their scent was strange, and made the skin tingle along my spine. One wrong word would mean death. They would kill me and leave my corpse in the sun for a day to putrefy, until it was fit to eat.

"We understand you, but the sound of your words is strange," he said at last.

"What clan are you?"

"Black Spring Clan. I am Alhazred."

They murmured at the name.

"We know nothing of this clan," the chief said, and crouched to leap at my throat.

"It lies across the sea to the east," I said quickly. "The leader of my clan is Gor. Here is his skull."

I pulled the knotted cord tied to Gor's skull from my belt and held the skull up in the moonlight, so that he could see its eye sockets.

He leaned forward until his misshapen face was a hand's-breadth from the skull. His eyes and the vacant sockets of the skull seemed to regard each other. The stillness of the night was marred by the sound of sniffing as he tested the scent of the skull.

"It is the skull of a ghoul," he said, more for the benefit of his clan than for my benefit.

The tension in the crouching shadows eased. The leader stood taller and allowed his fingers to curl and his arms to return to his sides. When I saw that he was no longer in the fighting stance of ghouls, I lowered my sword, but kept it naked in my hand. The skull I returned to my belt.

"Come with us, Alhazred of the Black Spring Clan. We will feed and talk."

He led the way, and the ring of ghouls parted for him, then closed behind me and guarded me on both sides, so that I had only one way of walking. The unspoken meaning was plain. Only a ghoul could tolerate the food of a ghoul. I must pass this last test before being acknowledged one of their race. They knew I was human by my scent and did not trust me.

The leader led me to a vertical fissure of shadow in the side of a hill. Turning his body sideways, he slid between the lips of stone. The others of the clan pressed close behind me and stood on either side of the cave to prevent my retreat. As a show of trust, I sheathed my sword, then slid my body between the rocks. It was an easier fit for me than for the ghouls who silently followed. Their chests were deeper than mine.

The cave ended after only a few paces. The leader had vanished. I stared around in the uncertain moonlight that shone through the gap at my back, looking for a bend in its length, but found nothing. The ghoul behind me made a harsh noise in his throat that I recognized as a bark of laughter, and pointed past me at a dark shadow at the end of the cave. When I bent close I perceived that it was an opening. Falling to my hands and knees, I crawled through.

The smell alone would have informed me that it was a ghoul's communal lair, even had I been blind. As it was, enough moonlight filtered down from a fissure in the roof of the cavern to let me see its general dimension. The roof was high, and the cavern shaped like a fish, sharp at its entrance and tapering toward the back, but wider in its middle. At some time in the dim past, rocks had fallen in at the center of the roof, and littered the floor of the space, forming a kind of elevated stage of irregular slabs that lay one on the other like a stack of books carelessly thrown together. Looking up, I saw stars through the opening. I sniffed the air, and above the putrefying stench smelled something else. Water. It came from the dark shadow at the rear of the cavern.

The leader waited until I satisfied my curiosity, then gestured for me to follow him. He mounted the pile of irregular blocks. I climbed after him, and saw that the top was flat. Gaps between the slabs had been filled in with sand, and the surface leveled and swept. The corpse of a woman lay naked in the center of the elevated floor, its intestines and viscera torn open and strewn around it. From the rotten odor I judged it to be three days old, perhaps four. Something moved in the cavity of the body, and I saw that maggots had made it their home.

He sat on the left side of the corpse, which lay twisted on its back, and gestured for me to sit on the opposite side. Other ghouls that I judged to be the strongest of the clan gathered round and formed a ring with the three of us at its center. On the cavern floor below I noticed several females and young ghouls staring up at me with hostile curiosity. It was almost certainly the first time a human being had entered their world. Unless my responses were exact, I would never leave it.

"Eat," the leader said, his eyes glittering.

I nodded to show my appreciation for his courtesy and lifted a blackened section of small intestine from the squirming mass of white maggots in which it lay. They shone silver under the moon, and had a curious beauty. There was no need to draw my knife. The flesh had putrefied to such an extent, that even without the claws of a ghoul I was able to tear off a section. I raised it to my face without hesitation and began to chew on it. The taste of rotten flesh brought back to me in an instant all the memories of my life among the Black Spring Clan, and at once I was no longer Alhazred the man but Alhazred the ghoul.

A murmur of appreciation ran around the ring of watchers. The leader took a section of intestine from where I had broken mine and fed on it. He nodded to one of the males in the ring, and the ghoul moved forward on his hands and knees with deference, and tore off a piece of flesh from the thigh of the corpse. One by one the surrounding ghouls approached and got meat. The cave filled with the sounds of chewing.

"I am Hakka of the Stone Valley Clan," the leader said when both of us finished our meat. He spread wide his arms. "These are my people."

"You have shared your meat with me," I said, remembering a scrap of lore I had heard from Gor on one of our long night hunts. "Your courtesy will be told to the young of the Black Spring Clan."

"Why did you seek us, Alhazred?" Hakka asked.

"I am dying," I told him without preamble. "Poison flows through my veins. It was brewed above the Second Cataract. There is a cure among those who made it. I seek to live."

In a few words I described the effects of the poison, and told what I knew about its use. Hakka showed no surprise when I mentioned the Order of the Sphinx.

"The necromancers who dwell beneath the Sphinx and their works are known to us. They possess dangerous arts. When we learn of their presence at Thebes, we avoid their approach."

"Are there any at Thebes now?"

"Three came up river last night."

He saw my expression of surprise and pulled his lips away from his yellow teeth in a grin.

"Nothing happens at night in Thebes without the knowledge of my clan."

"Do you know where the three are lodging?"

"They stay at a private house owned by one who is sympathetic to their work, and who serves the purposes of their order."

He named a street and described a house in such a way that I would be able to locate it. From his description, I judged it no more than a minute's walk from the inn where Martala had rented our room. I still held the hope that she had met with some harmless distraction that had prevented her from keeping our meeting in the market place, but it seemed more likely that the three who had tried to burn the *Elephant's Foot* had taken her captive, or murdered her and hidden her corpse. They would be seeking my location, so it was possible that they had kept her alive, temporarily. So I told myself, at least.

"Do you know anything of the antidote to this poison?"

"Nothing at all."

The ghoul spoke without emphasis. Death was not a horrifying stranger to his race, but a nightly companion.

"Then I have come here for nothing," I said, unable to keep the heaviness from my voice.

"There is one who may be able to guide you. An ancient oracle lost to the memory of men, but known to my people."

"How may I consult this oracle?"

I listened with attention to his directions. As he spoke, my heart sank further. It seemed little more than a fool's errand to attempt to consult this oracle.

"I will try to do as you suggest," I told him. "What choice do I have?"

He stood to indicate that my audience with him was at an end.

"I wish you well on your quest, Alhazred of the Black Spring Clan."

"If I live, the hospitality of the Stone Valley Clan shall not be forgotten."

Two of his warriors escorted me to the mouth of the cavern, between rows of gawking and silent women and children. The young were not so bold as those of my own clan, I observed, then corrected my thoughts—my former clan. Beside the exit was a round stone that could be rolled on its edge like a wheel over the opening. When it was in place, no one standing in the shallow cave on the other side would see anything other than a wall of rock. By this clever trick the lair of the ghouls was kept secret from men, even though it was so near the outskirts of Thebes.

My guards, or escorts, allowed me to leave the cave and make my way down the slope of the hill to the valley floor alone. The breeze had died, and the night air hung heavy around my shoulders, almost like a cloak of fine silk. There was nothing to indicate that any living thing other than myself existed on the earth. I felt a twinge at my neck and raised my hand by reflex. Wetness touched my fingertips. Drawing my hand away and gazing at it under the moonlight, I saw a smear of blood. Some night-flying insect had bitten me. Another token of the hostility of this valley, which had nothing beautiful in its aspect, even under the moon.

As I walked with care between the loose stones that littered the path, following it back the way I had entered, I became aware of three shadows behind a low ridge. I stopped and gazed at them without attempting to conceal myself. They had already seen me, and even with their eyes closed would have heard my approach over the pebble-strewn ground. The moonlight was clear, and it puzzled me that I could distinguish no more than their outlines, until I realized that each wore a black robe and a caul of black silk over his face. Only the gleam of naked steel from their drawn daggers showed clearly. I made no attempt to unsheath my sword. They were trained assassins. Before I could kill one, the others would take my life. I wondered if the ghouls watched from a safe distance, waiting to see which of us would be their meat for the following night.

"How did you find me?"

The leader stepped forward until he was within striking distance, and answered in Greek.

"I followed you to the house of the trader. He told me where you were going after you departed."

"What of the other two?" I asked casually, ignoring his dagger.

He turned and nodded to the men behind the ridge. They bent and dragged into view what looked like a sack of old rags. When it stood upright, I saw that it was

Martala, hands bound behind her back, her mouth gagged. Her eyes, so white in the moonlight, met mine with an expression of apology.

"She would not tell us where you keep the scroll," the leader said.

"Has she been damaged?"

"Not severely. Not yet. Before we kill you both, we want the scroll. If you tell us where you have hidden it, your deaths will be painless."

There was no pretense that he would allow us to live. He believed pretense to be unnecessary. In this matter we were in agreement.

"Had the *Elephant's Foot* burned, the scroll would have burned with it."

He shrugged with indifference.

"Our orders are to destroy it or return it. And to kill both of you."

"I am an agent of Nyarlathotep."

"Perhaps he will protect you."

Nyarlathotep cared nothing for my death, now that I had served his purpose. Feisel must have said as much to the head of the assassins. The speaking of the god's name did not frighten him.

I touched my coat with my left hand over the hidden inner pocket that held the scroll, and felt the rounded knob of its roller under my fingers. The assassin noticed the motion. He extended his hand.

"Give it to me now, and save yourself the humiliation of having the coat cut from your back."

Wordlessly, I took the scroll from its hiding place and extended it. He reached out for it, then flinched and cursed, drawing back his hand. When he again reached for the scroll, I saw a few drops of blood behind his middle knuckle.

One of his men slapped himself on the forehead.

"Hellish insects are hungry," he said to his companion, and the other gave a short laugh.

As the leader reached again to take the scroll, I dropped it, grabbed his arm and pulled him off balance toward me. In an instant I stood behind his back with my dagger across his throat.

"Release your knife. Tell your companions to do the same."

"Fool. We do not fear death."

He stabbed back at my thigh with his dagger. As I twisted my body to avoid the thrust, he was somehow able to writhe out of my grasp. I felt his strength as he pivoted away, and knew that he would be a formidable opponent. The other two rushed forward to kill me. Martala's legs had been left untied for walking. That was a mistake. She hooked a toe around the ankle of one man, and both she and the assassin fell together in a heap. The other two closed upon me, and I knew my death was near. The night felt so heavy, I could hardly breathe. It seemed to press upon me like an invisible blanket. I wondered if it was an effect of the poison, then heard the gasps from the assassins as they struggled for air.

We are attacked, Alhazred, Sashi said in my mind.

"Tell me something I don't know," I muttered aloud, drawing a forearm across my face in an effort to clear my sight, which was strangely darkened as though by a shadow, even though nothing blocked the rays of the moon.

The two assassins hesitated and faltered. They looked around in confusion and raised their arms as though to ward off invisible blows. Blinking at them, I saw small rents appear in their exposed skin as though by some magic. They were of a size such as might have been made by the sharp beaks of crows, but no sound of wings was heard on the stillness, only the grunts of pain of the two who stood reeling before me, and the curses of the third on the ground as he sought to disentangle himself from Martala's legs.

Something cut my left arm just below the shoulder, and I felt a similar slash on my left ankle, like the bite of a rat. Ignoring these pricks, I stepped forward and thrust the point of my dagger between the ribs of the assassin closest to me. As my hand neared his chest, it seemed to pass through a layer of thickened air, and immediately the back of my hand was covered with tiny cuts that gushed blood but caused no pain.

Drop to the earth, Alhazred.

I obeyed Sashi without question. The third assassin managed to kick Martala away with his boot, and stood with a murderous rage. For a moment he stared at his companions, as one flailed the air with his hands like some lunatic and the other slowly crumpled to his knees. His trance was brief. He cried out and covered his cauled face with both his hands, which gushed blood in the few seconds I watched from the ground. He began to slash at the air with his dagger, uttering cries that echoed from the indifferent hills.

I crawled beside Martala and began to cut her bonds with my blood-soaked knife. When her arms were free, her own knife appeared in her hand, and I had a moment to wonder that the assassins had not discovered its hiding place. She started to struggle to her feet, but I held her down with an arm across her waist.

"Stay low," I whispered. "Don't move."

We lay with our chests flat to the ground, watching the mad gyrations of the black-robed men. They behaved as though stung by a swarm of wasps, spinning and flailing their arms, yelps and grunts escaping between their barred teeth. The dagger of one man flew through the air as he forgot in his agonies to tighten his fingers on its hilt. I looked again, and saw that he had no fingers, only stumps that streamed blood. The blood-soaked silken caul was torn from his face as he spun on his heels, and he had no face. The other two fell to the ground, but the jerks of their bodies as they spasmed in agony showed that they were still under attack.

What are they? I asked Sashi silently in my mind.

They are vampire wraiths. I have never encountered them before, but have heard of their existence. They hunt in swarms, and feed on the life force in freshly flowing blood.

Are they djinn?

They are creatures of spirit, but not as I am.

If we lie still, will they ignore us?

I do not know, my love.

Can you defend us?

Perhaps, but it would mean leaving your body, and the poison has grown strong.

I leaned across to Martala, moving slowly so as not to attract attention to us.

"We will have to try to run," I whispered into her ear. "Are you strong enough?"

She nodded, eyes meeting mine. Her mouth was still gagged, and I noticed absently that the rag had dried blood on it. I wondered how badly they had tortured her.

All three assassins lay in heaps of bloody flesh on the stone-strewn ground. Nothing moved but the air around them, which had the appearance of black smoke, so thickly did the wraiths cluster above their bodies, seeking blood.

"Now," I said, and leapt to my feet.

Almost immediately, I felt the air thicken around my head. Without turning to look behind, I ran along the path toward the mouth of the valley. Martala's footfalls and her snorts of breath through her nose told me she followed close at my heels.

As we ran, we left the oppression in the air behind us. It seemed that these creatures could not pursue their prey swiftly. We would have faired well had not Martala set her foot on a loose stone and stumbled. I heard her fall and stopped to help her to her feet. It was the work of only a few moments, but it was enough to allow the invisible fiends to close the gap. They attacked my eyes and I was forced to cover them with my hands to protect them, rendering me blind and incapable of flight. I heard Martala's muted cries of terror beside me as we sat upon the ground and hunched our heads and shoulders in a futile effort to defend our faces.

Something left my body. Fatigue and pain descended upon my limbs like the hammer of a blacksmith. At first, I thought I could not move. It was a great effort just to take a breath. When I gathered my wits, I was able to open my eyes. I saw that the black smoke hung all around us, swirling and churning with fury, but some invisible barrier kept it at bay. Poor Martala's face was covered with small cuts, but her eyes had not been damaged. At least her beautiful lips were protected by the gag. As I watched, she struggled to work her fingers beneath its edges to tear it away, but it was too tight.

"We must keep running," I said, my words strangely slurred. The earth spun beneath me.

I struggled to my feet and would surely have fallen had Martala not caught me beneath the arm. We began to run once more, slower than before, but whatever barrier Sashi had erected around us was sufficient to keep most of the tiny flying devils away from our flesh. A few got through to vex us, but not so many as would sap our strength. We had little strength to spare, either of us. In spite of her torture and bondage, Martala was the stronger, and I realized how much Sashi had been doing over the past few days to protect me from the poison. Every joint in my body ached as though transfixed by a red-hot spike.

We stumbled from the valley, our feeble strength exhausted, and fell together to the ground. I raised my weary head and looked back, but there was no sign of any pursuit in the moonlight. Whether I could have seen the things in the air at that distance, I had no way to know. I only knew that we would run no further until we had rested. Martala laid her head upon my chest and put her arms around my shoulders. She could only gasp little puffs of air through her flared nostrils.

Making the painful effort to move my arm, I drew my dagger and cut the gag from her face. She gasped the cool night air with gratitude as the dirty rag peeled away from her sweating and blood-stained cheeks.

"Are we safe?" she asked.

I made no answer, since I knew no answer. Something surrounded my body, and for an instant fear leapt into my heart. Then I realized it was Sashi, returned to me. As she penetrated my skin, the pain diminished to the dull ache I had grown accustomed to, and my strength returned. No, not my strength, I corrected myself, merely an illusion of my strength. I had witnessed that night how thin was the illusion.

Martala licked her dry lips with the tip of her tongue.

"The scroll."

"I'll retrieve it in the morning, if it is still there," I told her. "As for the rest of the night, we have work to do."

She stared at me as though I had gone insane.

"We must consult the oracle of Amun in the temple of pillars. The ghouls say it will know where the antidote to the poison may be found."

Chapter 28

We washed the blood from our faces and hands at the first public well we encountered after returning to the city. The damage to Martala's face appeared severe, but when the blood was wiped away, I saw that the cuts made by the wraiths were tiny, no larger than the end of my fingernails, and curved in little crescents. They were thin, with smooth edges, like the cuts of a razor, and slow to cease bleeding, but when they did stop at last, they left little trace other than a hair-thin red line.

The well stood in a walled square, deserted due to the late hour. It was in a little-traveled section of the decaying city of Thebes. I made Martala take off her dress and chemise upon the elevated stone platform that surrounded its sides. She did not wish to expose herself, but I wanted to see what the assassins had done to her. Her belly and breasts were covered with bruises, though no bones were broken. The insides of her thighs were also bruised.

"How did they miss your dagger?"

She laughed scornfully, forgetting her embarrassment in the memory.

"They held me down on my back on the floor of our room and raised the hem of my dress over my head so that I was blinded and my body exposed. The fools never thought to look at my arms."

"Did they rape you?"

She scowled and turned away, snatching back her chemise and putting it on with impatient motions.

"What does it matter? I told them nothing."

"They are food for ghouls."

She smiled at the thought and slid her dress over her head, then smoothed her long dark hair with her hand as she fitted her head scarf and tightened the embroidered band around her waist.

"Follow me."

I stepped from the well platform and strode across the square to an archway leading to a more populous section of the city.

"Where are we going?" she asked, skipping behind me to catch up.

"We need workmen."

Laborers were not hard to locate, even at that late hour. The wine shops were filled with them. It soon became apparent that we would find no workmen who were sober, so I hired two that were drunk, a fat man with strong shoulders, and his younger and more slender brother. From their incessant chatter, I gathered their names were Yamas and Han. Both agreed to dig for us, and swore that they owned tools for digging. We followed behind them out of the wine shop and through the dark streets to their hovel of a house, where they kept their picks and spades. They walked ahead of us, singing loudly, each with an arm around the shoulder of the other. The song was unfamiliar, but I noted that the fat man had a fair voice, though the wine slurred his words.

As they slung their bags of tools over their backs, I caught the attention of the older man.

"How can we get across the river?"

Yamas blinked at me. I repeated the question twice. At last he grinned, showing surprisingly even white teeth.

"My brother has a boat."

The skinny one, who listened with his mouth partly open, nodded.

"Take us to the boat."

Again we trailed after these singing louts, who made enough noise to wake the dead from their winding sheets. I felt annoyed that we were attracting so much attention, then reflected that we would be dismissed as a band of drunken fools. It was a better concealment than if we crept through the shadows.

The boat was the most miserable thing I have ever seen borne upon water, apart from the excrement of pigs. It was made in the Egyptian style of sodden reeds tied together, with a sweeping bow and stern that rose to the height of my head as I balanced uneasily on the loose and rotting planks that lined its bottom. Han waved impatiently for the girl to go next. When Martala climbed aboard, it sank an alarming distance.

"Are you sure it will hold the four of us?" I asked the fat man.

"Yes, yes," he said with impatience, throwing his sack of tools down beside our feet.

He climbed ponderously over the bundled reeds that formed the boat's rounded edge, and it swayed and dipped until the surface of the Nile was no more than a few finger's breadth lower than the lowest part of the side.

At least his brother showed familiarity with the craft. Han cast in his tools and hopped into the stern with accustomed ease, in spite of his drunken state. The boat shuddered and sank again until the water kissed the top of its sides. Sitting on the bench in the bow, I noticed wetness in the bottom through the soles of my boots, and glanced at Martala beside me. Her eyes were saucers of milk in the moonlight.

"Sit down before you tip us," the younger brother grumbled at the elder.

The fat man sat abruptly with a faint splash in the wetness at our feet. The boat wobbled and shipped silver streaks of the river over both sides. With a curse, he pushed himself up and backward until his broad buttocks rested on the woven reeds of the middle bench. The little craft steadied and ceased to fill.

"There's a tin pan under your seat," the young man told me casually as he set the tiller into place and worked it back and forth to propel us away from the dock.

I passed the pan to Martala and she began to bail with a will. It was the only thing that kept us above the surface of the river, since the water seeped and slopped in as fast as she cast it out.

The side to side motion of the long oar was not quite enough to maintain us against the current of the river, but through good fortune the wind was in our favor and blew us across toward the eastern bank, while partially sustaining us against its flow. Even drunk, the slender brother knew what he was doing. Much to my surprise, we reached the other shore.

Martala hiked up her dress and chemise around her waist, giving the fat brother a clear view of her white flanks as she leapt out. She splashed through the shallows with no regard to how wet she became, so thankful was she to be on solid ground once again.

"No need to get wet," Yamas called after her. "I would have carried you."

I debated whether to risk having the corpulent oaf carry me to dry land on his shoulders, then decided it was safer to splash through the mud after the girl. Stripping off my clothes, I bundle them onto my head and stepped like a crane through the nodding reeds. I dressed while the brothers pulled the bow of the boat up on the bank, tied it securely to a rotting stump, and lifted out their tools.

"Where are we digging?" Yamas asked. The boat ride had begun to take the warm glow off his drunkenness, and his voice was both clearer and less cheerful.

"Do you know where the temple of pillars lies?"

"The big temple of Amun, you mean? Everyone knows it."

I gestured broadly for him to lead the way. He walked past us, looking at me curiously. His brother began to sing once again, but he did not join in.

Martala moved closer to me.

"Where are we going?" she asked in Greek.

I glanced at the brothers. They gave no sign of understanding what she had said.

"The leader of the ghoul clan told me where to find an oracle that knows the antidote to the poison."

"What is this oracle?"

"I know nothing about it, only where it lies hidden."

We walked along a broad paved avenue lined with statues toward the entrance of the greatest temple I had ever seen. Even comparison with the alien wonders accessed through the star chamber of portals did not diminish its grandeur. Its massive pillars soared to the heavens, and it extended back further than my eye could follow in the uncertain light of the waning moon. Although the roof had fallen in, most of the temple remained standing. To walk among its pillars was to enter a forest of stone, ancient beyond the reckoning of years.

The two Copts rolled their eyes fearfully. Even the younger brother felt the weight of centuries and fell silent. It was easy to imagine that ghosts walked between the pillars, unseen but not unperceived. Every so often a chillness touched my face, like the brush of wet silk.

I had no leisure to gawk in wonder with the others. I reviewed the directions given to me by Hakka and led my nervous little band deeper into the shadows, counting the pillars as I went. When I was sure I had found the right spot, I stomped a large flat paving stone with the heel of my boot. The clink of the stone echoed from the walls.

"Lift this stone and dig beneath it," I told the fat workman.

He studied the stone and grunted to himself. Most of his drunkenness had departed. Drawing an iron bar from amid his bag of tools, he fitted its pointed end under the edge of the stone and began to pry. His brother lent his back to the effort, and the stone groaned protest as it lifted and was levered to one side several inches. The stone was too heavy to lift, but by repeating this prying action the brothers contrived to slide it away, revealing the raw earth that lay beneath it.

They began to dig, and I saw that I had chosen well, for as limited as their minds were, they were skillful at their tasks and did not shirk the labor even when the sweat began to stream from their naked torsos. Early in the digging they stripped to the waist. The moonlight gleamed on their slick backs. The bite of spades and picks into the soil was the only sound. They worked at a measured pace without pausing to speak.

"Hakka said the oracle was hidden by the priests at a time when Egypt was invaded, but he did not remember who the invaders were," I whispered to Martala in Greek.

"My nation has been invaded many times," she said with a trace of bitterness.

"The ghoul said the oracle was not deeply buried, for the priests worked in haste."

Even as I spoke one of the spades clinked against something harder than stone. Yamas waved his younger brother aside and tapped around the spot with the tip of his shovel.

"Have a care not to damage it," I told him in Coptic.

He glanced at me but did not bother to answer. Gesturing for his brother to resume digging in a certain place, he began to gently scrape away the loose soil and small stones that turned up.

The statue lay on its side, no more than a cubit beneath the surface that had been covered by the paving stone. It had the gleam of gold, and its feet were attached to a small pedestal of the same metal. It was man-sized, human in both the shape of its limbs and the features of its face.

Han scraped away the dirt from its belly, and broke into loud, braying laughter. His brother also laughed, but with more restraint. Leaning over the pit, I saw the reason for their amusement, and heard Martala draw a noisy breath. The recumbent god had been uncommonly well endowed by the artist who made it, with a prick almost as long and thick as my forearm. It also gleamed with gold, but I saw that in places the gold had flaked off, exposing bronze beneath. Yamas saw the same thing.

"It's not gold, it's only bronze," he said in Coptic with disappointment.

Han continued to giggle to himself as he dug, until his older brother cuffed him on the back of the head with his open palm, knocking off his turban. Han bent and replaced it.

"It must be the god Amun himself," Martala breathed. There was both terror and wonder in her voice.

"How do you know? He has no ram's horns."

"Amun was the creator of all life, or such was the belief of those who worshiped him."

The brothers grasped the statue by its head and shoulders, and worked it from the dry soil. As it tilted upright on its pedestal, the dust fell away from its face, and I saw that it still possessed eyes. They were finely crafted of obsidian and lapis lazuli. With effort, the workmen rocked the statue from the hole and some distance away from its edge, then continued to dig. I did not tell them to stop. There might be other treasures buried beneath the god. With the lust for buried gold alive in their hearts, they paid no attention to me or the girl.

Walking slowly around the statue, I studied it and wondered how to go about asking a question of an ancient oracle. Perhaps whatever god or djinn had animated it in past times had faded away to nothingness while buried under the ground for so many centuries. My gaze returned to its eyes. They were so lifelike, I expected to see them move. They regarded me with tranquil indifference. How did one activate an oracle?

Martala reached out and timorously laid her fingertips on the phallus of the god. She caressed its length wonderingly, then suddenly drew back her hand.

"It's warm."

With a curious awkwardness, I laid my palm on the bronze prick. It was warm, but the heat faded quickly under my touch.

"Put your hand back on it," I told Martala.

She rested her fingers beside mine, and the warmth returned and strengthened.

"It is drawing nourishment from your body," I told her. "Keep your hand there."

Releasing the phallus, I returned my gaze to the obsidian eyes of the god. Something stirred in the depths of my mind, a presence or awareness that was both distant and powerful.

Oracle, I have a question, I said within my mind.

Ask.

The word came like a sigh of wind in no language that I could identify, yet I understood its meaning.

Are you familiar with the poison used by the Order of the Sphinx?

There was a pause as the intelligence within the bronze considered the matter.

It is a concentration of the venom from the black scorpion of the wastelands.

Do you know its antidote?

The poison is brewed by the shamans of the Besari tribe, above the Second Cataract. They also concoct its cure, for their own protection.

My mind raced. Was this enough information to locate this people, I wondered.

How shall I find the Besari?

Again the pause, briefer this time.

They dwell in villages along the west bank of the river. They are traders.

Martala continued to keep her hand upon the prick of the idol, but an expression of pain gathered in her face. I saw that wisps of steam arose from the shoulders of the idol, and touched it on its bare chest with my fingertips. It was hot—not yet hot enough to burn, but with the heat of new bath water, or freshly spilled blood.

Words walked through my mind, tickling like an insect on my skin.

Where are the priests of the temple?

The oracle was asking me, its humble petitioner, a question. At another time, this might have aroused amusement, but the pain beneath the words removed any impulse to smile.

Dead, and fallen to dust.

All of them?

Yes, all.

Dismay washed through me, radiating from the face of the idol. I felt the awareness of the being within the bronze expand in every direction, as for the first time it came fully awake after its long sleep. Martala grunted with pain but did not remove her hand from its prick.

Desolation, desolation, the end of days; the glory of god is put out like a reed torch in the river water, and the roof of the house is fallen.

Something thin and white flew up from the crown of the head of the statue with a wailing sound like the cry of a distant night hawk. Martala released the prick of the god with a gasp and pressed her palm to her dress to cool it.

Yamas looked up from his digging.

"What was that?"

"I heard nothing." I turned to the girl. "Did you hear anything?"

"Me? Nothing at all."

Yamas stared around with uncertainty. He met the vacant eyes of his brother.

"Well I heard nothing, either," Han said.

With a grunt, Yamas resumed his digging. I allowed them to continue for the space of a quarter hour. When the hole was up to their breasts, and they had still found nothing other than the bronze statue, I ordered them to stop, and told them to return the statue to its place and fill in the hole. I wanted no sign that the floor of the temple had ever been disturbed when the morning light shone between its pillars. They obeyed without reluctance, having satisfied themselves that nothing more was to be found, and that their only treasure of the night would come from my purse.

We had barely enough time before dawn to get back across the river and return to the inn. The wife of the proprietor was already awake and working in the kitchen. I persuaded her to reheat the bath water that had cooled from the previous night. The warm water felt so soothing as I washed the dried blood from my skin, I almost fell asleep in the round copper tub. Martala woke me from my stupor to demand her turn in the water. As she stripped, I was glad that the innkeeper's wife had placed the tub behind a folding wood-panel screen in the corner of the kitchen for our privacy. Her slender body was a mass of bruises and tiny crescent-shaped cuts. As she sat leaning forward in the tub, washing her long hair, I knelt behind it and used a rough rag to wash her back and shoulders. I described what the oracle had told me.

"Have you ever heard of the Besari tribe?"

"No." She frowned in thought. "I know little about what lies above Thebes, only a few fables my mother used to tell me."

"What were the tales about?"

She shrugged her slender shoulders beneath my hand.

"It is said to be an evil land, having many sorcerers. Those who go there suffer misfortunes."

"At least we won't be troubled by Farri. His power doesn't seem to extend above Memphis."

"He has no need," she said. "He knows we will have to come back down the Nile eventually."

This was something I had not considered, but I saw the sense in it. Above Thebes lay only a wilderness of black-skinned barbarians, so anyone who traveled up the

Nile must eventually travel down it again. The south offered no escape. Farri could afford to be patient.

Before returning to the ship, we went to the valley of the dead to retrieve the scroll. I felt confident that we would not be attacked by wraiths in daylight, and Sashi agreed with me that it was unlikely. As I expected, the bodies had been removed by the ghouls, along with their weapons. The scroll lay where I had dropped it. I opened it to be sure it was undamaged, then returned it to my inner coat pocket. The sun stood just above the uneven rim of the hills, but the shadowed floor of the valley retained the coolness of night. Gazing around, it was difficult to see any threat in those steep slopes. I wondered how many travelers had been lulled into complacency by their benign appearance in daylight.

We arrived at the dockside well before noon, only to discover Critias preparing to leave the dock. The gangplanks had already been drawn up, so we were forced to leap from the dock into the boat, a jump of no great distance.

I found the familiar deck of the *Elephant's Foot* strangely comforting. While aboard the ship, we were safe from the agents of both Farri and Feisel, since it was unlikely that Feisel would attempt another fire arrow attack after the first had failed and made us wary of small boats, even if he had additional assassins following us up river.

Without regret, I watched Thebes diminish behind the ship. Travel along a river, I had discovered, was much like moving through time. Ahead lay the unknown future, and behind, the past sliding into oblivion. Only the river itself seemed real. The rest of the world was a carnival of illusions, of pleasant dreams and nightmares best forgotten. The poison in my blood began to sing to me. I heard it in my ears as a high whine, rising and falling like the wings of an insect that at times drew near to circle my head. The remaining term of my life was brief, yet the length of the river could not be diminished by any art of necromancy. It required a full day and night of sailing to reach the First Cataract, and another two days to travel from the First to the Second Cataract.

I closed my eyes as I held on to the rail of the ship, feeling its gentle roll beneath my feet.

Sashi, can you control the poison for another three days?

Her beautiful face formed upon the darkness, her expression sad. I asked the question three times but she refused to answer.

Chapter 29

Someone shook my shoulder. Pain lanced in hot needles along my spine and through the sockets of my hips. I groaned and made the effort to force my swollen eyelids open. The brightness of day scalded my brain, but I kept my eyes parted as memory slowly returned.

We had left the *Elephant's Foot* at the base of the First Cataract, since a ship of its vast bulk could not be drawn past the roiling white water, and had hired a smaller boat above the turbulence to take us to the Second Cataract. It was then that the poison began to show its strength, in spite of all efforts of Sashi to quell it. I lay awake at night, unable to sleep from the pain in my limbs and vitals, only to doze fitfully throughout the day as I shivered and sweated in the bottom of the boat.

Two full days we sailed beneath the sun and stars, the banks of the river growing ever more wild, the cultivated fields becoming fewer until they dwindled to nothing and the rank tangle of the jungle ruled unbroken along both sides of the Nile. The boat master steered well clear of crocodiles and the monsters known as behemoths who watched us with deceptively tame brown eyes, the tops of their heads and comical little ears alone breaking the river surface, the rest of their vast bodies hidden in the murky depths. Birds hung upon the air like great clouds of colored silks, their shrill cries making speech impossible until they passed. Each time we tacked near the banks, swarms of biting flies pursued us, only to fall behind when we sailed into the midst of the Nile.

With the aid of a rough walking staff that Martala bought from a beggar for a bronze fil, I was able to walk the path that circumvented the Second Cataract. Above it was only a small fishing village of black-skinned savages who went nearly naked due to the heat. It was unlike the heat of the Empty Space, which is wholesome to a man with sufficient water. The air hung thick on my tongue and clogged my throat, choking me so that at times I thought I could not breathe, and had to stop and gasp while my body was racked with coughing. Even so, I was not warmed by my blue camelhair coat, but trembled with chills that sank to my very bones.

A few of the inhabitants of the village knew Coptic. One fisherman agreed to take us up the river to the chief town of the Besari tribe. Martala paid too much. I saw that his boat was filled with dried fish, and knew he had intended to sail up river to sell them at the town, so it was little cost to him to add us to his cargo. I said nothing. When I talked, the coughing returned. Sometimes it was many minutes before it ceased.

Martala bought a potion against sickness from an old woman in the fishing village before we departed. I drank it, reflecting that it would not kill me any faster than I was presently dying. It seemed to lessen my urge to cough. She also bought a filthy blanket and wrapped it around my shoulders. The inhabitants gazed in wonder to see a man shiver under the heat of the sun, though his body was wrapped in wool.

With impatience I thrust aside this tangled confusion of recent memories, and raised my head to look around the boat. I found that I lay upon a mound of dried fish that dug sharply into my back and neck. Martala held her hand under my head and gazed down at me, worry expressed in the vertical line between her gathered brows. I tried to smile, but my lips cracked and began to bleed. The blood tasted sweet on my tongue.

The reed fishing boat was tied to a crude wharf constructed of rough and irregular logs driven into the mud of the river, the bark still clinging to them. The space behind this barrier was filled with stones and sand to make a platform for unloading the small boats that bobbed on the flow of the river, bumping gently against it as the wind shifted. I counted seven such boats, similar in design, with broad beams for carrying cargo and large triangular linen sails for fighting up river against the current.

In the bow of our own boat, a black fisherman, naked save for a skirt of woven grasses around his hips, sat amid his catch with arms and legs extended, eyes wide and jaw slack with terror. I blinked at him as I slowly became aware of his expression, puzzling over what might have caused him such fear, then noticed his gaze fixed unwaveringly on my face.

"You neglected the glamour," Martala murmured into my ear in Greek.

The urge to mirth arose within me. I tried to suppress it, but had no strength of will. My laughter rolled out, strong and full, echoing over the river about the noises of the docks.

This was too much for the boatman, who scrambled to his bare feet in the sliding slabs of dried fish, gave a faint scream, and leaped from the boat to the wharf. Without glancing back, he ran toward the gates of the town, arousing curious stares from the other fishermen who worked on their sails or handled their catches.

When my bitter amusement at my pathetic condition exhausted itself, I raised my right hand and weakly made the gestures and spoke the word of the glamour.

"We should leave before he returns. I have already paid him." Martala said.

She helped me to my hands and knees. In my weakened state, the greatest difficulty was the transition from lying to standing. Once on my feet, I could keep them under me unaided for a brief period. She leaned over and grasped the rough logs of the wharf, drawing the boat slowly inward until the reeds of its side scraped their bark, and held it while I crawled onto the wharf. Jumping out of the boat, she put her arm under mine to help me stand, then returned to the boat for the walking staff I had used at the Second Cataract. I was ashamed to lean on it, but was forced to acknowledge to myself that I needed the aid of its support.

The fisherman had called the town Tyroon. It was little more than a scattering of round wattle huts with pointed roofs of bundled reeds, but it boasted a fortification wall of mud bricks as tall as a man, and crowned with sharpened stakes set irregularly along its top. As crude as this defense appeared to civilized eyes, it was unlikely that it had been constructed without a purpose. Life in Tyroon could not always be so harmonious as it seemed this bright morning.

The wooden gates of the town hung open, facing the fish market on the wharf. As we drew nearer, I saw that the massive log forming the lintel of the gate was decorated along its top with rotting human heads. Whatever its shortcomings, the town enjoyed the rule of law. The solitary guard leaning on his spear eyed us disagreeably as we passed beneath the head-studded log, but he said nothing and made no move to challenge us. He was dressed in a simple skirt of woven grasses dyed with red and green pigments, and wore nothing else except a wide collar of beaten brass disks that rested on his broad shoulders and hung over his chest. Patterns of scars crossed his thighs and surrounded his upper arms. They were not the scars of battle, but some form of ritual marking.

Tyroon, I perceived, was constructed in the shape of half a wheel, its fortification wall forming a circle that was interrupted by the gated straight section that bordered the Nile. Not all of the buildings were as inconsequential as they appeared to be from the river. An avenue lined with palms extended from the market square inside the gate to a long house of red brick with a rounded roof of thatch. Around it were placed other structures of carved wood logs cunningly fitted together, or made of the same red brick. They could only be the houses of nobles or wealthy merchants. Poor though they were to civilized eyes, they dwarfed the huts lining the other streets that radiated from the market.

A low building of white stone with a flat roof that stood near the long house had the appearance of a temple. It honored a serpent god whose sinuous effigies were carved boldly upon its pillars and walls. As I paused to study it, I realized that similar designs decorated the door of every house. It must be the image of Yig. Dimly I remembered reading in a book of arcane history that Yig was the supreme god of Khem, the black land. I paused to marvel at the simple elegance of the temple. It would not have been out of place in the sphinx-lined avenues of Memphis or Thebes. The only structure of the town made wholly of stone, it appeared much older than the other buildings.

We made our way across the open marketplace, ignoring the cries of the merchants and beggars, and found a public drinking house by following the smell of warm beer that drifted over the stalls. The tavern had no walls, merely a sun-bleached linen awning held aloft on four carved posts set in the earth, beneath which were tables and benches. The beer was ladled from clay pots by the proprietor, a small black man with white hair who seemed unable to speak.

Martala helped me to sit at an empty table and went to fetch two wooden cups. She returned and laid one on the table before me. I gazed into its liquid without enthusiasm. It was green. Small particles floated to the surface from its depths as I watched. Reminding myself that I was a ghoul, I drank it without drawing a breath, merely so that I would not have to look at it. Martala sipped her cup and made a face of disgust, but did not spit it out.

"We need to find a shaman," I said to her in Greek.

"Wait here," she said, rising from her seat. "I will ask questions in the market-place."

I allowed my mind to be lulled by the drone of conversation in the tavern and the more distant cries of the hawkers in the market. The little proprietor of the drinking place cast me a suspicious glance from time to time as he bent over his sweating clay vats, but made no attempt to approach my table. All the other patrons of his noxious brew were natives of this land. They ignored my presence as though my table were empty. I had not seen a single Greek or Copt since leaving the fishing boat, which surprised me. This was not a poor land, to judge by the wares in the market. Why would the Greeks not trade here? I shrugged to myself. Perhaps there was a law prohibiting foreign traders. In my present condition, it was a matter of no interest. Were the market peopled with a thousand Greeks, it would not have helped my circumstances.

As I brooded about my fate, I became aware of a man standing next to my table. I raised my head to examine him. He wore a breastplate and helmet of beaten brass, and little else apart from a woven skirt and sandals that laced to his calves. In his hand he carried a short spear with a long copper point. He stared down at me, dark face expressionless. When he saw that he held my attention, he spoke softly in a language strange to my ears, but due to my recently acquired gift for tongues, I understood his meaning.

"You must follow me."

There seemed little reason to argue. In my weakened condition, a child of ten might have knocked me down and stolen my purse. I nodded and pushed myself to my feet on my walking staff. He waited patiently until I was able to hobble around the bench, then led me slowly across the market square and along the palm-lined avenue toward the sprawling house of red brick that I had noted upon entering the town. Several times he paused and waited while I stopped to catch my breath, for which I gave him silent thanks, but he did not embarrass me by attempting to take my arm and assist me. Martala was nowhere in sight.

Inside the shadowy long house, the air felt cool on my cheeks. I quickly saw why. Two young boys, both naked, sat working the paddle levers of large fans with their feet. The levers were attached to the fans by ropes, and the fans moved back and forth above a throne occupied by a barrel-chested man in a tall feathered headdress and voluminous white robe that concealed his feet and all but the tips of his fingers. Each time the rectangular vanes of the fan passed above him, the red and white plumes bent and trembled. The throne was of wood, but could not be mistaken for any other kind of seat. Its arms were carved in the shape of coiling serpents, its high back decorated with two extraordinary elongated skulls studded with innumerable teeth. They must be the skulls of crocodiles, I speculated, for I could think of no other beast with a head so oddly formed. In his right hand, the man bore a short mace of polished black wood, topped with a globe of smoky crystal as big as a fist that was enclosed in a standing gold ring.

He was eating as I entered, and did not immediately look at me. A young woman with naked breasts fed him sweetmeats from a gold tray. She smiled each time she popped one into his mouth. Several gray-haired black men stood behind the throne, which was guarded on either side by soldiers in brass breastplates. Spears were their only weapons. My escort indicated that I should stand in the open space before the throne, then left the long house.

When the girl wiped the seated man's thick lips on a white cloth and removed the tray, he finally turned to me with a pleasant smile. Like most of the others in this land, his chin was beardless.

"Welcome to Tyroon," he said in a resonant voice in perfect Greek. "I am N'golo, king of the Besari. It is not often that we receive visitors from the north."

I bowed, leaning on my stick to keep my balance.

"My name is Alhazred. I am a traveler from Yemen."

His eyes widened with interest.

"A man of Islam. I have spoken with only a few of your kind. Your Prophet was a great warrior."

I bowed again to indicate my appreciation.

"Tell me, Alhazred, what is your purpose in coming to the land of Khem?"

For a moment, I hesitated, wondering if I would gain or lose by being truthful. The king seemed to have no hostility in his manner.

"By a mischance of fate, I was poisoned with the black ichor that is said to be brewed only by the shamans of your tribe, great king. I have come seeking a remedy before the poison corrupts my body to death."

He stared at me with interest, then gestured for me to approach. I came close and stood between his knees. His guards tensed and shifted their grip on their spears, but made no other movement. N'golo reached out a hand and gently lifted my eyelid, peering at the white of my eye beneath. Again, I marveled at the power of the glamour, which concealed my deformities even from his touch, for when his hand brushed my cheek he felt no scar. He turned in his throne and murmured into the ear of an aged advisor with a white beard who bent close. The old man whispered back to the king.

"This is most extraordinary, Alhazred. My advisor tells me that no man has survived the black ichor for more than a quarter of an hour. Most die in the first minute or two."

"I was fortunate, majesty. The poison barely scratched my skin."

His expression was skeptical, but receptive. He might be the king of a tribe of savages, I thought, but he himself was an educated man. I wondered where he had acquired his perfect Greek speech.

"The shamans of my people are not forthcoming in the display of their arts, and are of uncertain tempers, Alhazred. I sympathize with your condition, but it might be better for you to avoid the shamans and allow your body to fight off the poison with its own resources. You seem to have some extraordinary natural immunity to its effect."

"Alas, your majesty, I have been informed by divine revelation that only the antidote of the shamans will save my life."

He was silent for several moments, then leaned close so that I felt the heat of his breath on my cheeks.

"For your own safety, I must order you not to seek out the shamans of this land."

A cackle of laughter split the quiet in the shadowed air of the long house. I turned painfully on my stick. Outlined in the light of the open doorway stood a man of such inhuman thinness, his silhouette appeared that of a skeleton. The light from outside obscured his face. I was still trying to discern his features, when I noticed that everyone in the large audience chamber had dropped to their knees and bowed their heads to the hard-packed mud of the floor. Even the two guards on either side of the throne knelt. The king rose behind me, and I hastened to step aside, thinking that he would order this skeletal maniac taken prisoner by his guards for intruding on his presence. Instead, the king himself knelt at the foot of his own throne and bowed to the figure in the doorway.

The skeleton approached, and the two naked black boys who had been operating the fans jumped to their feet and ran out the door behind him. No one else rose from their postures of abasement. He was a black man of some forty years of age, dressed in feathers and bones, carrying a white wand that appeared to be a human thigh bone, with a ring of black feathers tied around its tip. From a thong around his neck hung a whistle made of bone. Apart from bands of red feathers encircling his upper arms and ankles, he wore only a loincloth of woven green and red straw. The top of his head was shaved in a broad strip from his forehead to the base of his neck, leaving two tufts of curly black hair above each ear. Red paint in the shape of lightning bolts decorated his hollow cheeks.

"What do you want with the shamans of the Besari?" he demanded in his own tongue, staring at me with bloodshot eyes that harbored madness in their depths.

I made no answer.

His lips were thin, his mouth small, like that of a child, and his tiny white teeth resembled a string of miniature pearls when he smiled.

"You have a spirit guardian who watches over you. It can hide your scars from these fools, but not from me."

He turned and in the tone a householder uses to command his slaves, ordered the king to stand. N'golo rose and faced the bony man. His handsome features remained expressionless, but beneath their surface resentment and hatred raged. Even so, when the other questioned him about me, the king answered truthfully, repeating what I had said to him. That I was still alive after being poisoned with the black ichor interested the thin man. He peered beneath my eyelids, as the king had done, and smelled my breath.

"There is power here," he murmured to himself, his eyes rolling.

Lost in thought, he seemed to forget that we stood before him for a time, and began to mutter and bark to himself in little yips, like a dog, turning in a circle as he wagged his head from side to side and extended his red tongue from the corners of his diminutive mouth. As ridiculous as this performance appeared, not a single person in the audience chamber laughed, or even lifted his head. I saw the curved back of one guard tremble, so great was his terror.

Recovering his wits, the bony man regarded the king with contempt.

"Bring him to my lodge. We will examine him to verify that he speaks the truth."

N'golo drew himself up. He was a tall man, at least several palms higher than the intruder.

"I am king of the Besari. It is not your place, Lo'oka, to tell me what to do."

The other man cackled again, flashing the tiny pearls of his teeth.

"Where is your favorite washcloth, N'golo? What has become of it? Did you misplace it? Was it stolen, I wonder?"

The face of the king paled under its dark skin. His broad shoulders sagged, and he dropped his gaze.

With a final glance at me that contained nothing but malice, the bony man turned and left the long house. It was a minute before the guards or advisors dared to lift their heads. The king sagged back on to his throne as though all the life had fled from his limbs.

"Who was that crazed fool?" I asked in Greek.

N'golo looked up quickly, face drawn with fear. With an effort, he controlled himself.

"Lo'oka is the chief of shamans in Khem. Those who defy him die."

"Even the king of the Besari?"

Anger flashed in his dark eyes. For a moment I thought he would leap up and strike me with his mace. He took a ragged breath and forced himself to smile, but it was bitter.

"Even the king has no defense against the walking dead. They come at night while we lie asleep and strangle us on our beds, then fall lifeless themselves into a heap of bones and putrefying flesh. Everyone knows they are sent by the shamans, but everyone is afraid to act against them. It has been this way in my land since the beginning of time."

"It is not my purpose to meddle in the affairs of shamans," I told him. "I only seek the antidote to the poison."

He stared at me as though I were mad, then shook his head.

"You know nothing of their ways, Alhazred. The chief of the shamans has set his glance upon you. Even were you not poisoned, you would be a dead man."

"Then I have no reason to fear attending him in his lodge," I reasoned.

"There are worse things than death," N'golo murmured.

His chief advisor leaned over his shoulder and whispered urgently into his ear. The face of the king became grim, but at last he nodded and waved the elderly man away from the throne. The advisor left the long house with dignified strides.

"I wish we had more time to talk, Alhazred. You might have instructed me in the teachings of your Prophet."

"Perhaps when the poison is cleaned from my veins, we will talk again."

N'golo smiled at me sadly, as a father might smile at a young child who boldly asserts that he intends to live forever.

The soft-spoken guard who had escorted me to my audience with the king returned in the company of the chief advisor.

"This man will show you the way to the lodge of shamans. May the great serpent protect you with his coils."

I bowed, and followed the guard from the long house into the sunlight. The shaman Lo'oka was not in evidence, but I noticed Martala watching me from behind a fluttering panel of red and green linen when we left the palm-shaded avenue and entered the market square. She stepped forward, as though intending to approach. I made a discrete motion with my hand. She withdrew so that only the left side of her face remained visible beyond the striped awning. The merchant of the stall spoke animatedly to her, convinced by her presence that she intended to buy his pots, but my escort gave no sign that he noticed her. If I truly walked to my death, there was no reason for the girl to walk beside me.

We followed a narrow and crooked street through the heart of the town, but to my surprise did not pause until we reached the westernmost limit of the bend in the fortification wall. Here there were few houses, and those appeared vacant and neglected. Set in the wall was a small but stout door of dark wood little taller than my head, but broad enough to admit two men side by side. In defiance of the prevailing serpent decorations that covered almost every post and wall in the town, the door was adorned only with the head of an enormous toad, carved deeply into its black planks. The monstrosity had an evil aspect, and almost appeared to grin forth from the portal in mockery.

The inner surface of the door possessed no bolt or bar to prevent entry, which struck me as odd, in consideration of how well the front gates facing the river were supplied with loops for wooden bars to seal them shut against assaults. It seemed foolish to defend the front door of the town, yet leave the back door unprotected. Granted, most attacks must come from the river, but what was to prevent raiders from making their way around to the rear of the wall?

As the guard fumbled with trembling fingers at the corroded brass ring set in the center of the door, just beneath the head of the toad, I glanced over my shoulder. From the back side, the town of Tyroon had a ghostly aspect. The only creature stirring was a dog that limped across the road on three legs.

The teeth of the guard chattered when he drew the door inward, and I realized he was almost overwhelmed with fear.

"Follow the path, and it will lead you to the place you seek."

"The king instructed you to lead me."

He rolled his eyes and stepped back as though he thought I intended to drag him with me through the doorway.

"I cannot pass through the Gate of Tsathoggua. All who pass through the gate die."

The name was familiar. Fighting off the poisonous clouds in my mind, I searched my memory. Tsathoggua was one of the Old Ones, not one of their lords but a lesser being of different blood. He had the form of a black toad with bulbous eyes and human hands. I had thought all the land of Khem ruled by Yig, the great serpent, but the shamans worshiped a different master. This was their private gate. They dwelled outside the town, beyond its wall.

Without hesitation, I stepped over the threshold. The door banged shut behind me, but there was no sound of a latch falling into place. Naturally not. Who would dare to hinder the entry of the shamans? If even the king of the land quailed before their leader, the common people must regard them as living gods.

Chapter 30

The narrow but well-traveled path wound beneath tall trees that cut off the light of the sun like a green curtain. So densely grew the undergrowth on either side a man would have found difficulty to force his way through it. At one place I encountered a great tree fallen across the path that no one had troubled to remove. I was forced to climb awkwardly over the moss-encrusted trunk with the aid of my walking staff, blood singing in my ears from the effort. I would have expected the canopy of trees to be filled with chattering birds, but the forest lay quiet, as though under a spell of sleep. The buzz of insects circling my head to bite my flesh was the only living sound not of my making.

There was a rankness in the heavy air of mingled pestilence and decay. I soon perceived the reason. The path undulated into a fen of evil-smelling pools and wet black mud. The floor of the forest became more open, but no easier to traverse. Anyone foolish enough to wander from the path into the swamps would quickly fall into some mud-filled sinkhole or hidden well and be lost forever. A mist hung like smoke just above the tall grasses, concealing the details of the ground from the eyes of those who might attempt to walk across it. The path was well marked by large white stones set at intervals on each of its sides, and in low-lying areas had been built up with rocks and earth so that it traversed the marsh like a meandering causeway. As I walked its length, I could almost imagine it to be the spine of the Great Serpent.

The lodge of shamans occupied a small island of firm ground in the midst of the fen. In form it was much like the long house of N'golo, but its walls were constructed of timber instead of brick. Smaller huts surrounded it. A rippling column of white smoke rose from a fire before one of the lesser structures, tended by a naked black woman who crouched on her heels and stirred with a stick the crackling embers beneath a sooty brass pot so that a cloud of sparks ascended through the hanging curtain of mist. Within the pot bubbled gray liquid. She was completely bald both on her head and between her thighs, but since she did not look much older than thirty years or so, I guessed that she had been shaved.

As I watched, a fly of the type that had so often bitten me along the path flew through the column of smoke and steam, and fell down into the pot as though it had struck a stone wall. She made a clucking sound in her throat and flicked the fly out on the tip of her stick. A younger black woman in the advanced stages of pregnancy, who was equally hairless and naked, emerged from a different hut with something that wriggled in her hands and proceeded to spit the thing on the sharpened point of a long wooden stake driven into the ground. When she stepped back, I saw that it was a large frog. It continued to struggle with the bloody stake extending out its gasping open mouth.

The older woman tending the fire looked at me knowingly and murmured to the younger, who laughed. I did not catch her words, but noticed that both of them appeared to have no teeth. I was more surprised by their lack of adornment than the absence of clothing, which was rendered additionally obscene by the smoothness between their legs. As I made my way past them toward the open door of the lodge, I looked around for dogs or children, but saw no signs of either. Nor were any guards posted. Faint groaning came from the interior of one of the huts, a dismal, tormented sound.

A young shaman walked around the edge of the lodge and noticed me. He approached at a casual gait, showing no surprise. A woven loincloth covered his groin. Rings of bright feathers around his arms and ankles were his only other apparel, apart from a necklace of finger bones. The top of his head was shaved down its center like that of his master. Stopping in front of me, he examined me with his dark eyes the way a farmer will examine his livestock. Had he attempted to touch me, I would have cut off his hand. I was prepared to be prodded by the king and the chief shaman, but not by any other inhabitant of this repellent land. He seemed to sense my antagonism and snorted to himself. With a negligent wave, he gestured for me to follow him and led me into the lodge.

The left end of the dim interior was dominated by a great statue of black stone carved in the shape of Tsathoggua, that rested on a low dais of gray stone. The god appeared to sit leaning forward in a throne, his curiously human hands curled over the arms of the seat, his bulbous eyes staring down in contempt, a superior and knowing smile on his grotesquely broad mouth. Before the statue stood a low stone pedestal with a shallow stone basin mounted on its top, filled with some noxious oily liquid that rippled as I glanced into it, as though aware of my attention. In color it was like a mixture of ink and blood.

Lo'oka's throne dominated the opposite end of the lodge. In size and shape, it resembled the throne of his god, and was carved from ebony. The chief shaman sat perched on the edge of its seat, his hideously thin body like that of a starved child in the seat of an elder. Behind the throne stood lesser shamans in parody of the advisors of N'golo. None carried a weapon. Near the throne, a naked hairless woman balanced a pitcher of glazed clay on the generous swell of her hip. Lo'oka held out the gold goblet in his hand without looking at her, and she filled it from the pitcher.

All eyes were on me as I entered, but no one spoke. The insolent young shaman who preceded me stepped around a post embedded in the clay floor near the center of the lodge, and as I blinked my eyes in the shadows, I saw that tied to it was a kneeling black man. His arms were bound behind his back around the post, and he hung facing Tsathoggua with his head dangling down from his shoulders, unconscious or dead. Patches of skin were missing from his back and the tops of his thighs. A triangle had been drawn on the floor around the stake with lines of white sand. As I followed the shaman past the stake, I took care not to break the line of the triangle, which pointed toward the statue of the toad god. The stake was daubed with blood, and the scent of drying blood hung thick on the air. Buzzing flies made the only comment.

Lo'oka upended his goblet and passed it back to the woman, then stood lightly from his seat and approached me. The other shamans gathered around us on bare feet in a circle, standing near enough that I might have reached out and touched them. It was some consolation that none of them wore a knife or sword. I tightened my grip on the walking staff in my right hand. A shiver ran through my body that I could not suppress. One of the shamans chuckled softly in the belief that I was frightened. His black eyes were without compassion. Glancing from face to face, I saw only amusement, mild interest, superiority, contempt. They looked at me as palace nobles might regard a deformed animal brought before them for their entertainment.

"I have come for an antidote to the poison known as the black ichor," I said in their language, coughing from the effort it cost me to speak.

"Look at his eyelids," Lo'oka said to the man beside him. "Do you see the shadows?"

The younger shaman nodded, eyeing me narrowly.

"Why is he still alive?"

"Enchantment," the chief shaman said. "Nothing else could stop the black death."

They began to murmur amongst themselves, speculating over what charms would be effective against the poison. One of them reached out to touch my face. I shrugged the woolen blanket from my shoulders, and with my left hand drew my dagger half out of its sheath. He stared into my eyes, then stepped back.

"Do you have the antidote?" I demanded of Lo'oka, who seemed to have forgotten that I stood before him.

He turned his malignant gaze upon me and showed the tiny gleaming pearls of his teeth.

"Why should we act to spare your life?"

"I have wealth. Jewels of uncommon rarity."

Tucking the shaft of my staff beneath my left arm for support, I opened my purse and poured several gems amid coins of gold and silver onto my palm, then held it up to the shaman. The greater number of jewels remained tied in a rag in my coat, but I had no intention of displaying them. His eyes narrowed in his skull-like face as he studied the glittering stones. Before he could pluck one between his fingers, I closed my fist and returned them to my purse. Anger flared redly in the depths of his gaze.

"Ugly man, I think we will take your jewels and let you die. We want to watch how long the ichor takes to kill you."

Thrusting through the ring of shaman, who made no resistance, I drew my sword. Lo'oka tittered, and I saw sly smiles on their faces. He raised his feather-ringed bone wand and began to gesture upon the air and mutter under his breath. From behind me I heard a gurgling, but did not dare turn my head.

"It would be unwise to kill a servant of Nyarlathotep," I told him. "It was he who sent me to the Besari to be cured."

The bony shaman stopped his incantation. The mention of the dark god's name caused the other shaman to draw away from me, as though the sound itself were a contagion.

"You lie."

I thrust my face forward.

"You have the sight. See his mark."

Lo'oka came nearer until his breath touched my lips. It stank of death. He stared hard, as though trying to see through a solid block of stone. For a moment I feared he would not perceive what others saw so clearly. At last, he stepped back, his expression thoughtful.

"He has the mark," he murmured to his companions, who stood in the depths of the shadows, watching me.

The young man who had led me into the lodge stepped forward.

"What of it? There is no love between Tsathoggua and the dark wanderer."

"Would you have the man with no face for an enemy?" I asked Lo'oka.

For several heartbeats he considered my words, then shrugged. He beckoned the woman, who had stood in the background, to come forward, and whispered into her ear. She glanced at me, nodded, and left the lodge. I felt the shamans in the shadows on either side relax and move slowly to the throne behind their leader. The burbling noise ceased. I risked a glance over my shoulder but could find no source for it. Within minutes, the hairless woman returned bearing with care between her hands a shallow clay bowl. She approached me, her expression passive and unreadable, and extended the bowl. I took it in my right hand and saw the dark surface of the liquid it contained tremble.

"Drink, and find the peace you seek," Lo'oka said.

Raising the bowl to my lips, I hesitated. Was it the antidote, or a poison? The woman before me met my eyes. I saw her nod imperceptibly. Her expression remained impossible to interpret.

It will kill or cure, Sashi, I spoke into my mind.

Drink deep, my love.

The words of the djinn decided me. I put the foul-smelling liquid to my cracked lips and filled my mouth, then drank it in a single swallow. Showing no emotion, the woman removed the empty bowl from my hand and walked with graceful strides from the lodge.

326

It burned in my throat. The burning spread to my stomach. I felt it seep through my flesh into my limbs, and in the space of a minute it reached my extremities. Even my breath felt hot as I gasped in shock. It was like being hit on the bare skin with scalding water, save that it flowed inside my body. I expected at any moment to fall dead, but the lack of exultation in the features of the chief shaman reassured me. The malice had not departed, but lay beneath the surface. He continued to watch as I balanced on my walking staff, struggling to keep my feet while the shadows slid sideways and the sound of rushing water came and went in my ears.

After a while I noticed that the burning had departed from my joints, and that I no longer shivered. Dizziness began to recede.

"Will I live?" I asked, my voice rough in the rawness of my throat.

The chief shaman came forward. I suffered him to peer beneath my eyelids and prod the sides of my neck. Smiling with his tiny slit of a mouth, he nodded.

"How much do you ask in payment?"

He waved his bony hand with a negligent gesture. I stared at him.

"You ask no payment for saving my life?"

He shook his head, and would not meet my eyes. Instead, he turned and went back to sit on the edge of his throne. He drew down one of the shamans standing behind him and began to murmur in conversation with the other man. Neither paid any attention to me. I realized that I had been dismissed.

Backing warily toward the doorway, I perceived that something had changed in the appearance of the kneeling corpse bound to the stake. For a moment my mind failed to register the difference. Then I realized that the bowed head of the corpse had been stripped of skin, exposing its bloody skull. Something bubbled before the altar of the toad god. I cast a glance at the stone basin and saw ripples on the surface of the dark liquid, though no breeze penetrated the entrance.

It was a profound relief to stand beneath the open sky. The sun resembled a red ball through the thickened curtain of mist that had continued to gather while I argued for my life in the lodge. Leaning on my staff, I walked with measured strides past the woman crouched before the fire. She did not raise her head to glance at me. Out of one of the huts came a faint mewing, but whether from a human throat or that of an animal, I could not determine.

When I traced with trembling steps the stone-lined path back to the fortification wall of Tyroon, I found Martala pacing nervously back and forth outside the opened gate of the shamans. She saw me with relief and ran along the path to help me.

"Another minute and I would have followed you," she said.

I waved her aside. Breathing deeply, I discovered that I no longer needed the support of the staff and gave it to her to carry.

"Did you get the antidote?"

"Yes. I am growing stronger."

Before I could prepare myself, she grabbed me around the neck and covered my face with kisses. I would have fallen, but she caught me under the arm and held me until my balance returned.

"I am sorry, Alhazred," she said with embarrassment. "I am happy that you will not die."

"Let's get out of this forest. I don't trust the shamans."

We passed through the toad-emblazoned door and shut it behind us. I wished there were some way to bolt it, but reflected that if the shamans wanted to enter Tyroon, there were probably a dozen ways for them to do so. The guard who had escorted me to the door had long since departed, Martala told me.

"Where is your blanket?" she asked.

I remembered shrugging it off my shoulders so that I could draw my dagger.

"It doesn't matter. I don't need it any longer."

"Come with me." She drew me along by the hand as though I were her aged grandfather. "I rented us a room for the night."

To call it a room was to accord it a level of distinction it failed to merit. It was a sleeping mat in the corner of a hut shared by the owner, his fat wife, and three squalling brats. The youngest never ceased to cry. I heard it from some distance as we approached the hut, a series of short piercing wails delivered as rapidly as the creature could draw breath into its tiny lungs. The two older children engaged in an obscure familial warfare that had no beginning or end, merely periods of uneasy truce. They ceased striking each other with their fists long enough to stare at me as I stopped in front of the doorway, with Martala holding my arm.

The owner was out, but his wife flashed me a gap-toothed smile and nodded affably from her seat upon the doorstep. She did not stand, but moved to one side to allow us to pass. We entered the dim interior of the small but odorous mud structure and stood over the dirty woven layer of river reeds that was to be our bed. The only amenity was a curtain of ragged brown cloth that hung on a cord, partially shielding the corner occupied by the mat from the rest of the interior. The sleeping mats of the family stood rolled up along a wall, but presumably would be laid flat on the floor beside ours during the night.

"Is this the best you could do?"

Martala frowned at me and stamped her shoe on the clay floor.

"Tyroon has no inns. No one ever comes to visit this place. At least it is a roof over us."

I looked around in resignation.

"I suppose a bath is out of the question?"

She smiled in spite of her petulance.

"Are you hungry?"

Pausing to reflect on the question, I discovered that I did have an appetite. Hardly surprising, since I had been able to keep no food in my stomach for almost two days. I nodded.

"Good. I will buy bread and fruit from the market. Wait for me."

She left before I could answer. Exhaling deeply, I went to the mat, and with the aid of the wall lowered myself into a sitting posture upon it. The clay of the wall felt cool against my back through my coat. Even though my body recovered rapidly from the poison, I was exhausted with a weariness that went so deep, it seemed to penetrate my very bones. I closed my eyelids to rest them for a moment.

The next I knew, Martala knelt beside me, holding a shallow wooden bowl to my lips. I drank from it and discovered that it held warm goat's milk. So great was my thirst, I had no impulse to spit it out. She set down the bowl and tore a corner from a flat loaf of bread. I took it from her and held it to my face to chew on it. My hand seemed almost to float independent of my body, such was the fatigue of my muscles. Everything ached, though not with the sharp ache of the poison, but the softer, more relaxed ache of a bruise that mends itself.

"Where will we go now, Alhazred?"

Closing my eyes, I leaned my head back against the coolness of the wall, and considered the matter.

"I have heard that many rare books are for sale in Alexandria. It may be possible to convert the scroll I stole from the Order of the Sphinx into something more useful."

"Didn't you steal the scroll to keep it?"

"What need have I for the scroll? I was the scribe who copied it. No, I took it because I knew it had great value."

"What does it teach?"

I recalled that Martala had not been able to understand the language of the ancient necromancer, even though she had been present during his questioning. Swallowing the last of the bread, I licked my lips and again closed my eyes. The floor seemed to move under my buttocks, but I knew it was only dizziness.

"The secrets of the necromancy used by the order, and much more besides. It should bring us a casket of gold in the book marts of Alexandria."

Her murmured reply was lost to me. I slept uneasily, recalling fragments of nightmare each time my mind stirred into a semblance of awareness. The first time I woke, I discovered that I lay on my right side with Martala curled in front of me, her head on my arm. She faced the room, where the red flame of an oil lamp flickered fitfully beneath the tattered hem of the curtain that concealed our mat. She had placed me so that my back was to the wall, and put herself in front for my defense. This realization brought a curious warmth into my heart. I tightened the arm that lay across her naked waist, and she patted with a sleepy gesture the back of my hand. I slid into sleep to the sound of the squalling baby and the soft clucks of its mother as she tried to quiet it.

When next I woke, the hut lay in near complete darkness. The only light came through the small, unshuttered window beside the door. Through the gap between the curtain and the wall, I saw starlight out the window. The baby had fallen asleep. Snoring came from the main part of the hut, but whether it issued from the throat of the mother or her husband, I could not determine.

There was something not quite right about the air, a faint scent of decay that I knew well from my days in the Empty Space. I strained my ears but heard nothing apart from the regular snores. Closing my eyes, I summoned Sashi. Her beautiful features formed on the darkness within my mind.

Sashi, is anything amiss?

She frowned and appeared to listen, then shook her head.

No spirits threaten your safety, Alhazred. I would have awakened you.

I know you would.

Opening my eyes, I peered around the edges of the curtain. Nothing stirred. My right arm had fallen numb from the pressure of Martala's head. I gently closed and opened my hand to make the blood flow to my fingers. My hand began to tingle as it regained sensation. I could have slid my arm away, but that would have awakened the girl, so I merely rotated it until her head rested on a different place.

While I did this, something caught my attention, a soft sound like the distant slap of a wet cloth against a river rock. I lay wondering what had caused it. There were no large rocks on the bank of the Nile that bordered the town, and in any case, no washerwoman would be doing her laundry in the middle of the night. Through the gap at the edge of the curtain, the stars in the window began to wink out. I squeezed shut my eyelids to clear my vision, thinking I imagined it. When I looked again the stars were back. Again, the faint slap came.

Cold ran down my spine like a dipper of well water. I reached my left hand to Martala's shoulder and squeezed gently. She stirred against my body, and made a faint sound with her lips, but my tightened grasp stopped it in her throat. Gently, I began to ease my arm from under her head, grateful that the girl had not wholly undressed me for the night. She had removed my sword and my boots, but my dagger still hung from its baldric at my hip. Outside the window came the murmur of a voice and quiet laughter.

Something scuffed in the room beyond the curtain. The snores ended with an abrupt snort. A sleep-laden man's voice asked who was there. A mat rustled, and the mother spoke a man's name. Suddenly he began to shout. The sounds of a struggle filled the darkness, mingled with the terrified and bewildered questions of the woman. The baby wailed, and for a few seconds the outer space was a milling confusion of unseen bodies. I gained my feet and pulled Martala up.

"Where is your weapon?"

"With my dress, in the corner. What's happening?"

I made no attempt to search for my sword, but gave silent thanks that the girl had not removed my dagger. Drawing it, I swept the curtain aside.

The dim light from the window showed two human shapes locked in struggle, while other forms danced around them. The man continued to shout, and his wife to scream, so that I wondered why their neighbors did not rush into the hut to discover the reason for the tumult. The frightened cries of the two older children joined the wails of the baby.

Above the din came a sharp snap, like the breaking of a dry branch, and one of the struggling forms crumpled slowly to the ground. A flash of light lit the hut. By its brief illumination I saw a black man sprawled across the disordered sleeping mats, his head twisted backward on his neck at a grotesque angle. Above him stood what I took to be another man, until I realized that the dark patches on his cheeks and mouth were not shadows, but holes. A second flash, and another, revealed the mother crouched over her oil lamp, attempting to ignite its wick with steel and flint, tears of fright streaming wetly down her round cheeks. In the corner, next to the crib of the infant, huddled the little girl and her older brother. Both were naked. He had an arm across her chest as though to shield her, but his eyes were vacant with fear.

Several more quick flashes of the flint showed the corpse that stood alone in the middle of the hut turning its worm-eaten face in my direction. The shriveled sockets of its skin-wrapped skull held no eyes, and I wondered how it could see its way. As I stepped forward, the wick of the oil lamp caught, and a red flicker illuminated the hut. Still the door remained shut. Through the open window I caught a glimpse of a black face, and recognized in that instant the young shaman who had argued for my death in the lodge of his master.

My dagger entered the heart of the corpse. It made no sound. When a man is stabbed in the chest, his breath hisses from his lips, and he gasps in pain. This thing did not breathe. I wrenched the dagger free and spun away to avoid its closing grasp, then slashed it across the arms. I might as well have been cutting the bark of tree limbs. It took no notice. From the corner of my eye I saw Martala, naked but carrying in her hand the long blade of her new dagger, as she circled around to approach behind the monster. I darted the tip of my own blade at its face. Several fingers' breadth of the steel entered its left eye socket. Before I could free my dagger, it got its hand on my shoulder. The strength in its bony, rotting fingers was unnatural. I tried to shrink away by bending my knees, but the tips of its fingers dug like spikes into my muscles, and I was only able to escape by hitting it an upward blow on the forearm with all the force of my arm.

Martala began to stab it in the back at the level of its kidneys. When this had no effect, she crouched and tried to cut the tendons at the back of its legs just above its heels. For a moment I had hope that this would bring it to its knees, but it continued to walk toward me, forcing me backward into the corner occupied by our sleeping mat. With the splitting of awareness that only comes in battle, I saw at the edges of my vision that the woman continued to huddle on the floor, holding the oil lamp up before her face as though it were a kind of charm. On the other side of the hut, the two children stood frozen in terror with their backs pressed against the wall.

"Alhazred, get out of there!"

Martala grasped the corpse around its waist and tried to pull it backwards, but its balance was as inhuman as its strength. It took no notice of her. All its attention remained fixed on me. I started to dodge to the right to get around it, but it was quick. For a moment I stood motionless, letting its arms extend over me on either side, then I ducked to the left. Its hand caught the collar of my coat. I struck at its forearm in a futile attempt to break its grip on the fabric, but before I could writhe my body out of the coat, its other hand closed over my right forearm.

Martala's cries of rage and frustration mingled with the unceasing squall of the infant. I heard her long blade slide into dead flesh over and over, but she stood concealed from my sight behind the chest of the corpse. Feeling the fingers of the thing grind through the muscle of my upper arm and grate against the bone, I transferred my dagger to my left hand and cut upwards into the rotting crotch of the hulk. Again I stabbed up, and heard its belly rip open. Something wet fell across the back of my left hand, and the stench of excrement filled the air.

It drew me closer, in spite of my effort to press it away. I heard Martala's fists beat against its back with impotence above her frenzied curses. As our faces drew near, I had time to reflect that the dead thing had a nose very like my own. I felt its blackened teeth in my throat, and the hot gush of my blood.

Then I died.

PART TWO

Chapter 31

The light was more than bright, it was an agony that poured through my brain like molten steel. Shrill screams rent the air, rising in pitch until they exhausted themselves with inarticulate babbling. My body convulsed and twisted around on itself. Something scraped my bare shoulder. I recognized the chill touch of stone. In the silence a voice spoke.

"Alhazred, don't be afraid."

I unclenched my eyes and opened the lids a crack. The pain was less intense. It receded along the nerves of my body like an ocean wave running off a beach. I saw my exposed knees and realized that my arms were looped around them. With a distinct effort of will, I forced them to relax. Rivulets of sweat trickled across my legs and chest, and I trembled as if with some ague. Over me leaned a shadow that became a woman's face. It wore an expression of deep concern, and something more in strange contrast. Exultation.

"Martala? Have I been sick?"

"Yes, you were ill, but you are better now."

Her hand touched my shoulder. I flinched. So sensitive was my skin, the coolness of her fingertips felt like ice. She helped me to sit upright on the flagstone floor. I became aware of my nakedness.

A single stone oil lamp burned on a low table of rough wooden planks. It was that flame that had seared into my eyes like the desert sun. The rest of the chamber lay under shadow. The walls were made of stone blocks, and the roof of vaulted red bricks, supported by two thick pillars of stone. In the corner I noticed a stone stair leading up into darkness. A kind of green mold grew on one wall darkened by a patch of moisture. Beyond the pillar in front of me, I saw a large copper kettle in a kind of open fireplace, the charcoal cold and black beneath it, a copper vent hood to remove fumes hanging over it. No one else was in the room.

The memory of the walking corpse returned. I grasped my throat, but found it whole and uninjured. Had it been nothing more than a dream?

"Can you stand?"

"Yes . . . I don't know, I think so."

Confused thoughts races through my brain. I remembered consulting with Lo'oka, the chief shaman, at his lodge on the island in the fen, and later being in the mud hut at Tyroon. This was no mud hut. It must be a vault beneath the ground, to judge by the cool damp air.

Martala helped me to my bare feet and guided me to a plain chair beside the table. I sat with relief, unwilling to trust the strangeness of my legs any longer. They were strong enough. The effects of the poison had wholly departed. Yet in some curious way they felt detached from my body, as though they were the legs of another man that I controlled at a distance. Everything felt both too intense and unreal.

Martala knelt on the floor at my feet and took my hand between hers. She wore a simple white linen dress unfamiliar to my eyes, with a broad embroidered girdle of the same color to close it around her waist, and her lustrous dark hair was knotted on top of her head in a fashion I had not seen her wear before. A comb of ivory held the coils in place. I wondered where she had acquired the dress. Her ice-gray eyes stared up into mine with concern.

"Where are we?"

"This is your house, Alhazred. We are in the cellar beneath your house."

I frowned and tried to still my racing thoughts.

"I own no house."

"Yes, you do." She smiled. "I bought it for you with several of your jewels."

By reflex I reached with my free hand to pat my waist where my purse usually hung, then remembered that I was naked.

"You took my purse?"

"I had to, there was no other way. I needed a place to work."

My laughter sounded strange in my ears. Martala flinched as though I had slapped her.

"If I were going to buy a house, it would not be in Tyroon."

"This isn't Tyroon."

Coldness washed over my heart. My breath caught in my throat, and I forced myself to exhale slowly while I stared at her face.

"Where are we?"

"Alexandria."

I nodded, considering the word, and remembered telling her that my intention was to travel down the river to Alexandria, after leaving Tyroon.

"How long was I dead?"

She blinked at the word, her face pale, then lowered her eyes and stared at my fingers for several moments, pressed between her own. When she raised her face to confront me, her expression was grim.

"Almost seven months."

Gently, I extracted my hand and pushed myself up with the aid of the table. My legs still felt odd, but they were once more my own legs. The vertigo that had gripped me was fading. It was an effort to stand on my own, but I could sustain it. I felt between my thighs to assure myself of the evidence of my own eyes. My manhood was still missing. I raised my hands to my head and slid them over the holes that should have been occupied by my nose and ears.

"Feisel was right," I murmured. "The process of resurrection cannot restore amputated flesh."

"It healed your throat," Martala pointed out, standing beside me.

"That is different. All the parts of my throat were still present." I chuckled to myself, prompting the girl to glance sideways at me as though in fear for my sanity. "A good thing for me the walking corpse didn't swallow what it bit."

"When it killed you, it fell lifeless beside your body."

"What did you do then?"

She shrugged.

"First I went to help you, but when I saw you were dead, I went a little crazy and cut the corpse that killed you with my knife. Then I heard the shaman laugh outside the window, so I ran out and caught him before he could run away, and forced him to go into the hut. By that time the mother and her children had fled."

"Did any people of the town come to your aid?"

"Those cowards?" She made a sound of disgust. "No one even opened their door to find out what was happening."

"They were terrified of the shamans."

She nodded. It was old information to her.

"At first the shaman laughed at me, but when I cut pieces off his body, he stopped laughing. I ordered him to restore you to life. He said that it was beyond his power. I thought he lied, but after a while I saw that he was too frightened of me to lie, so I wept while I sat on his chest with my knife at his throat, and my tears fell all over what remained of his face."

"The shamans have the power to animate corpses, but not to restore the dead to life," I said gently. The thought of her weeping for my death touched my heart.

"I made him tell me how he controlled the corpse before I killed him. It was with this."

She reached into the neck of her householder's dress and pulled forth a leather thong from which hung a bone whistle. It was the same as those I had seen hanging from the neck of Lo'oka and his disciples.

"To remove life from the walking dead, the shamans blow upon it like this." She raised the whistle to her mouth, then paused. "It took me weeks to learn how to play it."

She blew a series of notes that echoed mournfully from the wet stones and arched bricks of the vault. I held my breath, wondering if the music would return me to dust, but when I saw that it had no effect, I relaxed. Martala perceived my concern.

"No, it only works on the truly dead. You are alive, Alhazred. You are as you were before."

Holding my hand up before my face, I flexed my fingers. They moved easily, and I felt the strength in them. They were as pink and as clean as the skin of a week-old babe washed in spring water. My fingernails as yet did not project beyond the ends of my fingers, but were immature.

"How did you get my corpse down the Nile?"

"It wasn't easy, but with wealth anything is possible. I searched your coat and found the scroll, and I saw how many jewels you had in your purse, and in the knotted rag in your pocket. I was able to hire fishermen to take your body to the Second Cataract, and from there a trading boat carried it to the First Cataract, where I placed it on a ship that sailed for Alexandria."

"You are a resourceful woman."

She shrugged, but the blush of her cheek showed her pleasure at the compliment.

"I pretended to be your daughter, taking you home to Alexandria for mummification."

"How did you keep my flesh from rotting away?"

"Bitumen. I had your naked body coated in bitumen both inside and out. It kept away the worms and beetles. When I was a child at Memphis, I saw them use bitumen to make mummies, so I knew it would not hinder your resurrection."

"The bitumen all boiled away in the vat?"

She nodded.

"The ancient necromancer's scroll was very helpful. I had watched what was done to prepare the mummies under the Sphinx, but without the instructions of the scroll, I could not have restored you to life."

"Just as well that I decided to steal it."

She brushed her hands over my chest, as though wondering to see me stand before her. I reminded myself that although it had seemed only an instant to me, she had endured more than half a year of labor and doubt.

"Were you in paradise?" she asked in a timid voice.

"No."

She caught her breath.

"Not in hell?"

I shook my head.

"Oblivion."

For a moment she considered.

"Perhaps you were in paradise, and you have forgotten."

I smiled at the notion of a necromancer finding his way into the paradise described by the Prophet. Hell seemed a great deal more likely.

"Either way, I remember nothing."

To banish the disappointment that settled on her face, I asked her to show me around my house. She brightened and led me up the stairs to a door that was not locked. On the other side was a clean and spacious kitchen, filled with the light of early morning that poured through two windows in the exterior wall. I glanced through the screen of one and saw a small enclosed garden, its flowers and trees well tended.

"Do you live here alone?"

She jumped to sit on the long table before the cooking fireplace and swung her legs like a little girl.

"A woman of the city comes in each morning to clean and cook. Her husband tends the garden and runs whatever errands I give him. At night I sleep alone."

I repressed the urge to smile at the double meaning of her last words. That she had been faithful to my memory, I had no reason to doubt. My very existence gave proof of it.

"Show me the rest."

In addition to the kitchen, the street level held a dining hall and a reception chamber for guests, as well as a store room. On the upper level were three bedrooms and a room that contained a reading table and two cases of books. I was surprised by the number of volumes. A scroll lay open on the table beside a brass oil lamp that had burned itself dry. It was the necromantic scroll from under the Sphinx.

"You worked all night, didn't you?"

She nodded.

"You must be exhausted. You should sleep."

"Soon. I must introduce you to Hatero and his wife when they come. They will arrive soon, and would be alarmed to find only a strange man in the house."

"I understand."

Picking up a book that lay open beside the scroll, I saw that it was a book of magic written in Greek. When I went to one of the bookcases, I found that most of its volumes were on the necromantic arts. They were dangerous books.

"Hatero and his wife cannot read," she said, perceiving the direction of my thoughts.

"Even so, the diagrams."

"Yes. I don't let them into this room. I lock the door while they are in the house. I lock the door to the cellar as well."

In wonder I gazed at the other case of books that stood against the outer wall on the opposite side of the small window. There must have been over a hundred books in each case.

"How did you acquire so many forbidden texts?"

She clapped her hands together in delight.

"You will love it here, Alhazred. The booksellers of this place have everything. If they don't have it, they can get it within a few weeks. I found all that I needed for my studies, and much more."

I smiled to see her enthusiasm.

"You are at least as much a necromancer as I am. Indeed, more so, for you have raised the dead and I have not."

"I was so frightened that I would make a mistake," she said, wringing her hands together.

For the first time I noticed the dark shadows under her eyes, and the gauntness of her face, and wondered how many hours she slept each night. A strange impulse made me draw her to me and kiss her forehead. The warm morning sunlight through the window screen dappled our faces. She did not pull away, but stood staring up at me with joy. Tears gleamed in the corners of her eyes.

"Thank you for giving me back my life."

"What is a good servant for?"

Into the sweetness of the moment came a pang of regret, and I wondered what caused it. There was something missing, an emptiness where there should have been fullness. When at last I realized, all the joy left my heart.

"Sashi. She is gone."

It surprised me that the absence of the djinn would be a source of such sadness, but I reflected, over time a man can become accustomed to anything. She was gone. Death had driven her from me. She wandered the desert, somewhere above the Second Cataract, alone, as she had been before our union. Yet why did Martala smile so strangely?

The girl leaned up on her toes and kissed me on the lips before I could draw away in surprise. I felt a rushing sensation as though breath were being forced between my lips, yet it was not a substantial force but more subtle. It spread from my mouth down my body until it pervaded my limbs with a familiar presence. Ending the kiss, I closed my eyes, and the lovely face of the djinn, the face she always chose to present to me, formed itself on the darkness.

I knew you would return to me, my love.

Did Martala carry you all this while? I asked in my mind.

Yes. We were good companions, but I am glad to be home.

And I am happy that you were not lost to me.

She smiled, and I felt her embrace my body and kiss me. The thought came to me that she was taller than Martala and her lips were more rounded.

Rapping sounded from below.

"Hatero and his wife," Martala said. "I must lock this room and the door to the cellar before I let them in. Come down with me to meet them."

I spread my arms. She giggled.

"Your clothes are in my bedroom. I had them laundered and mended. Get dressed while I lock the library door, and I will show the servants their new master."

"Will they be surprised to see me here?"

"I told them last week that I expected you to arrive in port any day. You come from the Lebanon."

She led me down the short hall to the open door of one of the bedrooms and pointed to a tall cabinet. Within I found my undergarments, blue Muslim coat, and weapons, hanging on pegs. I patted the coat and felt the rag containing the dried white spiders in its usual place. There, too, my purse lay on a shelf, somewhat lighter than I remembered, and my empty water skin. Leaving them where they rested, I caressed the smooth surface of Gor's skull with delight. From the hallway, a key rattled in a lock.

"Another thing," she said from the hall as I hooked the thong of the skull through my belt beside the scabbard of my sword. "We are married. And you are a Christian."

"Naturally. We mustn't shock our neighbors."

Her head poked momentarily around the edge of the doorjamb as the rapping sounded again at the front door. She wore a head scarf of bright purple silk that hung over her hair and shoulders. I marveled at the change in her appearance. Seven months of toil and care had transformed her from a girl into a woman.

"Don't forget to put on your face."

I performed the spell of glamour while listening to her open the door below, and the sounds of footsteps across the slate floor. Had she not reminded me, I would have forgotten.

The servants were not overly surprised to see me descend the stairs. Hatero was a short and somewhat fat Egyptian who wore his hair like a Roman, in little curls across his forehead. His wet brown eyes glided up and down my body as I stepped off the last tread to stand with my arm around Martala's shoulders. No doubt he thought it strange that a Christian would wear the habitual garb of a Muslim, but it seemed unlikely he would be familiar with the customary dress of Lebanon, rendering an explanation unnecessary. He and his wife both bowed deeply, and after a few words of greeting, I sent them off to perform their daily functions.

"You should sleep," I reminded Martala when we stood alone in the entrance hall.

"Not yet. I have to see a man about a book. Now that you are alive, you can come with me. If you feel strong enough."

I laughed, causing her to smile.

"After seven months on my back, I'm ready to dance in the marketplace."

When we stepped from the front door into the street, the sunlight made me realize how alive I felt. There was no trace of fatigue in my new body. It tingled with reserves of energy. Part of this was due to the presence of Sashi, I guessed, but it went deeper than that. My body had not merely been restored, it had been remade. The vitality I felt was that of a newborn child, unhampered by the weakness and pain an infant suffers after birth.

By some sympathy, the world around me looked and sounded as new as my body felt. Even the sour smells of the city did not rob the scene of its wonder. There was beauty in the shadows cast by the houses on the cobblestones, beauty in the children who ran between the slow moving donkey carts and horses, even beauty in the house matron across the way who cast the golden contents of her chamber pot into the street through a slanting beam of sunlight.

"What makes this book so special?" I asked her, as we worked our way together down the slope of the street toward the harbor, walking to the left of the central gutter along which trickled a thin stream of slops.

"It is a scroll written entirely in the language of the Old Ones. But that is not what makes it so special. I have read a rumor that it contains information about the restoration of lost limbs."

I touched the right side of my head, where my ear should have been.

"If it can restore a limb, then perhaps it can bring back a nose and an ear as well."

"That was my thinking," she agreed.

We continued north along the prosperous and crowded residential street until the blue of the Mediterranean appeared on the horizon between the houses, and the scent of salt filled the air. I saw the masts of ships, and knew we must be close to the docks. Overhead, the cries of wheeling sea birds penetrated the babble of voices and the rumble of cart wheels. On the untended open green before a decayed temple of Hermes that was set back from an intersection of the streets, we paused to let a herder and his young son drive his goats along the cobbles toward the ships.

The green was dominated by a square pillar surmounted by a bearded bust of the god, so eroded by the salt air that his features were almost worn away. We sat on the crumbling edge of the stone block that formed its base.

"Where are we going?" I asked Martala. It was necessary to raise my voice above the general din.

She pointed at a board on the opposite side of the street that hung from chains above the heads of those who passed. Weathered by age and the salt air, it showed the image of a bird with a great fan of a tail, painted in green against a rust-colored background. The imposing three-level building attached to the sign dominated the corner where the streets met. A narrow alley on its opposite side gave it an air of free-standing pride that had begun to sag with the weight of years. Its front was sheathed in a layer of white clay that had flaked away in places to reveal the raw brick beneath. Its narrow windows, framed in dressed marble, stood uncommonly tall to let in the light. A gull in search of beetles pecked into a tuft of browning grass that sprouted in its lead roof gutter.

"The proprietor of that inn promised to contact a man who knows the Jew who keeps the scroll. I'm confident the man is the Jew's servant."

When the goats had passed, leaving a scattered reminder of their presence, we picked our way across the street to the inn of the Green Peacock. Its common room held a handful of seamen and laborers. They glanced at us with mild curiosity as we entered, but I saw nothing sinister in their eyes. The same could not be said of a lean man who sat alone behind the door, beneath a window, his shoulders hunched over his table, a cup of wine almost invisible between the interlaced fingers of his large hands. We were seated at our table before I noticed him. His gray eyes, like chips of charcoal, lingered on me from beneath the rim of his fur-trimmed cap as I looked at him, but he dropped his gaze with a deliberate show of disinterest.

I leaned across the table toward Martala.

"Have you seen any of Farri's men in Alexandria?"

She glanced at the man by the door.

"Not one of them since I came here. At first I was sure Farri would try to kill me, so I hired a bodyguard to walk with me whenever I left the house, but after three or four months, I dismissed him. I was paying him for nothing."

"Maybe Farri has forgotten about us. It has been a long time."

"Yes. Except . . ."

I waited for her to finish.

"It isn't like Farri to forget a grudge."

The proprietor of the inn passed a wooden tray of filled tin cups to a serving girl and came around the counter that divided his wine casks from the tables. He was a short Greek with gray hair spilling out from the faded blue turban on his head, and a full gray beard. His sun-creased face and the missing little finger from his left hand suggested that he had once been a seaman. Small scars covered his knuckles. I watched him wipe them dry on his apron as he stood beside our table, leering at Martala's unveiled face. She chose to ignore him.

He glanced at me keenly, dislike evident in his sour expression.

"You said you would come alone."

"This is my husband, Alhazred, who recently arrived from the Lebanon. I was acting as his agent, but now you must deal with him."

The Greek stared at her, then at me.

"Well?"

"Well, what?" I inquired mildly in his own language.

"The money. Have you got the money?"

"I have it," Martala said.

Glancing around the inn to see if anyone watched our table, she drew her purse from the ornamental girdle around her waist and hefted it so that the coins inside clinked. She loosened its drawstring and tipped its contents onto her palm, and I saw by their golden gleam that the coins were dinars. With quick motions she returned them to the purse, cinched it tight, and replaced it in her girdle.

"It better all be there," he said. "These people don't like to be cheated. Make one mistake, and you are both dead."

I laid a hand on his hairy forearm.

"When do I see the owner of the scroll?"

His snort of amusement was not pleasant.

"Never. No one ever sees him. Nobody knows who he is, not even the men who work for him."

"Then how will we—" Martala began.

He was not listening. He looked with a meaningful expression at the lean figure behind the door and nodded, then stepped back until my hand fell from his arm. As though he had already forgotten our existence, he barked a few harsh words in Coptic to the serving girl and returned to his wine casks.

The lean man stood and crossed the straw-strewn floor to our table, then sat on the long bench beside Martala without being asked. She drew away from him as far as the bench would allow. He exuded an aura of menace. His cap, and the coarse linen weave of his brown tunic that was so travel stained around its hem, set him apart from the seamen, nor did he have the look of a common dock worker. I saw at the neck of his tunic that he wore over his white shirt a vest of fine chain mail. His narrow face was seared on the right cheek, and the fire had left an ugly red patch almost the color of blood. He had tried to cover it with a close-trimmed beard, but the curly hairs did not grow high enough on his cheek to hide all of it. Strands of gray in the beard contrasted with the glossy dark curls hanging beneath the trim of brown fur around his cap.

"Don't talk, just listen," he whispered, voice like the scrape of a knife. "I'm here to give you instructions. If you want a chance to copy the scroll, you'll do as you're told."

"Copy?" Martala interrupted. "No, we want to buy the scroll, not copy it."

He turned slowly toward her. In spite of herself, she flinched away, then gathered her courage and faced him with a defiant expression.

"The scroll is not for sale. Didn't that fool tell you anything? You buy the time to make a copy of it."

"I have no supplies to do the work of a scribe," I told him.

"You need nothing, except money. How much are you prepared to pay?"

"One hundred dinars," Martala said quickly.

"Show me."

Again, she removed the purse and held it on her palm. He snatched it almost savagely and hefted it to feel its weight, then dropped it onto the table.

"Is this all you can pay?"

"This is our life savings," she lied. "We had to sell our lands in the Lebanon to raise so much gold."

He stared at her, then turned to me. I kept my expression neutral.

"Very well. It may be enough, but I make no promise. You, husband, stay at the inn and wait. The owner will give you a room. Take it and remain here alone. We deal with one person, not two."

"How long am I to remain here?"

"Until I come for you."

He stood from the bench, and I realized he was about to leave.

"What about the gold?"

"Keep it safe. If we come for you, and there is no gold, we will take our payment in blood. Understand?"

"Very clearly."

He left the inn with a curious sliding gait that made no sound on the scattered straw. I glanced at Martala, then drew her purse across the table and hooked the knobs of its drawstring through my belt.

"He's an assassin," she said.

"Or a mercenary. Probably both."

"He knew we lied."

"It doesn't matter. He expected us to lie."

"I don't like leaving you, Alhazred. You have so recently returned from the dead."

"Even so, I feel strong in health. Do not be afraid for me. I am curious to see this fabulous scroll of the Old Ones."

"I have prepared for this event, but you have not. I had a plan to ensure my safe departure with the scroll."

"Describe it to me, and I will fulfill it in your place."

She frowned in consideration. My mild smile reassured her, as I intended that it should. Leaning across the table, she spoke quietly for several minutes. As the innkeeper approached our table, she drew from inside her girdle a glass vial no larger than my little finger and passed it to me, using her body to conceal the action. I hid it in my left hand.

"Which of you is going to stay?" he asked in an impatient tone.

"I am your guest," I told him.

He nodded, as though he had anticipated as much. With a jerk of his hand, he indicated for me to follow, and started for the steep flight of stairs at the back of the inn.

Chapter 32

My days at the Green Peacock passed with excruciating monotony. I used them to put my scattered thoughts in order. The transition from life to death, and from death to life, had done no harm to my body, but I discovered that it had unsettled my mind. From time to time images of horrifying presence flashed before my sight, gone before I was able to distinguish their contents. Whether they were memories of dreams or something more, I could not guess, but they awoke a vague terror in my heart that was difficult to placate. In their after images I sometimes thought I could distinguish the outline of the dark man.

After the first day in my room above the drinking hall, the noises and smells of the inn passed unnoticed. I spent my time lying on my back on the bed, staring at a nest of spiders in a corner of the ceiling beam, or sitting on a wooden chair gazing down from the window into the street. I found the activities of the spiders interesting, but the comings and goings of the people on the cobblestones offered greater variation. Though my eyes looked outward, my attention was reflected inward, as though the bustling scene were no more than a mirror. From time to time I was summoned to meals in the common dining hall on the lower level of the inn, and an unwashed serving girl entered to empty my chamber pot and to replenish the water in the pitcher beside the washing basin.

I am uncertain how many days passed. Two, at the least, perhaps three. It was characteristic of my condition that whereas my days were troubled by flashes of fearful imagery, at night I slept as soundly and deeply as a babe in its crib. If I dreamed, I retained no memory of it after waking. I found myself wondering, in an idle way, whether the Jew who owned the scroll had decided that my payment was insufficient, and had forgotten about me. It seemed unlikely that the sour owner of the inn would continue to tolerate my presence unless someone was paying for my room.

On the afternoon of the second day—or it may have been the third—I noticed a young harlot in a green dress and green head wrap, lounging across the street on the ragged patch of browning grass in front of the ruined temple of Hermes. The lower part of her face was veiled beneath a black mesh boshiya from which hung strings of silver coins, but I judged her age to be around eighteen years from her posture. She leaned with a jutting hip against the column of the god, and made a show of flipping the hem of her dress to flash her red silk surwal and silver ankle bracelets at the merchants and ships' officers who passed, but her location was too far back from the street to encourage conversation. It did provide an excellent view of the front door of the inn, and of the alley that led up the side to its rear yard. From time to time, she raised her head and stared directly at my window.

The persistent presence of the harlot helped to draw my thoughts outward from the dark depths of my soul. What if Martala was mistaken about Farri? Perhaps he had merely set a watch on my house, waiting for my return before he put his plan for revenge into motion. If so, he would know of my presence in Alexandria, and might even now be in the city, drawing a net tight around Martala while I waited helpless in this pestilential inn. These fears were probably groundless, but for the first time, I felt the prick of impatience. I decided that I had waited long enough. If I was not summoned this night, in the morning I would give my regards to the innkeeper and return to my house.

With the setting of the sun, the traffic on the street grew thin, and the harlot in her emerald dress departed like a shadow. I prepared myself for bed, my thoughts on Martala, who did the same alone and unguarded. That she could defend herself I knew well enough, but little skill availed against the attack of several street-hardened villains, well accustomed to working in darkness. They would not kill her. They would truss her in bonds like a hen for market and carry her back to their master.

For a time, my troubled thoughts kept me alert. I heard the watch cry the tenth hour of the night. When sleep came at last, it was deep and dreamless.

Alhazred, wake.

I opened my eyes without moving my body on the straw-filled mattress, Sashi's voice still echoing inside my head. The only sound in my ears was my own breathing. At the foot of the bed I saw two dark shapes. The light that came through the window was so dim, I could barely distinguish the shadowy outlines of their cloaks from the gloom. I glanced across at the chair, and wondered how I could have been so careless as to leave my sword and dagger on it. If these were Farri's men, my resurrection had been brief.

"I know you are awake," whispered a harsh voice. "Get dressed."

The voice of the lean man, unlovely though it was, caused me to relax. I slid the sheet off my body and went to the chair to don my garments. When I put on my dagger and sword, the brooding shadows made no objection. I glanced down through the open window. The street was black. The slanting rays of the quarter moon did not penetrate to its depths, and no lamp burned at this late hour. As I drew my face away, I thought I heard the scuff of boot leather on the cobbles, but it was faint enough that it may have been no more than imagination.

"Give me your purse, Alhazred," the lean shadow murmured.

"Take it."

He came around the foot of the bed and took the purse Martala had entrusted to me, then poured its contents onto his palm, which he held close to the window to take advantage of the weak moon glow. By that light I saw that he wore a leather mask over the top half of his face that left his nose and mouth unobstructed. I wondered why he went masked, then reflected that he might not wish to be identified by passersby when he took me to the place the scroll was kept. After he satisfied himself as to the number of gold dinars, he grunted and slid them into a small pouch of sailcloth, then tucked the wooden knobs on the drawstring of the purse into my belt.

"Would you leave a foreign traveler in a strange city without a single coin?"

He opened his own purse and passed me a Sassanian dirham of the largest size. I placed the silver coin into the girl's purse.

"You know my name. It's only fitting that you tell me your own."

He cocked his head as though considering this novel proposition. When at last he replied, his voice held a trace of dry amusement.

"Call me Altrus. It's as good a name as any."

352

We descended in stealth to the rear of the inn, where the proprietor waited beside the open back door. No light burned. I recognized him more by smell than by sight. He said nothing, and barely looked at me.

"Wait." A hand fell on my shoulder. "Put this on."

A piece of cloth was thrust into my hands. Feeling its edges, I found an opening.

"Am I to be blinded like a goat staked out for wolves?"

"If we wanted you dead, you would never have left your room."

The truth of these plain words caused me to draw the hood over my head. It had a rank smell of old sweat. The vague shapes around me were blotted out.

"Put your hand on my shoulder. Walk where I walk."

Someone took hold of my left hand and raised it to Altrus' bony shoulder, but whether his silent companion or the proprietor of the inn, I could not tell. I was guided forward, half stumbled on the threshold of the door, then found myself walking on the rutted ground of what I assumed was the alley that ran up the side of the inn. This surface gave way to smooth cobblestones that were easier to walk over. The journey seemed to last forever. I reflected that anyone who passed us in the street would dismiss me as no more than a blind leper, hooded to conceal the ugliness of my face. It was just as well that I had renewed the glamour before sleep. The true horror of my features would remain hidden when the hood was removed.

At last we stopped. There were hard stones beneath my boots, so I knew we still stood within the walls of the city.

A knock sounded upon a door—three raps, followed by one, followed by three. A bolt rattled on the other side of the panel.

"Now we leave you. Tomorrow night at this time we will return and guide you back to the inn. Don't take off your hood until the door is shut behind you."

I reached toward the sound of his voice and caught his arm. He tried to shrug loose but I held firm, tightening my fingers into his flesh.

"One thing you must know before you depart. If you plan to defraud or murder me, you will not enjoy the consequences. I am under the protection of a powerful man. Perhaps you have heard of him. His name is Farri al-Asadi."

"I know no one of that name. Release me."

"He leads the beggars of Bubastis and has many dangerous agents at his command. The life of your master is not worth a bronze fil if you betray me."

With a final jerk he pulled his arm from my grasp. I was shoved roughly across a threshold, and would have fallen had not strong arms caught me on the other side. The door banged shut in its frame, and the hood was pulled from my head.

Blinking owlishly, I saw by the light of an oil lamp burning on a long oak table in the middle of the room two men who had the appearance of scribes. Their hair was cut so short, it was little more than a fuzz upon their scalps, and their shaven faces had the pallor of those unaccustomed to the harsh rays of the sun. Both were thin, with sunken cheeks and bloodless lips. They may have been brothers—there was a similarity in the shape of their dark eyes and hooked noses. One was my own height, the other considerably shorter. On top of their tan linen robes they wore leather belts around their hips that supported the scabbards of short, broad-bladed swords.

The taller scribe who had caught me released his grasp on my forearms and moved around me to set a wooden bar into place in iron brackets in the door through which I had entered. On the opposite end of the room I noticed a second door, shut. His less imposing companion removed my sword and dagger, and carried them through this rear door, which he locked behind him with a key hanging around his neck when he emerged.

The room was not large. Tight-fitted boards shuttered the only window on the inside, making it impossible to see either out or in. There were three oak chairs with the heads of lions carved upon their arms, one at the side of the table just beneath the shuttered window, and one on each end. A stack of blank papyrus leaves had been set on the table in front of the middle chair, beside a reed pen and an open inkwell. A corner of the room was occupied by a gray earthenware chamber pot. Against an otherwise vacant wall stood an ebony sideboard, its polished surface supporting rolled sheets of papyrus that were tied with green silk ribbons, two unlit brass lamps, an assortment of new reed pens, and several bottles of ink. In the front of this elegant piece of furniture, two shallow drawers with brass pull rings occupied the space above a closed cupboard. I wondered what the cupboard might contain.

"Where is the book of the Old Ones?" I asked in Greek.

"Before you may see the scroll, there are certain formalities," murmured the scribe by the door in a surprisingly mellow voice.

He gestured with a finger to his companion, who went to the sideboard and took from the drawer on the right a piece of parchment covered with writing. This he spread on the table. He returned to the drawer and extracted from it a miniature dagger of the sort that court women use to carve fruit and cheese when dining. I leaned over the table to examine the parchment. It was lettered in Greek, and had the appearance of a legal contract. Red sealing wax impressed with a geometric design occupied the lower-right corner of the sheet. The seal exhibited a disquieting animation when I looked at it, so that I found it prudent to remove my gaze.

"This is an agreement stating that you will in no way and under no circumstance disclose to any other human being the contents of the scroll you will copy, or cause copies to be made of your own copy. The penalty for deliberate violation of these terms is death."

I laughed lightly, drawing a sharp glance from the man with the knife.

"It is well for you to know that I enjoy the protection of a powerful man. His name is Farri al-Asadi, and he has the appearance of a gray-bearded beggar, but this is merely a deception. No man of greater authority dwells in the city of Bubastis."

"That is of no concern to us. Do you accept the terms of the agreement?"

"Very well, I agree. Where do I sign?"

"You do not sign," the tall scribe murmured.

"What mark do you wish of me, then?"

His silent companion grasped my left hand, and before I could react, used the needle-like point of the knife to prick my index finger. I cursed and snatched my hand away. The other man made a placating gesture and caught both my hands. He applied the drop of red blood welling from my left finger to the ball of my right thumb and covered it with wetness, then pressed my thumb firmly down upon the parchment beside the animated seal of red wax. When he withdrew my hand, a perfect impression of the ridges on the face of my thumb were left upon the sheet.

I wiped my bleeding finger on the rough camelhair of my coat. The prick was shallow. No more than a drop had welled forth. Already the blood began to clot.

"A signature would have been easier," I muttered with a trace of annoyance that I could not repress.

"The agents who enforce this agreement require blood," the taller scribe said.

The other man returned the knife to the drawer, and bent to remove from the cupboard a glazed blue bowl and a white pitcher of water. While the tall scribe unlocked the rear door with a key that hung on a chain around his neck, and carried my oath of silence into the room that lay beyond it, his companion washed my hands with care, using a soft linen cloth scrupulously white. The sureness of his touch showed that he had performed this curious act numerous times in the past. After patting dry my skin, and turning my hands back and forth to assure himself that all traces of dirt had been removed from around my nails, he rubbed and gently squeezed the cut on my finger. It did not bleed. This seemed to reassure him. He methodically placed the cloth, pitcher, and basin back into the cupboard.

When the tall scribe returned empty-handed and locked the door shut behind him, the other nodded, and they exchanged a look laden with significance. I watched with bemusement, wondering what other tricks or trials they would impose upon me. Together they went to a trunk of dark oak bound with iron straps that rested on the floor in the corner. It had the appearance of a strong box. With difficulty, for it was quite heavy, they each grasped an iron ring and lifted it to one end of the table. Taking a second key from the chain around his neck, the taller man unlocked the brass pad-lock that hung from the iron hasp of the trunk and opened it, then withdrew from its dark interior a small carved box.

My interest quickened as I studied it in the flickering shadows cast by the flame of the lamp. It had the dull sheen of polished ivory, but its color was a green tending to pink, like no form of ivory I had ever seen. Deeply carved upon its lid and all four of its sides were unearthly creatures, beasts that could only be found in the darkest of nightmares. They twisted and writhed over the surface of the box as though alive, showing glaring eyes and gleaming teeth amid the riotous confusion of their limbs. The only thing I had ever seen remotely like it was a nest of vipers.

I reached out to touch its surface, and paused. Its two attendants did not hesitate. They grasped the box and with sure fingers unlatched the three clasps of beaten and tarnished silver that held it shut, then opened it on its silver hinges. Its interior was filled with red silk embroidered with golden thread. Together, with reverential care, they unfolded the cloth like the petals of a rose, and from the middle of this rich nest took out a scroll of papyrus. The taller scribe extended it to me.

Taking it from him with some impatience, I laid it upon the table and unrolled a cubit of its length. Its roller was not ivory, as I first assumed, but bone. I recognized it as part of a human thigh bone, much yellowed with age. The scroll itself appeared in remarkable preservation, in view of its antiquity. That it was genuine, I had no doubt. During my time at the palace in Sana'a I had gained good experience at rec-ognizing forged books and documents. Many traders had mistaken my youth for credulity, though they only made this mistake once. At the top of the scroll the fig-ure of a dragon, in red and green inks edged with gold leaf, looped back upon itself, its serpentine tail extended down the left side next to the text, which was all in Greek, lettered in a small yet precise hand, with few scribal contractions.

"You may begin to make your copy," the tall man murmured.

His silent companion went to the chair at one end of the table and sat with his back straight, watching me while I positioned myself on the seat before the lamp and prepared to begin my transcription of the text. It was long since I had done this kind of work, but I found that my hands remembered it well enough. After the passage of an hour, my eyes began to water, and I asked that a second lamp be lit. This was done promptly. The brighter illumination made the work easier. For a time the tall scribe stood behind my right shoulder with his hands clasped at his groin, watching me work with evident interest. Eventually, he sat upon the remaining chair. Each time I glanced at either attendant, I found his eyes fixed unwaveringly upon me.

When I had completed several hours of the work, I examined the length of the scroll, and saw that the span of a day was just long enough to copy all of it, for a quick worker who did not pause to read its contents. Half the lines were meaningless, and could not be understood, although it was possible to sound them out since they were written in Greek letters. The alternate lines were penned in an antique but perfectly clear Greek poetic meter that had the rolling grandeur of Homer's epics. What little I read stirred coldness in the depths of my soul, and it was with difficulty that I broke my gaze away from the narrative and continued my lettering. At the left edge of my vision, the sinuous green and red tail of the dragon endlessly undulated.

The passage of hours ceased to hold any meaning. All my awareness contracted to the blackened tip of my pen. Once I heard a cock crow, and dimly in the back part of my mind I realized it must be morning. Every so often, the watchers rose to stretch their legs and make use of the chamber pot, or went through the locked rear door to the mysterious room that lay on the other side. I could only guess what might be done there. No sound emanated from the closed portal. On one such occasion, when the shorter man was absent and the taller momentarily turned his back, I seized the opportunity to renew the glamour of my features.

When I had labored without rest for some eight or nine hours, I asked for food and drink. The silent scribe arose at once, as though he had expected this request, and left by the rear door. In a few minutes he returned with a large silver tray that brimmed over with all manner of delicacies beside a glass pitcher of strong red wine. He began to fill a silver goblet with wine, but I perceived the hidden purpose of this extravagant abundance and laid my hand upon his wrist to stop him.

"No wine," I said with a tight smile. "Water. And bring brown bread. These foods are too rich for my stomach."

If he felt disappointment, he took care not to show it. Without a word he removed the platter, and returned with a smaller plate of wood that held only a single bun of bread and a leather bottle of clear water beside a plain tin cup. So keen was my hunger, I enjoyed the bread more than I would have savored the delicacies, and the water tasted as sweet as any wine on my parched tongue. I wasted no time eating, but finished as quickly as I could chew and returned to my work before the plate was removed from beside my elbow.

It was in the interests of the Jew who owned the scroll to limit the number of accurate and complete reproductions, I reflected as I continued to labor. The fewer perfect copies of the book that existed in the world, the more value possessed by the original. If his clients could be induced to waste their precious time sampling his delicacies or addling their brains on his fortified wine, so much the better. Their copies would be unfinished, or would contain errors. Idly, I wondered what agents enforced the terms of the contract that carried the imprint of my blood. I could not drive the movement of the wax seal from my memory, and when I thought of it my pen was apt to pause. There was something more than natural in the lines of the symbol impressed on the red wax. I judged that it would be imprudent in the highest degree to make a copy of a copy of this text.

Some inner sense warned me that my time grew short. Several cubits remained at the base of the scroll to be transcribed. I increased my pace, so that my pen flew across the papyrus sheets. Those I had completed formed a substantial pile and numbered over a hundred. They were penned only on one side. It seemed foolish to be economical with my materials, when I was given an endless supply with which to work. I developed a watery blister on the inside of my middle finger, where the pen rested, but took no notice of its sharp twinges. Of more concern was the cramping of my right hand. Every few minutes it became necessary to release the pen and flex my fingers, so that I could go on with the copying. My eyes were hot in their sockets and itched, but I knew they would not fail me. I have always had good eyes for reading and writing.

At last I saw the tip of the dragon's tail, and set the final line upon the middle of the last numbered papyrus sheet. With a sigh of relief, I set down my pen and straightened my back. My spine emitted a series of cracks, and sharp needles of fire pricked at the muscles below my shoulder blades. After a few moments, the pain subsided. I had been sitting in the same position for hours without moving. My heart leapt like a bird from a cage when I laid the last sheet upon the pile.

"Have you finished?" the tall scribe inquired in a tone of surprise from his chair at my left side.

I reached into my coat and drew forth the tiny vial of green liquid that Martala had given me in the common room at the inn. Pretending to cough, I plucked out its stopper with my teeth and drank its contents, then slid the empty vial and stopper back into my pocket. The potion felt like peppermint on my tongue, both hot and cold. I was aware of it spreading down my gullet and expanding in my stomach.

As the scribe rose from his seat and approached behind me to examine my work, I stood and turned in one movement to confront him. Parting my lips, I exhaled so that my breath touched his face. It issued from my lips like green smoke, but melted to nothingness an instant after it touched his cheeks. He stopped, his eyes vacant, and stood expressionless. I stepped back from him as though puzzled and turned to the other attendant, who stood slowly from his chair with his hand on his sword hilt. I shrugged and spread my hands in a gesture of bemusement.

With slow steps, he approached, eyes narrowed to slits. I saw him glance at the scroll on the table. Deliberately, I stepped away from it, and held my empty hands from my body in a posture that I hoped would look harmless and docile. His attention turned to his companion. He reached out and touched the taller man on the shoulder. The entranced scribe swayed slightly but made no response. While he puzzled over this, I moved closer with an expression of concern, and exhaled upon his face. The thin green smoke writhed around his cheeks and nose for a few seconds before dissipating. All awareness left his eyes. He stood with arms slack at his sides, unblinking.

Speaking quickly but clearly, I uttered the words of the charm conveyed to me by Martala at the inn. Animation returned to the features of the two men. They looked at me with interest, but no trace of hostility.

For the space of a dozen heartbeats I considered my circumstances. Martala had known nothing about the contract of the blood oath, or she would have mentioned it at the inn. That was the first matter to be corrected. The tall scribe made no protest when I drew the key chain off his neck and carried it to the rear door. Taking care to make no sound, I unlocked and opened it. I half expected to see a bearded Jew sitting behind a desk on the other side of the portal, and almost felt disappointment when the light of a single lamp hanging on chains from the ceiling revealed only a windowless storeroom. There was a door on the far end of the room, but when I tried it I found it locked. Neither of the keys on the chain fitted it. The shelves that lined the walls were empty save one, which held various foods on plates and several flasks and pitchers, along with an assortment of cups. The silver tray laden with delicacies rested beside them. Next to my sword and dagger lay a large leather wallet.

Sliding the wallet toward me, I undid the red ribbon that bound its flap and flipped it open. It held a single sheet, my contract. I drew it out and regarded it. The urge was strong to break into pieces the wax seal, but some instinct warned me against this action. Instead, I carefully tore away the corner of the papyrus sheet that bore my thumb print, then returned the contract to the wallet and sealed it before sliding it back to its original position on the shelf. I left the room, locked its door behind me, and returned the keys to the neck of the tall scribe. Holding the scrap of papyrus over the flame of one of the table lamps, I let it burn until the fire had completely consumed my blood mark, then carried the still-flaming remnant across to the chamber pot in the corner and dropped it in. It hissed when it struck the piss in the bottom of the pot and sent up a final wisp of smoke.

The two entranced scribes watched all this with placid expressions on their faces. Rounding the table, I stood before them and waited until I was sure their attention focused upon my eyes.

"All is as it should be. You remember nothing from the moment I completed the copy until now. You will watch me pick up my copy of the scroll from the table. Do you both understand?"

Both men nodded.

They turned to watch me as I rolled shut the dragon scroll on its bone roller and placed it into an inner pocket of my coat.

"Return the original scroll that rests upon the table to its box, then forget that I have spoken these instructions to you."

When I stepped back from the table, they reverently rolled up my copied sheets and placed them into the carved box, closed its three silver clasps and returned it to the chest of oak, then locked its brass lock. In a quiet voice I spoke the single word of release the girl had taught me. A slight shudder passed through the bodies of the two men. They blinked and gazed around as though waking from a dream.

I had finished my work with some little time to spare. I asked if the platter of delicacies that had been offered previously could be brought out once again. The silent scribe cast a glance of inquiry at his companion, who shrugged his shoulders. With a scowl, the first man went into the rear room and returned with the savors and wine. I began to sample each type. Some were strange to me, but others I recognized. Lark's tongues. Goat's eyes. Sugared orange slices. The wine was as good as any I have ever tasted. I offered the pitcher to the scribes, but they frowned with ascetic distaste and left me to my enjoyment. I was still eating when the measured knock came on the front door.

Chapter 33

No time was wasted on formalities. As soon as I reclaimed my weapons and donned the hood, I was pulled into the street and heard the door of the copy room bang shut behind me. Someone put my left hand on the familiar lean shoulder of Altrus. Through his cloak and tunic I felt the steel rings of his chain mail vest. I allowed myself to be guided along a maze of empty streets, the only sound apart from our footfalls the infrequent bark of a dog, or cough of a late reveler staggering back to his bed.

When we had walked a quarter hour or more, boots scuffed the cobbles with quickened pace. Altrus cursed and stepped out from under my hand. Someone stumbled against me, and I would have fallen had my shoulder not struck a brick wall. I stood blinded by the hood, wondering what to do. The clash of steel against stone decided my action. Tearing the hood from my head, I drew my sword.

Four shadowy figures confronted my masked companions, who stood on either side of me with swords extended. Our accosters wasted no time in talk, but attacked in unison before I could view their dim faces under the weak glow of the moon. I found myself fighting the smallest of the four, who pressed his sword strokes like a demon from hell. It took all my skill merely to ward them off. They descended on my good Damascus blade like a flock of hungry sparrows on a piece of bread.

From the corner of my sight, I perceived that Altrus at my left was as able a fighter as I had presumed him to be. Already he had wounded on the arm one of the two foes who pressed him, and I saw the tip of his sword cut the other man on the thigh. The protector on my right side handled his blade less artfully. He cried out in pain and staggered to one knee. I did my best to shield him with my sword parries, but he took a second slash somewhere on his body that drew a howl from his lips.

My sword met the sword of the slightly built shadow who attacked me with such passion that sparks were struck. By their momentary light I recognized the square-jaw and thin lips of Farri's daughter, Zayna, who had tried to kill me with her bow at Memphis. At the flash of the next spark she met my gaze with mocking dark eyes, widened in battle passion, then her face was lost in the night.

No more than a minute passed between the first and final blow, but to my aroused perceptions, it seemed the battle endured an hour. Altrus thrust his sword through the chest of one of the four with a bellow of triumph. They drew away from us like savage wolves that snap their jaws in frustration when driven from their prey. I had my first chance to take a complete breath. With surprise, I realized that I had not been cut. The masked hireling at my right still crouched on one knee, clutching his ribs with his free hand while extending his sword in defense. Altrus did not look injured, but in the dim moonlight it was impossible to be sure.

While the woman stood on guard, two of our foes lifted by the arms the limp body of the one struck through the chest. He was either unconscious or dead. His head lolled on his neck. They stepped backward and melted into the darkness. We listened to the stealthy brush of their boot soles until they passed out of hearing. Only then did Altrus help his companion to his feet. The injured man trembled with weakness, one bloody hand against the wall at our backs.

"I thought your master Farri protected you," Altrus said.

There was cynical amusement in his voice, and something more, a deep joy. I realized that what had just passed was what he lived for.

"Someone must have overheard Farri speak about the book he intends to buy from me."

"Either that, or he decided to save himself the price of purchase and steal it from your corpse."

I shook my head.

"I can't believe that of my master. He is an honorable man."

He pulled the leather mask from his sweating face and grinned at me as though I were a fool, his teeth white against the darkness of his beard, the burn on his cheek black in the moonlight.

"You know that if you reveal the contents of your copy of the scroll to any other, your life is forfeit?"

"I know it now," I said, putting bitterness into my tone. "I did not know it when I agreed to acquire the book."

He laughed at my predicament and clapped me on the shoulder in a companionable way.

"It's my job to get you safely back to the inn. After that, you're on your own."

"I can't go back to the inn. They'll be waiting."

"That may be so, but I'm not paid to take you anywhere else."

"Leave me, then. You have discharged your duty, and more, by defending me."

He paused to consider. A moan of pain from the clenched teeth of his companion decided him. With a grunt of disgust, he wrapped the right arm of the ailing man over his shoulders, so that his own right hand would remain free to reach his sword.

"Go, then. Watch your back."

Leaving the two agents of the Jew to make their slow way together where they would, I hurried in the opposite direction, my ears alert for footfalls. All the streets looked strange to me. I knew only the way Martala and I had walked from my house to the inn, and even that must appear completely changed under the weak light of the quarter moon. Before long I regretted not allowing the mercenary to complete his assigned task. Even were Farri's agents lurking in the street of the Green Peacock, at least I would have been able to find my way from there back to my house. Now that Farri had revealed his presence in Alexandria, it seemed certain he would attack the house, if he had not already done so.

For more than an hour I ranged back and forth across the great city of Alexandria, searching for some landmark that was familiar and cursing beneath my breath at my stupidity. Eventually, I found myself on the waterfront, and made my way with care along its length. Each time I came to a street, I followed it into the city, and when I saw nothing I recognized, retraced my steps back to the docks to try the next street. The Green Peacock was near the ocean, that much I knew. The vastness of the place amazed me. It was many times the size of Sana'a, and greater in size than any other city I had seen in Egypt. I began to despair of finding the accursed inn before daylight. Sashi sympathized with my distress, but admitted sorrowfully that she did not know the way.

I stood near a large dock, uncertain which street to search next, when retching broke the stillness of the night. It came from an alley behind a storage building. The alley ended on a blank brick wall with no other exit. It was very dark. For a moment I thought I had been mistaken, until my nose caught the scent of vomit. A shadow moved near the ground. My boot slipped in something wet, so that I had to catch the wall to keep my balance. A drunken mumble was cut off by another paroxysm of violent vomiting. Nothing splashed forth onto the cobbles. The stomach of the wine-sotted fool was already empty, but the heaving would not subside. At last I heard the sound of several spits, and the shadow pushed itself to its feet, holding onto the wall with both arms.

"Can you help me find my way? I'm looking for the Green Peacock."

"Peacocks? I don't have any peacocks."

It was a woman's voice. Too impatient for manners, I grasped her by the arm and dragged her roughly to the mouth of the alley, where the moonlight revealed her face. Her red dress and the heavy lines of kohl around her eyes, together with her safflower-reddened lips, told her profession. She was a dockside whore. A trail of wet vomit stained her dress between her breasts. Blinking up at me, she wiped her mouth with her hand. When she saw I was a man, she attempted to smile. There have been few occasions when I have been grateful to be a eunuch. This was one of them.

"Which way is the street of the Green Peacock?" I asked, speaking slowly and clearly in Coptic, which appeared to be her tongue.

She shook her head.

"The inn of the Green Peacock. An inn across from the temple of Hermes."

At this she nodded. Some glimmer of sense came into her eyes.

"I know the old temple of Hermes."

"Where is it?"

She looked from side to side, then raised her hand and pointed across the open square at the mouth of a street.

I released her. She swayed, but continued to stand. Putting her hand on her hip, she attempted to strike a pose of allurement.

"You're a fine-looking young man. Want a little fun?"

She reached out and held the wall with her left hand, then bent and drew up the hem of her skirts with her right. She wore no surwal. I saw the black triangle of her pubic mound against the pallor of her thighs. Not bothering to reply, I took my purse and felt for the solitary coin within, then cast it onto the cobbles without looking at it. It rang as it struck. With an inarticulate cry in her throat, she fell to her knees and crawled after the sound, fumbling the shadows with her fingers.

"Where did it go? Did you see where it went?"

Feeling no confidence in the accuracy of her direction, I crossed the square and entered the street. To my surprise, I recognized the outline of the ruined temple of Hermes on the left side of the deserted thoroughfare, and saw that I stood almost beneath the sign of the Green Peacock. I would have been easy prey had the inn been watched, but Farri's men must have decided that I would not return that night. Or they were occupied with other matters. This last thought spurred my steps past the darkened inn and up the street, in the direction of my own house. I almost ran, but controlled myself. It would do no good to arrive exhausted of strength.

The way from the house to the inn had not been convoluted. I remembered making two turns, and was reasonably sure that I found them in the darkness. Even so, it was a relief to recognize the front step of the house, where I had stood admiring the sunlight a few days earlier. The house had a different appearance in the night, but I recognized it by the narrow alley that separated it from the larger building on its left side, and by the diamond carving on the screens of its second level windows that overlooked the street.

I paused at the corner and studied the street. Not a cat stirred. Stilling my breath, I listened but heard nothing. The hour must be very late, at least three of the clock. Relaxing my shoulders, I approached the door, my hand light on the hilt of my sheathed sword. Martala would not expect me to come in the night. I wondered how I could wake her without waking her neighbors. It was only then, as I stood on the elevated platform of packed clay that extended across the front of the house and separated it from the cobbles of the street, that I saw the black line of shadow along the edge of the door.

My sword made no whisper as it left my scabbard. With its tip, I pushed the door inward slowly to avoid the squeal of hinges. The darkness beyond was absolute.

Do you see anything, Sashi?

The space beyond is empty, my love.

I entered without sound, struggling to retrieve from my memory the arrangement of the rooms and furniture on the lower level. Martala was probably gone, taken by force while I wasted my time wandering the streets of Alexandria. The urge to shout in frustration made me clench my teeth, and so quiet was the night, I heard the faint grit of their edges. With gliding steps, I moved from room to room and satisfied myself that no one lurked behind the doors. The stairs creaked when I ascended to the second level. There was no way to prevent it. Each tread made its own unique noise. When I stood upon the landing and heard nothing, I allowed myself to relax. Martala was certainly gone. I decided to find a lamp and strike it aflame with my tinderbox to examine the rooms for any signs of her abductors.

They waited for me in her bedroom. A hood was snatched from a lantern as I entered through the open doorway on soft steps, filling the room with candlelight. I saw Martala naked on the bed amid a tangle of sheets, her eyes closed. Farri sat beside her in a careless posture, his weight on his left arm, watching me with alert brown eyes. His right hand reached across to press the edge of a curved dagger to the girl's throat. It was like the knives used by fishermen to gut fish. Blood reddened her dark hair at the temple and seeped in two thin streams from her nose. She did not move when the light flashed out from the lantern.

At almost the same moment this image registered in my mind, my arms were seized from both sides and I was thrown facedown on to the floorboards at the foot of the bed. Someone ripped the sword from my grasp and rolled me over roughly. Other hands patted my body until they found the dagger at my waist and pulled it from its sheath. I felt the knobbed ends of the drawstring of Martala's empty purse jerked loose from my belt, and the dragon scroll of the Old Ones removed from my inner pocket. The scroll lay on the bed beside Farri when his hired villains lifted me to my feet.

Zayna grasped my right wrist, her fingers surprisingly powerful. She was dressed in the black cloak and tunic I had seen her wear at Memphis, but her head was bare. She shook a lock of short hair from her eye and smiled at me with her pale mouth. The man on my left I did not recognize, but I was confident he had not been among my attackers earlier that night. He showed no sign of sword wounds. The emotionless eyes in his sullen bearded face looked black in the glow from the soot-dimmed glass port of the lantern.

"Bring the light closer," Farri said.

Someone standing in the dark corner by the window stepped forward and grasped the handle at the base of the lantern, elevating it from its table so that strange shadows danced over his features. Without surprise I recognized Hatero, my portly gardener. I wondered if his wife lurked elsewhere in the house.

Farri took his dagger away from the unconscious girl's throat and sheathed it at his waist, then picked up the scroll and examined its contents. He wore the expression of a man who savors honey upon his tongue.

"I was told you made a copy of an ancient book," he murmured in Greek. "This isn't a copy."

What was the purpose in talk? I shrugged as I watched his eyes.

"The value of this, coupled with the pouch of jewels I found earlier in the cupboard and the gold and silver in your other purse, is almost compensation enough for the trouble you caused me."

"I kept the girl by force," I said, merely for the sake of saying something. "She never betrayed you."

He laughed. None of the others joined in his merriment.

"By force? No one has ever forced this she-devil to do anything."

"It was a charm. I am a necromancer."

"I believe you, the part about you being a sorcerer," he said, his grizzled face suddenly serious. "If you begin to mutter a charm, I will kill you at once, and then the girl."

"What do you want of me?"

He looked at the others with wide eyes, gazing at each in turn. His daughter smiled and again jerked her head to move the hair from her eye.

"What do I want? You stole what is mine. No man has ever done that and lived. You won't be the first."

"You have the jewels, the scroll, even the girl. Why should you kill me?"

He leaned forward so that his face brightened in the glow of the lantern.

"Satisfaction," he hissed.

I saw my death in his eyes. Nothing I could say or do would change his purpose. Relaxing in the grasp that held my arms apart, I drew a deeper breath. I felt no fear. Perhaps when you die once, the fear of death departs. To my memory, my first death had occurred only four days ago. It seemed unkind of the fates that I should die twice in the span of a single week. I prepared myself like a true philosopher, and waited with complacence for the blade that would slit my throat or pierce my heart.

Farri saw my thoughts written across my face, and shook his head with a smile.

"You won't die by the blade. I have a much more interesting end planned for you. I want Martala to see it. We'll wait until she wakes. It seems only fitting that the woman who gave you life should witness your death."

He nodded at my surprise, enjoying our circumstances.

"I know what she did for you. One of my men recognized your corpse as she brought it down the Nile. I was curious about what she wanted in Alexandria with your bitumen-coated remains, so I had this house watched, and discovered the books she bought and the alchemical substances she had delivered to her door. I knew she planned some necromancy, so I ordered my agent to make a copy of the text you stole from the Order of the Sphinx."

I glanced at Hatero. If he felt any satisfaction at his act of betrayal, his face did not show it.

"Yes, I know about that scroll, too. I could have had Martala killed at any time in the past seven months, but I wanted her to bring back your life, so that I could end it again."

"Only a fool harbors so much hatred inside him."

"No one has called me that in many years."

"Why did you attack me on the street? Why not wait for me to return here?"

"Why take the chance that you would not return? I preferred to bring you here by force. As it happened, you returned on your own."

It was so quiet, I heard the candle gutter inside the lantern. Martala exhaled a long breath that sounded loud in the stillness. Her head rolled to the side.

"Wash her face with cold water," Farri told Hatero. "She's slept long enough."

The gardener replaced the lantern on the table and drew from beneath it a white clay pitcher and brass basin in which a towel lay folded. He poured water into it to wet the towel, then walked around the bed with the basin in his hands and proceeded to wipe the blood from the nose and mouth of the girl. The cool touch of the cloth caused her eyelashes to flutter open. She looked directly at me, yet gave no sign of dismay or fear. Her composure surprised me. Perhaps she had only feigned unconsciousness and had been listening all the while.

Farri winced as he pushed himself up from the bed. His years pressed on him, I perceived, so that the joints of his crippled leg stiffened when he sat long. He tossed the priceless dragon scroll onto the mattress and made his way to the footboard. His daughter and his hired man drew me to the side and tightened their grasp on my arms as he confronted me. Though he was a small man with a hunched back, dressed in the dirty tunic of a beggar, he stood with a confidence that demanded attention.

He glanced at Martala, who managed to sit up.

"Hold her."

Hatero set the basin on the bed and took her left wrist in his two hands. She made no attempt to resist or to cover her nakedness. Her eyes never left me. I turned to look at the spiteful face of Zayna.

"I like you better in your green dress and red surwal. They suit you," I said, merely for the sake of saying something that might delay for a few moments the inevitable.

"You should have died at Memphis," she hissed.

Studying her face and that of her father so close together, I saw the resemblance of blood. They had the same small brown eyes in which danced the light of fanaticism, the same tight mouth devoid of compassion.

"You were clumsy," I said in a taunting tone. "A pity about the house matron."

"I'm glad she failed," Farri said. "This is better."

"What do you intend?"

"It is written in the holy books of the Jews that man is raised up from the dust, and to the dust he returns. Or perhaps I should say, to the salts."

The needle of fear that stabbed my heart could not be hidden from his keen gaze. He savored it.

"Long have I pored over the necromancy that raised you from the dead, studying and practicing its incantation. How fitting that it should be used to return you to the grave."

He raised his hand, and I stiffened my body for a blow from his fist, but he merely drew a symbol upon the air that I recognized with dread in my throat. It was the *coda draconis*. His words became plain. By the Head of the Dragon are the dead raised from their salts, and by the Tail of the Dragon are they returned to them. He began to murmur in the language of the Old Ones the words of the incantation that would deprive me of my brief second life. Despair overwhelmed me. There was no time, no time for anything.

As he finished the chant and stared at me with a look of the purest hatred mingled with triumph, I held my breath, my body rigid as stone. The thuds of my heart in my chest counted the seconds. Slowly, I released the air from my lungs. Farri's joy became doubt, then confusion. He repeated the symbol and the chant, with the same result.

Martala's laughter made him turn with the quickness of an old wolf.

"Had you spent more time studying the art of necromancy, and wasted less memorizing your copy of the scroll, you would have learned that there are two ways of restoring the dead to life. The priests under the Sphinx use the first method, but I used the second."

Only then did I remember a fragment of conversation between Feisel and his son. Dru had spoken about a way of giving natural life to the dead, life that could not be revoked by symbol or word. The priests made no use of it, since it was not suited to their purposes. It was more convenient to them to be able to return a resurrected body to its salts for easy keeping.

Farri started toward the bed with a murderous expression, then restrained himself and straightened his back, as much as his crooked back could be made straight.

"You are a clever girl, Martala. That is why I do not kill you. In the past you were useful to me, and you shall be useful again."

He turned to me, a veil of amusement concealing his frustration.

"Nothing has changed, necromancer. I will still return you to dust, but with this."

Drawing his dagger from its sheath at his waist, he extended it at the level of my heart for a killing thrust.

Chapter 34

"You have something that belongs to me."

The quiet words drew Farri around in a fighting crouch, a snarl on his unlovely lips. Altrus leaned against the frame of the open door, his crossed arms exposed through the gap at the front of his cloak, which also revealed his sword hilt. He stepped forward into the flickering glow of the lantern and glanced around the room. Everyone stood as though staked to the floor. His appearance had the suddenness of an apparition. I wondered how he had mounted the stairs without causing the treads to squeak.

"You must be Farri," he said, his keen gaze settling on the old beggar. "You were imprudent to make an enemy of my master."

Farri straightened from his crouch and relaxed.

"Your master?"

"He has a deep purse and a long memory. Did you really imagine you could send this fool to steal from him? Did you think the loss of the scroll would not be noticed?"

Farri's smile was deadly.

"There is only one fool in this room. A dead fool."

Farri's daughter released my wrist to draw her sword. She sidled toward her father, moving on the toes of her boots with the grace of a dancer. Altrus continued to stand with arms folded. From the corner of my eye I saw Hatero get up from the bed and draw a dagger from his belt. The naked blade trembled in his hand as he held it ready near his thigh. I caught Martala's gaze and glanced at the lantern. Understanding passed between us.

She leaned forward and picked up the brass basin of water that had been used to wash her face, then in a single motion hurled it across at the lantern on the table. Its edge shattered the glass ports and its contents quenched the flame of the candle before any other person in the room could think to move. I spun and drove my knee upward into the groin of the heavyset bearded man who still clutched my left arm. His meaty thigh deflected the blow, but as I expected, he released me to draw his sword. The steel made a familiar sound in the darkness as it slid over the brass guard of his scabbard, a sound repeated from the doorway.

"Kill him!" Farri cried.

Boot leather scuffed the floorboards, and steel struck on steel. The murk was almost absolute. All I could discern were vague outlines of blackness on deeper blackness. I slid my body along the wall to the corner of the room, then across to the head of the bed. Martala stood beside it, invisible in the gloom, but I smelled her sweat and felt her heat. When my hand brushed her, she flinched aside, then clutched my arm with chill fingers. I pressed her cheek with my palm in reassurance.

A shrill whistle cut the air, and in moments boots thundered up the staircase. They belonged to more than one, but how many more and whether Farri's men or companions of Altrus I could not judge. The room became a very dangerous place.

Martala felt for my hand and pressed something hard into it. I recognized the leather-bound hilt of my Damascus blade. She must have marked its location in her mind before putting out the light, and then seized it in the darkness. Its balanced weight brought reassurance, though I dared not extend it before us. One touch of its point would draw a furious attack impossible to parry in this ink.

The battle would surely have caught us up, were it not for the reluctance of Farri and Zayna to move from their places. The only way to distinguish each other was by remembered location and by their harsh shouts. Altrus suffered no such constraint on his movements. He said nothing, but darted and slashed among the others. The fight milled this way and that, making escape impossible. Curses, grunts, and cries of pain were punctuated by the occasional spark of steel on steel, flashing a vivid picture on the darkness. While the combat grew more heated, my eyes adjusted to the dim moonlight sifting through the diamond-patterned window screens. I pulled Martala toward the far corner, where I hoped the light would not reach.

Cries of alarm echoed in the street amid a swelling babble of excited voices, as the clash of swords attracted the attention of neighbors and brought them out of their houses.

"Stay close behind me," I murmured into Martala's ear.

Stepping to the bed, I pulled the sack of the feather mattress from its box and tilted it upright, holding its edges in both hands. The grip of my right hand was awkward since I did not dare release my sword. With a murmured curse at the absurdity of human existence, I ran forward toward where I knew the door to be. The mattress hit the flailing body of a man and drove him back into another. I used my weight to push them through the open doorway onto the hall landing. Outside the room, darkness was complete. My foot tripped on the edge of the mattress and I fell forward. The bodies on the other side of the soft barrier thrust back, and I found myself tumbling through the air down the stairs. By good fortune I ended my descent on top of the pile rather than beneath it, still clutching my weapon.

"Martala?"

"I am here." Her voice came close behind me.

Pushing to my feet, I groped in the darkness until I found her hand, then drew her toward the dim rectangle of the open doorway and into the street. The bewildered gathering of neighbors, most of them barefoot in their sleeping caps and gowns, parted with frightened faces to let us pass. They stared after us at the girl's white buttocks as we ran down the street. She grasped something in her free hand but I did not stop to look at it. I took the first turning to the left, and when we had gone far enough to leave the muffled curses of the fight behind us, I drew the girl into an alcove of shadow that was the entrance to a house. The locked door came as no surprise. I had not hoped to gain entrance, but only to avoid the gaze of any who chanced to pass.

"What did you bring with you?" I asked Martala.

"Only this."

I felt the hardness of the bone roller of the scroll of the Old Ones.

"Clever girl. That was quick thinking."

Sliding my sword into its scabbard, I took the scroll and put it away in the usual pocket of my coat. It amused me to think that neither Farri nor Altrus had the scroll, yet. They would come searching for us, that was certain, but it would take them a while to disengage from each other and gather their men.

"We must leave Alexandria with what we presently bear on our backs. With what I bear on my back," I corrected myself.

"Yes, we must leave this place, but we are not so destitute as you believe, Alhazred."

I clutched the slender shoulders of the girl in hope.

"It is wise to be prepared," she said. "Follow after me, before we are noticed."

Through narrow and crooked streets she led me. I did my best to remember the way we came, but at last was forced to admit to myself that I was as lost as I had been at the docks. From time to time we stopped and listened in the night for the sound of footsteps behind us, but heard nothing other than the bark of dogs. Martala pressed me ahead of her into the mouth of an alley so narrow, the brick walls brushed my elbows. At its end was a wooden door. In the darkness I was able to trace its edges with my fingers. I felt for its latch and found that it was locked.

Martala slid her slender body past mine while I pressed my back to the rough bricks. A key rattled in the lock. Wooden hinges creaked. She pulled me stumbling over an elevated threshold onto floorboards, then closed and bolted the door. The smell of dust nearly choked me at the back of my throat.

"What is this place?"

"A house of safety. Let me light the lamp and I will tell you about it."

I heard her feel her way into the room, then scratch steel on flint to ignite a tinderbox. She applied the flame to the wick of a brass oil lamp. By its glow I saw that we stood in a room some five paces square. For furniture it boasted no more than two chairs with woven reed seats, a table supporting the lamp and tinderbox in the middle of the floor, and a closed cabinet against the wall on the left. A heavy tapestry hung on the wall nearest the door, its faded pattern obscured by dust. I lifted its edge and saw behind it a shuttered window. On the other side of the room a flight of steep stairs led upward into shadow.

"A single bedroom above," Martala explained.

"Does any other person know of this house?"

She shook her head, regarding me with satisfaction. Her complete lack of nervousness calmed my fears. I forced the tightness out of my shoulders and neck and sat in one of the chairs at the table.

"Not long after coming with your corpse to this city, I judged it would be wise to have a place of concealment, in case Farri showed himself. I rented this house for a year, after assuring myself that the owner would not return in that time or make troublesome inquiries. I visit here seldom, only to keep the lamps filled and the cabinet stocked with food and water."

"Where did you hide the key to the door?"

She blushed in the lamp glow and set the key on the table.

"I have worn it night and day."

For a moment her words puzzled me since I had noticed no key hanging about her neck. Then I understood.

"You are wise beyond your years. You say there is food here?"

She opened the cabinet and took out a round loaf of flat brown bread and a block of hard cheese, then set a wicker-bound beaker of wine and a pewter goblet on the table. The bread was like stone, but not moldy. I clinked it against the tabletop and broke it with difficulty between my hands, filling the goblet twice before my thirst was quenched and I felt able to pass it to the girl. She made a face as she sipped. Wine was never to her liking. The dry old bread resisted my teeth. She did not even attempt it, but sat nibbling a piece of cheese, watching me.

"We cannot go back to your house," I said, my mouth full of crust flakes.

"Your house," she corrected.

"Yours, mine, or the Caliph's, if we go back there we will surely be taken. I wish we had the jewels, but they are lost. We must make our way with what we carry, a familiar condition that does not trouble me."

"Even so, we are not completely lacking resources," she said with a glint of amusement in her ice-gray eyes.

She returned to the cabinet and opened its left side. From its depths she took two daggers and two swords and laid them across the table. The larger curved dagger nestled in a sheath of ivory trimmed with silver and possessed an ornately carved hilt of the same material. The smaller straight blade had a plain sheath of black leather. One sword was shorter and lighter than the other. I saw that the cabinet also contained a shelf of folded clothing, and two pairs of boots.

"Stout travel tunics and cloaks," she explained. "And there is this."

She laid a leather purse on the table between the swords. I snatched it up, and could not mute my pleasure when I felt its contents. With eager fingers I loosened the knobs of the drawstring and poured several of the jewels into my hand.

"I took a small number of them and hid them here, Alhazred. When I awakened you from death I meant to tell you about it, but there was no time."

"With these we can buy horses, or passage on a ship."

"We? You mean to take me with you?"

I looked at her with surprise. Her voice held childlike uncertainty.

"A man must have a servant when he travels."

The beginning of a smile touched the corners of her lips. She hid it behind the goblet as she sipped from its rim, eyelashes lowered to the wine.

"Where will we go?"

I sat back and pondered the question.

"Egypt is no longer safe for either of us. I cannot return to the land of Yemen, and have had my fill of wandering the desert. Let the dark man keep it for his own. We must go forward, across the sea."

"Yes, but where?"

From my pocket I took the scroll of the Old Ones and unrolled it. There was a passage toward the end that I had noticed in the course of copying its contents. It was not a part of the original text, but had been added in pen by a later hand—perhaps by one of the owners of the scroll prior to its coming into the possession of the Jew. The gloss was written in tiny Greek letters between the text of the scroll itself, and it was a commentary on a reference in the text to the alchemical mutation of human flesh. I was forced to tilt the papyrus to catch the light of the lamp before I could read it aloud.

"In a valley between the rivers Euphrates and Tigris lies the Well of the Seraph, the waters of which restore to wholeness flesh that has been withered or struck off. The location of the well is forgotten, unless perchance it is known to the wisest head of Babylon."

"Babylon? Does it refer to the fortress at Fustat?"

"I think not. The rivers are far to the east, and Babylon is a city there."

"I have heard of this other Babylon," Martala murmured. "It was once a great kingdom."

"What is its head, do you suppose?"

She frowned in thought.

"When I was a child, a magician at Memphis kept an oracular talking head made of brass in a cedar box. My father heard it speak. But he said the head was a fraud. A boy spoke into a long brass tube so that the head itself seemed to utter words."

I rolled the scroll and put it back in its pocket. Drawing the dagger from its ivory sheath, I studied my face in its polished steel. The glamour had passed. I saw myself as I truly appeared, realizing for the first time that the girl had been looking upon the unveiled horror of my face without a qualm. She had grown accustomed to her monster.

"It is not my wish to remain a eunuch the rest of my life—my second life. If there is a charm or spell that can restore my manhood and my face, I intend to find it. Then I will go back to Sana'a and kill that fool, the king, and take his daughter for my own."

A shadow passed over Martala's eyes. She regarded me evenly while I removed the woolen baldric with its empty leather sheath from my shoulder and fitted the new dagger and sheath to my belt.

"We travel to Babylon?"

"Yes. We will seek out the head, whatever it may be, and learn from it the location of this well."

"Babylon may be far enough to escape Farri's wrath," Martala said. But her voice held doubt.

"Farri has concerns of his own. The rich Jew who lost the scroll believes Farri his enemy, thanks to certain words I uttered. Let them occupy each other while we make our departure from this land."

We ascended the almost vertical stair, the girl going first with the lamp in her hands to light the way. The sway of her naked buttocks as she climbed made me regret the empty space between my thighs. The room above boasted the same dimensions as that below. The low ceiling was no more than slats of wood supporting the red clay tiles of the roof, but the walls had been plastered and whitewashed around the year of my birth, though the whitewash had faded to gray and the plaster was flaking off in sheets. The room held a narrow bed, a low wooden stand with a crockery basin for washing and a stoppered clay beaker filled with clean water, a brass chamber pot, a peg board on the wall, and a single stool. I saw that the plain boards sealing the window would admit scant light during the day, but, what was more important, they would let little of the glow from the lamp escape at night. The same smell of dust that choked me in the room below hung on the air.

I stripped and did my best to wash my body in the basin. As had been her custom before my death, Martala dried me with a towel. Her gentle touch soothed my nerves. Only after my body was clean did she wash the dried blood from her head and upper lip. I made use of the pot. When I lay naked upon the bed sheet on my back, she climbed onto the narrow mattress to press her skin against my right side. I put my arm under her shoulders. Beyond the shutter, the sun must have been about to rise in the east. It had been thirty hours since I had last slept.

With the strange clarity of mind that sometimes comes in fever, I knew that I dreamed but could not awaken myself. I walked alone across the desert at night, as I so often did during my dreams. The flat land was ridged with small ribs of wind-blown sand and speckled with stones the size of plums that turned treacherously beneath the soles of my boots. I began to run in haste, fleeing something that I could never see when I paused and looked back to scan the horizon. The moon hung low above the distant hills, and sent my long shadow rippling in front of me over the sandy ridges. I wondered if it was the moon I tried to escape, then realized that no man could outrace the moon.

Turning from the silver crescent at my back, I saw him standing before me and stumbled in my haste to stop before I ran into him. He stood with his arms raised and outspread, his black robe and cloak flowing on the night breeze. I tried to look up into his face, but lacked the courage or the strength of will. Each time I struggled to raise my eyes, a terror gripped my heart and forced my gaze to the sands at his feet.

"Why do you flee me, Alhazred?"

Hollow amusement rasped on his sibilant voice. He spoke a strange language, but I understood it.

"You frighten me, lord."

"You are my servant. There is nothing to fear."

Again I fought to lift my face, but found that I could not see. As I tilted up my head my eyelids closed. No effort would open them for so long as my face was turned to his. I spoke blindly to him.

"I thought you had abandoned me."

He laughed, a sound that turned my bones to well water.

"Your life is bound up with my purposes. There is a new task for you in the lands of the east."

"What would you have me do?" I asked meekly. All resentment or rebellion left me like a passing shadow. My heart trembled, and I longed to get away from him, as a child yearns to be released from the critical inspection of his tutor.

"My enemies are massed in the east. They have sealed their stronghold against my sight. You must learn their purposes."

"How will I know them, lord?"

379

No answer came. I found that I could raise my head and keep my eyes open. The vast desert stretched empty to the starry horizon. Again I knew that I was dreaming, and this time forced myself awake.

Martala sat on the stool with her feet together and hands on her knees, watching me with a serene expression. In the dim splinters of sunlight slanting through the cracks in the window shutters, one half of her face was bright and the other half shadowed. She might have been the statue of a goddess such as I had seen in Memphis, so still she sat.

She had put on a tunic of pale blue linen richly ornamented at the neck, hem, and around the narrow sleeves with bands of yarn dyed in muted shades of pink, gray, lime, and lemon. Or perhaps the colors had faded due to numerous washings. It bore the curious arabesques so common to the tunics of the Copts, embroidered on its shoulders and front panels at the level of her shins. These were square, the more common shape, although round arabesques were also to be seen in the street. Such was its length that it would have covered her feet, but the leather belt at her waist drew it up to reveal the toes of her new boots. At her waist I noticed the small dagger in its sheath and the smaller of the two swords from the cabinet. She had bound up her hair and hidden it beneath a round hat of dark green felt that extended low in the back, so that she gave the appearance of a slender boy.

A fine mist of sweat covered my body. The unmoving air in the bedroom would soon become unbearable as the sun continued to beat down on the roof of this dwelling. I watched dust motes dance in the slivers of sunlight.

"What hour is it?"

"Near ten of the morning."

I listened to the noises of the street that came down the narrow alley. They might have emanated from another world. How long, I wondered, could we stay safe in this place? With a sudden determination, I forced myself to sit.

"I must find us passage on a ship sailing north. That is the quickest route to the headwaters of the Euphrates, which will carry us to Babylon."

"What port do we seek?"

I tried to visualize a map of the eastern coastline of the Mediterranean in my mind. It was not a region I had ever studied with intent to travel there.

"As far north on the eastern coast as we can reach."

I stood. She rose with me and stepped forward to put her hand on my bare chest over my heart.

"Let me make the arrangements, Alhazred. You know nothing of the streets. I have formed associations that will be useful in gaining information without being observed."

What she said was true enough. I was apt to become lost, and even if I found my way would be conspicuous wandering the docks trying to secure passage in a ship. Both Farri and Altrus would expect us to attempt to flee by sea, and would have agents watching for me. The girl was less noticeable in her new tunic, with her hair coiled up and hidden beneath her hat. Farri would recognize her in an instant, but his daughter might overlook her in a crowd, and it was likely Altrus would be watching for her long black hair.

I nodded my assent and without another word she left me and descended the stair. I heard the door open and shut. She had been waiting only for me to awaken, to gain permission to act on whatever plan she had made in her own mind during the night. There was little else for me to do but trust in her cunning.

After relieving my bladder and washing the sweat from my limbs with a towel moistened in the basin, I went naked down the stair and took the remaining tunic from its shelf in the tall cabinet. It would be prudent to change my clothing, since my dark-blue Muslim coat was easily recognized. The boots I ignored. I had no intention of giving up my old footwear, just when my boots were beginning to fit my feet. The girl had left the lamp alight, and I saw that the leather purse no longer rested beside it. The green cloak was also missing from the cabinet. No doubt she had chosen the green cloak because its color matched her hat, leaving me the black cloak.

I studied at arm's length the sand-colored linen of the tunic in the lamp glow. It bore the characteristic pattern of the Copts, four square arabesques, and embroidered bands of brown, black, and white at its neck, sleeves and hem—less colorful than the tunic of the girl, but more eye-catching than I would have wished. Perhaps Martala had picked the garments for this very reason. They did not resemble the clothing of two people who sought to hide. These reflections were in my mind while I put on the linen undershirt that had been folded beneath the tunic, then slid the tunic over my head.

I returned with thoughtful steps up the stair to gather my boots, belt, and other things, but retreated as swiftly as I was able from the heat that radiated down from the exposed tile roof like the prickle of glowing iron. The upper room was not for the living during the hours of day. An open window might help cool it, but I doubted it would be pleasant to sit in no matter what was done. For a time I considered removing Gor's skull from my belt. Farri would know it at a glance, as would Altrus. In the end I allowed it to remain. So long had I worn it, I would feel strange unless its hardness tapped against my thigh. I started to place the scroll into my new tunic, then realized that it had no opening in the front, and in any case, no pockets. The scroll and the rag that contained the white spiders would have to be carried elsewhere.

When she returned in late afternoon, I sat reading the scroll of the Old Ones at the table by the glow of the oil lamp. The rattle of the door drew me up from my chair like a fish on a hook. I stood behind the door with my back to the wall, dagger drawn. Her solitary shadow in the rectangle of daylight upon the floor reassured me. She set her heavy wicker basket on the table and smiled, her face expressing the success of her mission.

"We depart on the evening tide, aboard the vessel *Sword of the Prophet*. Her captain is a Syrian named Ravicar, who makes Tyre his home. He trades all along the eastern coast and has agreed to take us as far north as the port of Iskanderun, in the Gulf of Issus."

"I wish I had a map."

She drew from the basket a folded parchment and spread it across the table on top of the scroll. It was a crude map of the eastern coast done in charcoal.

"The captain drew it for me when I asked him if there was any port farther north."

Rough though it might be, the map had been drawn by a man who knew the making of charts. The names of a dozen ports were written along the coast in Arabic script. It even had a scale in Roman miles. I saw that Iskanderun was located on the easternmost side of the Gulf of Issus. The only other town shown in the gulf was Issus itself, but it was at the head of the gulf and further to the west. The line of the Euphrates river had been drawn in more vaguely than the coastline, but if the scale of miles was accurate, there would be a journey overland of some one hundred Roman miles from the port to the river. This matched my own vague recollection of the maps I had studied in Sana'a. I remembered that Iskanderun stood near the Syrian Gates, a pass through the mountains that ran along the coast, and for this reason the port was the western end of a caravan road that conveyed cloth and spices from Baghdad and the lands further east.

"The captain is a faithful follower of the Prophet," Martala said, leaning over my shoulder to look at the map. "He did not want more passengers, but I told him that you were a countryman of his, the eldest son of a noble family, fleeing the wrath of wealthy Egyptian Christians. I presented myself as your Egyptian serving boy. I think he believes I am your lover."

"Why not? You have attractive features for a boy," I murmured, folding up the map. "I hope you did not pay with jewels?"

"Have I earned the name of a fool?" she asked with indignation. "I exchanged two of them for a purse of dinars and dirhams before going to the docks."

"It is a risk. They know we have gems."

"We needed gold and silver."

I nodded. Risks must be taken. She had done well.

"What else do you have in that basket?"

"A feast." She drew out fresh fruit and newly baked pastries. "Enjoy it, Alhazred, it is the last meal we will eat in Egypt."

Seeing the wisdom of her words, I sampled a pastry, which was still warm from the oven, and discovered shreds of spiced goat meat at its center. While I chewed, I wondered if it would be our last meal in this world.

Chapter 35

The cry of the ship's boy high overhead woke me from dreamless sleep. A cool breeze fanned my eyelashes and stirred the hairs on my chest. I opened them and saw the pale light of morning reflected from the stripped yellow and green cotton awning that acted as the roof of my sleeping place. Strung on part of the ship's rigging, the awning angled up from where it was pegged to the deck and opened toward the sea, so that it gave the illusion of privacy to those who lay beneath it.

Not that such a thing existed on a ship, as I had learned on the *Eye of Mecca*. The awning fluttered softly. With automatic gestures and a muttered word, I restored the glamour of my appearance and slid across the sleeping rug toward the rail.

The naked boy, no more than nine years of age, clung like a monkey to the tip of the mast that projected above the crossbeam of the sail, both legs and an arm wrapped around the slender pole. The other arm gestured to someone below who stood on deck, concealed from my sight behind the awning. The boy's round face beamed with cheerfulness.

The heat of the sun made clothing a burden, but the laws of Mohammed were strict on the matter of modesty. No one except the boy was permitted to walk the deck naked, although the seamen shed as many garments as they thought Ravicar ibn Anas, captain of the *Sword of the Prophet*, would tolerate. Having no wish to invite his disfavor, I imitated their example during the day, but slept in my own skin at night for the sake of comfort.

Martala stepped around the awning as I hung from the rail with my bare buttocks projected as far as was physically possible beyond the side of the ship. The captain was particular about cleanliness, and wore an unhappy expression for hours after I fouled his planks on the first day of our voyage.

The sight of her disguise still startled me, although I should have become used to it. She had bound her breasts flat, and the green felt cap pulled over her head completely covered her long hair. So slender was her body, the slight swell of her hips below her belt was unlikely to be noticed, and few would ever guess she was other than the youthful scholar she pretended to be.

Wrinkling her nose, she waited for me to wipe myself with a scrap of cotton rag and watched it float behind the product of my bowels.

Sea air agreed with her. Enthusiasm glowed in her cheeks and brightened her pale gray eyes.

"Alhazred, the captain was right."

"Iskanderun?"

"The boy saw it first from the top of the mast. Come and look."

She raced away before I could respond. The previous afternoon during mealtime, Ravicar had predicted that his ship would reach the port by morning, even though land had not been sighted for two days. Cheerless and strict though he might be, he was a competent navigator.

I ducked beneath the awning and pulled on my loose linen undershirt, then unrolled my tunic, which served as my pillow at night. Thrusting my head and arms through its narrow openings, I belted on my sword and dagger, adding Gor's skull and my purse, and slid my feet into my boots. The scroll I left in the woven hemp bag the girl had bought to hold our meager possessions before our departure from Alexandria. Whatever the faults of the crew, dishonesty was not among them. I found Martala with several seamen in the bow, peering forward with her eyes shaded against the glare of the rising sun. One man clapped her on the back with good nature, and she made some indistinguishable comment that caused them all to laugh.

I glanced back at the stern. Ravicar stood in his usual place by the steering oar. Indeed, he had scarcely moved from it in our fifteen days and nights at sea, apart from meals and brief periods of sleep. Old enough to be my grandfather, he met my eye with no hint of greeting in his grizzled face. I was grateful to him for bearing me safely out of Egypt, but he was not a man to inspire affection. His black tunic only emphasized his solemn manner.

The entire crew believed Martala to be my lover. This might not have troubled Ravicar so much had she not disguised herself as a youth. He made no effort to conceal his religious prejudice against such connections. My uncovered head and shaved chin also annoyed him since they conflicted with the sartorial code laid down by the mullahs.

Instead of going to the bow, I made my way back and leaned over the port rail, where it sloped upward toward the stern, to scan the horizon to the south and west. It stretched unbroken between the perfect blues of sea and sky.

Sashi, do you see a sail?

The sea is empty, my love.

I allowed my grip on the rail to relax. No doubt I worried needlessly. For the past three days a sail had followed in the wake of our ship, never near enough for me to see the hull to which it was attached. The sight of fishing boats and galleys along the coast was common, but this sail troubled me with its persistence, and it was unusual for vessels to venture as far from shore as had the *Sword of the Prophet*.

Ravicar cast me a sidelong glance from beneath his turban.

"She may have passed us in the night," he murmured.

We had not spoken about the sail, but I should have known he would notice my interest in its movements.

"Could it travel so much more quickly than your ship?" I asked in surprise.

"The wind is capricious. We were becalmed last night. If she found the wind when the *Sword* lost it, she may already be in port."

He offered no other comment. Martala had given him the tale that I was fleeing Egypt from persecution. No doubt he believed the ship to carry my persecutors.

I returned to the bow, moving with accustomed ease to the gentle roll of the sand-scrubbed deck. The last two weeks at sea had taught me the trick of it. Even the milk goat that wandered free and the Egyptian cat were no more sure-footed.

Martala caught my hand and drew me to the rail, causing one seaman to grin at another and wink.

"There." She pointed with her other hand. "See the whiteness of the stones? That is what they call a breakwater."

"Iskanderun lies behind it?"

"So they say."

There were dozens of ships moored in the harbor when we glided in on the morning tide. I studied them closely, but with their sails furled I could not tell if our pursuer was among them. The large white stone blocks of the docks and the sea walls gave the port an appearance of aged strength, yet it seemed cramped in comparison with the bustling expanse of Alexandria. By the time the side of the ship touched the dock, the efficient crew had struck our awning and stowed it below the deck. Martala had paid our passage before our departure from Egypt. Nothing remained except to gather our travel cloaks and the hemp bag with our possessions, and debark. A gang plank was rattled across to the dock for our benefit. The barefooted seamen did not bother with it, but leapt from the rail to the stones while they finished securing the ship.

Ravicar approached, his hands clasped before him at his waist in his habitual manner, his face grave. I half expected him to make some disapproving remark at our parting, but to my surprise he merely bowed his head.

"Go with God," he said.

I returned the words, reflecting that even a strict follower of Mohammed could be a man of honor. We left him at the rail, watching us pass into the walls of the city.

Iskanderun was much like Alexandria save for the absence of Egyptians. The streets were thick with cheerful and drunken seamen, most of them Arabs and Greeks, who stopped in knots to laugh and banter words with the red-robed whores, or made their way purposefully carrying packs or pulling wagons. The air hung heavy with the stench of rotting fish, and was rent by unceasing screams from sea birds that wheeled in the cloudless heavens, or pecked at trash in the gutter with no concern for the humans who shared the cobblestones.

I watched a trio of naked street urchins, none as old as the ship's boy, creep up on a gull as it worried with its beak the flattened corpse of a rat crushed beneath a cart-wheel. They burst with shrill cries from behind a wagon and threw pebbles at the bird and ran after it, waving their arms like wings.

Touching Martala on the shoulder to attract her attention, I bent my head close so that I would not need to shout above the din.

"Find us a room. We will spend the night here." I opened my purse and gave her two small dirhams. "Buy food and drink for yourself, if you wish."

"My lord is too generous."

Her voice carried a hint of mockery. I had taken for my own the purse that held the remaining jewels and the coins acquired at Alexandria, leaving her with no more than a few brass fils tied in a rag at her belt.

"A good servant has no sense of humor," I reminded her.

"Where will you be, Alhazred? How shall I find you?"

"Meet me in the marketplace. There are items I must purchase for our journey to the Euphrates."

I left her to her task and climbed the slope of the street. It twisted from side to side like the back of a great serpent. The market square of any town is easy to locate. All roads lead to it, if you follow them far enough. This one had no wall, but was completely enclosed by the sides of buildings, apart from the streets that led into it. As was not uncommon, an elevated well of carved stone adorned its center. Three women knelt on the steps of the well, washing garments in a large wooden tub. The slap of the wet cloth against the worn stone steps sounded across the square above the voices of the hawkers in their stalls, and the milling tread of buyers. The stench of fish had remained behind at the docks, and in the air hung the savor of baked bread.

Most of the sellers were Greeks, but a few Jews plied their trade among them. I wandered around the square, glancing at their wares and ignoring their cries, until I found a table of leather goods and saw what I had been searching for, a water skin. All the time since fleeing from my own house at Alexandria, I had been uneasy without the familiar water skin I had carried in the Empty Space. It was foolish to be concerned about water when so much of it was free for the taking, but I knew I would not rest easy in my own heart until I carried water.

I selected a large new skin hanging on a peg at the side of the stall and slung its strap over my shoulder. Its weight felt reassuring, even though it was empty. The Jew seated behind the table smiled, showing a set of even white teeth through the well-oiled black beard that covered his lip and chin.

"Does my lord travel east with the caravan? Perhaps I can provide you with other necessities."

Nodding, I studied his wares. There were saddles and saddle bags, whips, bridles, soft-sided bottles, belts, empty scabbards, and other articles of leather.

"Do you have any travel packs, for carrying things on the back while walking?" I asked in Greek, the common tongue of the port.

He spread his hands in apology and shook his head.

"They do not use such things in this land. No one walks. Everyone rides."

"Why should they not walk?"

"The distance between wells on the caravan road is too great. One who walked would surely perish. And there are many bandits on the road. A man on foot would be easy prey."

Had I traveled alone, I might have ignored this well-intentioned advice, but Martala was not hardened to the desert. It would be best, I reflected, to purchase horses for the many days we must spend on the road. We haggled over the price of the water skin without ill feeling, and I made him add a small leather purse to the bargain, for the girl. After paying the amount agreed upon, I had him direct me to a stable where I could buy mounts. He tried to sell me new saddles but I declined, thinking that the stable owner would surely have used saddles at a much better price.

The weight of the well water in the skin bumping at my side comforted me. I was pleased that the skin did not leak. The stables were located inside the city wall near the eastern gate. Had I not been given such good directions by the Jew, I could probably have found them by following my nose. They were filthy. In Sana'a, any stableman who kept his stalls in such a condition would have been whipped through the streets—King Huban had always held great fondness for horses and prohibited their mistreatment. A pity for me that his tenderness of heart did not extend to men.

Accustomed as I was to the royal stables, even the best mounts the proprietor had to offer seemed to me poor beasts. He was a fat unwashed man in a stained leather apron that covered the entire front of his body. For modesty's sake he wore a sleeveless shirt that hung down to his knees, and sandals that were almost the same black color as his feet. Not too many days before he had burned his forearm, and the sear mark had turned an interesting shade of purple around the red crease. He sweated in the growing heat of morning, black hair plastered tight to his forehead.

I picked out two horses, one a gray gelding and the other a tan mare, that did not look as through they would drop dead on the first day of riding. He named a price that was easily four times their value.

"If you don't wish to sell your horses, I can always walk the caravan road," I told him in irritation.

His small dark eyes widened in horror.

"No one walks. It would be certain death. If you did not die of thirst, you would be killed by bandits."

This seemed a popular theme in Iskanderun. Glancing around the stable, I noticed a row of saddles resting across a rail in the shadows at the rear.

"I will buy your horses for half your price."

He thrust out his lower lip and glared at me. I met his gaze with a mild expression. His resolve softened.

"But only if you supply those two saddles as part of the bargain," I added, pointing at the rail.

As is true of most men who bluster, once he had expressed his initial indignation, he became more reasonable, and we settled on a price that was only slightly higher than what I had named. As I turned to leave the stench of the stables, he caught my arm.

"My lord, forgive me, but I cannot allow you to travel east with only a single companion. It would be your death. You must go with a caravan for your own protection."

"When is the earliest caravan departing the city?"

"Not for six days."

"Then I must go with only my servant. I cannot wait that long."

"If you must leave before the caravan, at least allow me to hire men to accompany you and guard you from bandits."

"For which you would expect a fee."

"A small fee," he agreed with an apologetic smile. "My wife's brothers are trained in the use of the sword. They often serve as bodyguards for noble travelers like yourself. You will need to hire at least four guards, or your party will be too small to discourage bandits. They are very bold, my lord. Just last month bandits killed an entire sect of religious zealots who made the mistake of trying to walk the road. They piled up their heads beside a well."

I considered the situation. No doubt he and his relations would overcharge me, but I did not wish to waste time searching for bodyguards. If the bandits truly were so notorious, it might be best to take precautions against them.

"Very well. Lead me to your wife's brothers. If I like their looks, I will hire them."

He raised his hands with the palms up.

"Alas, they are not at home, but they will return at some time during the night."

"I cannot wait here until the middle of the night. I need to rest before setting out from the city."

"If you wish, I can hire them for you when they return home, and they will be waiting for you here with your horses when you and your servant are ready to begin your travels in the morning."

He named an exorbitant price, as I expected. I was too impatient to be gone from that pestilential stable to haggle. My easy acceptance pleased him, and put him in a better humor. He agreed to stock saddle bags with grain and water for the horses, and when I mentioned beds he added two sleeping rugs without asking an additional fee. All would be ready at dawn, he assured me. I counted out the pieces of gold and silver, and from the corner of my eye saw the tip of his tongue dart over his fat lips.

Martala was eating flat bread and strips of goat meat grilled over glowing charcoal when I found her in the market square. I bought more of the same and sat with her on the lower step of the well, the glistening grease on our lips as we chewed. She was pleased with herself.

"So many ships are in the harbor, there is not a room to be had in any inn. A scribe took pity on me, imagining me to be a fellow scholar, and directed me to the house of his married sister, who is willing to let us use an outbuilding for the night."

The vision of a rat and cockroach infested storage shed arose in my mind.

"What kind of outbuilding?"

"What do you care?" she asked. "It has four walls and a roof. And it was cheap."

After we finished our meal, I returned to the stall of the leather merchant and bought two wallets that I had noticed earlier. They were not as capacious as packs carried on the back, but were made to be worn over one shoulder and wrap around the body, with a pocket in front at the chest and another pocket behind. The pockets had leather strings on their inner corners so that they could be tied together beneath the opposite arm to prevent the flat strap from slipping off the shoulder. We went around the market, filling one pocket of each wallet with hard black bread, salted strips of meat, and dried fruit for our journey.

Despite my misgivings, the outbuilding had a floor of boards, and even a bed of sorts. It had been newly made with clean white sheets. When I kicked the leather mattress bag with my toe, nothing squeaked or scurried away. The shed was located behind the house of the scribe's sister, beneath a spreading cedar. The tree kept the sun from its tile roof during the day, so that when we entered it at twilight it was already cool.

Martala fell quickly into sleep. I lay listening to her deep breaths beside me, hands behind my head, the cotton sheet pleasant against my naked limbs. Faint light came through a wide gap above the door. The shed had no window. The breeze stirred the boughs of the cedar above the roof and made a soft rustle in the darkness. Somewhere in the midst of the tree an owl sounded its melancholy call. My thoughts began to drift.

Sashi came toward me through the darkness, her face serene and lovely, as it always was when I saw it in my mind. She smiled. Her lustrous hair was plaited elaborately on top of her head, her body clothed in transparent silk that opened at the waist. Red henna dyed the tips of her fingers bright crimson. Black henna darkened her palms and the soles of her feet. Tonight she had a ring of silver through the side of her nose. She did not always wear this ring. Silver bracelets enclosed her wrists and ankles.

There was no need to speak. She knew my thoughts. Her round thighs opened and straddled my waist, settling on my erect prick, as long and hard as ever it had been in life. She reached behind her head and drew out combs of tortoise shell, so that her hair fell in cascades down her shoulders, then leaned forward and draped it around my face, a scented veil of mystery. Her kiss drew out my breath with indescribable sweetness, so that I panted with my desire. My hips rose and fell in rolling rhythm. I found the tip of her tongue with mine and stifled a groan as my seed erupted. She drew her face away from mine, so that the world was filled only with her eyes.

A slight sound beside me made me turn my head in languid ease and peer into the darkness. My eyes had grown accustomed to the shadows. I saw Martala watching me with an expression of curiosity.

"Did you have a dream of love, Alhazred?" she whispered.

"Not a dream."

Comprehension came into her eyes. She thought for a moment, and smiled.

"I am glad for you. The Goddess has given you this mercy because you have suffered so terribly."

"Why would the Goddess show me mercy? I, who have given her nothing?"

"That is her way," she replied with simple faith. "She gives help to those who suffer."

Resting her cheek against my bare shoulder, she sighed and closed her eyes. In moments she was asleep. I soon followed her, and did not wake again until the first light of dawn glowed through the gap above the door.

We dressed and lashed the wallets into place over our cloaks. The weight made me give silent thanks that we would ride instead of walk. I was not accustomed to carry the provision of many days. While among the Black Spring Clan, I had carried my meat in my distended belly. It comforted me to have a secure place to put the scroll. I slid it in the front pocket of the wallet, along with the rag of white spiders, and lashed shut the flap.

True to his word, the stableman had the horses saddled and standing ready when we reached the yard. I saw with approval that the saddle bags bulged with grain, and that the water skins were full. Tightly rolled sleeping rugs nestled behind the saddles. The horses looked more promising in the chill light. They widened their eyes and trembled with eagerness to be off.

The fat man eyed Martala up and down with a knowing leer.

"My wife's brothers are waiting. I will call them out."

He raised his voice in a shout that made the gray gelding snort and shy away from him. He gave the reins an impatient jerk without looking at the horse. I decided to take the gelding for my mount. I had ridden many high-spirited horses from the royal stables at Sana'a. The smaller and more docile mare was better suited to the girl.

With murmurs and rough banter, the brothers led their horses out the open door of the stable. As they saw me, they fell silent. Misgiving stirred in my heart. They were an unpromising band. Their horses had the road-weary look of animals ridden too many miles in too few years. Their tunics were faded and travel-stained, the fur ragged around their leather helmets. Three wore vests of chain mail, and the other, who appeared to be the eldest, a tarnished bronze breastplate. All bore swords and poniards at their broad belts, the scabbards raw from use.

The man in the breastplate passed the reins of his horse to one of his companions and came forward, meeting my eyes. His face held no emotion. A scar ran through the corner of his lower lip, evidently caused by a blade. He was bearded, as were the others except for the youngest, who cast his eyes over Martala as a man will look at a women, even though she was clothed as a youth.

"This is Hassan, my wife's eldest brother. He will keep you safe on your journey."

"I have protected many travelers," Hassan said in a deep voice. "Not one has died from a bandit's blade."

I considered my misgivings. Now was the time to make other arrangements, if they were to be made. We could wait almost a week and depart with the next caravan, or we could go alone, and take our chances with bandits. I reflected that anyone who performed the job of professional bodyguard for hire was apt to look uncouth and menacing. It seemed unlikely that these four could continue to get work if they were as unreliable as they appeared. All this passed through my mind in an instant.

"Very well, we will trust ourselves to your care," I told him.

He nodded and turned away. Taking back the reins of his horse, he swung into the saddle. The others followed his example wordlessly.

"You are in skilled hands, my lord," the stableman said with a smile that showed discolored teeth.

I glanced at Martala. She raised her eyebrows slightly and I shrugged. Mounting the gelding, I watched her swing herself lightly onto the back of the tan mare.

Hassan led the way from the dung-strewn yard into the street, moving at a slow walk toward the gate that would put us outside the walls of the city and on the long road east. A brother rode beside him. The other two fell into step at our rear, the beardless young man taking his place behind Martala.

The Syrian Gates were less impressive than I expected, from their fabled reputation. One pass between rocky hills is much like another. The sea fell behind us, and we wound our way beside hanging cliffs and across stony ridges. After the lushness of Egypt the land seemed barren. The road itself was passable, in most places broad enough for two laden camels to walk abreast. Hassan set an easy pace. Perhaps he thought we were not accustomed to long days in the saddle and wanted to avoid exhausting us. I was thankful for his prudence. Even though I was skilled on horseback, I had ridden for sport alone in Yemen, and my legs and buttocks began to complain before the sun reached the zenith.

Twice we paused to water our horses and rest our legs. As the sun sank low to the hills at our backs, casting our shadows before us across the uneven road, we reached a slope of dusty pebbles beside a great boulder larger than a house that had been used many times in the past as a stopping site. The charcoal of numerous ancient cooking fires spotted the ground within crude circles of loose stones. No doubt the caravans stopped here. The enormous stone gave shelter from the night wind, and from the stealthy approach of ghouls or wild beasts, allowing an easy watch to be set.

I had chosen the food that would go into our wallets with care. It was all of a type that required no preparation, and might be eaten from the saddle. Hot food is better than cold, but cold food is better than none. I did not wish to be encumbered with wood for cooking fires. Since our guards had brought no pack animal laden with sticks, I thought they meant to eat the same kind of meal, but to my surprise the young man with eyes for Martala drew forth a brass cooking lamp from his pack and used his tinderbox to light its wicks. Upon this he set a copper pot which he filled with water, and proceeded to add salted meat and dried vegetables and herbs to make a kind of thick stew.

While we unsaddled our horses and gave them water and grain, the pot bubbled. The odor that arose was seductive to an empty stomach. Martala crouched on her haunches beside her sleeping mat, gnawing with her eyeteeth on a strip of salted meat that was as hard as uncured leather. She gazed wistfully at the brothers as they held out bowls to receive the steaming stew.

"We should have brought such a lamp," she murmured to me in Coptic.

"It is too heavy. Look at all the oil it burns. Why not carry a bread oven, and have fresh loaves each morning?"

From her expression, I saw that she was not convinced by my argument. She would make a poor ghoul.

The youngest brother cast a sidelong glance at her. Smiling, he got up from his place beside the stove and approached her. He extended his wooden bowl in offering, nodding his head.

"Eat, eat," he said in Greek. "We have more than enough."

Martala glanced at me. I nodded. Eagerly, she took the bowl and tipped it to her lips. A bright smile illuminated her face. As an afterthought, the young man, who looked only a year or two older than Martala, turned to me.

"Let me fill a bowl for you, lord. We will eat together."

I showed him the strip of dried goat meat I was chewing.

"Will this add to the pot?"

He smiled and nodded. Taking our offerings, he cut them up with his knife and dropped them into the steaming pot, then ladled out a bowl for me while his brothers watched in silence. They did not object, but neither did they voice approval.

As darkness fell around us, Hassan and two of his brothers lay upon their sleeping mats, leaving a bearded man to sit watchfully gazing across the barren hills to the south. From his place he could see a stretch of the road extending east and west, while the towering side of the great stone acted as a wall to guard his back. I settled on my rug beside Martala, reflecting to myself that this armed watcher and his companions were a luxury, it was true, but a luxury I could well afford. Feeling easier in my mind than I had felt all day, I drifted into a deep and pleasant slumber.

How many times the watch was changed during the night, I could only guess, since I did not wake until bright daylight. The brothers were already stirring about their horses, saddling them and lashing on their saddle packs and mats. Martala tossed me a piece of black bread from where she sat cross-legged. Apparently no oil was wasted on a morning meal. The cooking stove had not been lit, but was already packed away on the rump of the horse belonging to the young brother.

I ate, pissed, and saddled my horse. Nor did I forget to reinforce my glamour when I found a moment of privacy. We set off eastward along the road without ceremony, not a word having been spoken to us by Hassan. He could scarcely be called a cheerful companion. Had it not been for the shy smiles cast by the youth at Martala, there would have been no cheer at all. She derived quiet mirth from his attentions, but she kept her amusement hidden save for the occasional wink she cast my way when his head turned.

As we rode, the land remained hilly, but the hills flattened and the space between them grew ever wider. It would not be many days before we left the coastal mountains behind us and entered onto the flat lands. It was not a true desert. Plants grew from cracks between stones. For me, there was only one true desert and nothing grew there. By comparison, this land was a lush garden. I could have lived upon its riches with ease, were I stripped naked and deprived of water and food. Even so, the constant jog of the new water skin beneath my cloak was a comfort.

We passed a well. Our guards stopped to fill a skin from its leather bucket. To my keen sense of smell, the water seemed poor, but it must be drinkable or the ruler of this land would have ordered the well filled in with stones. Perhaps boiling removed its brackish flavor.

It was late afternoon when we heard the first cry. It came from beyond the hills that lined the road to the north. It was harsh and drawn out, but a human voice.

I glanced at Martala to see whether she had heard it over the clank of the bridles and the rattle of pebbles beneath the hooves of our mounts, then at Hassan, who turned in his saddle without stopping his horse. His scarred mouth was grave.

"Bandits," he said.

Chapter 36

Another shout sounded, followed by a faint clash of steel. The noises echoed between the hills, making it difficult to perceive their origin. Hassan reined to a halt and stood in his stirrups, scanning the stone ridges on either side of the road. I could see no movement at their crests. He rode a few paces away and motioned for his brothers to follow. They bent their heads over the necks of their gathered horses and murmured amongst themselves. Hassan cast a glance back at me, then gestured toward the northern side of the road. The two bearded men in chain mail rode away at a canter without another word.

"I have sent them into the hills to determine the number of the bandits," Hassan told me when he and the young man returned. "We will ride on."

"Will the bandits attack?" Martala asked.

He smiled at her, the scar on his lower lip twisting his mouth into a grimace.

"Attack is certain. They would not have alerted us to their presence otherwise. When we learn their number, we will know whether to stand and fight, or flee."

"Why would the bandits want us to know about them?" I asked. "Why not attack us in the night while we lie asleep?"

Hassan shrugged his broad shoulders.

"It is their way. They hope to terrify us, so that we will do something foolish."

Before I could speak, he jerked the head of his horse around and set off along the road at a brisk walk. We let our mounts fall into step behind him, and the youth took up his customary place behind Martala.

The hills drew close on either side, so that in places outcroppings of rock overhung the road where it skirted their bases. Countless ravines and gullies offered concealment for armed men to lie in wait. It was ideal for an ambush. I wondered that Hassan could ride into it with such a display of unconcern. He was braver than I would have believed, certainly braver than me. I felt invisible eyes on my back every step of the way. Whether they were real or only in my imagination, they made the skin over my spine crawl.

We had not ridden more than a quarter of an hour by the clock when the babble of a man's voice floated to us on the still air. His indistinguishable words, if they were words at all, gave way to broken sobs and short cries that the stony hills threw in all directions. Hassan raised his hand and halted to listen, his face hardset. The voice fell silent, and a moment later we heard a scream that was abruptly cut off by a harsh gurgle. Martala's eyes went wide, but not so wide as the eyes of the smooth-faced youth behind her. I had heard such a sound before, and knew it for the gurgle of blood in a slit throat.

A different voice began to beg for mercy, its shrillness mounting, until it too became a death scream.

"They killed Habib and Kesof," the boy cried out.

He turned his horse and started to spur it up a gully on the north side of the road when Hassan, riding with surprising quickness for so big a man, cut off his path and grabbed the reins from his hand. He struck his younger brother brutally in the mouth with his open hand.

"They are both dead," he said, glaring at the trembling youth. "We will come back for them when our work is done."

Stifling a sob with his knuckles, the boy nodded and bowed his head on his chest. Hassan gave him back the reins and looked at me.

"We must return to the city."

"No. I paid you to take us to the river."

"Are you mad? The bandits will be waiting ahead. It would be certain death for all of us."

"How do you know they aren't waiting behind?" I countered.

He brushed the question from the air with his hand.

"We are closer to the city than the river. There is no shelter to the east for six days."

I considered for several moments. There was nothing for me in Iskanderun. If we went back to the city, we would only need to ride over the same road again, and who could say that the danger would be less?

"I am going forward to the river with my servant. I release you from your duty toward us. You may return to the city if you wish."

He set his teeth stubbornly and started to speak, then turned to squint at the northern hills. At last he shook his shaggy head.

"No, you hired us to protect you. We will not abandon you to the bandits."

This sudden display of honor surprised me. I might have expected it from a nobleman, but not from a rough mercenary. I nodded my appreciation.

"If we live, I will double your fee."

"Keep your money," he said with contempt. "We have been paid."

We urged our horses to a canter. It would have been madness to ride with greater haste through the heat of the day. The already weary beasts would collapse within a few miles from thirst and exhaustion. The breeze created by our progress cooled my face, but white flecks of sweat formed on the neck of my gelding.

When I began to hope we had left the bandits behind, a solitary rider emerged from his hiding place behind an outcropping and barred our path. The place was well chosen for ambush. Although the hills on either side were not very high, their steep slopes, treacherous with loose pebbles, pressed close on either side. A horseman might ride down by sliding in the loose stones, but it would be difficult or impossible to reach the crests from the road.

A black cloak covered him completely from his shoulders to below his stirrups, and a sack of black cloth with eye holes cut in its side concealed his face. By the bulk of his shoulders and the way he overhung his mount, I could see he was a mountain of a man, as tall as Hassan but easily twice as broad. He drew a long blade from its scabbard at his hip and held it up to catch the sunlight on its polished side.

"Throw down your swords or you will be killed," he roared with the voice of a bull.

The clatter of hooves behind us drew my attention over my shoulder. Two riders similarly cloaked with faces concealed in black sacks approached cautiously, swords extended.

"If we disarm ourselves, you will surely kill us," Hassan responded.

"No. You have my oath. By the Prophet, if you cast down your weapons, you will be released unharmed. If you refuse, you will surely die."

I urged my gelding beside Hassan.

"They are only three men," I whispered.

"Are you a fool? There are many more in the hills."

"Why do they not descend?"

"If they show their faces, they must kill us to avoid our witness against them. Be thankful you have not seen them. You may have a chance at life."

I gazed up at the hills. If men waited there behind the crests, they could descend on us in moments. I saw the wisdom of his words, but the thought of giving up my Damascus blade made me sick inwardly. Even before my chastisement and expulsion from the palace, I had never trusted a spoken pledge. Words melt on the wind the way water sinks into dry sand. To place my life in the hands of bandits was difficult. Yet there was sense in the mercenary's counsel. Why would the bandits be hooded if they intended to kill us outright? Why would most of their number remain concealed in the hills?

Their leader approached, brandishing his great sword easily in his hand, as though it weighed no more than a stick of kindling. I slid my blade from its scabbard and prepared to cast it onto the ground, when my eye caught a flash of purple on the bandit's exposed forearm. I recognized the purple-ringed burn mark I had seen at the stables on the arm of the fat stableman.

"Martala, it's a trick. They are all against us!"

Hassan's hand caught the reins of my horse and drew back its head while the hooded stable master rode forward and put the tip of his sword against my throat. I heard Martala struggle and curse behind me.

"I have him," the bare-chinned brother said with a laugh. "Don't wriggle so, young scholar, or your master will be killed."

"You fool," Hassan hissed at me. "Had you kept silent, you would have been released to walk back to the city."

"So that is your game. Pretend to guard travelers, then rob them disguised as bandits and let them return to Iskanderun to swell the rumor of the dangers on the caravan road."

"Naturally," the fat man said with a laugh.

He pulled the black sack off his head. His gleaming face was flushed, the linen of the hood sodden with sweat. The other two removed their sacks, revealing the bearded faces of the supposedly murdered brothers.

"No traveler hearing the tales of robbers on the road will venture outside the walls without an armed escort."

"Which you are happy to provide for a price."

"It has been a good living for my family for years. I regret that we must kill you. It is something we try to avoid."

"Are there really bandits on this road?"

He smiled in a pleasant manner.

"Perhaps. Who knows? But not so near to the city."

The time for talk ended. I saw the corners of his eyes tighten, and his fingers flex on the hilt of his sword. I wondered if I could beat his heavy blade aside before it cut my throat, and before the youngest of his kin killed Martala. My own blade hung half-lowered at my right side. Hassan had a hand occupied with the reins of my gelding. It was some help since it forced him to lean in his saddle, putting him off balance.

A soft hiss sounded in the air behind me. For a moment I thought of a knife cutting through silk. The fat man looked past my head, and his blade dropped a hand's-breadth from my throat. A gurgle made me turn in time to see one of the bearded brothers fall from his saddle, the point of an arrow projecting through the front of his chain mail vest, which became visible through the opening in his cloak as he slid sideways.

The youngest brother held Martala half pulled from her saddle, one arm around her throat and his knife at her belly. He stared in wonder at the dead man, then at me, as though I were responsible.

Beyond his white face, small in the distance, I noticed two horsemen approaching along the road from the west at a brisk trot. The rising heat from the road made their forms shimmer and dance, as though reflected in water, yet still I recognized them. The slightly built figure on the left who sat so straight in the saddle was Farri's daughter, Zayna. Beside her, more at ease in his posture, rode Altrus.

As I watched in wonderment, Zayna drew an arrow from a quiver at her saddle. Only then did I see that she held a bow. She notched the arrow to its string and rose in her stirrups to draw it.

With a curse, I jerked my reins from Hassan's slack fingers and spurred my gelding in the ribs with my knee so that it reared skittishly to the side. He remained motionless, as though entranced, watching the approaching riders. The arrow missed my back and buried itself in the stable owner's fat thigh.

He roared in mingled pain and rage. For the moment both Martala and I were forgotten. Zayna moved without haste to draw another arrow from her quiver.

"They are only two men," Hassan cried in fury. His outrage spurred him to action.

Martala pushed away from the bewildered youth. He did not bother to try to recapture her, but turned his horse with the others and galloped at the strangers, his dagger waving above his head in his fist. I felt thankful for their enthusiasm. Zayna had aimed at my back, of that I was certain.

The third arrow struck the stableman in the chest but failed to unhorse him. I suppose it was lost in the thick layers of suet that covered his torso and did not find his heart.

"Catch the horse," I told Martala, who was nearer the frightened beast.

She rode up to the mount that had formerly carried the slain brother and grabbed its bridle as it reared, pulling it forcefully back to earth. I reached her and took the reins. Without another look at the charging brothers or the two who continued forward at an unhurried pace to meet them, I urged my nervous gelding into motion, drawing the riderless horse after me until it began to trot. Martala positioned herself on the other side of the creature and reached to take the slack of its reins. With both of us holding them drawn tight on either side, we were able to gallop eastward away from the battle, the riderless horse between us.

"Why do you want the horse?" Martala asked after the shouts and the clash of steel on steel fell behind us.

"I don't. We need its water."

She looked at me with puzzlement.

"If we don't have to stop at the wells, we can travel more quickly."

Understanding came into her frost-pale eyes.

"Zayna and Altrus will not stop," I continued. "They will have all the water on the other horses, after they kill the fat man and his brothers-in-law."

"Are you so sure they will win the battle?"

I remembered the way Altrus handled his sword, and the joy that came into his hard face when he fought.

"They will win."

The hills soon concealed the cloud of dust that arose from the fight. We slowed to a canter to rest our gasping mounts. Soon we would have to stop, no matter how much danger it entailed. The horses needed rest and water or they would drop dead between our knees.

A ledge of bare rock scattered with loose pebbles extended south, gently rising through a gap between the hills. It seemed as good a place to leave the road as any. I reined to a halt and sat listening above the snorts of my gelding. The other horses stood silent. No clash of battle reached my ears, only the soft sigh of the wind that blew sand between the stones.

"How did Farri's daughter come to ride with the Jew's mercenary?" Martala murmured, as though afraid her voice might carry to them.

"Farri must have spoken with Altrus after we fled the house, and discovered my trick to make them enemies. It's too bad. I'd hoped they would kill each other."

As I spoke, I leaned in my saddle to unload the water bags from the riderless horse and slung them over the haunches of my gelding. Taking the reins from Martala, I let them fall and slapped the beast on its flank. It bolted in terror along the road to the east and disappeared around a hillock. For a time we listened to the clatter of its hooves. Turning the head of the gelding, I urged it up the expanse of rock with my knees. Martala followed.

Progress through the hills was more difficult than along the road, but we had come far enough from the sea that their slopes were passable. Eventually, as we traveled east, they would give way to plains. Or so I had gathered from maps I had studied years ago of the river valley of the upper Euphrates. We had only to continue eastward and we would eventually encounter the river. It was possible that Altrus would not see where we turned off the road, and would pass us and lose our track, but I had no faith in such a rosy fortune.

"We might turn and wait for them to reach us," Martala mused, as though speaking to herself.

"You saw what Zayna did with that bow."

"If we came upon them from behind, before she could use it?"

"Altrus would kill us both. I am no match for him with a sword."

She pouted, her cool gray eyes turned away. It was not difficult to guess her thoughts. My words were those of a fearful man who ran and hid, not those of a bold warrior. I nearly laughed. When had I ever made pretense to be a warrior? The best battles were those that did not need to be fought, and next to those the battles that were easy to win. I wanted no test of skill with Altrus.

We continued to work our way through the hills, tending eastward when we could, but often forced to make our way south or even west to circle impassible ridges. The land held no welcome. From time to time lizards of a dusty brown color darted between the legs of our horses and ran into cracks amid the rocks, their needle-like black claws skittering over the hard stones. A lone hawk circled in the cloudless blue sky, no larger than a fly speck.

When we had ridden for an hour or so, I judged it safe to risk a brief stop. The heads of the horses drooped with exhaustion. We gave them water in a shallow leather bag shaped to allow them to drink, then fed them a small amount of grain from the flats of our hands. There was not a blade of grass for forage.

I sipped from my new water skin, seated on a boulder beside the silent girl, and considered the choice I was forced to make. Either I could continue to flee eastward in the hope of staying beyond the reach of Altrus and Zayna until they lost our track and abandoned the chase, or I could attempt to approach them undetected and kill them. Neither course held any appeal.

My pursuers would continue hunting us until they got the scroll of the Old Ones. If they had talked to Ravicar while in Iskanderun, or questioned one of the brothers before killing him, they would know we were bound for the Euphrates, and might easily guess that to be our destination in any case, since the caravan road led to the river. From there it was no difficult work of the brain to assume that we would travel down the Euphrates by boat toward civilization. We might shake them from our heels at the ruins of Babylon, but not before.

"I could carry the scroll of the Old Ones back to them and let them capture me," Martala said.

"They would kill you."

"Not at once. I am a woman. Altrus would have a use for me, before he cut my throat, and Zayna would enjoy my screams."

I considered her plan. If I could come upon Altrus without his sword, occupied in raping the girl, I might be able to slay him by stealth. Reluctantly, I abandoned the notion. Even if the girl swore to him that she had murdered me for the scroll, he would not believe her and would remain cautious of an attack. Zayna might be young enough to fall for such a lie, but Altrus was more likely to kill Martala outright, take the scroll, and then kill Zayna.

"We will find another way," I told her.

The slender shoulders of the girl fell with relief, though she tried to hide it from her expression.

We continued through the hills into the late afternoon, keeping the road no great distance away on our left side. From time to time we glimpsed it between the ridges of rock. When I judged we had come far enough to make immediate discovery difficult, I found a sheltered hollow for the horses. We removed their saddles, fed and watered them, then tied them so that they would not wander off. Leaving the grain and most of the water with the horses, I went on foot with Martala over bare rocks that left no mark of our passage until I located a deep cleft between large stones. It was spacious enough to lie within protected from the sun.

I squeezed through the slot of the entrance, then leaned out and motioned for the girl to follow. She made a wry face and hesitated. I realized she was fearful of vermin.

"It's empty," I told her with impatience.

Compared to some of the scorpion-infested holes where I had slept while in the Empty Space, it was a palace. She shuddered and slid her slender body into the shadow.

"We will sleep here until after dark. I do not believe that Altrus will find the horses, but even if he does, he will not find us."

From the front pocket of my wallet I drew forth the knotted red and green silk rag that held the white spiders. Untying it with care upon my palm, I regarded the small pile of dried creatures with a kind of amazement that they had traveled so far with me without mishap. It was fortunate the girl had not discarded the rag after my death, thinking it worthless. I ate three spiders, then counted three more.

"Hold out your hand."

Martala watched me in revulsion. When I did not speak a second time, she extended her palm with reluctance and accepted the three spiders.

"Eat them."

Her face might have been comic, were I in a different frame of mind. As it was, I felt only impatience at her display of reluctance. At last she put the spiders into her mouth and ground their dried legs between her teeth, then swallowed them. I uncorked my water skin and let her sip to clear her throat. She coughed once and wiped her lips on the back of her hand.

"Try to sleep. I will wake you when it is time."

Sleep came to me with ease. Now that I was certain in my mind what I would do, I felt no disquiet. I possess the trick of waking when I wish, if only I tell myself beforehand when I should wake, so I knew I would not sleep beyond midnight. The distant bark of a desert fox reached my ears when once again I became aware. I lay listening in the darkness to the regular breaths of the girl curled up against my left side. The night air felt cool on my cheek after the heat of the day.

She woke with a start when I touched her shoulder. We worked our bodies out through the narrow cleft. I expected a strong response from the girl to her first experience of the second sight, but still she surprised me. She made a soft sound of wonder as she turned a complete circle, staring at the narrow ravine in which the cleft lay hidden.

"Did the spiders do this?" she whispered. "It is so beautiful."

I followed the direction of her gaze. Tiny sparks of cool light glowed in the rocks. The bodies of desert night creatures shone like stars against this background. Here and there the ghosts of trees and bushes long dead stood transparently above the places of their vanished roots. A snake glided across the ground, as silent as a silver ripple on a moonlit pool.

Sashi, I said inwardly.

Yes, my love?

Leave me and locate where Zayna and Altrus have camped for the night.

It will be as you say.

I felt her slide through the pores of my skin and stream from my eyes, nose-hole, and parted lips. Martala cried in terror and jumped back, drawing her dagger. Perhaps I should have warned her.

"This is Sashi," I said when the djinn crouched on a rock before us, glowing with an eerie luminescence.

Martala stared speechless at the spirit, who waggled her grotesque head at the girl before loping away on her long hind legs in the direction of the road.

"Is that truly how she looks?"

"It is," I said, then corrected myself. "It is her true appearance while she is outside my skin."

We started on foot toward the north, where the road crossed through the hills. Without the second sight, progress over the loose stones and uneven ground would have been impossible. The only natural light came from the stars. Not even a sliver of moon rode the heavens. It was as dark as night ever became in the absence of a storm. I hoped that the darkness would provide the advantage I needed over Altrus.

As we crawled on hands and knees to peer over the crest of a hill at the glowing ribbon of the caravan road that wound its way below, the shining body of the djinn returned through the night air, moving in quick little darts from side to side as though dancing weightlessly across the stones. I stood with open arms and let her enter my flesh.

They are camped for the night in the northern hills, not far along the road to the east.

"Tell me when we are close."

I will do so, my love.

We descended to the road as noiselessly as we were able and followed its bright path eastward. The warning of the djinn enabled me to find the place where the two assassins had entered the hills. Remnants of their footprints still glowed on the ground. It was a natural canyon of no great depth. Brightly shining piles of old charcoal showed that its floor was often used as a stopping place by travelers. Their horses were tied to a small pile of stones.

Altrus lay on his woven sleeping mat near a wall of rock at the rear of the canyon, covered with a blanket. Zayna sat further away with her back to the rock, legs crossed, her sword naked on her knee. As I watched, she slapped at her neck and cursed softly. The flying insect that had bitten her evaded her hand and escaped with her blood, glowing like a tiny lamp to my second sight. The horses stirred with unease and drew their tethers taunt. I wondered if they smelled our sweat.

Saddles and packs lay piled in a heap next to the horses. Among their brightly radiant forms, the bow Zayna had used to attack the bandit brothers leaned unstrung across a saddle, its string wrapped around one of its curved ends. The quiver of arrows rested upright against the saddle. It was a poor way to handle such a fine bow. The string and the fletching of the arrows would be wet with night dew.

For a time I considered the puzzle. Altrus lay closer to the horses than Zayna. If I attempted to get beside Zayna to cut her throat, I must pass near Altrus, and I had no confidence that I could do so without waking him. If I tossed a pebble to draw Zayna out from her place, the mercenary would wake. I wondered how well Farri's daughter could see in the shadowed canyon, with only the stars for lanterns.

Gesturing for Martala to remain where she crouched, I worked my way closer, approaching the campsite directly behind the horses. My movements were hidden by the restless stirrings of their legs, or so I hoped. The eye of the nearer animal rolled as it regarded the darkness with unease. I stood motionless as a pillar. The spiders gave me the advantage of seeing every loose pebble in my path, for the stones were impregnated with the bodies of tiny ancient creatures that glowed like flecks of silver in ink. Zayna cast her glance toward the horses with a frown on her face. She heard them moving but perceived no reason for their unease.

Taking the bow into my hand, I withdrew a step behind the horses and set one end on the ground to string it. As I put pressure on the tapered and curved wood, it gave forth a small crack. I cursed silently to myself. A bow always complained when it was strung. Usually it was done so quickly that the sound passed unnoticed. Tonight I could not afford to make so familiar a noise. I slowly increased the strain on the bow, bending it down the width of a thumbnail before pausing.

What at first had seemed like a good idea soon became a nightmare. Sweat dripped from my face and hands as I held the tension on the bow, using the weight of my body to bend it by tiny degrees so that it would emit no recognizable sound. The further the bow curved, the more strongly it resisted my push. When I became impatient and bent it more than I intended, it cracked softly, causing Zayna to glance at the horses. I waited for her to lose interest, then continued in the same way. My relief when the loop of the string finally slipped into place over the grooved end of the weapon was so great, I almost cried out. For several minutes I stood trembling, sweat running down my body.

Martala had not moved. I saw that she held the naked blade of her little dagger next to her knee. With exquisite care, I stepped to the side of the horses and reached forward to slide an arrow from the quiver. It made no sound. I notched its fledged end to the string and aligned it against the first knuckle of my left hand where I gripped the leather lashing of the bow.

Zayna jumped to her feet when she heard the bow bend as I drew the arrow to my ear. I shot her through the center of the chest where she stood. A groan escaped her lips, loud in the stillness, and her sword clattered on the stony ground. Altrus threw off his blanket and sat up, peering around in the darkness, which I knew must seem almost absolute to his eyes. He felt for the sword at his side and grasped the hilt.

"Zayna, what is it?" he hissed.

He heard the woman's corpse crumple to the earth. A horse neighed in alarm, and I saw him stare straight at me. As I fumbled for a second arrow, he found his feet and started toward me. I knew I must draw and fire quickly, unless I wished to find myself fighting for my life. When I pulled the arrow to my cheek, the dew-wetted string of the bow snapped with a force that jarred the bones in both my hands.

Altrus was almost upon me before my sword cleared its scabbard. How he fought in the darkness is a mystery. He seemed able to feel my blade as I cut the air, and he blocked it with disquieting ease. Had it not been for the excited prancing of the horses at the ends of the tethers, driving us apart, he would have killed me within moments. Even so, I would surely have died had I fought him alone.

I heard him cry out in agony, and for the first time realized that as we battled, Martala had worked her way behind him. She pulled her dagger from between his shoulder blades, brightness dripping from its edge to the stones. Of all the things that shine in the second sight of the white spiders, nothing shines brighter than fresh blood. I felt the resistance of his robes give way beneath the slashing stroke of my sword, and the hardness of his ribs against the thrusting point of steel.

Maddened by the scent of blood, one of the horses broke its tether and stumbled between us. Altrus grasped its streaming mane in his left hand and threw his right leg over its back. When it bolted from the canyon in terror, I saw him clinging precariously to its side, only partially upon its back, the tip of the sword he would not release trailing the ground and casting up sparks where it struck on stones.

Chapter 37

The next five days passed monotonously, a pleasant change of pace. I am not a man to complain about lack of excitement. Boredom never killed anyone. It seemed prudent to choose campsites that were easy to defend from approach in the darkness, and we kept watch in turns, one asleep while the other sat listening to the night sounds. There was little wood along the road for the making of fires, so we ate our travel provisions cold. The girl did not complain.

She spent the early hours of the first night restlessly shifting on her sleeping rug, starting at pebbles rolled by the hooves of the horses and the squeak of rats. I almost felt sorry for her when I gave her the second watch and lay down beneath my cloak. In the light of morning it was clear to see that she had not slept at all. The next night I told her to take the first watch, on the assumption that she might sleep if she were tired enough, and we continued this practice to the river.

Altrus we neither saw by day nor heard by night.

"Maybe he returned to Iskanderun," Martala said, speaking her thoughts aloud.

We guided our dusty and fatigued horses along the road as it wound its way over the plain of brown grasses and low shrubs that replaced the hills when we neared the Euphrates. Out of habit I scanned the horizon for movement. We were alone. Over the entire journey we had encountered only a single caravan, making its way to the sea with its score of camels heavily laden with bags of spices and bolts of silk.

"He was badly wounded," I observed. "He must have been or he would have killed us by now."

"My dagger struck deep," she said with satisfaction.

"Let us hope he lies crawling with maggots and flies amid the hills."

"May the Goddess make it so."

Not for a moment did I believe it, and neither did she.

On the fifth day after our battle with Altrus the grasses became greener and taller. Flocks of birds flew overhead with uncanny precision, turning and diving through the air in unison like a single creature as the sunlight flashed on the white of their angled wings. I smelled the river before we saw it. The smell was rich and muddy, with a tang of decay.

The Euphrates was as much a disappointment as the Syrian Gates. From its ancient reputation as a great river, I expected it to have the same broad majesty as the Nile, but it was narrow and twisted, with rocks projecting above its swiftly moving waters. They were green with the slime of the innumerable reeds and lilies that grew in shallow pools at its edge. The more traveled branch of the road followed the river southward, divided from the water by a barrier of dense green willows, their leaves so thick in places that I could not see through them, even from the back of my horse. The flies had no trouble penetrating them. I sweated and cursed as they drew my blood.

We came upon a gathering of buildings thatched over with sun-yellowed reeds. The lower part of the houses were of unmortared field stones, the upper part of irregular reddish mud brick. It would be pretentious to call it a town, although it boasted a wall of sorts. The road continued along the river bank, but no man with sanity travels by land when he can travel by water. I glanced at Martala and inclined my head toward the gateway of the place. She nodded and turned her horse after mine, too tired to speak.

The inhabitants surprised me by their physical beauty. Many had reddish hair and fair skin. They were tall and of well-proportioned limbs, the remnant of the Greek army of Alexander, perhaps. The women wore no veils, but stared at us without shyness when we rode into the marketplace. The men paid little attention, and the children watched in respectful silence. Even the dogs refrained from barking or nipping at the heels of our travel-weary mounts.

We left our horses to be cared for at the public stable and continued on foot across the marketplace to the river. It was a relief to stretch my legs after so many hours in the saddle. The wooden docks supported by massive piles were extensive enough to have served a much more populous village. Numerous flat-bottomed river craft floated on the water, some much larger than others, their bows tied to vertical poles inserted into the mud beneath the river. Both bow and stern upturned in much the same way as the Egyptian reed boats, but these were made from wooden planks overlapped like the scales of a fish. Short masts with furled sails extended from the middle of their decks. It puzzled me to imagine what use a sail would serve in this swift current.

Walking to the very end of the docks, I peered down the stream and saw a donkey on a beaten track that followed the edge of the water, pulling one such vessel on a rope against the flow, while two boatmen assisted its progress and kept it away from the reeds with long poles. Both wore white linen robes trimmed with pale blue that resembled thawbs, having loose sleeves that hung down below their elbows, and brimless white caps that clung tight to their heads. They appeared impervious to the biting flies that swarmed up in clouds from the shallows at the edge of the river, disturbed by the ripples.

The girl who rode the donkey could not have been older than seven or eight years. She minded the flies no more than the men, even though they lit and crawled over the dark hair that cascaded in waves down her back. A blue dress protected her arms with its long sleeves, but the skirt ended at her knees, and the ungathered cuffs of her white surwal left her ankles and feet bare. She grinned when she saw my eyes upon her, showing teeth like pearls.

As we stood idly watching the cargo bales from one of the larger vessels unloaded onto the dockside, amid much cursing and rough talk from the boatmen, I noticed the pilot of the donkey-drawn craft eye us with a shrewd glance. He stood uncommonly tall, with a back as upright as the shaft of an ash spear, and a flowing white beard and bushy white eyebrows that seemed to burst forth like cat's fur from under the tight rim of his cap. His hollow cheeks accentuated the noble thrust of his nose, its bridge as sharp as an axe blade. He turned to help his passengers, evidently a merchant and his wife, onto the dock. While his crewman unloaded the merchant's belongings, he approached us with an inquiring expression.

"Are you seeking to hire? My name is Yarku and my boat is the best on the river." This was said without pretension.

The language he spoke rang strange in my ears. Thanks to the finger of Nectanebus, I had no trouble comprehending his words, but out of long habit I pretended not to understand, and he repeated his question in Greek. I admitted that we intended to hire a boat to take us down the river, and eyed his vessel doubtfully. It was so narrow, I could have touched both gunnels by lying across it, without the need to stretch out my arms.

"Will it hold the two of us and our horses?"

He made a gesture with his hand, dismissing my concern.

"Only two horses? I've taken four."

"When can you be ready to depart?"

He raised his bushy eyebrows in surprise.

"You wish to leave today?"

I smiled tightly, wondering to myself how this old fellow came to have so much nose while I had none at all.

"Your town is charming, whatever may be its name—"

"Meskene."

"But we have no dealings here," I finished.

"What is your destination?"

"We seek the ruins of the ancient city named Babylon," Martala said in a pleasant tone. "Do you know of them?"

His tanned cheeks paled beneath their web work of wrinkles. The boatmen laboring nearby fell silent and eyed us with unease.

"I know it," he admitted with reluctance. "It is a place accursed. Only a madman would go there."

I smiled to disarm him, but he only hardened his mouth, thinking that I mocked his warning.

"What is the nature of this curse?"

"Death." He spat the word at me. "All who go there die."

"Even so, that is our destination. If you are frightened of the place, you can put us on land some distance up river, and we will ride the last few miles."

"That isn't necessary. The ruins are not on the water, although they are close to it."

"Will you take us there?"

He hesitated, then shrugged his bony shoulders. The unspoken words were plain. If we were mad enough to go there, he would bear no responsibility for our fate.

We fixed on a price, and he promised to have the boat ready for us, with our horses and belongings loaded, in an hour. There was just time to visit a tavern and buy a cooked meal of fresh river fish fried in a pan and newly baked bread. The tavern beer tasted good after the dust of the road.

"How long do you think it will take us to reach the ruins?" Martala asked with her mouth full of crust.

We sat at a small table in the corner of the shadowy common room, away from the ears of its other patrons. So many were travelers like ourselves, we attracted not a glance.

"At least two weeks, but probably nearer three. It is a long distance. Ask that bearded Cassandra when we board the boat."

She laughed, and had to push the bread back between her lips with her fingers.

"Aren't you frightened by his prophecy?" I said with a grim smile.

She snorted and drank from her wooden flagon, then wiped her lips with the back of her hand.

"We're necromancers. What fears can death hold for us?"

Her bold words surprised me, but I admitted to myself they carried some truth. Why should a man resurrected from his own corpse fear death? In my heart I did not feel so cheerful. Only a fool ignores a warning of danger.

When we returned to the dockside, the food suddenly became leaden in my stomach. Not only had Yarku loaded our horses, but also his donkey. The little girl sat astride its back in the stern, which seemed sensible, for I could not see an open place as wide as my hand on the flat deck planks in the bottom of the vessel for her to stand. It rode so low in the river, the ripples washed no more than half a cubit below the midpoint of its gunnels.

The bearded old man saw my expression of dismay and hurried over to us with a reassuring smile that Charon must have given the shades of the dead just before they crossed the Styx.

He ushered us into the boat with gentle proddings of his long fingers.

"Your places are in the bow. No, young sir, pass between the horses if you please, along the keel."

Martala, who had been about to crawl past the horses along the outmost side, pushed their rumps apart and squeezed between their barrel chests to the front of the little craft. I followed, and saw that amid the boat's supplies and our saddles and packs, there was just enough room for the two of us to sit. The other boatman, who stool on a small platform in the bow holding a long pole, smiled at us and nodded. He had clear gray eyes like those of the little girl, and a reddish beard that was only half as long as that of his master.

"This is Yuga, my son, and this is Kaleia, his daughter," Yarku said in introduction. The little girl nodded at the sound of her name, a bright gleam of mischief in her glance. She leaned forward and whispered into the ear of the donkey in her own language, speaking too low for me to understand. No doubt she told it what cowards we were, to fear the river.

The boat wobbled alarmingly when the two men untied it from its post and pushed away from the dock with their poles. The horses tossed their heads and looked around with alarm at the receding shore. Their unease was no greater than my own. I saw that the steering oar in the stern was lashed into place. Yarku and his son made no effort to unfurl the square sail tied to the angled yard of the mast, but guided the boat with expert nudges of their poles at the bottom of the river. When we did not capsize, I began to breathe more deeply.

"Do you mean to carry your donkey all the way to Babylon?" I asked Yarku in Greek.

He shook his head. His granddaughter turned to ask him what I had said, and he explained my question to her in his native language. She broke into peals of bright laughter, staring at me with delight. Her father chuckled from his perch in the bow behind our backs.

"Only to the end of the path," Yarku explained in Greek, a reluctant smile on his lips. The laughter of the child was difficult to resist. "This part of the river is too swift and narrow for sail. Below these rapids the donkey is not needed."

As the shadows lengthened on the sliding banks, the girl began to sing a folk song in her own tongue. She sang softly at first, then grew more confident when she saw we were not displeased. Martala took up the chorus in harmony with her, after she heard it repeated a few times. Her singing voice was better than I would have expected, given the stridency of her speech. I sat listening, my eyes on the donkey path that followed the edge of the river, lulled into a kind of trance. The swiftness of our progress kept the flies away. Half a dozen times we passed boats being pulled toward Meskene against the current.

Night fell almost before I was aware of the darkness. While there was yet a hint of gray in the sky, Yarku poled his little boat toward a crude gathering of huts on the bank and lashed it to a post against the tug of the stream, so that the side of the boat bumped against the rough trunks of trees driven into the mud to retain the earth of the landing area. I saw that the donkey path had reached its end. Here, the river was wider, its surface more placid. The child said her farewell to Martala with a smile, and repeated it to me with a more serious expression, then kicked the sides and tugged at the ears of the donkey until the uncomplaining animal stepped over the gunnel of the boat onto the ground. With a wave of her hand to her father and grandfather, she rode around the side of the huts and out of sight.

Yarku explained that we would spend the night on shore. I left him with his son to care for our horses, and went with Martala to explore the rough little hamlet. It boasted an inn of sorts, a single long building composed of red mud brick to the level of my waist, supporting walls of split wooden planks that held up the thatched roof. The interior was divided into two rooms, the larger chamber a common room for food and drink, the other a sleeping place filled with rough woven straw mats that rested directly on the earthen floor. The wife of the innkeeper found us a late meal of greasy joints of lamb, dried brown bread, and soft cheese, made palatable by more of the excellent beer of that land.

After we had eaten by the light of a smoky oil lamp, the stink of which did not improve the flavor of the food, we were shown sleeping mats in the other room by the serving slut, who spoke not a word to us and did not trouble to smile.

A naked infant howled in the arms of its mother. She sat upon a mat with her dress opened at the top and her breasts exposed, trying to make it suck. Mingled scents of curdled milk and excrement emanated from its discarded swaddling cloth. Little wonder the rag was soiled, since there appeared to be no other. Beside the frustrated woman, a young man with the look of a scribe sat with his back against the mud brick wall, long hair trailing over his flat cheeks as he drank from a wine skin and laughed softly to himself, his eyes dazed and unfocused. He may have been the woman's husband. If so, I felt pity for her.

We were forced to step around a prosperous traveler in a white silk turban and splendid red silk coat, beneath which was a tunic of red and gold, who stood with booted feet wide-planted, arguing with the innkeeper, his fat hands sawing the air while his face above the chestnut curls of his beard gradually assumed a darker shade of purple. From his choice of words I took him to be a physician.

"I cannot possibly sleep on the ground," he roared in Arabic. "The dampness will unbalance my humors. Are you trying to kill me? Do you want my blood to coagulate in my veins? Are you trying to give me an ague? You pool of camel spit, I want a bed."

The innkeeper minded this blast no more than a cat attends to the calling of its name. He nodded, a slight smile on his thin lips.

"As I have told you, good doctor Bassarius," he said when the fat man drew breath, "there are no beds. No mattresses. No feather pillows. No sheets of silk. There is only what you see here."

A barrage of curses followed. The innkeeper weathered it with a shrug and left the physician fuming in the middle of the room, an object of distaste for his fellow wayfarers, who probably enjoyed the crude mats no better, but had more sense than to complain. Damning the innkeeper to Shaitan, he waddled over to the mat beside my own and plunked his fat buttocks down upon it.

With fatalistic melancholy, I realized that he was to be my sleeping companion. I thought of asking Martala to trade her mat for mine, but on the other side was the infant, at last hungry enough to take suck of its mother's teat. I deemed the physician less likely to wake howling and squalling in the middle of the night than the child, and so determined to accept my lot.

Sleep took me easily, as it always does. In the dream, I walked beneath a star-shot sky across a dusty plane scattered with loose stones. It was not the fine sand of the Empty Space, but dried mud that had turned to dust, although the grit of sand was mingled with it. A great shadow loomed above the horizon and shut off the stars. At first I thought it must be a mountain, but as I walked nearer I saw that its sloped sides divided into terraces. It was a pyramid of human construction, different in shape from those I had seen in Egypt. Time had wrought much decay upon it, so that its lower parts were almost obscured by slides of debris from the perished bricks above.

A figure of human shape stood at its base, awaiting my approach. With sinking heart I recognized the cloak of the dark man, my master. I had begun to hope that I would never see him again, waking or sleeping. My heart thudded painfully in my chest and my legs trembled as I stopped before him. He spoke no word, but parted his cloak and raised it up behind him with his outspread arms, like the black wings of some hellish bat, so that it concealed the pyramid.

Light flickered and glowed over the inner surface of the cloak, and over his very body, opening into a kind of window filled with so many stars, they had the appearance of wreaths of smoke against the blackness of the heavens. I stared in wonder at its vastness, larger than the sky that arched above my head from horizon to horizon.

For some moments nothing stirred within the infinity of space. Then innumerable forms approached from the distant stars, amorphous and changing their shapes with restless hunger. Only their eyes remained unaltered, black and clear and darkly burning.

The horde of specters descended toward a beautiful sphere dappled with blue and green and brown. It was a barbarous world of monstrous plants and even stranger creatures. The largest was shaped like a cone, with a small round head and arms that resembled the claws of a scorpion. A kind of trumpet extended from the head, the bell of which moved and closed like a valve, and I realized that it was the creature's mouth. Into these nightmare beings the misty ghosts with the bright eyes entered, each possessing one of the beasts in the way a demon will possess a man.

The picture in the cloak of the dark man moved and changed with bewildering rapidity. Mountains rose and were worn away, the outlines of oceans receded, the plants grew up with different shapes, and even the sun that sped across the sky from east to west became more dim. As these transformations slowed, I saw a green river valley inhabited by men human in appearance, but of barbarous aspect. One night while they lay asleep under the stars by their campfires, the wraiths from between the stars descended from the sky and entered into their bodies, as they had entered the cone-shaped beings of more ancient times. There were not so many as before. Whereas the first descent had numbered in thousands, the second was no more than hundreds.

Again, time raced forward. The men possessed by the wraiths were rendered deathless, and became wise in all the arts, and took women to wife and bred many sons and daughters. They built an empire by conquering all the neighboring tribes and enslaving them. Using the labor of the slaves and the wealth of conquest, they constructed pyramids from red brick on the fertile plane beside the river. At intervals they ascended to the flat tops of these artificial mounds and lit fires and made sacrifice. Above the fires, portals opened in the air and objects of unguessable purpose passed through.

The vision became more distant, and I saw as through the eyes of an eagle that flew high above the land all the towers built by the sons of the immortals arrayed like place marks on a map. Silver rays of light radiated from them along the surface of the ground like the lines of a spider's web and converged on to a single point close to the river. The image descended. The rulers of the empire stood gathered around a steaming vent in the ground, some lost in discussion, others using survey sticks to mark out the ground in a square grid that enclosed the vent. Time sped forward, and

I watched a pyramid with stepped sides arise over the vent. It was larger and more impressive than those that had been built earlier. At intervals, the workmen stopped to allow the immortals, whose bodies glowed with inner fire, to place with care patterned bricks into the construction.

A multitude of people gathered at the newly built pyramid, surrounding its base and lining the stairways that wrapped around it even to its flat summit. The leaders of the immortals began a ritual of invocation and lit a fire upon the stone altar. At once a great beam of light ascended from the altar to the heavens and a gateway opened above the flames. The chanting of the worshippers gave way to shouts of joy and they began to dance upon the steps, but this soon turned to cries of dismay, and then terror, as the very earth itself trembled. A lightning bolt, brighter and larger than any I had ever seen, struck down at the pyramid and blasted its upper half into fragments. Those who had not fled from it at once when the shakings started were burned black like sacrificial offerings.

Again, time moved a rapid pace of years. The broken pyramid became cloaked in dust, and crumbled under its own weight as its disordered bricks decayed. It resembled little more than a hill of rocks and dirt. The glorious city at its base fell into ruin and was lost from sight, all except a few low foundations. The descendants of the immortals who had been so numerous grew few. Barbarian hoards overwhelmed them in their poor villages along the river, slaughtering the men, enslaving the women and children.

The veiled dark man closed his cloak and brought the dumb show to its end. He turned and gestured with his hand at the tumbled ruin behind him. Something glowed within the wreck of the pyramid, something bright that lay deep between the crumbled bricks. I began to walk toward the place. In the darkness the light was like a beacon that could not be mistaken. As I drew near to the fissure from out of which it issued, I began to see the shape that made it. I reached out my hand.

The squalling of an infant woke me. Martala was not on her mat. By the dim morning glow that found its way through the latticework of the east-facing window, I saw the mother of the night before attempting to placate her baby by offering it a piece of red coral. The infant thrust the offering away repeatedly with its tiny hand, a glare of fury on its wrinkled reddened face. Thanking the Goddess that I was childless, I rose and set about determining what place was deemed appropriate for voiding the bowels.

My nose-hole led me to the rear of the sleeping room, where a door opened onto a kind of courtyard with a low wall of bricks. Into the clay of the ground two depressions had been dug. They were separated by a partition of narrow wooden boards supported by two posts, with many gaps between the slats. Already the flies had begun to gather upon the contents of the holes. I added my own offering, annoyed that I had brought nothing with which to wipe myself. At last I used my left hand, and scraped it clean on the wooden partition, as I saw many others had done. With my right I remembered to renew the glamour of my face. This had become such an habitual action, I did it without thought.

Martala sat sipping broth from a clay bowl as I entered the common room, the steam of its contents rising past her cheeks. She dipped a piece of bread into the hot liquid and ate it. I obtained similar fair from the wife of the innkeeper, who sat next to the fireplace, ladling it from a large iron cauldron into wooden bowls that were stacked on the hearth at her foot. Bearing the bowl and my piece of bread with care back to the table, I sat opposite the girl. She had retained her disguise. Her hair was hidden beneath her green felt hat, and no sign of her breasts deformed the front of her tunic.

"You can become a girl again, if you wish, now that we have left Altrus behind us."

"And terrify poor old Yarku?" She sniggered, laughing with her mouth closed to avoid spitting out her broth. "He would believe that I was transformed by some djinn, and would jump into the river from his own boat."

The broth was better than I expected. It contained no treasures of meat, but fresh herbs floated in its depths, and strengthening grease pooled in yellow puddles on its surface, testifying that the bones of some beast lay boiling in the cauldron at the fire. I imitated my servant and dipped a corner of the hard bread, softening it in the bowl before chewing it. The salt in the broth was well received by my stomach.

"The boat is waiting for us when we finish," she said, tipping the bowl to drink.

"So early?"

"Yarku told me he does not travel by night when he can avoid it, so he likes to make the best of the daylight hours."

"I had a dream last night," I said, surprised at my hesitation to mention it.

She looked up and met my gaze.

"The dark man again?"

I nodded, and told her of my vision in his cloak.

"That tower you describe sounds familiar." She bit her lower lip in thought.

"The tower on the golden plate in the hall of pillars, beneath the tail of the Sphinx."

"Of course," she said. "The tower struck by lightning. It must be the same. But what does it mean?"

I shrugged in annoyance, draining my bowl as I tilted it to my lips.

"If the dark man wishes me to know, let him tell me. He has a voice, and most unpleasant it is on the ear."

A full stomach made my heart lighter as we paid for our breakfast and left the inn to return to the riverside. It fell again when I saw the fat physician in red silks of the previous evening, sitting in the place in our boat that had formerly held the donkey. The change was not an improvement, I reflected, since donkeys cannot talk. He turned and scowled at the sound of our approach, no gladder to see us than we were to see him. The horses had already been loaded. We stepped into the bow of the boat.

Yarku untied the boat and his son pushed it with his pole from the still water near the dock into the flow of the river. As it began to drift downstream, Yuga untied the bindings on the dirty square sail and hoisted the tilted spar to the top of the mast. He fussed with the ropes that held the sail at the desired angle while his father sat in the stern with one long leg projected from his robe and slung over the steering oar. It appeared an awkward posture, but I saw that he could recline that way for hours, moving the oar back and forth without effort as the wind required. The bare foot of the old man, its sole black with dirt, waggled ludicrously in the air.

The horses interposed on either side of the mast made conversation with the physician unnecessary, although we sat facing each other. As the sun rose and the river glided its placid way between the green banks, it became apparent that the fat man had no wish to remain silent. The warmth and the gentle breeze softened his features. He nodded to me between the flanks of the beasts when I chanced to look his way. I pretended a sudden interest in the sail, which flapped slightly as the boat rounded a gentle bend. He was not a man to be discouraged once he formed his intention. He cleared his throat, a deep noise like the thrumming of a frog. I glanced at Martala, who smiled at me behind her hand while pretending to adjust her hat. The harrumphing and thrumming kept up for a time, increasing in loudness, until at last I met his eye. He stretched his fat lips and nodded.

"My name is Bassarius," he said in Arabic.

"I am called Alhazred." There was no need to introduce Martala, who was only a servant.

"How comes it that a young man of noble family, as you clearly are by your bearing and speech, travels this fly-infested river?"

Resisting the urge to speak sharply at his impertinent question, I adopted an affable and, I hoped, slightly stupid expression. Perhaps if he judged me of low intelligence he would lose interest.

"My family in Yemen wished me to see the world. They would have sent me by caravan, but I loath the desert. Water travel is so much more civilized."

He nodded indulgently, and wiped his face on the corner of a white silk kerchief that hung around his neck. The glistening sweat on his brow made a dark patch on the cloth.

"I hate travel by river or road, but there is no help for it. The Amir of Persia has offered me the position of physician to his court at Baghdad, and I must get there some way."

"A royal appointment?" I tried to make my expression suitably impressed. "You must be a man of substantial reputation."

This pleased him. He smiled and shrugged his rounded shoulders beneath his red coat.

"I was fourth personal physician to the Caliph at Damascus, but the Amir offered such generous terms I could not deny him."

Reading between his words, I guessed that he had been expelled from the court at Damascus, and had taken this journey in the hope of finding a place of wealth and ease in Baghdad.

"You have no family?"

"Sadly, no," he said, pursing his lips and gazing down into his opened palms. "My wife died last year. Such a pretty young thing she was, always laughing and dancing, but no stamina. The slightest chastisement with a whip or rod upon her back sent her to her bed."

He blew a gust of air between his lips at the memory and shook his head. I imitated the motion, wondering without great curiosity what this fat monster had done to his young bride that had so shortened her life. Whatever it may have been, it was no affair of mine.

I can be such a fool in my optimism. During the next ten days Bassarius, who I learned was the product of a Greek father and an Arab mother of high family, regaled me with the intimate details of his family history, his marital life, his work as a healer of the sick, his service to the Caliph, the daily life in the court at Damascus, the personal habits of the Amir at Baghdad, the breeding of horses for racing, the purgative nature of sulphur, the care of fine leather boots, the price of silks in Alexandria compared with their price in Constantinople, the difficulties in training a competent cook, and a host of other matters about which I had no interest of any kind. Once the man overcame his brief and uncharacteristic initial reticence, there was no way to stem the flow of his words. They poured forth like the Euphrates itself, and were equally unending.

On the tenth day at the fall of twilight, after the boat had been tied up to a tree growing at the very edge of the water, and the horses had been led off hobbled to browse the soft green grasses, I turned to Martala.

"If that fat fool doesn't stop talking, I will cut his throat tomorrow morning. I can bear no more of it."

I heard the faint note of desperation in my own voice, but she only laughed. My suffering had been a constant source of quiet mirth to her. I suspected it was also a joke shared between Yarku and his son when they were out of my hearing, since the two cast amused glances at me when they thought I was occupied with other matters.

"The man is inhuman. Indeed, I do not believe him to be a man at all but some kind of hellish djinn. All men stop talking from time to time. The human voice is not constituted to speak without interruption from dawn until dusk, day after day."

She paid me no heed, but laughing softly to herself, set about unlashing our sleeping rugs. There was no hut to shield us from the stars that began to wink on like candle flames in the deepening purple of the sky. Fortunately, the camp place was elevated above the riverside, and removed far enough from its edge to avoid the flies that dwelled amid the reeds.

Bassarius returned from the grove of trees, tugging at the backside of his tunic through his open coat with his left hand as he waddled like a goose toward our sleeping rugs. The boatmen were preparing a fire in a circle of blackened stones some distance up the side of the little hill and paid us no attention. I suppose we were merely cargo to them, little different from the horses, except that our purses held gold.

"It is a strange thing, friend Alhazred, the way the bowel behaves at various hours of the day. An elderly physician of Damascus wrote a treatise on the subject, in which he describes the constitution of the dung of a man at each hour of the day and night, relating its softness, hardness, color, odor, and other qualities to the seven wan-dering bodies, which as you know are allotted to the hours of the day and night . . ."

My fingers unconsciously tightened around the ivory hilt of my dagger, and I heard a grating noise from my teeth. What might have happened next, I cannot judge, for my mind was inflamed with hatred, but any action I felt germinating in my heart lacked time to flower.

A shadow covered the physician. He took no notice and continued toward me. Puzzled, I looked up in time to see a dark shape of indeterminate outline descend like a stooping hawk upon its prey. The droning voice ceased with a squawk. There was a soft sound of flapping, like the wings of a bat that flies past the ear, and Bassarius was gone.

Chapter 38

As I gazed in wonder at the bare hillside where the fat man had stood, the bent grass crushed beneath his boots slowly straightened in the last dim glow from the dying light of the sky. Only then did I think to raise my eyes and look around. A black shape raced low along the horizon on the opposite bank of the river. Before I saw it clearly it was gone over the crests of distant hills.

I turned to Martala. She stared at me with an expression of puzzlement on her pale face, gray in the gathering darkness. Only the western horizon glowed. The rest of the sky was shot with stars.

Approaching footsteps drew my attention to Yarku.

"The fire is burning. We'll have something boiling in the pot in a few minutes. Where is the physician?"

He looked from my face to the girl, then back to me. An expression of horror stole across his features and he spun wildly, trying to peer on all sides and upward through his cat-tail eyebrows at the same moment. It might have been comical were his terror not so genuine.

"The Beast took him," he whispered. He made a gesture with his right hand that I recognized as the Elder Sign. My interest quickened.

"What do you know of this Beast?"

He ignored me. Stumbling back up the hill to the fire, he began to babble and gesticulate at his son, who made soothing sounds and tried to calm the old man with his hands by stroking his shoulders and arms. The expression of fear on Yuga's bearded face made a mock of his words. He was as terrified as his father. I approached with Martala beside me. The uneasy tingling between my shoulders almost forced me to look around but I resisted the impulse.

"What is this Beast?" I asked Yuga.

"No one knows what it is," he said, glancing at the darkening sky. "It comes at dusk or in the early hours of the night, and takes a man away with it. Sometimes it takes a child or a woman, but never a horse or donkey."

"It is an evil from the abyss," his father added. "They say it lives in the depths of the ruins of Babylon, and ventures forth for its prey."

"Does it take more than one a night?" Martala asked.

They looked at each other. Yarku exhaled and relaxed his tense shoulders. He made an effort to master his emotions. A portion of his dignity returned.

"I have never heard that it takes more than one."

"Then we are safe," I said by way of emphasis.

"I think so, yes."

They could tell us nothing useful about the Beast. No boatman had ever seen it. The creature descended silently from the sky and was gone in moments. Sometimes those it captured and carried away had time to cry out, but usually they made no sound. I remembered once as a boy seeing an owl swoop down on quiet wings to seize a mouse. The mouse let out a single squeak of surprise before the talons of the owl crushed it. None of us expect danger to fall from the empty sky. That is what makes it so terrifying. The gods cast down their wrath upon the heads of men. The heavens are a place for birds and gods, not for us.

We shared a solemn meal, each avoiding the gaze of the others. After so many days of endless chatter from Bassarius, the silence felt strange on my ears. The bowl intended for his use sat beside the hearthstones on the stiff grass where Yarku had placed it. When we were done, he collected it with the rest and packed it away. I felt no anxiety of heart as I unrolled my sleeping rug and positioned it where the warmth from the dying embers reached my side. The hardships of the desert had made me philosophical. If Yarku was correct, the monster would not return and we were safe; if he was wrong, still there were four of us and it could only carry one. Comforted by this reflection, I slept deep and awoke refreshed.

The dark circles under Martala's eyes testified to her wakeful night. The two boatmen began the day as blear-eyed and short of temper as the girl, but were soon mollified to discover that Bassarius had hidden a money belt of gold dinars at the bottom of his travel trunk. It is an evil wind indeed that blows no good. Yarku did not offer to share the gold with us, and since I saw no reason why he should do so, I said nothing. We sailed swiftly south on a favorable wind, passing several boats laden with cargo for the villages along the river. I sat in the elevated bow, gazing across the dry plains at the horizon, for the margin of green plants that lined both sides of the river was narrow and quickly gave way to dust and rock.

Dotting the distant expanse, mounds of crumbled stones interrupted the flat monotony. Yarku thought they were ancient temples to gods of fire, but apart from the stories of djinn that inhabited the ruins and killed unwary travelers who ventured near, he could tell me little that was useful. Before the Prophet brought his teaching to this land, his people had worshipped fire as a living force. Many tribes still followed the ancient ways, and there were sects of degenerate priests who made the mounds their temples, and burned fire under the stars. When I asked him to what purpose they lit their fires, he shrugged. He was not a man of religion, and the ways of the gods held scant interest for him.

That night, he tied up his boat on the western bank well before sunset, and made our camp in the hollow of a rock ledge that overhung our sleeping place, affording some protection against whatever evil might choose to descend upon us. The place was removed from the riverside and elevated, to escape the biting flies that otherwise would have made sleep impossible. I sat long, gazing across the river toward the east while the others slept. They were exhausted from their previous sleepless night. The fire died to embers that dimmed until its red glow was only visible when I looked upon it from the corner of my eye. In the distant eastern plain a flickering red spark danced atop one of the mounds. Someone had lit flames to the gods of the sky.

Wake me if danger approaches, Sashi, I said inwardly.

I will watch over you. Sleep deeply, my beloved.

In spite of Sashi's comforting words, I was not deceived. A monster that came from nowhere and fell like a thunderbolt could not be watched for, since the moment of its arrival was the moment of death. Curling on my side upon my sleeping mat, I let my mind drift into oblivion with the reflection that danger was ever present in the world.

All through the following day, the anxiety of Yarku and his son increased. Even if I had not known that we approached the ruins of Babylon, I could have guessed it from the fearful glances they cast at the eastern bank of the river, which they avoided as far as the shallows would allow, hugging the west bank with their boat the way an infant clings to the skirts of its mother. In the afternoon, Yarku muttered a prayer in his own strange tongue and resolutely turned the steering oar of the boat so that the little vessel cut across the stream of the river to the eastern side, where there was a landing area of sorts.

Yuga jumped from his place in the bow with a line to tie up the boat to a large boulder. The lazy current carried the stern around until the boat pointed in the opposite direction, up river. As he knotted the rope, he looked over his shoulder through the thin band of willows that divided the river from the plain. I followed his gaze but saw only dusty leaves rustle in the breeze. Yarku set about getting the horses off almost before his son was finished making the boat fast, such was his haste. He made no attempt at conversation.

"Where are the ruins?" I asked, unloading our saddle packs from the bow.

He pointed to the east without looking at me.

"How are we to find them?"

"You will find them," he snapped. Fear had drawn his lips into a thin line. "Ride east. They are near."

"Too near," Yuga murmured in his own tongue, which I pretended not to understand.

We stood beside our horses and watched the men pole away from the bank and catch the breeze in their sail. The boat moved slowly north against the current of the river, close to the western bank, but at last passed from sight around the bend. I slapped my neck with my hand and cursed. The sleepy air beneath the trees made my skin prickle with sweat inside my cloak, and the familiar reek of the river muck sickened me. I had seen enough of this river, and its vermin, and felt relief at leaving it behind for the wholesomeness of the barren plain. Where there is life there is always corruption.

"They were both terrified," Martala said with a slight shake of her head.

I swung into the saddle of my gelding and waited for her to mount her mare. What was there to say? For a moment I found myself wishing that I sat in the boat with the two men, sailing up the river and away from this accursed place. Annoyed at my weakness, I shook this fantasy from my thoughts. The north held nothing for me, no hiding place to escape the horror of my mutilated body or my enslavement to the dark man. I must go onward, fear or no fear.

We rode out of the willows and across the plain. It was not perfectly flat, but undulated to the horizon in low hills from which heat danced and made the distant air shimmer like beaten silver. A small mountain loomed no great distance away. Following the terse directions of the boatman, I headed east toward the foot of the mountain, wondering how the ruins of the greatest city of the ancients would look after the passage of so many centuries. I anticipated impressive pillars and statues like to those I had seen in Memphis and Thebes, but when we reached the outskirts of the ruins, I gazed upon them with disappointment.

Here and there lay scattered the remnants of foundation walls. The bases of a few pillars of stone stood like solitary watchmen, but many more lay on their sides. They were not of the impressive dimensions of the pillars at Thebes, but smaller and ugly in shape. Not a single roof survived. The flat paving stones of streets showed where the wind stripped the dust from them. Low outlines of buildings extended to the horizon. Only the sheer number of the ruins testified that here had once stood a great city. Little wonder travelers avoided the place. The wind sighing among the fallen stones sang of despair and desolation.

We picked our way through the puzzle of carven blocks and crumbling bricks, eyes alert for vipers, but saw nothing living apart from large beetles with backs like polished jet that made their lumbering way through the dust, leaving characteristic tracks behind them that resembled some obscure written script. These tracks were everywhere, so that the entire city seemed the book of a madman, scribbled with mute folly in words that could no longer be read. My heart sank in despair. We made a slow circuit of the ruins and returned to our starting place.

As the sun fell low on the western horizon, the light slowly changed and the shadows of the stones grew long. I chanced to look across to the north at the nearby mountain, and stopped my horse to brood. It had a familiar aspect.

"A fool's errand," Martala said in disgust.

"So it would appear."

"I see no head of any kind."

"Nor do I."

"Who are we to ask about the Well of the Seraph?"

I bit my tongue. Cursing the girl would not bring me the information I sought. With impatience, I dug my heels into the flanks of my horse and sent it trotting back toward the margin of the river. Martala followed me more slowly. When she reached the willows, I had the saddle and bags off the back of the animal, and its forelegs hobbled with a length of woven leather cord.

"We will let the horses browse on the grasses and drink from the river."

Silently, she dismounted and removed her packs and saddle, laying them beside mine, then set about hobbling her mare. The tails of the horses flicked across their flanks as the flies gathered in a swarm, attracted by the smell of our sweat. A dozen moving black dots spotted the tan rump of the mare.

"After we finish our meal, we'll come back and lead them away from the river before this infernal vermin makes its meal of them."

She nodded and bent with me to pick up the packs that held our sleeping rugs and utensils. I pulled forth a small copper pot before slinging my pack over my shoulder, and filled the pot half full with water at the edge of the river. This I carried with care to avoid slopping with the intention of making a stew with salted strips of goat's meat. Seeing my purpose, the girl began to gather an armful of the scattered sun-bleached wood that had washed up from the river in time of flood.

As we turned with our burdens to leave the willows and their flies behind, a cry sounded on the stillness of twilight. It was like the distant scream of a hawk when the falconer casts it upward to begin the hunt. I resisted the impulse to throw the pot aside and cower under a bush. Instead, I looked between the leafy tops of the willows, and realized that the sun had set on the western horizon. Already the brightest stars were emerging from behind the veil of the dying day. We stood almost touching and listened with our breath stilled in our throats. Other than the uneasy whinny of my gelding, and the faint rustle of the leaves in the treetops, there was no sound.

"It might be wise to remain under the trees," Martala murmured.

A fly whined in my ear and bit the side of my neck. I crushed it under my hand, then cursed when I realized I had spilled half the water from the pot.

"We can't stay here all night. We'll be eaten alive."

I returned to the river to refill the pot, then carried it with a display of assurance out of the willows and toward the distant ruins of the city. She followed me with her armload of sticks, making no further comment, but her eyes continued to scan the sky over each shoulder. I had to resist the urge to glance up, and felt annoyed with myself. If this Beast wished to kill me, it would surely do so. When we were midway between the river and the ruins, I looked around for a likely place to build a fire and unroll our bed mats. The ground rose gently to the left. We climbed the rise and made our fire on its crest in a circle of stones. When the fire burned strongly, I set the pot across two stones and began to cut pieces of dried goat meat into it. The girl scattered in a handful of dried herbs from her own pack.

While I crouched at the pot, stirring it with the blade of my knife, I noticed the mountain before me. It seemed to glow in the light from the rising crescent of the moon, which was a few days past full. Something in its outline awakened a memory. My hand stopped and my eyes narrowed. Hearing the scrape of my knife cease, the girl looked up from the fire.

"That little mountain," I said, pointing with my chin behind her. "It's the pyramid that was in my dream of the dark man's cloak."

She turned and studied it, then shook her head.

"It looks like only a hill to me."

"It is the pyramid. I recognize it in the darkness."

We ate our thin stew with dried bread, saying little. The desolation of the rocky plain discouraged conversation. It had a blasted appearance under the moon, as though in the distant past all softness of life had been swept from it by fire, leaving only a few green things to struggle pitifully for their existence along the river. What else could account for the loose stones that lay scattered everywhere?

I scoured my wooden bowl clean with a handful of pebbles, then set it on my pack and stood to stretch my legs.

"You can stay here beside the fire, if you wish," I told the girl.

As I approached the base of the pyramid, I heard her footsteps. She fell into step beside me on my left side. I said nothing, but her presence comforted me. I must be growing sentimental, I reflected. In the Empty Space I had needed no comfort.

It was an eerie experience to approach the ruined pyramid under the stars, as I had approached it in my dream. I scarcely knew whether I woke or slept. Only the absence of the dark man spoiled the illusion. We climbed awkwardly up the lower slope, slipping in the loose till that showered down around our ankles with a dry clatter at each step. A broad ledge extended around the top of the base. The higher sides of the pyramid lay crumbled almost beyond recognition. Unlike the Egyptians, who constructed their monuments of stone to last the ages, the people of the river had built predominantly with brick. Some of the pieces were glazed. I picked up a fragment and squinted at it, but could not tell its color in the glow of the moon. It clinked like a shard of pot when I tossed it aside.

A scream froze my blood. I looked upward, sure that the wings of the Beast were closing to enfold me. From a fissure between the bricks of the sloping side of the pyramid came a flurry of movement. Something hit me in the chest and knocked me from my feet. The back of my head struck a brick, and I lay blinking, all strength gone from my limbs. I saw the dull flash of a blade arc upward, but before it could reverse its course, the weight that pressed on my chest was thrust aside. Martala's curses rang on the night. I heard her dagger strike again and again into flesh. For a moment I must have lost awareness, for when next I opened my eyes, soft hands were helping me to sit up. I found myself able to move my limbs once again.

"A madman," she said as she probed the back of my skull with her fingertips.

I winced at her touch, and felt the place. It was wet with blood beneath my hair. My head throbbed like a drum, but my wits were returned. Rolling to my knees, I crawled over to the crumpled shape that lay beside me, and heard a gurgle of breath.

He had the wild beard and hair of a madman. Even under the moon I could see its grayness. A ragged sleeveless tunic closed with a knotted sash was his only garment, other than a rough pelt of fur tied over his shoulders like a cloak. I brushed the dust from it and saw that it was the fur of a wolf. The stench that rose up from him was worse than any corpse. He gasped for air, blood bubbling at his lips, and revealed teeth so rotten, they were no more than blackened stumps lining his gums. Martala put her hand over her mouth and drew back her head, but I ignored the smell.

"Why did you try to murder me?" I asked in Greek.

He glared and groped across the ground at his side with his clawed hand. Glancing over, I saw that his dagger lay a cubit beyond his grasp.

I repeated my question in Arabic. He snarled and cursed me in a language strange to me, but similar to the language of the boatmen of Meskene. The desiccated flesh of the finger of Nectanebus gave me perfect knowledge of it, and I asked the question a third time in his own tongue.

"This place is sacred," he said, eyelids drooping as the life ran out of his body. "Only the priests of fire may come here."

"Are you a priest?"

"I am the last priest. Now there is no one to light the holy flame."

His eyes began to close. I grasped his shoulders and shook him roughly. He choked on his own blood and coughed, meeting my gaze with hatred.

"What do you know of the wisest head of Babylon?"

He licked his lips, and blood welled from his mouth.

"You seek the head?"

"I seek it," I said grimly. "Tell me where it is, and I will give you water."

The rasping gurgle of his laughter surprised me.

"Go to the gate in the eastern part of the city. There you will see a pit between two fallen pillars. One of the pillars lies broken into three fragments. Descend, and you will find what you seek."

"Why do you help me?" I demanded.

He made no answer, and I saw that he was dead. I let his reeking carcass fall from my hands and pushed myself to my feet. My head throbbed painfully and the stars spun around, making me stagger. Martala caught my arm and held it.

"You should sit, Alhazred. You are not fit to walk."

Ignoring her gentle words, I pushed my way up the slope of rubble that led to the base of the fissure from which the madman had emerged. It split the pyramid as though cleft by some gigantic axe. The image was clear in my remembered dream. I saw in my mind the place where the ray of light had shone forth, and worked my way toward it, leaning upon Martala for support. At the back, the fissure narrowed so that I was forced to crawl into it on my hands and knees. The girl could not follow. Even the murk of indirect moonlight gave way to total darkness. I made my way by touch, following the image in my mind. Stretching on my belly, I reached my arm downward into a crevice. There was just enough light on the back of my cloak for the girl to see what I did.

"Are you mad? That hole may be filled with scorpions."

I felt over the dusty bricks and between the cracks at its bottom. Bitter disappointment welled in my heart. The dark man had deceived me. The hole was empty. As I began to withdraw my hand, my fingertips brushed something that clinked with a metallic sound. Stretching my arm so far that I feared it would dislocate from its joint, I touched a smooth metal edge, and was able to fit it between two fingers. With great care I withdrew it from its resting place. Not until I closed my fist around it did I allow myself to breathe.

Martala helped me work my way out of the fissure. With every passing moment my head became clearer, although the pain did not diminish. I felt the back of my skull with my left hand and found that my blood had ceased to flow. When we stood on the broad terrace beside the corpse of the mad priest, I opened my fist and looked at my prize. Martala caught her breath in amazement.

Beneath the moon it had the appearance of silver. It was a medallion no more than an inch in diameter, with a beaded edge and a loop for hanging it around the neck. One side was covered with a spiral of obscure hieroglyphs unlike those of the Egyptians. I could make nothing of them. On the opposite side the Elder Seal had been deeply cut. Its five branches, like the branches of a tree limb, gleamed in the moonlight.

"That is what the dark man wanted you to find?"

I nodded, fingering its engraved surface.

"But why?"

When there is no answer to make, it is foolish to speak.

We returned in silence to the campsite and renewed the fire with fresh wood, then led the horses away from the flies of the river. The night wind blew strong from the distant ruins, which could be seen from the hill, but it carried no refreshment. We settled ourselves on our rugs near the fire. For a long while I studied the medallion. In the firelight I saw that it was gold, not silver. There was a strangeness in its workmanship, and the metal felt unnaturally cold on my fingers, as though it sucked the heat from my flesh. I wondered if it truly was gold, or some unknown alloy of metals forged by ancient alchemy. With the disk in my hand, I drifted into uneasy sleep.

Chapter 39

The echo of a distant cry woke me. I lay wondering if I had heard it with my ruined ears, or in a dream. I sat up and saw the sun just rising above the ruins of the city. The long shadows cast by its slanting rays outlined with startling clarity the streets and buildings that had once existed. Many features were defined by nothing more than irregularities in the ground, and would have been wholly invisible under any other light. The ruins were much more extensive than I had imagined. They led around the base of the broken pyramid, and extended even to the river. I realized that we had made camp within the city itself, and that the hill upon which I sat was probably the remnant of some great temple or public building. The ruins that had survived best the passage of centuries were those constructed of stone, such as the fallen pillars and the fragments of carved statues. The much more numerous buildings of bricks, formed from dust in their making, had returned to dust, or almost to dust.

Martala stirred in sleep and broke my reflections. She yawned and stretched, blinking the dryness from her pale eyes. When she saw me watching her, she smiled with a curious expression.

"We live to see another morning, Alhazred."

Cheese and hard bread formed our simple breakfast. I find little use for heated food, and did not intend to waste an hour of the day preparing a fire and cooking what could be eaten cold, in spite of Martala's repeated wistful glances at the copper cooking pot. In the night, a camp fire serves other useful purposes, such as light for defense and warmth for sleeping, but to light a fire in the day merely to heat food is a foolish extravagance. The girl did not complain.

When our horses were watered and fed, I unbraided a length of the fine leather rope that we used to hobble their forelegs, and hung the gold medallion around my neck from one of its slender plaits. For a moment I wondered whether to leave it outside my cloak, but feared that it might be hooked and pulled away by some passing obstruction without my awareness. I slid it down the front of my throat and felt it cool against the skin of my chest over my heart. The coolness persisted, as it had in my hand. My conviction grew that it was no ordinary metal.

We had ridden past the fallen eastern gate of the city without taking particular notice of it on our first broad circuit of the ruins. This morning, we rode directly to the place. Each side of the gate was an elaborately carved pillar of stone wide enough at its top to lie upon. They were shaped like sitting lions, with jaws agape and a forepaw raised as though in warning. Once, the pillars must have towered like great cedars, but presently they rose no higher than a man could reach with his upstretched hand. Everything above had been overthrown in the wreck of the city, including the arching span of stone blocks that had formed the top of the gateway. Of the massive external fortification wall in which the gate had been set, no trace remained. The destroyers of the city had razed it to its foundation stones.

I wondered why they had left the lions, then realized that each was a single enormous block of stone. Their snarling faces showed marks where men had beaten them with hammers, but the stone must have been unnaturally hard, for the faces of the lions could still be distinguished.

Some way behind the gateposts lay two long pillars that touched at their ends like the spread first and second fingers of the hand. The pillar to the south had shattered in its fall to three pieces. Between them the earth sank downward, sloping toward the meeting place of the pillars and vanishing into shadow.

I dismounted and approached the pit with caution. Some subsidence in the ground had opened this cavity between the pillars. It did not have the appearance of a passage dug by men. I bent my eyes close to the sloping entrance. The wind that never fully ceased to blow in this accursed place had drifted dust over it, but there appeared to be a regular series of marks leading downward into the pit. They resembled the tracks left by the black beetles that wandered elsewhere amid the ruins, but enormously magnified. I laughed to myself at the fancy.

"What is so amusing?" Martala demanded.

Her tone held irritation. I realized that she missed her hot breakfast. Women can be frail creatures.

"Tie the horses to the broken end of that pillar and follow me."

If I expected anything in the pit, it was the sight of some natural cavern that had collapsed at the roof and fallen in. Such caves, carved out long ago by flows of water, are not uncommon in the desert. To my surprise, I found a well-shaped vault of brickwork tall enough to allow me to walk upright and as wide as my outspread hands.

"What is this place?" the girl asked, hurrying up behind me while I stood peering into the darkness.

"A storage cellar, perhaps. Who can say?"

When we advanced into the shadowed depths of the passage and found no end to it, even when the light from the pit was a small patch on the slope of ground behind us, I knew it must be something other than a chamber. Martala laid her hand on my shoulder. It was too dark to see. We progressed more slowly by touch, feeling the way before us with our toes to avoid falling into an abyss. I stopped when we came to an opening in the wall, the mouth to a tunnel of much the same size and shape as the one we walked along. Martala felt past me until her hands touched the brickwork of its edge.

"Which way do we go?"

I stood listening. How far did these tunnels extend? And how many were there? A rat squeaked. At least we would not starve, if we became lost. From the side passage I smelled a faint odor of decay mingled with excrement.

"We will go this way," I told her, leading her into the new tunnel.

"Why?"

"I smell death this way."

She thought about this for a moment.

"Shouldn't you be leading us away from it?"

"Where there is death, there is also life," I explained with patience. "Flesh decays. Every creature must eat, and if it eats, it defecates."

Following the stench, I made my way deeper into the bowels of the tunnels. They interconnected with each other like the web of a spider. At intervals, the roof had cracked or fallen in, allowing shafts of daylight to penetrate. We were not far below the surface. As I stood gazing at the wall beneath one of these ruptures, I realized where we walked. A white line ran across at the height of my waist, formed by salts that had leeched out of the bricks. The tunnels had once conveyed water. There were too many of them to be an aqueduct, so they could only be an ancient sewer system.

Without the indicator of the sun, it was impossible to guess how much time passed. Several hours, at least. The tunnels were a true maze, and at last I acknowledged to myself in irritation that I must be leading us in circles. My nose, what remained of it, was not so sure a guide as I had supposed. My stomach rumbled with emptiness. I found reason to regret not humoring the girl with a hot breakfast. Licking my dry lips, I paused beneath a thin shaft of daylight from a crack in the roof and took off my water skin to drink.

"Alhazred, rats!"

Martala gave a small involuntary shriek and danced behind me as four large rats approached nervously, their noses twitching. The light from above made their eyes resemble tiny amber beads. She drew her dagger. At a glance it was obvious to me that the rats were merely curious. I corked the water skin and slung it on my shoulder, turning my back to avoid alarming them.

"They are coming closer!"

Their faint inquisitive squeaks allowed me to gauge their distance. They had few predators in the tunnels or they would not be so tame. With a practiced motion I twisted and crouched, snatching up the nearest rat in one hand. It squealed and struggled to escape my fingers, but before it could bite, I broke its neck against the wall of the tunnel. The others fled in confusion. Here was something new, a killer of their kind in their safe familiar tunnels. I slid the tip of my dagger down the belly of the dead animal and stripped off its skin with a twist and pull of my hand, then cut the meat away from its sides.

As I gnawed the raw meat, dripping with blood, I noticed Martala staring at me. I offered her the other strip of flesh. She looked at it with her lips parted and swallowed her spittle, then shook her head, stepping backward. I shrugged and finished the first piece, then began to chew the second. It was saltier than was desirable, but I had an ample supply of water.

While I gnawed the tough meat, I wondered how to best find my way through the maze of tunnels. We could easily waste the entire day wandering in loops and tracking backward over passages we had already traversed. I fell into a meditative study as I chewed. To my surprise, Martala did not interrupt my thoughts. Usually she was more talkative.

A faint breeze stirred the tiny hairs on my bare cheek. It had been there all the while, but so soft was its touch, I had not noticed. I soon determined that it did not blow from the source of the ever-present stench. It must be the wind on the plain forcing its way down the pit between the pillars. The angle of the fallen pillars, coupled with the slope of the ground at the entrance of the pit, would form a natural funnel for the moving air.

I tossed the skinless corpse of the rat aside with regret. There was still good meat on it, but I had consumed the best portions. With care, stopping every few paces to test the faint breeze, I increased the distance from the pit entrance. It was delicate work, for the cooling air was faint and hard to feel, but eventually I was rewarded by a thickening in the foulness of the stench that found its way to us against the current. How strong the smell would be, were the breeze not present to counter it, I could only imagine. The tunnels descended in a gentle slope, taking us deeper under the center of the city.

We emerged into a large circular chamber lit with the dull green luminescence of decay. The air hung almost too rank to breathe. I heard Martala choke and fight to keep her gorge from rising in her throat.

"Tie a kerchief around your face."

She fumbled in the front pocket of her leather wallet and pulled forth a red cotton cloth, which she wrapped around her mouth and tied behind her head. It would have no effect on the stench, but it would cause her to feel that she had done something to make it bearable.

The chamber was thirty or so paces across, vaulted with a shallow dome of bricks arranged in concentric circles. We stood on a narrow walkway that ran completely around its diameter. Five other openings similar to the one through which we had emerged interrupted the curved wall at regular intervals. The catch basin that formed the center of the chamber was almost completely filled to the level of the walkway with excrement, in which was embedded bones, armor, and bits of clothing. They shone with greenish fire as I looked at them. I saw swords, helmets, and shields amid the charnel mound. The bronze blades of the swords were bright with verdigris. I wondered how many centuries they had lain there.

My eyes fixed on a large mass of a dark red color, similar to a clot of dried blood, at the center of the heap. At first I thought it was blood. I stepped forward off the edge of the walkway to see it more clearly in the dimness. As my boot grated on the bones, it stirred and turned its heads, opening its eyes to regard me with awareness. Before I could act, it sprang with terrible haste and bore me backward to the wall. I heard Martala cry my name, felt the needle-sharp daggers of its claws prick my chest, and saw the gray wedge of its massive beak gape.

It hesitated. I held my breath, not daring to move. A deep sound, like the puffing of a bellows, came from its open beak. I realized that the monster was tasting my scent.

"Alhazred?"

Martala's voice came softly from my right side.

"Stay back," I murmured quietly.

With excruciating slowness, I reached my hand to my throat and drew forth the leather thong to reveal the gold medallion. The heads of the beast regarded it in turn, their eyes rolling, as they twisted on their sinuous necks, which writhed like the arms of an octopus. Its foreclaws released me, and it backed up with an air almost of deference until it sat once more on its mound of phosphorescent shit and bones. It settled itself as I had first seen it, and its heads drooped.

"Stay close to me," I told the girl as I inched toward her, unwilling to remove my gaze from the monster. "The medallion may not protect us both if we separate."

How could a creature so large move with such quickness? I studied it as I felt the girl's arm slide around my waist. She trembled against me.

Its body was the size of a large horse, though more compact. Each leg ended in a claw armed with four talons a span in length that curved like the waning moon. Its rear legs were longer than its front and heavily muscled. A whip-like tail curled around its hip to its knee, the end barbed and black like the talons. Scales covered all of its reddish body apart from its black wings, membranous like those of a bat and folded on either side of its spinal ridge.

I found it impossible to look away from its heads. They were seven, all of them human in appearance but no two the same. In unceasing motion, they melted and merged, forming on the ends of the necks the way fruit swells on the vine, to persist for a time, only to shrivel away to nothingness and be replaced by a different head, a different face. They swelled and diminished by turns in a process of growth and decay that was almost liquid. In their fullness they were perfect in every detail, with hair, beards, even eyelashes. Most were the heads of men, but some were women, and there were even a few children. They murmured uneasily, eyelids almost closed, as though in troubled dreams from which they could not wake.

The Beast settled upon the bones to resume its interrupted sleep. A deep rasp came from the parted gray beak at the base of its necks, below its amorphous heads. I realized that in its own way, it was snoring. Anyone coming upon it like this, who had not seen it move, might make the error of judging it harmless. The mistake would be fatal. Only the medallion had prevented it from tearing my body to pieces as easily as I stripped the hide from a rat.

"This is the Beast the river men feared," Martala said softly into my ear.

"It can be no other," I agreed.

"The mad priest sent you here to be killed."

I remembered his words and his dying laughter.

"We should leave this place while it still sleeps."

"We came to consult the head of Babylon."

"What head?" she said in contempt. "There is nothing here. We've walked the tunnels and they are empty, apart from the rats."

When I did not speak, she withdrew from my side in irritation. Blows and harsh words she might tolerate, but not being ignored. Lost in my own thoughts, it was a few minutes before I realized that she stood some paces away.

"Come here, fool," I hissed.

She returned with a petulant expression, her lower lip pressed outward. I held up the Elder Seal.

"Without this you are a corpse. Can you form the Elder Sign with your hand?"

Reluctantly, she shook her head.

With my right hand, I showed her how to make the sign of protection.

"Tip of the index finger touching the tip of the thumb, second finger crossed over third, little finger raised straight upward. Do it."

Awkwardly, she formed the sign with the help of her other hand. She did not yet have the trick of crossing the second finger over the third unaided.

"If we are separated, use this. It may save your life. Stay near my side and pray you never need to test it."

I lowered myself to the walkway and sat with my back against the wall. The girl imitated my posture, but asked no questions. There was a strange fascination in watching the dreaming heads rise from the flesh of the Beast's shoulders like fungoidal growths, only to shrink to nothingness. Each endured less than the tenth part of an hour. Since there were seven necks, a new head appeared almost every minute, providing constant novelty to the eye. Most heads came forth only once, but a few emerged repeatedly, and seemed more aware than the others even in their dreaming.

The head of a bald and beardless man grew with regularity, so that it was seldom absent from one of the necks. It was of small size, the skull rounded and the brows of delicate shape, the cheekbones high. Fine webs of lines creased the yellowish skin on his cheeks. His intense dark eyes never closed for longer than a moment, and seemed to regard me from beneath their drooping lids. Even in sleep they held veiled awareness that was akin to the mind of a man drugged with the gum of the poppy.

The head of a young woman of considerable beauty slowly parted its long lashes as though waking, and gazed at me with an expression of the most abysmal despair. She rolled her eyes to peer around the domed chamber so that their whites shone in the lambent glow of the bones. Tears seeped from their corners and made wet tracks down her cheeks. Other heads began to open their eyes. A bearded old man cursed and made the motion to spit with his lips, although no spittle came forth. He began to sing in a thin tuneless voice, but so badly I could not distinguish the words or even the language of the song. A younger man with a scar on his cheek twisted around on his neck and snapped his teeth with a sharp click in front of the elder's nose. The old man fell silent, glaring his hatred at the younger head.

The scaled body of the Beast stirred restlessly and stretched like a cat, with its shoulders down and hips in the air. As it came to life, the animation of its heads increased. They began to babble in different tongues, crying out names, reciting prayers, begging for mercy from some oppressor only they could perceive. It was evident that most of the heads were insane. Those who took notice of us sitting on the walkway either cursed or mocked us. Their voices echoed from the bricks of the dome and filled the round chamber with a sound that was like the noise of many birds nesting in the reeds.

"You must help me," cried the head of a balding man of middle years, who wore a short beard flecked with gray. "I will pay you."

He spoke in my own language, or I might not have distinguished his words over the confusion of voices.

"Tell my wife, the gold is hidden in the well. Go to her with this message, and tell her to give you ten dinars for your trouble."

"What is the name of your wife?" I asked in Arabic.

The ears of the head had already melted into the neck as I spoke. He gave one last look of dismay before his face dissolved and was replaced by that of a small boy, who at once began to scream for his mother.

The Beast circled on its pile of dried excrement with restless paces, then sat on its haunches. Every few minutes it stood and repeated the action, like a wolf in a cage waiting to be fed. I realized that it must be waiting for the sun to set, so that it could fly through the heavens in search of prey. It gave no attention to Martala or to me. Either it had forgotten our presence, or the power of the Elder Seal turned away its awareness. Neither did the voices of its own heads distract it, although it used their eyes to see its way, forcing them to turn at its will where it placed its steps.

The heads held little converse between themselves, but contested for the chance to pray or sing or speak without being overwhelmed by the other voices. They did this by snapping their jaws in a menacing way, and making savage expressions, as well as with screams and curses. They twisted their lips into snarls and widened their eyes until the white showed all around, so that they resembled the masks of demons more than the faces of human beings. Never did I see a head bite another head. It was all threat and bluster. Perhaps some power of the Beast prevented them from harming each other.

I began at last to grow weary of the ceaseless displays and quarrels among the heads. They seldom appeared more than once, save for the sallow-cheeked elder with the keen gaze, but behaved in much the same way, bemoaning their fate and cursing their neighbors during their brief presence. My attention wandered to the Beast itself, and its black wings that were like the folded sides of a portable tent. They appeared too small to bear up such a weight upon the air.

"Alhazred, do you see?"

The girl dug her pointed fingernails into my shoulder. A head newly formed on the lowermost neck blinked and stared around with a dazed wonder. I recognized the bearded face of Bassarius at once. The likeness was perfect. His brown eyes turned to me in puzzlement.

"Alhazred, what is this place?"

Even his voice was so like that of the fat physician, had I closed my eyelids I would have seen him in his coat of red silk. I pushed myself to my feet, moving slowly to avoid arousing the attention of the Beast.

"Do you remember nothing?"

His expression grew thoughtful and uncertain, like a man overcome by wine who tries to recollect his actions of the night before. Comprehension of his plight came slowly, mingled with equal measures of horror and fear. He craned his sinuous neck from side to side to view the scaled haunches of the Beast, and stared with revulsion at the other heads that screamed and chuckled and babbled. All but two, who were most in madness, turned to glare at him with expressions of malicious glee.

"I stood on the hill beside the river at dusk," he said in a voice that trembled. "Something caught me up into the air and carried me to a distant hilltop. Allah be merciful, it held me to the ground and bit open my chest—"

Horror overwhelmed him. He began to scream repeatedly, his voice rising higher and higher amid the laughter and jeers of the other heads, until it was no more than a breathless shriek stretched thin and shrill. Martala clutched my arm and pressed her face into my shoulder. Her hot breath penetrated my garments and warmed my skin.

Some shadow of sanity returned to the physician's expression. Awareness of his fate gave place in turn to desperation, sorrow, anger, bitterness, and at last to hope and strengthening resolve.

"Kill me, Alhazred, for the mercy of Allah. Use your sword. Cut at my throat and release me."

I looked into his eyes and shook my head. I might as well have struck him with my fist.

"I beg you to kill me. I have gold in my trunk. Take it all, only free me from this hell."

When I made no move to draw my sword, he fell to begging and cursing me by turns. He felt his head being drawn into the fleshy neck that supported it and wailed. The other heads jeered, turning on their necks to gaze at him and savor his torment. Only one of them, that of the hairless old man, remained silent. His bloodless mouth twisted in an expression of sardonic amusement, but his dark eyes watched me. In another moment the head of the physician was no more, replaced by the idiot grin of an old woman who wagged her head from side to side with a grunting noise so that her long white hair fell over her face like a veil.

"Why did you refuse to kill him?" Martala demanded, pulling away from my touch. There was accusation in her gaze.

Before I could answer, a high clear voice spoke in Greek, penetrating the babble the way a flute sounds above the thunder of many drums.

"It would serve no purpose."

She stared in surprise at the Beast. The yellow head nodded, watching us.

"Strike off a head, and it grows back. We cannot die."

Martala glanced at me.

"You knew this, Alhazred?"

I studied the cynical eyes of the yellow head. There was no madness in their depths, only a bitter amusement mingled with contempt. As I watched, the head melted into its neck and vanished, replaced by another. I turned to the girl, and tried for the sake of politeness to keep the irritation from my tone.

"Why should I be fool enough to strike at such a monster with my sword, to comfort a fat physician who did nothing for me during life but annoy me with his endless talk?"

Her expression hardened.

"Sometimes I think you have no feeling in your heart."

"Then you think rightly, if you equate compassion with acts of charity toward fools."

"What is a man without human kindness?"

"In the Empty Space, he is a man who lives."

We argued in this way for several minutes. I became aware that the head of the yellow-skinned ancient had reformed on a different neck, and was watching us.

"You are the one I have come for," I said, pointing at the head with my finger. "You are the wisest head of Babylon. Deny it if you can."

He pursed his mouth in reflection, regarding me with catlike ease.

"Is that how they call me in the outer world? The wisest head of Babylon?"

I nodded.

"Then you have found what you seek."

"Who are you?" Martala asked, her irritation at me replaced by curiosity.

He considered her question and decided to answer it.

"In life my name was Belaka. A score of centuries ago, I was a necromancer who dwelled in the lands east of Persia. I came to this accursed city seeking wisdom. I was arrogant in my own power, and took no precautions. The Beast caught me sleeping. Its claws severed the cord of my spine when it lifted me up, so that I felt no pain but was unable to move my arms and legs. It carried me many leagues into the distant hills before setting me on a peak and tearing out my entrails. It was an amusing circumstance. I watched it feast on my blood and flesh without pain or feeling of any kind, until at last it set its beak into my exposed throbbing heart. I awoke as you see me now, and have been this way for over two thousand years."

"We also are necromancers," Martala said.

"Are you indeed?" He fixed his glittering gaze upon her, and imitated her smile. "Necromancers? Like me?"

"I have questions for you, Belaka," I said with more harshness than I intended.

"Ask them swiftly, fellow necromancer, for the sun falls, and soon the Beast will leave this place to hunt."

"How did you become a part of this monster?"

He seemed to shrug, although he had no shoulders. His finely drawn eyebrows, as black as painted lines of kohl, arched up the merest degree.

"It is a drinker of blood and an eater of souls. Perhaps the souls enter it with the blood. Who can say, save the one that created it and her kindred."

"Tell me the name of its creator."

"Shub-Niggurath is its mother. As for its father . . ." He laughter was like the tinkling of small bells. "Shub-Niggurath was always a whore."

"A spawn of the Old Ones," I murmured to myself. "A child of the Prolific Goat."

He nodded, eyes fixed on mine.

"You have little time, young necromancer. Tell me what you really wish to learn. You did not come to this place to gossip about the Old Ones. What has a slave of Nyarlathotep to do with the plaything of Shub-Niggurath?"

I did my best to conceal my surprise. If the mark of the dark man upon my forehead was so plain to his eyes, what else might he see?

"What do you know about the Well of the Seraph?"

"Ahhhh," he breathed, nodding with comprehension. "Now I understand. You seek the restoration of your face and manhood."

My private question was answered. He saw, not only the mark, but the true condition of my face and body.

"Tell me what I ask."

"If I choose not to answer, what will you do to one who is deathless?"

He mocked me, but whether to test my determination or merely for his own amusement, I could not judge. I might lie open to his understanding, but his true thoughts remained hidden.

I stepped to the edge of the walkway and bent to pick up a splintered thighbone. The beast moved swiftly toward me with a threatening aspect, a hiss escaping from its beak. Remaining still, I waited for it so settle on its haunches once again, then took up a rag of faded silk that must have been some rich garment centuries in the past. This I wrapped around the end of the bone and tied it into place. Belaka watched with polite interest, but I could see that he was inwardly laughing at me. I took the tinderbox from my wallet and struck sparks to ignite the tinder. The Beast shifted restlessly on its legs at the smell of the flame. It was fully alert. The sun must be almost set.

"You cannot die, but you can feel pain," I told the ancient necromancer, holding the blazing tinder just below the rag.

He laughed aloud as he had before, with the sound of tinkling silver bells.

"I do not believe the Beast would allow you to apply fire to its flesh. Your amulet might not be strong enough to restrain its rage."

"I am willing to make the experiment," I told him, lighting the rag.

It blazed impressively, casting a flickering red illumination throughout the chamber that seemed like daylight in comparison to the feeble corpse shine. The Beast cried out like a hawk, and started forward, then hesitated and stood at the edge of the pit, its barbed tail lashing from side to side in annoyance.

"No, stop, you will kill yourself, and your pretty companion along with you. I can't let that happen, since I have a need for your services."

I moved the torch behind me so that my body shielded its light. It was already dying down as the flames consumed the rag to ashes.

"If I perform this service you seek, will you tell me what I wish to learn?"

Again, he made his strange, shoulderless shrug.

"Why not? Your purposes are nothing to me. Although it would amuse me to thwart the plans of the dark man, whatever may be their shape."

"His plans are not my plans."

He appraised my expression as a jeweler tests gold on a touchstone.

"In that event, the world is more interesting with you alive. Bend close, there is little time. I will tell you what you must do."

Chapter 40

The Beast stood and shook itself like a dog so that the skin of its wings slapped against its back. With a resolute motion it came forward and stepped from the refuse heap onto the walkway that surrounded the pit. I drew the girl behind me, having care to stay beyond the limit of its restlessly sweeping tail. It bent its heads and fitted its massive shoulders into the opening of the tunnel from which we had emerged. In a moment, it was gone. We waited until the brushing sound of its progress began to diminish, then went after it. I had no difficulty following its trail through the darkness. Its stench led me by the nose.

When we emerged between the fallen pillars by the east gate, I cursed in vexation. The horses had bolted, as I should have known they would upon sight of the monster rising out of the ground. The Beast reared upright on its hind legs, facing the glow of the western horizon with its black wings opened. Already the sun had set, and the brightest stars flashed in the heavens.

I watched the wings of the Beast expand, as Belaka had foretold, until they were like the vast sails of a great ship. It beat them in the air to stiffen them, leaning forward with eagerness.

"When we have gone, try to find the horses," I murmured to the girl. "Until then, do not move."

The Beast was most dangerous at dusk, with its mind alert, its hunger sharp in its belly.

Leaving her near the mouth of the hole, I approached the creature from behind. It gave no sign that it sensed my presence. This was due solely to the power of the medallion. I wondered how long the golden disk at my breast would protect Martala, now that she no longer stood close to my side. There was no help for it, we must separate. I hesitated, studying the place where the wings spread from the back of the monster. There seemed little to grasp with the hands.

"Courage, young necromancer," spoke the faintly amused voice of Belaka. His small dark eyes watched me over the shoulder of the Beast, his head twisted backward on its long neck.

With a silent curse, I ran forward past the swishing barb of the tail and set my boot on the bent thigh of the Beast's rear leg. Before it moved, I threw myself flat on my belly across its back between its wings. All seven heads swung around to regard me. A shriek of fury came from its beak. I felt rather than saw the whip of its tail poised above my back, ready to strike down like a dagger.

The heads became still. As Belaka had predicted, the power of the amulet turned away its irritation. The tail withdrew from my back. Sliding my body forward so that my elbows were bent and my face pressed just behind the writhing mass of heads, I slid my legs down its sides and tried to squeeze my boots tight against its loins.

The Beast began to sniff the air through its beak. It bent its wings and turned back toward the entrance to the sewers, where Martala stood. Like a crow at a carcass, it hopped across the ground toward her.

She fumbled to make the Elder Sign with her right hand. For a moment, her fingers became tangled, but she sorted them out with her left hand and held the Sign up before her. The Beast hesitated, its breath coming in rapid pants. It snapped its beak several times, and the teeth of its heads imitated the motion. Over its shoulder, I saw Martala's terrified expression. She waved the Sign in the air, but it continued to hop forward.

"Back up into the hole," I told her.

She needed little instruction. She was already slipping backward on the treacherous loose dust. The shadow of the dark tunnel hid her from view in the failing light from the sky. The Beast stopped at the slope and considered the situation. When I thought it was about to enter the hole, and made up my mind to slide off its back to protect the girl, it turned with a hop and faced the wind, wings expanding to their full stretch. It ran forward on swift leaps of its long hind legs and with a shriek, launched itself into the air, its wings beating with powerful strokes that thrummed on my ears.

The tightly overlapping scales of its back were even more difficult to keep from sliding across than I had anticipated. Like the scales of a serpent, they felt cool and dry, but were as slick as polished leather. Once it attained its height, its wings ceased to beat so strongly, and held themselves level. Their satin surface was not so smooth as the dark red scales, and gave some purchase for my outstretched chest and abdomen at their base. It was sorely needed when the Beast turned in its flight, and its entire body leaned to one side.

With caution to avoid unbalancing the creature, I peered over the leading edge of its right wing. The rushing wind made my eyes water. Shadows covered the plain and merged its details into a gray obscurity. The moon was not yet risen. I caught the reflected gleam of starlight and guessed we were flying above the river, although I could not see it clearly.

"It always hunts first."

I looked up. The hairless head of the ancient necromancer watched me, neck arched backward so that the sharp ridge of his nose almost touched mine. His breath smelled foul, even in the forceful wind.

"Does it always kill?" I shouted, blinking the tears from my eyes.

"Not always. Sometimes it goes hungry, and other times it kills just before it returns to its lair, and drags the body with it so that it can feast without being interrupted by the rising sun."

"That explains the many bones."

His laughter tinkled on the wind.

"Some are the bones of foolish seekers after knowledge. They did not enjoy the protection of the dark man."

"The skulls were cracked."

"It pops the head in its beak, like the shell of a nut, and eats the brain."

"How many have you watched it kill?"

"Too many to number."

How long we flew, I could not judge. My attention was occupied by the necessity to constantly shift my body to prevent it from sliding off. It was like trying to ride a galloping horse without a saddle. I became aware that the river was closer, and that we flew more slowly, gliding along with only an occasional beat of the mighty wings. We passed over a cargo boat tied up at a landing place for the night. The Beast wheeled and returned. I saw a dim solitary shape near the river, collecting dried wood thrown up on the bank by past floods. Upon a nearby hill, a campfire burned with several shadowed figures seated around it. As we slid over the wood gatherer, we drew near enough so that I could see it was a young boy of ten or twelve years.

"Run, you fool," I cried.

Startled, he dropped his armload of sticks and looked up. I heard voices from the campfire. As the Beast drew away I turned and saw him running toward the fire. The Beast cried out in frustration. Tremors ran through its muscles, as though it yearned to throw me from its back and tear me to pieces with its talons before I reached the ground. It circled, and I saw several men with swords drawn, standing beside the campfire, the boy huddled among them. I thought the Beast would attack the group, but it must prefer to take its prey by stealth. It passed over and flew onward.

"So you do have human feelings," Belaka said. His voice held a faint disappointment.

"If this monster stooped like a hawk to seize that child, how could I maintain my place upon its back?" I shouted at him against the wind.

He said nothing, but merely raised his thin eyebrows as his face dissolved into its neck, and the neck withdrew.

The Beast left the river and flew across the plain. I saw the pale ribbon of a caravan road, but it was empty of travelers. After following it for what seemed an hour, the Beast began to circle, gaining height. The stars grew brighter, the air more chill. It set off in a new direction with a determined purpose. I could not see the earth below, but something felt different. At last I chanced to glance up, and noticed that the rising moon was larger than it should have been, and tinted with a redness as though eclipsed. Stranger still, it showed the wrong face. It should have been in its third quarter, but instead approached fullness. I had read in the scroll of the Old Ones that a few among the children of Shub-Niggurath have the power to move between the worlds. This moon did not resemble the moon with which I was familiar.

We flew for hours. Time extended endlessly into the darkness that wrapped on all sides, broken only by the blood moon and glittering stars above. My mind drifted in a waking trance. The wind striking my face grew so cold, it almost turned the tears on my cheeks to ice, and the thin air made me gasp. The thought came to me that should it fly where there was no air at all, I would strangle and fall from its back, a frozen corpse. Perhaps this was what Belaka intended. Perhaps all that he had told me was a lie.

A distant shadow loomed, darkness against deeper darkness. The Beast flew directly toward it. For a time it appeared to draw no nearer, then all at once it towered in front of us, a vast wall of black rock as sheer as the side of a pillar. The Beast circled it, gaining height with each beat of its wings, and I saw that it was a mountain. We ascended over the rim of its windswept top. With a cry, the Beast extended its hind legs and fluttered its wings, landing the way a hawk lands on the crown of a tree.

It shook its wings and folded them, hopping forward across the tufts of browning grasses that grew up between the stones. As the wings began to shrink, I slid from its back and stepped quickly away from its restless tail. The heads all shouted and laughed and wept, as though possessed by a common madness. Belaka's face was not evident among them. I turned to examine this strange plateau. It sloped gently, with a stone-filled gully across its middle where water must flow during periods of rain. Most of it was flat grassland, but at the higher elevation a ridge of rock rose like an irregular wall. Here and there, a black boulder projected half its bulk above the thin soil.

In the middle of the plateau, in a slight depression, stood a pillar of stone. It was not of the same kind as the rock of the mountain. That was a dull black, but the pillar caught the moonlight on its irregular surface and reflected it like glass. Approaching to examine it more closely, I saw that it was striated with veins of dark red that seemed to glow or pulse. I touched it but snatched my hand away. It felt warm, almost like flesh. It had not been shaped by any chisel, but was of natural formation, slightly wider at the top than at its base, and angled at its crown, so that it resembled a great nail of black glass stained with streaks of blood, driven into the mountain to half its length. As tall as the pillars of blue stone I had seen in the temple at Albion, it bore no symbol or mark to reveal the intention of whatever intelligence had placed it there.

The wind keened through the stiff tufts of grass around its base, making them nod their heads. I saw among them the tiny white flowers Belaka had described, each no larger than the nail of my smallest finger, shaped like a star with five points. They grew in clusters on a low plant with thick dry leaves that appeared gray under the feeble moonlight. The taller grasses protected the gray plants from the worst of the wind, yet still they trembled in its harshness. I walked across the plateau to the gully, but found the plant only near the base of the pillar. The flowers grew in a broad depression three paces wide that surrounded stone, and nowhere else.

Quickly, I bent and pulled several dozen of the flowers up by their roots. Their leaves and stems had a furred texture that was unpleasant against the hand, but their roots yielded easily and came up intact. In shape they were like a carrot, but smaller, no more than the length of my middle finger, and white like the flowers. I broke off the leaves and stems and sorted the roots into a pile on the ground, then took a rag of blue silk from the front pocket of my wallet and tied the roots into it. If what Belaka claimed was true, these little roots were worth more than their weight in precious jewels. They would need to be dried with care to preserve them.

The Beast snorted out its breath like a horse. Looking across at the edge of the plateau where it stood, I saw that its wings were folded tight against its back. The heads had fallen silent. In my interest in the roots, I had failed to notice. Their eyelids drooped as though in sleep. The head of the necromancer had not emerged. It seemed that Belaka's will was overwhelmed by the purpose of the Beast, preventing him from forcing his head to form. On its four legs, the Beast approached the pillar.

It stood facing the great dagger of black glass with its heads lowered almost to the ground, as though in silent prayer. There was something solemn and majestic about its serene pose. At last it roused itself and began to walk around the pillar with slow steps in a circle that bent to its left. I found a convenient boulder and sat upon it, watching the circumambulation of the monster. It seemed tireless in its single-minded purpose. It came into my thoughts that its feet had worn the depression in the hard ground over centuries, or even eons of walking. Every so often, a piece of dung dropped from its hindquarters, and its claws treaded it into the grass and worked it around the circle.

The unnatural moon set, and the sky began to pale at the horizon, revealing a distant line of jagged mountains that thrust up like black swords. At last, the Beast stopped and turned its heads toward the light. It shook itself and walked back to the place on the edge of the plateau where it had landed. Facing the chill wind, it opened its wings and stood fanning them up and down to inflate their size.

"Alhazred, come here quickly."

Belaka's bald head had returned, along with his dry voice. I pushed myself stiffly to my feet and rubbed my buttocks, which had gone numb against the icy stone. Without haste, I approached. His head extended over the shoulder of the beast and regarded me impatiently.

"There isn't much time. Did you get the *u'mal* root?"

"Is that what it's called?"

"Yes, yes, did you get it?"

I withdrew the blue rag and untied a corner. Taking out a root, I held it up for him to see in the pallid light from the east.

"Excellent. Place it into my mouth."

I twisted the white root between my thumb and forefinger, admiring it. Such a small thing to be the object of so great a desire.

"The Well of the Seraph? Where shall I find it?"

"I do not know its location," he said peering at the root as though afraid I might drop it and lose it amid the grass.

With a curse, I closed my fist around the root.

"You promised me the well. Are you nothing but an idle boaster, like the rest of these heads?"

Several of the other heads laughed and snapped their teeth at me. Belaka ignored them.

"I do not know where the well is, but I know how it can be found. Give me the root, and I will tell you."

"Tell me, and I will give you the root."

He scowled at me, his expression murderous. His anger lent the Greek he spoke a strange accent. He cursed me, and I realized with surprise that I did not know the language of his curses. It must have been a tongue unknown to Nectanebus, for all his fabled wisdom. When he saw that I did not mean to give him the root until he spoke, he mastered his fury and forced a smile upon his thin lips.

"Ride east from the ruins of Babylon into the land of the Persians. Ride until you come upon the river Tigris, where the two courses of the river fork. There you will find a school of philosophers who call themselves the Sons of Sirius."

"How will this help me reach the Well of the Seraph?"

"Listen, fool, and I will explain. In the library of the school is a book. In the book is a gloss that describes the location of the well. Find the book and you will find the well."

"Which book? What is the name of it? Who wrote it?"

"These things I know not. I only know what I hear spoken by the heads that are taken by the Beast. They all like to talk, before they go mad. If they know anything of interest, I listen to them. A head told me of this book a century ago."

This was not the answer I had hoped for. I frowned in thought. It might be no more than a fool's errand. I remembered the words of the dark man concerning his enemies in the east, and wondered if he had meant this school of philosophers. The Beast flapped its wings and stretched them in the wind.

"Hurry, the Beast is almost ready to fly. Give me the root."

Extending it in my hand, I held it just away from his extended lips. They writhed in a snarl.

"What does the root do? How do I know it won't give you the power to slay me?"

"It is a medicine, nothing more. It heals disease, and restores vitality. When eaten once each cycle of the moon, it extends life and confers immortality."

My interest quickened. I looked at the pale root with greater respect.

"Will it heal mutilations of the face and restore manhood?"

The hairless head laughed his tinkling laugh.

"If its powers were so great, it might grow me a new body to go with my head. No, it cannot restore flesh that has been struck off."

"Why do you need it?"

Belaka hesitated and averted his glittering eyes. He almost appeared to be embarrassed.

"Those who are slain by the Beast return as its heads exactly as they were at the time of their deaths, with all their infirmities. They do not age, or sicken, but neither do they heal."

"What are you saying?" I asked with impatience. "Are you afflicted with some sickness?"

Again he hesitated. When he saw that I did not mean to give him the root until I was satisfied, he sighed.

"When I was killed, I suffered from a toothache."

"A toothache?" I laughed. "Is that all?"

"Foolish child, you do not understand. I have suffered from that same toothache both day and night for over two thousand years."

I considered this, and nodded. The prospect of ending such ceaseless torment would be attractive. Extending the root, I placed it between his lips, taking care to keep my fingers well back from his teeth, which were blackened at their roots. I realized now the reason for his foul breath. His teeth were rotten. He chewed the tough root.

"Quickly," he said as he held the root in his mouth. "Take your dagger and cut your arm so that I can suck your blood."

"This was not part of the bargain."

"The root requires fresh blood from the veins of another human being before it becomes active. Alone, it is without value. If you mean to keep your word, you must give me your blood."

Reluctantly, I took out my dagger and made a small cut on the inside of my left wrist. Blood welled forth and trickled down my wrist on to the heel of my hand. The Beast snorted and trembled as it caught the scent of blood, but did not drop its wings, which had expanded to their full size. There was little time to waste. I offered my wrist to the head. Belaka pressed his small mouth over the cut and sucked noisily, his eyes wide. After a few moments, I snatched my arm back.

"Do you mean to suck me dry, vampire?"

He tinkled merrily, his good humor restored by the flavor of my blood, and licked his reddened lips.

"I can feel it working like fire within me. It is healing my teeth."

He spoke the truth. They were no longer black at their roots, but yellow. In appearance they remained unchanged, but the corruption was gone from them.

"A precious root indeed."

"With what you have gathered, you can buy a king's palace, if you sell it to those who know its worth."

"I should gather more," I said, looking over my shoulder.

The Beast cried out, and lifted itself on its hind legs for a moment, before dropping back to its forelegs.

"No time. Get on its back, or you will be left behind."

"Maybe it would be better to remain a day in this place. I can always climb upon the Beast when it returns tomorrow night."

Belaka laughed, but not unkindly. The ending of his pain made him benevolent.

"I should leave you here. When the Beast returned, you would be nothing but bleached bones. In this place, the hours of daylight pass more slowly. One of our days is here a thousand years."

This information made me tie up my packet of roots and climb with haste upon the Beast's back. The prospect of spending a thousand years on this windswept plateau, with nothing to eat but grass and *u'mal* root, did not appeal to me. No sooner had I stretched out on my belly and gripped the edges of its wings with my hands,

456

then it stood on its hind legs and took three hopping steps toward the edge of the precipice. Without pause, it leaped over into the void, and we fell with a rapidity that made my stomach rise to my throat. I pressed the toes of my boots into the muscular loins of the creature and hoped I would not slide forward.

It leveled its flight and sent itself rushing through the air with the light of dawn behind us, as though fleeing the sun that would soon rise above the broken teeth of the mountains. Below, I saw countless similar peaks, rising like needles with no space between their steep sides. They were barren of life. Hours we flew, yet the light at my back became no stronger, for the beast outraced the sun of that strange land. If anything, it became darker, and the ground below fell under a veil of shadow. When at last this began to lift, I saw that it was the familiar plain beside the river Euphrates.

We raced along the winding length of the river, the stars vanishing overhead one by one until only Venus remained visible, shining with bright beauty in the east, lonely herald of the dawn. I saw the mountain that was the remains of the pyramid of Babylon rise above the horizon, and in moments we were beside it. The Beast circled the ruins of the ancient city and landed near the pillars at the east gate. With relief, I slid my stiffened limbs off its back and moved with care out of the range of its tail.

"Alhazred!" Martala's voice sounded across the ruins. "Thank the Goddess you have returned."

She stood beside a low wall at what she believed to be a safe distance, holding the horses by their reins. I cursed her stupidity silently to myself.

"Shut up, you fool," I shouted, hoping to distract the Beast with my voice.

Hunger gnawed at its vitals. Its heads turned toward the east, and it hesitated, but the lure of fresh food proved too strong. It hopped toward the girl with its wings still half extended from its shoulders. Each gliding hop carried it a dozen paces. I ran after it but knew I could never get there in time.

The horses went mad with terror at the sight of its approach. The mare rolled its eyes and reared up on its hind legs to lash out with its hoofs. The Beast tore open its exposed breast with a single sweep of its talons, and without pause reached for Martala.

As has often been the case, the courage and quick thinking of the girl surprised me. Instead of fleeing on foot, she threw her leg over the back of my gelding and dug her boots into its flanks. The spur was unnecessary. It bolted as if all the demons of hell were at its heels, the Beast following after it with shrieks that split the morning air. I fumbled at the throat of my tunic for the gold medallion, only to discover that it no longer hung from my neck. Nothing gleamed on the ground behind me. There was no leisure to search for where it had fallen. I ran on, cursing the stiffness of my legs. By the time I reached the girl it would be over.

I found them in a hollow. The gelding lay dead, its belly torn open and its entrails strewn over the dusty ground like a nest of blood-splashed vipers. The girl crouched behind a broken pillar, the Elder Sign made with both hands. As the Beast snapped at her with its beak or struck with its talons, she danced aside, keeping the column of stone between them. Before my aching legs could reach them, the Beast gave a forlorn cry and turned to look full at the east. The first rays of the morning sun blazed above the horizon. The sunlight redden the jagged top of the pillar behind which the girl cowered. With an impotent scream of rage, it turned from her and loped past me as though I were not there, moving in the direction of the east gate.

One of its seven heads gazed back at me across its flanks, and I saw the gleam of gold in its grinning mouth.

"Keep the girl," the voice of Belaka cried, his words slurred by the pressure of the medallion against his tongue. "She will bring you good fortune."

"She already has," I replied.

"One last thing." His voice grew faint as the distance increased. "When you travel east, avoid the valley of the—"

The rest of his warning, whatever it may have been, was lost on the wind.

Chapter 41

Breathing heavily from my run, I approached the girl and gazed with distaste at the still quivering corpse of my gelding. Already the large black beetles that roamed the ruins in such numbers had found the pool of its blood, and were delicately dipping their mouthparts to drink. Soon would come desert foxes and crows and rats. In a day there would be nothing left but scattered bones, which the ants would pick clean. I took my dagger and cut fresh meat from its haunch. The sleepless night on the mountain plateau had left me nearly as hungry as the Beast.

Martala watched in distaste while I chewed the raw flesh. Knowing her fastidiousness, I did not bother to offer her a piece.

I told her of my experiences while we gathered what possessions we could carry on our backs from the slain horses. She stared in wonder when I opened my small store of *u'mal* root.

"You should try it, Alhazred. That evil wizard may have lied to you from malice."

I did not believe Belaka had lied, but there was sense in her words. Better not to place trust in another, when there was no need.

"Very well," I agreed.

Placing one of the roots in my mouth, I chewed it. The taste was bitter and faintly sour, but not excessively unpleasant. It made the saliva gush from my cheeks.

Martala bared her arm by sliding up the cuff of her narrow sleeve and pressed the blade of her little dagger against her skin. Her blood welled like a row of rubies in the golden sunlight. I put my mouth to the place and sucked, tasting its salty and metallic flavor on my tongue.

Fire coursed through my limbs and into my belly. It was like drinking strong spirits of wine. At once the stiffness and fatigue left my legs. My body felt lighter. I reached my hand to my face, and shrugged with regret. There was still a hole where the end of my nose should have been. I felt over my cheeks, my ears, and finally lowered my hand to my groin.

Martala saw my disappointment. Her shoulders sagged.

"Still, it was worth the attempt," I told her, keeping my voice light to disguise my bitterness of heart.

We made our way on foot southward along the meandering bank of the Euphrates. From the air I had glimpsed a village on the river, not more than half a dozen miles downstream from the ruins. By late morning we reached it. The place was named Hilla, as we learned when I spoke to a man plowing a furrow behind his ox across an elongated field of turned earth. The plowed field, and others like it that stretched along the bend of the river, were kept from turning to dust and blowing away on the wind by means of irrigation ditches that extended on either side from a primary canal. A dam at the end would be opened each evening to allow the water to flood the fields. I had observed similar arrangements of irrigation ditches in the Nile Delta, but the black soil of Egypt was infinitely richer than this poor red clay.

The score or so of mud brick huts scattered amongst the fields boasted no feature of interest. The village elder, a tall and beardless man with a wild mass of curling white hair upon his head, greeted us with hospitality, but was unwilling to sell us anything to ride. Horses he had none, and donkeys he could not spare. When I showed him a handful of dinars, he admitted with reluctance that the village kept a solitary camel left there months ago by a passing group of travelers to recover from sickness. So great was his distress to part with it, the camel might have been one of his own children. We paid separately for the ragged blanket and worn saddle that had been left behind with the elderly and half-blind creature, and bought several small bags of fresh vegetables and dried fruit, then rode our stumbling mount back to the ruins in order to retrieve the remainder of our possessions, apart from the equipage of the horses which we could not carry.

The ruins oppressed my spirit. I was sick of the sight of the crumbled bricks and fallen pillars, and of the countless beetles that wrote their secret verses in the dust with their feet. Without the medallion of the Elder Seal around my neck I mistrusted the Beast. By nightfall it would be insane with hunger. I wished to get as far away as possible from the cursed place before the setting of the sun, but knew it would be irrational to start forth so late in the day. After pondering where to spend the night, I spurred our complaining camel, loaded down with the girl and our saddle bags and sleeping rugs, to the ancient ruin of the pyramid.

It was no easy task inducing the stupid creature to climb the slope of loose rubble that led to the first terrace. I had to drag upon its reins while Martala whipped its buttocks with a length of leather rope. When it smelled the corpse of the priest, it tried to turn and run back down the hill, but with curses we managed to drive it to one side and hold it against the wall of bricks. I left the reins in the girl's hands and approached the corpse. Carrion birds and rats had gnawed its face, so that little remained. Indeed, its features were somewhat uglier than my own. I grasped it by the ankles and pulled it toward the edge of the terrace. A cloud of angry flies arose from its blackened skin. They followed it over the edge as it tumbled down to the plain.

The camel would be safe from wolves on its own in this elevated place. The Beast hunted only human prey for food, and was unlikely to kill it without provocation. I reasoned that since the mad priest had lived for years in the fissure of the pyramid, so near to the lair of the Beast, yet had not become one of its countless heads, the cleft would probably protect us for the night. With our sleeping rugs in hand, we crawled in as deep as we could penetrate with comfort. In my exhaustion, I fell asleep almost at once and did not awaken until the next morning. If the Beast hunted us, it suffered disappointment, but I thought it possessed insufficient intelligence to remember an injury or sustain a hatred.

We set out in the early morning, riding directly toward the red ball of the rising sun. After sitting on a horse for so many days on the caravan road, the pace of the camel surprised me. I had forgotten how much ground was covered by the long legs of these ungainly animals. Its gait was ideally suited to the low and rolling hills of the dry plain. As long as I took care to guide it around the more troublesome stones, it placed its hoofs without stumbling. A milky cataract covered its left eye, but it had learned to hold its head turned to the left in compensation. Every dozen steps it let out a groan at the stiffness of its limbs. Old age had brought disease to its joints.

"The poor beast," Martala said behind me after a particularly piteous complaint. "Alhazred, we should get down and walk."

I laughed so heartily and so long at this notion that she fell into a sullen silence. After a while, her arms tightened around my waist.

"Why don't you give her an *u'mal* root? Perhaps it would cure her."

"Are you mad? Each root is worth a hundred pieces of gold. A thousand pieces."

"If she collapses and dies under us, we will have to walk the rest of the way with packs tied to our backs."

This was food for thought. The girl had only spoken to get her own way, but her words held truth. I felt no desire to walk where I could ride. I wondered if the root would have effect on a mindless brute.

We stopped and dismounted in the middle of the barren plain, the ripples of heat rising off the rocks around us and making the air shimmer and dance. With care, I removed the smallest root from the blue rag and cut from it a piece as long as the end joint of my thumb before replacing it and returning the bundle to my wallet. Martala held the head of the camel steady by shortening the reins in her fist. I inserted the root between the soft lips of the startled animal. It began to chew. Moving swiftly, I drew the point of my dagger across my bared left forearm, some distance above the cut I had made for Belaka, and pressed the welling blood to the mouth of the camel. It licked my skin and snorted at the taste of blood. Martala had to drag its head down as it tried to dance away.

For several minutes there appeared to be no change, apart from its increased restlessness.

"Hold her head still," I told the girl.

The milkiness of the cataract covered only half the surface of the left eye, where before it had completely obscured it. As I watched, the white cloud shrank and became less white. In a dozen breaths, it vanished. I reported this change to Martala, who laughed with delight. We made the animal kneel and climbed onto its back to resume our journey. It walked at the same pace it had walked before eating the root, but it ceased to stumble and uttered no more groans.

The girl began to sing an Egyptian folk song softly in my ear. I did not reprove her. She sang well, in a voice strong and pure of tone. It was long since I had raised my own voice in song. I remembered a song of Yemen that had been a favorite of the Princess Narisa. When the girl fell silent I began to sing it, wondering where the princess walked at that moment, and if her mind held an image of me as I had looked before the day of my mutilation.

When I finished, Martala rested her cheek against my back and began to hum to herself. I felt the soft burr of her voice in my spine.

"I don't care what fate awaits us," she said. "I am happy."

For three days we rode from sunrise to sunset, meeting no other travelers and seeing no human habitations. Nothing moved in the plain apart from the hawks that passed high overhead and an occasional desert creature.

At the end of the third day we stopped to watch a fox chase a hare. The fox ran with the brush of its tail streaming behind it, pursuing the hare with determination borne of hunger. It ran faster than the hare, but the hare possessed greater agility. Each time the hare dodged to the right or left, the fox overshot it snapping frustration at its heels, and had to loop back to resume the chase. The hare led the fox eastward toward a line of rocky hills with slopes that were almost vertical. The sun low at our backs made the racing beasts easy to see even in the distance, although the heat rising from the plain caused their forms to waver, as though they ran through shallow water.

Abruptly, the hare vanished. A moment later, the fox also vanished. I continued to watch, wondering if my eyes had deceived me.

"Where did they go?" Martala asked. "It looked as if they ran into the cliff, but there's no opening."

She echoed my own thoughts. I stirred the camel to life, and we began to ride toward the place where the hare had disappeared. I expected to see some small cleft revealed as we drew nearer, but the rock face remained unbroken.

"Where did they go?" I repeated to myself in a low voice, eyes narrowed.

They ran into the gap between the hills, my love.

Sashi thought I had asked the question to her.

"There is no gap between the hills," I pointed out.

There is a gap. Can't you see it, Alhazred? It is quite narrow.

I studied the distant line of hills. It stretched in an unbroken wall to the left and right, curving away on both sides. There could be no mistake. The setting sun behind me shone full on the rock.

Mulling on this puzzle, I suddenly remembered a passage in the voluminous writings of Ibn Schacabao, concerning a valley three days to the east of the river Euphrates. He called it the Valley of the Speaking Mouth, and asserted it to lie behind a wall of impassable cliffs, its entrance concealed by enchantment. What else had he written? I searched my memory. Within the valley resided something called the seat of wisdom, a place of great danger, but what this seat did, or who had made it, Ibn Schacabao did not venture to reveal. There was something about a serpent with venom so poisonous, it could be diluted to an almost infinite degree, yet still retain the power to kill. The other things he had written about the valley were lost to me. I had given little attention to the fable. Ibn Schacabao was surnamed the Boaster by later commentators, and was held to be an unreliable source.

If there was a glamour on the hillside, there might be a way to remove it. From the front pocket of my leather wallet I drew forth the scroll of the Old Ones and opened it in my hands, scanning its text for the remembered lines. It took several minutes to find the passage, but Martala sat with admirable patience behind me and allowed me to concentrate. There it was, the formula of banishment in Greek translation and in the guttural language of the Old Ones, transcribed in Greek letters. I found the starting place and read the strange words in a clear voice. They vibrated on the air and sprang forth from my lips like living things.

For several breaths I stared at the hills. Nothing happened. Disappointed, I lowered the scroll to return it to my wallet. When again I looked, I saw a gap in the wall of reddish rock. It was as Sashi had described it, quite narrow. Whatever glamour had been laid upon it was directed at human eyes, not the eyes of beasts, or those of djinn. Wider in the middle than at its top or bottom, it gave the appearance of a mouth turned on its side. As I watched, it seemed to open and close as though speaking silent words. The illusion was startling.

"The heat rising from the plain makes it appear to move," I told Martala.

"Will you enter it?" Her attempt at indifference could not conceal her apprehension.

"It may lead through the hills. If we ride around, it will add days to our journey."

Before the power of the banishment failed and the veil of glamour descended once more to conceal the entrance between the hills, I urged the camel forward at a trot. As we drew nearer, the gap assumed a more natural appearance and ceased to open and shut.

It was wide enough at the elevation of our saddlebow to allow our passage without the rolled sleeping rugs brushing both sides at once, though so narrow at its dusty floor that the camel had to pick its steps with care to avoid tripping on its own hooves. At the top it opened to the sky, but in places its sides almost touched far above our heads. It wound like the body of a snake, making it impossible to see ahead more than a few paces. Should it end abruptly, we would be forced to lead the animal out backwards by its tail, since there was no space for it to turn its body. I studied the soft dust but saw no footprints, or tracks of horses or camels, only the marks of small desert creatures. No one had walked here for a long time.

A projection of rock from the left side of the passage forced me to bend forward until my face pressed against the neck of the camel. I felt Martala's body fit itself against my back. The camel lowered its own head and stepped forward. The overhang rubbed the back of the girl and squeezed her hard against me. I exhaled and bent still lower.

We emerged into a narrow defile with steep sides of broken rubble. After the knife cut through which we had passed it appeared spacious. Stones loosened by sudden floods had spilled down the slopes and completely filled up the floor of the defile in places. We climbed over them with care. They were treacherously balanced and apt to turn underfoot. In this way we made a slow progress eastward in the gathering twilight. The walls of the defile drew apart on either side, and we found ourselves at the top of a hill, overlooking a valley. I stopped the progress of the camel and sat studying the geography of the place.

Completely surrounded by hills, it extended from west to east in the shape of a boat, narrower at each end. The densely forested floor lay under shadow, making it difficult to see its features, but the setting sun lit the crests of the distant hills with a ring of fire. At the western end, not far from us, a spring bubbled vigorously up from the naked crown of a low hill, the noise of its waters loud in the still air of twilight. It divided into four streams that flowed in separate courses across the slope of the valley floor to lose themselves from sight beneath the canopy of trees.

I narrowed my eyes and studied the eastern end. The waters must exit the valley somewhere, but I could discern no opening in the hills, only a shadowed oblong mass almost obscured by the gathering darkness. It was necessary to descend quickly, before we lost the last of the light. I urged the camel down the grass-covered slope and under the tall trees. Some resembled palms, but were larger than any I had ever seen. Others were strange in shape, arising from the ground like great ferns to spread their curving boughs over our heads as we passed.

As we moved further away from the rushing waters of the spring, the voices of birds reached our ears, chattering and squawking with a bewildering cacophony as though in competition with each other. I could not see them among the trees, but they were all around us. The hooves of the camel sank into the soft green floor of the forest. The air beneath the trees brushed my face with cool fingers, and the tall grasses gave way to low plants and ferns that grew in a carpet of dense green moss.

Despite the near absence of a breeze, I realized we were not under attack from swarms of biting flies. This was scarcely to be expected in so lush and wet a valley. Insects flew past our heads with soft drones from time to time, but ignored us. The dense overlapping canopy high above the mossy ground kept it free from under-growth, while the immense thickness of the gnarled and vine-cloaked trunks that sup-ported it testified to the vast antiquity of the forest. It was strange not to see the stars emerging in the heavens. Soon it would be so dark, I would not be able to find our way. I urged the camel toward a tributary of the spring. It snorted and hesitated, uncertain what to do with it, but at last was encouraged by a combination of curses and kicks from my heels to step into the water, which did not rise higher than its knees.

On the other side, we dismounted and used the last of the dying light to find a knoll upon which to spread our rugs. So green and moist was everything, we could not have made a campfire even had we been inclined to do so. The vague shadow of the hobbled camel cropped the lush ferns with evident pleasure, to judge by the sounds from its jaws, which seemed loud now that the birds had fallen silent for the night. From curiosity, I broke off a fern head and chewed it. The water-filled stem, cool and pure on my tongue, held no bitterness. Sitting on our rugs, we shared some of the dried fruit and vegetables we had purchased at Hilla by touch, for it was already too dark to see each other.

The tranquility of the forest conveyed a sense of harmlessness that caused me to neglect to set a watch. It is difficult to know what I could have watched for in that utter blackness. A deep weariness closed my eyes almost before I lay upon my rug. I slept without dreams and awoke refreshed in the soft light of morning, alert and lis-tening. Regular breaths from the girl indicated that she continued to sleep. The for-est noises gave no hint of what had disturbed me, but my body held an unnatural tension.

What is it that woke me, Sashi?

Someone watches you from the stream, my love.

Where the stream divided the trees, enough light reached the forest floor to encourage the growth of low shrubs dense enough to hide within. I rolled my eyes to my left without turning my head, and saw leaves tremble. Wide brown eyes peered out at me. It looked like the face of a young boy.

Yawning and stretching my arms as though just awakened, I stood and walked in a sleepy fashion in the opposite direction among the great pillars of the trees, as though looking for a place to void my bowels. The moment I passed from observation behind a moss-covered fallen log, the twisted roots of which towered above my head, I bent my course and traced the edge of the stream back to the bush where the watcher lay on his belly.

His bare feet and naked brown legs projected into the sunlight. Drawing my dagger, I crept forward with care to avoid rustling the tall grass and grabbed his ankle in my left hand.

He cried out in surprise and kicked so hard, I could not hold him. In a flash of copper-colored skin he slipped under the bushes. I forced them apart and stumbled through, annoyed at my clumsiness. The shadowed depths of the forest betrayed no movement. The camel stood rubbing its hindquarters against the irregular bole of a tree. Martala lay propped on her elbow on her sleeping mat, squinting and blinking at me.

I told her about the watcher. The information did not surprise her.

"He probably hoped to steal from our packs while we slept," she said, yawning.

"There must be a village. Maybe it lies hidden behind that black wall I saw from the hillside."

After eating a frugal breakfast, we bathed in the stream. The water was unnaturally cold, as though it flowed over ice deep within the earth before issuing forth from the spring on the rocky hillock. It felt delightful against my bare skin. The dust and dried sweat of travel turned to mud and washed away as I dipped my cupped hands and flung the silver droplets over my arms and shoulders, standing knee deep with the swift current tugging at my shins. Martala danced naked beside me, laughing and splashing herself with the icy spray.

We decided to wash our garments, not knowing when we would get another chance to be clean. Plunging them deep to get them wet, we found a boulder that projected above the surface of the water and beat them until the dirt no longer ran from them. All this while, I kept an eye upon the place where I had laid my wallet containing the precious rags of spiders and roots along with the scroll of the Old Ones. That we were watched, I had no doubt. I sensed several sets of eyes upon me. Sashi confirmed this feeling.

They are in the trees, Alhazred.

"How many, Sashi?"

I see four of them.

"Warn me if any venture near our wallets."

Martala made no remark at this one-sided dialogue. She was accustomed to hear me address Sashi aloud. She seemed curiously unconcerned about our watchers. The sunlight and chill current intoxicated her and made her giddy. While we waited for our undershirts and tunics to dry, she danced up to her knees in the middle of the stream like a young child, scooping handfuls of smooth pebbles from the bed and throwing them into the air so that they made circular ripples where they fell that were swept away in a moment.

It was easier to lead the laden camel behind us through the trees than to ride upon its back. Progress was slowed in spite of the openness of the forest floor by many fallen trees. The gaps in the canopy created by their fall allowed sunlight to shine down and gave rise to saplings and dense brush difficult to penetrate. The irregular patches of sunlight provided some sense of where we were going. I tried to keep moving northeast, toward the middle of the valley, but when the boughs closed overhead and shut out the sky, it was impossible to be certain of any direction. We crossed a tributary of the spring. I could not judge whether it was the same one we had bathed in, or another.

Once, an antelope no larger than a dog walked in front of us and stopped with its foreleg raised to regard us with curious brown eyes. I approached, but to my astonishment it did not run away. When I extended my hand, it leaned forward and sniffed my palm, wrinkling its moist nose. Only when I tried to lay my hand upon its neck did it leap backwards. It walked slowly away from us on stiff legs, pausing several times to gaze back over its shoulder before it was lost from sight among the trees.

Birds showed the same lack of fear when we approached. We saw many varieties, some the size of peacocks with richly colored plumage of red and green and blue. They did not move aside until we were about to step on their backs, and even then did so only with squawks of protest, as though annoyed at having to make the effort. It appeared to me that they had never been hunted. The only animals to behave in a more natural manner were the small wild pigs that we heard rooting amid the trees. They took care to keep their distance, and when they chanced to wander near enough for us to see them, they turned and waddled away with quick motions of their short legs.

In the afternoon we came upon a forest path and followed it in what seemed to be an easterly direction. It opened into a clearing filled with thatched huts. Fearing an ambush, I hesitated to enter the village, but when at last we made our way cautiously to the center, we found it deserted. Nothing stirred, not even a dog. I ducked my head into several of the doorless huts. They were small in size, their openings no higher than my chest, their thatched roofs too low for me to straighten my back while inside. Woven baskets filled with dried strips of some dark meat, and others containing figs, nuts, or berries sat beside several of the entrances. At first glance I thought the baskets made of coarse cloth, so fine was the weaving. They were decorated in green, yellow, blue, and red with complex geometric patterns that displayed no right angles.

Beside a wooden bowl partly filled with a kind of coarse flour I noticed a mortar and pestle of sorts. The pestle was no more than a rounded rock, and the mortar a depression in a flat stone. Near them lay a stone knife with a handle of woven grasses. The blade was elegant in shape, the weaving done in crossing diagonal bands that simulated the scales of a serpent. From the end of the handle extended a woven loop with a slip knot. For the first time I noticed that there were no fireplaces, not even a single circle of fire stones in the center of the clearing.

"These people are savages, Alhazred," Martala said, eyeing the knife.

"So it appears."

We sampled the berries and nuts, and examined the woven works. Not even the crudest strip of cloth or leather could we find in any of the huts. Weaving of grasses seemed to suffice for all the needs of this tribe. I wondered what they wore as clothing.

My curiosity was soon satisfied. Martala spoke my name quietly and pointed behind me. I turned to see a group of about a dozen men, if they can be called such, working their way cautiously into the village, each with a stone knife held high as if to strike. None stood taller than my chest. They were slender of limb, so that they resembled young boys, save for the wrinkles around their eyes and mouths which betrayed their adult years. In color, their skin was like newly beaten copper, more yellow than red, except for their cheeks and beardless chins which were tattooed in geometric designs with a dark blue pigment. They wore their black hair in three braids down their backs.

All were naked. No, not naked, I realized. Around their necks and ankles many wore strings of red transparent beads that caught the sun. The beads could only be amber, but of a darker and richer color than any amber I had seen in Yemen. I wondered where they procured it, and how much they had collected.

As they drew nearer, Martala stepped beside me and drew her dagger, her preferred weapon. I unsheathed my slender Damascus blade, but held its point downward in a manner that did not threaten. The leader, whose braided hair showed streaks of gray, spread his arms to halt the other villagers and came forward alone. Fear was evident on his features. He kept glancing from me to the girl to the camel. The beast fascinated him, so that he had difficulty looking away from it. I wondered if it could possibly be the first camel he had ever seen.

He stopped when he stood near enough to strike with his knife. Its point angled in the direction of my heart. I resisted the urge to raise my sword. Upon the air I smelled a spice strange to me, but pleasant, akin to cinnamon. It was several moments before I realized that the fragrance came from the little savage.

In a soft voice, much like the voice of a child, he spoke a few words, then repeated them, his intelligent dark eyes fixed on mine. It was a language unknown to me, and equally unknown to the dead Egyptian necromancer Nectanebus, whose desiccated flesh was my flesh. More than this, it did not resemble any language that I had ever heard.

I glanced at the girl, who shook her head to indicate that she did not understand. When I looked back, the dagger was moving forward. The flinch of my muscles came automatically, but by good fortune my sword was not in a position to strike. Before I could raise it, the little man dropped his eyes, and still murmuring in so soft a voice that I could barely hear him, bent to his knees on the hard-packed mud of the clearing and laid his knife at my feet, with the point directed at himself.

Chapter 42

Silently, the other savages imitated their leader, and knelt to lay their stone knives on the ground, their heads bowed.

I stared at them, perplexed. In the throne room at Sana'a I had often watched the king receive foreign delegations. The message of these little naked men could not be mistaken. They wished peace and friendship with us. Though I tried not to show it, I was greatly relieved. Small they might be, but had they wished they could have overwhelmed and killed us.

"Put away your dagger," I told Martala in a mild voice.

Sheathing my sword, I gently touched the man at my feet on the shoulder. He started and trembled, but held his gaze down. Only at my insistent nudges did he at last look up and allow himself to be raised to a standing posture. I gestured for the other men to stand. They watched me covertly with their heads bowed, but not one stirred until their leader spoke a few quiet words. They got up and stood gathered together in silence.

Bending, I picked up the stone dagger and passed it back to the leader, hilt first. This gesture pleased him. He smiled and turned to show the others what I had done. They nodded and grinned with approving noises, then retrieved their knives from the ground. Following the example of their leader, they slid their arms through the braided loop at the end of the hilts and pulled the slip knots tight above their elbows, so that the knives hung point downward from their upper arms.

It appeared an awkward way to carry a weapon, but perhaps they did not regard the knives as weapons. With their downcast eyes and quiet voices, they formed an uncommonly peaceful group of savages. None of them would look at my face for more than a moment except their leader, and even he wore an expression of awe. I was glad that I had renewed the veil of glamour out of habit earlier in the day, or they might never have left the forest.

Their initial terror abated by degrees. They were fascinated by the camel, and stood around it, caressing its hair. Its belly hung just lower than their heads, so that with only a slight bow and a bend of their knees, they could walk between its legs from one side to the other. The placid creature refrained from biting or kicking them.

Women and children began to emerge from the trees. The women were as naked as their men, but in addition to the strings of amber beads, they wore colored bands of woven grasses in their hair, interlacing numerous fine braids. Their faces, which were attractive in a childlike way, bore no tattoos. The tiny breasts of the older girls and younger women stood away from their chests like the breasts of Nubian slave girls. Only in the older women did they sag. None had more than a small tuft of dark hair on her lower belly that failed utterly to conceal the outline of her sex. Their bodies were like those of normal women, but reduced in size, giving the curious illusion when I looked at them that they stood further away than was true.

The women gathered around Martala and around me with the same enthusiasm the men displayed toward the camel. They chattered in their soft language and touched our tunics beneath our open cloaks with their fingertips. I realized they had never before seen cloth, and believed it to be an exceptionally fine weave of grasses.

"Show them your silk scarf," I told Martala.

When she drew the red silk from her leather wallet, they gave exclamations of wonder and delight, holding the silk up to their eyes. They were fascinated at being able to see through it so easily. I noticed several sniff the silk and wrinkle their faces in disgust. Even though it had been washed along with the rest of our garments, it still smelled faintly of sweat, whereas every member of this tiny race smelled of spice.

I discovered the reason for their odor of paradise when they invited us to share their food. The spice formed a staple of their diet. They probably ate it every day, and it mingled with the sweat on their skin, scenting it with a kind of perfume. We sat on small round mats of grass, woven with beautiful colors, that were arranged in a circle. The leader sat at my right side, Martala at my left. The men of the tribe took their places with crossed legs on the other mats while their women laid out wooden bowls and plates of various foods in the center, then sat down facing the men and ensured that everyone could eat what he wished by passing the vessels around the circle.

As a sign of hospitality, I took off my wallet and offered them portions of our own rations. They made noises of appreciation at the figs and other dried fruit, but spat out the tiny bits of dried meat they tried on their tongues. In return for a taste of their spice, I let them sample the salt in our salt cellar, and this they also rejected. I judged that none of them had ever tasted salt in its concentrated form. Their own variety of fig was different in flavor from ours, having less sweetness. When I gave them sips of wine, they made faces but did not refuse a second drink.

It was evident that of wine or beer they knew nothing, and possessed no milk other than what flowed from the breasts of their women. They kept no livestock of any kind that could be milked or butchered, and no fowl from which to gather eggs. Their diet appeared to consist in the main of soft roots, nuts and berries gleaned from the forest trees and plants. This they varied with uncooked patties shaped from coarse flour, made by grinding the heads of wild grain in their mortars, and allowing the pastry to rise by some natural process on flat stones in the heat of the sun.

My speculation about the origin of the dried strips of meat we had found in the huts was satisfied when a group of laughing children dragged a wild pig, squealing in protest, from the forest on the end of two braided grass ropes that encircled its neck. Flowers of white and red petals that were bound to its ears, tail and legs gave it a festive appearance. Smiling, the leader of the tribe gestured for us to rise from our places of honor on the mats. The entire tribe stood up from the bowls and baskets of food and formed an irregular line in pairs behind the pig, while the leader of the tribe took up his solitary place in front. The children handled the ropes in such a way as to guide the grunting and squealing beast where they wished.

I glanced at Martala and shrugged. We were their guests, and it was evident they wished us to accompany them. We fell into step behind the headman. The procession undulated along a well-beaten path through the dark forest, beneath the overarching boughs of massive trees, to another clearing of compacted clay at no great distance from the huts. The clearing was roughly circular in shape, with a standing stone in its center. I studied it in surprise, for it was remarkably similar in color and shape to the pillar adored by the Beast of Babylon on its lonely mountain plateau, although this stone was only the height of a man. No mark of ax or hammer marred its irregular squared surface. It rose from a flat disk resembling a millstone, made of the common rock of the valley. Rusty stains surrounded the base of the pillar, and flies swarmed over it in unusual numbers. I recognized the scent but said nothing to the girl.

I wanted to approach the pillar to see if it held the same fine veins of ruby running through its shiny jet surface as the larger pillar of the Beast, but the reverence shown to the stone by the savages made me hesitate. They came no nearer than a crescent of eleven smaller boulders of common brown rock that had been placed on the north side of the clearing. For a time I puzzled over their arrangement, then realized that they were set at the limit of the shadow cast by the central pillar. It was evident from their behavior that the clearing served them as a kind of temple.

The excitement of the children overwhelmed their respect for the black stone. Laughing and crying out with delight, they dragged the uncooperative pig toward the pillar by pulling the ropes past it on either side, until the head of the pig touched the irregular glassy surface. The rest of the tribe gathered close to the crescent of small rocks that had the great stone at its focus. The leader went forward with a grave expression and raised his palms. He began to chant. I did not understand his words, but it seemed to my ears that the language was different from what he had spoken to me, both more ancient and harsher in its tone.

When he finished, the members of the tribe began to sound a strange keening noise in their throats. This rose in pitch and intensity as the leader slid his stone knife down his arm and stepped behind the pig. Using a practiced motion, he grasped the pig by the snout and pulled back its head, then slit its throat so that its blood gushed out upon the base of the pillar. The other members of the tribe, including the children on the ropes, gave a final shout as the legs of the animal buckled and it fell dead.

Martala stared at the blood with horror. I caught her eye and shook my head to warn her not to speak or show any sign of revulsion. She nodded her understanding and mastered her emotions as four women went forward and surrounded the body of the pig with their knives. In minutes they had cut from it numerous long strips of meat, which they laid in a wooden bowl. We returned with them and the majority of the men, leaving the children and a few of the elders to dispose of the remains of the carcass.

In the village, the strips of raw meat were first sprinkled with dried herbs, then beaten on flat stones with rounded rocks. This was done with ritual precision, but with much talk and expectant laughter. We resumed our places on the mats of the feast circle. In due time, strips of pig flesh were brought to us on a wooden platter. I sampled it without hesitation, but without much expectation. The taste was a pleasant surprise. The beating had rendered the meat tender, and the herbs provided an agreeable sharpness to the taste. Even Martala did not refuse the offering. It was evident from the expressions of delight on the faces of the feasters that the meat of the pig was their greatest delicacy.

While the meat was being enjoyed, some of the women went out of the feast circle and gathered a short distance away to sing in sweet high voices, surrounded by the younger children, who sat at their feet listening with avid expressions on their upturned faces. The song, if it was a song, extended itself in bewildering complexity without repetition. My mind was divided between the singing, and the soft conversation of the head man sitting beside me with the village elders, who did their best to make his meaning known to me by gestures and repetitions of his words.

"What is he saying?" I murmured to Martala when I could do so without being impolite.

"You are the speaker of lost tongues, you tell me."

"A good servant refrains from impertinence."

She rolled her eyes, and pondered the gestures for a moment.

"I think he is asking whether we fell from the sky."

At once the meaning of his hand motions became plain. I shook my head and held up my hands with the palms flat as though pushing away. After a moment he seemed to understand. I pointed in the direction where I knew the fissure lay, and formed the shape of a narrow slit with my cupped and joined palms. One of the men on the other side of the circle laughed like a braying donkey, but the leader of the tribe silenced him with a word. He studied my hands and at last widened his eyes in comprehension. When he spoke softly to the men gathered around the circle, they fell quiet and stared at me with curious expressions, mingled awe and dread.

By his repeated speaking of the words, I gathered that the name of the headman was Enoki, and that the valley or the village was called Edena in their tongue. By pointing at the strips of pig flesh and mimicking the shape of the black pillar, I drew forth the name Yad, which I took to be the name of the pillar, or of their god, or perhaps both. In curiosity, I uttered several names of the Old Ones, but they drew no reaction. This race knew nothing of them, or at least, nothing of their common names. On a chance inspiration, I voiced the name of the god of the Jews, Yahweh. In horror, Enoki touched his fingers to his lips. Several other elders did the same. This name they recognized, but it was not to be spoken aloud.

The onset of twilight came without any attempt by the savages to murder us, which I took as a sign that our responses at the feast had been acceptable. I made no protest when Enoki led us to an empty hut and offered it to us in his gentle voice. Whoever was its owner, if this tribe understood the meaning of ownership, he gave no sign or word of displeasure when we passed through the doorless entrance with our own sleeping rugs, having entrusted the camel to the care of the children of the village.

In the morning we were greeted with casual good humor by the savages, but without awe. The formal honors of the day before were not renewed. After eating from our rations, supplemented with some of the flat uncooked bread of our hosts, we left the camel and most of our supplies in the village and set off with our leather wallets on our shoulders in an easterly direction along one of the paths that led away from the clearing. I wished to explore the black wall that I had glimpsed from the mouth of the fissure. Without communication, but with a smiling countenance, Enoki accompanied us. I wondered if he was merely curious about our purpose, or felt an obligation to guide and protect us.

Whatever his thoughts, a guardian proved unneeded. We kept to the winding but well-trodden path, and met nothing that threatened along the way. Once, a wild pig stopped on the path directly ahead and gazed over its shoulder at our approach with its weak eyes. When it caught Enoki's scent, it snorted in alarm and darted through the tall ferns with an agility surprising for a creature of its shortness of limb. We stood and listened to the fading rustle of its progress.

The forest felt warm and cool by turns as we moved from patches of sunlight into depths of shadow. All around us, the chatter and cries of unseen birds continued unceasing, mingled with the lazy drone of flying beetles and the occasional green and gold dragonfly. We walked in a line, me in front, followed by the tiny savage, and then Martala, who had not been comfortable when he tried to fall into step behind her. From time to time, Enoki gestured for us to stop and showed us some plant with an edible root, or a bush bearing berries. I made no objection to these delays. It is always wise to know how to live from the wildness of the land.

His face was a curious mingling of youth and age. It would have been easy to mistake him for a child, both by his small stature and his nimbleness, but the gray streaks in the upper half of his three braids, and the fine lines at the corners of his eyes when he smiled, showed that he was a man of middle years. Even had they been absent, there was a knowingness in the depths of his brown eyes that could only be acquired by the experience of life.

He was fascinated by my water skin. When I paused beside a stream to fill it, after drinking deeply of its contents, he laughed out loud and clapped his hands in the rapture of his amusement, his dark eyes sparkling. The concept of carrying water in this valley of pure cool streams seemed so outrageous and absurd to him that it overcame his natural good manners. The skull of Gor on my belt also drew his attention. He tried not to look at it when my cloak fluttered open, but his gaze returned to it repeatedly, and once he brushed the rounded surface of the bone with his fingertips, as if by accident.

The path grew narrower, the bushes encroaching on either side, as we traveled further east. The mood of our escort also changed. He spoke and laughed less often, and began casting nervous glances between the shadowed pillars of the trees. The crack of a twig from the forest floor or the knock of one wind-blown branch against another overhead made him flinch and listen with his ear cocked. His unhappiness was plain, but he said nothing until we reached a fork in the path. The better-traveled track on the right bent south, but the thin and almost invisible left track continued east.

When I took the left side, Enoki could no longer contain himself. He began to babble softly and make earnest apologetic gestures with his copper hands, indicating that we should turn southward. The other path he pushed away violently. The fear in his eyes was no longer concealed by the thick lashes on his half-lowered eyelids. He licked his lips and tugged gently at my sleeve, reminding me of a dog trying to communicate its wishes to its master.

I shrugged away with impatience. The black wall lay somewhere in the direction of the left path, and I had no intention of being turned aside by a nervous savage. When he saw that we were determined to defy him, his face took on an expression of sadness mingled with resignation. He followed after me, head bowed, with the gloom of a funeral marcher.

Abruptly, the forest ended. There was no gradual thinning of the canopy above us. We stepped out from the trees into the sunlight as though exiting the door of a house. On the other side of a clearing of no great width rose the wall I had seen from the fissure. It was just that, a wall the height of a tall palm tree, having no features other than a closed gate some distance to the north. On the opposite side, not far from where we stood, I saw that a tributary of the spring that watered the valley flowed beneath the wall at its corner and vanished beyond.

I turned to speak to Martala. Enoki stood trembling so severely, he could only with effort sustain himself on his feet. Knees drawn together, he hugged his chest and stared past me at the wall with utter terror. He seemed to forget that Martala and I were with him until I laid my hand on his shoulder. At my touch he screamed and clutched my sleeve. Some sanity returned into his face as he met my curious gaze.

"Poamala yaida raas," he said, pointing at the gate, and repeated the words over and over.

When he saw that I intended to approach the wall through the tall grasses and thorny plants that grew in the clearing to the height of our waists, he made a motion to leave us and return into the forest. I caught his elbow and shook my head, indicting as well as I could that I wanted him to stay. It occurred to me that his knowledge might prove useful. He writhed in my grasp like a child, but made no attempt to strike me with his fists or stab me with his stone dagger. With tears springing into his brown eyes, he let me pull him into the clearing.

It was curious that the thorns pricking my thighs through my cloak grew no where else in the valley that I had seen. The grass showed little evidence of the passage or browsing of large beasts. I stopped ten paces from the wall and examined it. No joints between its blocks were visible. It seemed to soak up the light of the sun and return nothing other than a dull luster similar to obsidian that has been polished with sand. Its surface was not perfectly flat, but rippled gently like a pool of black water frozen in its motion. The thought came to me that the wall had been poured into place, but I dismissed this notion as fanciful.

I had to drag the trembling Enoki northward through the thorns toward the gate. Over and over he babbled *poamala yaida raas*, and sometimes he added in his shrill voice *oxiayal teloc*, but what these strange words might mean I could not guess. They were not in his own language, so much I could judge from their sound. As we neared the gate, his legs failed him. He lay rolling in the grass and the thorns, keening like a frightened child. Nothing I could do would force him to his feet, even though the thorns cut his naked skin and made him bleed in innumerable places.

I turned to study the gate. It stood twice the height of a man and equally wide, its double doors of black wood bound with what appeared to be heavy iron straps, although they showed no appearance of rust. The heads of the nails that secured the straps of the hinges to the massive planks were as large as my fist, and in shape like a pyramid. It was evident from the undisturbed growth of grass and thorn bushes that the gate had not been opened for many years.

"I do not like the look of it," Martala murmured.

"What is to like or dislike? It is a door."

The brooding black surface of the ebon planks and the threatening points on the nail heads mocked my careless words.

There was little hope that I could force the gate, even should it be unbolted and open inward, yet I determined to make the attempt. I looked around in the grass for a stone, and dug one half-embedded from the sod that was so heavy, I could only with difficulty hold it in one hand.

"I will bang on the gate and try to arouse a gatekeeper, if there is such a being."

Enoki must have divined my intention from my purposeful motion toward the gate, for he could not have understood my words. He leaped to his feet with a scream and ran past Martala before she could move to catch him. He ran back toward the forest along the track we had made in the grass. When he was near the trees, he turned. His head and shoulders were visible above the grass. Anger replaced terror on his childlike, yet strangely knowing, countenance. He pulled his stone knife from his arm and held it pointed toward me. Babbling in his own tongue, he made thrusting gestures that conveyed his meaning. We were no longer welcome in his village.

Replacing his knife, he turned his back upon us and walked with dignity into the shadows of the trees.

I paid little attention to his departure, but turned to search for an easy approach to the portal. The grass was taller, the brambles thicker, at the base of the gate, and in addition there grew a profusion of bright red flowers on wiry stems. I started to press them apart, trying to avoid the thorns that pricked and pierced my cloak.

Martala grasped my shoulder and jerked me back a step, just as I raised my hand to the amazingly smooth planks. I shrugged off her grasp with annoyance.

"Alhazred, the flowers."

Her words meant nothing to me, but her tone of warning was plain enough. I met her gaze, then turned to look past her at the clearing. Not a single red blossom grew elsewhere amid the tall grasses.

"What makes the flowers grow?" she asked, as though posing a riddle.

"The dung of the camel, or the horse," I murmured thoughtfully.

"Or the dead flesh of beasts," she said, finishing my thought.

I dropped the stone, and bent my knees so that I crouched amid the grass. Taking care to avoid thorns, I parted the shoots to expose their roots. Amid them were innumerable bones of animals, some small, others large. Many were the bones of birds, but I saw what appeared to be the skull of a wild pig. With care, I stood and backed another step away from the gate.

We set out walking north through the clearing with the wall on our right side, and in time reached a corner similar to the corner in the south under which the stream ran. Rounding it, my heart fell. The wall continued eastward into the distance, unbroken by door or window.

"If we walk to the far end, we might find another gate," Martala suggested.

"Yes. And it might be as treacherous as the first. I am hot, and not in a humor to walk for miles through this thicket."

I retraced our way along the path we had beaten down, continuing past the gate, and past the place where the track of our feet bent into the forest. Martala followed without comment. I stopped on the bank of the stream. As I had hoped, there was a space between the surface of the bubbling water and lower foundation of the wall, the footing of which extended but a little way into the soil of the plain.

For the sake of satisfying my own curiosity, I squatted and clutched the sod with my hand as I let my boots slip off the lip of the bank and into the icy water. It swirled around my thighs. I waded to the opposite bank and with difficulty pulled myself out. As I had suspected, the black wall beyond the corner extended just as far and as straight as it had in the north. It must enclose a rectangle of considerable land. Martala waited patiently until I returned to the stream and slid my legs into its waters. Silver fish darted away from my heels, flashing as they rose near the surface of the swirling dark flow. This was a favorable omen. What did not kill the fish would not kill us.

I started wading through the water toward the wall. With a shrug, Martala let herself into the stream and followed. There was little reason to fear the wall itself, since no flowers grew along its base. Even so, some undefined dread made me hesitate as I extended my hand to touch its lower edge. The chill surface lay inert beneath my fingers.

Untying my wallet, I doubled it and slung both pockets over my shoulder with its strap in my left hand. I bent forward and crawled beneath the wall, half floating on the current, my free hand clutching the slime-covered domes of submerged stones. The underside of the wall rubbed my wallet and the water lapped at my face and blinded me. Through the swirl of bubbles I saw a patch of brightness ahead and pulled myself along in that direction, letting the swiftness of the stream carry me forward.

The wall could not have been more than ten paces thick, but seemed nearer a hundred. With intense relief, I lifted my face from the icy kiss of the stream and shook water from my hair and ear-holes.

In spite of my lack of expectation, I felt disappointment. A short distance from the bank grew a forest of tall trees, in every visible respect identical to the forest on the other side of the wall. The stream wound its way in a northeasterly direction between the trunks, the overhanging boughs of the giants almost cutting off the blue of the sky above it.

I pulled myself out on the northern bank and sat in the short grass to empty my boots. Martala sputtered and cursed as her face broke the surface, then began to cough. She threw her wallet down beside me and sat on her rump to pull off her boots, which were uncommonly tight. How she could walk in them was a mystery to me, but she had sworn several times in the past that they fitted her well. I decided to take advantage of the small patch of sunlight that reached the banks where the stream exited the wall, and drew off my cloak and tunic to dry them. If we walked in our wet clothing amid the deep shadows of the forest, we might not be dry before nightfall, or even by the following day.

The shriek of the girl made me clutch the place where the ivory hilt of my dagger should have been as I whirled on my bare heel. She sat squealing her delight, a sodden boot in one hand, and in the other a stone the size of a grape that gleamed like old wine in the sunlight. Laughing, she raised it to her eye and looked at me through its rounded sides. I stared at her and cursed. We both dove for the stream at the same instant, and for several moments floundered around in its chill depths with our faces beneath its surface. When I unbent my back I held five lumps of amber in my left hand and three in my right. Martala's cupped palms overflowed.

Chapter 43

The sun moved slowly past its zenith. Its strong rays drove the water from the linen tunics and raised wisps of steam from the darker cloaks. I let my thin undershirt dry on my body, but the girl stripped to the skin and carefully laid all her garments in a row along the grassy bank with the fastidiousness of her sex. Her limbs gleamed in the sunlight, singing a wordless song of vitality and youth.

The amber lay in heaps on the grass. There was more than we could carry on our backs. It littered the bed of the stream, some pieces larger than my fist. I decided to select the best lumps of a convenient size for trade and of the highest quality. We could come back for what remained with the camel, assuming we were able to persuade the savages to return our mount. I picked the piles over while Martala watched, then divided the chosen stones and put half into my wallet wrapped in a scrap of rag to protect them from scratches. The girl loaded her wallet with the rest.

A female antelope of the same diminutive kind that we had seen on the other side of the wall came from the trees while we were occupied with the amber. She glanced once at us, then went to the edge of the water and spread her front legs, stretching down her long neck to drink. She raised her head, wiggled her enormous ears, and walked back into the forest without sparing us a second glance. I wondered if she had ever seen a human being.

We dressed without haste and followed in the same general direction. The forest floor was open and easy to walk upon, apart for wind-downed trees that lay like moss-covered leviathans, their supine trunks higher than our heads. The upper canopy of leaves was hidden in shadows, save here and there, when the sun forced its slanting way through some small gap, illuminating the mists like smoke. I was able to judge the passage of the hours by the angle of its rays. Moss swallowed the sound of our footfalls. We heard many birds but saw only a few, when they chanced to flit through sunbeams from one treetop to another with flashes of their brightly colored wings.

At length, we came upon a path, or more properly a road, for it was ten paces broad, and made from enormous brown paving stones each wider than a man is tall. So tightly were they fitted, not a single blade of grass or tuft of moss grew up between them. The overhanging trees covered them in deep shadows, so that the stones felt cool to the touch. The path was broad enough to accommodate a marching army. Since we had encountered no trace of humanity within the wall, I wondered what creature walked it, and hoped that other affairs occupied it today.

We followed the paved path as it wound between the great trees, and came to a place where it divided into two branches. Without hesitation, I took what I judged to be the more easterly way, for I wished to penetrate to the east end of the enclosure to determine it if possessed a gateway that might lead to a passage out of the valley. It was no simple task to maintain a direction, for the path wound back upon itself like the body of a dragon. Repeatedly we encountered branches on the walkway that led into the shadows. It was with relief that I recognized the gentle gurgle of the brook somewhere beyond sight on my right. The waters of the valley flowed eastward, so I knew we must still face that direction. It was all too easy a matter to become lost amid the maze of the pathways.

I had given up all expectation of anything but forest inside the black wall, when without warning the trees ceased and gave way to a large meadow with two gentle grass-covered hills, between which flowed along a deep crease the swift waters of the brook. We stood at the edge of the clearing and gazed at it in wonder, for it was not a natural landscape, but had been crafted by some cunning mind. The hills were exactly equal in height, their rounded domes like soft breasts on a reclining woman. On the crest of each hill grew a single enormous tree, larger even that the trees of the moss-cloaked forest behind us. The tree on the left hill was green with leaves and flourishing, but the tree on the right hill projected into the blue heavens like a skeleton, its leaves and bark long since perished, leaving only naked limbs that resembled bones. Branches broken from it by the wind littered the ground beneath it like the ribs of some ancient monster. Between the hills, a stone bridge with an ornately carved panel arising at the center of its parapet spanned the brook in a shallow arch.

At the limit of the forest the paved walkway ceased. The grass in the meadow grew no higher than our ankles, and had a mowed appearance, being regular in its height. No boulders or stumps marred its smooth expanse. Surely it was a kind of park maintained by a keeper, or saplings from the forest would have covered it within the span of a dozen years. As we walked from beneath the long shadows of the trees at our backs, I looked for a caretaker's house, but the vast meadow stretched to the margin of the wood on either side and gave no sign of occupation. At the east end the grassy expanse was limited by a black wall, unbroken by any gate. The water-course flowed beneath it and in this way passed out from the enclosure. The hills of the valley rose steeply just beyond the wall in two distinct peaks.

"What is this place, Alhazred?" Martala asked in a hushed whisper.

Having no answer, I said nothing. The meadow possessed the solemnity of a holy place and impelled deference. The wall of leaves behind us dimmed the cease-less cries of birds. Even the gurgle of the brook was muted by its deep course between overhanging banks. The warm air lay still and hushed. I welcomed the sun after the gloom under the trees, but felt unease in my heart. Every instinct informed me that I did not belong here, that it would be in the interests of my health to depart at once.

As we approached the northern hill with the living tree, I saw that ripe red fruit weighed down its massive boughs. So many globes grew on each limb that the lower branches brushed the grass.

Martala went forward to pick one that hung within easy reach. Some memory caused me to stop her with a harsh word. She turned with a look of inquiry. Behind her shoulder, a slender serpent, its ebon body spotted with irregular patches of orange and yellow, slid over the curve of the pear-shaped fruit she had been about to take between her fingers. At the sight of the serpent, I remembered.

"This place is described in a book by Ibn Schacabao that I read several years ago while at Sana'a. The sage reports that the fruit of this tree is poisoned by the venom of serpents, and is deadly to eat."

She returned her gaze to the tree, and flinched away from the viper that extended its bobbing head toward her. The distance was great enough that the snake could not strike, but she stepped quickly back. As though in disappointment, it curled its lurid body around the fruit. A single blue drop fell from its open mouth and ran down the sun-warmed side.

The entire tree was filled with snakes. Now that our eyes were looking for them, we saw them everywhere amid the thick leaves. Each red globe had its own guardian. In places, tangled masses of newborn serpents writhed like the head of a gorgon, watched over with maternal care by the one that had given them birth. The babies were like worms, but even the fully-grown vipers extended no more than a cubit from nose to tail.

"Schacabao wrote much concerning the virtues of their venom as a poison, the details of which I will not bore you with. It is enough to know that it is deadly to consume, and that a single scratch from a blade steeped in it will bring death in seconds."

"I am no longer hungry."

We laughed from nervous relief. It would have been so easy to plunge our arms into the foliage of the tree seeking the luscious fruit. Such are the practical benefits of scholarship, where information gained in hours of leisure may prove useful during times of uncertainty.

Did you see the serpents, Sashi?

Of course, my love.

Yet you said nothing.

You were not in danger, dear one.

This remark, unheard by Martala, I set aside on the shelf of my memory for future consideration. What affection or lack of it Sashi felt toward Martala was not a matter into which I had troubled to inquire, but it might become necessary to do so. The girl was useful to me, and I would regret to have her killed through the negligence of my spirit lover.

"I wish we had some vessel into which we could collect this poison," I murmured. "Schacabao writes that it dries in the sun into blue crystals that may be diluted to a near infinite degree without loss of potency."

"Why would we want it? You are not a poisoner."

"No. Poison is a weapon of the royal court, not of the countryside. Its use on a blade is an expression of malice, nothing more, since common poisons act too slowly to determine the outcome of a battle. However, this venom is uncommon and would be a valuable commodity for trade."

"I have nothing that would hold it," Martala said with complacency.

"Perhaps if I emptied out the salt cellar—"

"Alhazred, no! We would have no salt with our fresh vegetables. You know the salt would spoil if you tied it in a cloth. Our sweat would turn it to a lump of stone."

Watching the serpents slide among the green leaves, I sighed with regret. It would be a hardship to give up salt on our journey. In any case, collecting and drying the poison would take hours. I had what remained of the jewels, the white spiders, the u'mal roots, the amber, and the scroll of the Old Ones for trade—although it was my intention to retain the scroll for my own study, at least until I exhausted its wisdom.

"Let us cross the bridge and see what the other tree offers," I told her.

"What does Schacabao write of the other tree?"

"Nothing at all." Memory stirred in my head. "He did write something about a wisdom seat, but what he meant was not clear to me."

We climbed the slope of the stone bridge, which was unnaturally wide, as though shaped for feet larger than human.

"Surely this is Schacabao's wisdom seat," Martala said, stopping in the middle of the bridge.

A large throne occupied the right side of the bridge, set into a recess in the parapet so that it did not project on to the walkway. We had not noticed it before since the ornately carved back of the seat concealed it from the western approach, and appeared nothing more than an architectural feature of the bridge. Nor was it prominent when viewed from the side, since the sun declining in the western sky and striking its back cast a shadow over it. The low arms were shaped like the claws of a hawk. Each claw grasped a stone ball. The back was carved into four feathered wings, two raised upward toward heaven, and two drooping to the earth. At their center rested an inhuman visage more than a cubit broad, with ribs or streamers extending from its opened mouth. Or they may have been intended to represent serpents. The stonework was greatly weathered by time.

In the forehead of the face, a single ruby occupied a golden frame shaped to resemble an eye. Both the gold of the frame and the polished surface of the jewel had resisted the action of sun and wind, and appeared as fresh as if they had been placed in the throne the day before. The stone looked almost black in the shadow of the throne's wings. I touched it with my fingers, wondering if so large a jewel could be real. It felt cool. The round ruby filled a circle in the center of the oval gold setting that was the size of a hen's egg. It was of greater monetary value than all the gems I carried in my wallet. The decision to investigate this enclosure had proved more rewarding than expected, even without the dried crystals of the viper venom.

Martala sat upon the throne and laid her hands on its sinister arms. She resembled an infant in the chair of its father.

"Not a very comfortable seat. It needs a cushion."

"It was not made for your buttocks, or those of any human being, to judge by the shape of it."

I continued across the bridge to the south side of the brook. She ran up behind me.

"Aren't you going to sit in it, Alhazred?"

"Perhaps later. I want to explore the rest of this place before we lose the sun."

It surprised me that the day had grown so late while we wandered along the convoluted paths under the trees. It had seemed that we had walked but a short time, yet the entire afternoon had passed away.

The white tree was as it appeared from the other side of the brook, no more than a bleached framework of naked limbs. There was no sign of decay. Some property of the wood preserved it, so that even small twigs that littered the ground beneath it did not rot. I picked up a stub of a branch. It felt unnaturally heavy and hard, more like ivory than wood. It seemed prudent to select half a dozen short sections of branches and put them into my wallet. The wood might possess properties of value, or might command a good price if we ever again walked among civilized men. Observing my activity, the girl did the same.

We made our way down to the place where the stream bubbled beneath the wall on the eastern side of the enclosure. The water looked black, with no gap between the base of the wall and its swirling surface. The stream backed up into a deep pool in which a small whirlpool turned. It did not appear to be a promising exit, unless we wished to emerge from the wall as corpses. I resolved to explore the exterior of the enclosure the next day, to see what lay on the other side of the eastern wall. The four tributaries of the spring left the valley, so there must be some passage through those looming hills, presently lit red by the setting sun as though splashed with blood.

I made our camp for the night in the middle of the bridge, on the consideration that if danger threatened, we would have a route of escape. The brook was too wide to leap across. Any enemy approaching from one side would need to use the bridge to reach the opposite side. By that time, we could flee safely back into the trees of the forest. Such was my thinking, although if asked what danger I imagined might appear, I could offer no answer. The sense of unease felt at our entry into the meadow had not lessened with time. It weighed upon the mind like a cloak of shadow with a pressure that was almost palpable.

We ate with little conversation. I pissed over the low stone parapet on the eastern side of the bridge into the gurgling water and unrolled my rug to sleep. In defiance of our usual custom, we did not remove our boots, but left them on along with our tunics beneath our cloaks, and placed our wallets and weapons where they could be grasped in the darkness. The twilight air barely moved, yet we remained untroubled by biting insects. I realized that we had seen no living things in the meadow other than the serpents, although there were undoubtedly fish in the brook. Perhaps the same oppression that weighed on my mind discouraged the presence of other creatures. I was grateful not to dream.

A glow filled the eastern sky when I woke. The girl lay on her rug, breathing easily with her arm across her face, her spine twisted, one leg bent double to her hip. How she could sleep in such an awkward posture was a source of puzzlement, but she often lay in even more ungainly positions. Her body appeared jointless in slumber. I shrugged to myself. The mysteries of this world were infinite, and there were infinite worlds to explore.

Washing my mouth with water from my water skin, I spat over the side of the bridge, then drank deep. The skin felt half empty. It would do no harm to fill it, I reflected to myself, and left the bridge for a place where the grassy bank dipped low near the surface of the stream. There I splashed icy droplets over my face, and filled my vessel.

I expected that the noise would awaken the girl, but to my surprise she still slept when I returned. Perhaps she had lain awake the previous night, and was recovering her lost slumber. The rising sun illuminated the edges of the line of hills that projected above the black wall along the eastern end of the valley. The two tallest peaks stood up like raised arms, and I saw that the sun would ascend between them. I opened my pack and made a light breakfast of salted meat and dried figs. The combination of flavors went surprisingly well together, to a man with an appetite. Still the girl slept. I found no reason to disturb her.

The edge of the solar disk crept above the hollow between the eastern peaks, orange enough to gaze at without strain on the eyes. Its rays struck the ruby and sent beautiful reflections of red across the walkway and parapet of the bridge. The effect was beyond the capacity of any artist to imitate with his brush, yet it had repeated itself every day for countless years, unobserved in this place of mystery. Ruminating in this way, with the taste of breakfast still in my mouth, I sat upon the seat to watch the sunrise.

The walls of my mind fled away into limitless space in all directions, and I felt myself falling through an infinite void. I was no longer in my body, but formless and without a center. Blinding white obscured my vision, a low roar that was like the rumble of a waterfall sounded in my ears from every side. I experienced a moment of utter terror similar to that of a man who steps forward in darkness with confidence, only to discover that his foot descends on empty air. The urge to scream rose within me but I heard no sound above the roar.

With desperation, seeking some firm image to cling to, I focused my thoughts on the bridge. At once I saw it as though floating in the air above it. Every particle of its stones shone with an inner illumination. I saw myself sitting in the chair, an entranced expression on my ravaged face—for I had not renewed the glamour that veiled my features. As I looked more closely, every wrinkle and hair and pore in my skin became visible. I needed only to direct my attention to a part of my body to see into it, through the barrier of my skin, and could count the particles of blood that pulsed through my veins with the throbs of my heart.

When I turned my attention to the girl, I saw that she was sitting on her rug, regarding me with curiosity but without alarm. I looked more closely and counted the hairs growing from her scalp. There was no effort, the number was simply available to my awareness. I wondered what she was thinking, and immediately heard her thoughts echo in my own mind.

So he tried the seat after all. I knew he could not resist. I wonder why he sits so silent? He must be thinking. I will not disturb him. What a pity about his face. He must have been so handsome.

My restless mind could not remain focused for long on any one thing. I turned my awareness toward the east, and sent it flying over the black wall, over the hills, and across the plain. There, somewhere, lay the stronghold of the magi who were the foes of the dark man. At once my mind flew like a hawk across the ground, and I observed every feature along the way. Beside a broad river I saw a walled fortress bordered on one side by cultivated fields and cottages, and on the other by a dockside with numerous river craft loading and unloading their wares. This occupied no more than an instant to my perception, yet I could easily trace every step of the path. It was impressed on my memory as a print of a hand shows itself in wet clay.

I wondered if Altrus still pursued us, or if he had died from his wounds, and at once my awareness flew in the opposite direction, toward the west, where I saw as from a great height a solitary man on a travel-weary horse, riding along the line of hills that guarded the valley, looking for some passage through their slopes. He was far from the fissure, and I knew with absolute clarity that he would never locate it. He would be forced to ride around the hills, which would take him days. I descended closer, and saw that his wounds had begun to heal, and contained no putrescence. He would recover. The vitality of his body surprised me. It burned with an inner fire that generated prodigious reserves of endurance.

Before I could examine him in more detail, my restless mind flew to the great desert of the Empty Space. I looked down upon the territory of the Black Spring Clan, and saw that it was occupied by a scattering of families from another clan of ghouls that I did not recognize. They lay within their dens, protected from the rays of the morning sun. I could see the bubbles rise and break on the inky surface of the spring, and remembered the taste of its water on my tongue.

My mind turned to the dark man. I wondered what his true purpose might be, and why he needed my aid when he was so great with power. This was a mistake. My awareness flew through a vast distance in a moment, and beyond space to another realm of reality, and there I found the dark man, but when my mind attempted to encompass him, it became bewildered in its failure. It was as though I attempted to pick up a smooth wooden sphere larger than my head in the fingers of one hand. My awareness slipped and slid when it tried to grasp the purposes of this Old One. Even the true form of Nyarlathotep was not revealed, for he possessed countless forms, each no less real than the others, and more than this, his forms changed and mutated in their interaction with the worlds he simultaneously inhabited.

He became aware of my attention, but his reaction was no more than mild amusement. I felt it brush my thoughts and burn them, so that I instinctively withdrew, but there was no hostility in the touch. Had he wished, I realized with the clarity granted me by the wisdom seat, he could with a single word have purged my mind of all thought and left me a drooling idiot. I withdrew from him in the way a man will stumble backward from a room in which he does not belong.

With a gasp of breath, I leapt up from the seat and stood trembling, covered with sweat, nausea twisting my bowels, the world spinning around me. Arms caught me as my knees buckled.

"Alhazred, what is the matter?" Martala asked.

She guided me to my sleeping rug and helped me to sit. I said nothing for a few moments, waiting for the sickness in my guts to subside. I knew that were I to part my lips to speak, I would surely vomit. A ghoul does not vomit. They view it as a contemptible weakness that men sometimes throw forth the food they consume. What a ghoul takes into his body remains always a part of him and is never given up. Such was the philosophy of the Black Spring Clan, strangely clear in my thoughts due to my memory of them on the wisdom seat.

When my head ceased to spin, I noticed that the sun had risen full above the eastern hills. What had seemed to me mere moments had consumed almost an hour. The ruby in the carven stone face no longer cast its colored panels of light across the bridge.

In a few words I told the girl what had transpired in my mind while I sat upon the seat. She glanced at it with respect mingled with aversion.

"I saw nothing while I sat upon the seat."

"The ruby was in shadow. In some manner the rays of the sun make it active and release its power."

I struggled to my feet. Silently, she lent her arm and supported me until I gained my balance. Strength returned to my limbs and my guts ceased to roll. It had not been a physical sickness that overcame me, but a reaction to the confusion in my mind. Now that my thoughts were ordered and limited in their usual way, my body ceased to complain.

When the girl realized what I intended, she pulled against me.

"Are you mad? You may be killed."

I shrugged her away in annoyance. Must I explain my every intention to this troublesome child?

Tentatively, I lowered my buttocks onto the seat and placed my hands on the balls held in the carven claws. The sun had warmed the stone. I no longer felt its chill penetrate through my flesh. As I suspected, nothing happened. I tried to cast my mind over the hills, but it remained firmly within my skull. Standing, I turned and touched the ruby. It, too, felt warm.

"Whatever activates the seat, it occurs only in the hour of sunrise."

I left the seat. The girl gave me a nervous glance, then gathered her courage and sat in it. After a moment, she stood up.

"A man who stayed in this enclosure and sat upon this seat every morning for a year would have all the wisdom of this world, and countless other worlds, at his command," I murmured.

"We can't stay here," Martala objected. "Don't you feel it? This place hates us. It wants to kill us."

I would have laughed, had I not struggled against the same conviction since entering the enclosure.

"There's no need to stay here. All the power of the wisdom seat is contained in this one jewel. If we take the jewel with us, we will possess the power of the seat whenever we wish to use it."

She regarded the ruby with doubt.

"It may not work without the chair."

"The chair is only carved stone. We can have another fashioned similar to it when we reach a place of civilization. I will remove the jewel and its setting of gold. Even if we cannot make the ruby function as it does in the chair, it is worth the wealth of a kingdom."

Drawing my dagger, I applied its sharp tip to the heavy rim of gold that formed the setting for the jewel. I did not wish to damage it, but intended to remove it from the brown stone of the chair's back intact or in pieces. It resisted the point of the steel blade with unnatural toughness. Perhaps it was not gold at all, but merely a metal that resembled gold.

As I felt the setting shift in the stone the merest trifle, a darkness covered the sky. Martala screamed. I stepped back from the chair and looked heavenward.

The sky gaped opened at the zenith as though torn, its blue parted to reveal the black of night beyond. Through this unnatural aperture descended a thing of nightmare of the kind that the mind refuses to confront, but mercifully blots from memory at the moment of waking. Seen without the protective oblivion of sleep, there was no escape from its horror.

The body of the thing appeared that of a woman, but a second look revealed its mockery of the human form. Myriad translucent streamers grew not only from her narrow head but from her naked shoulders and back, spreading outward in all directions to wave with sinuous grace as plants dance in the sea, in continual motion, changing with bright colors. They spread so wide that they covered the sky and seemed to draw warmth from the air itself. Her feet were like the talons of a hawk bent to clutch its prey. How many arms she possessed I could not count. They were many, and long, but their unceasing movement made their number uncertain. From her fingers grew slender filaments black in color.

Her face held an expression of fury. In her high forehead was set a single enormous eye, its midnight center glittering with stars. When she parted her lips, the air trembled with her cry. Streamers of light expanded from her open mouth, and on their tips formed droplets of flame. These fell like burning oil. In moments the entire sky filled with points of flame.

Awareness of our immediate peril came to me and to the girl at the same moment. She stared at me with terror, but seemed to gather strength from my eyes.

"Tie on your wallet. Quickly."

My words were almost lost on the shrieks that rent and shivered the sky. I glanced upward. Each cry of the monster sent a thousand additional streamers erupting from her mouth, dripping with fire.

"Leave the cursed sleeping rug. Get your sword."

Without waiting to see if she understood my words, I ran off the bridge and along the southern bank of the brook toward the black wall. The girl was close behind, and in a dozen paces she passed me. Something touched my cheek and burned like an ember from a fire. Another similar pain stabbed my shoulder through my cloak, and I smelled the stench of my burning hair. The girl's head and back were soon covered with points of flame that did not extinguish themselves, but continued to blaze with the vigor of burning sulfur. Smoke streamed from her green felt hat as she ran.

Before we crossed half the distance to the wall, tiny flames covered the grass of the meadow. They burned brighter the longer they rested there. As more and more fell, they began to link together. The grass itself was burning now, and giving off plumes of gray smoke that danced in the morning breeze. Even through the leather soles of my boots I felt the heat. I did not dare turn my head, but the glare of the guardian of the wisdom seat on my back was as tactile as the flames, and pressed nearer with each of my steps.

When Martala reached the pool of dark water at the base of the wall, the little fool turned to wait for me. Her wide pale eyes went past me and upward, and she became motionless in her terror. I did not pause, but opened my arm and caught her to my chest as I dove into the swirling vortex.

Chapter 44

Neither of us had time to draw a deep breath. The water felt blissfully cool and soothed the pains of my burns. The current carried us forward. I felt a jut of stone bruise my shoulder, and scattered pebbles under the kicking toes of my boots. The girl I kept beneath my arm. She clawed at the water and helped to draw us along by pulling at the rocks on the sides and bottom of the passage. Something hard and flat grated against my head. I pushed downward from it and kicked more strongly.

The passage narrowed and the rush of the water quickened, so that it would have been impossible to resist even had we wished to turn back. The darkness became absolute. Only the current provided a sense of direction. My lungs began to ache. The yearning to breathe grew so powerful, I could not resist drawing small amounts of water in through my nose, although I kept my lips tightly locked. I felt the girl convulse against my chest, and knew that she had tried to breathe.

My head broke the surface in a black space, and I coughed and gasped simultaneously. We were in some kind of cave beneath the hills. I turned all around but of light there was no trace. I fought to touch the bottom with my feet, then thrust against it to lift the girl upward. She sputtered and drew a whoop of air. The flow of the stream carried us gently along as we held each other and regained our breath. It was shallow enough that my feet touched the bottom from time to time, even though my legs were bent at the knees.

There was no way to estimate how long we floated in absolute darkness on that icy stream, pressed and rolled over the rocks of the passage by its varying force. Where the way narrowed, the water flowed more swiftly and became impossible to resist. I soon discovered that it was best not to fight the current, but to yield to it, taking care only to avoid with outstretched hands any jutting points of stone that might project from the walls or roof. We spoke little. The swirling water filled our mouths when we opened them. At times we suffered acute terror, when the roof lowered so much that no space for breath remained. These sections of the underground water course were mercifully few and of no great length.

I began to fear that the stream had no outlet, but flowed ever deeper into the subterranean world. It was with joy of heart that I glimpsed a glow of light reflecting from the rocks through the clear water. Martala cried out when she saw it, so great was her relief. In minutes the stream vomited us forth into the rocky plain at the base of a range of steep hills.

We climbed from its depths on hands and knees and lay unmoving on the stones, content to allow the sunlight to warm our numbed limbs. My body shivered uncontrollably, so much so that when I threw off my cloak and tried to unbind my belt, my hands were not equal to the task. The girl shook in the same way. When I found the strength, I rolled toward her and gathered her into my arms to share my warmth with her. She pressed her face into the sodden shoulder of my tunic, and I realized from the heaves of her back that she sobbed in silence.

For a time I slept. When my awareness returned, the shivering of my flesh had ceased. I sat up. The rays from the sun, high in the heavens, had driven out most of the water from my clothing. The girl stood naked beside her outspread green cloak, hat, and other garments, regarding the contents of her travel wallet. She turned to me with a rueful smile.

"I dropped my sword and dagger in the caverns."

"No matter. We can buy others with the smallest of those pieces of amber."

With efficient motions I stripped off my boots and tunic, setting them where the sun would deprive them of dampness. Unlashing the front pocket of my wallet, I took up the scroll of the Old Ones and unrolled a portion of it with great care. I expected to discover a solid pulpy mass, but the water had done no damage that I could see. The inks were of a type that resisted moisture, and the papyrus needed only to be dried to restore its original strength. I did not attempt to unroll more of it, but left it exposed on the rocks to sun and breeze.

To my surprise, I found myself growing cheerful. True, my body ached from a dozen bruises, and showed red patches where the droplets of flame had settled on my skin or burned holes through the shoulders and back of my cloak, but I was still alive, and the contents of our wallets had suffered little loss. The salt cellar was impervious to dampness, the tinderbox could be dried, the salted meat and dried fruit had not greatly noticed their bath, other than a slight softening. I put a fig in my mouth and chewed thoughtfully as I turned the stripped silk rag that held the white spiders so that its underside would catch the air.

"What was the thing that attacked us?" Martala asked. "Did the sage write about it?"

"Not a word. I doubt Ibn Schacabao ever saw the wisdom seat with his own eyes. He probably heard some traveler's tale of it repeated in the tavern."

"Do you think it will pursue us?"

I shook my head.

"It is the guardian of the jewel. It will never leave it merely for the pleasure of killing us."

When the sun finished its work, we dressed and set off through the rising columns of heated air that shimmered like transparent fountains above the irregular plain. We passed a decayed pyramid on our left near the horizon, but I had no inclination to investigate its dismal heap of scattered bricks.

My spirits were strong. We had survived the valley and emerged from it greatly enriched, with only a few burns that would heal in a week or two. The damage the fire and underground stream had done to our clothing, coupled with my burnt hair and the sear marks on our faces, made us resemble beggars, but in this uninhabited land we suffered no criticism. My water skin hung full and our wallets held enough food to carry us across to the Tigris. The scroll of the Old Ones, once again banging against my chest in the front pocket of my wallet, had been improved by its dunking, as the waters had removed some of the dust and finger marks from its surface.

When our shadows lengthened before us and the air ceased to dance like the blast from a blacksmith's forge, Martala began to sing one of her Egyptian folk songs that I had come to know well. I joined in harmony, and the notes of the ancient tune floated across the baked clay and tangled stone-choked gullies to startle the desert foxes, who stopped running and stared at us with their enormous ears upraised and turned toward us like fans.

We made camp at twilight. One place seemed as good as another in that broken but monotonous landscape. I chose a flat slab of stone elevated several cubits above the plain, on the consideration that its warmth would be welcome when the chill of night descended full upon us. There was not enough wood to make a fire, even had the tinder in my tinderbox dried sufficiently to attempt to ignite a spark. Our sleeping rugs were still on the bridge, and would no doubt puzzle the next traveler who sat upon the wisdom seat, should another man ever have the misfortune to do so.

By morning the rock had cooled, and we woke shivering. It was not long before the rising sun heated our faces. The quality of the land began to change in slow stages, becoming greener as we continued our trek eastward. In low-lying hollows the grass-covered ground was soft beneath my boots, betraying water not deep beneath the surface. Here and there, groves of trees cast cool patches of shadow. Martala welcomed the growing things that reminded her of the lushness of her homeland, but I looked upon their gathering density with disapproval. They made walking more difficult, and with moist earth and green plants came the inevitable swarms of biting flies that are one of the plagues of humanity.

They seemed to enjoy the taste of my sweat. For some reason the girl was less afflicted by them.

With a curse, I swatted my neck for the third-score time and glared across at her. Not a single bead of moisture clung to her serene brow beneath the brim of her felt hat, her skin white as milk after its bath in the stream.

"Why is it that these devils bite me and not you?" I asked, unable to restrain myself any longer.

She smiled, and I saw that my discomfort was a source of amusement for her. She raised her hand with its back to me and wiggled her fingers to draw my attention to the points of her fingernails.

"They are obedient to the Goddess. The Goddess watches over me and protects me from those creatures that worship her."

Her words, or perhaps her good humor, made me scowl. I had not renewed the glamour of my face, so my expression must have been truly horrifying. Her explanation displeased me, but I could conceive no other reason why the flies would bite me and not her, so I said nothing, but merely brooded on the injustices of the world.

When we came upon the northern end of a vast lake, the breeze that blew across the water and drove the swarms that had followed us for miles back into the trees was like a blessing from heaven. A small fishing village occupied a headland to the east. The white triangular sails of its boats dotted the expanse of blue water, and I saw a distant flash of silver as a fisherman cast his net over the side of one vessel. The air to the south was thick with flocks of water fowl, flying and diving in unison as though with a single mind. The expanses of green reeds along the margin of the lake provided ideal homes for such birds. I had seen similar flocks in Egypt on the delta of the river, but none so large as these.

We approached an ancient fisherman sitting beside his upturned boat, mending his net. From time to time he raised his head from his bone needle to observe our progress along the shore. I had completely forgotten my face, but the whisper of the girl reminded me. I turned as though to look behind and applied the spell. The old man's eyesight was poor enough that he failed to notice the change. When we drew nearer, I hailed him and asked if he knew the location of a monastery of wise men.

His Persian was so corrupt, the linguistic skills of Nectanebus were nearly unequal to the task of translation.

"You mean the Order of the Sons of Sirius," he said, squinting at me. "Everyone knows them in this land. They buy our fish and give us fair prices. They are honorable men, every one of them, and great warriors."

Once started in conversation, he was difficult to stop. I listened with what patience I could muster to his babbling. When he paused for breath, I turned to Martala.

"He says the fortress of the magi lies to the east, nearly a day's brisk walking from his village," I interpreted for Martala. "There is a road, but not a very good road."

"Perhaps we can buy horses in his village."

I surveyed the shabby cluster of huts, half of them built on posts so that they hung over the shallows of the lake, and shook my head.

"What use would poor fishermen have for horses?"

The old man confirmed my surmise. Neither horse nor camel were to be had in his village. There was a man who owned a donkey, and for gold he might be persuaded to part with it, even though its loss would break the heart of his wife, who regarded the beast as fondly as though it were her own child.

"I don't believe we will cause the woman grief," I said to the girl as we continued our way toward the village. "What use is a donkey to us, when we have nothing for it to carry?"

"It is better than walking," she murmured. She was in an argumentative humor.

"One donkey?"

"We could take turns riding."

"Have you ever ridden a donkey? I'd rather be beaten on the buttocks with a club."

She stopped and put her hands on her hips, and I almost felt sorry for having spoken.

"I have ridden many donkeys. What of you, O resident of the royal palace of Sana'a? Have you ridden a donkey?"

I brushed her question aside with my hand.

"Anyone can see to look at the creatures that their legs are too short to be of use for riding. We could walk with greater ease."

She made a sound of derision in her throat.

It was true, the royal hunting expeditions of the king had not involved donkeys, nor were they stabled at the palace, and my direct experience with the creatures was limited. My father had been too poor to own such a beast. I turned over my words in my mind, looking for weakness in my argument, but it appeared no more than reasonable.

Even so, I found myself haggling behind one of the huts situated on dry land over the purchase of a beast so old, it threatened to collapse on its trembling knees before my business could be concluded. A fat woman of middle age sobbed and caressed the hairy nose of the donkey as she watched with wide eyes her avaricious husband demand more gold. At first I tried to rent the donkey, which pleased the woman, but the sneering owner refused, saying there was no one to bring the beast back when I finished with it. My promise to hire a boy to ride the donkey home did not satisfy him, and I perceived that he wished to sell it merely to spite his wife, so I paid his price.

I wondered if the peasants of this disagreeable land saved all of their sickest and most ancient beasts of burden to sell to travelers. I had no intention of wasting another piece of precious *u'mal* root on this infirm creature. If it dropped dead beneath the girl, so much the better. It would teach her to mind her tongue.

We bought a small bag of salted fish and some flat loaves of unleavened bread. The girl searched for a dagger all over the village, but the fishermen only possessed fishing knives and could not by any argument be persuaded to part with them for a reasonable exchange. I refused her request that I bribe them with amber. It was too precious to waste. Instead, to sooth her mind, I gave her my dagger. She seemed content to have its ornate ivory sheath belted to her waist.

She made little argument when I insisted that she ride. Her feet almost brushed the ground on either side of the narrow rut that served as the road mentioned by the old fisherman. To my surprise, the beast did not fall dead, but plodded along at a walking pace, making little complaint. Several times through the afternoon, Martala offered to give up her seat to me, but the prospect of bouncing along on the bony spine of the beast did not appeal. I declined with what grace I could manage and attempted to ignore the ache in my legs. The progress of the animal was quicker than the pace I would have chosen for myself.

By the time we reached plowed fields and heard the lowing of cattle in their pastures, darkness had almost descended around us. We climbed a low rise and stopped upon the crest. I saw that we had entered the bend of a broad river that could only be the Tigris. It wrapped its crescent course around extensive farmlands before continuing its journey southward. Trees and brush grew densely along its banks and defined its channel to the horizon.

A thousand paces would bring us across the fields to the outskirts of a well-populated village of flat-roofed buildings located near the river at the head of the bend. Many of the houses stood taller than a single level, and were of more elaborate construction than the usual hovels of country folk. Behind them loomed the wall of a fortress of impressive dimensions. It appeared gray in the gathering twilight. I saw a sentry with a bow slung over his shoulder, no larger than an ant in the distance, walk along its battlements between two square towers that stood at its corners.

"That must be where the wise men keep their school," Martala murmured, pale eyes wide with interest.

"It is larger than I expected, and uncommonly well defended for a place of learning."

"Let us go and look at it," she said in an eager voice.

I caught her arm before she could strike the flank of the donkey with her switch. For several minutes, I stood in silent thought.

"We will walk around the fortress and examine it. Stay in the shadows and keep your head bowed. Say nothing to anyone."

My serious mood banished her bright spirits. We went forward at a modest pace. A dog began to bark, and another, and then another. I expected a group of villagers to confront us as we passed down a cart track between the houses, but the barking was ignored. The reason became apparent as we rounded the southern side of the fortress and approached the river. Several inns occupied the road, which became paved with well-cut flat stones beneath our feet. The passage of strangers must be a nightly occurrence.

An impressive system of docks stretched along the buttressed bank of the river, piled high with cargo from numerous boats tied against its side. On the broad paved plaza that occupied the space between the docks and the east-facing gates at the front of the fortress, dozens of brightly clothed men and women walked and conversed. It was a kind of open marketplace, and the sellers were just closing their stalls for the evening. We attracted no particular attention as we moved along the edge of the docks with our heads bowed, keeping our distance.

We continued around to the corner. I was struck by the contrast between the two sides of the fortress. The inns under the southern wall were respectable establishments in which to sleep and eat, but on the north side a scattering of poorer structures hugged the shadow at the base of the wall, and I saw that several of them were the huts of harlots. Loud laughter and the babble of voices issued from the open doorway of a wine seller. The men who staggered past us, leaning on each other for support, ignored us. Some had the look of farmers, others were boatmen, while a few appeared by their rich clothing to be prosperous merchants or travelers. Near the bank of the river I could see and smell piles of garbage, the detritus of this thriving community.

A woman left her lighted doorway and approached Martala, thinking her a young man. She ignored me. No doubt she thought me a slave or servant, since I walked on the opposite side of the donkey. Only the poor walked. Had she been able to clearly see the disreputable condition of our robes in the growing murk, she might have ignored both of us. She babbled in Persian, and when Martala made no response other than to glance at her, she pulled open the top of her red dress and exposed her naked breasts, then cupped them in her hands and squeezed them, laughing. Her teeth were not good.

Martala made a gesture with her left hand that carried universal meaning. The harlot stepped back as though slapped and spat on the ground, then covered herself and returned to her doorway.

We went on to the end of the wall and passed between the more honest dwellings of the village before making our way into the fields. Behind a grove of nut trees we stopped, and the girl dismounted from the donkey. She tried to conceal her relief and rubbed her buttocks when she thought my eyes looked elsewhere. It was some consolation that her backside ached as much as my legs, but I drew no attention to it.

"There are more people here than I expected," she said.

"Indeed. This is a prospering port. The fortress must provide protection against bandits and river raiders."

"Did you notice the two guards at the gate?"

"They were wearing armor. Chain mail shirts over their tunics, and steel helmets. The Sons of Sirius must keep their own army."

"They must be wealthy."

The same thought had occurred to me. The signs of wealth were everywhere. The dockside exhibited good repair, and this could only be achieved by constant maintenance. Several cargos unloaded from the boats were costly trade goods of silks, ivory, and sandalwood. The merchants I had seen in the plaza and coming out of the ale house wore their prosperity on their backs, and their heads—their turbans were enormous. I had no taste for such ostentatious display. It was my own view that ten additional cubits of silk wrapped around the head denoted a fool.

"Perhaps they throw open the gates during the day."

I shook my head, lost in thought. The guards had been too watchful. These were prudent men, these magi. Gaining entry into the walls of the monastery might prove more difficult than I had imagined.

Through the deepening gloom I studied the ground beneath the trees. The dry grass had not recently been grazed.

"We will sleep here tonight. Tomorrow we will attempt to breach the walls of their keep."

How this was to be accomplished, I had no notion. Perhaps the dark man would visit me in my dreams and offer me the key to the gate, I thought wryly. He had been anxious that I should learn the secrets of the magi, but silent as to how this was to be accomplished. No matter, my own purposes required that I gain access to their library. That was spur enough to my imagination.

I woke in the glow of morning with no memory of dreams, and the scent of fresh dung in my nostrils. Our donkey had chosen to relieve itself, and the girl had tied it too near our sleeping place. It was fortunate that its rope was not longer. Slapping the girl on the rump through her cloak to wake her, I cut short her curses with a finger to my lips.

"We must find a place to conceal our wealth before the village wakes," I told her.

Leaving the donkey to browse the dewy grass, we walked far enough past the fields to be reasonably assured that the spot we chose was seldom traveled. I emptied our wallets and shifted all the precious items into my wallet. This I hid beneath the overhang of a large rock, where there was a small gap of shadow. Our food and common items I pressed into the girl's wallet until it bulged, and gave it to her to sling on her shoulder. The ground showed little sign of our passage. I was satisfied that I would recognize the place again without difficulty by day or night, but that no one else would see that we had been there.

"Belt this to your waist," I said, passing her my sword in its scabbard.

"What is this all about?" Martala murmured in a surly tone as she put on my sword. She did not like being kept in ignorance.

My mind still working, I made my way with swift strides to the donkey while the girl trailed after me with a pout, and untied the rope from around its neck. When I retied it around my own neck, she looked at me as though I had suddenly gone mad.

"I am your feeble-witted older brother," I told her. "You must lead me by this rope to prevent me doing injury to myself."

"Indeed?" She put her hands on her hips. "How came this misfortune?"

"As a child of three I was kicked by a donkey, and ever since I have been unable to speak, or make any sounds other than a kind of braying. Like this."

I demonstrated what I considered to be the noises of a madman. The girl smiled in spite of herself.

"I can feed myself and perform simple work, but I drool and I cannot be trusted to cut my nails or clean my own anus."

She frowned.

"Surely you are not that feeble of mind?"

"Yes, I fear I am. You must be with me at all times to assist me in such necessary functions. But you do not mind, because you promised our father before he died that you would always take care of me."

"Where do we come from, and why are we here?"

"Good questions. I wonder if the truth would serve?"

"I have never known it to do so," she said simply.

"Nor have I."

503

I cast my eyes eastward. The sun was just rising above the lip of the world. It lit the wall of the fortress with red light, and I observed that the wall was composed of clay bricks. Never had I known a land so fond of bricks.

"We are from Alexandria. You were forced to flee with me out of Egypt when your uncle sought my life, as the rightful inheritor of our father's fortune. You had reason to believe that you would find security at Baghdad, where dwelt the father of our dead mother, but recently you learned that he had succumbed to a lingering sickness." I stopped and regarded her face. "Too complex?"

"No." She mused a moment. "Why aren't we rich?"

"Pirates stole what little gold we could carry away from our wicked uncle. They tortured me until you told them where it was hidden aboard the ship, and disfigured me, and deprived me of my manhood. Now we make our way with only the clothes on our backs and this sorry animal, which we purchased with our last bronze fil."

"It is plausible. A little romance is useful when spinning a tale. It occupies the mind."

I unfolded the few remaining scraps of my plan to her as we made our way toward the gates of the fortress by way of its northern side, she upon the donkey, tugging me at the end of my rope. Several farmers and their wives glanced at us curiously as we passed through the village, but they recoiled when they saw my face. I projected my tongue at the corner of my mouth and made braying noises in my throat.

"Tell me if I overact," I whispered to the girl.

She jerked the rope and choked me, struggling to suppress her amusement.

As we had agreed, she rode across the plaza and dismounted next to a stone post that stood beside a round stone basin filled with water. She tied the tattered bridle of the beast to an iron ring of the post. A horse stood tied to another of the rings. It ignored the donkey with a sublime display of indifference borne of its own sense of superiority. Tugging me along at the end of my own tether, Martala went to watch the merchants open their stalls.

I took a little wooden bowl from my belt and began to perform the part of a fool. My antics attracted a small group of village children who had no better occupation while their parents prepared their farm wares for sale. To my surprise, they were not mean of spirit. They merely stared at me in wide-eyed fascination, and laughed when I made faces at them. A little girl, who could not have been older than five years, was so terrified of my face, she remained hidden behind the body of her older brother the whole time, hugging his waist, and peeked at me through the space beneath his armpit.

From time to time, a passing merchant or boatman dropped a bronze fil into the wooden bowl between my hands. When this happened, Martala immediately removed the coin and thanked the charity of the giver. I smiled with vacant delight and bobbed my head in the imitation of a bow, making noises as though attempting to speak.

When the sun rose well above the horizon, and the plaza began to bustle with buyers and sellers intent on their own business, a small door no taller than the entrance door of a house opened in the left iron-bound panel of the main gate of the fortress. A young man of my own age or less, dressed in the white turban and white robe of a scholar yet wearing a sword belted at his waist, emerged and made his way toward two rows of stone benches beneath a spreading shade tree, on the side of the plaza away from the noise of the market where perhaps a dozen men and two women sat waiting. All had fat purses, to judge by their fine clothing and freshly oiled hair. I had watched them gather with curiosity, having no notion of their purpose, but it soon became apparent they were students.

He began to declaim to them in Greek concerning Aristotle's *History of Animals*, walking up and down before the benches, quoting long passages in the work of the Stagirite from memory, and emphasizing his points with gestures of his hands. At times he paused to allow his pupils to ask questions. He engaged in dialogue with them, but his tone remained unemotional, almost detached, as though he knew the topic so well, it no longer had the power to challenge his mind.

All this while, men exited from the small door to transact business with merchants or to purchase food stuffs from the stalls, counting out dinars or dirhams into the eager palms of those who waited for their appearance. I observed that at no time did anyone pass into the gate who had not already emerged from it. The sages carried through the doorway their own baskets of fish, eggs, and other provisions, and used wheeled carts to convey cut firewood into the compound from a stack that had been erected at no great distance from the wall by those selling it.

At any instant there might be a dozen men from the fortress in the plaza, not including the two guards who stood like stone images with their pikes perfectly upright. Some were dressed as warriors, wearing conical helmets on their heads and chain mail vests over their tunics, or even breastplates, while others wore the long white robes of scholars, yet even the scholars carried weapons. I did not see one who lacked a sword at his belt.

Martala drew me away from the stalls and nearer the benches, feigning an interest in the lesson. In this, we were not alone, for a scattering of merchants and other travelers idling in the plaza gathered around behind the benches to hear the words of the young teacher. I was not assured from the expressions of their faces that every one of them comprehended the subject, or indeed the Greek tongue itself, but they remained respectfully silent, a tribute to the inherent dignity of the speaker. The women hearers appeared particularly impressed. He was a handsome youth, almost as attractive as I had been, with curling black hair and lustrous brown eyes, but his narrow chin and small mouth made his face both sensual and weak.

During a pause longer than usual, Martala hazarded a question. The young scholar blinked at her in surprise, impressed by the intelligence of her inquiry, or by the excellence of her Greek, perhaps both. He glanced at me and I stuck out my tongue at him. This ruffled his dignity though he strove not to show it. He gave the girl an excellent answer and went on with his teaching, from time to time casting her an appraising glance.

When the lesson concluded, the seated pupils gathered close to him and, with a word or two of praise for his work, put coins into a silver cup that he held out. I reflected that he and I were in the same profession, but that his coins were silver, whereas mine were bronze. Some of those who had stood listening behind the benches also came forward and placed dirhams of the smallest size into his cup.

Perceiving an opportunity, Martala gave a little tug on my rope and went forward to drop into his cup one of the bronze fils I had begged.

"If I could offer more I would do so," she said in a modest tone, her head lowered. "Never have I heard such wisdom spoken so well."

His serious expression softened. He removed the fil from the cup and held it out to her.

"I can see that you need this more than my order. Please, do not impoverish yourself. Use it to buy a loaf of bread."

Martala lifted her head with pride.

"I was not always poor. Do not deprive me of what little dignity remains in my life."

What else could the scholar do, but ask for the story of her life? She told it without enhancement, as though ashamed of its details, and with such conviction that I almost believed it myself. I had to remind myself to grunt and drool, I was so captivated by her artfulness. She added details that I would never have conceived to make our implausible tale more convincing. When she came to the part about the pirates, the young sage turned to study my face and shook his head.

"A double tragedy, that your brother should have been deprived of sense at so young an age, and then had his beauty stolen as well. My heart sorrows for your fate, but we derive strength from our misfortunes, and I see that you are a boy of brave spirits."

For the next six days, we made ourselves at home in the marketplace during the day, and slept in the woods beyond the fields at night. On the second day Martala sold the donkey to a farmer for less than a tenth of what I had paid for the beast. This allowed us to buy what we needed of fresh food and drink from the vendors without arousing suspicion. I continued to dance and crawl on all fours, and my wooden bowl seldom went empty. Travelers passed through the port daily, moving with the boats up or down the river, so there was always a new audience. I began to enjoy my antics. Success in my deception was determined by how many coins I received.

Each day, Martala listened to the lessons beneath the tree. Several members of the order, all of them young and beardless, taught various subjects such as mathematics and rhetoric. I discovered that some of the regular students had traveled from far lands to sit at their feet. At the end of the lesson the girl never failed to place her pathetic bronze fil into the silver cup, although she never sat on a bench but always stood respectfully at the back.

On the seventh day, the first scholar she had addressed, who bore the heroic name Baruch, smiled at her as he accepted her offering.

"You must accompany me into the monastery. I have told my brothers about you, and your thirst for knowledge, and our leader Rumius wishes to speak with you."

Chapter 45

The timbers that composed the great gate were cedar beams of impressive thickness, I observed as we were escorted through the small door by Baruch. Even the little door itself was secured behind us by four heavy iron bars that ran completely across it from one side to the other, making it as strong as any other part of the gate. It would take a siege ram to batter it down.

As we left the entrance a line of men, some young and others of middle years, ran past with heavy packs on their bare backs. They grunted and laughed with effort, arms and sides glistening with sweat. A man in a helmet and chain mail vest stood to one side and encouraged their steps with a short whip having many leather tassels on its end. At first glance I mistook them for slaves. Then I realized they were monks exercising their bodies. Further away, pairs of men engaged in swordplay under the watchful eye of a gray-haired teacher, and others who were completely naked wrestled in the Greek fashion, by using only the arms and upper body, within circles of packed red clay.

There was more open space inside the walls of the monastery than I had expected, most of it closely mowed grass shaded by overspreading trees and crossed by numerous paved paths, with here and there a stone bench for sitting. On the nearest bench, a bearded elder watched our progress with an expression of mild curiosity. The entry of those not of his order must have been an uncommon event. I let my gaze wander, impressed by the splendor of the place, which would rival the walled garden of an emperor.

Three great buildings dominated the enclosure. The largest was made of stone, and occupied the northern side. In its upper two levels, glass windows with many tiny panes caught the sunlight and glittered. Two wings extended outward like the paws of a reclining lion, so that between them was formed a small courtyard paved with red sandstone blocks that held at its center the bronze statue of a slender woman. Naked to the waist and bearing as a crown the horns of the crescent moon, she stood with proud posture upon a stone pedestal, one arm elevated as though to pluck something from the sky. She evoked an echo in my memory that eluded me when I sought to recall it.

The many small shuttered windows in the great brick edifice to the west gave it the look of a dormitory. The lack of pretension in its architecture suggested that it had been built to house the largest possible number of inhabitants. Indeed, it was an ugly building, its rust-colored facade stained with streaks of soot that rain had washed off the flat roof. It did not press its back against the wall, but stood out from it a considerable distance. A tall board fence enclosed the space behind it. I heard the lowing of a cow beyond the fence, and my unglamoured nose caught the distinct scent of stewed cabbage. The kitchens that would feed so many men must be extensive.

The noise of hammers beating on metal sounded from the smaller building against the southern wall. As we continued across the lawn, I noticed columns of black smoke coil upward from its many chimneys. It was of mixed construction, its ground level of roughly dressed stone, its upper two levels of heavy timbers. Small fired bricks glazed with blue and green filled the spaces between the timbers. Windows were few and of small size, their carved screens all fastened wide to catch the breeze.

At the side of this foundry, as it seemed to be by the racket that emanated through its open windows, a group of archers wearing white robes shot arrows at straw targets made in the shape of men. They used black bows of a design unknown to my experience, and larger than any bows I had ever seen, that sent the long black arrows completely through the targets and deep into tightly bound bales of straw piled behind them. I stopped to watch in amazement the power of the bows, until Martala gave a short jerk on the rope around my neck to remind me of my idiocy.

We were led past the statue of the curiously familiar goddess, through a double door sheathed in hammered brass. The hall within was floored with polished red marble. Gleaming columns of a similar stone stood at intervals, supporting the upper floors. Monks passed us silently in their soft-soled shoes, bearing scrolls in their arms, intent on their own affairs. In spite of their discipline, they could not refrain from a curious glance. I tilted my disfigured face to display the drool on my chin. Their composure never wavered, and I was surprised to see compassion in their eyes.

Ascending a broad marble staircase to the second level landing, we went down a hallway on the left paneled from floor to ceiling in dark wood. The rooms on either side occupying the main body of the building were filled with shelves of books greater in number than I had ever seen gathered in a single place. I realized that this enormous pile of stones was a library, and my mind reeled. There must be more books under its roof than could be found in the entire city of Alexandria, the book mart of the world.

We turned the corner into the west wing, and I saw that on this level it was given over to smaller rooms with desks and tables, at which monks read, wrote, or conversed in small groups. Many doors were closed for privacy. Our guide stopped at one such door and knocked on its panel so softly, I barely heard the raps. A sonorous male voice on the other side gave permission for him to enter.

The room proved to be a private study. A Persian carpet of no great size occupied the center of the waxed floorboards. Books stood in shelves against two walls. Small oblongs of slanting sunlight from the glazed window in the east-facing wall, which overlooked the courtyard, dappled a desk of ornately carved blond wood, illuminating scattered parchments that almost covered its broad surface.

The black-robed man seated behind the desk did not look up until he finished the sentence he wrote. I saw that the language was Arabic, but could not read the inverted script. His long hair and flowing beard, both the color of sun-bleached cotton, combined with a prominent Greek nose to give his head a noble aspect, like that of a biblical patriarch. He set aside his goose quill and gazed at Baruch with keen blue eyes.

"These are the men I told you about, Rumius," said the young monk in Greek. "This is Amed ibn Anas of Alexandria, and his unfortunate older brother Idi."

Martala nodded when the name she had chosen for herself was spoken, but I merely lolled my head to one side with my lips parted, the way a dog will perk its ears when it hears a familiar word.

He stood and came around the desk to study us. His pale eyes pierced so deeply into mine that I found it difficult to maintain my vague expression. He was almost a giant of a man, at least a head taller than me, with a back perfectly straight. When he extended his hand, I saw loose threads hanging from the sleeve of his worn black robe and stains of dry ink on his long fingers.

He gathered my hand gently into his own and held it.

"It is as you said, Baruch. A great tragedy."

At the urging of Rumius, Martala told the same story she had given the young monk, changing only as many minor details as would serve to make it more plausible. She was wise enough in the ways of deception to realize that no man told the story of his life twice in exactly the same manner. Rumius listened with interest, now and then expressing sympathy or asking a question. His questions were calculated to reveal deception, particularly those concerning the city of Alexandria, but Martala had learned enough about the city during the period of my resurrection to answer them without pause.

"This young brother tells me that you have an interest in our lessons," he said at length to the girl.

"My own education was cut short by the misfortunes of my family. Yet still I thirst for knowledge."

"A noble thirst. What languages can you speak, other than Greek?"

"Coptic, which is the common language in my country. A little Arabic. A little Latin."

He tested her language skills, and she gave evidence of an ability greater than she had indicated. From the corner of my eye, I saw that Baruch was impressed.

"Can you read and write?"

"I read and write my own tongue and Greek. I can read Latin and Arabic also, but cannot write them."

"But you would like to learn?" he prompted.

"Of course."

He laughed easily.

"Here is one who wants to learn everything," he said to Baruch, who smiled in answer.

"Admission to our order is not easy," he told Martala. "There is a period of probation and study. I am informed that your brother can do simple work, such as sweeping a floor or emptying slops."

"That is so, noble father," she replied.

"Here we have only the names we choose for ourselves when we join the Order of Sirius. I am Rumius within these walls, nothing more."

My heart rejoiced so greatly, I scarce heard his words. We were to be admitted to live within the walls of the monastery. It was more than I had hoped for, though undoubtedly the interest the young monk felt toward Martala accounted in large part for our favorable reception. I realized that the decision to admit us had already been made. Rumius was merely conducting the necessary formalities.

"Tell me, Amed, do you desire to learn the motions of the stars in the heavens, and the secrets of the gods that have been hidden from common men since the dawn of time?"

"Yes, Rumius, with all my heart." Her face glowed with ardor.

He slapped her in good nature on her slender shoulder.

"Baruch will find a room for you and your brother, and will tell you more about our work. This is a time of probation. You are free to decline membership in the order for a full cycle of the moon. You will be bound by a vow not to disclose what you have been shown here, but otherwise you will be allowed to leave the gates at any time during the coming month, if that is your desire. After you take your vow and receive your order name, you cannot leave us except by death. This is necessary to preserve our secrets, which would be dangerous to release into the world at this time in its troubled history. It is needless to add that your brother is not bound by our laws, due to his infirmity of mind."

"Will I be permitted to keep my brother with me always? For I have sworn to protect him."

His face softened.

"We are not an uncharitable order. You are best suited to see to his needs, so naturally he will be permitted to stay with you."

"Then I would like nothing better than to become a brother of your order, like Baruch."

The young monk blushed when she cast her bright gaze full upon him. This was scarcely to be wondered at, for I had seen not a single woman within the walls of the monastery, and Martala made an uncommonly attractive youth. I wondered if the growing affection of the monk, which had served us so well in gaining entrance to this place, would be of use to us in the future.

Baruch led us out the doors of the library and into the sunlight.

"What is that statue?" Martala asked as we passed the bronze figure on its pedestal.

"She is the goddess Ishtar, who reaches up to pluck from the heavens Sirius, the Dog Star. She embodies in her qualities the grace and wisdom we strive to attain, but we do not worship her."

"What then do you worship?"

"Truth. Beauty. Wisdom. Justice. Harmony. We worship all these things and none of them. We have no god or goddess set above us."

I wondered why the armies of Mohammed had spared this place from the sword, for it was obviously a stronghold of infidels. Perhaps they had not had leisure to lay it under siege in their haste to march eastward. Even so, the days of the monastery were numbered, for the Caliph Yazid at Damascus would never tolerate its existence once its barbarous creed became known to him.

The young monk led us across the lawn to the ugly building of red bricks. As I had suspected, it was a dormitory for the brothers of the order. Beyond its modest front door, the main hall was narrow and low of ceiling. We ascended to the third level and the rooms assigned to the newest admissions to the monastery, being the least desirable because of the stairs. The rooms varied little in size or appearance, as I saw through the open doorways we passed. Each was long and narrow, with a bed of no great size, a wash stand, a wall rack for hanging up clothing and towels, a copper pot in the corner for piss, and beneath the single tiny window a small table for study.

I sat on the bed, a look of vacant contentment on my face, and bounced up and down. The thin mattress rustled. Straw. Well, it would hardly have been filled with feathers. Knotted ropes supported it on a simple frame of wood.

Baruch eyed our leather travel wallet, which Martala hung by its broad shoulder strap from the wall rack.

"You should know that once you join the order, all your property and possessions become the common property of the monastery. In your case, this is only a formality. I'm sure you will be permitted to keep your pack and its contents. The other side of the coin is that all new members share equally in the wealth of the order, without distinction of age or social rank."

"Is the order very wealthy?" Martala asked with a charming smile.

"Our greatest wealth is our knowledge." Baruch laughed. "But as to that, we have gold enough for our needs."

The girl's gray eyes lit up at the word like the eyes of a wolf, but she concealed her enthusiasm beneath lowered lashes. So charmed was the monk by her manner, he failed to notice. He stuttered and shuffled his feet, wanting to stay but having little reason to remain with us.

"Nothing is expected of you for the rest of the day," he said at last. "Explore the grounds. A brother will bring new robes and shoes to your room while you are away. Tomorrow I will come for you at first light and escort you through the routine of our lives. It is not difficult to learn."

"Must you leave us?" Martala pouted.

"I have duties," he said with regret. "If you need anything, ask one of the brothers and he will help you."

The nape of his neck burned a bright red as he left the room. Martala shut the door softly after him.

"The fool is in love with you," I murmured, slipping the noose of the rope off my neck with relief. I rubbed my throat. Where the prickly rope pressed, it always itched.

"Nonsense. Really?"

She giggled like an empty-headed maiden, enjoying the thought more than was necessary. I reflected that the monk was uncommonly handsome and well spoken.

"You must tell them that I can work without your presence," I went on. "It will give me greater freedom of movement."

"Of course. You are bewildered by strange places, but once they become familiar, your confusion passes and you can be trusted to do simple tasks on your own."

"I need to get work in the library. That is where the scroll will be that identifies the location of the Well of the Seraph."

She nodded her understanding.

"Did you recognize the figure of the goddess in the courtyard?" she asked.

"No, but it was oddly familiar."

"Well it should have been. It was engraved on one of the golden tablets in the hall of pillars beneath the Sphinx."

I clapped my hands together, more loudly than I intended.

"Of course. That is where I remember it."

One of the tablets had illustrated the fallen pyramid on the plain. Another showed the goddess Ishtar reaching upward to capture the Dog Star. I wondered if all the images on the plates pertained to this ancient land between the rivers, and once again regretted not prying them out of their places.

For the rest of the afternoon we wandered around the compound and visited its buildings. The monks were cheerful but modest in their greetings. They all seemed to know that we were to be admitted to the monastery for a period of probation. As I suspected, the kitchens were located behind the dormitory, and were possessed of their own pens of livestock. Chickens were kept for meat and eggs. Cows were maintained for milk, and were permitted to graze on a part of the lawn out of the way of the exercise of the monks. There was even an ingenious marble bath house large enough to accommodate scores of men at one time. Its water, heated in the undying fires of the kitchens, was diverted to the bath through a series of lead pipes by means of copper pumps.

The water for the monastery came, not from the river as I had supposed, but from a great cistern fed by a perpetual spring in the southwest corner of the grounds. A small but fortified building protected the mouth of the well that gave access to the water. When Martala inquired about it, she was told that the cistern was always full, and that the overflow from the spring was diverted through a culvert to the river. Unlike the sourness of the river water, that drawn from the spring tasted sweet on the tongue. I reflected that with sufficient food in storage, the monks could withstand a siege of many months, or perhaps even years. As I learned by listening to the girl's conversations with various brothers, the monastery had been assaulted by armed forces several times in its long history, but never had it been conquered. The monks regarded it as impregnable.

They had good reason for their confidence. Each was trained with rigorous discipline in the fighting arts, and exercised daily to maintain a fitness of body. Their principal weapon was the great black bow that they made in their workshop—the building of smoking chimneys at the southern wall. They were beautifully lacquered and decorated with filigrees of gold leaf on either side of the wound leather handgrip.

The power of these bows astonished me. One of those engaged in archery practice handed his bow to Martala, but she could only draw it half of the way. The monk assured her that after a few months of practice she would gain the strength to use it. The arrows were almost as long as my arm and finely crafted, yet the storehouse attached to the workshop overflowed with them. I could well believe that four-score of archers ranked along the walls could hold off an attacking army of thousands.

The monks also used the sword and pike, but regarded them as inferior weapons. The ability to strike at a distance with the bow held for them an almost mystical significance. They likened their black arrows to thunderbolts, the weapon of divine judgment in the fables of the Greeks. A monk intimated to Martala that the arrows were intended, not to defend the monastery against any mortal foe, but to fend off the attack of unholy forces. He was about to speak further, but his companions drew him away, as though he had already said too much.

When we retired in the evening, we possessed a better understanding of the monastery buildings and their functions, but had learned almost nothing about the true purpose of the order. That they loved wisdom for its own sake, I did not doubt, but there was something more that drove their relentless quest for perfection in arms.

"We must gain access to their records," I murmured to Martala.

The monks retired early, and the hall outside our closed door was quiet. I did not wish my voice to carry.

"They intend to instruct me in their wisdom. Surely the lessons will be taught in the library," she whispered.

She lay beside me on the narrow bed, naked as I was against the warmth that radiated down from the roof. The shutters of the window stood wide, but little night breeze entered our stifling room. A thin layer of sweat covered my chest, not enough to run down in rivulets but slick to the touch.

"Have you considered what to say about the bath?"

I felt her body stiffen.

"Goddess, no. Alhazred, what am I to do?"

"You cannot bathe with the other monks, that's certain."

We lay considering this problem without voicing a solution until sleep took us.

The dark man came in my dream. I walked at night across the sands of the Empty Space, as I so often did in sleep. The waxing crescent of the moon cast my shadow before me, and the drone of flying beetles filled the air. I heard their gentle buzz all around as they went on their night errands, oblivious to my life. My heart felt peaceful in my breast. I noticed a second shadow beside my own, rippling like an ebony serpent across the ribbed sands, and became aware that the dark man walked beside me on my left side. He had been there for some while, keeping pace with my steps, before I took notice of him.

"You must learn the purposes and plans of the monks," he said in his hollow voice. "That is why I have led you to this place."

"I will learn what I can learn, once my own purpose has been satisfied," I said, greatly daring at my insolence.

"My purpose is your purpose. Without achieving it, you will never know the location of the well."

"You would conceal it from me?" I felt anger rise in my breast. "I am not your slave."

He laughed without malice. My words had not touched his emotions. I was not important enough to arouse his anger. Suddenly he turned and grasped the hem of his cloak, sweeping it over me. I cried out in terror, the cold of it biting through my skin to the bone. When he pulled it away, we stood in a small valley before a low mound of flat stones that was half covered by blowing sands.

"A token of my good faith," he said in a mocking tone. "Here is the well you seek."

I stared around, trying to fix details of the moonlit landscape in my memory, but one hill looked like another, each stone like all other stones.

"Where it is?" I cried. "How can I find it again?"

"Don't expect me to do everything for you without a price, Alhazred. Fulfill my purpose, and you will be led to this well."

"I will do as you say, lord," I told him, my voice shaking with emotion.

Beneath this humble pile of flat stones lay my face, my manhood, my only chance for happiness with the princess Narisa.

A touch on my shoulder woke me. Martala leaned over me with sleep-narrowed eyes.

"You cried aloud," she murmured.

"A dream, nothing more," I said, my heart still hammering in my chest.

The light before dawn illuminated the narrow chamber with gray. It was early, but since we both lay awake, we left the bed and relieved ourselves in the heavy copper pot that occupied the corner, then did our best to wash the sweat from our skin in the wooden basin with the clay pitcher of water and the single small towel on the washstand.

When Baruch knocked on our door, we were both dressed in the new garments that had been left in our room the previous afternoon. They were unadorned white linen robes similar to his own that hung over our bodies almost to our feet. A belt of quilted linen drew them close at our waists and provided support for the sword and dagger worn by the girl. I remained unarmed, since a fool cannot be trusted with a weapon. White turbans wrapped our skulls. Our boots had been exchanged for shoes of soft leather that rose no higher than the bones of our ankles, and tied about our calves with two leather thongs after the manner of Roman sandals. I found this scholar's uniform surprisingly comfortable.

The rising ball of the morning sun painted a rectangle of cinnabar on the wall beside the open door. I squinted at it through our small window while the monk and the girl exchanged their blushing greetings behind my back. Like splashes of fresh blood, the sunlight caught the polished spiked helmets and gilded shoulder-guards of the armored sentries who paced the battlements between the towers, just finishing their final night watch. It spilled across the end of the lawn, and for a moment I had the fancy that each blade of grass had withered to the same rust-colored clay that composed the bricks of the walls.

We were led into a great hall in the ground level of the dormitory, where hundreds of men milled around rows of long tables and matching benches. The hall was not wide, but was one of the longest chambers I had ever seen. Baruch showed us where to sit, at the end of the row nearest the entrance door, among the younger brothers. None were less than sixteen years or older than twenty. At the other end of the hall, where stood an elevated platform, the bearded elders sat at their tables. All brothers might be equal, I reflected, but not all were equally placed at meals.

The food was simple, as might be expected for the early meal of the day, brown bread and a bowl of soup in which floated more vegetables and herbs than pieces of meat. I allowed Martala to feed me, after making an ineffectual attempt to guide the wooden spoon to my lips without aid. A few of the younger brothers shook their heads in sorrow. As we ate, one of the elder monks at the far end of the hall left his table and ascended to the platform, where he began to declaim a lesson in a booming voice that easily carried to my ears, for the monks all fell silent. It concerned the virtue of moderation in all things, and was delivered in Greek, the common tongue of the monastery.

There was no division of the monks at the table by race, only by age. The beards began midway down the hall. Where I sat, the younger members of the order had smooth chins, but the further along I cast my eyes, the longer grew the beards. From their faces, more than half the monks appeared to be Persians. The next most numerous race were Greeks, and after that came a scattering of all peoples. There were a score or so of Egyptians, and even three men of black skin who may have been Nubians.

Rumius sat at the head of one of the tables nearest to the platform. His features were difficult for me to interpret. In part he appeared Persian, but he had the nose and eyes of a Greek, of the type that dwells in the land of Macedonia. At one time his hair may have been golden. The historians say that the descendants of Alexander the Great were scattered across the eastern lands, even to fabled India. I wondered if their blood ran in the veins of this giant of a man, who more than any man I had ever met possessed an indefinable air of divinity.

"In the mornings you will practice with the sword and bow, and exercise your body by running. Then, after your cleansing bath, you will join the other younger brothers in the lesson room, which is located in the lower level of the eastern wing of the library."

Martala stopped on the path and jerked me to a halt beside her with a tug on my rope. Baruch turned with a expression of inquiry. We had been on our way to the library, after finishing our meal.

"I cannot bathe in the bath house," she said.

He smiled with reassurance.

"It is our custom to bathe every morning after exercise. I know it seems strange to those who come from outside, but the water is not harmful. Those who say that bathing causes sickness are mistaken."

"It is not for myself, but for my brother, that I cannot bathe."

I glanced at her from the corner of my eye, wondering what story she would come up with that would excuse her from having to strip naked in the company of three score monks.

"Does your poor brother fear the water?"

"That is it, exactly," she said with a bit too much emphasis. "Ever since the kick of the donkey, he has had an unnatural dread of water."

The monk gazed at me with wonder.

"What you describe is a form of the disease the Greeks call hydrophobia, but I see no signs of this disease in your brother."

"It is not a sickness, only an irrational fear. Watch what happens when I say the word in my own tongue." She spoke the word water in Coptic.

I cried out and covered my head with my hands, staring around with wild eyes, then crouched to the ground as though fearful of being beaten. With soothing words and touches of her fingers, Martala induced me to stand and lower my arms to my sides.

"You see? I must bathe my brother with my own hands, and it has become my custom to wash myself at the same time. This we can do using the wash basin in our room."

The monk was disappointed. He had looked forward to the sight of Martala's nakedness. No doubt they washed each other in the bath house. It would give him the excuse to caress her skin. That he could never be permitted to do, or they would surely put us both to death. I expected him to argue that some other brother could bathe me, but this made so little sense that he held his tongue. We continued on our way toward the library.

"I will show you the lesson room. In the afternoon, you will divide your efforts between copying texts in the scriptorium and manual labor in the workshop. We make all our common tools and furniture with our hands, and even weave our own linen and woolen cloths."

"I know how to use a loom. My cousin was a weaver."

He gave her a curious look.

"An unlikely occupation for the member of a wealthy family."

"It was a diversion for him, nothing more," she said without hesitation. "An eccentric amusement."

After viewing the lesson room, we mounted the marble staircase and continued onward to the third level of the library. The doors along the hallway were shut. A monk came out from one door carrying what appeared to be a collection of brass plates bound together at one edge by rings of wire. I realized that it was a book of some kind, but unlike any book I had ever seen. Over his shoulder I caught a glimpse of tables heaped with oddly shaped scroll cases and books, before he shut the door behind him. We trailed after the silent shoes of this monk.

"This is where we keep our most precious and dangerous texts," he said to Martala. "They are in strange tongues, and are translated into Greek to make them more easily read, and to preserve them from decay. You need not concern yourself with this work. You will be assigned the task of copying the less sensitive of the reports that we receive from all across the world from various agents, so that they are gathered together in a single document for the study of our elders. Once you have passed your period of probation, you may be entrusted with more secret communications."

We followed the monk with the brass book through another small door, and I stopped in wonder, forgetting to play the fool as I gazed around with hungry eyes. Monks sat hunched over long slanted tables, writing on leaves of parchment. At their elbows rested an astonishing collection of books. The leather and wooden spines, bound with green brass or blackened silver, breathed a palpable odor of age. Some were not even books as we know them. I saw a monk copying text from a collection of ivory disks which he drew for the purpose from a leather pouch similar in shape to a money purse. Another transcribed from strips of bark, each as long as his forearm but no wider than three fingers. The characters written on the bark were like none that I had ever seen, nor were they known to the flesh of Nectanebus.

This was the scriptorium of the Order of Sirius, where surely I would discover those secrets that so interested the dark man. Here, too, I might find the directions to the Well of the Seraph and the salvation of my second life.

Chapter 46

The following two months passed with surprising swiftness. In spite of the super-ficially changeless appearance of the monastery, it was a center of ceaseless activity that went on below the surface of the orderly round of day-to-day tasks. Monks were forever dispatched on mysterious errands, some dressed as scholars, other dis-guised to resemble merchants or mercenaries. There was an underlying sense of urgency to this clandestine work, like that of an army preparing for a great battle that pressed upon them.

At the end of Martala's period of probation, she was accepted into the Sons of Sirius with a simple yet dignified ceremony, in which she declared her order name to be Timonius and gave oath that she would willingly accept death should she by mal-ice or error betray its secrets. Rumius presided over the ritual. I was permitted to attend, but my idiocy made me unfit for induction, and I kept my former false name. At the end, Rumius took Martala by the shoulders and kissed her on each cheek. Tears welled from poor Baruch's brown eyes. It was a touching scene. I picked my nose-hole solemnly as I watched and sampled the taste of my finger, until one of the monks swatted me on the back of the head with his hand.

For the first few weeks the monks set me to work cleaning the stables and emp-tying the chamber pots into the long communal outhouse behind the dormitory, where a constant flow of water from the overflow of the spring carried the wastes through an underground passage to the river. They were infinite in their patience, but eventually concluded that I did not possess the wits for such work. I had a distressing tendency to fling manure onto the backs of the horses in the stable, and splash piss down the staircase of the dormitory. To their surprise, I proved adept at the use of a broom, particularly when I was working in the library.

I contrived to spend as much time as possible in the scriptorium, by feigning a simple pleasure in the books. The copyists became accustomed to the sound of my straw broom on the floorboards, and sometimes let me carry piles of books from their benches back to the central table, where they were sorted and filed away. All the books judged important enough to copy were kept on the third level of the library for the sake of convenience. This included strange books from far lands written in languages completely unknown to me. Some of these curious volumes did not appear shaped for the use of human hands.

The acquisition of books was an unending expense for the order. Rumius paid fantastic sums for rare works on philosophy or magic, an eccentricity that was known from the headwaters to the mouth of the Tigris. Every day a few scrolls or bound sets of parchment were acquired in the marketplace from the boat masters, and when a dealer's consignment arrived from Baghdad or some other city, the books were pushed through the little door in the gate piled high on wheelbarrows, like so many turnips.

The brothers grew casual in their acceptance of me, and treated me as they would their own dim-witted kin, with rough kindness. They ignored my presence when they talked amongst themselves, and by leaning on my broom and listening I began to gather an understanding of the true work of the Order of Sirius. They believed themselves a defending army of light that would preserve humanity in a great war of destruction against the forces of darkness. For reasons unclear to me, they were convinced that this conflict was imminent. Hence their zeal to train their bodies and minds before the battle.

Early in the third month, not many days after the new moon, I stood sweeping an open space of the floor of the scriptorium that was so clean, a white towel drawn across it would not have shown a shadow. The room was almost deserted. Most of the monks had descended for the evening meal in the dining hall. In the far corner three bearded monks stood talking, oblivious to my presence. I swept a little closer.

"Rumius knows my opinion," said one. "The weapon of lights will never be powerful enough to destroy the spawn of Cthulhu."

At the name of the Old One, my breath caught in my throat, but they were so intent on their topic they failed to notice the sound.

"The last two experiments put the lie to your words," said the youngest of them with indignation. "A combination of rays was found that burned the hide of that thing in the vault beneath our feet. Smoke arose from its body."

"Yes, but it healed in minutes. It was no more than an irritation to it."

"I stay far away from that thing," the third said darkly. "My mind is not strong enough to resist it."

"No one's mind is strong enough," the elder of the three said. "That is why we take care to never go to it alone, but always in groups of three, so that if it seizes one of us the other two can restrain him. It can only control a single mind at a time."

"It should have been destroyed long ago. It is dangerous to keep it here."

"Dangerous, but necessary," the younger monk said. "How can we combat an enemy we do not understand?"

"I am not certain we could kill it even if we wished," said the elder. "It has the power to reform itself, like the evil demon from which it came."

They left the scriptorium still in heated argument. I set the broom against a bench. This was what I had waited for. The times when the scriptorium emptied were few during the day, and it was not possible to visit it at night without risking discovery since all monks save those with special duties were expected to be within their rooms in the evening hours. Though no watch was set over the dormitory, a few elders always stayed in the library until dawn, studying by the light of lamps. I found the period of the evening meal the best occasion for private research. Attendance at the tables was flexible, but I had only a short time in which to work. Were I to fail to appear for my meal, someone would be sent to look for me.

I went quickly to the cupboard that held the letters of correspondence from the covert agents in the hire of the order. They were in a dozen different languages, from all nations of the world, for the arms of the Sons of Sirius were long, and dispensed dinars the way a farmer scatters golden seed into the furrows of his plowed field. It was one of the tasks of the scribes to translate them into Greek and compile them for the study of Rumius and his senior advisors. They had served as my main source of information concerning the hidden activities of the order, for the monks seldom spoke of secret matters.

I scanned through the documents, picking up a shred of information here, a fragment there, and filing them in my memory for future consideration. The order was particularly strong in Persia, as might be expected, but it also had many agents in Constantinople and Rome, and even in Damascus. One was an advisor to the Caliph, and stood ready to end his life on a word from Rumius. Similar sleeping assassins were placed in other palaces. Had Rumius wished, he could kill half the leaders of the civilized world with the stroke of a pen.

A dirty scrap of papyrus caught my eye. It was from the agent in Yemen, placed within the palace at Sana'a, and was dated only two weeks ago. I smiled when I read the words in Arabic scrawled across its surface, and knew a moment of intense satisfaction:

"Gracious Lord, the work you set me to do in your most recent communication has been accomplished. Let me be the first to inform you of the news that will soon travel throughout the world. King Huban of Sana'a is dead. While conducting his customary walking inspection of the grounds of his palace, he was struck upon the head by a loose tile that dislodged itself from a roof just as he passed beneath it. His personal guard immediately surrounded him and carried him into the throne room to the care of his physicians, but they could do nothing to prolong his life. A search was made of the building from which the tile fell, but it was found to be empty, and no sign of tampering with the roof was discovered. The following day, word of the king's death having spread throughout the palace, the crown prince Yanni declared it an accident of fate and proclaimed himself the new ruler of the land, with the approval of his generals and advisors. His coronation ceremony passed without incident.

"It is undoubtedly an act of divine wisdom that removes from this world so highly placed a worshipper of the Old Ones, for with the temporal power of the throne of Sana'a joined in common with their ancient evil, no wickedness would be beyond contemplation. Your promise of additional payment, made in the coda of your most recent letter, is unnecessary. The Order has been generous. I exist only to serve its holy purpose."

The message was unsigned to ensure the safety of the agent who wrote it, should it be intercepted, but bore a small symbol of identification in its lower corner. These symbols were recorded on a scroll, beside the names of the agents they identified. There were hundreds of them. When an agent ceased to report, his name was crossed out with a pen. New agents were added to the bottom of the scroll with their assigned symbols.

Tearing the papyrus into small fragments, I scattered them behind a bookshelf where, if discovered, they would be dismissed as the gnawings of mice.

Not long after gaining entrance to the monastery, I had discovered the correspondence of this agent, and had on a sudden impulse added a coda to the bottom of the latest communication from Rumius, informing the agent that King Huban was a secret worshipper of the Old Ones. This was wholly untrue. It was my certain knowledge that Huban was a faithful follower of the teachings of the Prophet. The false addendum to the letter of Rumius had been an act of speculation on my part, a casting of bread upon the waters if you will, for I had no way of knowing what the outcome would be. It was gratifying to find it so richly rewarded.

The first occasion I found to talk to Martala came when we prepared for sleep that night within our room.

"What do you know about a weapon of lights?" I murmured. It was necessary to speak in a low voice in the evenings.

She pulled her robe upwards and off her head, then shook out her dark hair, combing it with her fingers. It was a relief for her to let down her hair, since throughout the day it remained tightly coiled beneath her turban.

"Why should I know anything about a weapon?"

"You spend most of your time in the workshop. If a weapon is being constructed, surely that is where they are making it."

"I spend most of my time in a small room on the lower level, seated at a loom. They have me weaving linen cloth."

I made a sound of disgust as I lay on the bed.

"Where's your curiosity? You should know everything that goes on in that soot-shrouded building by now."

"Twice last week I tried to go up the stair," she said, sliding onto the bed beside me. "Both times an elder asked me what business took me to the upper levels, and did I know they were forbidden to all but those monks assigned to work there. It would be dangerous to try a third time."

I related the conversation overheard in the scriptorium.

"They have been talking about lenses a great deal lately," she mused. "How they cannot get the right kind of glass, and the difficulties in coloring it, and how the lenses must be ground and polished."

"See what you can discover tomorrow, but don't take any foolish risks," I told her.

That night, the dark man came to me. We stood in the scriptorium at twilight, when gloom lay piled like folds of transparent black silk in the corners and beneath the tables. He walked around the room, examining everything with mild curiosity mingled with an air of contempt. He pulled a book from a shelf, and I noted that it was a book I had looked into several days before. He read through the secret communications of the agents that I had studied the previous afternoon.

"We are not in the scriptorium," I said with sudden conviction. "We are in my memory of the scriptorium."

For the first time, he turned his hooded shadow of a face toward me.

"What have you learned about the plans of these warrior monks?"

I related the scraps of information I had overheard or read, without adding my own conjectures, which I judged of no interest to Nyarlathotep. He remained indifferent until I spoke of the weapon of lights, and the thing in the vault.

"So it is not dead," he murmured in so low a voice that I barely heard. "You must gain entrance to its prison and examine the bonds that bind it."

"What is this creature?"

He turned and spoke, but for some reason his words failed to reach my ears. Before I could ask again, my eyelids opened on the pale glow of morning. It was the practice of the monks to rise before the sun at first light, in order to extract the most use from the day. For this reason alone I would have felt little fondness for them. I preferred to rise at my leisure, when it suited my own purposes.

After the morning meal I was assigned to sweep the library stairs, as was my usual practice. The scribes that passed up and down with their scrolls and books had grown so accustomed to the sight of me, they barely noticed my presence. I contrived to work my way to the foot of the staircase, and when unobserved, slipped into the east wing past the door of the school room, where Martala and the other young brothers listened to a lesson on Roman history, to judge by what words of the speaker echoed into the hallway. If nothing else, our stay within the monastery would profit her education, I reflected.

The brooms, mops, and wooden buckets were kept in the cellar, which was reached through a door at the end of the east wing that was never locked. I had been shown how to open it and where to find my broom and other cleaning tools not long after our coming to the monastery. It was unlikely anyone would notice my absence from the stairs, and if they did, the cellar was a reasonable place for me to wander in my idiocy.

Descending the rough steps, I paused to listen for the sound of footfalls on the brick floor of the cellar, which ran the full length of the library foundations. The only light came from four oil lamps that hung from the ceiling on chains, and were kept perpetually filled and burning. Above each, a great patch of black soot attested to the diligence of the monks in this matter.

When I perceived that I was alone, I cast the broom aside and began a thorough search for a trap door in the floor. The air felt cool and dry on the back of my neck as I bent and peered downward, but carried less dust than might be expected. The floor bricks were almost as cleanly swept as the marble tiles of the level above. Uncleanliness was equated by the monks with evil. They hated the sight of any dust or stain, even in the concealed places of their little world.

I had searched the cellar several times in the past, but never with this degree of thoroughness. Even so, I almost missed the door. It was located in the extreme western end, where the shadows were blackest. I discovered it by touch. Chancing to run my fingers across the stone blocks of the cellar wall, I felt wooden planks, and traced the heavy frame of a door that was no higher than my shoulders. It was bound with thick straps of metal that had the chill of iron. I felt the projection of its hinges, and knew from this that it opened toward me. On the right side, midway down its length, a latch stood out above a square iron plate with a keyhole at its center.

Gently, I tried to lift the latch. It clicked but the door remained fast in its frame. I laid my ear against its boards. Was it my imagination, or could I hear a voice on the other side? I straightened and withdrew to the other end of the cellar, where I retrieved my broom and ascended the steps to resume my task of sweeping the already spotless floor of the front hall.

The young brothers filed out of the school room at the usual time. They wandered past me, talking amongst themselves in pairs and small groups, ignoring me as usual. When Martala failed to emerge through the open door, which I could see from my place at the foot of the stair, I wondered if she had remained behind in order to communicate to me in private some information of importance. I swept my way down the hall, and when no monk was in sight, glanced into the school room. It appeared deserted, but I heard a faint sound that caused me to project my head around the frame of the doorway.

In the corner, beyond the benches, Martala and Baruch stood in a close embrace, kissing with obvious passion. I had neglected to look for the teacher of the lesson among the emerging students, or I would have realized that there must be two remaining in the room. With half my mind, I reproved myself for carelessness, while the other half gaped at the spectacle.

By good fortune, Baruch stood with his back to the door. I saw Martala's face over his shoulder but her eyelids remained closed. I withdrew, and with my thoughts in confusion, went to sweep the far end of the great hall. How could I have missed the evidence of her growing affection for the smooth-cheeked cow-eyed monk? His infatuation with her had always been apparent, but never had it occurred to my thoughts that she would reciprocate. Did he know that she was a woman? No, it was impossible. His vow to the order would force him to report her deception to Rumius. He must still believe her to be a youth.

For the first time since awakening to my second life, I contemplated the inconvenience of losing her. So accustomed had I grown to her presence, I found the idea of her absence distinctly unpleasant. Nothing bound her to me, other than her desire to learn the forbidden wisdom of the necromantic arts, and her need to get as far away as possible from the malice of Farri. Yet I felt betrayed. I almost laughed aloud at my own folly. Was it possible that I held affection for the faithless little slut? I was a man without manhood. I should not have expected her to behave in any other way.

It was some consolation that she could not betray me to the order without betraying herself. Rumius was a compassionate man, but he had a will of iron. We would both be put to death were our true purposes discovered.

I gave no sign in the dining hall of anything amiss. When we retired to our room that night, she faced me with an expression of excitement.

"I saw the weapon," she breathed in a quiet voice.

Without making a reply, I continued to wash my face over the basin. My lack of response disappointed her.

"Alhazred, did you hear? I saw it. A machine of shining brass with wheels revolving inside wheels, and polished gems that glow with their own inner fire. Their light is projected through sets of glass disks that are mounted on revolving brass plates."

When I continued to say nothing, she looked at me strangely.

"How did you get close to it?" I asked, merely to say something that would lull her unease.

"One of the monks is an alchemist." She laughed. "He is always talking about his sealed vessels, and his experiments. When I pretended to be interested, he almost dragged me by the arm up the stairs to show me his work. The machine sat in the corner, partly covered by a piece of sail cloth."

"Give me your dagger," I said in a dull voice.

"Why do you want my dagger?"

"I have a use for it."

Shrugging, she drew the blade from its ivory sheath and passed it to me, hilt first. My fingers closed around the hilt. I saw my knuckles go white, and made the effort to relax my hand. Not a word about Baruch. Well, what should I expect?

I slid the gently curved blade under my linen belt and sat on the side of the bed, staring at the black square of the open window. Voices carried in the night air. It was natural that Martala would be heard to murmur to her idiot brother, but it would not do for the other monks to hear her brother make an intelligible response. She sat beside me.

"What did you discover in the cellar?"

Bending my head close to hers, I described the door in the western wall.

"It can only lead downward. There is nothing on the other side of the foundation but open lawn."

"How will you get the key to the lock?"

I touched the hilt of the dagger.

"This is my key. The lock is heavy, but of the simplest kind. There were locks like it in the palace at Sana'a. I used to move from locked room to locked room, with nothing more than a dagger."

The memory recalled the face of the princess Narisa, and the pain of her absence stabbed like a needle through my heart.

"Do you wish me to come with you?"

I shook my head. Tonight, I wanted to be alone. That was impossible within the confines of our room. I gave silent thanks for the excuse to leave it.

It was necessary to wait until midnight. Most of the monks who observed the heavens from the towers of the monastery and from the library roof retired then, in order to keep to their usual custom of rising before the dawn. Only when some special observation was needed that did not appear in the heavens in the early hours would a scattering of them remain awake all night, peering upward along the edges of their enormous protractors and measuring the separation of stars with their dividers. I hoped that no such special observation was planned for tonight.

The girl undressed and lay on her back on the bed. She draped an arm across her eyes and pretended to sleep. She had been hurt by my coldness, but did not know its cause, or how to speak about it. She would dismiss it as nothing more than a mood, I told myself.

Hours passed slowly. I listened to the movements within the dormitory as they grew increasingly few. From time to time, a monk rose and the sound of piss striking the bottom of a copper pot carried clearly through the open shutters. The separation between the windows of the rooms was not great. I crossed to the opening and looked up at the night sky. The moon in her first quarter had already fallen below the western horizon, but the stars themselves illuminated the lawn well enough to distinguish gray outlines of the buildings and dark masses of trees.

Lamps burned at the sides of the towers that stood at the corners of the great wall. Somewhere between the towers paced guards with their black bows, ever watchful, always listening. I could not see them on the battlements, and with luck that meant they would not see me. I doubted they would be able to hit a moving target in the darkness, but even to arouse an alarm would be fatal to my purpose.

I left the window and walked with quiet steps toward the door.

"Alhazred?"

I stopped.

"Take care."

Opening the panel slowly so that its hinges did not squeal, I left the room. No one passed me in the hall or on the stairs. I knew the steps well enough to avoid those that creaked. The front door was never locked, but I let myself out through the kitchen door as there was more concealment on that side of the dormitory. The smells of the animals in their pens that hung on the warm night air gave an odd reassurance, they were so familiar.

It was easier to reach the library than I expected. Shade trees offered hiding places from the towers. When necessary to dart across an open patch of grass, I took the chance that the guards had their attention directed outward, not inward, and hoped they would hesitate to shoot at a moving shadow without knowing its identity. Even so, my imagination painted vivid pictures of those long black arrows passing completely through my chest and pinning my corpse to the lawn. My turban I had left in the room, but the white linen of my robe shone pale in the starlight.

The cellar beneath the library had an exterior door that enabled stores to be moved in and out without the necessity of carrying through the great hall. As was true of almost all the doors in the monastery, it was never locked. I made my way into the courtyard. The statue of Ishtar seemed to frown down upon my back. The cellar door was located in the west wing near the inner corner, deep in shadow. It creaked when I tried to open it, and I cursed my carelessness in not having applied a little butter to its hinges earlier in the day. I found it impossible to open without noise. Every time I drew it back an inch, it gave a loud crack. After each I waited in silence, the sweat beading on my face, and listened for a cry from one of the towers.

It was almost with surprise that I realized I had opened the door far enough to slip my body through without alerting the sentries on the walls. The lamps still burned in the cellar with low steady flames. Once, Martala asked Baruch why lights were kept burning throughout the night in all buildings, and the monk had replied that it was to ensure that during any surprise attack, there would not be confusion. It had always seemed to me foolish to carry this extravagance as far as the cellar of the library, but that was before I knew that the cellar served another purpose beside the storing of brooms and mops.

Entering the gloomy western end of the cellar, I located the small door by touch and tried the latch. As I expected, it remained locked. The keyhole was large enough to admit my little finger, which I used to explore its wards. It was of the simplest design. A bent piece of wire could have been used to open it. The narrow tip of the dagger served admirably for the purpose. I took care inserting it to avoid scratching the plate, even though it was unlikely scratches would be seen in this murk. The door opened without noise.

Light burned from somewhere below, enough to reveal the outlines of a narrow flight of stone steps that wound their way downward. Trailing my left hand along the curve of the wall, with the dagger held ready in my right, I descended the steps with care. They were so steep, a fall might result in a crippling injury, or even death. The light grew stronger at the base of the stair. It came from a lamp hung on chains from the vaulted ceiling of a corridor. I advanced with soft steps in what I judged to be an easterly direction, listening for the sound of voices or footfalls. The floor of the corridor sloped downward at an angle revealed by the chains of the hanging lamps, which burned at intervals and cast barely enough light to banish the shadows between them. The reek of their untrimmed wicks clogged my throat, and something else, a more repulsive stench.

The corridor ended on an archway that opened into a vast circular chamber with a domed roof. Lamps flamed in brackets on the wall, illuminating a cage of black iron shaped in the form of a ball composed of three interlocking rings. It was a massive thing of many tons of weight, yet it hung suspended high above the center of the floor on three iron chains bracketed into the stones of the dome. Each link of these chains was big enough that I might easily have slipped my hand through its opening, had I been able to reach them.

The curve of the dome, as well as the antiquity of the stonework, suggested to my eye that it had been built by Romans, but what the armies of Rome might have wanted with this distant land, and why they would build so large a chamber beneath the ground, would puzzle the wits of an antiquarian. The surface of the dome was painted with numerous arcane symbols in various colors. Similar tokens of magic adorned the stones of the floor.

I might have studied the symbols more closely, but my gaze was drawn to a slight movement within the iron cage, and I realized for the first time that it held a prisoner. It was oddly difficult to focus the eye upon it, in part because its translucent flesh let the light from the guttering lamps pass through, but also because its shape was so shocking to the mind that it resisted comprehension. The thing crouched on its haunches, massive shoulders and folded, unfledged wings almost filling the space within the riveted iron bands. Huge clawed hands rested over its knees. It was like a finely crafted sculpture carved by a madman from a single piece of rock crystal, highlighted within by gleaming silver threads and patches of smoke.

A claw twitched as I regarded the monstrous hands. I searched for the head of the creature, and found only a mass of quiescent tentacles, above which gleamed tiny eyes like rubies, three on either side of its softly throbbing skull. My mind refused to comprehend its face. I could not hold it in my memory for even a few moments before it was rejected with violence, in the way the stomach vomits forth something unwholesome. I wondered if the creature noticed me on the floor below, and whether it possessed the power of speech.

Numbness overcame my thoughts. I shook my head to clear it, and realized with terror that I stood almost beneath the sphere. Another step would put me within reach of those terrible claws, yet I held no memory of moving from my place at the entrance. For a moment my flesh refused to obey me. With an effort of will, I raised my left hand and made the Elder Sign, uttering under my breath words of power. The invisible chains that bound me fell free. Like a mouse that leaps from a closing trap, I jumped backward, bruising my buttocks on the flagstones. In the extremity of my anxiety I did not even try to stand but scrabbled away, my eyes fixed on the twin triangles of blazing rubies. I felt it watching me, and sensed its detached amusement, beneath which lay a fiery lake of hatred.

Thoughts echoed in my mind, as precise and heartless as the beating of a hammer on an anvil.

Slave of Nyarlathotep, have you been sent to free me?

Chapter 47

The monster within the iron cage spoke inside my skull. It knew I was in the thrall of the dark man. Yet it could not read my thoughts, or why would it bother to question me?

That is not quite true. I am able to read those thoughts that lie on the surface of your mind. Or how could you communicate with me?

Blinking and averting my gaze, I saw my dagger on the floor some distance from where I sat and found the strength to regain my feet and retrieve it. I slipped the curved blade beneath my belt. It felt like a tiny thing in my hand, and I wondered if that was my own thought, or the thought of this spawn of Cthulhu. For such it must be. I recognized in its shape the carved statues of the deathless dreaming god that I had seen in my soul travels beneath Irem.

Drawing a long breath that shuddered in my chest, I forced myself once again to look at it. It represented danger, but also opportunity.

"Can everyone see the mark of the dark man on my face except me?"

Its amusement touched me like cold air from a cave of ice.

It was not made for your eyes, but for mine, and others like me.

I gathered my thoughts. With what small dignity I retained, I knelt on the floor and made the ancient sign of obeisance to the Old Ones, covering my eye sockets with the heels of my palms and bending forward until the backs of my hands touched the stones.

"Mighty servant of Cthulhu, Nyarlathotep sends his greetings. He wishes you to tell me all you know concerning the plots and weapons of the Sons of Sirius. And to teach me what arts of necromancy may be of aid in my work."

The last I added for my own benefit, as an afterthought. It is always useful to acquire knowledge of magic.

It made no response, but stared at me with its unwinking eyes. The tentacles on its face rippled like the many legs of a centipede.

There is a second mind within you. It flees from me when I try to touch it.

For a moment I did not understand the meaning of the creature. Then I realized that it meant Sashi.

"It is a djinn, my sworn companion through life, and of no concern to you. Do not seek to divert my attention with trifles. How do you answer the demand of the dark lord?"

I will give your lord the knowledge he seeks, because it serves the purpose of my lord who dreams in death. First, free me from this prison.

"No, " I said at once. "You would kill me. I can feel your anger. You lust to destroy and slay."

It grasped the iron bands of its prison in its claws and shook them, and I expected them to shatter, but the great chains that supported the ball merely clanked with a dull sound. More than iron held it. The painted symbols on the dome were its primary bonds.

Release me, or I will tell the monks what you do.

"Why should you help those who torture you? If you tell the monks, I will never be able to release you."

For several moments its fury blazed like an open furnace. Then it mastered itself.

Very well. Ask what questions your feeble brain can conceive. I will answer them.

"What trap did the Sons of Sirius use to capture you?"

My mind echoed like a hollow drum. I realized the thing was laughing.

I was here eons before the monks.

"Did the Romans build this place?"

When this cage was made, Rome was no more than mud huts on the side of a river.

"Then who built it?" I asked with impatience at the evasiveness of the creature.

They have been forgotten. You would not know their name.

As it spoke, I felt it tug at the fabric of my mind, attempting to unravel its corners and find an entrance to the places of my secret thoughts. Again I made the Elder Sign. The pull weakened but did not relent.

"If you don't stop trying to control me, I will leave and not return."

That would not serve the purpose of your lord.

"Nyarlathotep has his purposes, and I have mine. One of mine is to stay alive."

Again the hollow laughter, like the beating of a drum inside my head. The worrying at my mind ceased.

I questioned it for several hours. It never gave a direct answer, but spoke obliquely in a rambling way. If it was insane from its long imprisonment and the torture of its translucent flesh by the light rays of the monks, its madness failed to dull its perception. It knew I was not alone in the monastery, and that my companion was a woman. It knew I had died and been resurrected. This seemed to amuse it. The casual way it plucked these secret matters from my memory made me feel like a desert hare beneath the shadow of a hawk.

I learned many things I did not seek to know concerning the Old Ones and their history, but gained little useful information about the plans of the Sons of Sirius. At first I thought the vagueness of its replies was due to the decay of its brain, but I began to realize that the evasion of my questions was deliberate. As long as it kept the knowledge I sought to itself, it held power over me.

I felt the approach of morning and told the creature that I must return to my bed. Pink light flashed through its crystalline limbs.

Release me. I have answered all your questions.

"You have wasted my time," I said with bitterness. "Where is the necromancy you promised to teach? What are the weaknesses of the Order of Sirius, by which it may be defeated?"

My hostility moderated its rage. It regarded me in the same way a fisherman looks at a fat fish only half impaled on his hook.

Return tomorrow night, necromancer, and I will give you the answers you seek.

Its thoughts went from my head, and I realized how great was the weight I had supported since entering the domed vault. The abrupt lightness of my brain made me dizzy. I backed toward the archway, my eyes never leaving the monster, but its attention had already left me, and flown far from its prison of iron.

Martala sat on the bed, waiting for me, when I returned to my room. I wondered if she had slept. She wanted to know all that had transpired, but my eyes burned with weariness that was more than mere lack of sleep. I stripped off my robe and shoes, and threw myself upon the straw-filled mattress. If she spoke again, I heard nothing.

The touch of her hand on my shoulder woke me. I forced open heavy lids and saw the infernal glow of dawn through the window. We talked in low voices while we prepared ourselves for the morning meal in the dining hall. I described the vault and the creature in the iron ball. When I told her how it had almost gained control over my mind, she became angry.

"You should have let me come with you. That is what the monk meant about this thing being too dangerous to confront alone."

"I don't want you there. I can keep it out of my mind, but it would pick your brain as a monkey picks lice."

"So you say," she pouted. "I can keep a secret."

Indeed you can, I thought, but let no change show in my face.

For the following five days I left my room each midnight and made my way to the vault, where I remained in conversation with the spawn of Cthulhu until the dawn threatened to overtake me. Each night the moon hung longer in the western sky, and filled her face with greater brightness, making it more perilous to cross the lawn beneath the watchful sentries on the walls. I became so deprived of sleep that I began to dream while standing with my broom in my lax hands.

The thing in the cage told me how to release it. If three of the symbols upon the walls of the vault were obscured with paint, or struck from the stones, the spell binding it would sufficiently weaken for it to shatter its prison and rise up through the earth to freedom. I agreed solemnly that I would bring hammer and chisel when I knew that it had taught me all that I required of it. As a mark of its good faith, it taught me the technique of transferring my awareness into the brain of another intelligent being. It was a useful trick worth knowing, since it required neither script nor potion.

In this way I have watched you and your companion from the day you entered the stronghold above.

"You see through the eyes of the monks?" I asked in amazement.

One of them is under my thrall. He is weak-willed and was easy to master.

"What is the name of this monk?"

Tell me your true name, the one you were given when you were born, and I will tell you his.

It was a trick intended to raise my given name to the surface of my thoughts. Names are potent in magic, containing as they do the essence of identity. It failed only because the name of my childhood was lost in the sands of the Empty Space.

The thoughts of the creature held the power to charm with their diversity and amaze with their profundity, but I never forgot the first night, how I had walked across the floor in trance, almost within reach of those swordlike claws. I cared little for the lives of the monks, but knew that were this thing from the depths of the world released, it would kill me first, before it killed the others, so that Nyarlathotep could not profit from the information it fed into my mind. Nyarlathotep and Cthulhu might be of the same blood, but they hated each other. I saw in its thoughts, which it believed hidden from my perception, the contempt of its master for the way the dark man slunk through the shadows and used frail humanity for his servants.

On the last night I asked the question I had waited to ask, but did not dare speak before I gained all that it was willing to teach about the purposes of the monks.

"I seek the location of a well. It is called the Well of the Seraph. Do you know its location?"

The thing pondered within itself for several moments.

The name is familiar. I saw it in the mind of an elder scribe who came to gape at me. It is written on a scroll that he glanced at many years ago.

"Where is this scroll located?" I asked, trying to control my excitement.

Why do you seek the well? What use has your dark lord for holy water?

I sensed suspicion in its thoughts and fought to contain my desire beneath the surface of my mind. I feigned indifference.

"Such information might be valuable. Perhaps I can sell it in Damascus for gold."

If I tell you where to find this scroll, will you then release me?

"I will release you," I promised solemnly with the conviction of my heart. I have found that a lie is more effective when the man who tells it almost believes it himself.

The colors of doubt flashed through its crystalline form like sparkles of the sun upon the water of a stream. Its body became smoky as it considered the matter. I cast my gaze over the arcane symbols on the wall, feeling the way a player at chess feels when he is about to checkmate his foe, and does not dare look at the board lest his eyes betray his intention.

Go to the room where scrolls are kept, at the western end of the hall.

"Which level?"

The highest level.

"How shall I recognize the scroll?"

Its roller is made of rosewood. The knobs are carved in the shape of rosebuds.

I tried to keep the exultation from my face. Since gaining access to the library I had searched every day for the scroll, without success. I understood now the obscure meaning of Nyarlathotep, when he said in my dream that I must fulfill his purpose before my own would be fulfilled.

"Tomorrow I will find the scroll and verify its text. If you spoke the truth, I will return in the night with chisel and hammer and strike off three of these signs."

I turned to go. As I passed through the arch into the passage, I heard its words in my head.

Betray me, and I will seek you out when I escape from this place. You will not have warning of my approach, for I can move unseen through the air. I will make your body resemble your face.

The drumbeats of its hollow laughter echoed in my skull as I walked quickly from the vault, my shoulders shivering at the contact of its malignant gaze.

Baruch waited for me as I entered through the kitchen door of the dormitory. I smelled him in the darkness an instant before he spoke.

"Not so great a fool as we were led to suppose," he whispered.

My dagger was in my hand before he closed his lips. Neither of us could see the other in the darkness, but his words revealed his position. I had the impulse to kill him at once, but mastered it. Had he betrayed us? If so, where were the other monks?

"I have watched you leave your room these past three nights, and go to the library cellar."

"How did you come to be watching the door of my room at midnight?" I murmured.

"So? It speaks as well. You play the idiot with skill."

"Who have you told?"

He remained silent. I considered my options. If I killed him and hid his corpse, I would gain an hour, no more. He would be missed at the morning meal in the dining hall, and an alarm would be raised. Then again, he might not be so easy to slay. All the Sons of Sirius were skilled in combat, even those who preferred the pen to the sword. If I allowed him to live, he held my life in his mouth. A single cry would bring the monks running from their rooms.

"Come with me," he said at last.

"Where are we going?"

"Your room."

We made our way by touch through the silent kitchen. A lamp burned on the upper landing of the stair. I saw that his face was bloodless, his mouth hardened into a thin line of resolve. His slender white hands clenched and opened as he climbed the stairs, but they held no weapon. I followed him to the third level landing and down the dimly lit hallway to the door of my room, my thoughts racing furiously. As he reached for the latch, I laid my hand on his arm.

"It is against the rules of the order for a monk to visit another monk in his room at night," I murmured.

He glared at me.

"You dare to tell me what is proper for the member of my order?"

I saw that my words had made him hesitate.

"At least let me go in first to warn my brother of your coming. He may cry out in surprise the moment he sees you and betray us all. In any case, it will shock his modesty for you to see him unclothed."

He considered this for a moment, and reluctantly nodded.

"If you try to keep me out, I will hammer on the door with my fist."

I opened the door and slipped through the crack sideways, closing it before there was any chance of him glancing past my shoulder. The first glow of morning through the window revealed the shadows of the bed and the washstand. As usual, Martala lay naked on the mattress. She sat up at the brush of the soft soles of my shoes across the floor, blinking her eyes. She had almost been asleep. I knelt beside her and touched her warm lips with my fingers. Her body stiffened.

"Baruch is outside the door. He knows of my deception, and wants to talk to you. I suggest that you get dressed."

She broke into a silent flurry of activity. As she threw on her robe and coiled her turban, I set my back against the door, in case the impatience of the young monk got the better of his discretion. It was as well that I did. The latch clicked, louder than I would have wished, and the door bumped my back. I pressed my toes against the floor, resisting the pressure. A single rap sounded on the door, not loud, intended as a warning of what would follow unless I let him enter.

"Have you no shame?" I hissed. "Let him cover himself."

The pressure relented.

When I opened the door, he did not even glance at me as he brushed past. He had eyes only for Martala. He drew her to the window so that he could see her face.

I closed the door softly and studied his half-turned back, judging where to place the point of the dagger to find his heart.

"How could you betray me, betray the order, after what has passed between us?"

"Would the order have taken us in if we had told the truth?"

"What is the truth, Timonius?"

"We are pursued by an assassin who followed us from Egypt. We needed the security of these walls."

"An assassin in the hire of your evil uncle, I suppose," he said with derision.

"There is no uncle. We stole something from a wealthy man, and he wants it back."

"Thieves. I might have guessed. Are you planning to rob the monastery?"

"We would never do such a thing," she said with passion. "The order has protected us. We owe you our lives."

I felt a moment of admiration for the conviction she put into her voice. I almost believed her myself.

"You told me you loved me," he said with bitterness, turning toward me. "Is this man even your brother?"

Martala hesitated, meeting my eyes.

"No."

"They why are you traveling together?" A thought darkened his face.

"I am a eunuch," I murmured quickly. "That much of our story was true."

He relaxed his shoulders, enough that I knew my words had reached him. Had he believed I was her lover, he would have sounded the alarm at once.

She took him gently by the arms and turned him to face her, staring up at him.

"Only you know, Baruch. We can go on as before. Nothing has changed."

He laughed and struck her hands aside.

"What was Idi doing under the library? There's nothing there except tools and supplies. Nothing except—"

His eyes widened, and I knew with regret that I would have to kill him.

"You went into the vault," he murmured, staring at me. "You talked to that thing in the cage. Why would you do that, unless you are in league with the Old Ones?"

With every word his voice mounted. It seemed impossible that it could pass unheard by the other monks. I raised my left palm in supplication, keeping my right hand, which held the dagger, at my thigh.

"It is not as you believe. I was merely curious."

542

"For three days? Or have you been visiting its lair longer than that? You have, I see it in your face. Traitors, both of you, liars and traitors."

His voice was much too loud. With a glare of determination, he stepped toward me. I extended the dagger to thrust.

Martala drew my Damascus sword from its scabbard with a flash of silver in the gray dawn glow and plunged its point into his back. He stopped and reached both arms up and over his shoulders in an attempt to touch the steel, his face convulsed. Blood filled his open mouth and ran down his chin, looking black against the pallor of his complexion. No more than a gurgling hiss escaped his throat. I caught his shoulders as he fell so that his body would not sound against the floorboards, and held him upright pressed to my chest while his knees sagged.

Martala stood framed in the light from the window, staring at me without expression as the sword drooped in her hand.

"Keep the blood from the floor," I hissed, nodding at the sword.

She came to her senses quickly, lifting the blade level so that blood would not drip from its point. I reached to take the sword from her and gave her the dagger.

"Get the towel. Cut it in two."

One of the pieces of cloth I stuffed into the mouth of the corpse. The other I pressed to the wound in its back. The point of the sword had not projected through the chest, but it must have pierced the heart, for death had been almost instant. The blood no longer flowed. In a few minutes, I knew, it would harden and the cloths would no longer be needed.

"Alhazred, your robe. It is soaked in blood."

I heard the horror in her voice, and saw her struggle to keep from retching. It is not every day that you kill a man you have kissed.

"What are we to do?" she said, pressing the back of her hand to her lips. "Merciful Goddess, what are we to do?"

I held up a finger for silence and listened. Nothing stirred in the hall outside the door. It was almost an hour before the time of rising. With good fortune, all the monks near enough to have overheard Baruch's voice lay asleep. The smell of fresh blood hung thick in the air, but the morning breeze would soon carry it away.

"It's too late to try to take the body elsewhere," I murmured. "Lift the mattress from its ropes."

She pulled the sack of the mattress out of its wooden frame. Still supporting the body, I leaned over to examine the space below the knotted ropes. It was deep enough. The sideboards of the bed did not reach to the floor, but were so low that no one would notice a body beneath the bed unless he got down on to his hands and knees and peered under. The monks did their own cleaning. There was little reason to enter the room of another brother during the day, unless invited, and entry was forbidden at night. Eventually the flies would betray us, but I hoped to be long away before that occurred.

She cleaned the blade of my sword on the robe of the dead monk, then slid the corpse under the bed while I stood at its foot and held it up at an angle. The legs were a bit long. I had to raise the bed a second time while Martala turned the corpse partly onto its side and bent its knees with her hands. When the mattress was in place and the sheets pulled over it, the bed appeared empty.

"I will get you another robe from the laundry," Martala murmured. "We should hide your robe under the bed—" She stopped herself before she said "with the body."

"It's too late. They will be awake soon. Do it after the first bell sounds. If anyone asks, tell them your idiot brother soiled himself."

She nodded, eyes downcast. Her shoulders trembled, even though she clasped her hands in front of her at her waist and tried to keep them still.

"It was necessary," I said, touching her cheek.

She glanced at me. Tears gleamed in her pale eyes but did not fall.

"I would have killed him in another moment, if you had not done it. He was about to betray us both. The monks would have executed us, but first they would have tortured us to discover our purposes."

"They may still do so," she murmured, and I smiled to hear some of her usual strength creep back into her voice.

"Were you in love with him?"

She shook her head slowly, then held it still, her face turned away from mine.

"He thought I was a boy. What chance was there for love?"

Chapter 48

The ringing of the morning bell woke the dormitory to life. Murmurs of voices and the shuffle of feet sounded in the hallway outside the door. Martala left to get me a clean robe and gather food from the kitchen for our departure, for it was evident that we must flee the Sons of Sirius before the discovery of the corpse. I occupied myself by hiding my bloody robe beneath the mattress and washing all traces of blood from my hands and chest. The water in the basin took on a distinct red tinge. I poured it into the chamber pot, and the piss and shit from the previous evening disguised its color well enough for a casual glance, after I stirred the mixture.

She returned with the robe in her arms, its folds filled with loaves of bread, a piece of salted pork, and dried dates and apricots.

"It was the best food I could steal. I could only stay in the kitchen for a few moments, and was never left alone."

"It will serve well enough," I said, putting my arms through the robe and tying its quilted belt. I slid her empty travel wallet and my flat water skin into the front of it through the slit of its neck. The bulge was noticeable, but could be disguised by bending forward and folding my arm across my belly. I regretted the loss of our boots. It would have attracted instant notice to wear anything other than the daily uniform of the order, and in any case, our boots had been taken away shortly after our admittance into the monastery and sold, the money they earned adding to the general coffers.

As expected, the absence of Baruch was noticed in the dining hall, and a young brother dispatched to look for him while the rest of us made a breakfast of fresh bread, boiled eggs, and ham. Toward the end of the meal, the brother returned with an apologetic posture and made his way directly to the head table, where sat Rumius and his fellow elders. I could not hear what question Rumius put to him, but he merely shook his head. Rumius dismissed him with an expression of concern, and bent in council with one of his advisors, who always dined at his elbow. This coming and going was not missed by the monks seated further down the hall. Suddenly Baruch became the focus of conversation at all the tables.

A general search was undertaken shortly before noon, amid growing alarm. Everyone knew that Baruch must still be within the monastery, which made his absence a mystery that verged on a wonder. He had been seen retiring to his room in the dormitory the evening before, or so the general gossip testified. Since the gate was locked at sunset, guarded all night, and not opened until after the morning meal, he could not be outside the walls, yet he had vanished. The initial assumption was that he had fallen into the cistern and drowned, but this was soon disproved by investigation, and the area of the search widened.

The search served my purposes better than I would have hoped. It drew most of the scribes out of the scriptorium, and many of the senior monks from their offices. I was exempt from the search due to my weak mind, and was permitted to carry on with my usual morning duty, sweeping the floors of the library. As soon as I could do so without attracting notice, I worked my way down to the western end of the hall on the third level. The scroll was still where the elder monk had placed it, after scanning over its contents. It would have been safest to steal the scroll and read it at my leisure when safely outside the walls of the monastery, but I dared not trust the words of the monster below. Fingers trembling with eagerness, I unrolled it.

The letters were Hebrew, the language Aramaic, a tongue well-known to Nectanebus, but obscure to most scholars of the present age. It was a work of no great interest that described various holy sites of the world, a kind of traveler's guide similar to the book of Pausanius the Greek. I let my eyes dance through it with impatience. What I sought was written in another hand at the foot of the main text, a gloss of no great extent. I read it with care, then rolled up the scroll and replaced it.

During my time in the library, I had taken notice of a number of valuable works on the necromantic arts, fixing their places of keeping in my mind. I went to them and gathered several scrolls that could easily fit into the pockets of the wallet. It was with regret that I passed over others too bulky to conceal on my person. Each was worth far more than its weight in gold to those interested in the arcane secrets of death and life.

As I descended to the landing on the second level, I saw that the door to the office where the library strongbox was kept had been left open in the confusion of the search. It was one of the few doors in the monastery with a lock. The temptation was too great for me to resist. The lock on the strongbox did not frustrate my efforts to spring it for more than a few minutes. It was of antique design, difficult to break but easy to pick with a penknife left lying on the desk. I reached in and took a generous handful of dinars, then stuffed them into the wallet with the scrolls. They would pay for the loss of my boots, I reflected, and be some compensation for the weeks spent acting the fool.

"What are you doing here, Idi? Don't you know this room is forbidden to you?" asked a cultured voice behind my back.

My blood turned to cold spring water, and I remained motionless with my hand still in the neck of my robe. Replacing the habitually foolish expression on my face, I slowly straightened and turned, cursing myself for not bringing the dagger. The blade of the penknife was no longer than my little finger. Still, it was a weapon of sorts. The bearded monk who faced me from the open doorway was of no great age. I recognized him as the youngest of those who carried out the administration of the monastery from these offices. His name came to me after a few seconds during which my mind remained as dense as a block of wood. Brother Adrian. I lolled my tongue at him and wagged my head as though confused.

His clear brown eyes strayed to the open strongbox. I wondered how difficult it would be to kill him with the little knife. Where would I hide the body? With the entire monastery engaged in a search of all the buildings, no corner would long remain safe from discovery, even were I able to drag his corpse down the hallway and stairs unobserved. Would his body fit into the strongbox? I cast my eyes in the same direction as his to measure its dimensions.

"You have been very naughty, Idi." His voice held a trace of amusement. "What would Brother Baruch think, if he could see you now?"

The use of the missing monk's name was so unexpected, I forgot myself for an instant and glanced keenly at him.

"Talk to me, Idi," he said. "Your secret is safe. Only I and Baruch know of it, and Baruch won't be telling anyone, will he?"

So the love-smitten monk had not kept his discoveries to himself, but had informed his friend. How many others had he told, and if so, why was I still alive? For a few moments I debated in my own thoughts the wisdom of continuing to play the fool, but the expression on the face of the monk was so knowing, I saw that it would be futile. At least I could straighten the curve of my back, and face him like a man.

"What did Baruch tell you?"

He laughed in delight at the change of my posture. I took a small step toward him, the penknife concealed in my left hand.

"He told me nothing. His infatuation with your companion was well-known among the brothers. When I learned of his disappearance, I made the natural assumption that he had discovered your nightly visits beneath the library, and that you had killed him to ensure his silence."

There was something uncanny about his face, a kind of blankness. When he smiled, the creases at the corners of his lips were not echoed by lines at the corners of his eyes. His face had the stiffness of a living mask, animated by wires from a distance. As if sensing the trend of my thoughts, he nodded. No, it was the thing moving his body like a puppet that nodded to me. I felt sickness mingled with relief. The situation had changed, and I would not have to kill. I forced bravado into my voice.

"So this is the monk whose mind you command at a distance?"

"A very weak mind it is," the creature said with contempt. "But his mind is of no importance. His eyes and ears serve me, and occasionally, his hands."

"Why not compel him to deface the signs on the vault and set you free?"

"He is not so clever with locks as you, and I cannot control his hands with the required precision. The brothers never visit me alone, but always in groups of three, for their own security. A wise precaution for them, but frustrating, since Adrian is not permitted to be with me in private, not even for a moment."

"I have not forgotten our bargain," I said.

"Are you sure?" The thing eyed me narrowly. "Why were you stealing gold from the box? What is that beneath the folds of your robe?"

548

"The search for Baruch gave me the opportunity to take what I have long intended to steal."

"Surely you know the thefts will be discovered? And where is the corpse of the monk hidden? That will be found, also, when it starts to rot."

"I will come to you tonight, as soon as the monastery is asleep," I said quickly, to distract the trend of its thoughts. "I have black paint from the workshop. Your release will be the work of a few minutes."

"No, I do not believe you will," it said slowly. "You mean to flee from the monastery today, before the corpse of Baruch is found. Why are you in such haste?"

"I swear to you, on the honor of Nyarlathotep, that I will fulfill my pledge to you."

It laughed until the tears started from the eyes of the entranced monk and coursed down his cheeks.

"Nyarlathotep is without honor. Why do you think he is so universally despised? You are his true servant, of that I have no doubt."

"If you betray me, I will betray you," I said in warning. "You will lose the use of this vehicle, and will no longer be able to spy upon the doings of the monks."

"I could kill you now," it said, and the fingers of the monk's hands twitched.

"What would that gain you? Freedom? Brother Adrian might be discovered, and then you would still lose your vehicle."

"What makes you think he is the only one who serves as my eyes?"

I had made no such assumption, but was merely arguing for my own security.

"Give me the chance to prove the worth of my word," I said with as much sincerity as I could muster. "Let me come to you tonight and set you free."

It pondered for so long a time, I thought it had lost control of the monk, and expected to see awareness return to Adrian's eyes.

"Very well, prove the honor of your bond. But know this, I will be watching you. If you try to leave the monastery grounds before you fulfill your vow, I will sound an alarm. You will be taken and tortured, and your little companion as well."

He watched while I closed and relocked the strongbox, then stepped aside to let me pass out of the office. I felt his gaze burning on my back as I shuffled down the hallway with my arms across my belly to conceal the scrolls. No one passed me on the stairs. I sat on the corner of the bottom step, as was my custom, to wait for the girl.

Martala came for me at the usual time, and we made our way to the dining hall. The noon meal was delayed by the general chaos of the ongoing search. Groups of unfed monks sat at the bare tables, talking in low voices. I saw expressions of fear on the faces of several of the younger brothers. The disappearance of Baruch, because it was inexplicable, seemed unnatural. Others speculated that he had fallen and hit his head in some obscure corner, and would be found before the end of the day. It would not be long before the talk turned to the possibility of murder. When that happened, all of the dormitory rooms would be searched with minute care. We must be long gone before the corpse was discovered.

We ate the delayed meal finally set before us with little appetite and left the dining hall in the midst of the general throng, Martala tugging on the rope around my neck to guide me, for it was her custom to lead me by the rope in any crowded public place. I walked bent over, as though something disagreed with my stomach. None of the monks noticed the bulge of my robes. Their attention was elsewhere.

No, I corrected myself, one monk had his gaze fixed upon us. Brother Adrian watched our exit from the dining hall, and started to follow after us as we approached the front entrance of the dormitory. Martala had not yet sensed his eyes on her back. I was relieved to see him stopped in the entrance hall and taken into earnest conversation by two bearded elders, no doubt concerning details of the search. He cast a glance of frustrated fury at me as I passed through the door, and I could not refrain from giving him my idiot grin.

"Did you get the wheelbarrow?"

"It is waiting," she murmured without turning to look at my face.

On any ordinary day, it was common for the younger brothers to go into the market square to teach lessons, or to buy meat, fish, vegetables, and other goods from the merchants. I put my faith in the strength of long custom, that Rumius in his preoccupation with the search had not thought to forbid the monks to leave the walls of the monastery, or told the guards to bar the door. As I pushed the wheelbarrow toward the gate, I was relieved to see a clerical monk enter with an armload of scrolls, which he had no doubt purchased from a master of one of the recently arrived riverboats.

Martala spoke to the guard who was about to draw the iron bars across the small door. We had often been outside the gate to the market, so our presence aroused no suspicion. He opened the door.

As we were about to pass through, the other guard put his heavy hand on my bent shoulder. My heart tripped in my chest.

"What's wrong with your brother?" he asked.

"Poor Idi," Martala laughed. "I can't keep him from eating apricots. He steals them from the kitchen. This morning he stuffed his belly with them and now he has cramps."

They laughed with her at my predicament. I grinned and lolled my tongue from the corner of my mouth, tilting my head to look at each of them.

Their attention was distracted by a monk who came running across the lawn, waving his arms like a madman and calling out to them. I did not need to look to know the voice of Brother Adrian. I had hoped that the thing in the vault would not betray me at the last, since it gained nothing by it, but the satisfaction of causing my discovery must have tempted it beyond endurance. While the guards were distracted, I leaned close to Martala.

"Whatever happens, say nothing and keep going."

I did not wait for her to respond, but cast my attention inward to Sashi.

Can you control this body of mine, if I leave it? I asked in thought.

Of course, my love.

Keep it moving beside Martala. Go where she leads you.

"Guards! Bolt the gate! I know the murderer of Brother Baruch!"

One of the guards glanced at the open door, then at Adrian, who had the appearance of a madman, stumbling across the lawn with widened eyes and disordered hair hanging from beneath the band of his turban. As the thing in the vault had indicated in the library, its control over the coordination of its host was limited. Perhaps this was the first time it had ever attempted to run.

Focusing my will and murmuring the required words under my breath, I sent my mind outward in the way the monster had taught me, and felt it touch the brain of the staggering monk. My unexpected thrust succeeded. At once, I ceased to inhabit my own body, and became a resident in the flesh of Adrian. Not the sole tenant, for his flesh was filled with the powerful presence of the spawn of the warrior god, whose will is strongest of all the Old Ones. We struggled like two wrestlers, while the body of the monk stopped and swayed, the words gurgling in his throat. He must appear to the approaching guards to be taking some kind of fit, I thought with a corner of my mind. The rest was occupied in a battle for survival. Now that the thing held my mind in its grasp, naked and unprotected, it intended to crush it.

551

The mind is curious in its ways. Mine was bound by chains of unseen iron. I could not begin to overthrow the will of the spawn, so much more potent than my own, yet my thoughts, which could not move forward or retreat, managed to escape sideways into memory. I found myself reliving the final wrestling match with my brutish foster brother, Yanni. My brother had always been stronger. Yet sometimes I was able to throw him to the ground by using his own force against him, by letting it carry itself past me without resistance and then adding to its momentum with my lesser strength. I did this in my mind against the thrusting, destroying force of the thing in the vault, and felt it lose its equilibrium and tumble out of the brain of the monk. Before it could return, I slammed shut all the gates against it. The brain was mine, and the body it controlled.

"Brother Adrian, what's wrong? Are you ill?" One of the guards held my arms near the shoulders to keep me from collapsing.

"I know the murderer of Brother Baruch," I repeated breathlessly, the spittle flying from my lips. "I did it, I killed him. Then I hid the body."

One of the guards glanced at the gate, uneasy about having left his post. I saw over his shoulder Martala lead Idi, who still pushed the empty wheelbarrow, through the open doorway. She did not look behind.

The other guard laid his hand on my back and studied my frenzied face with concern. I began to grapple with them both, pulling them close, and let madness creep into my voice. They restrained me, the gate momentarily forgotten.

"Do you know what you are saying, Brother Adrian?" the second guard asked, not unkindly.

"It was jealousy. It drove me to madness. Baruch was my lover but he ceased to care about me, so I killed him and hid his body where you'll never find it. No, I won't tell you where it is."

My hold on the mind of the monk began to slip. I felt pressure as the thing in the vault probed the surface of his brain in search of a crack through which to pour itself and resume command. I tried to hold on for as long as possible while the body of the monk slowly collapsed to the grass in the arms of the guards. As the creature cast me out of the monk's skull, I looked directly into the eyes of the guard who held me close, his face no more than a hand's breadth away. With a tremendous effort of concentration, I framed the words of power and forced my escaping awareness into the head of the guard.

His mind was not so highly educated as Adrian's but his will was stronger. I had control for only a few moments, for he almost immediately began to push back against the rushing flood of my will. It was long enough to grasp the hilt of his dagger and thrust its point through Adrian's chest. The surprise and fury in the face of the dying monk might have made me laugh aloud had I still possessed a mouth, but I was ejected from the brain of the guard before the blade ceased to slide between the monk's ribs.

I found myself whirled through a roaring cataract of darkness. The impact of my awareness entering my own brain made my body jerk as though stung by a wasp. I drew a gasp and saw that I pushed the wheelbarrow through the market square. My body felt chill beneath my robe, and I tasted the salt of sweat beads on my upper lip. Martala glanced across at me with concern in her wide pale eyes, but gave no other sign that she noticed the violence of my return.

The market was more than usually crowded with new arrivals from the boats. The few monks bargaining at the stalls paid us no attention, since we were a familiar sight. We left the wheelbarrow near the gate and walked quickly toward the corner as though having business at one of the inns on the southern side of the wall. I felt a prickling between my shoulder blades, but refrained from turning to look at the guards on the battlements. The numerous travelers who walked and pushed carts along the road that led through the village made our passage inconspicuous.

We went quickly across the fields and through the trees to the rock where I had concealed the leather wallet containing our precious possessions and my money purse. The weather had done it no great harm, apart from a small patch of mildew on one corner that easily brushed off. The smooth surface of Gor's skull beneath my fingertips filled me with fondness. I transferred the pilfered gold to the purse, and slung the wallet and my empty water skin on my back, after giving the other wallet with the stolen scrolls and food to Martala. It was a credit to the common sense of the girl that she asked no questions. With a single glance through the trees at the looming wall of the monastery, I led the way toward the rutted track that led west.

As we retraced the road that had brought us to the monastery, I explained how close we had come to betrayal by Adrian, and how I had diverted suspicion upon the monk.

"Was it necessary to kill him?" she asked.

"The spawn of Cthulhu was sure to deny the confession and name us both as murderers. It would have led the elders directly to the corpse, and Rumius would have dispatched horsemen at once to ride us down and capture us."

"You gained us a few hours, at least," she said with understanding. "Unless the monster can betray us through another monk."

"I do not believe it has any other under its power, or it would surely have managed to free itself from its cage. Adrian's mind was uncommonly weak, and he made the error of visiting the thing in its vault. The spawn was able to forge an enduring link with him."

She shivered.

"If it ever escapes, it will kill you."

"It will have to await its turn," I said lightly.

In early afternoon we left the road and went behind the brow of a low hill to eat some of the food Martala had stolen from the kitchen.

"It is time we changed our identities," I told her, and used the spell of glamour to disguise the horrors of my face.

"Good. I've grown tired of being a boy."

She stripped off her turban and shook out her long hair, then folded the band of the turban and slid it into the front of her robe, withdrawing from the same place a scarf of blue silk she had somehow obtained and draping it over her head. I attached Gor's skull and my sword to my belt but left the dagger with the girl. There was little we could do about our plain white linen robes. If we bought different clothing in the fishing village beside the lake, the fishermen would tell the monks when they came searching after us, as they surely would when our absence from the evening meal was observed, and they located the corpse in our room by its smell and the buzzing swarm of flies. It might take them longer to discover the loss of the gold and missing scrolls, but the thefts were the least of the reasons Rumius would seek our return.

We came upon the lake at sunset and made a wide circle around the fishing village, then followed the lakeshore southward in the darkness to gain as much distance from the village as possible before stopping for the night. While we were still on the margin of the lake I filled my water skin, and felt reassured by its heaviness. The weight of water always gave me confidence.

It still hung from its leather strap on my shoulder when I walked down the lee side of an enormous dune in the Empty Space, the sand blowing over my boots and concealing my toes as though I walked through moonlit mist. The dark man walked at my side, and I knew when I saw him that I dreamed.

"What have you learned, my resourceful spy?" he said with a kind of hollow chuckle.

I dug into an inner pocket of my thawb, which I saw was my old cream-colored thawb that I had stolen from the corpse of the Bedouin so long ago, and passed over a packet of parchment sheets. He took them and unfolded them. They were closely written on both sides in the language of the Old Ones. A part of my dreaming mind remembered writing them in my dreams, while another part knew that they did not exist in the material world. It was merely a device by which my mind conveyed its knowledge to Nyarlathotep. He read them as we walked to the bottom of the dune and began to mount toward the crest of the next.

"You have done well," he murmured, putting the phantom sheets away beneath the folds of his black cloak.

"What is my reward, lord?" I asked, unable to keep a sardonic lilt from my voice.

"You already have your reward, ungrateful wretch."

"If you mean the location of the well, I discovered that through my own efforts."

"I mean your life."

He stepped in front of me and turned, quick as thought, forcing me to stumble to a halt to avoid walking into him. I felt coldness emanate from his dark body in the same way it flows from ice that is brought down from the mountains.

"Do not question my methods. Seek only to obey my commands, and I may allow you to live a little longer."

"Is that to be my only reward?" I asked with bitterness that overcame my fear. "Only life?"

"Only life," he echoed. "Yet I promise you this, Alhazred. Your life will be interesting."

Chapter 49

After leaving the lake behind, we walked west for a day, then turned south. It was a desolate region, possessing neither the clean severity of the desert, nor the lush and rampant greenery of the Nile valley. Our way was obstructed by hillocks, fissures, ridges, and occasional bogs in hollows, where springs found their way to the surface and made the stinking ground suck around our soft leather shoes at each step. The land seemed uncertain whether it wanted to be dry or wet. We encountered many small animals and birds, but no travelers or human habitations.

By the close of the second day, my spirits rose. If the monks had any notion of where we were going, we would have been overtaken by riders. The spawn of the Old One must not control another mind, or it would surely have found a way to betray my purpose to Rumius. I concluded that we had escaped their search, and began to sing as I walked. For once, Martala did not join in, but listened with a slight smile on her lips.

"What landmark are we looking for?" she asked when I fell silent.

"Two rounded hills rising from the plain. The valley of the well lies somewhere between them."

"Tell me what was written in the scroll."

This was the first time she had asked about the gloss. I saw no reason to withhold its contents from her.

"It relates a legend of the Jews. You know that in the reign of Nebuchadnezzar, their city of Jerusalem was conquered and its people led away to Babylon as slaves to serve his empire?"

She shook her head, squinting into the sunset as she searched the horizon. I reminded myself that her education, although considerable in a woman, was of uneven quality. She had acquired it piecemeal, in a sense stealing it from those around her, and had not enjoyed the benefit of tutors other than the teachers in the schoolroom at the monastery.

"The legend relates that the priests of the Temple at Jerusalem took away one of its holy objects before its destruction by the Babylonians. It does not say what it was, only that it was divided into pieces so that it could be more easily concealed on the journey to Babylon, where it was reassembled. The priests could not bear the thought of its discovery by their conquerors, so one night they took it out of Babylon on the back of a camel, and carried it southeast for three days to a long-disused well known only to the barbarous tribe that inhabited the region. The well had been poisoned for generations, and was all but forgotten."

"The Well of the Seraph?" she murmured.

"Yes. But it was not called that by the hill dwellers. Six men went out of Babylon in the darkness, prepared to defend the holy object with their lives. They found the well and uncovered it, then lowered the sacred thing into the depths on ropes. To their amazement, the water far down in the well began to glow with a golden light. It sent a column of radiance into the heavens. The eldest priest, eager to investigate the cause of this wonder, had a pail lowered into the well to sample the shining water."

"Did the water still glow when it was taken out of the well?"

"So the legend relates. When the white-bearded priest found the courage to taste it, he discovered that it was pure and sweet on the tongue. The poison had been purged away by the golden light. More than this, it possessed restorative virtue. On the journey out of Jerusalem he had fallen from a horse and broken his arm, and the bones had knitted poorly, making his arm useless. The glowing water caused his entire body to shine as though illuminated by the sun, and his twisted arm became whole and straight."

"A powerful virtue indeed," the girl said with a trace of amusement. "You should have been a storyteller in the marketplace, Alhazred. I liked the detail of the white beard."

"He was an old priest, he must have had a white beard. Be quiet while I finish the tale. Seeing these wonders, and emboldened in their courage, the other priests also drank from the pail. The water strengthened their bodies and washed away their travel fatigue. More than this, it healed their infirmities. Scars were erased from their skin. One who was deaf in his left ear regained his hearing. The youngest among them, who had lost a finger, watched with amazement as the finger regrew itself."

She made a sound of understanding, and looked at my face. It lay concealed beneath its glamour, but I knew she could see its scars with her scrying gift.

"The u'mal root can restore vigor and heal disease, but cannot replace a finger," she mused aloud. "Only the water of the Well of the Seraph is fabled to regrow an amputated member."

I smiled at her discreet use of the word. There was one particular member I was most anxious to restore, and it was not my nose.

"The priests covered the well with stones so that it would remain hidden, then made their way back to Babylon. On the journey they were attacked by bandits and all were killed except the youngest, who carried the tale of the well to the Jews in the city."

"Why is it called the Well of the Seraph?"

This made me pause. It was a question I had never bothered to consider.

"The name was not explained in the gloss. Perhaps it is a title of honor bestowed on the well because it holds the sacred object."

While I puzzled over this question, she drew my attention to the north. My heart, so recently lightened with song, became heavy. On the horizon gleamed a star of light. It glittered and went out, then returned. It could only be the slanting sunlight reflected from polished metal, such as the dome of a breastplate, or the point of a spear. We no longer walked alone through this desolate land.

"Whoever it is, they are too far away to see us. They are following our tracks."

"It must be a search party sent out from the monastery."

I nodded agreement, but continued to watch the flashing star. There was only a single point of light. After a short while it went out and did not return.

We made camp for the night without building a fire. The girl offered no complaint. She realized the necessity to remain unseen. A fire, even if concealed by the ledge at our backs, would have been too great a risk. The final dying of the sun was marked by a long howl that sounded almost human. It carried across the plain from a great distance through the still air, and fell to a soft gibbering. As I lay down beside the girl, I wondered what djinn haunted this land, and on a whim put the question to Sashi.

Many spirits, my darling. They are all around us, but they keep their distance.

She was potent enough to guard us from lesser djinn who might otherwise have sought to trouble our sleep, thanks to the vitality she drew from my living flesh. I closed my eyes and settled myself on the warm slope, reflecting that at least it was one less foe to trouble my dreams.

The following day, we moved quickly and did our best to remain concealed from the north behind whatever scant cover we could find. I took care to walk on rock where it offered a path. I had a new reason to curse the soft soil of the hollows. Our footprints might as well have been our signatures, so clearly did they identify our passage. Many times we stopped and cast our gaze behind us, to the northern horizon, but without the rays of the setting sun to highlight the armor of our pursuer, we saw nothing to confirm our unease. I had become certain in my own mind that we were followed by a single rider, and that I would recognize his face when we saw it. I sensed that the girl held the same opinion, but neither of us voiced his name, as though to speak it would be to call its possessor upon us.

In the afternoon, a hill rose on the southern horizon to the east of our direction of travel. I did not bend our feet toward it, as it appeared uninteresting in every respect, but as we walked, its rounded crest divided itself into two domes that gradually drew apart, the further we went forward. I realized that these must be the hills called in the gloss the Breasts of the Goddess, although if these were her breasts, the rest of her body would be of little interest to anyone. They were barely high enough to distinguish themselves from the general landscape.

It was twilight before we reached the shallow valley that nestled between the hills. Everywhere were piles of stones and solitary boulders, thousands of them. I slapped a fly dead on my cheek and brushed away its twitching corpse, surveying the mounds of stones over the rim of the valley.

"How are we to find this well?" the girl asked, voicing aloud my own thoughts.

"There," I said, pointing at a stone that stood upright, like a rough pillar.

"Is that the well?" she asked doubtfully.

"No, but it will lead us to the well in the morning."

I did not trouble to explain myself. I was tired and my feet ached. The leather shoes of the brotherhood were fine for shuffling along the halls of the library, but poor things for walking over sharp stones or through patches of wet mud. When the monks traveled across the land on their secret missions, they wore more sturdy boots better suited to walking or riding. What I hated most about the apparel of the order was the lack of pockets in the robes. We had to carry everything in our travel wallets or at our belts. It was fortunate that the girl's wallet had not been taken from us, since one alone would not have held all our possessions.

I took off my turban, belt and shoes, but left on my robe for protection against biting flies. Sleep was difficult to find. The hills sheltered us from the wind, giving the unseen insects ample opportunity to feast on my blood. As usual, they did not trouble the girl. I began to believe her superstition that her goddess shielded her. Protection from things that bite in darkness is not the worst reason to worship a deity, I reflected, as I lay listening to the night sounds of the valley.

A stone tumbled, ticking other stones as it rolled. I came fully awake before the noise ceased, and strained with every nerve for the fall of a horse's hoof or the brush of a boot against the dust. The moon had risen to bathe the valley in silver, and I realized that I must have dozed for several hours. The girl slept on, her slow length-ened breaths unvaried. I stood quietly to avoid waking her, drew my sword from its scabbard, and with its naked blade in my hand, picked my careful steps up the side of the nearest of the two hills.

When I had climbed midway to its crest, I turned and dropped to one knee, searching the moonlit stony hollow with both my eyes and my ears. For a long time I crouched motionless in this uncomfortable posture, breathing through my parted lips to avoid any whisper that would betray my location. If someone lurked at the edge of the valley, there was a chance he would choose to approach, thinking me no more than another of the numerous boulders on the hillside.

The noises of small animals came clearly through the night air. I heard a rat dig-ging in the sand. The rustle of wings overhead marked the passage of some night hawk. From time to time the drone of a flying beetle reached my ears. None of these noises was out of place. It was my usual practice to ignore them all, but this night my alarm made my ears sensitive to even the slightest tick or rustle in the dark. I became like a piece of stone, cold and stiff. Only my thumb moved, as I stroked the rounded dome of bone that was Gor's skull in an habitual gesture that had become for me a kind of meditation.

Does anyone watch us, Sashi?

She remained silent for a moment.

If he was near, he has withdrawn himself. I see or hear no one.

Perhaps an hour passed, or even longer. When my knee and back were afire with stiffness, I finally pushed myself to my feet and returned to the sleeping place, one of my legs so numb I could barely use it. I returned my sword to its sheath and lay beside the girl, a thousand needles pricking my leg as blood started to flow once again through it. I ignored the unpleasant sensation while continuing to listen to the night. If anyone prowled outside the valley, he moved with so great a skill that I could not detect him. At last fatigue began to lull my mind into sleep.

Wake me before the dawn, Sashi.

I will, beloved.

If you detect the approach of a man, wake me at once.

That I would do without being told. Sleep deep, Alhazred. I will watch over you.

The hours left no sense of their passage. Sashi's loving face dispelled my vague dreams like drifting mist. She smiled at me, and I kissed her tenderly on the lips, then opened my eyes. The dawn was well advanced. Already the first rays of the rising sun splashed blood across the crests of the hills. Sashi had let me sleep longer than I would have wished, but I voiced no complaint. Martala nodded to me. She sat on a flat stone, chewing a piece of bread. I pushed myself erect. The leg I had abused the previous night still ached as I tied on the laces of my shoes and my linen belt.

"Now we will find the well, if the gloss in the scroll is accurate."

She followed me across the valley and up its eastern slope to the standing stone. As I approached it, I saw that its top was indeed cleft, as described in the text. The crack was no wider than the flat of my hand. I looked across the boulder-strewn hollow and traced the shadow of the pillar, elongated hundreds of strides by the slanting sunlight.

"What are we looking for?" the girl asked.

"When the sun shines through this narrow cleft in the pillar, it will mark the place of the well."

We watched the shadow of the pillar shorten and move across the valley as the disk of the sun ascended above the horizon.

"Suppose it is the wrong time of year, and the sun is not at the right angle?" she asked, still chewing on the tough crust of the bread.

This was something I had not considered. I mulled the idea, and found myself displeased by it, and irritated with the girl for having voiced it.

"If the locator of the well was dependent upon the time of year, don't you think that would have been mentioned in the gloss?"

"I don't know," she said mildly. "Would it?"

"We will stay in this cursed valley until we find the well, even if it means staying here all year."

Whatever remark she might have made was distracted from her mind by the appearance of a narrow splinter of sunlight, resembling the blade of a crooked sword, in the upper part of the shadow of the pillar. Its point touched the middle region of the valley, nearly an equal distance from both hills. The tip did not lie upon a pile of stones, but there was one of no impressive size midway along the length of the blade.

"Quickly, run over there and stand by that pile of stones."

She hurried across the valley floor, following the shadow of the pillar, and positioned herself beside the low pile of sand and rock, which rose no higher than the middle of her shins. I continued to watch the shadow as it moved slowly to the right, the morning sun warm against my back. My own shadow stretched almost to the feet of the girl, for the pillar was of no great height. As the shadow moved, the blade of sunlight began to narrow, and in a brief time vanished utterly. I saw no other pile of stones marked by the moving blade, although similar piles lay scattered all around.

Squinting over my shoulder at the brightness of the morning, and alert for any sign of movement, I walked slowly down to the girl.

"Either the well is here, or the pillar does not mark it."

We began to dig with our fingers into the wind-blown dust and small pebbles that had sifted between the cracks of the flat stones, covering their edges. When we cleared away the loose earth, we drew the stones aside one by one. They were heavy, but not so large that four strong hands failed to shift them. This gave me hope. If the well mouth had been covered, I reasoned that those who concealed it had used stones they could drag without too much difficulty. No laborer makes unnecessary work for himself.

The stones continued beneath the level of the valley floor, and I realized as I brushed sweat from my forehead with the back of my wrist that the wind had drifted the dust over them for centuries. It was a wonder that the entire mound had not been covered up. It became more difficult to shift the slabs, now that their edges were below the surface of the ground. Our fingers were not strong enough to force between the tight cracks between them, so that we could pry them apart. I looked around for something to use. I did not wish to blunt or bend the points of my dagger or sword on such work.

Telling Martala to rest, I went across to where our wallets lay and got from mine several of the white pieces of wood that I had collected from the base of the skeleton tree in the valley of the wisdom seat. These were as hard as ivory, and their jagged ends made them ideal as wedges. I used a small rock as a hammer and pounded the points of several white shards into the crack between the flat stones. This forced them apart, as I had hoped, far enough for me to insert my entire hand. I was able to reach deep and get a good grip on the lower edge of one of the slabs. When I had it raised partway, I nodded to the girl to help me. Her added strength was enough to fold the stone over, exposing a black hole.

Eagerly, I fell to my knees and put my face near the opening. The air that touched my cheeks was moist and cool. I pressed my face lower. As my head and shoulders obscured the opening, I saw a dull light far below that shifted and brightened as I looked at it. I sat up, blinking at the brightness of the blue sky, and met the eager gaze of the girl.

"It is the Well of the Seraph."

She let out a cry of delight and began to dance, waving her arms in the air like a child. I felt enthusiasm well up in my own heart as I watched her, but restrained myself from jumping to my feet and capering about. I had played the fool enough at the monastery to fulfill my ambition in that regard for a lifetime. I scanned the rim of the valley. No movement apart from the girl caught my eye. Even so, I had the uneasy sensation of being watched.

We labored like slaves the rest of the morning to clear the remainder of the overlapping stones from the well mouth. It was of no great size, being under four cubits across and circular. Two of the largest stone slabs had been slid together to touch at their edges over the center of the opening, and these had provided the support for the others. Though not broad, it was as deep as any well of my desert homeland. I dropped a pebble into the darkness, and waited several heartbeats before hearing the faint sound of the splash. The glow of the water was invisible now that the entire opening lay exposed to the light of the sky.

She approached me with a stricken look, as though she had swallowed a spider.

"Alhazred, how are we to get water from the well?"

I smiled. The same question had formed part of my meditations for the past three days, and I had arrived at only one possible solution.

"If we cannot draw the water up to us, I will have to descend down to the water," I told her.

She quickly fell to her belly and extended her head and shoulders over the edge of the dark hole, leaning downward until I could not resist putting the toe of my foot on her buttocks, it looked so likely that she would overbalance and fall in. In her excitement, she did not even protest.

"I see notches in the stones, cut into the side." Her voice had a hollow echo. "They descend in a spiral course."

"Naturally. All wells need to be cleaned at intervals. The builders often make a way to descend to their depths."

She sat up, shrugging aside my foot.

"I'll come with you."

"No. I don't want the both of us in that hole at the same time. In case of some mishap."

She glanced quickly around the rim of the valley. She knew what kind of misfortune worried my mind, and made no protest. Were a man who wished us harm to come upon the well with both of us in its depths, it would be an easy matter to pick up stones and simply drop them into the hole until we were both dead. We would be utterly helpless.

There was no reason to delay my descent, with the well mouth gaping, yet as I sat on its rim and lowered my heels to the level of the first hollowed stone, I felt a sense of unease press on my chest like an invisible hand, making it difficult for me to breathe. If Martala noticed my hesitation, she said nothing. Turning my body and supporting myself by my arms on the rim of the well, I let the hollow step receive my full weight. It was wide enough to accept both feet, and seemed firm. I stepped down to the next hollow, and continued in this way into darkness. It required care to ensure that the smooth leather soles of my shoes did not slide off the rounded edges of the stone slots, but the notches had been cut at such a pitch that my hands were able to grip the upper track of the spiral while my toes felt blindly for the lower steps.

I came to a place where a notched stone had fallen out, leaving only a hole. The air had grown cooler, and the side of the well beneath my curled fingers felt damp. I looked up and realized how far I had come. The mouth of the well was no more than a small circle that resembled a startled eye. In the deep blue of the heavens I saw a star twinkle, even though the hour was near midday. When I turned my gaze downward the golden light shone brightly, illuminating the lowermost depths of the shaft. It shifted and flared almost like a living thing. Perhaps a spring bubbled at the bottom of the water, giving it movement, I speculated while testing the toe of my shoe in the hole left by the missing block.

At last I reached the water. Its brightness dazzled my eyes and made me shield them with my arm. Not one lamp, but a dozen or more seemed to flash and dim in its depths, shifting their places with liquid grace. The glow was oddly fatiguing to the sight. I felt reluctant to put my feet into the water. The spiral of the stair continued beneath its surface, but how deep it might be, I could not judge, as the dancing lights made it impossible to see the bottom. It would have been difficult to bend over double to reach the water with my hands without tumbling in head first.

With the philosophical reflection that the girl could always fish out my corpse, at last I slid my feet beneath the rippling surface. It felt warmer against my ankles than I anticipated. Shivering in spite of this heat, I lowered myself and probed for the next step with my toe. I should have known it would be slick. My foot slipped off the rounded edge, and I found myself up to my neck, coughing out the drops from the splash that had gone between my open lips.

"Alhazred, are you hurt?"

Martala's voice echoing from the stones sounded far away.

"I fell in, but I am not hurt," I shouted with what little breath I retained.

Cursing with surprise, I began to spit the water from my mouth. So much for the accuracy of the legend. Whether or not the water in the well was poison, it had an uncommonly foul taste. I floated, clinging to the notches of the stair with my hands, my chin up and my head tilted back, and wondered if I should risk drinking any of it. I had tasted water from many bad wells, brackish pools, and polluted springs, and was not particular about the savor on my tongue, but this well had an unwholesome thickness at the back of my throat.

Even as the question occurred to me, I realized that my hesitation was pointless. Having come this far, I was not about to leave the well without trying the healing virtue of its water. I steeled my resolve with the reflection that I was a ghoul, and drank a mouthful. As soon as I swallowed the water, my throat constricted. The cramps began in my belly. Faintness took the strength from my limbs. Had I not been floating in the water, I would have fallen from the side of the well. Touching my face with one hand, I laughed bitterly, the sound of my laughter echoing from the dank stones with mockery into my ear holes. My face was unchanged. Where my nose should have been, there was only the familiar hole. I did not need to grope between my thighs to know that nothing hung there.

"Why are you laughing?" the girl shouted in her tiny, distant voice.

"I am amused at my own folly. Forget about me. Keep watch for the approach of anyone."

The shadow outline of her head withdrew from the staring eye of the well mouth.

I had barely finished speaking when the vomit erupted from my lips. This induced another burst of laughter from my chest. I spat the sour contents of my stomach from my mouth. It would probably not be a wise idea to rinse it out with the water of the well, I thought.

For several minutes I hung suspended in the glowing pool, watching my feet through the turbid water as I kicked them gently and pondered my fate. The water of the well was not to be the answer to my unspoken prayers. Well, what of it? I would find some other way to restore my face and manhood. In the greatness of the universe some method must exist by which I could be made whole. Damascus was the home of many necromancers and sages. Perhaps the answer was known among them.

The most prudent course would have been to climb my way out of that poison pool, but disappointment made me reckless. I wondered if the other parts of the legend were also lies. If a holy relic of value lay at the bottom of the well, it might be worth at least a look. Perhaps it was of such a size and shape that I could carry it out on my back. Drawing a deep breath, I plunged my head into the water and turned my body, then pulled myself downward on the notched stone steps.

The water was of no great depth, though more than deep enough to drown a man. In the shimmering shifting yellow light that was so difficult to look upon, I saw a kind of box about the size of a travel trunk, its flat sides covered with gold leaf. Carved figures rose up on either end. These also appeared gilded, and were probably made of wood, but the loops on its sides attracted my attention. They looked like metal, and might well be solid gold. No trace of corrosion or rust detracted from their smooth and shining surfaces. Pulling myself forward through the murky water, which was obscured by sediment stirred up by the motions of my limbs, I reached out to test the nature of one of the loops.

Something slid from behind the box, or perhaps through its surface. I did not see its place of origin amid the clouds of mud. It flowed forth and uncoiled itself like a gigantic serpent of golden light, winding around and around the side of the well so that it encircled me. It thrust its head at my face and regarded me with its shining eyes. I released bubbles of my breath and paddled backward with my hands. Its face was human, resembling the face of a beautiful woman, but terrible in its severity, its eyes void of mercy or any other emotion. It opened its finely shaped lips, and its elongated teeth were like countless needles of ivory.

Before I could kick off from the muck at the bottom of the well toward the surface, the shining glowing coils of its body fell all around me. They looked material to the sight, but their touch was insubstantial, like the brush of a silk scarf. Yet wherever they touched my limbs, they drew from them the heat of my body and left me numb. My terror mounted with my need to breathe. I became entangled in the coils of the creature as I fought. In desperation, I reached for my sword, only to remember leaving it on the ground beside my wallet.

My fingers closed on something hard. It was a stick of the white wood I had used as a wedge to move the slabs of stone that covered the well. I jerked it from my belt and stabbed at the creature. To my surprise, the stick did not pass through its body, as my fists did, but sank into flesh. It emitted a kind of shriek under the water, either of pain or rage, and its coils withdrew from me. Still stabbing wildly in all directions, I found one of the steps on the side of the well with my hand and pulled my head above the surface. I wasted no time enjoying the air, but scrambled as swiftly as my body would move up the spiral stair until I hung wholly above the accursed pool. In my haste, the white shard of wood fell from my hand. It was so dense, it did not float but sank like a stone.

My legs felt as though they were filled with lead, and my bowels still twisted with cramps. I spat the taste of the foul water from my mouth and started to climb up the notches. I took my time ascending, so that it was twice as prolonged as my descent. It would not have been wise to slip and fall back into the pool, for the thing that protected the box would surely have drowned me. All the while I muttered a string of curses under my breath. My mood was murderous. I had hung all my hopes on the virtues of this well, and in reward for my faith had nearly left my corpse in it.

Martala helped me climb out of the well mouth. I shook her off. Something in my eyes made her step back and keep her silence. I looked around, and found what I sought, a stone the size of my head. Picking it up in both hands to my waist, I shuffled over and dropped it into the well, then listened with deep satisfaction to the sound as it struck the water. It was followed by a thrashing, as though the water in the well began to boil. I chuckled, and found another rock.

After dropping a dozen large stones into the well, my fury began to dim. Fatigue overcame me, and I staggered to one of the flat slabs that had covered the opening and sat upon it. Martala came close but did not touch me. I would not have knocked her hand away. My anger spent, I was left with only a wry appreciation of my own folly.

"The water is poison," I said. "The holy thing is a box. Some spirit or angel of the Hebrews protects it."

"What will we do?" she asked quietly.

I spat. The taste of the well water still fouled my mouth. My guts rolled and I repressed the urge to vomit, knowing that my stomach was empty.

"Leave this accursed place. We will travel west, to Damascus. That is where all the great necromancers of this world dwell, or so it is said. Maybe one of them knows the secret of restoring limbs that have been cut off."

She accepted my decision with her usual lack of argument. She enjoyed bickering about small things, but seldom opposed me on matters of importance.

I gathered up the scattered sticks of white wood and carried them back to our sleeping place. How much they would bring in the markets at Damascus, I could not guess, but one had saved my life, and I was disposed to value them. As I bent over my travel wallet to replace these sticks within it, a mocking laughter floated across the valley.

Dropping the wallet, I snatched up my sword and whipped it in an arc to send its sheath clattering across the stones. The girl drew her dagger, eyes wide with dread. We both knew the voice.

Chapter 50

Why Altrus chose not to kill us both at the well puzzled me more with each day that passed. I could imagine no reason for him to withhold his sword. Had it been any other mercenary, he might hesitate to face both of us at the same time, but I knew that Altrus possessed the skill to kill us with ease. In any case, timidity was not a part of his nature. He followed us to gain the scroll of the Old Ones. It made no sense to me that he would delay the achievement of his purpose.

After the sound of his laughter faded, we waited with our backs touching for his approach. When he failed to come, I began to explore the rim of the valley, and at last climbed to the crest of one of the hills. He had withdrawn himself with such swiftness and skill, no trace remained to betray his presence. I searched the ground for footprints but found only my own and those of the girl. Even so, it was several hours before I felt confident enough to return for the scabbard and sheath my sword. The weight of it was a mockery at my waist. Altrus could beat the blade from my hand with a dozen strokes.

We traveled west, moving with haste, doing our best to conceal our tracks, and sleeping in hollows and caves when we found them. It was not until we left the ferry that carried us across the Euphrates that I began to hope we had escaped his pursuit. The river marked the boundary of the land of the Persians. I welcomed the dryness of the hill country after the green monotony of the southern plain. Even though we traveled far from Yemen, I felt that I was returned to the land of my own people. Those we encountered spoke Arabic more often than not.

Ever westward we worked our way through the barren hills, until we encountered a caravan road that was said to lead to Damascus. I debated with myself the wisdom of following the road, knowing that Altrus must be somewhere behind. There was no real faith in my heart that we could shake off his dogged pursuit so easily. At length, I decided that it would be wiser to keep to the road, but to disguise ourselves amid the many caravans and riders who used it. Alone in the hills we would be easy to track, but amid the multitude of scholars, mercenaries, traders, pilgrims, and wanderers who followed the road, we might indeed lose ourselves and remain hidden.

From the first caravan we overtook we were able to buy apparel better suited to the long journey that lay in front of us than the scholarly garments of the Sons of Sirius, which had become so filthy with mud and dust that their color was more brown than white. One of the merchants possessed a store of used robes, scarves, turbans, hats, and footwear, bundled in sacks over the backs of two camels. When I asked where he had acquired such an abundance of secondhand garments, he said he had bartered for them the day before from a passing wagon. By his satisfied expression, I gathered that he had paid an uncommonly low price, but he took pains to charge me as much as my temper would bear.

Martala did not attempt to disguise herself as a boy, since there seemed little to gain by the subterfuge, but let her dark hair hang freely over her shoulders beneath a new silk head scarf of a deep blue scattered with golden stars. She chose a loose-legged surwal and a simple chemise, both of white cotton, worn beneath a woman's thawb deep blue in color and richly embroidered with beads at the neck and down the front. The thawb was wool, as was the black cloak that covered it and hung down almost to her feet. With the autumnal equinox passed, cooler nights had forced travelers to change from summer cotton to winter wool.

The voluminous cloak was cut in the Persian fashion, with square corners and a hood that hung down in the back. It concealed the new short sword belted at her waist, which I purchased from another merchant of the caravan who traded in edged weapons. The width of its blade made me hesitate to buy it, fearing it would be too heavy for the girl to use, but when I had her make practice cuts in the air, I saw that her arm was strong enough to swing its weight. I took back my ivory-hilted dagger and bought Martala a dagger with a short straight blade of the kind she preferred. She slid its sheath into the furred top of her right boot.

For my part, I rummaged in the bags of clothes so long, the merchant began to roll his eyes with impatience, until at last I found a thawb with an open neck slit down the front that had inner pockets. It was an ugly color midway between green and yellow, with overbold tiraz bands at the sleeves, but its deep pockets were sufficient compensation for my injured sensibilities. To wear beneath it, I chose a white cotton shirt with a long tail, and over it an outer cloak of brown camel hair that was cut round at the corners, as are all sensible cloaks. I purchased a broad belt of leather for my sword, preferring a belt to a baldric, which tended to swing about.

I refused to sell our castoff scholar's robes to the greedy merchant, who sought them for the value of their linen. At the first chance, I went into the hills and hid them beneath a stone along with the infernal shoes, the thin soles of which had worn in holes. It was certain Altrus would recognize the robes, even at a distance, both from their lack of ornament and their slender cut. For several minutes I debated in my mind whether to hide the leather travel wallets along with the robes, but at last decided with reluctance to keep them, since we had no other way to conveniently carry our possessions.

We returned to the road and made good speed in our new boots, which showed little wear from their former owners. Martala swore that hers fitted perfectly. Mine pinched the small toe on my left foot, but not enough to be troublesome.

The way ran uncommonly broad for a caravan track, each section well maintained by the local ruler, so I was not unduly surprised when we passed three wagons drawn by teams of dust-caked weary ponies. It was proof of the high quality of the road that it could be traveled by wagon. They were of a design I had not seen in my wanderings. Each was painted bright yellow, and enclosed by an arched wooden canopy, so that it resembled a little house. At the front of the canopy, above the seat of the woman who held the reins, was drawn in red paint a sign that resembled an eye, but turned on to its corner so that it stood upright.

The wagons moved slowly, rocking from side to side, accompanied by small herds of bleating goats driven along the open margin of the road by dirty-faced children wielding switches. Men of varying ages walked next to the enormous spoked wheels, which at times became trapped in ruts, so that the shaggy little horses needed help from their masters to free them. The men wore no weapons of any kind, unlike their women, who kept long knives in their richly embroidered girdles. On each wagon a woman controlled the horses from a bench at the front. Other women rode within, but occasionally projected their scarf-covered heads through the side windows or back door to harangue the men in their strange tongue. It had an eastern taste in my ear, but was unknown to the flesh of Nectanebus. The swarthy race of the wagons also spoke Arabic, but uttered it with a barbaric accent that made their words difficult to comprehend.

"Have you ever seen wagons like these?" I asked the girl as we made our way past them. They also traveled westward, but at less than a walking pace.

"There is a people that go in wagons up and down the roads of the Delta," she said, squinting through the cloud of dust at the leading conveyance. "They are like these, but different."

One of the men by the huge rear wheel tilted up his head and eyed her from beneath the broad brim of his felt hat. Malignancy glittered in his black eye. I looked at him with a mild expression, wondering how the flesh of his corpse would taste.

"They are traveling tinkers and fortunetellers, a harmless folk always welcome in the villages of Egypt because of the trade goods they carry."

"These men do not look harmless," I murmured so that only she could hear.

"These wagons are different. I have never seen this ugly yellow color, or this red eye, along the Nile."

"Perhaps they are a different clan, and these are their clan markings."

She had no answer. We left the lumbering wagon and its surly brood behind us, but the puzzle of their nature stayed in the back of my thoughts. When we overtook a group of seven pilgrims walking single file on their way to Damascus, I asked their leader about the piss-colored wagons.

"Stay away from them," he said, making the sign of the evil eye with his hand as we walked beside him.

"Are they dangerous?" Martala asked. She had veiled all but her eyes with her scarf to avoid the disapproval of these holy men.

He wagged his head with vigor, making his long black beard ripple on his chest.

"They are thieves and murderers. Some say even worse things about them, that the women divine the future with evil stones, and imprison the souls of their enemies in glass bottles, and that the men sell their first-born sons to Shaitan."

"Shocking," Martala agreed. "Why does the army of the Prophet not put them to the sword?"

He spread his hands, the joints of his fingers knobbed like plums with the disease of stiffness.

"None are more adept in the ways of deception. Do not talk to them, for you will get only lies, and like as not, a knife in your back."

When I had verified to my satisfaction that he knew nothing more about the wagon people than these few bits of gossip, we moved onward, passing another great caravan before the onset of twilight. Our pace carried us faster along the road than most of the traffic. None except those mounted on horseback overtook us. Altrus almost certainly traveled by horse. Our new cloaks concealed us well, but we were betrayed by our number. He had only to keep alert for a man and a woman, or a man and a boy, moving along the road without company.

As full darkness descended, we left the road in search of a place to sleep. I noticed one of the yellow wagons drawn up under a tree in an open patch of ragged grass, the ponies tethered and the goats within a rough stockade of stakes driven into the ground. No one moved near the wagon. Mindful of the warning of the holy man, I kept my distance as we started past. The sound of a deep male voice intoning words within the canopy floated to us on the still night air. Other voices answered in unison, in what had the quality of a religious rite. With perfect clarity, I heard the words *a'ai y'gatu l'il ro'kanah Shub-Niggurath.*

Had the Goat With A Thousand Young herself risen from a fissure in the earth, I would not have been more amazed. To hear the name of Shub-Niggurath chanted by these homeless vagabonds was surprise enough, but to hear it spoken in the language of the Old Ones defied rational explanation. I stopped and listened to the rest of the rite, straining to make out every word. Most of it was in the language of the wagon people, which I did not understand. At the end of the rite, I left the wagon and led the girl into the hills, where we found a hollow with a ledge of rock at its back that was difficult to approach without being seen.

We made a cold meal from our travel wallets in the darkness. There was sufficient dry wood for a fire, but I wanted no beacon to attract Altrus, should it happen that he followed so close behind us.

"Why did you listen at the wagon?" the girl asked.

"Didn't you hear the language of the Old Ones? They spoke the name Shub-Niggurath."

She digested this, along with the fig she chewed. I heard it squishing between her teeth.

"What did they say in the language of the Old Ones?"

I searched my memory, wishing there was sufficient light to study the scroll in my wallet. My ear for tongues had always been good, but the inhabitants of the wagon voiced the ancient words with a thick accent.

"It was an injunction to Shub-Niggurath to fulfill her covenant with the crafty race," I ventured at last.

"A bold folk, to give orders to one of the Old Ones."

"Indeed."

"What is the crafty race?"

I shook my head, realized that she could not see me in the darkness, then did not bother to answer, since I had no answer to make.

When we descended from our hiding place in the early morning, we found the people of the wagon preparing to rejoin the road. A boy and two girls, one older and the other younger than him, pulled up the sticks of the stockade and bundled them on a rack beneath the rear of the wagon. The boy eyed me as we approached. He was no more than twelve years of age, but his face had the blank stare of an adult, giving nothing and expecting nothing in return. The girls glanced at us, but otherwise pretended we did not exist. Their silence was unnatural in children. The bleats of complaint from the goats made the only sound on the still morning air.

I stopped beside the wagon and waited. After a few minutes, the boy went to the back and said something through the open door. A woman poked out her head and glared at us. From beyond her, I noticed two men approaching, their backs heavy under bundles of sticks bound with ropes. They were dressed after the manner of horsemen, in short belted tunics and leather surwals the legs of which tucked into the tops of their high black boots.

"What do you want?" the woman demanded in Arabic.

Another woman with gray hair left the wagon without glancing at us and went to the smoldering cooking fire. She began to poke its embers with a burnt twig. In moments, flames raised their heads around the iron pot that sat across the hearth stones. She took off its copper lid and stirred its contents with the same blackened stick.

"We have heard it said that you foretell the future by lines in the palm," I told the younger woman.

She shrugged a long strand of black hair from her eye and proceeded to bind her head with a striped yellow and white scarf. Her body was slender beneath her dress of gold-embroidered red silk, her face attractive in an angular kind of way.

"What of it?"

I decided to take a more direct approach.

"We have silver."

This made her pause. She eyed me in an appraising manner, not neglecting to study the bulge of the wallet over my shoulder.

"I have a little time before the morning meal," she said, jerking her head in the direction of the cooking fire. "Come inside."

Martala followed silently at my heels as I approached the wagon. The men ignored us. They deposited a few of the sticks next to the fire, and began to tie the others to wooden brackets at the side of the wagon. The boy gave Martala a knowing smirk that was out of place in a child of his years and flipped up the hem of his ragged shirt. To her credit, she restrained the urge to box his ear, though I sensed it was an effort for her.

Within the wagon, the woman opened a small circular table with folding legs. I saw three narrow cots fixed on the left wall, one above the other, and on the right side a large cupboard secured at the top by ropes stood with its doors wide, revealing upper shelves filled with all manner of cooking implements, spices, and jars. The lower shelves held bottles, clothing, and other household articles. At the rear of the wagon, beneath the window that opened on its exterior driver's seat, stood an ornately carved cabinet of blond sandalwood. It had the look of a portable shrine, and was of unexpected richness. I wondered if it had been stolen from the house of some wealthy landowner. The shadowed space within the wagon possessed a distinct odor that was a mingling of spices, wood smoke, and stale sweat.

She nodded her kerchief-bound head to a row of stools that hung along the wall. I took one and Martala took another. We sat at the round table, and the woman seated herself on the opposite side with the sandalwood cabinet at her back. Her keen black eyes glanced from my face to that of the girl with startling penetration. They returned to stare at me with a trace of amusement. I wondered what she saw.

Taking out my purse, I jiggled it to make the coins within it clink, and drew forth a silver dirham of the middle size. She held it up to the light from the open door to examine the beardless profile of the old Sassanian emperor Yazdegerd, and put it into her broad girdle.

"Give me your hand," she commanded.

I did not know which hand she might prefer, so I extended my left. She grunted, but accepted it. As her fingers touched mine, I felt a tingle. She released my fingers and stared at me, speaking words in her own tongue.

"I cannot understand your language," I told her.

"You are one of us," she said. "How can this be?"

I glanced across at Martala, who shrugged her shoulders. The elder of the two men put his head around the corner of the wagon and looked at us from beneath the brim of his hat, but his bearded face betrayed nothing. He withdrew when the woman waved him away with an impatient jerk of her head.

"You are not alone," she said, nodding with a kind of smile.

"This girl is my servant."

She made a noise of disgust in her throat.

"You know what I refer to, the one you carry inside."

Can she mean you, Sashi? I thought.

She sees me, Alhazred. She has the second sight that you receive from the white spiders. She has something more, a djinn inside her.

This quickened my interest.

What kind of djinn?

I cannot identify it. The spirit is like none I have ever encountered. It will not speak to me.

The woman seemed to listen to my very thoughts as Sashi talked within my mind. She frowned and withdrew herself slightly.

"I was wrong. You are unlike us. You carry a companion, but she is not of the Mother."

"Your words are curious," I said, affecting a dull-witted smile. "I do not understand them."

"No matter," she said brusquely, dismissing my curiosity. "Give me your hand."

She grasped it firmly and studied its palm.

"You were born into poverty, but were raised up to a high estate. You provoked the anger of a great man and suffered the penalty."

As she said this, she glanced at my face, and I knew she saw its mutilation beneath the veil of glamour.

"You fled into the wilderness, and for a long time you wandered in search of wisdom. Many men seek your death."

She drew a harsh breath, and stared into my eyes.

"You died and were reborn. Now you search for a way to regain the love that you lost. Someone watches you, a dark man of the desert. He is not your friend, but neither is he your enemy."

"These are matters of the past and present. What of the future?"

She squinted at my hand, shaking her head and mumbling, then released it with a gesture of dismissal.

"I cannot see your future. It is veiled, just like your face."

I nodded. A more honest teller of fortunes I had never encountered. An understanding of sorts passed between us. I knew that she knew more than she was telling, and she knew the same about me. As an act of good faith, I decided to reveal myself, and used the word and gestures of the glamour in their reverse order to strip away the veil of illusion from my features. Her eyes narrowed, but she betrayed no other reaction.

"Why did you really come here?"

"We are pursued by an assassin who has seen both my faces. Alone on the road we are easy to identify, and vulnerable to attack. I wish to travel with your wagon, so that the assassin will not find us and will pass over us on the road."

"Cannot you lie in wait for this assassin and kill him?"

"If you knew the assassin, you would not ask such a thing," Martala muttered.

The woman ignored her.

"We do not travel with those not of our own race," she said.

I lifted my purse and let it fall on the table with a rich clink of coins. She eyed the purse, and many thoughts passed through her mind. I did not need the power of second sight to divine their trend. If we were close, and misfortune befell us, the contents of the purse would be fair game for the first person quick enough to seize it up from my corpse. She named an amount in gold, and I counted it out and gave it into her hand.

"Very well, you may walk beside the wheels, and eat with us if you wish, but you must sleep outside the wagon at night."

"What name are you called?"

"We are Thugians. In our own language, the name signifies the wise race, for we are knowing in the ways of beasts and men."

"No, you misunderstand. If we are to travel together we must know what to call you." I told her my name and the name of the girl.

"I am Naleen, wife of Belok who is the tall man with the bushy beard you have seen. The younger man is his brother, Ell. The old woman heating our stew is Belok's mother, Urga. My son is called Rakk, my older daughter is Pula, and my younger daughter Leti. Now you have our names, and power over us. And I have your names."

The threat was not voiced, but was plain enough. Any magic I might work with their names would be matched by magic against us using our names.

A faint tinkling came from the lower shelf of the open cupboard. I looked for its source but saw only a row of tall bottles of clear glass that appeared to be empty, although they were tightly sealed with corks and wax. They were in shadow, but I observed a kind of mist swirl in the nearest bottle. Without haste, she stood from her stool and shut the doors of the cupboard, securing them with the wooden latch. Her posture indicated that our business was concluded.

I left the wagon with the girl. The horror of my face provoked as little reaction from the men and children as it had evoked from the witch. They glanced at me, then looked away. I found their lack of surprise at the change in my features unnatural. We sat on a flat stone some distance from the fire, where we could talk without being overheard.

"She plans to slit our throats while we sleep," Martala murmured, voicing a thought that had passed through my own mind.

"I don't think so. That she would kill us for our gold I have no doubt, but not while we are traveling with the wagon. That would be poor hospitality."

"Not every race is as mindful of the rules of hospitality as your own," she said.

"I wonder what they keep in that shrine?"

"Ask the bitch. No doubt she will show you, if you pay enough gold."

"You may be right. But not today. First, we must gain their trust."

She laughed scornfully.

"We could travel with these cutthroats for a year and not gain their trust."

"I grant your superior knowledge of thieves and vagabonds," I said patiently. "Even so, I mean to travel with the wagon. It is the best chance we have of avoiding the notice of Altrus. If he does identify us, he will be reluctant to attack in the presence of so many people."

She could not argue with the good sense of my words, but they did not change her opinion of the Thugians. Perhaps she recognized in their nature a muddy reflection of her own image, and disliked the reminder that until joining me, she might have passed as one of the children of the wagon.

The stew was better than I expected. Sitting in the covered pot overnight had not hurt its flavor. As the level dropped, the old woman added water from a water skin, and used her knife to cut onions and parsnips into it. A rabbit, freshly caught and skinned by the boy, also contributed to its contents. At the end of the meal, she covered the pot and took it off the embers, but did not empty it. I wondered how long the same stew had been eaten and replenished. The fanciful idea came to me that it might be older than the gray-haired hag that stirred it.

While the men wordlessly harnessed the small horses to the wagon, the children gathered the goats into a tight, milling mass by cutting the air with their switches and hissing like snakes. This noise seemed to subdue the animals. They waited with docile expressions on their long faces for the wheels of the wagon to lurch into motion. The road ran no great distance from the camp site. We found ourselves moving along beside the turning wheels, which exerted a kind of entrancement on the mind. When the wagon wheels became trapped in deep ruts of soft sand, we put our hands to the spokes with the two men and the boy, and urged them free. This was hard work, but it came at infrequent intervals, and by walking far enough to the side of the wagon we were able to avoid the worst of the dust.

It soon became apparent that Naleen led the family of wanderers. Belok grunted and cast her dark looks when she ordered him about, but he never failed to do what he was told. No one contested her words, not even the children. She was an impressive woman with proud breasts that showed no sign of sagging beneath her long-sleeved dress of red and gold, and wide hips that accentuated her slender waist, well displayed by her broad embroidered girdle. Had it not been for the expression of malice that settled around the drawn corners of her mouth, she might have been beautiful.

None of the women of the wagons wore veils, but all went about shamelessly with their faces exposed like men, presumably because it was more practical for travel along the road. The deep-blue Persian cloak and starry head scarf worn by Martala blended well with the bright clothing of the Thugian women. My own brown cloak looked a little drab in comparison. To better play the part of a wanderer, I tied around my forehead a yellow kerchief striped with white that I bought from the eldest girl, Pula. This seemed to be a kind of emblem for the Thugians. Almost all the men of the wagons we passed on the road, and many of the women, wore such a yellow and white cloth around their heads, or necks. I saw Belok cast me a long glance when I put on the kerchief, but he did not order me to remove it.

At noon we stopped to rest and water the ponies, and to have a brief uncooked meal of bread and cheese. Martala made herself useful by helping the men care for the little horses. I sat on a hillock as I finished my crust and watched the children at play, if it can be called that, for they conducted themselves with utmost seriousness.

While Pula stood staring off into the distance, affecting indifference, Rakk crept up behind her with his yellow kerchief twisted between his fists. When he was close enough, he threw it over her head and around her neck, and proceeded to choke her with it. She fought him vigorously, and if she managed to twist out of his grasp, she taunted him until his cheeks burned. If he managed to hold her until she tapped upon his fists with her hands in a gesture of submission, he released her to gasp for air, then strutted around like a breeding cock to show his superiority. The younger child watched these exertions and urged her sister to greater efforts. It was a strange game that I found disquieting in its implications.

At the approach of evening, we camped outside a village. The wagon attracted the inhabitants, who came in small groups or pairs to trade and have their fortunes told. I noticed that none approached the wagon alone. The villagers treated the travelers with barely disguised contempt, yet were eager to barter with them for spices, dried roots, charms, amulets, rings, glass beads, bright kerchiefs, and other magpie treasures. Many came with shameful faces seeking potions from the witch Naleen. Love philters and medicines against impotence were no doubt a popular purchase in this remote land. I wondered if she also sold poisons.

Leaving Martala with the wagon, I walked into the village at twilight to draw water from the well that occupied the center of the market square, which was no more than a beaten patch of bare ground surrounded by stone and wattle huts. As I filled my water skin from the well bucket, I discover that my presence was unwelcome. A dozen dirty children in rags gathered, jeering at my face which I had not troubled to conceal. When their number was great enough to give them courage, they threw stones until I withdrew myself. They followed me to the edge of the cultivated vegetable gardens that surrounded the huts, but went no further, for the shadows of night had fallen.

We continued along the road in this manner for three days, and might have gone on without incident all the way to Damascus, when we came to a place where the road crossed a narrower track that extended in a more northerly direction. The wagon was compelled to stop and wait for the passage of an uncommonly large and wealthy caravan. I guessed by the silver bells on the equipage of the camels and the gleaming ceremonial armor of the mounted guards that it was a royal procession of some sort. Two-score mounted and armored soldiers protected three wagons, their interiors enclosed by hanging curtains of silk embroidered with gold and silver thread. The central wagon, larger than the other two, was covered entirely in gold leaf. Dozens of camels bore heavy loads, tended by innumerable well-dressed slaves.

"They must be carrying home the corpse of some prince," Martala muttered.

Her mood was soured by the clouds of fine dust raised by the hooves of the camels and horses. I glanced at Belok, who stared at the gold leaf on the sides of the big wagon with an avaricious glint. His eyes widened and his lips parted in amazement, causing me to look back at the passing wagon.

A woman of exquisite beauty held the side curtain wide to gaze out with a bored and impatient expression. Her arm was covered by a sleeve of transparent silk of a delicate pink, and a silver bracelet adorned her wrist. She blinked against the brightness of the sun, her gaze passing over the yellow wagon, and for a moment her eyes met mine.

"What a haughty expression on the face of that slut," Martala grumbled. "Who does she think she is?"

"She is the Princess Narisa of Yemen," I said, my voice hollow in my own earholes.

Chapter 51

Martala regarded me as though I had plunged a dagger of ice into her breast. "This is the woman you love? The woman you speak about?"

I nodded, barely hearing her words. Since my expulsion from the palace at Sana'a, I had contemplated Narisa's perfect features a thousand times in memory, yet to look upon them with my eyes made them appear unreal, a face viewed in a dream. I drank her beauty with the thirst of desperation, trying to fill the emptiness in my heart. When she let the embroidered curtain fall shut and withdrew her white hand, I almost cried out, so keen was my frustration.

She had gazed directly at me, yet no hint of recognition had stirred in her brown eyes. I told myself that the horror of my mutilated face deceived her memory. I must get closer with my veil of glamour in place, so that she would see me as I had looked while her lover at the palace. Then she would know me and express her joy. A thought rose like an eel from the depths of my mind and I pushed it away, yet it returned, no matter how often I repulsed it. Where was my own joy? Where was my love? I felt only a strange numbness, an unfulfilled expectation.

Naleen showed no haste to continue on the Damascus road after the last heavily laden camel of the caravan passed, but sat with the reins in her hands, watching it diminish in the distance. Belok came close to the wagon seat and they murmured together in their own tongue. I paid them scant attention. My mind was occupied with the question of whether to follow the caravan immediately, or to wait until after the fall of darkness. I must see the princess face to face. How was I to approach the caravan without arousing the suspicions of her armed guard?

While I debated this matter, the wagon was driven to the side of the road, and Belok and his brother set about unhitching the horses. It was a curious time of the day to stop, still early afternoon. Had I not been distracted by the ache in my heart, I flatter myself that I would have comprehended their purpose more quickly. As it was, I only understood after they put saddles on three of the shaggy beasts. They had changed their clothing, and wore hats to cover the striped yellow kerchiefs on their heads. Even the boy wore a different shirt.

Approaching Belok, I laid my hand on his arm as he was about to swing himself into his saddle.

"Let me come with you. I can be of service."

He stared at me, his expression opaque.

"You know what we do?"

"Yes. I know you intend to rob the rich caravan that passed. I will help you."

"They saw the wounds on your face. They would recognize you."

I made the passes of the charm and spoke its word. He nodded grudgingly as my features changed.

Martala watched me from a distance, hugging her arms across her chest, the hurt still in her eyes. Belok glanced at her.

"We have only four horses."

"The girl will stay behind. If I fail you, she will suffer your punishment."

He grunted, probably wondering how much affection I had for the girl. At last he handed the reins of his horse to his son, and walked to the wagon to confer with his wife. To my surprise, she decided in my favor. Belok took back the reins and swung himself into his saddle. Without a glance at me, he ordered Rakk to saddle the fourth horse.

Martala approached while we watched the boy carry the saddle from the wagon and throw it onto the back of the animal.

"If you do this thing, no good will come of it," she murmured, standing near me. "What has changed for you, since last you saw her?"

"It is none of your affair," I snapped. "Stay near the wagon. You are their hostage lest I betray them. If you flee they will surely kill me, and kill you when they catch you."

"I understand. I will wait for you, Alhazred. Do what you must, but remember my words."

Had she demanded to know what lay in my mind, I could not have told her. My thoughts roiled with empty longing and confusion. Determination warred with doubt, pushing the balance first forward, then back. I threw her words away, unwilling even to consider them for fear they might weaken my resolve. After so many months, fate had reunited me to the woman I loved. This could not be an accident of chance, I told myself. There must be purpose to so improbable a conjunction.

We walked the horses at a moderate pace, following the wheel tracks of the caravan. In late afternoon, we overtook the straggling camels at its rear and swung wide to the left side of the road, as though to escape the dust that hung in a cloud behind the plodding beasts. This was opposite the side we had occupied while the caravan passed the wagon. The riders on the left would not have gained a clear look at any of our faces, though it was unlikely even those who rode on the right would recognize us, so little attention had they given us in their passing. I noticed other solitary riders and small groups, following behind or to the side of the camels. By their appearance, they did not belong to the caravan.

"Riders alone or few in number always seek security in the shadow of an armed caravan," Belok explained when he observed the direction of my gaze. "It is considered an uncharitable act to drive them away."

From the ease of his manner, it was not the first time he had worked this deceit. His brother sat his horse equally relaxed, but the boy's face shone with excitement. I guessed it was his initiation into serious thievery. He felt my gaze upon him and glared with challenge. I smiled mildly and looked away, reflecting that ghouls were younger when they went on their first hunt. The test of manhood always came, sooner or later, and had only two outcomes—glory or shame. This was Rakk's day of trial.

I could not resist separating myself from my companions and riding forward until I was almost abreast of the gilded wagon. The mounted guards cast their eyes upon me, but said nothing when I made no attempt to approach. To my surprise, the curtains were parted to take advantage of the rays of the setting sun, which made the gold leaf on the side and wheels flash like flame. Narisa reclined on a bed of cushions, her unveiled face to the opening, her cheeks painted with golden light. Beyond her I saw two handmaidens. One knelt and massaged her naked foot with oil while the other read aloud from a book.

I stared at her face, willing her to notice me. She felt my eyes upon her and glanced at me with disinterest. For a dozen heartbeats, our eyes remained locked. Something stirred deep within her gaze, and her eyelashes fluttered. I knew with certainty that she recognized me. I forced a faint smile upon my lips, feeling like a fool, wondering why my heart beat like a leaden bell. She frowned and her rouge-reddened lips became hard. Without turning her head, she spoke several words to the servant at her feet. The girl reached over and drew shut the curtains of the wagon. They closed across an expression of disdain on the face of the princess, an expression I knew well, but one reserved for her slaves and servants, never before cast upon me.

One of the guards noticed my interest in the wagon and made a curt gesture with his hand, warning me to drop back. I let the pace of my pony slow, and fell back into step with Belok and his kin. I was scarcely aware of what I did.

Narisa had recognized me, of that I was certain. I had anticipated that she would struggle to contain her joy, would laugh aloud, weep, rise from her seat, call out my old name, but I had seen only reserve and irritation in her countenance.

She has forsaken you, my love.

Sashi's inner voice held a note of satisfaction. I tried to ignore her words, refusing at first to consider them. She was a jealous creature, that I already knew, and would say anything to weaken my love for Narisa. Yet, as I searched the image in my memory in vain for any trace of welcome or affection in the dark eyes of the princess, I realized that Sashi spoke the truth. Was I so greatly changed from my ordeal in the desert that I no longer stirred her love? Or had her mind broken after being compelled to witness my punishment, and rejected all affection for me?

My thoughts grew so troubled, I scarcely noticed Ell in casual conversation with one of the mounted guards of the caravan. He rode back to rejoin us and caused his mount to fall into step beside his brother.

"This is the bridal caravan of a princess of Yemen." He spoke in Arabic for my benefit. "She goes to be united with her husband in Constantinople. A marriage of political convenience, arranged by her brother, the king. The caravan carries her dowry."

At this final word, Belok's dark eyes widened.

"The wealth carried on the backs of these camels must be great," he said. "No wonder there is so strong a guard."

The words of the younger brother brought blood pounding in my ears. I tightened my hands on the reins of my mount to keep my balance in the saddle, and fought down sickness in my belly. Narisa was pledged to another man. The marriage contract had already been signed, and now she journeyed to consummate her union with her husband. Reason enough to reject me. Yet still I wondered that she had shown such coldness, and what action I should take. Martala's words returned to me. Nothing had changed. I could never be a husband to Narisa in my present state. Even so, how could I allow her to give herself to another man and lose her forever?

The evening camp of the caravan occupied a large space, with a dozen fires burning at intervals around the gathered wagons. When we left our horses hobbled and sat at the edge of a fire, the soldiers who tended it made no attempt to drive us away. They shared their bread with us, and Belok gave them some of the salted goat meat he had brought on the journey. The soldiers laughed and joked among themselves, for the most part ignoring us. Their numbers made them careless. Apart from two posted guards, who stood leaning on their javelins, few bothered to glance out at the surrounding darkness.

Belok leaned over to speak to me in a low murmur.

"Can you move without noise?"

The absurdity of a man asking a ghoul whether he could move silently through the darkness almost caused me to laugh aloud. Repressing this urge, I nodded with a solemn expression.

"I am going to teach you a great secret of my people. It is the only way you can serve us."

"I am honored by your trust," I lied.

He turned his body as though to warm his back at the fire, and I did the same. In the shadow of our backs, he passed me a slip of parchment. Opening it, I distinguished a curious symbol inscribed with what appeared to be blood. The fire's glow that passed between our bodies lit a prick of red on the tip of his index finger, and I knew it was his own blood on the parchment. He made a gesture with his hand. I watched closely while he repeated it, then imitated it.

"Good," he nodded with satisfaction. "Now listen closely."

He spoke a word in his own language. I let him speak it a second time, then repeated it. He made me repeat the word several times until he was satisfied with my way of speaking it.

"Our goddess has given us power to steal from those who are not her worshippers. Those near enough to hear the word of her charm fall into a deep sleep."

"I have heard of such a trick used by necromancers," I said. "A hand with candles
on its fingers, made from human fat."

He spat on the ground.

"This is a holy thing I teach you, not a trick."

Chagrined by his manner, I felt my irritation mount.

"Why am I not asleep? You spoke the word to me."

"First we speak the word, then we make the motions of the hand. That causes the
charm to function. If the gesture is made before the word is uttered, there is no
effect. How else could we teach this charm?"

I could not argue with this reasoning. I wondered if the charm would work for a
man that failed to worship his goddess, who could only be Shub-Niggurath. If so, it
would be a useful magic to acquire.

"The sign on the parchment gives power for only one night beneath the moon,"
he added, as though reading my thoughts. "The rays of the sun frustrate its working."

"What if the moon is below the horizon, or does not show her face?"

"No matter. As long as the sun has set, the spell will work."

The hour grew late, and the campfires burned down to embers. The soldiers and
slaves wrapped themselves in their cloaks and settled onto their sleeping mats beside
the warm circles of stones. The murmur of voices diminished, until only the grunts of
the camels as they shifted against their restraints could be heard, mingled with the
faint but ever-present night sounds of the stony land. I lay beside Belok, his brother
and son on his opposite side. He gave a skillful imitation of a man asleep, breathing
gusty sighs interrupted with the occasional snort from his nose.

These deceiving snorts ceased, and I felt his finger touch my thigh in the darkness.

"It is time," he whispered.

I saw the vague bulk of his shadow rise up and work its way around the edge of
the glow from the dying embers of the fire toward a night guard, who stood with his
face turned away. He moved with almost no sound on the small pebbles and loose
sand, not as silently as a ghoul, but with greater skill than I expected. When he was
near enough to the guard to touch, I saw his mouth move. The guard began to turn,
and he made the gesture. Slowly, the knees of the soldier buckled and he collapsed
with a soft sound to the ground.

Ell and Rakk immediately gained their feet and began to move around the camp-fires, whispering the word of the charm and making the gesture over the sleeping forms of the soldiers and slaves. The few who stirred into wakefulness at their approach were stilled with the charm. They kept well apart from each other. I realized that if one were to speak the word of the charm and make the gesture within hearing of the other, the hearer would be put to sleep, and I took care to move far enough away from them as they worked to avoid overhearing the word. The other night guard stood watch on the opposite side of the wagons. The Thugians worked their way around the encampment. Soon, everyone outside the wagons lay entranced.

Rakk moved toward the gilded wagon of the princess. I approached quickly and set myself between him and its curtain.

"This wagon is mine," I murmured.

There was enough glow from a nearby hearth to illuminate his face. He smirked in that knowing way of his, so unnatural in a child.

"She is beautiful. Do not take too long, or my father will become angry."

He left me for the next wagon. Belok and his brother were occupied with the piles of packs that had been removed from the camels, evidently content to allow the boy to put the occupants of the wagons into trance.

I tried to part the side curtains of the gilded wagon, realized they were tied shut from the inside, and used my dagger to slit them apart by sliding its blade up the gap where the curtains met. Through this opening I reached my arm and released the ties at the bottom of a curtain by touch, so that I could pull it aside. Gentle breathing came from within the wagon. With utmost care, I eased my body through the opening and knelt until my eyes adjusted to the faint ember glow from the hearths that found its way into the interior.

There was more space in the wagon that I would have guessed. The princess slept on the cushions of her bed beneath a blanket of soft wool. Her handmaids lay on the floor, one beside her and the other at the foot of the bed. I crawled to each slave in turn and whispered the word of the charm into her ear, then made the gesture. Neither showed any change, leaving me to wonder if the charm had worked. Moving with caution, I raised myself and sat upon the side of the bed. I did not know what I intended to do or say. For several minutes I did nothing except sit and gaze at the shadow of her face, which grew brighter as my eyes became more accustomed to the gloom inside the wagon. She had the face of an angel.

Upon a table next to the bed I noticed a brass lamp, and beside it what could only be a tinderbox. Some impulse made me open the tinderbox and strike its flint on steel. The flutter of flame on the tinder seemed bright. I touched it to the wick of the lamp. A steady glow filled the wagon. The handmaidens continued to lie unmoving upon the floor, giving me some hope that the charm was effective. In the warm light of the lamp, I studied the features of my beloved. A vague dissatisfaction stirred in my heart, but I pushed it away.

Her eyes fluttered open, lazy with sleep. They rolled from side to side, then fixed upon me. I touched my fingertips to her parted lips. She seized my wrist in both her hands, her long nails digging into my skin, but continued to stare at my face, making no attempt to thrust my hand away.

"I came back for you, Narisa," I said, sliding my fingers off her lips.

"Whatever you want, take it and go. If I scream, my guards will kill you."

Her manner puzzled me. Beneath her fear was a gathering resolve. I saw no expression of love, yet I knew she recognized me, as she had earlier in the day.

"Can you speak this way to your lover?"

"My lover is dead," she said coldly. "He died in the Empty Space. I am traveling to join my husband."

Her feigned indifference should have driven me to fury, but I felt nothing apart from a distant sadness.

"Don't you remember our pledge? We swore to be faithful to each other forever."

"Children say foolish things," she hissed, anger gathering in her eyes. "I am a married woman. I do not know you."

My own anger rose in response. I took the glamour away from my face.

"Do you know me now?"

She spat into my face and started to rise. I held her down, and she began to struggle and kick.

"You are no more than a thief. I will call for my guards."

As she filled her lungs with air, I spoke the word of the sleep charm in a quiet voice and made the gesture. Her eyes closed, and the breath slowly sighed from her lips. Her face softened into the face of the child I remembered, the child I had loved once, but loved no longer.

Some impulse made me search the cupboards and boxes in the wagon. In her jewel case I found what I sought, the pendant I had given her as a token of our undying pledge. Holding it in my hand, I studied the large sapphire within its circle of smaller diamonds. It seemed impossible that less than two years before, we had gazed together into its blue depths with a single hope and happiness. Now I felt nothing as I looked upon it. My confusion and doubt were replaced by a vast emptiness of the soul.

Cupping my hand to the lamp, I blew out its flame, then slid the pendant into a pocket of my thawb. I worked my body through the gap in the curtains and walked across to Belok, who stood over a small pile of valuable things gathered from the opened packs. His brother and son were beside him.

"Are they asleep?" Belok asked without glancing at me.

"They sleep."

"We take nothing from the wagons," he said. "Only from the sealed packs. If we are lucky, it will be days before anyone notices that anything is missing."

"That is wise," I told him, fingering the hardness of the pendant through the side of my thawb.

"Why did you light the lamp?"

"I was curious to see what the wagon held."

He grunted. Rakk laughed and smirked at me in his usual way.

"You were quick," the boy said.

His father hit him in the side of the head with his open hand. The boy gave no indication that he noticed the blow.

I left them opening the sealed leather packs and investigating their contents. None paid attention to me when I walked from the dull red glow of the sooty hearths into the night. I moved as I used to move in the Empty Space, pleased to see that my old skills had not deserted me. The fancy came into my mind to keep going away from the caravan camp, away from the Thugian thieves, away from Martala, until nothing but the cleanness of the desert surrounded me. I rejected the impulse with impatience. It arose from weakness. A ghoul was not permitted the luxury of being weak. I stroked the smooth dome of Gor's skull beneath my cloak and continued to hunt through the rocks until I found what I sought.

Returning to the camp, I saw that my absence had caused no concern. Belok and his brother packed away the precious articles of gold and silver into the sacks tied across the rumps of the little horses. I had wondered about the purpose of the sacks. The boy carried armloads of loot from the diminishing pile on the ground and stood waiting while it was lifted with care and fitted away so that it did not make a sound. They worked efficiently but without haste, secure in the power of the sleep charm.

I entered the gilded wagon, but did not bother to light the lamp. The princess slept as I had left her. An impulse made me arrange her arms more gracefully across her breast. I smelled her perfume while bent across her body, and could not resist kissing her softly on the lips. They parted at the pressure from my kiss. Her breath touched my face as I withdrew.

Looking around the dark wagon, I located the oblong shadow of her jewel box and opened it. From a pocket I took a rolled rag and unfolded it with care. As its last fold fell open I released one side of the rag. A black shape the length of my finger dropped into the jewel box with a soft click and remained motionless for a moment. In the dimness I saw it turn its body and open its claws, its envenomed tail curling up in preparation to strike. Smiling to myself, I closed the lid of the box without a sound.

When I emerged once again, the three thieves had the loot of the caravan stowed onto the backs of the horses and were making certain that the large leather packs of the camels were closed in such a way that no one would notice that they had been opened. Belok studied the arrangement of the piles of packs with a critical eye, and directed his brother to move packs this way and that until he was satisfied that they looked as they had looked before being disturbed. Rakk loitered beside the horses, holding their reins in both hands. Evidently Belok intended to leave the caravan before morning. Such unannounced departures of stragglers were probably common enough.

The sound of stumbling footsteps in the darkness turned the four of us to stone. A man staggered into view and approached the horses. He wore a puzzled expression. I saw that it was one of the slaves responsible for handling the camels. The boy dropped the reins of the horses, and as they milled around in unease he confronted the slave. Belok and his brother covered their ears with their hands. Realizing what was about to happen, I imitated them. Rakk spoke the charm and made the gesture. The man, who was evidently drunk, blinked at him, looking around at the four of us. The boy repeated the charm, but without effect. He looked at his father in puzzlement as Belok lowered his hands.

The eyes of the slave settled on the fat packs across the backs of the ponies and his eyes widened with comprehension. He began to make loud but inarticulate noises with his throat, rolling his eyes. He stared at Rakk, then stumbled away from him and ran toward a sleeping guard. Picking up his javelin, he brandished it in a menacing way, still lowing and bellowing like a bull with cramps in its belly. Before I could react to this extraordinary display, Belok rushed across and knocked the wavering point of the javelin aside with his foot. He nodded to his son.

The boy drew out a yellow kerchief from inside his shirt and twisted it into a rope, as I had watched him do in the game played with his sister. Belok grasped the spear and tore it away from the deaf and dumb slave, while his brother wrapped his arms around the slave from the front, pinning the slave's arms to his sides at his elbows. Rakk stepped behind the slave and looped the yellow noose over his head. He drew it tight. The eyes of the drunken slave bulged. Saliva gurgled deep in his throat. He tried to throw off Ell's grasp, and Belok came to help his brother while Rakk finished the task of strangling him.

The boy kept the noose tight until there was no doubt that the slave was quite dead. Without a word between them, Belok and his brother picked up the corpse by its wrists and ankles and carried it out of the camp. The boy put away his kerchief, took up the javelin, and returned it to the sleeping guard. He glanced at me as he came back to gather in the reins of the horses. Pride glowed in his face. The beasts had not run far. Perhaps this was a common event for them. From Belok's saddle he drew forth a short pickax with a broad blade and carried it casually in the direction the men had gone with the dead slave.

I followed out of curiosity, although I had little doubt what I would see. Behind a low hill some distance from the road we found them. I saw in the faint starlight the dead slave lying naked on his belly, his clothes and shoes in a pile. Belok took the tool and dug a shallow grave. When it was two cubits deep, his brother and son tumbled the corpse into the hole, and helped him cover it with earth by kicking in loose stones and sand with their feet. He took a few minutes to smooth the ground and scatter the excess dirt around. After the wind blew, there would be little trace to show that anything had been buried. Ell gathered up the clothing of the murdered man in his arms.

Belok saw me watching him. He wiped sweat from his forehead with the sleeve of his tunic and grinned fiercely, showing all his teeth like a wolf.

"We do this in honor of our goddess, who ensures our good fortune in perpetuity."

"Why did you let your boy kill the deaf mute?"

He slapped the grinning Rakk on the back and gathered him close with an arm around his neck.

"He is no longer a boy, but a man."

"A'ai y'gatu l'il ro'kanah Shub-Niggurath!" chanted his brother in a voice of exultation.

The father and the boy repeated the chant. Not wishing to feel like an outsider at this emotional moment, I said it with them.

Chapter 52

The sun had not yet risen when we returned to the wagon, but the sky glowed with the chill light of early morning. Martala squatted beside the cooking fire, encouraging it to burn by poking it with a crooked stick. When she heard the approach of our horses, she stood and peered anxiously through the grayness. Her face relaxed into a smile as she recognized me.

Belok called out in his deep voice and roused the women and girls from the wagon. They milled around the horses while we dismounted, chattering their questions. Little Leti, who had not yet dressed herself, clung naked to her mother's cloak, shifting from one foot to the other in her excitement. Rakk said something in their language, and groans of approval came from Naleen and the old woman, who took the boy's face between her hands and kissed him on the lips. I left them untying the heavy sacks of stolen goods from the saddles.

"I didn't know if you would come back," Martala said as we walked together back to the smoking fire.

"You were right. There was nothing for me in the caravan."

She remained silent to encourage me to speak, but I had said all I wished to say. Belok came over and slapped me on the back with good humor, his bristly face beaming.

"I told my wife you bring our wagon good fortune."

I felt tired, and was ill disposed to be jovial. He did not seem to notice my dullness.

"I thought your goddess ensured your fortune."

"So she does, but we can never have too much luck."

Laughing, he left us and returned to his son, who talked in their language with much animation, his mother and sisters for an audience. They made approving sounds at appropriate pauses. Ell unsaddled the horses, and the old woman tended to the morning meal.

As we continued to make our way along the road in the days that followed, the attitude of Naleen changed toward me. Whereas she had barely spoken a dozen words before the raid on the caravan, she now sought me out in the early evenings after making camp, eager to acquire what techniques of necromancy I could teach, for she was always seeking to enlarge her power. I learned much concerning the history and beliefs of the Thugians, and their tribal pact with Shub-Niggurath. In return I taught her what small charms I knew. I thought she might desire to learn the names and nature of the Old Ones, but she was indifferent to this knowledge because it could not be turned by her to practical advantage.

Martala resented this apparent intimacy between me and the witch. She need not have concerned herself. It was based on nothing more than mutual gain. If Belok shared her resentment, he gave no expression to his feelings. I believe he knew his wife well enough not to feel jealousy. In any case, it was not his place to criticize her actions. He respected her authority, and more than this, he feared her wrath. They all feared her, even the boy, who obeyed without a word when his mother ordered him to do a task. Perhaps they loved her as well, but their love was not as evident as their fear.

For ten dinars, I persuaded her to show me the mystery that was kept hidden behind the closed doors of the sandalwood shrine. This she did on a misty morning when the men hunted rabbits in the hollows, and the children were occupied outside the wagon with Martala and the old woman, washing soiled undergarments in a wooden tub. As she closed the door at the back of the wagon, I saw Martala cast me a troubled glance. I made a gesture with my palm downward behind Naleen's back to show that she had no reason for alarm.

"That girl guards you like a brooding hawk," she said as she turned.

The flame of an oil lamp lit the sharp planes of her angular face, severe and beautiful at the same time.

"She is a faithful servant."

"Is that all she is to you?"

I indicated the holes of my missing nose and ears.

"What else could she be?"

She shrugged and moved further back into the wagon to the shrine. It rested on a low table, its arched roof on the level of my heart. The peak of the roof was surmounted by a wooden ball, in which was carved a lidless eye turned on its point. Winged beasts like dragons, but with the beaks of birds, entwined on its front panels, their claws upraised in warning. They seemed to move in the flicker of the lamp.

"What I show to you now is our most sacred mystery. Belok and the others must never know that you have seen it."

"I understand."

The doors of the shrine were not opened by a key, but by means of small studs that projected from the carved panels and appeared to be nothing more than details of the design. She passed her slender fingers over them, pressing here and there too swiftly for my eyes to follow, then pulled open the doors.

The polished black limbs of the stone idol within the shrine were frozen in the posture of dance. She stood upon her pedestal on one foot, the other upraised, her arms askew, her eyes staring with insane glee, her thick lips writhed away from her ivory teeth, and her tongue extended in a silent scream of ecstasy. In the middle of her forehead a third eye glared. An ivory necklace of exquisitely carved human skulls hung from her naked torso below the level of her full breasts. Her hairless and obscenely exposed vulva had been shaped by the artist in complete detail. Inset between its lips glowed a rounded emerald of the deepest green. Her vulva seemed to gape as though about to give birth to the jewel, and this same impression of pregnancy was conveyed by the dome of her belly.

"She is the giver and taker of life," the witch murmured with awe. "All my powers of divination and spirit vision come from her. So does the favorable luck of my race, without which we would not have survived wandering through these hostile lands."

"Why do you call her Shub-Niggurath?"

She hissed and glared at me, her face for a moment resembling the face of the idol.

"Be silent, fool. To speak her name is to invoke her. Do you want her to kill you, and me along with you?"

I wondered what the goddess would look like when evoked to tangible appearance. The images of Shub-Niggurath that I had come across in my studies and my wandering did not resemble this dancing pregnant woman. Perhaps she took different forms to different worshippers, as was the practice of Nyarlathotep. It was a question I felt no great haste to answer. A single Old One in my life was enough for this incarnation, and for the last, and the next.

"She is the mother of all births. Were she to break her covenant with my race, our women would become infertile and our goats would cease to breed. The goat is her chosen beast, because it is so ready to copulate at all times."

"How did the crafty race come to have a covenant with this goddess?"

She glanced at me and seemed to consider whether to speak on this matter, then shrugged.

"At the beginning of the world, the fertile mother tried to give birth to the human race, but each time she sent a man forth from her loins, he was killed by a great monster that dwelled in the ocean. She battled the monster with her sword, and would have defeated it, but from the drops of blood that fell from its wounds it spawned creatures shaped like itself, though smaller in size, that vexed her and distracted her from her purpose. Being wise, she saw that she could not overcome both the monster and its devilish spawn. From the sweat of her brow she formed two brothers, the first of my race. She tore strips of cloth from the hem of her dress and gave them to the brothers, commanding them to strangle any demons that arose from the monster's blood during the battle. The men strangled its offspring as quickly as they took shape, and in this way the mother was able to send the monster beneath the waves. As repayment, she gifts the bloodline of the brothers with fertility and good fortune for so long as their descendants continue to make sacrifice in her honor."

"So that is why Rakk strangled the deaf mute at the caravan," I murmured.

"The men of my people are forbidden to shed blood, for it was from the drops of blood shed by the monster of the sea that its spawn arose. They must strangle a man once a year, or the goddess turns away from them and their good fortune is ended. This obligation cannot be shirked after the sixteenth birthday, but no law prohibits them from taking it up at a younger age."

"A heavy price to pay for luck."

"It has other compensations," she said. "Those who are sacrificed give up their possessions to us. We sell their boots, weapons, and clothing, and keep their gold and silver."

I remembered the camels laden with old clothes, from which I had bought boots and garments for myself and the girl. The glaring eyes of the black idol watched me with gleeful madness.

"Does the Mother have the power to restore my face and manhood?"

The witch considered my face with a speculative eye.

"I have never heard of such a thing. Anyway, no one may enter the covenant with the goddess but those of my race."

"Do you know of any spell or charm that can restore a lost limb?" I asked, taking another approach to the matter that was central in my life.

She shook her head, a smile twitching the corners of her thin mouth. My unfortunate state was a source of amusement for her.

"It is beyond my ability. I have heard that the necromancers at Damascus possess strange spells, and have delved deeply into the wellsprings of this world in search of knowledge."

"It is to them that I journey."

"So I assumed. They dwell in the northern quarter, in a street called the Lane of Scholars, but they do not encourage the approach of strangers."

This bit of information I put away for later use. The deep voice of Belok alerted us to the return of the men from their hunt. She shut the doors of the shrine and ushered me out of the wagon.

"Say nothing of what you have seen and heard," she hissed at my back.

I nodded without turning.

That night we did not camp alone, but in an enclave of five other yellow wagons. It was the largest gathering of the travelers I had seen, and as I learned from Martala, had not occurred by chance.

"There is a ritual tonight," she told me while we watered and brushed down the backs of the tired horses. "The older girl called it the rite of the companion."

"What is its nature?"

"I'm not sure. It sounded like what the Christians do with their babies."

"Eat them, you mean?" I asked with a smile.

She snorted in laughter.

"Christians don't eat babies. That's just a fable. They eat their god."

The wagons were not on the side of the road, but drawn together in a ring in a hollow sheltered between low hills. The existence of a long-established hearth of blackened stones in the middle of the hollow showed that it had been used many times in the past. The hearth was larger than usual, too large to accommodate a pot. It was furnished with firewood, but it had not yet been ignited.

While we cared for the shaggy horses, Belok stood apart with the men of the other wagons and talked to them in a low voice. From time to time, the men cast dark glances at us. I did not like the spark in the depths of their eyes, but said nothing to alarm the girl. Belok left the group and came over to us, a smile on his broad face.

"The elders have agreed to allow you to witness the rite of the companion tonight. You are the first outsiders ever to see it."

"We are honored," I told him.

He nodded, glancing from me to the girl.

"Say nothing during the rite, and keep to the background. The less you are noticed, the better."

As night fell, wood piled upon the open hearth was ignited. The crackling fire drew all the inhabitants of the wagons into the open. Some of the younger men carried flutes of curious construction, that appeared to my eye to be made of bone, and others flat drums inset around their rims with silver bangles. As the celebrants stood watching the sparks from the blazing fire ascend toward the stars, straw-covered flasks were passed from hand to hand. Each man or woman who received a flask took a drink from its open mouth and passed it on. The children were not denied the flasks, although the younger ones coughed and made wry faces after they swallowed. A youth who drank and laughed at the same time sprayed his mouthful of liquor into the fire, which roared up with the voice of an angry dragon, to the delight and amusement of the throng.

The musicians began to beat the drums with curved sticks and make a trilling music with the flutes. The rest milled about, talking and laughing, faces flushed with excitement. Some of the older girls and youths began to dance around the fire, leaping from one foot to the other and raising their arms while shouting in unison.

"I wonder what is in the flasks," Martala murmured with a wistful note.

We sat together on stones beside Naleen's wagon, a few paces outside the circle of revelers.

"Fortified spirits of wine," I said, watching four of the older bearded men approach the fire. "Do not drink it. I want your wits about you tonight."

The four elders arranged themselves around the fire, so close that its flames must have been painful upon their bare cheeks and hands. One looked to be at least four-score years. His humped back did not disguise the vigor of his body, nor was there any weakness of age in his keen gaze. He turned toward the far side of the circle, and the music raggedly ceased. Following his gaze with my own, I saw a man carry a naked infant toward the fire in his outstretched hands. The baby lay cradled on his palms.

He took his place at the fire with the four elders, standing close to the flames but holding the baby near his chest in the shelter of his arms so that its tender skin was not singed by the heat. The music resumed in a more rhythmic and purposeful way. A woman began to sing in a nasal voice. Soon other women joined in the song, their voices rising and falling with the trilling of the flutes. I could make out no words. The song was composed of extended vowels voiced deep in the throat and chest, so that they caused the night air to vibrate.

The white-bearded elder with the hump between his shoulders began to make an invocation, raising his hands skyward while the musicians and singers swayed their bodies from side to side. He chanted in the tongue of the wagon race, his words unknown to me, save for the single repeated refrain *a'ai y'gatu l'il ro'kanah Shub-Niggu-rath*, which was spoken in the language of the Old Ones. As the chant rose in power, the father of the infant passed it through the flames and smoke to another elder, holding the child high to avoid burning it. A great shout went up from the gathering. The baby began to bawl in protest and kick its tiny naked feet. The second elder passed the child through the flames to a third, and another shout arose. In this way the babe was exchanged above the fire five times and returned to its father's hands.

So intense was my concentration on what was being done around the fire, I did not notice the goat until it bleated, its thin cries rising above the music. It was led into the circle on two ropes that were tied to its forelegs. Each rope was held by a girl dressed in a white gown, with a wreath of flowers and greenery about her fore-head. One of the girls was Pula. Her face bore an expression of nervous expectancy. The goat, too, was wreathed in flowers, its coat so spotlessly white that I wondered if it had been treated with chalk. It moved without resistance as though in a daze.

As the music quickened, the wordless keening of the singers intensified. A woman not much older than Martala left the throng and stepped to the side of the goat. She drew her long knife from her embroidered girdle. All the onlookers seized up metal pots, wooden bowls, and dry sticks which they had waiting beside them and began to bang them together, making a deafening din. The father of the infant turned from the fire and knelt on one knee, holding the baby close to the bewildered animal as the woman pulled back its head and slit its throat with a single stroke. A scarlet fountain gushed upon the naked infant, covering it with red from head to toe. The goat dropped to its knees, then collapsed dead before the pulses of blood from its throat ceased.

Amid the bang of pans and the shouted voices, two of the elders picked up the carcass of the beast by its limp legs and cast it directly upon the fire. A crackle went up from its blazing white hide. The hump-backed senior took the baby out of the hands of the father. He elevated the blood-drenched infant directly above the flames, holding it as high as his arms allowed to avoid the worst of the heat, which must still have been intense upon the backs of his hands and forearms.

Martala touched my arm. I glanced at her, and she pointed upward. High above the fire, a kind of mist formed in the night sky. It mingled with the rising smoke yet was not of the same color. Nor did it ascend and disperse with the smoke, but coalesced and fell downward in an unnatural manner. A tongue of this pale mist extended itself toward the infant like the inquisitive head of a serpent.

The moment the mist touched the infant, the crowd of watchers ceased their clamor, and the wail of the baby was cut off as though smothered. In the eerie silence that followed, the mist formed a mask over its tiny face and entered it through the seven openings of its head. As the last tendril of mist curled between its lips, it turned its head to the side with strange precision, and its small eyes shone with awareness in which there was no trace of innocence. It seemed to gaze directly at me with a malicious intent that sent a shiver of dread along my spine.

A yellow and white cloth was given to the woman who killed the goat. She took the silent baby from the bent elder and wrapped it with loving care. I realized that she must be the mother of the child. The father came to her and they gazed down at the babe in her arms with expressions of bliss.

Once again, the music began, but more carefree and less purposeful than before. The effects of the straw-covered flasks made the beat of the drums irregular. The gathering broke into couples and small groups. Men gave women leering glances and drew them away from the light of the fire, or tumbled them to the rough grass and rolled on top of them. It was a scene Bacchus would have approved.

The white-bearded elder took a young man of some fifteen years by the hand and led him over to Pula, who stood in her white gown, trembling. He smiled and joined her hand with the hand of the youth, who leaned forward and whispered something into her ear. She blushed, but her eyes flashed with pleasure. They walked together away from the fire and into the darkness beyond the ring of wagons. The old man laughed and went to Belok, who stood watching with an expression of drunken good humor.

"Where is he taking the girl?" Martala asked.

"That is a foolish question."

All the travelers were drunk, even the children. No one watched us. Men chased the women like satyrs, their tunics hiked up to reveal their lust, and the women were too dizzy to run far even had they wished to escape.

Martala's eyes widened with comprehension.

"She is only thirteen years old."

"Old enough, to judge by the stains on her linen," I murmured. "Didn't you notice them when her grandmother boiled her clothes?"

She shook her head, an expression of outrage on her face. From this response, I guessed that she remembered her first experience of love, which had not been agreeable.

"I am going to follow them. Pula may need my help."

"As you wish," I murmured, glancing around to see if we were being watched. "Guard your back. I dislike the way the men talked together before the ritual. Stay close so that I can find you quickly."

She nodded and slipped away in the darkness, moving with moderate skill in the direction taken by the blushing girl and her lover.

I made my way to the back of Naleen's wagon. By good fortune it was turned slightly away from the fire, so that its doors were in shadow. Reaching to open them, I hesitated. The witch had vanished at the end of the ritual, probably in the company of some lusty young man, but I had not noticed her departure. If she was inside the wagon, I would have to kill her. This I was happy to do, but it might arouse an outcry and bring the entire encampment down around my ear-holes. I was almost certain the witch was not in the wagon. Grasping the latch, I lifted it and opened the right side of the door, then climbed the step into the dark interior and closed the door behind me.

Enough light from the fire came through the window in the left side to show that I was alone. I went directly to the sandalwood shrine and laid my hands on its doors, feeling the wooden studs.

Sashi, do you remember which of these projections the witch pushed?

Of course, dear love.

Press them.

I felt her flow into my arms and hands like a cool trickle of spring water. My fingers tingled and twitched. She took control of my hands and used them to manipulate the locking mechanism of the doors. With a soft click, they fell open.

I stared long into the shrine, deep in thought. What I was about to do was irrevocable. It would force me to flee the wagons before the rising of the sun, or Naleen would have me strangled, along with the girl, if she herself did not slit our throats. Yet it was time to leave. Damascus could not be more than a few days' travel. Once inside the city walls I wanted nothing to do with the yellow wagons or their fanatical inhabitants.

In my nervous state of awareness, the glaring eyes of the black idol seemed to watch me with malice. I felt repugnance to touch its stone surface, but found it dry and warm as though heated by some inner flame. I drew my dagger from its sheath and used its point to pry at the silver setting that held the emerald in the rolled lips of its vulva. It popped out and I caught it in the palm of my other hand. It was the size of a small grape. After glancing at it in the light from the window to assure myself that I had not damaged it, I slipped it into a pocket.

The loot from the caravan was kept in two large oak strongboxes strapped to the underside of the wagon. They were bound with black iron and locked. Even were I able to force the locks, I could not have lifted their lids without unstrapping them from their places beneath the floor. Nor could I have carried more than a fraction of the precious objects away. Putting the treasure chests out of my mind, I looked around the interior of the wagon for something else worth stealing. It was a disappointing search. The few books of the witch were of no interest to me and possessed scant value in the marketplace. Her store of herbs and stones were the common stock of any village wise woman, apart from a few substances that I did not recognize.

I cast my eyes over the crowded shelves of the cupboard. As I suspected, the emerald was the only thing of outstanding worth in the wagon. With a noise of disgust deep in my throat, I began to shut the cupboard doors. A loud tinkling arose from the bottom shelf, and I remembered the row of glass bottles. Words the holy man had spoken on the road tickled the edge of my memory. It was something about souls. I had not listened after dismissing his ramblings as empty gossip.

I knelt on the floor and bent my head low. There were seven bottles on the shelf, identical in size and shape, cylinders of clear glass that narrowed slightly at their broad mouths, which were stoppered with cork and green wax. The bottle on the right end of the row appeared brighter than the others. I peered close at its side. A weight of some kind hung inside from the rim on a thread, just above a small pool of noxious amber liquid. As I watched, the weight moved and tapped the inside surface of the glass. Cloudiness filled the space above the liquid, forming a fine condensation on the inside of the bottle that ran down in rivulets.

Sashi, what is inside this bottle?

She was silent for several moments.

A spirit, dear heart. The spirit of a man.

Can you understand what it is trying to say?

Of course. It wishes to be released.

How should I release it?

You must break the bottle. That is all you must do.

I sat back on my heels, listening to the annoying tinkle of the weight against the glass while I considered this odd request. I cared nothing about the magic of the witch. Who she chose to imprison in her bottles was none of my concern.

Does each of these bottles contain a soul?

Yes, my love. The others are asleep. They dream.

Why is this one making so much noise?

Its will is stronger than the others.

Tell it that if I break the bottle, it may attract the notice of the witch.

As I spoke these words in my mind, the tinkling became more violent. I could not hear its thoughts, but it could hear mine.

I have no reason to help you, I thought, and several reasons not to help.

Ignoring the tinkling, I began to close the doors of the cupboard.

Alhazred, it says that you are in great danger. If you release it from its prison, it will tell you how to save yourself.

Again I leaned back on my heels and regarded the smoky cylinder of glass, my hands still on the doors.

Tell me what the danger is, and then I will release you.

The tinkling slowed, then ceased for a moment before resuming.

It says that it has no reason to trust you. How can it be sure you will fulfill your pledge?

I laughed with bitterness.

"You have no more reason to trust me than you do the witch," I murmured aloud. "Yet consider that I care nothing for your fate, while it is evident that the witch hates you."

The silence lasted for a score of heartbeats. Then the tinkling resumed with a methodical rhythm. Sashi's face swam before my sight in the dimness of the wagon, wearing an expression of alarm.

The spirit says that the men of the wagons intend to strangle you and the girl in the morning, before returning to the road. You must flee tonight.

"I thought we had gained their trust," I murmured. "Why would they kill us now?"

She cocked her lovely head to the side as though listening to the tinkle of glass.

The old man with the bent back and the white beard demands your death. He thinks you have seen too many of their secrets, and cannot be trusted. He has authority over the others. Naleen and Belok cannot defy him.

The old man had moved with assurance among the travelers, and had presided over the rite of the companion. It was not to be wondered that he possessed the power to issue judgments. Every people must have its lawgivers, even a race so diverse and free as the Thugians.

"Tell me this, did the witch try to change the mind of the old man?"

Sashi listened, then solemnly shook her head.

I had expected as much. The friendship offered by Naleen extended only as far as her acquisition of my store of useful bits of magic. In her eyes, how could I be more than a sacrifice for her goddess? Those excluded from the covenant with Shub-Niggurath were lesser beings, scarcely above the beasts.

"Your warning is meaningless," I told the spirit. "I have already determined to depart this place."

I am the enemy of your enemy.

I considered my options, and made my decision.

"I will free you."

The weight in the bottle tinked three times against the glass and became silent. I gathered up all seven of the bottles in my arms and carried them out of the wagon beneath the drape of my cloak. They were an awkward handful, but I took care not to drop them on the hard ground. Glancing around the clearing, I saw that no one watched me. A few girls danced drunkenly to the notes from a solitary piper. Men lay on the grass where they had fallen, snoring in their sleep. From beyond the range of the firelight floated a woman's wild laughter. It ascended in a shriek of delight.

I walked to the fire and knelt as though to warm myself. With quick movements, I placed the bottles into the bed of embers, pressing them down so that they would not be noticed by anyone who chanced to pass.

There was little time. I went from the circle of wagons in the direction taken by Martala. She met me as I walked down the slope of a low hill. Weak light from the waning crescent of the moon illuminated her face. Recognizing me, she shook her head with disapproval.

"That girl has the soul of a whore," she muttered. "You would not believe what she is doing with the young man. Come and look."

"We have no time for entertainment. We must leave at once."

In a few words I told her the warning given by the spirit in the bottle. Her eyes widened in alarm.

"We will go south into the hills, then bend our path westward. When I'm sure we are well in front of the wagons, we will rejoin the road. Have you all your possessions on your back?"

She nodded. As a precaution, we had agreed days before to keep ourselves in a state that allowed us to leave the wagon without a moment of warning. She had not allowed her vigilance to lapse. My water skin was slacker than I would have wished, but I reflected that I could fill it at the next well on the road.

Behind us, a great explosion rent the night, followed almost immediately by another, and then others. I turned and saw over the crest of the hill I had just climbed several strange shifting lights in the sky that were paler than the glow of a fire. Voices shouted in alarm. Then came screams. I recognized the terrified whinny of a horse, but the rest of the cries were from human throats. We stood listening to them in the darkness. It was many minutes before they diminished to silence, giving me occasion to reflect that I might not need to concern myself with pursuit from the wagons.

605

Chapter 53

It was tempting to return to the wagons for the treasure in the strong boxes, but I rejected the impulse. The travelers had scattered throughout the hills, either to get drunk or engage in indiscriminate mating. The seven angry spirits were unlikely to find them all in the darkness, even if they possessed the vitality to slay them. Hearing the cries, the men would gather their wits and stagger back to the wagons. Pula was safe, for I had seen no spirit glow fly in her direction, but her mother was almost certainly dead. The spirits would never rest until they sought out and killed the one who had imprisoned them.

We did not wait for daylight but moved between the hills by the light of the waning moon. Through long experience I found this no difficult task. The girl turned stones beneath her boots and cursed the darkness at regular intervals.

"How can you walk without a sound through this miserable country?" she exclaimed in vexation.

"It is a skill all ghouls possess," I murmured. "Keep your voice low."

"We are miles from the wagons. And you are not a ghoul, you are a man."

"Once I was a man. My body still bears the shape of a man. But my soul is the soul of a ghoul."

"Is that why you carry that skull at your belt?"

"It is a token of respect. You would not understand."

She made a rude noise with her lips.

"We may be able to return to the caravan road more quickly than I anticipated," I said, ignoring her criticism. "The travelers will believe we fled the spirits into the hills and were killed. I doubt they will waste time searching for our bodies, if many of their own lie dead. As long as we stay ahead of the wagons on the road, we will be undetected."

Even as I spoke these words, a stone rolled somewhere in the darkness behind us. We stopped and held our breaths to listen. Only the insect sounds of the night reached my ears. I saw the gray patch of Martala's face turn to me, and laid a reassuring hand on her shoulder. We moved off with greater care, listening at our back, but the noise was not repeated.

At dawn we stopped and ate a cold meal, then slept in a narrow fissure between two juts of rock until near midday. I did not dare stay longer for fear the wagons would somehow get ahead of us on the road, and we would find ourselves overtaking them from behind. They moved at less than a walking pace, and would not have left the enclave until dawn at the earliest, so it was unlikely they could pass us, despite the hindrance of the irregular ground over which we traveled.

We emerged from the hills in the early afternoon and continued on the road westward. The increase in traffic, coupled with the larger size of the villages, indicated that we were moving through a more populous region. I restored the glamour to my face as we approached a solitary Thugian wagon from behind, on the consideration that the travelers who had seen me at the gathering would look for a man badly disfigured. Belok and his family knew that I had two faces, but it was unlikely the others had been told. This precaution proved unnecessary. None of the scowling men who walked beside the wheels looked familiar. They made a display of ignoring us as we passed.

The road descended the gentle slope of a barren rock-strewn valley and ascended the opposite side. As we climbed the crest of the hill, I looked behind and saw on the far side of the valley a lone horseman. His head hung down, so that his turban concealed his face, but where his long cloak fluttered open, his breastplate caught the sun and glittered. The rider was too far behind on the road for me to distinguish any details of his appearance. His cloak was dark blue, his horse a pale gray. I judged him a mercenary by his posture in the saddle, which was erect but careless. The horse was large enough to be a horse of war.

It was not unusual to be passed by horsemen on the road, but they seldom traveled alone. Either they rode in pairs or groups for greater security, or if alone, they stayed near the edges of a caravan to profit from its armed guard. Martala turned and walked backwards, gazing behind, but did not speak. We shared the same thought, without need to voice it aloud. The rider might be Altrus. If so, it was probably too late to retreat into the hills. We would leave tracks easy to follow in the sand. We could not hope to outrun a horse in open country, or elude detection in daylight.

If the lone rider was Altrus, I expected him to overtake us swiftly. Yet minutes passed, and no sound of hooves came from behind. The road wound this way and that, denying us a clear view back along its length. It was not until late afternoon that we found ourselves on a long and straight section. To my amazement, I saw that the rider had not advanced, but was the same distance behind us.

"He is keeping pace with us," Martala murmured, wiping sweat from her eyebrows with her fingers.

"His horse may be weary, or lame," I speculated.

Everything I knew about Altrus told me he would fall upon us like a whirlwind and slay us before we could draw our blades, yet if this was Altrus, he declined to approach. I could conceive no reason for hesitation. In another man I might suspect fear, but that was an emotion unknown to this mercenary. I told myself it must be some weary traveler whose horse had gone lame, but in my heart I did not believe. My heart told me that Altrus was toying with me as a cat plays with a bird. Yet above all other qualities, the mercenary was a practical man, and to inflict torment for its own sake seemed beneath his dignity.

I waited until dusk fell before leaving the road to find a place to rest for the night. Not even Altrus could track footprints in the dark. We continued over the rough ground through the fading twilight, then hid ourselves on the top of a ridge that was a sheer cliff in the back and impossible to climb blind from that side. If the mercenary did locate us by some magic, I wanted him to have only one approach, and that as difficult as I could make it. The steep slope in front was littered with loose stones. We lay behind a boulder and I told the girl to sleep.

"Wake me at midnight, and I will listen until dawn," she whispered.

It was near midnight before I heard her deepened breaths. I let her sleep until morning. There seemed little point in both of us being exhausted from a sleepless night. With Altrus out there, wandering the darkness, there had been no prospect of sleep for me. I would sleep on the road, while I walked, a trick I had learned from Gor. I stroked his skull, and the smooth bone comforted me.

The dust and flies were more tormenting on the road the following day than they had been since leaving the river Euphrates. It was easy to account for the dust. The increased traffic stirred up the bed of the road and ground it to a find powder that drifted upward in the slightest breeze. For a time the flies puzzled me, until I noticed them rising in clouds from the piles of dung dropped by the passing camels and horses. An increased number of travelers meant more food cast to the side of the road to rot, more animal excrement, more breeding places for maggots, and hence more numerous flies to vex me, and me alone. As usual, Martala walked through the swarms almost untouched. Now and then a fly would land on her head scarf or shoulder, but it did no harm and soon flew away.

I took the striped yellow and white scarf that I had kept from the wagon and wound it around my head and face so that only my eyes were visible through its slit. This helped keep the dust from my throat and the flies from the pit of my severed nose, where they liked to burrow. I fell into a rolling pace, letting my mind drift in the way I had been taught by the ghouls, so that I dreamed while walking, and saw visions pass on either side from the corners of my eyes. I kept only enough attention on the road to avoid the piles of dung that came into my narrowed field of view at irregular intervals.

It was late afternoon when the girl tugged my sleeve, waking me from my moving dream.

"Alhazred, look," she said with excitement, pointing ahead.

The wall of a great city floated on the horizon, and beyond it, the gleam of gold-covered minarets. It could only be Damascus, the navel of the world, whose gates it was said all pilgrims were destined to pass through at least once in their lives. As I gazed upon it, shimmering in the rising heat like some mirage of the desert, tears welled into my eyes. I had not realized how road-weary I had grown. I was sickened with walking. The prospect of a warm bath and a night spent in a bed seemed like some vision of paradise.

We reached the open gates just before twilight. Above the shadowed battlements of the wall, the western sky shone with fire and gold from the setting sun. The guards standing on either side of the road eyed us as we passed between them and entered the city but gave no challenge. The double gate was less impressive and smaller in size than I expected, yet sturdy enough in its construction to withstand a siege. All the fables about Damascus read in my youth had caused me to imagine it the wonder of the world, yet after all I found it was only a city. Filth lay in pools along the gullies in the middle of the cobblestone street. Some of the buildings needed to be washed with lime, or were missing glazed tiles from their facades. The smells were those of any city, excrement and rotting cabbage and smoke.

A black dog danced around our heels for a time, barking itself hoarse, then wandered off along the crowded street in search of more interesting amusement. We passed a harlot in a dirty red dress, hands on her broad hips, bawling out words to another woman who leaned from a second-level window across the street. She felt my eyes upon her and gave me a yellow-toothed smile. I shook my head and dropped the scarf from across my englamoured face to smile politely. She sneered a response and went back to her conversation.

"So this is Damascus," Martala said. "It looks no greater than Fustat to me."

"This is the home of the Caliph Yazid," I reminded her. "Damascus rules Fustat."

"Egypt ruled the world before Damascus had a name," she said with a tartness in her tone that surprised me.

"Perhaps," I conceded. "But that was centuries ago, and we must live today."

Beggars were as numerous as flies along the narrow and winding streets, and never ceased to try to make us stumble over their feet or legs, so that they could stop us long enough to beg for alms. Beneath my brown cloak, I kept one hand on my purse and the other on the hilt of my dagger. We made our way to the marketplace by following our nose and our ears. It was a mad mill of human bodies garbed in every imaginable kind of clothing, and the babble of commerce made it difficult to talk, or even to think.

One young man in the market showed uncommon persistence. He leaned on a stick due to a clubbed foot that twisted inward, and looked as thin as any desiccated linen-wrapped corpse of the Nile. Strings of ragged greasy hair hung over his unwashed face, which betrayed on its chin the beginnings of an unimpressive beard.

"Anything your heart desires, noble lord, I can procure for you. I am called Ani, the resourceful one. Remember my name. If you want food, Ani will bring it. If you seek wine, Ani can find the best in the city. If you need a room to rest the night, you need only ask, and for a trifle I will have your bed filled with the most beautiful girl you have ever looked upon."

Martala listened with a frown and growing impatience, until at last she had heard enough. She bent and picked up a handful of pebbles, then began to throw them at the smiling and nodding youth, one by one, with unerring accuracy. He backed up, a pained expression on his thin face, struggling to maintain his happy countenance as the little stones bounced from his forehead and cheeks.

"Be gone, rogue. We need nothing from you. Do you think we are fools? Take your lies away."

I put a hand upon her arm.

"Wait, Ani, let me talk with you."

He returned with the swiftness of a stooping hawk that falls upon its prey, ignoring the presence of the girl as if she had ceased to exist.

"Yes, great lord, anything you need, I will find for you. To name it is to have it in your possession."

"For tonight we will need a room at a good inn that has a tub for bathing the body, and hot food."

"That is the easiest thing, lord. I know just the inn, only a few streets from the market. Other inns have bugs that bite in the beds, but this inn is as clean as the palace of the Caliph himself. The rooms are large, so large you would never believe their size—"

I raised a hand to cut off the flow of words, which showed no sign of stopping.

"Then I would like to rent a house in a street called the Lane of Scholars."

The expression on his face became fixed, and a paleness came under his skin that made his cheeks gray in the failing light.

Before he could respond, he was distracted by a crush of bodies that pressed against us. Other procurers of the market, most of them young men, saw that Ani had gained my interest and surrounded us with clamoring voices, eager to turn some of our silver into their upraised palms. Ani flew into a flailing whirlwind of curses, using his stick to beat the rival procurers savagely away, his face a snarl of rage. With reluctance, they withdrew before his onslaught. He turned back to me and regained his toothy smile with the ease of long practice.

"That is possible, my lord. It can be done without difficulty, only the houses in the Lane of Scholars are large and of no small price."

"Find the best house that is available and make inquiries on my behalf," I told him, taking out my purse and giving him a dinar. "When you know which houses are for rent, make arrangements with the owners to show them to us tomorrow."

He almost kissed my hand when he took the gold coin, so great was his delight. I noticed the hollows in his cheeks and wondered when last he had eaten. The gold would buy many loaves of bread, and probably a few skins of wine and a harlot as well.

"What am I to call you, noble master? The agents for the owners will wish to know your name."

"I am called Alhazred. This is my servant, Martala."

He led us out of the market and through the streets of Damascus as though protecting two fragile babes, his eyes darting ceaselessly around, ready to beat off the approach of any other procurer. Above the front door of the inn hung a sign painted with the image of a white bird standing on one leg in a pool of blue water. As I expected, the Inn of the Stork was ordinary, but it did boast a copper tub in an unused room beside the kitchen that the mistress of the house would fill with warm water for a nominal fee. After being shown our bed, I sent Ani off to inquire about houses, and ordered the matron to put her kettle on the fire for the tub.

Martala was inclined to sulk in the bath chamber.

"You gave that smelly wretch too much money," she said with a pout. "He would have done what you asked for bronze, and you gave him gold."

"I wanted to ensure his loyalty and his enthusiasm. I may have need of him in future."

Slipping off my dust-encrusted undershirt, I threw it into a chair on top of my mustard-colored thawb and stepped naked into the hot steaming water, which came up to the level of my knees. The tub was not large around, but delightfully deep. As I sank down, the water rose to my shoulders and almost covered the domes of my bent knees.

"Ask the innkeeper's wife if we can get our clothes washed before the morning, and if she has something we can wear in the meantime."

"Why bother?" she said. "You throw gold around like bits of chaff. Why not just buy new tunics in the market tomorrow?"

"Because I do not wish to put those filthy things on my back after my bath. And because we need no new clothes."

She snorted, shaking my garments as she folded them, so that the road dust floated over the bath, making me sneeze.

"Empty the pockets and put the things into my wallet."

She began to do so, but not without much banging and grumbled words.

"A good servant does not complain. What are you saying?"

"You will probably stay in that tub until the water is cold, and then what pleasure will there be left for me?"

"Come into the tub with me, then."

This caused her to smile in spite of her wish to maintain her ill-temper.

"So I would, if the tub were larger. We would force out all the water onto the floor."

Her exclamation of surprise caused me to open my eyes. She held up Narisa's sapphire and diamond pendant by its fine gold chain, admiring it in the light from the window screens.

"Where did you get this?"

"I don't remember. Do you like it?"

"It's beautiful."

"Accept it as my gift."

To drown her squeals of joy, I managed to slide down in the tub until the water rose above my ear-holes.

By the time I emerged, my relaxed limbs smoking with warm mist, Martala had found simple but clean robes for us both, and the woman who ran the inn had agreed to have our travel garments washed and ready for us by morning. I suspected she intended to wash them herself in the water of the tub, as soon as Martala finished with it. The water was still warm when the girl stripped and slid into it with a soft sigh, the sapphire pendant around her neck. I sat and watched her splash like a happy child and toy with her bauble. She truly was a child in years, though wiser in the ways of life than many men twice her age.

When she finished, I helped dry her with a towel, then held her white cotton robe while she stepped into it and belted it at her waist.

"Why are you being so attentive?" she asked playfully, all traces of her pettishness gone.

"If that was Altrus behind us on the road, I do not wish to be separated from you. Or our wallets."

We took up the wallets and our weapons and proceeded to our room. It was on the second level of the inn, not far from the top of the stair. One of the better rooms, to judge by what I saw through open doorways. Ani had probably told the innkeeper that I was a man of wealth despite my squalid appearance. I wasted no time, but bolted the door behind us, threw off my robe and boots, and cast myself beneath the sheet of the large bed. I was asleep so swiftly, I did not feel the girl lie down beside me.

The morning sunlight streaming through the open window across my face woke me. I felt refreshed, apart from deep aches in my muscles that came from so many days of hard walking. There was no memory of dreams. Martala stood by the open door, unfolding my thawb and cloak to lay them across the back of a chair. She wore her clean clothes. The leather wallets and my water skin hung from pegs on the wall, newly brushed and oiled. On a table lay our swords and knives out of their sheaths, and I knew by the smell in the air and the gleam of the steel that the girl had oiled the blades and the leather of the sheaths. Even the carved ivory sheath of my dagger appeared whiter.

"You've been busy this morning."

"Your breakfast awaits you in the common room," she said briskly. "I did not know if you wanted it brought to the room. Ani is sitting outside on the step."

"Why isn't he sitting in the common room?"

"The innkeeper's wife threw him out."

"I should buy him a meal while I eat," I said as I yawned and stretched under the sheet. "He may die from starvation before he takes us to view the house."

"He is vermin. Waste no more money on him."

"I thought followers of the Goddess were more charitable."

She glanced at her fingernails.

"It is only that I know his kind. I used to be like him."

I renewed the glamour on my face and dressed. We put the wallets on our shoulders, and belted our blades to our waists. If it became necessary to flee, I wanted nothing of value left behind.

"I filled your water skin," she murmured as she slung its strap over my head. "I know it comforts you."

"You may become an adequate servant."

She projected her tongue at me, and we descended to the common room, where a breakfast of boiled eggs, fowl, and fresh bread waited. The wine was better than I expected—another sign that the innkeeper planned to give me a large bill when I left his roof.

Ani jumped to his bare feet when we emerged from the inn.

"Master, I have found such a house for you, a house fit for a prince," he said with excitement. "Such spacious rooms. Such a broad courtyard. Such a garden with fruit trees and roses."

"Does it come with its own staff?"

"Of course. They have been with the house for many years, and are as discreet as you would wish."

"Why would I wish them to be discreet?"

He stopped for a moment, unable to find words. He reminded me of a dog that knows it has displeased its owner, but does not know how.

"Everyone in the Lane of Scholars seeks discretion," he said at last with an apologetic bow of his head. "All the householders are private men of wealth and reputation. They want no gossiping servants."

We followed him westward through the heart of Damascus. At length we passed on our right a high stone wall, with gilded towers rising on its far side. Guards in full armor stood with pikes at the closed gate, already sweating in the morning sun despite the lateness of the season. I imagined how hot their leather tunics and chain mail vests must become at noon, and almost felt sorry for them, in spite of the surly looks they gave me from under their visors as we walked by.

"That is the palace of the Caliph, Yazid ibn Muawya," Ani said with mingled pride and awe. "He is the ruler of the world."

The Lane of Scholars ran through a quiet part of the northwestern quarter of the city that was almost entirely made up of houses within walled enclosures. Each house sat on its own private plot of ground. From the street, nothing gave indication of their existence but small featureless doors in the brick walls that ran continuously on either side along the winding road, which was so narrow, two ox carts could not have passed upon it. The bustle and din of the marketplace and the busy thoroughfares of shops and professions might have been in another land. The only sound was the scuff of our boots and the chirping of birds in trees on the far sides of the high walls, which were so tall that I could not reach their tops with my extended fingers.

"Be careful," Ani warned. "Iron spikes are set in the mortar at the tops."

"The householders in the Lane of Scholars cherish their privacy," I murmured.

The only thing to distinguish the doors from each other was their bright colors. They were unmarked by names or numbers, and boasted no windows or viewing slots. As if by way of compensation, their unsocial owners had painted their bare planks with shades of red, blue, yellow, green, and every other pigment available to the artist. Each door wore its individual color as though proclaiming ownership, and no two doors that I passed were painted the same tint.

We stopped at length before a door bearing the brightness of spring grass. Ani seized the knob of the brass chain dangling through a slot in its lintel and pulled. The sound of a bell came from the opposite side of the wall. After a brief wait, the bolt rattled across the panel and it swung inward.

The man who faced us was dressed as a scholar in a white robe and white turban, with soft leather shoes laced on his feet. He was of middle years and no great height, wore a serious expression on his long and bearded face, and carried himself with exaggerated dignity. I wondered whether he was the owner or a servant, and how I should address him. Ani perceived my difficulty and made our introductions.

"This is the agent for the owner of the house, who has agreed to show the house to you, and to rent it to you if it meets your needs, and if the terms are agreeable to you," he said with unexpected eloquence.

"I am Alhazred, and this is Martala," I told the scribe.

He smiled coolly and bowed an almost imperceptible bow.

"The owner of the house wishes to remain nameless," he said in a cultured but thin voice. "I am called Theon. The owner has empowered me to rent the property to a suitable tenant."

"Theon is a Greek name," I said.

His made an effort to conceal his irritation, but his expression hardened.

"My father was Greek. I have embraced the teachings of the Prophet, may he be blessed."

I did not need to ask who qualified as a suitable tenant. It would be anyone willing to pay the rent demanded.

We followed him through the doorway into a court paved with widely spaced blocks of unpolished pink marble, between which grew well-watered grass that had recently been mowed. Amid the manicured ornamental trees, marble statues of female figures adorned the court on granite pedestals. They were Greek and bore an ancient look, the loot of decayed temples. Pagan sculptures in marble and bronze were to be had for no great price to anyone willing to pay the cost of transporting them, there were so many temples abandoned and fallen to ruin. If they were goddesses, I failed to recognize them, although I could not help admiring their voluptuous naked limbs.

The front door stood beneath a projection of the upper level of the house that was supported by a row of graceful pink marble pillars. The panel of the door was sheathed in plates of beaten brass secured by an ornate floral pattern of large brass nails. A design of leaves and flowers had been engraved into the brass sheets, so that the brightly polished door presented an almost festive appearance. It opened on well-greased hinges. The floor of the hall beyond continued the theme of marble, but was of a cream color and reflected the light from the windows almost as well as a mirror.

A veiled housemaid with linen in her arms bowed her head and lowered her eyes as we passed, her back against the wall. Her modesty was admirable. She resisted the impulse to stare after us. Theon ignored her. With quick steps he paced us through the ornate rooms on the lower level, and showed us the kitchen and the house of defecation in the back garden. It had been recently cleaned or was long disused, for it had almost no odor. Not far from it was the mouth of a well. I tasted its water and found it good. The garden was larger than I anticipated from the facade of the house. It ran back for a considerable distance between high walls that divided it from the gardens of the neighboring dwellings.

Not a murmur of voices reached my ears over the walls as we walked around, examining the fruit trees and flowers. Near the rear was a pleasant bower overhung with roses, and behind it more utilitarian structures for storing firewood and gardening tools. The old gardener bowed his head and reported to the agent that everything was in order, as was obvious from a brief glance. We went back into the house and ascended the marble stair to view the servant's quarters at the rear and the larger rooms in the front of the house. I decided that I might as well look at everything, and had Theon show me the cellar.

To my surprise, the cellar was not dank with cobwebs and mold, but revealed signs of regular use. The walls above the lamp brackets were black with soot, and the floors well swept. Ani lit a brass hand lamp and carried it before him through the cellar from room to room. Roman arches and thick stone pillars supported the weight of the house above. The floor was paved with flat stones tightly fitted together. There were many utilitarian tables and shelves, all empty. In one room I saw chains hanging from the wall with iron cuffs at their ends.

"Servants sometimes need to be disciplined," the agent murmured, observing the direction of my gaze.

I let my eyes slide over the brown-stained stones of the wall but made no comment. Perhaps the stains were rust from the chains, although the air of the cellar was exceedingly dry. It was of no concern to me how the former tenant had entertained himself. The rooms would be useful for work that required privacy from household servants. I made my decision.

"Would the owner be willing to sell the house outright, rather than rent it?"

Theon blinked.

"Perhaps. He has not discussed the possibility with me. The price would be high."

"Please inquire on my behalf, and give Ani the details when he contacts you."

As the agent led us from the cellar, Martala bent her head close to my ear.

"You really mean to buy this great pile of stones?" she asked, excitement in her voice.

"It is private and easy to defend," I murmured. "After all, a man cannot wander forever."

Chapter 54

The next morning, Ani was again waiting at the step of the inn. When I finished breakfast I went out to talk to him. Martala had gone off to buy writing instruments in the paper-seller's shop. I thought it useful to have means of writing letters, now that I had become a man of the city. The clubfooted youth greeted me with his usual enthusiasm. I saw that he wore a clean if somewhat faded tunic, and that his hair had been cut. At least some portion of the gold coin had gone to good use.

"Theon says his master is willing to sell the house, but he asks for a great deal of gold."

"How much gold?"

He named a sum large enough to buy a country estate with a thousand goats in Yemen. When I hesitated in thought, Ani became anxious and wrung his thin fingers.

"Theon says the house is all the property his master holds in the world, and he must get a good price for it if he cannot rent it. He had expected to live on the rent."

"I understand. Do you know a good gem trader in the city?"

He blinked at this shift in our conversation.

"Yes, lord, I know many dealers in precious stones."

"I will need to exchange several rare gems for gold, if I am to purchase the house."

His thin face broke into a smile and he nodded.

"I know just the man. He deals in very fine jewels and pearls. He is a Roman from Constantinople who has embraced the way of the Prophet."

"Take me to him."

It was in the interests of any foreigner to declare faith in Allah, if he sought to live and trade in Damascus, where the administrators and officers of the Caliph watched all that went on and received bribes for facilitating questionable transactions.

The criers were calling the people to prayer as we left the inn and headed north through the streets. It would be some while before I knew my way around Damascus. It was an ancient city, some of its streets no more than paved donkey tracks, with the houses so close on either side that I could reach out both arms and brush their doors with my fingertips. The only streets that ran straight and broad were near the palace of the Caliph.

A soldier put his hand upon my chest and stopped me in midstep. Looking around with interest at the antique architecture, I had not noticed his approach. He possessed the body of a bull and the eyes of a pig. Sweat streamed down his forehead from beneath the band of his steel helmet, which looked too tight, as though it squeezed his brain inside his skull.

"Why are you not at prayer?"

Ani stepped forward with an anxious expression and bowed so low I thought he intended to kiss the soldier's boot.

"My noble lord has important business to transact that cannot be delayed."

The guard grunted with displeasure. My rough travel cloak and leather wallet did not give me a prosperous appearance.

"Are you a native of Damascus? What is your name?"

"Alhazred of Yemen. I only recently arrived in your beautiful city," I said, spreading my hands in apology. "I do not yet know all your laws, but this man is helping me to learn them."

He nodded. It was probably not the first time he had been told a similar story.

"In Damascus we obey the teachings of the Prophet, may he be blessed. When we are called to prayer, we answer. Those who are slow to go to the mosque are beaten through the streets with sticks."

"A useful encouragement to piety," I said in a mild tone.

He glared at me, uncertain whether I mocked him. Then he spat near my boot, and stepped aside.

We continued on to Goldbeater Lane, a short street lined with unassuming shops. Ani led me to the smallest and most weathered door and knocked. A tiny old man with a bald head and long white beard, who wore a leather apron with pockets over his linen tunic, peered up at me with an unreadable expression. His head did not reach my chin. A lens of glass in a brass frame hung from a fine chain around his neck. He stepped back and allowed us to enter the dim shop. Beneath the window to the right of the door was a table and chair. Two other chairs rested against a wall, along with a closed cabinet. Otherwise, the front room was bare. A closed door in the rear wall no doubt led off to other rooms in the shop.

"My master wishes to trade with you," Ani said, smiling his toothy grin.

The old man ignored him. He looked at me and raised a black eyebrow. I turned and took from the front pocket of my wallet the rag that held my supply of jewels, considerably diminished in the course of my travels. It still contained more than a dozen excellent stones. Three of the smallest I removed, and also the great round emerald I had pried from the idol of Shub-Niggurath. The last stone I concealed in the folds of the palm of my hand as I replaced the rag. With a careless gesture, I laid the three jewels gathered from beneath the lost city of Irem on the bare boards of the table in the morning sunlight.

The interest of the old man quickened. He sat and bent his head over the stones, examining them closely without touching them. Then he took up each between his thumb and forefinger and turned it under the lens, which he held near his face.

"These are uncommon stones," he said in a cultured voice in Arabic with a Latin accent. "How did you come by them?"

"A legacy from my father at his death. He was captain of a ship in the Red Sea and acquired many curious treasures."

He chewed his lower lip as he continued to study the stones. I wondered if he had ever encountered this type of jewel before, but did not wish to appear overly inquisitive.

"They are such beautiful gems," Ani said, hovering near his shoulder. "Look at them sparkle in the sunlight. I have never seen such gems in all of Damascus."

The dealer cast me a penetrating glance over his shoulder, and named a sum. It was less than a tenth of the gold I needed to buy the house. I allowed my face to express disappointment, and gathered up the jewels with regret.

"That is not enough," I said. "I am selling these gems to buy a house and need more gold."

621

"Have you no more stones to sell?" he asked.

I paused, as if the thought had not occurred to me, and made a display of uncertainty.

"There is one jewel, but I could not sell it for ten times what you have offered. It was my father's most prized possession."

"Devotion in a son is admirable," he murmured, watching me. "Yet when a father dies, the son must make his own way in the world."

"Your words are true."

Heaving a sigh of reluctance, I pretended to take from a pocket of my thawb the emerald, and set it before him. He gazed at it in silence for many heartbeats, and I realized that he had ceased to breathe. His fingers trembled slightly as he picked it up and studied it beneath his magnifier. The sunlight shining through it did not diminish the green within its depths. When he looked at me, his face held a pallor that was disquieting in a man of his years.

"Where did you get this?"

"As I explained, my father was a captain of a ship—"

He made a sound of disgust and frowned, then turned back to the stone. It seemed to attract his gaze as polished amber draws a wisp of straw. He named a price in gold that was ten times his first offer. Ani beamed from ear to ear.

"For this, and for the other three," he added.

"For the emerald alone," I said.

He frowned in thought. I made a motion of impatience, and he closed his fingers around the stone.

"Agreed."

We left the shop with a small wooden strongbox that Ani carried on one shoulder as he limped along with the help of his stick.

"We should hire an armed guard," he said in a low voice. "This is a lot of gold."

"I trust you to safeguard it," I told him.

The expression on his face approached bliss. It was probably the first time anyone had ever said such a thing to him. Naturally it was a lie. I trusted that I could outrun him, with his crippled foot, but my trust extended no further than that. I am not by nature a trusting person.

As we rounded a corner, I felt eyes upon my back and turned quickly. A man in a blue cloak, his head bowed so that I could not see his face beneath the band of his turban, stepped between two buildings into an alley. I walked quickly back to the mouth of the alley, my hand on the hilt of my sword, and peered around the edge of the wall. It opened at the far end into the adjoining street. I saw men and women walk past its exit, but no trace of the man in the blue cloak.

Ani eyed me curiously when I returned but said nothing.

We reached the Inn of the Stork without challenge. I had Ani carry the box up to my room, where the girl waited. Martala stared with delight at the golden gleam of the dinars in the open box, letting them run through her fingers, and expressed surprise that I had bargained so well in her absence. I said nothing, but I wondered if I had received even half of what the sea-green jewel was worth. The Greek had been too eager to acquire it. He had looked upon it with recognition, almost as though he knew its origin.

In the afternoon we took the strongbox with the greater part of its gold to the house of the green door in the Lane of Scholars. The surplus of the gold hung heavy in my purse. A servant opened the door without speaking and escorted us into the hall. Theon waited in one of the rooms on the lower level beside a large man wearing a chain mail vest over his leather tunic, who I took to be his bodyguard, and a slender young scribe, who spread several parchments out on a large and highly polished table.

The scribe counted the gold with efficient motions of his fingers and nodded to Theon, who closed the strongbox and gave it to the guard. I signed in the indicated places on the parchments, which were three in number—one for the anonymous owner of the house, another for me, and one for the civil bureaucracy of the Caliph, whose meticulous administrators kept filed away all exchanges of land or property within the city walls. The owner had placed his mark next to the signature of the agent.

"It is a pity I could not meet your master face to face," I murmured as I accepted one of the rolled parchments, held shut with a knotted red ribbon.

"That is not possible," Theon said, watching the scribe gather his pen and other implements into his portable writing desk, which he hugged to his shallow chest.

"May I know the reason for your master's shyness?"

He looked at me without warmth.

"No, you may not."

I accepted the keys without speaking, and watched the three leave my house. If its former owner wished to conceal his identity, it was of no concern to me.

"Ignorant pig," Martala said, her arms folded on her breast.

"What can you expect from an infidel?" Ani said.

We turned to look at him, and he nervously stepped from foot to foot as he leaned on his stick.

"Go and ensure that linen has been spread on the beds in the two best rooms, and ask what the cook has prepared for the midday meal," I told him.

His grin of pleasure appeared genuine. He tapped his way from the room on his errands.

"This will serve nicely for a library," I told Martala, gazing at the blank walls of the chamber. There was ample space for book shelves and scroll racks.

"Do you no longer wish me to sleep in your bed?" she asked in dejection.

I turned to her with curiosity, surprised at the emotion in her words.

"Don't you want your own room, with your own bed?"

"No."

I shrugged.

"If you prefer to sleep on the floor at the side of my bed, it is of no concern to me. You will be sooner ready to help me dress in the mornings."

To my surprise, she nodded with a complacent look.

"What about Ani? Do you mean to keep him?"

"For the present. He knows Damascus and we do not."

"He will betray you," she said with assurance.

I thought she was probably correct, but did not give her the satisfaction of admitting it.

The next three days were among the most pleasant I have ever experienced. I reacquainted myself with the luxury I had known in the palace at Sana'a, but with the difference that all of it was purchased with my own gold. This gave me a curious satisfaction. A similar sense of well-being arose from being a householder. True, the house at Alexandria had been mine by name, but I had not bought it, and had little enough time to get to know it. This was my house. I felt as though I belonged within its walls, beneath its roof. I drank the water of its well, and ate the food cooked on its kitchen fire.

Every morning Ani and Martala went to the shops or the marketplace with several of the servants, and returned with cartloads of rugs, hangings, furniture, books, pots, and other necessary items. The previous owner must have endured a period of difficulty, for much of the furniture had been sold, and there were bare patches on the walls to show where paintings and tapestries had formerly hung. The silverware had been pawned, leaving only wooden and brass eating implements. The remaining ill-assorted plates were of wood or lead. Drinking cups of gold, silver, or crystal there were none. I wondered why the statues in the courtyard had not been sold, then reflected that it might be difficult to auction off the images of naked pagan goddesses in Damascus, the city most loyal in all the world to the strict injunctions of the Prophet.

I was anxious to make the acquaintance of my neighbors, but this was not so easy to accomplish. They rarely ventured beyond their closed doors. Ani was of no use to introduce me to men of wealth and power. If this was a street of necromancers, there was nothing to reveal it. By day the houses appeared deserted, until their doors opened briefly to release a servant on some errand. These servants were dour of face and disinclined to speak to Martala. I could not address them in the street myself, since it was beneath my dignity as master of my house. As I had learned in my boyhood at Sana'a, such proprieties, foolish though they might seem, must be observed in society.

The traffic on the street at night took on a more sinister aspect. Groups of hooded men wheeled small carts laden with tied linen bundles that were man-sized and reeked of the grave, or brought strange alchemical flasks and distilleries. Sometimes solitary messengers came and went on stealthy errands. It was obvious by their appearance and manner that they did not belong to the household staffs. Strange chemical scents floated past me on the breeze, and in the late stillness more than once I heard a faint shriek that could only be from the throat of some tormented creature.

I saw all this on the third night as I walked the twisting Lane of Scholars after moonset, trying to get a sense of who lived behind the other doors. I had left Martala curled up and asleep under the silk sheet on my bed. As I had anticipated, her enthusiasm for sleeping on the floor waned after the second night, and I did not object when she slipped under the sheet beside me. The bed was large enough to sleep six. In any case, I had grown accustomed to having her soft snores in my ear.

I returned back along the serpentine length of the street, keeping a discreet distance behind a two-wheeled cart pushed by a pair of laborers who muttered to each other as they tried to hold their awkward burden balanced over the wheels, yet prevent it sliding off into the street each time the cart tipped. My interest quickened when I saw that they intended to take it into the brown door of the house beside my own. Someone waited for their approach on the other side of the door. One of the men knocked lightly twice with the knuckle of his index finger, and the door imme-diately swung open on well-greased hinges. The cart disappeared and the door shut silently. Not a word had been spoken.

Should I wait until the laborers emerged with their empty cart and question them about their business? Like as not, they would try to murder me and make me their next delivery. As I stood wondering what to do, I noticed a shadow move near the wall. The movement was slight. Most men would never have seen it. As I stared at the place, wondering if I had imagined the slide of darkness over darkness, the hood of a black cloak opened to reveal the face of a ghoul. His eyes studied me with keen attention.

"You see me," he said in the language of the ghouls. "How can such a thing be?"

"Nothing so strange, that a ghoul should see a ghoul in the night," I answered in the same tongue.

The strangeness lay in the cloak he wore, and his presence here amid the houses of men. Ghouls preferred to go naked. They detested the rasp of clothing against their smooth dry skin, and could move more silently without its encumbrance. They seldom venture within the walls of a town, where the pairs of watching eyes were innumerable and the places of concealment few.

His surprise at hearing me speak his own language was not so great as I expected. He approached me with care, emerging from the shadows as he drew nearer, and I smelled the carrion of his breath.

"Why do you call yourself a ghoul?" he asked.

His black fingernails gleamed as he flexed his large hands, and I saw that he was about to tear out my throat.

"I am Alhazred of the Black Spring Clan," I answered with haste. "Where we show courtesy to those of other clans who venture into our territory."

"Your clan is unknown to me." He spoke without warmth, but withdrew his hands beneath his cloak. "This is not my territory."

"What are you called, and where do you dwell?"

"My name is Uto, of the White Skull Clan. We dwell beyond the walls of this city in one of its burial places."

"You have business with a necromancer of this street," I said, divining his purpose.

"That is no concern of yours, Alhazred of the Black Spring Clan."

"It may be in future." I gestured at the green door, only a dozen paces further along the street. "That is my house."

"Ah! So you are the necromancer who bought old Hapla's house. I thought your name sounded familiar. You are the latest gossip of the city."

"What do they say about me?"

"Merely that you possess jewels of great rarity, and that you purchased Hapla's house outright with a chest of gold. You are presumed to be fabulously wealthy."

"How is it known that I am a necromancer?"

The ghoul's shoulders shook, and he made the rasping noise that is laughter for his kind.

"Everyone who lives in the Lane of Scholars is a necromancer. Surely you knew that before you bought the house?"

"I was told something to that effect," I admitted. "What do you know of the previous owner of my house?"

Uto shrugged beneath his cloak.

"Little enough. I had no dealings with him. He was said to be wrapped up in the magic of portals, a very deep study of many years."

"He must have been successful, for he is gone."

Again the ghoul laughed.

"For a human, you have a good sense of humor," he said, his sharpened teeth projecting over his lower lip. "I almost like you."

"If Hapla did not vanish into one of his portals, what caused him to sell his house?"

Uto scowled.

"As I heard the tale, he was given a choice by the Caliph Yazid. Either to leave the city or be arrested and executed."

"What has the Caliph against necromancers?"

"He is afraid of your kind. If it lay within his power, he would have his guards break down all these doors, kill you while you slept, and burn your houses to the ground. He may yet do so, on one of these dark nights. As it is, he moves against those individuals who draw his displeasure. Last month it was Hapla. Next month it may be you."

"Who dwells there?" I asked, gesturing toward the brown door.

"There lives the greatest of you, or so the gossip says. It was with him that I had business."

Before we could speak further, the brown door opened to emit the cart, empty of its linen-bound burden. The laborers pushed it back along the street, and the ghoul floated like a shadow behind them, unseen by the two men, who did not notice my presence in the shadows. It was evident that Uto had only been there to ensure the safe delivery of the corpse, for such it surely must be. I wondered what use the inhabitant of the house beyond the brown door would have for such an object.

My encounter with the ghoul occupied my thoughts the following day, but I found nothing in his discourse to turn to my advantage, other than to remind myself that it would be foolish to annoy the Caliph Yazid, and this I had always known. He was said to be quite mad, and to spend all his time in a drunken stupor amid his concubines and eunuchs, playing on the flute and composing love songs. If this was so, there was little to worry about, but I reflected that even a drunkard became sober from time to time.

Martala occupied herself with Ani and the household staff, seeing to the display of her latest purchases for the house. I sat at a table beneath a shade tree in my garden, reading the scroll of the Old Ones and trying to understand some of the more obscure points of grammar in their difficult language, which was several times more complex than any language spoken by men. In truth, it was a human language, since the primal tongue of the Old Ones could not have been comprehended by the human brain, but it was a human language that most closely conveyed the essence and potency of their true tongue. It had not been created by men, but by the Old Ones themselves for the use of their slaves.

A babble of childish laughter drifted over the wall at my back. It seemed an incongruous sound to emanate from the same house that had received a wrapped corpse on the night before, but my thoughts were elsewhere and I paid it scant attention as I formed the arcane words and sounded out their Greek letters. My mind was drawn back to itself by the impact of a leather ball upon the surface of the table. The ball was not solid, but a bladder filled with air. It bounced twice on the grass and came to rest at the base of a tree.

"Father, my ball! I lost my ball!" a child's voice cried out in Arabic from the other side of the wall.

"Lost it?" a man's voice said in good humor. "It was here a moment ago. How can it be lost?"

"Perhaps I can supply the answer," I called out.

There was silence from the other side of the barrier. I stood and picked up the ball.

"What was reduced to nothing can be made to reform itself," I said, and tossed the leather sphere into the other garden, which I could not see, for the wall was much higher than my head.

"Indeed it can," said the man's voice. "May I ask the name of the one who has performed this miracle for my daughter?"

"I am Alhazred, late of Yemen, but now a resident of Damascus."

"A fortuitous acquaintance, Alhazred. The girl would have shed tears all afternoon without your intervention."

His voice was cultured and deep, that of a scholar and teacher. The child giggled. By the sound, she could not have been older than five or six.

"I am known in this city as Harkanos," the voice continued. "And I am indebted to you. Will you come to my garden and share wine with me?"

"With the greatest delight."

A servant ushered me from the street through the brown door into a courtyard that was similar in size to my own, but lacked the adornment of Greek goddesses. Waiting for me at the foot of the front steps was a man some twenty years my senior, who wore a dark green robe of shimmering silk decorated at its collar, hem and cuffs with double strips of cloth of gold. At the open throat of the robe over his plain white undershirt hung a silver medallion of curious design, in the shape of a crescent moon with the two horns turned downward. From the point of each horn dangled a seed pearl. His brown hair was cut short to reveal his ears, and curled over his broad forehead. Like me, he went with his head uncovered and his chin shaven. He smiled, showing even white teeth.

"I have been wishing to become acquainted with my new neighbor," he said, studying my englamoured face with warm interest.

"As have I."

"So Uto told me." He saw my look of surprise. "He returned to me after you left the street and related your conversation with him."

His clear gray eyes held only frankness and a mild amusement.

"Was it chance that your daughter's ball found its way over the wall?"

He laughed and put his hand on my shoulder in a friendly way to guide me into his house.

"Let us go into my study where we can converse freely."

The room was filled with books, charts, and mathematical instruments. It occupied the left side of the house on the lower level. I recognized an astrolabe, several astronomical instruments for measuring the stars, and a celestial globe, but many of the finely crafted tools of brass were unfamiliar.

"You are an astrologer?"

He saw that I was looking at several freshly made horoscopes on his desk, and nodded.

"There are wealthy men who pay large amounts of gold to have their futures divined in the stars. It is a frivolous occupation, I grant, but it pays for my more serious studies."

Crossing to a cabinet, he opened its doors and poured wine into two slender goblets of smoky transparent glass. He gave me one of the glasses and indicated that I should sit on a cushioned seat beneath the window, which opened onto his back garden. I saw the child running through the grass, naked as Eve, when I sat. He sat beside me and drew his leg up to turn and face me. I sampled the wine. It was a kind of mead, as good as any I had ever tasted.

"I was sorry to hear about Hapla," I murmured. "It is my hope to cease my wandering and make Damascus my home."

"The Caliph makes life difficult for us all," he said, sipping from his goblet with his eyes closed to savor the golden wine.

"For you as well?"

He shrugged.

"He employs me to draw up horoscopes for his concubines and various princes and men of power with whom he has dealings. Thus far he has not threatened me."

I remembered the unfortunate fate of an astrologer to King Huban's court at Sana'a. Not many months after I began living at the palace, the king had taken a dislike to his predictions and had caused him to be impaled on a stake just outside the gates of the city.

He studied my face closely as though looking at the details of a painting. When he noticed my attention, he smiled disarmingly.

"That is a well-wrought glamour. Do you mind?"

I shook my head, wondering what he intended. He made several fluid gestures and muttered a few words. I felt the veil of glamour fall from my countenance. He did not flinch away, but his eyes held pity.

"I see why you wear the glamour. You have suffered much, Alhazred. Perhaps at some future meeting you will tell me your history."

I spoke the word of the veiling spell and restored my mask while he watched the motions of my hand with interest.

"Perhaps. And in return, you may tell me about your real work, that causes you to receive the bodies of the dead in the night."

He nodded.

"Trust between men cannot be won in a moment, or with a few words."

I left his house with my mind filled with unanswered questions. Was he married? If so, I had seen no trace of his wife. How close was he to the Caliph? Did I dare trust him, or any man of power, with my true history? King Huban was dead, but I had no doubt that his son Yanni would enforce his late father's decrees. Yet it would be useful to have as a friend a man with the same interests and skills. When next we conversed in private, I resolved to ask him about magic that would restore lost limbs.

A captain of the Caliph's guard and two foot soldiers waited for me in the courtyard when I returned to my own house. Martala ran across and put her arms protectively around me.

"They have come to arrest you, Alhazred," she said, her voice breaking with emotion. "You are to be taken before the Caliph and judged."

Chapter 55

Yazid was a man whose body had gone soft from too much indulgence for too many years. It was said that his age was thirty-nine, but he looked older. His skin, deprived of sunlight, had acquired a sickly pallor and a scattering of dark moles. Broken blood vessels reddened his nose, and blue pouches hung beneath his blood-shot eyes. A ragged beard that resembled a worn shaving brush decorated the tip of his chin. His small white hands fluttered like ensnared birds when emotion overcame his exaggerated dignity.

"Do you think me a fool? Do you think I know nothing of your ways?" he shrieked. Echoes reverberated from the domed ceiling.

No answer helpful to my situation arose in my mind, so I remained silent. I had been forced upon my knees on the mosaic floor tiles by the two helmeted guards who stood at my elbows with their arms folded on their breastplates. In addition to the royal bodyguard, several dozen advisors, servants, and courtiers were gathered in the lofty audience chamber of the Caliph, watching me with impassive expressions. I was merely one of many men that Yazid would judge this day, to be forgotten as quickly as the others.

Yazid leaped from his throne in a passion and took several nervous steps across the polished tiles on his pink satin slippers.

"How do you explain this?"

He thrust out his hand. On his palm rested a large emerald. With sinking heart, I recognized it as the stone from the vulva of the Thugian idol.

"It is an emerald," I said, licking my swollen lower lip.

The guards had not been gentle while escorting me from my house to a waiting room at the palace. They had found ways to make me stumble, and when I stumbled, had used that excuse to strike me.

His eyes bulged and he ground his teeth.

"Where did you get this stone?"

If he expected me to deny knowledge of the emerald, he was disappointed. That he held the stone meant that he had questioned the gem dealer, who would have repeated all that I told him.

"It belonged to my father, who was a captain on the Red Sea for many years. How it came into his possession, I do not know, but when he died it was passed on to me, as his only son."

Clutching the emerald in his fist, he hit me across the face with a backhand blow, his knuckles catching me on the cheekbone.

"Lies! This stone is from an idol of the wagon-dwelling vermin that infest my roads. It is an evil thing anointed in blood to honor their obscene goddess."

"Of these matters I know nothing."

He raised his fist as though to strike me again, but restrained himself. Instead, he wiped the sweat from his flushed face with his sleeve. The odor of his body, only a step away, was uncommonly foul, and I noticed with an absent mind the dried vomit stains on the breast of his ornately embroidered purple silk robe.

"Nothing? Nothing?" He stared around at his courtiers with raised eyebrows. Several of the bolder sycophants laughed. "I suppose you know nothing about the forbidden arts of necromancy?"

"Necromancy is a crime against the laws of the Prophet, may he be blessed, and those who practice it are punished with banishment or execution."

"Indeed they are." He stared at me with an idiotic expression of exultation, and I wondered if he were mad. "Tell me, necromancer, why should I not order you put to death?"

Looking around the audience room, I saw no sympathy in the eyes of those assembled to watch this vulgar display. I might attempt to take possession of Yazid's mind, but if I failed I would have no recourse. He was undoubtedly a fool, but it did

633

not necessarily follow that he had a weak will. In any case, the moment I released him he would have me recaptured and put to death.

"Harkanos, your advisor on matters celestial, will speak for me, and testify to my good character," I said quickly.

This made him hesitate. His eyes narrowed.

"You know Harkanos?"

"He is my closest friend in Damascus."

"He will speak for you?"

"He will testify that I am ignorant of all forbidden arts."

"Why in the name of the Prophet do you dwell in the Lane of Scholars?"

I shrugged.

"The house was for sale, and it was next to that of my friend Harkanos."

He withdrew and huddled with several of his advisors, who cast me dark looks as they talked among themselves in low voices. At length he returned and drew himself up, recollecting his dignity as Caliph.

"I do not believe you, but I have no further time to waste on you. Since you invoke the name of Harkanos as your protector, I will be lenient. You have three days to rent or sell your house, remove your possessions, and leave Damascus. If you are within the walls when this period of grace has elapsed, you will be taken to a place of public execution and beheaded by the sword. That is my judgment."

He jerked his chin so that the role of fat beneath it jiggled. The guards at my sides seized my arms and lifted me to my feet. My legs were numb from kneeling on the chill tiles. The guards prevented me from collapsing as they marched me out of the audience chamber and to the front gate of the palace, where I found Martala and Ani waiting with anxious faces.

In answer to their questions, I merely shook my head, lost in my own thoughts. We walked back to the house in silence. I did not speak until we stood in my study, away from the curious ears of the household staff.

"The Caliph has ordered me to give up this house and leave Damascus. I have three days."

Martala took the news stoically. She had heard worse things in her life. By contrast, Ani reacted as though stabbed in the heart. He began to moan and beat his forehead and his chest with his fists. I presume he lamented the end of his luxurious new life.

"I must talk to Harkanos, our neighbor. I was forced to involve him to save my own life."

When I told the impassive servant who came to answer the bell at the brown door that I must speak with his master, Harkanos himself returned to the door to admit me. I recounted in a few words my arrest and the decree of the Caliph, and with some embarrassment, told him that I had used his name to save myself. To my surprise, he was not angry. He nodded and laid his hand upon my shoulder.

"You acted wisely to save your life. If there is need, I will testify to your good character, but I do not believe that will be necessary."

"As long as I have not placed you in danger by linking you to my misfortunes, I am content."

"Nonsense, nonsense, you are one of us now. It is time we acted together for the good of all."

He motioned for a servant to approach and murmured in his ear, while I puzzled over his words. The servant bowed and withdrew.

"Can you return here at midnight?"

"Of course."

"Do so, and I hope to have better news for you."

It was with great curiosity, and some trepidation, that I returned to his door at the agreed hour. The same wordless servant admitted me from the street and ushered me into the house. I expected him to lead me to the study of his master, but instead, he went toward the rear of the house, where a modest door of plain boards opened upon a stone stair that led downward into the cellar. I found it similar to my own cellar, though less bleak. The stone walls were adorned with tapestries, and rugs took the harshness from the flagstone floor.

A short corridor opened upon an oblong chamber with an arched roof of red brick. A single oil lamp hanging from an iron bracket on the wall cast a dim light. The room contained a table and little else apart from shelves on one wall that held various obscure receptacles of brass and glass. The table was a rough workbench, stained by chemicals and perhaps by blood, but wooden chairs were arranged around it. Harkanos sat at its head. Four other men sat along the far side, their backs to the wall, and three on the side nearest the door. At the foot of the table sat the ghoul Uto, his eyes narrowed to slits against the glow of the lamp. He grinned at me, showing his sharp teeth against the blackness of his lips. I recognized none of the men. They watched me without speaking as I entered the room, and the door shut behind me.

Harkanos rose from his chair and gestured for me to come forward.

"Take a seat, my friend."

There was one vacant chair at the near side of the table, on the end. I slid into it, gazing around at the others with keen interest. The youngest, who sat at the left elbow of Harkanos, looked a few years older than myself, and the eldest, who sat across from me, might have been my grandfather. They were all men of dignified bearing and intelligent countenance.

"It is best if we do not exchange names, in view of our purpose," Harkanos said.

Several of the men nodded, and I wondered what our purpose might be.

"These are all your neighbors, and no doubt in time you will come to have acquaintance with them. Uto, you have already met."

He turned to the others.

"As I told you in my messages, this is the man who bought Hapla's house. Today he was commanded by Yazid to give up his residence and leave Damascus."

"Did the Caliph give a reason for his judgment?" asked the elder, whose white beard descended below the edge of the table.

"He accused me of necromancy," I said, meeting his pale blue eyes.

"No other crime? Merely the practice of necromancy?"

"Only that."

An angry murmur rounded the table.

"This is intolerable," said the bald man beside me, who I took to be an Egyptian by his accent. "One by one, Yazid has us banished or executed. He will not stop until we are all cast out of the city. Yet we have done nothing to earn his displeasure."

"He is terrified of magic," said the ghoul. "He sees demons under his bed and finds curses written in lampblack on his ceiling. Drunkenness has stolen away his reason."

Harkanos raised a hand for attention.

"Are we agreed that Yazid intends to banish all necromancers from Damascus?"

They solemnly nodded, and after a moment of consideration, I added my assent.

"Then we have only to decide what action to take in our own defense."

"We might hazard a bribe," the bearded ancient said. "If it was large enough, Yazid would be tempted."

"Would that allay his irrational hatred of necromancy?" asked the youngest man at the elbow of our host.

"No," admitted the eldest. "It might turn his ire away for a year or two, but it would not solve the problem."

"Why should we throw away good gold on that besotted pig?" demanded the Egyptian.

Several others voiced agreement with his view.

"We might try to frighten him," Harkanos mused. "Yet he has grown so irrational in his mind, a threat could cause him to move against all of us at once."

"For too long have we bent like reeds to his bluster," the Egyptian continued. "I say we end it. For if we turn our faces away and let this newcomer suffer his fate, the next time it will be one of us who is driven from his home."

To this view there was general accord.

"You are but recently arrived in Damascus," the Egyptian said to me. "You don't know what it has been like, to be mindful of every action or word, lest it trigger the anger of the Caliph."

"The last three years have been difficult," the ghoul agreed.

"Yazid must be eliminated," Harkanos said. "How are we to accomplish it?"

"Poison?" the younger man on his left murmured. "Simple, but effective."

"I've heard that he has food tasters who sample everything he eats or drinks," said the ghoul.

"Whatever way we choose, it must be certain," Harkanos said. "If we fail and it becomes known that he was attacked by necromancy, we are apt to face even greater oppression."

"A demon," the Egyptian began in a musing tone, gazing at his fingers, which he joined at the tips, "would be messy," he concluded.

"That's an understatement," said the bearded ancient. "There would be parts of Yazid scattered through half a dozen rooms of the palace."

We all sat in silence, considering the ways of murder.

"It is not necessary that Yazid be killed," the Egyptian said. "Only that he be sent away."

"Far enough away that he can never return," the ancient agreed.

"I know of a portal spell," I murmured. "It was taught to me by . . . one well versed in such magic."

In a few words I described the spell of opening the portal between worlds by means of a whirlwind that was shown to me so long ago by the dark man in the desert. They were an attentive audience.

"The difficulty with such portal magic is control," the ancient said. "Easy to open a portal, but difficult to know where it leads."

"What matter where it leads, as long as it is to some other plane of reality," observed the Egyptian.

This evoked chuckles from several men at the table. They found the idea of Yazid cast off into an unknown void amusing. I admit, it brought a smile to my own swollen lips. I remembered the different worlds I had visited in soul flight while beneath the lost city of Irem. Any one of them would serve for Yazid's exile. The Plateau of Leng seemed especially appropriate for a man of his vulgarity.

"We would need a way to open the portal at a distance," Harkanos said.

"That is not beyond possibility," said the ancient, his cold blue eyes glittering beneath his snowy eyebrows.

Other ideas were brought forward, but none held as much appeal as opening a hole in the fabric of space itself for the drunken Yazid to tumble into.

We spent an hour discussing the mechanical aspects of the portal ritual. The spell taught to me by Nyarlathotep was to be used as the foundation. I did not see the need to admit the origin of the spell to the necromancers. Harkanos was able to provide the locator for the spell by using an astrological birth chart of Yazid. A birth horoscope was as distinctive as a portrait. He also possessed a scrap of underclothing stained with the Caliph's semen, no doubt purchased from one of his concubines.

Four of the men carried the heavy table to one end of the room and stacked the chairs on top of it. The Egyptian drew a ritual circle around us using blue chalk that glowed in the dim light from the hanging lamp on the wall. Harkanos himself inscribed within the circle a sigil to Yog-Sothoth, the god of portals, and placed the horoscope and stained scrap of cloth in its center. Nine of us stood upon the circle, our hands joined, with Harkanos at its center. The ghoul was on my left. I took his dry hand into mind with a sense of familiarity. It had been long since I had touched a ghoul. We began to chant in the language of the Old Ones, projecting the power we raised into Harkanos while he concentrated his will upon Yazid. The air inside the circle took on a glow, as though filled with countless fine golden particles that danced together.

This was the first time I had practiced my art in the company of other necromancers, and each was at least equal to my skill. I found the chant intoxicating. The power of the guttural words lifted me up and expanded my astral body, until I felt myself a league in height, my head among the stars. Around me stood the others, giants whose feet spanned the arc of the world. Our united voices caused the very fabric of the firmament to shake, or so it seemed to my exalted senses.

There was no leader of the chant, yet we all stopped at the same instant. Silence stretched for a dozen heartbeats. Harkanos stood with his head bowed, his body flickering with balefire. He cast up his arms and uttered dread words of consummation in the forbidden tongue.

"Yiii, n'galas g'h Yog-Sothoth, reg'hi n'gl lohk!"

A shaft of light lanced upward, draining the circle of its vitality so utterly that I had to fight to keep my knees from buckling. I felt as though I had just recovered from a long sickness, both weak and nauseous. I saw cold sweat gleam on the faces of the other necromancers and knew they suffered the same loss of vital spirits. Only the ghoul appeared unaffected.

"It is done," Harkanos said, his face a gray mask in the flickering lamp light. "We must wait to hear the outcome."

Fatigue made us indifferent to conversation. There was nothing to talk about until we learned the effect of our magic. By unspoken agreement we prepared to leave the house. Harkanos erased the circle and put away the relics of the Caliph on a shelf, then helped to carry the table back to the center of the room. He summoned his taciturn servant by means of a bell cord. I had been the last to arrive, but was the first to leave the house. The dark street held an air of desolation. Not surprising, since most of its inhabitants were still in my neighbor's cellar.

I had left the street door to my house unlatched, so that I could return without waking anyone. This was not so much a courtesy intended to preserve their rest, as a desire to avoid the notice of the servants. The brass-sheathed front door of the house itself remained locked, so there was little to fear from robbers, who in any case would have been mad to steal from anyone living in the Lane of Scholars. I shut the green door and gently slid its iron bolt into place. My weariness made me anxious to reach my bed. I wondered if Martala lay asleep or waited for my arrival to hear the events of the night.

As I turned to cross the courtyard to the front step, I became aware of a presence in the shadows. Without thinking, I drew my sword. Its blade gleamed silver in the weak starlight, for the waxing crescent moon had already set, and only the faintest glow from a street lantern found its way over the wall.

"How long I have waited for this night," said a voice that I recognized all too well.

He stepped from behind one of the marble statues, and with a sickness of heart I saw his sword in his hand. I gathered my shreds of courage. I had known this encounter would come eventually.

"Welcome to my house, Altrus," I said with as much bravado as I could simulate.

"You have done well for yourself, Alhazred," he rasped. "A pity I must take all this away from you."

"I have gold," I said, easing to my right with my back close to the outer wall.

"You know that is not my way."

He sprang forward, and I met his blade on my own, dancing away from the wall to the center of the courtyard so that I would not be restricted in movement. He advanced one step after another, slashing at my sword.

We both stopped and drew breath. To my astonishment, I was still alive. I had not even suffered a wound. I blinked and narrowed my eyes, trying to penetrate the shadows. Something was wrong with his body. For a moment it puzzled me. Then I saw that his right arm hung limp at his side. Altrus had always held his sword in his right hand, not his left, but tonight he clutched it awkwardly in his left fist. One of his legs was not normal. The knee did not bend when he stepped forward.

"I had to wait until you were alone, before I could kill you," he said with bitterness. "I am not the man I was. When you and that bitch attacked me on the caravan road, you did some injury to my spine."

"That is why you did not kill us at the Well of the Seraph."

He laughed, an ugly sound.

"Had I been able to draw a bow, you would both have been dead a hundred times over."

"If you do kill me, let the girl go," I said.

He shrugged.

"I care nothing for the girl. I want the scroll to take back to my master, and your death as retribution for its theft."

Again he lunged, catching me off balance, but his instincts were better than his skills, and his damaged body refused to obey his will fast enough. I beat aside his point, which had been aimed at the pit of my throat, and danced back.

The servants slept in their rooms at the back of the house. We made little sound apart from the occasional clash of our blades. I resisted the urge to cry out and summon aid. In part it was because I did not wish to endanger the girl, who newly risen from sleep might stumble into Altrus' sword. Yet the main reason I held my tongue was a sense that it would be contemptible to call for help. This was a duel between two men.

My skill with a blade is equal or better than that of most men trained in the sword, who do not make the sword their living. The old Altrus was many times my superior, but this strange crippled Altrus who fought with his left hand was no more than my peer. His body had lost its vigor. I saw that he tired quickly, and deliberately gave back before his attack, leaving an opening. As I expected, he lunged, and I took the point of his blade through the folds of my cloak. My own point buried itself upward beneath his breastplate, above his left hip. It was a deep thrust that grated on bone.

He fell to his knee like a sacrificial ox, his bad leg splaying out from him, then toppled slowly backward. His sword clattered across the paving stones, and he groped blindly for it with his left hand, eyes fixed on my face. I approached and angled my sword for a killing thrust through his throat. There was no fear in his expression, only a curious tranquility.

"You fought well," he said, his breathing labored.

"Had you not been injured, I would never have beaten you."

"True."

I hardened my resolve for the thrust. I could not take my gaze off his eyes. He appeared resigned, even eager, to meet his death. I reflected that it could not have been an easy task, to track me across half the world with only one arm and a leg that would not bend.

"What are you waiting for? Kill me," he rasped. "Or do you want to watch me die slowly?"

Some madness made me lift up the point of my sword. I cannot explain it. I felt possessed by an essence that moved through my mind and body, filling me with that most foolhardy and dangerous of emotions, compassion. He must have seen a shadow of it in my face. He frowned and stared hard at me.

"Suppose I were to spare your life and heal your body?" I said softly.

"A cripple is no use as a mercenary. I would have killed myself, except that I had a job to finish."

"No, you misunderstand me. Suppose I were to heal you of all your injuries and make you as you were when we first met? Would you give up your quest for the scroll, and cease trying to kill me?"

He thought for several heartbeats, a solemn cast to his features.

"No. I was hired to kill you and retrieve the scroll."

I wiped my sword blade on the inner lining of my cloak and slid it into its sheath.

"Your determination is admirable, but your loyalties are misplaced."

He shrugged and attempted to smile.

"A mercenary has little enough in this world. Would you take away his honor as well?"

Damn his soul, I did not wish to kill him. Cursing under my breath, I left him lying in the middle of the courtyard under the indifferent stars, and unlocked the front door of my house. What I needed was in my bedroom with my travel wallet, which I had not yet completely emptied. It hung on a peg beside the door. I entered the room silently, but the girl was already awake.

"Alhazred? I thought I heard the clash of steel. Was it a dream?"

"No dream. Get dressed and help me."

She slid out of bed and put on one of my new white shirts with a tail that hung down to her knees. Not bothering with anything else, she belted her sword and dagger to her waist. When she came to me, I had the contents of my wallet spread across the writing desk that occupied a corner of our bedroom. I found the rag that held the dried pieces of *u'mal* root and used my dagger to cut a section from one root that was as long as the last joint of my index finger.

"What are we doing?"

"Saving a life."

When she saw Altrus lying on his back in the courtyard, she hissed between her teeth and drew her dagger. She would have slit his throat had I not caught her wrist. She stared at him, then at me, an expression of horror gathering in her face.

"You cannot mean to heal him."

"It is my decision."

"He will kill us both."

Altrus laughed weakly. His laughter turned to a retching cough, and I saw blood on his lips. My sword had scraped past his rib and pricked the lowermost lobe of his lung.

"The girl is right. Don't be a fool, Alhazred. Kill me while you have the chance."

"Everyone chooses to give me advice," I said, kneeling beside him. "I do not choose to take it."

"Fool," he whispered.

I pushed the piece of *u'mal* root between his teeth.

"Chew and swallow this while you have the strength."

His jaw began to mechanically grind the tough root. He shut his eyes with exhaustion. I drew my dagger, cut my left forearm with a curse, and held it over his face.

"Open your mouth, and swallow."

He parted his blood-stained lips. Perhaps he could not taste my blood, mingled as it was with his own.

For several moments nothing happened. I began to think the potency of the root had departed with its juice, in spite of what Belaka, the wisest head of the Beast, had told me. Then his body seemed to soften, like wax held near a flame. A kind of glow appeared beneath his blanched skin that pulsed with the rhythm of his heart, and I realized that it had its origin in his blood. His right arm twitched, unbending at the elbow, and the fingers of his right hand closed into a fist. He opened his eyelids and regarded his right hand with an expression of wonder.

"The pain has stopped," he murmured.

Martala drew her sword and stepped back, balanced on the balls of her bare feet.

"You are a fool, Alhazred," she said, her eyes fixed on the mercenary as though he were a viper bent to strike.

In my own mind I agreed with her, but the instinct to heal Altrus had been strong, and even though it made no rational sense, I could not have denied it.

"If you will refrain from killing me for the present, I will help you to bed, so that you can rest."

He said nothing but accepted my arm. I pulled him to his feet. His formerly stiff knee bent with ease as he walked with my aid into the house and up the stairs. I put him to bed in the bedroom I had intended for Martala. All the while she watched narrowly at our backs, her sword extended. In spite of the vivifying effects of the *u'mal* root, his near meeting with death had left the mercenary exhausted. He was asleep almost before his back touched the sheets of the bed. I worked the boots off his feet and unbuckled his breastplate, sliding it aside and laying it on the floor in the corner of the room.

"What are you going to do now?" Martala breathed, staring down at the sleeping face of the mercenary in the golden glow of the oil lamp.

"Go to bed. I am more tired than I have ever been."

It was full daylight when I awoke in my own bed, my body still aching from the strain of my duel with Altrus. The sound of boots marching in the street and harsh cries came through the open window. I pushed myself up on one elbow and saw Martala sitting in a chair beside the closed door, still wearing my shirt, her naked sword across her lap.

"It was good of you to watch over me," I said gently. "You know that Altrus can kill us both any time he chooses?"

Her face hardened, and I realized that Altrus would have a fight on his hands if he attempted to take my life.

"What is that infernal din on the street?"

She shook her head.

"It has been going on since first light. I'm surprised it didn't wake you."

"I was too exhausted to wake."

I swung my feet out of bed. She set her sword aside and brought the brass chamber pot for me to piss into, then covered it and put it back in its corner. As she helped me dress, Ani burst into the room followed by Altrus. I scarcely recognized the mercenary, so improved was his appearance. His hair and close-cropped beard were darker, and the ugly red sear on his right cheek had healed. He almost looked handsome.

"Master, you must come downstairs at once. The soldiers are demanding to talk to you."

"More soldiers," I muttered.

The Caliph vanished through the portal, I thought to myself. That would explain the unrest in the street.

Leaving Martala to dress herself, I went with Ani and the unspeaking Altrus to the front hall. A captain of the Caliph's guard and two soldiers stood waiting near the open door.

"Are you the owner of this house?" the captain demanded, looking at Altrus.

"I am Alhazred, the owner."

He turned his attention to me.

"By order of the Caliph Yazid Ibn Muawya, none of the residents of the Lane of Scholars are to be permitted to leave their houses. Guards will be posted outside your street door and in the alley that runs behind your house, both day and night, until the Caliph has determined your judgement."

"What is the meaning of this outrage?"

He glared at me.

"An attempt was made upon the life of the Caliph last night. It failed. The Caliph intends to find those responsible and make an example of them to the people of Damascus."

Chapter 56

After the captain and his soldiers left my front hall, we stood staring at each other. Several servants hovered in the doorways and watched us with nervous eyes. I suppose they wondered what their fate would be, and whether it was bound up with mine. I could not expect loyalty from them since they had served me less than a week. I gestured for Martala, Altrus, and Ani to follow me into my study, and shut both the door to the front hall and the door on the opposite side that exited to another room.

"What is this all about, Alhazred?" Martala asked.

"Were I to speculate, I would guess that a group of necromancers used their magic in an attempt to assassinate the Caliph, and failed. He must believe that they dwell in this street."

"So that's what you were doing last night in the house next door," said Altrus. "I wondered why you tarried there so long."

"You tried to kill the Caliph?"

Martala put her hand to her face, and Ani's eyes grew round, although he did not speak. The Caliph was Allah's emissary upon the earth, or so the people believed.

"I must consult with my neighbor, Harkanos." I looked at each of them. "You need not concern yourselves. If the blade falls, let it fall upon my neck."

When I left the study and made my way down the rear hall and out the back door, they trailed after me. I looked behind the gardener's shed and found what I searched after—a wooden ladder. Carrying it to the side wall of the garden, I angled it slowly upward so that its top would not project far above the stone wall. Both the street in front and the alley behind the house were narrow, and bordered by high walls. I reasoned that the soldiers standing guard would not be able to see me climb out of the garden at the side, if I kept my head low.

Altrus helped me fix the foot of the ladder into the sod so that it would not slip down the wall.

"Are you sure you want to help me?"

"Why not?" he said with a grin. "If I let the Caliph kill you, it would deprive my master of his retribution."

"You could slay me now."

"I am in no hurry."

I glanced at Martala and Ani.

"You should stay here, in case the soldiers return asking questions."

"I'm coming with you," the girl said. I had heard that tone before, and knew it would be futile to argue.

Ani licked his dry lips, staring at us.

"I will come too," he said after a hesitation.

His display of loyalty surprised me. I reflected that it would not matter who was missing from the house if the soldiers returned. They would want to talk to me, no one else. The only worry was that one of the servants might go into the street and inform the soldiers of our absence. This seemed unlikely, since they would not wish to draw attention to themselves.

I climbed to the top of the wall. Short iron spikes ran along its rounded cap of mortar. There was enough space to kneel between them. I could not see the guards in the street in front or the alley behind, so I presumed they could not see me. In the other garden, the little girl stood watching me with curious eyes, a rag doll in her hand. Today she wore an embroidered pink dress that fell to her ankles, showing her bare feet beneath its hem. She dropped her doll and ran into the open back door of the house.

Altrus came up the ladder easily and knelt on the opposite side. We helped the girl climb and lowered her into the other garden. The drop to the soft grass was not great. She kept her footing. Ani fell more awkwardly and landed on his side. Altrus threw his walking stick down beside him. We grasped the ladder and lifted it over the wall, keeping it flat, then tilted it down on the other side. He descended its rungs and held it steady while I followed.

By this time, Harkanos had emerged from his back door and stood watching our intrusion, his hands clasped serenely at his waist, hidden beneath the folds of his gold-banded green sleeves. He smiled at me when I caught his eye and came over.

"Do you know what took place at the palace?" I asked.

"Our attempt failed. The portal opened, but Yazid was in the midst of his women. They knocked him flat in their terror to escape. Several who stood over him were pulled through, but the weight of the others lying across his back anchored his body and prevented the whirlwind from drawing him into its vortex."

"Why does he blame us?"

"Yazid blames the residents of the Lane of Scholars for every work of magic."

"This time he means to act against you," Altrus said. "I looked into the street when the soldiers arrived. They are not a token force, and they are well armed."

"What will you do?" I asked.

"Day is not the best time for works of necromancy," Harkanos mused. "I doubt we could gather the others here without being discovered by the soldiers."

"You tried necromancy and it failed," Altrus said.

Harkanos eyed him keenly. I was surprised the mercenary did not quake before his gaze, so deeply did it penetrate, but Altrus appeared untroubled.

"It is time for the sword," the mercenary said.

"How will we get into the palace?" the clubfooted procurer asked in a whine. Fear was naked on his narrow face, and I regretted not ordering him to remain at the house.

"I am the Caliph's astrologer," Harkanos mused. "I know a little-used door at the rear of the palace that leads into the back chambers, behind the seraglio."

"Is it locked?" Altrus demanded.

"Of course. But I was given a key."

He lifted a heavy key ring from his belt and took from it a brass key of simple design. I laid my hand on his as he was about to pass it to Altrus.

"If we use this and are killed by the palace guard, your own life may be forfeit."

"It is too late for such concerns. Once that madman Yazid gathers his wits and his courage, he will order his guard to move against our houses. He will probably lock us inside with our servants and set them ablaze. Whatever we do must be done at once."

648

A shadow of care crossed his face as he glanced behind him. His daughter stood in the back doorway, clinging to the door latch and watching us, her thumb in her mouth. He give the key to Altrus, and described how to reach the door it opened.

"But how are we to get to the palace?" Ani asked.

"You should go back to the house," I told him. "You do not need to accompany us."

"No, I will come with you," he said. "If you die, I have nothing."

This was too sensible a statement to deny.

"There is a way out of this house that will bypass the guards in the rear alley," Harkanos said to me. "It is sometimes useful for deliveries at night."

He led us into the rear hall. With a quiet word he told his daughter to go to her room, and she obeyed without protest, bending to look at us over the banister as she slowly climbed the main stair. When she was out of sight, he escorted us to the cellar door and we descended the stone steps. I saw no servants, and presumed that the necromancer had ordered them into another part of the house before coming into the garden to speak to us. He took a burning oil lamp from its bracket on the wall and made his way to the right, in a direction opposite the room in which we had worked the ritual. At the end of the corridor a set of four steps led down into a depression that accommodated a small oak door, which was set in the wall at a level lower than the floor of the cellar. The door could not have been more than three cubits in height, and had a dank air of disuse.

"Take this," he said, passing to me the brass lamp, its chains dangling. "The passage exits in the back of a stall in the stables across the alley behind the house. No one will challenge you when you emerge. The front of the stables is in the next street, and should not be under guard."

The iron hinges of the door groaned with rust as Altrus forced it inward with his shoulder. I passed the lamp to him, and we followed its light through a low passage lined with brick, its ceiling supported by a Roman arch. I judged it had not been used for at least several months. Mold on the damp floor clung to the soles of my boots. Altrus cursed under his breath and used his dagger blade to brush away the hanging webs of spiders. I walked at his back, and behind me trailed the girl, followed by Ani, his stick tapping with unease on the bricks in the darkness.

We climbed a steep stair and emerged at the back of a horse stall. The door was disguised to resemble part of the vertical slats that made up the rear of the stall. The horse shifted its hindquarters but did not kick. Altrus soothed it with a few quiet words and laid his hand upon its neck until we were all out, and the door to the tunnel closed behind us. A stableman spreading fresh hay on the floor of the barn saw us leave the stall, but merely watched in silence. No doubt Harkanos had paid him well to be blind to such comings and goings.

The street wound its way south. For a short distance we followed it, then turned east and worked our way toward the palace, walking without haste and showing little obvious interest in what was behind us, even though we strained our ears for the sound of a shout or the rush of boots on the cobblestones. It was unlikely any soldier of the guard would recognize us, but there was always a chance that one of the men who had arrested and brought me before the Caliph would walk past. Altrus and Martala showed an admirable ease of manner. By contrast, Ani sweated silver beads on his forehead and had the look of a thief, his eyes darting nervously from side to side.

"Relax," I murmured without looking at him.

"Easy to say," he replied. "Do you know what the Caliph will do to us if we are caught?"

"Nothing worse than I have suffered already."

"He will kill us, slowly and with exquisite torments."

By crossing from street to street, we made our way around the palace to its northern side. Somewhere not far beyond the high wall that confronted us, the concubines of the Caliph lay in silken luxury, awaiting his drunken summons. The unguarded door had the appearance of a disused servant entrance. The planks of its surface were unbroken by any latch, bell pull, or knocker. Four broad iron straps extended from its hinges and held it together with heavy iron rivets. A small escutcheon midway down the left edge indicated the place to insert the key. The look of disuse was a deception. There was no rust on the iron. The key turned easily in its lock, and the door swung soundlessly inward with a light thrust.

I expected to step through onto the rear palace grounds, but to my surprise we passed into a dim corridor. On this side of the compound the palace pressed directly against the outer wall. It was a convenient and inconspicuous access for the Caliph and his courtiers to the streets of Damascus, when they wished to leave the palace without ceremony. I wondered how many held a key similar to that given to Harkanos.

The only light came from the open door behind us. Altrus had left the oil lamp at the end of the tunnel when we exited to the stable. It had seemed natural to allow

Altrus to lead while he carried the lamp, but in darkness I knew my own skills were superior. I stepped in front of him.

"Put your hand on my shoulder," I told him. "Martala, put your hand on Altrus' shoulder, and Ani, you do the same with the girl."

Ani pushed the door shut behind him with his heel. The click of the latch sounded loud in the darkness. A single ray of daylight shone through the keyhole. All else lay covered in pitch. I started down the corridor with caution, using my keen senses of hearing and smelling to guide me, trailing my hand along the rough wooden paneling of the wall. Dust hung in the air. The floor was not swept with regularity, which reassured me that the passage was vacant most of the time. I passed several open doorways, but from the dead air that lay beyond I judged them storage rooms.

The narrow corridor bent to the left, then to the right. I almost stumbled over the bottom step of a wooden stair, and stood for a few moments at its base, feeling its shape with my hands. The mercenary's fingers flexed on my shoulder.

"Why have you stopped?" he whispered.

"Be quiet. Listen."

From above came the sound of voices and distant laughter, so faint that I wondered if I imagined it.

"I hear them," Martala breathed.

At the top of the stair was a small landing. Light shone through the crack under a door. I felt over its surface but could find no latch or keyhole. Reflecting that it must be designed to be opened in the darkness, I slid my hands over the frame in which it was set, and was rewarded by a faint click when I pressed a wooden lever. The door opened toward me, forcing me to step back. We passed through, and I saw that it was a secret panel set in the wall of a hallway of no impressive dimension. The door was cunningly concealed. It was angled to shut against its spring under its own weight, and when closed appeared nothing more than a part of the wall.

We stood at the end of a short passage illuminated by a single guttering oil lamp that hung from a wall bracket. Immediately to the right a door was set in the wall. I tried its latch and found it locked, then laid my ear against it but heard no sound from the other side. Advancing down the passage with the others close at my heels, I listened at the door set in its end wall. Murmuring voices approached. I stepped back and put my hand on my dagger. The voices diminished. I tried the latch and the door opened easily. Through its crack I saw the backs of two men in conversation, walking away along a broad hall decorated on its walls with patterned tiles of white and black. The men wore the plain white robes of scribes. I shut the door.

"This is madness," Ani said. "The first person who sees us will raise an alarm."

"Go back if you wish," I snapped. His whining grated on my nerves.

It was evident that beyond this unlocked door lay a well-used section of the palace. We could not walk into it without the risk of immediate discovery. I went back down the passage to the locked door, set in the side wall, and listened again. Still no sounds. Drawing my dagger, I fitted the fine point into the keyhole and felt for the wards of the lock.

Altrus looked on with some amusement. I suspected he could have picked the mechanism just as easily.

"A useful talent, should you ever return to a condition of poverty."

"No study is ever wasted. It has served me well."

The lock clicked, and the door opened easily when I lifted the brass latch. The room beyond lay in shadow. My spirits fell. As like as not it was just another disused storage chamber. We entered, leaving the door open for light. It was an odd room, long and narrow, with a kind of boxed bench running the length of the left wall. At the far end was yet another closed door. It held no furnishing of any kind, but above the bench were a series of small panels set in wooden tracks to allow them to be slid to the side. Each had a knob. I stood on the bench to get a closer look at them, and realized that was the purpose of the bench. It raised my face to just above the level of the panels. Sweat and dirt on the knobs and the panels themselves showed that they were in frequent use.

From the panels came the faint sound of babbling voices and lazy laughter that I had heard while on the lower level, at the foot of the stair. I looked at Altrus, who stood beside me at another of the panels. He shrugged, and together we grasped the knobs and slid the panels to the side. The brightness blinded me for several moments. I had to look away and blink until my eyes adjusted to the glare. The voices were louder. I found myself peering through the fretwork of a finely carved wooden screen, at what might have been a view of paradise.

We gazed down upon a great chamber illuminated by crystal windows set in a ring just under a domed roof of polished marble, so that they admitted the golden rays of the sun from all sides as it moved around the heavens. The windows were above our peepholes. Just below us was a circular balcony of polished marble that ran completely around the chamber, with numerous doors leading off it, and a marble stair in the shape of a spiral that wound down to the lower level. On the marble floor far below was a circular bathing pool, made to resemble the shape of the dome. The water shone like sapphire. Women swam in the pool, or lay on cushions placed around its edge, or stood talking and laughing in groups as they drank wine from golden cups and ate dainties from silver trays supported in the hands of Nubian male slaves. The slaves were clothed in loose silks of many colors, but most of the women were completely naked. As I watched in wonder, two women who floated in the pool swam together and kissed in a way that suggested more than friendship.

"What are you looking at?" Martala asked with impatience.

"Horrible things," Altrus told her. "Best for you not to look, or you will never sleep again."

She snorted, and naturally climbed onto the bench and opened another of the panels, standing on her toes since she was a little shorter than those for whom they had been constructed. I heard her draw a breath, and Altrus chuckled. I almost felt a liking for him.

"What is it? What do you see?" Ani asked. He got onto the bench and opened the last remaining panel. After that he said nothing.

"Why are there four panels?" Martala murmured.

"Whoever watches here likes to have company," I said.

The male slaves must be eunuchs, I mused to myself. Not the worst labor in the world for a man bereft of his manhood. Perhaps frustrating at times, but a feast for the imagination. Sashi's face came momentarily before my interior sight, her beautiful lips pursed in an expression of disapproval, but she did not speak.

"I can't see the Caliph," I said.

"Nor do I," Altrus agreed.

We closed our panels, and after a few moments Martala and Ani did the same. The door at the far end of the peep chamber was not locked. It opened on a narrow corridor that curved gently to the left, unilluminated save for light that shone around the edges of similar sliding panels, which were set at intervals in its left wall. Beneath each panel was a small bench. It was not difficult to divine their purpose. I climbed onto one and opened the panel above it.

Through a wooden screen I saw a well-apportioned private sleeping chamber, illuminated by light from a circular window in the center of the domed ceiling. The silk sheets on the bed had not been made up, and trailed upon the marble floor, which was warmed by several rugs. Various articles of clothing lay scattered about.

Hangings of Bacchic scenes in which nymphs and satyrs played the primary parts adorned the walls. Above a small table was a mirror of considerable size and uncommon clarity. It must be pure silver, and to remain that clear would have to be polished every day. Such is the price of vanity.

Altrus watched me with curiosity. I stepped off the bench and let him look.

"A private woman's chamber," he murmured, stepping down.

Martala took her look, and after her, Ani.

"It seems that the Caliph enjoys keeping a secret watch over his concubines," I said.

"Perhaps he does not trust their fidelity," Martala suggested.

We continued along the curving passage, and I realized that it must wrap completely around the great bath chamber, which was ringed on its upper level by the sleeping rooms of the concubines.

More bedchambers must be on the lower level, since there were not enough in the upper circle to accommodate half the number of the Caliph's women, but the rooms were of such size and luxury, I suspected they were given to his most favored lovers, as a reward for their efforts in stirring his lust.

It was impossible to resist peeping into each room as we passed. Most were empty. In one chamber, two women lay locked together in lovemaking, their groans of passion clearly audible through the screen. In another, one of the concubines sat on the edge of her bed while a turbaned eunuch with skin black as ebony knelt between her parted knees and gave her satisfaction in the only way available to him.

Altrus cursed softly when he looked. He saw me watching him and shrugged.

"It's been weeks since I last had a woman."

Ani tittered. His arousal was apparent. Martala shook her head with disgust.

"This is accomplishing nothing."

"On the contrary," I said. "We can watch half of the Caliph's seraglio through these panels, and if we wait long enough surely he will visit a woman in one of these chambers."

"But we have no way of reaching him even if we see him," Ani said.

"Too bad that I did not bring a bow," Altrus murmured. "I might just be able to shoot an arrow through one of these screens."

"Perhaps he will come back here to spy upon them," I mused.

"We can't wait here," Martala said with impatience, arms crossed below her breasts. "By the time the Caliph comes, if he does come, every house in the Lane of Scholars may be burning."

Altrus met my eyes. What she said could not be denied. Had we enough time, we could wait until nightfall and explore the palace while it lay asleep, but whatever we did must be done in the next few hours, before the Lane of Scholars came under attack. If Yazid planned to burn the houses as Harkanos believed, I suspected that he would launch his assault at dusk so that the fires of their burning would be all the more spectacular.

We continued along the corridor of portals to its end. To my disappointment, there was no access into any of the sleeping rooms. They might as well have been in Mecca. Yazid could stand laughing at us on the other side of the screens, and we would be powerless to harm him by physical means since the openings were too small to crawl through. It might be possible to kill him with magic. In my mind, I ran through the spells I had acquired. None of them was ideally suited to kill a man. Pure magic is seldom used to accomplish what can be done with a sword, and with good reason—a sword is more reliable.

At the end of the curved secret passage, a stair ran down to the lower level and another concealed panel that opened on a richly adorned hall decorated with gilded statues and cloth of gold on the walls. The cool air barely stirred, and the sounds of the women in the bath chamber were so faint that I would not have recognized them for human voices, hearing them for the first time. We moved along the hall, away from the women and into the silence, our swords drawn and ready to strike at an instant, yet we encountered no servants or guards, to my great surprise. I expected our presence to be discovered from moment to moment, and had long since given up our effort to kill Yazid as hopeless although I did not express my pessimism.

From the end of the corridor came the faint scream of a woman, high and drawn out, like the cry of some strange bird. I hesitated and looked at Altrus and Martala, but there was nothing of value behind us. We must move forward. We reached the end of the hall and passed through an open arch into a chamber unfurnished apart from a splendid Persian carpet that filled almost the whole of the sizable room. Beyond lay yet another broad hallway illuminated by lamps on the wall. We crept along it on our toes, the sounds of whimpering and pleas for mercy becoming clearer at each step. There was the sharp crack of a hand striking flesh, followed by a drawn out shriek.

At the end of this corridor was another open arch, but the room beyond it was not deserted. On a cushioned couch a naked woman lay on her back, her arms and legs pulled wide by tight chains attached to the four posts that supported the strange bed. Yazid knelt beside the couch on a footstool padded with red satin. In his hand he held a razor, the shining steel of its blade stained with fresh blood. At his elbow, a table supported a crystal decanter and a crystal goblet, both filled with red wine. He leaned forward on his stool and licked along one of the red lines that decorated the golden thigh of the young woman, who was not much older than Martala. Then he reached behind him and drank from the goblet.

The eyes of the tortured woman grew round as she saw us, standing in the archway, but she did not speak. Yazid had his gaze on her skin, not her face, and failed to notice her attention. Her body was slender, her breasts small and round, but her skin was the most perfect I have ever seen, apart from the bloody cuts that marred its purity. I looked quickly around, hardly daring to believe that we had been so fortunate. There were no servants, no guards, only the Caliph and his lover. The door at the opposite side of the room was shut, and I hoped, locked. Yazid must prefer privacy when he indulged in his more unusual passions.

"You have a strange taste in wine," Altrus said in a dry voice.

Yazid whirled around, a look of incomprehension on his puffy, sweating face. Blood smeared his thick lips and clotted in his sparse beard. He parted his lips in a kind of snarl, and I saw that his teeth were red-stained as well. With a shriek, he jumped to his feet and stared around, as though expecting men to rush to his defense. It was several moments before he realized that he was without protection. He began to back toward the door on the other side of the room, crying out with all his strength.

"Guards! I am being murdered! Save me!"

Altrus moved forward and tripped him, so that he fell on his back, and continued to try to crawl away like a crab. Fists began to pound the door behind him. It rattled on its hinges but did not open, and I saw that a brass bolt had been slid into place by Yazid. Privacy would be the death of him.

His bloodshot eyes fixed on mine and an expression of pure hatred twisted his face.

"You! I should have had you killed."

"We all must suffer the consequences of our errors," I said philosophically, raising my sword.

656

Yazid began to shriek, and the woman chained to the bed joined in with her own screams. I found it difficult to tell which were higher pitched. Altrus stepped close to Yazid. I noticed hanging from the neck of the Caliph a large green stone on a gold chain, and recognized it as the Thugian emerald. The glimmer of an idea came into my mind.

"Don't kill him," I said. "Not with the sword."

Altrus looked at me curiously but drew back his blade. I went to Yazid and jerked the emerald from his neck while he continued to shriek. The slender gold chain from which it hung broke easily. I sheathed my sword and used my dagger to pry the stone loose. Pocketing the stone, I cast the empty socket and broken chain on the floor beside the Caliph. With half my mind, I noticed Martala go to the woman on the bed and attempt to sooth her. The woman did not even see her, but stared past her with blank eyes, lost in some maze of horror in her own mind.

"Hold his arms," I told Altrus, and drew from the pocket of my thawb the yellow and white scarf that I had bought from the Thugians. I twisted it into a rope, and he saw my purpose. However, Yazid was not an easy man to grasp. He kicked with his satin-slippered feet whenever Altrus bent over him, and twisted his body on the tiled floor to prevent my approach from behind.

The blows against the bolted door were thunderous. It shook in its frame, yet looked strong enough to resist the attack of the guards for a few minutes. Altrus caught both of Yazid's feet at the same time, and at last I was able to slip the scarf over his head and around his fat throat. His womanly shrieks changed to gurgles and his eyes bulged even further from their sockets as I set my knee behind his neck and pulled.

The sweeter the ointment, the more likely it is to attract a fly. I had my attention on the elusive Yazid, and did not notice Ani until Martala cried out.

"Alhazred, the door!"

It was too late. The clubfooted procurer had the bolt in his hands. Casting me a murderous glance, he shot it open, and the door burst inward. Armed guards poured through like angry wasps.

Chapter 57

Altrus released the feet of Yazid, leaving me to my own devices, and stepped quickly toward the door. Ani was already moving behind the advancing wall of guards, but his club foot made him a little slow. The point of the mercenary's dagger, thrown with the left hand with unerring accuracy, buried itself in the back of Ani's skinny neck, and he fell as though hamstrung. At the same time I felt Yazid give a final shudder against my knee and go limp.

The guards closed on Altrus, who stepped back and danced to the side. One soldier fell clutching his throat, blood spurting between his fingers.

"Save yourselves," he cried without turning. "I can hold them."

I gave a final vicious pull on the scarf and released its ends, leaving it coiled around Yazid's neck. Martala matched swords with one of the guards, who beat her back toward the archway with the strength of his arm. Two others approached me, and I fell back before them, hard pressed to avoid both their blades at the same time. From the corner of my eye, I saw Altrus surrounded. Two more guards came toward me.

Cursing, I whirled and slashed at the exposed back of the guard who cut so viciously at the girl. He screamed with pain and fell as the strength left his legs. She stepped forward and caught a blade on her guard that would have taken off my head, had it fallen free. Together, we backed through the arch, driven along the hallway, unable to advance against the strength of steel wielded against us. Their armor gave them an advantage. Only the corridor, which was not wide enough for more than two men to fight abreast, preserved our lives. Each time one of us cut down an attacker, another came from behind to take his place.

They almost killed us in the empty chamber with the carpet, but we were able to retreat fast enough to keep from being completely encircled. We reached the entrance to the narrow stair that led up to the secret passage on the second level, and encountered another difficulty. It was not obvious how the panel opened from this side. Fighting off our attackers with an arm that was becoming weary, I watched the girl feel around the edge of the panel without success.

"Use your sword," I cried.

She began to hack at the wall. After a few cuts, a hole appeared in the wooden panel and she widened it with the heel of her boot. I watched from the edge of my vision as she slipped through, then in one motion backed and ducked through the hole, to the obvious amazement of the guards, who hesitated to follow me into the darkness.

We were at the top of the stair before I heard them splintering the remains of the panel away from its frame.

"Run," I told her.

We ran along the curved passage, guided by ribbons of light that leaked through the cracks around the sliding covers of the peep holes. The alarm had not reached this part of the palace. There was no sound of a search from ahead as we darted across the long spy chamber above the bathing pool and out through the open door with the lock. I stopped and drew my dagger. My anxious haste made my fingers clumsy, and it took me twice as long to relock the door as it had taken me to open it. We stood on the other side, breathing hard. The muffled thuds of approaching footfalls came through the locked door, but I heard nothing from beyond the other door at the far end of the passage.

We had enough time to locate the concealed latch for the hidden panel in the wall. When it closed behind us, I felt relieved. It was likely that not many in the palace knew its secret. At the least, it should delay pursuit. Sheathing our weapons, we made our way down the stair and along the corridor to the outer door. Only then did I remember that Altrus still had the key. It was not difficult to pick the lock with my dagger, but I cursed myself for failing to take the key from him. Yet how were we to know which of us would escape, and which would die in the palace?

The first hints of alarm began to show in the streets as we made our way to the stable. Bells were rung. Groups of soldiers ran past, keeping a tight formation with swords drawn. They ignored us. The common people began to gather in the doors of the shops and speculate about what was happening in nervous voices. No one noticed a man and a girl walk past with their heads bowed. The stable was deserted when we reached it, apart from the horses. We entered the tunnel unseen, and found the brass oil lamp still burning where Altrus had left it. The taciturn servant of Harkanos was waiting for us at the other end.

He bowed when I emerged through the little door in the cellar and led us into the large vaulted chamber with the long table, where Harkanos sat in conference with three other men I recognized from the portal ritual. One was the bald Egyptian, another the bearded ancient with the pale blue eyes, and the third a portly man with a cheerful face who resembled a merchant, and who had said nothing the previous night.

"Only two?" Harkanos asked with sadness, looking from Martala to me.

"They have your key," I said. "It was with Altrus."

"Ani betrayed us," Martala added. "Altrus killed him."

"What of the Caliph?" asked the Egyptian.

"Dead. Strangled by a Thugian scarf, and the Thugian jewel he wore around his neck pried from its socket."

I dug into my inner pocket and held out the jewel.

Comprehension came into their eyes. The bearded ancient smiled and nodded.

"Very clever. Will the jewel be missed?"

"One of his concubines saw me tear it from his neck. She will remember, if she remembers anything. But if the key is noticed, it may have been for nothing."

"Do not worry so much about the key," Harkanos said. "Others were given similar keys by the Caliph. Now that he is dead, it may not be easy to identify all their owners, who will naturally be reluctant to admit to possessing a means of secret access to the palace."

"How did these men come here?" I wondered.

Harkanos laughed, and the others smiled at the memory.

"We used your trick with the ladder. But we may not need it again. Shortly before we descended to the cellar, there was the sound of much running in the street. I did not look out my door, but I suspect the guards have departed."

"We passed them. The soldiers set to watch over the Lane of Scholars must have been recalled to the palace."

This proved to be true when we emerged from the house into the courtyard and unbolted the brown door to peer into the street. It was completely deserted, the soldiers gone, but the population of the Lane of Scholars afraid to leave their houses in violation of the Caliph's order, for fear that the armed guard might suddenly return.

"You have done a good work this day," Harkanos said, putting his hand on my shoulder as we stood together near the street door. "For yourself and for all of us."

The other three necromancers nodded. They watched us pass into the street, and Harkanos closed the brown door behind us.

"Where now? Home?" the girl asked.

"Presently. I want to learn what the reaction of the city is to the Caliph's assassination."

We walked toward the marketplace, where gossip is always more recent and plentiful. The people in the streets passed hurriedly with nervous expressions, their eyes darting this way and that, but there was a curious sense of elation that grew stronger as we entered the market. The din of voices could be heard for some distance outside the market walls, louder than usual. It swelled to a roar as we passed through the open gate. Trading had almost ceased. Everyone clustered and talked about the current situation at the palace, which was said to be ringed by guards and impossible to enter or leave.

Some of the merchants had family who served in the Caliph's guard, and from them we learned that the Caliph was either dead or gravely wounded, having been attacked by a strong force of professional assassins in his private chambers while engaged in the act of love. Two of the assassins were slain, but the others had escaped. Traitors within the palace were suspected, for how else could the assassins have made their way to the Caliph without detection? His chief advisor of state had assumed command of the guard, and at present no challenge had been made to his questionable authority. It was generally agreed that Yazid's son, Moawiya, would succeed to the throne should Yazid be dead. Moawiya was presently on a hunting expedition in the hills outside the city. A messenger had been sent to find his hunting party and give him word of the tragedy.

The stories were many and conflicting, which cheered my heart, since it meant that the true details of the attack remained confused. Nothing was said about a key, nor was any connection made in the marketplace between the assassination and the Caliph's action against the Lane of Scholars. On the contrary, it was generally whispered with nods and knowing looks that his son, Moawiya, was responsible for the assassination. I voiced the rumor that a Thugian scarf had been found on Yazid's body, and that the travelers in the yellow wagons were well-known to strangle their enemies with such scarves. This proved quite a popular theory, and I found myself repeating it many times around the market. The Thugians were universally despised as thieves and cutthroats. It required no effort to turn the thoughts of the people against them, and it was fortunate for the travelers that their wagons were banned from entering the walls of the city, or they would have been torn to pieces by the mob.

From a distracted merchant we bought a small amount of brown sugar and some barley flour that the girl said was needed in the kitchen, and carried these home. By this time, a few nervous souls had ventured into the Lane of Scholars on pressing errands, or merely to satisfy their curiosity. I had nothing certain to tell Harkanos, so I made no return visit to his house. The hours passed from afternoon into evening without event, and it became obvious that the ire against the Lane of Scholars had been forgotten in the chaos at the palace.

That night as I lay naked in my bed, the girl in a similar state at my side beneath a white silk sheet, hope for the future predominated my thoughts. The question of the key still troubled me, but there was nothing to be done about it, so I thrust it aside. I felt regret over the death of Altrus, who had given his life to save mine. Even though he had been my enemy, I had never been able to resist an admiration for his reckless daring and sword skill. More than once, I cursed myself for trusting Ani.

"You were right," I murmured aloud when we had rested side by side for several minutes.

"Hmmm?" the girl said, already drifting into sleep.

"Ani did betray us."

"I told you he would."

"I am a fool. It's a wonder I have been able to stay alive this long."

"A fool?"

"The jewel," I said in disgust. "How did the Caliph come to possess the emerald?"

"I don't know," she murmured softly, her breathing slow and deep. Soon I would be talking to myself in the darkness.

"Ani saw me sell it to the Roman gem trader. When Yazid presented the emerald to me, I should have suspected Ani at once. Why did I not suspect him?"

She mumbled something.

"What was that?"

"I said you trusted him because you believed him dependent on you."

What she said was true. In my vanity I had believed Ani's future prosperity bound up with my own. It never occurred to me that Ani, in his ambition and greed, might perceive the Caliph a better patron.

The breaths of the girl lengthened into sleep. In a few minutes my thoughts became random, and I drifted into a similar state. The dark man waited for me in my dreams. He stood in the chamber of the palace where I had killed Yazid. The body of the Caliph lay twisted on the floor, his tongue purple where it hung from his mouth, his eyes staring into oblivion. Otherwise, the room was unoccupied.

The dark man stood over the corpse and stared down at it in silence. He turned the shadow of his hooded face toward me and pointed a bony black finger at Yazid.

"You have deprived me of one of my servants."

A chill of dread passed over my heart, but I gave no sign of it.

"How was I to know Yazid served you?"

"True. I neglected to tell you. Yet how was I to imagine that you possessed the audacity to take his life? By the time I realized what you intended, the deed was accomplished."

"In what way did Yazid serve you?"

The dark man kicked the corpse gently in the ribs, so that it rocked. It was almost a gesture of affection.

"His mind was weak, and his lusts made him easy to control. I fear the next Caliph won't be so soft."

"He planned to kill all the necromancers in Damascus," I said.

The dark man shrugged beneath his black cloak.

"What do I care about the fate of necromancers? Your kind are an irritation to me, nothing more."

"Then have you finished your dealings with me?"

He chuckled, the hollow rasp in his voice making my teeth clench.

"On the contrary, Alhazred, I have come to reward you."

He stepped over the corpse and walked toward me until he stood near enough to touch. I looked into his hood but as usual saw nothing.

"It is within my power to restore your manhood and your face."

"You would do this?" My heart quickened.

He nodded, then raised his bony ebon hand with his index finger extended.

"In return for one trifling additional service from you."

I took an involuntary step backward, my suspicions aroused.

"What is this service?"

"I want you to murder Harkanos. He defies me, and he is leader of the necro-mancers in Damascus. I find his scruples an obstruction to my purposes."

A dizziness threatened to engulf my mind, and the darkness of his cloak expanded until I could see nothing apart from the corpse of Yazid, its face turned to me with an obscene leer. My thoughts raced. To achieve the end I had sought with such longing for so many months, for the life of a single man. It seemed a small price to pay. Yet Harkanos had offered me friendship and treated me with trust. To kill him would be to cast aside any remaining shred of honor I might possess and be forever damned. A part of my mind argued that I was damned in any case for my dealings with the Old Ones, but this argument did not convince.

What Nyarlathotep asked of me was so base, I wondered if the death of Harkanos could be his only motive. To submit my will so completely to his purposes, and defile myself beyond redemption, would be to place my soul under his power. At present I was his unwilling servant, but if I did this vile thing I would become his slave. I thought of Martala's contempt, should she learn that I had done such an evil deed, and to my surprise the opinion of the girl mattered.

The darkness withdrew, and I found myself standing naked in the desert beneath the light of the moon. Nyarlathotep pointed at my groin.

"Consider well, fool, for I will not make this offer twice. Serve me in this one small act, and I will restore your beauty and your potency. Deny me, and you will remain as you are now forever, the contempt of men, the mock of women, the horror of children."

"I know what I am."

Turning my back upon him, I walked without haste across the blowing sands. My heart grew serene within my breast as I left all doubt behind me in my footprints. I heard his roar of rage, was buffeted off my feet, and awoke in the darkness with a jerk, all my muscles rigid and my naked body covered with sweat. My heart raced as though I had been running. I drew deep breaths and waited for it to slow before relaxing my head upon the pillow. The girl continued to sleep. She was accustomed to my nightmares.

Morning brought the news from the marketplace that young Moawiya had returned to the palace during the night. There had been a brief battle between his personal guard and a small force of the palace guard loyal to Yazid's chief advisor, after which several of those closest to the late Caliph had been put to the sword. The new self-proclaimed Caliph declared the day to be a day of celebration. A feast was to be held in the evening on the palace lawn for the leading men and women of Damascus. Prisoners in the city jails had already been set free as a display of clemency. I was told by Harkanos that this was not uncommon when a new ruler assumed the caliphate.

"It bodes well for us," he said, passing me wine. "If Moawiya wishes to make a show of kindness, he is less likely to have our houses burned."

I sat beside Martala on the padded divan in his study. He had dismissed his solemn servant after the man brought the silver tray with the wine, and both doors of the chamber were shut.

"There is quiet rejoicing along the street," he said, sipping the golden liquid with appreciation. "With the threat of Yazid ended, we will be able to resume our more serious studies."

"What do you know of magic that can restore lost limbs?" I tried to keep my voice careless, but the tremble in my hand as it brought the smoky glass goblet to my lips betrayed me.

He set down his own glass and regarded me with gravity. There was pity in his eyes.

"I know nothing of such magic myself," he murmured. "I will make inquiries, and consult my texts."

I nodded and drank to hide my eyes beneath lowered lids. It was the answer I had expected.

"There is one thing that may interest you," he said. "When you have finished your wine, I would like to show you something."

We followed him from the study and into the cellar with silent curiosity. He led the way to the vaulted chamber. A linen-wrapped bundle lay upon the long table, stained with earth and wound tightly with hemp cord. My nose told me that it was a corpse before my eyes made sense of its shape. It smelled of soil and damp, beneath which hung an odor of putrefaction.

Harkanos took a knife from a shelf and began to cut the loops of cord, loosening the linen as he went. When he had cut midway down the corpse, he unfolded the linen to expose its head and shoulders. Martala drew a sharp breath. On the table, Altrus lay as though asleep, his face bloodless but unblemished. The same could not be said for his shoulders and neck, which had suffered several wounds.

"Uto brought this to me last night. The new caliph, Moawiya, had it buried without ceremony or marker in the graveyard where the White Skull Clan dwells. It is my belief that he wished to remove all traces of the assassination as quickly as possible, so that its details could not by any artifice of his enemies be turned against him.

"They didn't even bother to remove his clothing," Martala murmured as she gazed down at his face. "But they stole his sword and armor."

"May I have the knife?" I asked.

Harkanos passed it over and watched while I cut the remainder of the cords, exposing the corpse to its knees. I parted the mercenary's blue cloak and felt along its inner lining. There were several pockets. In one I found the key. I held it up and smiled at our host.

"Either they never bothered to search his body, or they thought this key of no significance."

He took it and put it on the key ring at his waist.

"I doubt I shall have occasion to use it again, but who can foresee the future? The new caliph may prove unsatisfactory."

"Is the body intact?" Martala asked, excitement in her voice.

"So far as I am aware. Let us examine it."

We removed the linen shroud and stripped the corpse. Apart from the many wounds that had caused his death, the body of Altrus was unmutilated. I touched the shoulder of the girl. She turned with a smile, and I knew what was in her mind.

"He may still try to kill me," I reminded her.

"Perhaps, but I doubt it."

"We will need to acquire a number of things."

"That is the advantage of living in Damascus," Harkanos said. "All things may be obtained, for a price."

"Very well," I told her. "We will attempt it."

"Any assistance that I or my colleagues can provide, you need only ask," Harkanos said.

"I have made many enemies in my travels," I murmured, staring at the face of the mercenary. "I will need a trustworthy bodyguard if I am to continue to live in this city in peace."

"You could not find another more capable," said the girl.

To my surprise, I realized that in some indefinable way and without my awareness of the change, Damascus had become my home. The desire to wander the world was gone from my heart. Here I chose to live, and here I would pursue my studies. The fancy came that at some future period in my life, I might even write down the events of my travels in the form of a book, for the benefit of other seekers after arcane knowledge, and as a warning to fools. I had acquired much curious lore that would be of interest to serious students of the necromantic arts.

My enemies would continue to search after me, and would never cease to make attempts on my life. It was dangerous to remain in one city, and dwell in one house. My identity would eventually become known to those wishing my death, and I would need to take stringent precautions to defend myself and my household. I gathered my resolve. So be it. Whether my remaining years were long or short, here I would stay and live the life of a necromancer, enslaved neither to men nor to gods, my own master until the end.

COMING FALL 2007
FROM LLEWELLYN PUBLICATIONS

WATCH FOR
THE
Necronomicon
TAROT KIT

FEATURING TEXT BY
DONALD TYSON

AND THE ARTWORK OF
ANNE STOKES